Lawrie Ryan and Roger Norris

Cambridge International AS and A Level

Chemistry

Coursebook

Second Edition

CAMBRIDGE
UNIVERSITY PRESS

CAMBRIDGE
UNIVERSITY PRESS

University Printing House, Cambridge CB2 8BS, United Kingdom

Cambridge University Press is part of the University of Cambridge.

It furthers the University's mission by disseminating knowledge in the pursuit of education, learning and research at the highest international levels of excellence.

www.cambridge.org
Information on this title: www.cambridge.org

First published 2011
Second edition 2014

Printed in the United Kingdom by Latimer Trend

A catalogue record for this publication is available from the British Library

ISBN 978-1-107-63845-7 Paperback with CD-ROM for Windows® and Mac®

Cambridge University Press has no responsibility for the persistence or accuracy of URLs for external or third-party internet websites referred to in this publication, and does not guarantee that any content on such websites is, or will remain, accurate or appropriate. Information regarding prices, travel timetables, and other factual information given in this work is correct at the time of first printing but Cambridge University Press does not guarantee the accuracy of such information thereafter.

....

Example answers and all other end-of-chapter questions were written by the authors.

Contents

| How to use this book | vi |

Chapter 1: Moles and equations — 1

Masses of atoms and molecules	2
Accurate relative atomic masses	3
Amount of substance	5
Mole calculations	6
Chemical formulae and chemical equations	10
Solutions and concentration	14
Calculations involving gas volumes	18

Chapter 2: Atomic structure — 24

Elements and atoms	25
Inside the atom	25
Numbers of nucleons	28
Isotopes	28
How many protons, neutrons and electrons?	29

Chapter 3: Electrons in atoms — 32

Simple electronic structure	33
Evidence for electronic structure	34
Subshells and atomic orbitals	37
Electronic configurations	38
Orbitals and the Periodic Table	40
Patterns in ionisation energies in the Periodic Table	41

Chapter 4: Chemical bonding — 48

Types of chemical bonding	49
Ionic bonding	49
Covalent bonding	51
Shapes of molecules	55
More molecular shapes	56
Metallic bonding	58
Intermolecular forces	60
Hydrogen bonding	64
Bonding and physical properties	66

Chapter 5: States of matter — 72

States of matter	73
The gaseous state	73
The liquid state	77
The solid state	78
Simple molecular lattices	80
Carbon nanoparticles	82
Conserving materials	83

Chapter 6: Enthalpy changes — 89

What are enthalpy changes?	90
Standard enthalpy changes	92
Measuring enthalpy changes	94
Hess's law	97
Enthalpy change of reaction from enthalpy changes of formation	97
Enthalpy change of formation from enthalpy changes of combustion	98
Calculating the enthalpy change of hydration of an anhydrous salt	99
Bond energies and enthalpy changes	99
Calculating enthalpy changes using bond energies	101

Chapter 7: Redox reactions — 106

What is a redox reaction?	107
Redox and electron transfer	108
Oxidation numbers	109
Redox and oxidation number	110
Naming compounds	111
From name to formula	112
Balancing chemical equations using oxidation numbers	112

Chapter 8: Equilibrium — 116

Reversible reactions and equilibrium	117
Changing the position of equilibrium	119
Equilibrium expressions and the equilibrium constant, K_c	123
Equilibria in gas reactions: the equilibrium constant, K_p	127
Equilibria and the chemical industry	129
Acid-base equilibria	130

Chapter 9: Rates of reaction — 140

Reaction kinetics	141
The effect of concentration on rate of reaction	143
The effect of temperature on rate of reaction	143
Catalysis	144
Enzymes	145

Chapter 10: Periodicity — 148

Structure of the Periodic Table	149
Periodicity of physical properties	149
Periodicity of chemical properties	154

Oxides of Period 3 elements	156
Chlorides of Period 3 elements	158

Chapter 11: Group 2 — 163

Physical properties of Group 2 elements	164
Reactions of Group 2 elements	165
Thermal decomposition of Group 2 carbonates and nitrates	168
Some uses of Group 2 compounds	169

Chapter 12: Group 17 — 171

Physical properties of Group 17 elements	172
Reactions of Group 17 elements	173
Reactions of the halide ions	175
Disproportionation	177
Uses of the halogens and their compounds	178

Chapter 13: Nitrogen and sulfur — 180

Nitrogen gas	181
Ammonia and ammonium compounds	182
Uses of ammonia and ammonium compounds	183
Sulfur and its oxides	185
Sulfuric acid	185

Chapter 14: Introduction to organic chemistry — 188

Representing organic molecules	189
Functional groups	192
Naming organic compounds	192
Bonding in organic molecules	193
Structural isomerism	194
Stereoisomerism	195
Organic reactions – mechanisms	196
Types of organic reaction	198

Chapter 15: Hydrocarbons — 201

The homologous group of alkanes	202
Sources of the alkanes	202
Reactions of alkanes	204
The alkenes	207
Addition reactions of the alkenes	208
Oxidation of the alkenes	210
Addition polymerisation	211
Tackling questions on addition polymers	213

Chapter 16: Halogenoalkanes — 217

Nucleophilic substitution reactions	218
Mechanism of nucleophilic substitution in halogenoalkanes	220
Elimination reactions	222
Uses of halogenoalkanes	222

Chapter 17: Alcohols, esters and carboxylic acids — 225

The homologous series of alcohols	226
Reactions of the alcohols	226
Carboxylic acids	231

Chapter 18: Carbonyl compounds — 234

The homologous series of aldehydes and ketones	235
Preparation of aldehydes and ketones	236
Reduction of aldehydes and ketones	237
Nucleophilic addition with HCN	237
Testing for aldehydes and ketones	238
Reactions to form tri-iodomethane	240
Infra-red spectroscopy	241

Chapter P1: Practical skills 1 — 246

Review of practical knowledge and understanding	247
Manipulation, measurement and observation	249
Presentation of data and observations	250
Analysis, conclusions and evaluation	251

Chapter 19: Lattice energy — 257

Defining lattice energy	258
Enthalpy change of atomisation and electron affinity	258
Born–Haber cycles	259
Factors affecting the value of lattice energy	262
Ion polarisation	263
Enthalpy changes in solution	265

Chapter 20: Electrochemistry — 273

Redox reactions revisited	274
Electrolysis	275
Quantitative electrolysis	276
Electrode potentials	278
Measuring standard electrode potentials	282
Using $E^{\ominus}$ values	284
Cells and batteries	293
More about electrolysis	295

Chapter 21: Further aspects of equilibria — 303

The ionic product of water, K_w	304
pH calculations	305
Weak acids – using the acid dissociation constant, K_a	307
Indicators and acid–base titrations	309
Buffer solutions	313

Equilibrium and solubility 316
Partition coefficients 319

Chapter 22: Reaction kinetics 324

Factors affecting reaction rate 325
Rate of reaction 325
Rate equations 330
Which order of reaction? 332
Calculations involving the rate constant, k 334
Deducing order of reaction from raw data 335
Kinetics and reaction mechanisms 338
Catalysis 340

Chapter 23: Entropy and Gibbs free energy 349

Introducing entropy 350
Chance and spontaneous change 350
Calculating entropy changes 354
Entropy and temperature 357
Entropy, enthalpy changes and free energy 357
Gibbs free energy 358
Gibbs free energy calculations 360

Chapter 24: Transition elements 366

What is a transition element? 367
Physical properties of the transition elements 369
Redox reactions 369
Ligands and complex formation 371

Chapter 25: Benzene and its compounds 381

The benzene ring 382
Reactions of arenes 384
Phenol 387
Reactions of phenol 388

Chapter 26: Carboxylic acids and their derivatives 393

The acidity of carboxylic acids 394
Oxidation of two carboxylic acids 395
Acyl chlorides 396

Chapter 27: Organic nitrogen compounds 400

Amines 401
Formation of amines 402
Amino acids 404
Peptides 405
Reactions of the amides 406
Electrophoresis 407

Chapter 28: Polymerisation 411

Condensation polymerisation 412
Synthetic polyamides 413
Biochemical polymers 414
The importance of hydrogen bonding in DNA 418
Polyesters 421
Designing useful polymers 422
Degradable polymers 425
Polymer deductions 426

Chapter 29: Analytical chemistry 433

Chromatography 434
Proton (^{1}H) nuclear magnetic resonance 439
Carbon-13 NMR spectroscopy 444
Mass spectrometry 446

Chapter 30: Organic synthesis 456

Designing new medicinal drugs 457

Chapter P2: Practical skills 2 464

Written examination of practical skills 465
Planning 465
Analysis, conclusions and evaluation 468

Appendix 1: The Periodic Table of the Elements 473

Appendix 2: Selected standard electrode potentials 474

Appendix 3: Qualitative analysis notes 475

Glossary 477

Index 486

Acknowledgements 493

Terms and conditions of use for the CD-ROM 494

v

How to use this book

Each chapter begins with a short list of the facts and concepts that are explained in it.

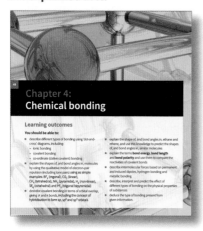

There is a short context at the beginning of each chapter, containing an example of how the material covered in the chapter relates to the 'real world'.

Introduction

In the last chapter we looked at the types of forces that keep the particles in solids and liquids together and make it possible to liquefy gases. In this chapter, we shall also consider how the closeness and motion of the particles influences the properties of these three states of matter (Figure 5.1).

Figure 5.1 The three states of water are ice, water and steam. The 'steam' we see from the kettle is condensed droplets of water. The real gaseous water is in the area between this condensation and the spout of the kettle. We can't see it because it is colourless.

This book does not contain detailed instructions for doing particular experiments, but you will find background information about the practical work you need to do in these boxes. There are also two chapters, P1 and P2, which provide detailed information about the practical skills you need to develop during the course.

Important equations and other facts are shown in highlight boxes.

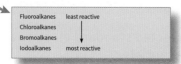

Fluoroalkanes	least reactive
Chloroalkanes	↓
Bromoalkanes	
Iodoalkanes	most reactive

METHODS FOR FOLLOWING THE COURSE OF A REACTION (CONTINUED)

The progress of some reactions can be followed by measuring small changes in the volume of the reaction mixture. For example, during the hydration of methylpropene, the volume decreases.

$$(CH_3)_2C{=}CH_2 + H_2O \xrightarrow{H^+} (CH_3)_3COH$$

An instrument called a dilatometer (Figure 22.4) is used to measure the small changes in volume. The temperature has to be controlled to an accuracy of ±0.001 °C. Can you think why?

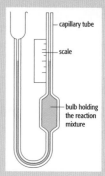

Figure 22.4 A dilatometer.

Questions throughout the text give you a chance to check that you have understood the topic you have just read about. You can find the answers to these questions on the CD-ROM.

QUESTION

2 a Suggest a suitable method for following the progress of each of these reactions:

i $H_2O_2(aq) + 2I^-(aq) + 2H^+(aq)$
$$\longrightarrow 2H_2O(l) + I_2(aq)$$

ii $HCOOCH_3(aq) + H_2O(l)$
$$\longrightarrow HCOOH(aq) + CH_3OH(aq)$$

iii $2H_2O_2(aq) \longrightarrow 2H_2O(l) + O_2(g)$

iv $BrO_3^-(aq) + 5Br^-(aq) + 6H^+(aq)$
$$\longrightarrow 3Br_2(aq) + 3H_2O(l)$$

b Why is it essential that the temperature is kept constant when measuring the progress of a reaction?

The text and illustrations describe and explain all of the facts and concepts that you need to know. The chapters, and often the content within them as well, are arranged in the same sequence as in your syllabus.

Calculating rate of reaction graphically

Rate of reaction usually changes as the reaction proceeds. This is because the concentration of reactants is decreasing. Taking the isomerisation of cyclopropane to propene as an example:

$$\begin{array}{c} H_2C \\ \;|\;\;CH_2(g) \longrightarrow CH_3CH = CH_2(g) \\ H_2C \end{array}$$

cyclopropane   propene

The progress of this reaction can be followed by measuring the decrease in concentration of cyclopropane or increase

in concentration of propene. Table 22.1 shows these changes at 500 °C. The measurements were all made at the same temperature because reaction rate is affected markedly by temperature.

Time / min	[cyclopropane] / mol dm⁻³	[propene] / mol dm⁻³
0	1.50	0.00
5	1.23	0.27
10	1.00	0.50
15	0.82	0.68
20	0.67	0.83
25	0.55	0.95
30	0.45	1.05
35	0.37	1.13
40	0.33	1.17

Table 22.1 Concentrations of reactant (cyclopropane) and product (propene) at 5-minute intervals (temperature = 500 °C (773 K)).

Note that we put square brackets, [ ], around the cyclopropane and propene to indicate concentration; [propene] means 'concentration of propene'.

Figure 22.5 shows how the concentration of propene changes with time.

Wherever you need to know how to use a formula to carry out a calculation, there are worked example boses to show you how to do this.

WORKED EXAMPLE (CONTINUED)

Step 1 Draw a graph of concentration (of hydrochloric acid) against time (Figure 22.13).

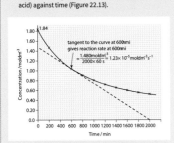

Figure 22.13 The concentration of hydrochloric acid and methanol fall at the same rate as time passes.

Step 2 Draw tangents to the curve at various places corresponding to a range of concentrations. In Figure 22.13 the tangent drawn corresponds to $[HCl] = 1.04 \, mol \, dm^{-3}$.

Step 3 For each tangent drawn, calculate the gradient and then the rate of reaction. In Figure 22.13, the rate corresponding to $[HCl] = 1.04 \, mol \, dm^{-3}$ is

$$\frac{1.480}{2000 \times 60} = 1.23 \times 10^{-5} \, mol \, dm^{-3} \, s^{-1}$$

(multiply by 60 to convert minutes to seconds)

Table 22.7 shows the rates corresponding to five different concentrations of hydrochloric acid.

Time / min	Concen- tration / mol dm⁻³	Rate from graph / mol dm⁻³ min⁻¹	Rate from graph / mol dm⁻³ s⁻¹
0	1.84	2.30×10^{-3}	3.83×10^{-5}
200	1.45	1.46×10^{-3}	2.43×10^{-5}
400	1.22	1.05×10^{-3}	1.75×10^{-5}
600	1.04	0.74×10^{-3}	1.23×10^{-5}
800	0.91	0.54×10^{-3}	0.90×10^{-5}

WORKED EXAMPLE (CONTINUED)

the $[CH_3OH]$ because if you look at the data in Table 22.6, you will see that the concentration of CH_3OH is decreasing at the same rate as the decrease in concentration of HCl.

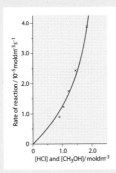

Figure 22.14 A graph showing how concentration changes of hydrochloric acid or methanol affect rate of reaction. The curve shows that the reaction is likely to be second order.

Figure 22.14 shows an upward curve. This indicates that the reaction is second order. But second order with respect to what? As the concentrations of both HCl and CH_3OH are decreasing at the same rate, either of these may be second order. The possibilities are:

- rate = $k[CH_3OH][HCl]$
- rate = $k[CH_3OH]^2$
- rate = $k[HCl]^2$

Further experiments would have to be carried out to confirm one or other of these possibilities. The only thing we can be sure of is that the reaction is second order overall.

Definitions that are required by the syllabus are shown in highlight boxes.

> Oxidation Is Loss of electrons.
> Reduction Is Gain of electrons.
> The initial letters shown in bold spell **OIL RIG**. This may help you to remember these two definitions!

Key words are highlighted in the text when they are first introduced.

> hydrolyse a protein and try to identify the amino acid residues present. This is when **two-way chromatography** is useful. In this technique, paper chromatography is carried out as normal but then the chromatogram produced is rotated by 90° and re-run in a different solvent. It is unlikely that the R_f values will coincide in two different solvents, so separation takes place (Figure 29.4).

You will also find definitions of these words in the Glossary.

> **two-way chromatography** a technique used in paper or thin-layer chromatography in which one spot of a mixture is placed at the corner of a square sheet and is developed in the first solvent as usual. The sheet is then turned through 90° and developed in the second solvent, giving a better separation of components having similar R_f values.

There is a summary of key points at the end of each chapter. You might find this helpful when you are revising.

Summary

- Each of the transition elements forms at least one ion with a partially filled d orbital. They are metals with similar physical and chemical properties.

- When a transition element is oxidised, it loses electrons from the 4s subshell first and then the 3d subshell to form a positively charged ion.

- Transition elements can exist in several oxidation states.

- Some transition element complexes exist as geometrical (*cis-trans*) isomers, e.g. *cis-* and *trans-*platin; others, especially those associated with bidentate ligands with co-ordination number 6, may exist as optical isomers.

- *cis*-platin can be used as an anti-cancer drug by binding to DNA in cancer cells and preventing cell division.

Questions at the end of each chapter are more demanding exam-style questions, some of which may require use of knowledge from previous chapters. Answers to these questions can be found on the CD-ROM.

End-of-chapter questions

1 The diagram shows an electrochemical cell designed to find the standard electrode potential for zinc.

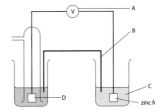

a Name the apparatus labelled **A** and give a characteristic it should have. [2]
b i Name part **B** and give its two functions. [3]
  ii Describe how part **B** can be prepared. [2]
c What is **C**? [2]
d Name part **D** and give its two functions. [3]
e Give the three standard conditions for the measurement of a standard electrode potential. [3]

Total = 15

Chapter 1:
Moles and equations

Learning outcomes

You should be able to:

- define and use the terms:
  - **relative atomic mass**, **isotopic mass** and **formula mass** based on the ^{12}C scale
  - **empirical formula** and **molecular formula**
  - the **mole** in terms of the Avogadro constant
- analyse and use mass spectra to calculate the relative atomic mass of an element
- calculate empirical and molecular formulae using combustion data or composition by mass
- write and construct balanced equations

- perform calculations, including use of the mole concept involving:
  - reacting masses (from formulae and equations)
  - volumes of gases (e.g. in the burning of hydrocarbons)
  - volumes and concentrations of solutions
- deduce stoichiometric relationships from calculations involving reacting masses, volumes of gases and volumes and concentrations of solutions.

Introduction

For thousands of years, people have heated rocks and distilled plant juices to extract materials. Over the past two centuries, chemists have learnt more and more about how to get materials from rocks, from the air and the sea, and from plants. They have also found out the right conditions to allow these materials to react together to make new substances, such as dyes, plastics and medicines. When we make a new substance it is important to mix the reactants in the correct proportions to ensure that none is wasted. In order to do this we need to know about the relative masses of atoms and molecules and how these are used in chemical calculations.

Figure 1.1 A titration is a method used to find the amount of a particular substance in a solution.

Masses of atoms and molecules

Relative atomic mass, A_r

Atoms of different elements have different masses. When we perform chemical calculations, we need to know how heavy one atom is compared with another. The mass of a single atom is so small that it is impossible to weigh it directly. To overcome this problem, we have to weigh a lot of atoms. We then compare this mass with the mass of the same number of 'standard' atoms. Scientists have chosen to use the isotope carbon-12 as the standard. This has been given a mass of exactly 12 units. The mass of other atoms is found by comparing their mass with the mass of carbon-12 atoms. This is called the relative atomic mass, A_r.

> The relative atomic mass is the weighted average mass of naturally occurring atoms of an element on a scale where an atom of carbon-12 has a mass of exactly 12 units.

From this it follows that:

A_r [element Y]

$$= \frac{\text{average mass of one atom of element } Y \times 12}{\text{mass of one atom of carbon-12}}$$

We use the average mass of the atom of a particular element because most elements are mixtures of isotopes. For example, the exact A_r of hydrogen is 1.0079. This is very close to 1 and most periodic tables give the A_r of hydrogen as 1.0. However, some elements in the Periodic Table have values that are not whole numbers. For example, the A_r for chlorine is 35.5. This is because chlorine has two isotopes. In a sample of chlorine, chlorine-35 makes up about three-quarters of the chlorine atoms and chlorine-37 makes up about a quarter.

Relative isotopic mass

Isotopes are atoms that have the same number of protons but different numbers of neutrons (see page 28). We represent the nucleon number (the total number of neutrons plus protons in an atom) by a number written at the top left-hand corner of the atom's symbol, e.g. ^{20}Ne, or by a number written after the atom's name or symbol, e.g. neon-20 or Ne-20.

We use the term relative isotopic mass for the mass of a particular isotope of an element on a scale where an atom of carbon-12 has a mass of exactly 12 units. For example, the relative isotopic mass of carbon-13 is 13.00. If we know both the natural abundance of every isotope of an element and their isotopic masses, we can calculate the relative atomic mass of the element very accurately. To find the necessary data we use an instrument called a mass spectrometer (see box on mass spectrometry).

Relative molecular mass, M_r

The relative molecular mass of a compound (M_r) is the relative mass of one molecule of the compound on a scale where the carbon-12 isotope has a mass of exactly 12 units. We find the relative molecular mass by adding up the relative atomic masses of all the atoms present in the molecule.

For example, for methane:

formula	CH_4
atoms present	$1 \times C; 4 \times H$
add A_r values	$(1 \times A_r[C]) + (4 \times A_r[H])$
M_r of methane	$= (1 \times 12.0) + (4 \times 1.0)$
	$= 16.0$

Relative formula mass

For compounds containing ions we use the term relative formula mass. This is calculated in the same way as for relative molecular mass. It is also given the same symbol, M_r. For example, for magnesium hydroxide:

formula	$Mg(OH)_2$
ions present	$1 \times Mg^{2+}; 2 \times (OH^-)$
add A_r values	$(1 \times A_r[Mg]) + (2 \times (A_r[O] + A_r[H]))$
M_r of magnesium hydroxide	$= (1 \times 24.3) + (2 \times (16.0 + 1.0))$
	$= 58.3$

QUESTION

1 Use the Periodic Table on page 473 to calculate the relative formula masses of the following:

   a calcium chloride, $CaCl_2$

   b copper(II) sulfate, $CuSO_4$

   c ammonium sulfate, $(NH_4)_2SO_4$

   d magnesium nitrate-6-water, $Mg(NO_3)_2.6H_2O$

   Hint: for part d you need to calculate the mass of water separately and then add it to the M_r of $Mg(NO_3)_2$.

Accurate relative atomic masses

MASS SPECTROMETRY

A mass spectrometer (Figure 1.2) can be used to measure the mass of each isotope present in an element. It also compares how much of each isotope is present – the relative abundance (isotopic abundance). A simplified diagram of a mass spectrometer is shown in Figure 1.3. You will not be expected to know the details of how a mass spectrometer works, but it is useful to understand how the results are obtained.

Figure 1.2 A mass spectrometer is a large and complex instrument.

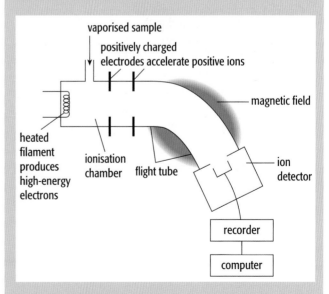

Figure 1.3 Simplified diagram of a mass spectrometer.

MASS SPECTROMETRY (CONTINUED)

The atoms of the element in the vaporised sample are converted into ions. The stream of ions is brought to a detector after being deflected (bent) by a strong magnetic field. As the magnetic field is increased, the ions of heavier and heavier isotopes are brought to the detector. The detector is connected to a computer, which displays the mass spectrum.

The mass spectrum produced shows the relative abundance (isotopic abundance) on the vertical axis and the mass to ion charge ratio (m/e) on the horizontal axis. Figure 1.4 shows a typical mass spectrum for a sample of lead. Table 1.1 shows how the data is interpreted.

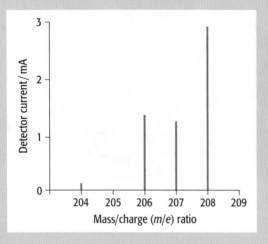

Figure 1.4 The mass spectrum of a sample of lead.

For singly positively charged ions the m/e values give the nucleon number of the isotopes detected. In the case of lead, Table 1.1 shows that 52% of the lead is the isotope with an isotopic mass of 208. The rest is lead-204 (2%), lead-206 (24%) and lead-207 (22%).

Isotopic mass	Relative abundance / %
204	2
206	24
207	22
208	52
total	100

Table 1.1 The data from Figure 1.4.

Determination of A_r from mass spectra

We can use the data obtained from a mass spectrometer to calculate the relative atomic mass of an element very accurately. To calculate the relative atomic mass we follow this method:

- multiply each isotopic mass by its percentage abundance
- add the figures together
- divide by 100.

We can use this method to calculate the relative atomic mass of neon from its mass spectrum, shown in Figure 1.5.

The mass spectrum of neon has three peaks:

^{20}Ne (90.9%), ^{21}Ne (0.3%) and ^{22}Ne (8.8%).

A_r of neon

$$= \frac{(20 \times 90.9) + (21.0 \times 0.3) + (22 \times 8.8)}{100} = 20.2$$

Note that this answer is given to 3 significant figures, which is consistent with the data given.

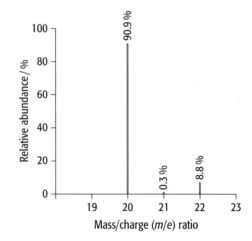

Figure 1.5 The mass spectrum of neon, Ne.

A high-resolution mass spectrometer can give very accurate relative isotopic masses. For example ^{16}O = 15.995 and ^{32}S = 31.972. Because of this, chemists can distinguish between molecules such as SO_2 and S_2, which appear to have the same relative molecular mass.

QUESTION

2 Look at the mass spectrum of germanium, Ge.

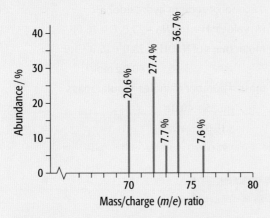

Figure 1.6 The mass spectrum of germanium.

a Write the isotopic formula for the heaviest isotope of germanium.

b Use the % abundance of each isotope to calculate the relative atomic mass of germanium.

Amount of substance

The mole and the Avogadro constant

The formula of a compound shows us the number of atoms of each element present in one formula unit or one molecule of the compound. In water we know that two atoms of hydrogen ($A_r = 1.0$) combine with one atom of oxygen ($A_r = 16.0$). So the ratio of mass of hydrogen atoms to oxygen atoms in a water molecule is 2 : 16. No matter how many molecules of water we have, this ratio will always be the same. But the mass of even 1000 atoms is far too small to be weighed. We have to scale up much more than this to get an amount of substance that is easy to weigh.

The relative atomic mass or relative molecular mass of a substance in grams is called a **mole** of the substance. So a mole of sodium ($A_r = 23.0$) weighs 23.0 g. The abbreviation for a mole is mol. We define the mole in terms of the standard carbon-12 isotope (see page 28).

One mole of a substance is the amount of that substance that has the same number of specific particles (atoms, molecules or ions) as there are atoms in exactly 12 g of the carbon-12 isotope.

We often refer to the mass of a mole of substance as its **molar mass** (abbreviation M). The units of molar mass are g mol^{-1}.

The number of atoms in a mole of atoms is very large: 6.02×10^{23} atoms. This number is called the **Avogadro constant** (or Avogadro number). The symbol for the Avogadro constant is L (the symbol N_A may also be used). The Avogadro constant applies to atoms, molecules, ions and electrons. So in 1 mole of sodium there are 6.02×10^{23} sodium atoms and in 1 mole of sodium chloride (NaCl) there are 6.02×10^{23} sodium ions and 6.02×10^{23} chloride ions.

It is important to make clear what type of particles we are referring to. If we just state 'moles of chlorine', it is not clear whether we are thinking about chlorine atoms or chlorine molecules. A mole of chlorine molecules, Cl_2, contains 6.02×10^{23} chlorine molecules but twice as many chlorine atoms, as there are two chlorine atoms in every chlorine molecule.

Figure 1.7 Amedeo Avogadro (1776–1856) was an Italian scientist who first deduced that equal volumes of gases contain equal numbers of molecules. Although the Avogadro constant is named after him, it was left to other scientists to calculate the number of particles in a mole.

Moles and mass

The Système International (SI) base unit for mass is the kilogram. But this is a rather large mass to use for general laboratory work in chemistry. So chemists prefer to use the relative molecular mass or formula mass in grams (1000 g = 1 kg). You can find the number of moles of a substance by using the mass of substance and the relative atomic mass (A_r) or relative molecular mass (M_r).

$$\text{number of moles (mol)} = \frac{\text{mass of substance in grams (g)}}{\text{molar mass (g mol}^{-1})}$$

5

WORKED EXAMPLE

1 How many moles of sodium chloride are present in 117.0 g of sodium chloride, NaCl?

(A_r values: Na = 23.0, Cl = 35.5)

molar mass of NaCl = 23.0 + 35.5

$$= 58.5\,\mathrm{g\,mol^{-1}}$$

$$\mathrm{number\ of\ moles} = \frac{mass}{molar\ mass}$$

$$= \frac{117.0}{58.5}$$

$$= 2.0\,\mathrm{mol}$$

WORKED EXAMPLE

2 What mass of sodium hydroxide, NaOH, is present in 0.25 mol of sodium hydroxide?

(A_r values: H = 1.0, Na = 23.0, O = 16.0)

molar mass of NaOH = 23.0 + 16.0 + 1.0

$$= 40.0\,\mathrm{g\,mol^{-1}}$$

mass = number of moles × molar mass

$$= 0.25 \times 40.0\,\mathrm{g}$$

$$= 10.0\,\mathrm{g\ NaOH}$$

QUESTION

4 Use these A_r values: C = 12.0, Fe = 55.8, H = 1.0, O = 16.0, Na = 23.0.

Calculate the mass of the following:

a 0.20 moles of carbon dioxide, CO_2

b 0.050 moles of sodium carbonate, Na_2CO_3

c 5.00 moles of iron(II) hydroxide, $Fe(OH)_2$

Figure 1.8 From left to right, one mole of each of copper, bromine, carbon, mercury and lead.

QUESTION

3 a Use these A_r values (Fe = 55.8, N = 14.0, O = 16.0, S = 32.1) to calculate the amount of substance in moles in each of the following:

  i 10.7 g of sulfur atoms

  ii 64.2 g of sulfur molecules (S_8)

  iii 60.45 g of anhydrous iron(III) nitrate, $Fe(NO_3)_3$.

b Use the value of the Avogadro constant (6.02 × $10^{23}\,\mathrm{mol^{-1}}$) to calculate the total number of atoms in 7.10 g of chlorine atoms. (A_r value: Cl = 35.5)

To find the mass of a substance present in a given number of moles, you need to rearrange the equation

$$\mathrm{number\ of\ moles\ (mol)} = \frac{mass\ of\ substance\ in\ grams\ (g)}{molar\ mass\ (g\,mol^{-1})}$$

mass of substance (g)

$$= \mathrm{number\ of\ moles\ (mol) \times molar\ mass\ (g\,mol^{-1})}$$

Mole calculations

Reacting masses

When reacting chemicals together we may need to know what mass of each reactant to use so that they react exactly and there is no waste. To calculate this we need to know the chemical equation. This shows us the ratio of moles of the reactants and products – the **stoichiometry** of the equation. The balanced equation shows this stoichiometry. For example, in the reaction

$$Fe_2O_3 + 3CO \longrightarrow 2Fe + 3CO_2$$

1 mole of iron(III) oxide reacts with 3 moles of carbon monoxide to form 2 moles of iron and 3 moles of carbon dioxide. The stoichiometry of the equation is 1 : 3 : 2 : 3. The large numbers that are included in the equation (3, 2 and 3) are called stoichiometric numbers.

In order to find the mass of products formed in a chemical reaction we use:

- the mass of the reactants
- the molar mass of the reactants
- the balanced equation.

Figure 1.9 Iron reacting with sulfur to produce iron sulfide. We can calculate exactly how much iron is needed to react with sulfur and the mass of the products formed by knowing the molar mass of each reactant and the balanced chemical equation.

3   Magnesium burns in oxygen to form magnesium oxide.

$$2Mg + O_2 \longrightarrow 2MgO$$

We can calculate the mass of oxygen needed to react with 1 mole of magnesium. We can calculate the mass of magnesium oxide formed.

Step 1 Write the balanced equation.

Step 2 Multiply each formula mass in g by the relevant stoichiometric number in the equation.

2Mg	+	O_2	$\longrightarrow$	2MgO
$2 \times 24.3\,g$		$1 \times 32.0\,g$		$2 \times (24.3\,g + 16.0\,g)$
$48.6\,g$		$32.0\,g$		$80.6\,g$

From this calculation we can deduce that:

- $32.0\,g$ of oxygen are needed to react exactly with $48.6\,g$ of magnesium
- $80.6\,g$ of magnesium oxide are formed.

If we burn $12.15\,g$ of magnesium ($0.5\,mol$) we get $20.15\,g$ of magnesium oxide. This is because the stoichiometry of the reaction shows us that for every mole of magnesium burnt we get the same number of moles of magnesium oxide.

In this type of calculation we do not always need to know the molar mass of each of the reactants. If one or more of the reactants is in excess, we need only know the mass in grams and the molar mass of the reactant that is not in excess (the limiting reactant).

4   Iron(III) oxide reacts with carbon monoxide to form iron and carbon dioxide.

$$Fe_2O_3 + 3CO \longrightarrow 2Fe + 3CO_2$$

Calculate the maximum mass of iron produced when $798\,g$ of iron(III) oxide is reduced by excess carbon monoxide.

(A_r values: Fe = 55.8, O = 16.0)

Step 1 $Fe_2O_3 + 3CO \longrightarrow 2Fe + 3CO_2$

Step 2 1 mole iron(III) oxide $\longrightarrow$ 2 moles iron

$(2 \times 55.8) + (3 \times 16.0) \longrightarrow 2 \times 55.8$

$159.6\,g\ Fe_2O_3 \longrightarrow 111.6\,g\ Fe$

Step 3 $798\,g$

$\dfrac{111.6}{159.6} \times 798$

$= 558\,g\ Fe$

You can see that in step **3**, we have simply used ratios to calculate the amount of iron produced from $798\,g$ of iron(III) oxide.

5   **a**   Sodium reacts with excess oxygen to form sodium peroxide, Na_2O_2.

$$2Na + O_2 \longrightarrow Na_2O_2$$

Calculate the maximum mass of sodium peroxide formed when $4.60\,g$ of sodium is burnt in excess oxygen.

(A_r values: Na = 23.0, O = 16.0)

b   Tin(IV) oxide is reduced to tin by carbon. Carbon monoxide is also formed.

$$SnO_2 + 2C \longrightarrow Sn + 2CO$$

Calculate the mass of carbon that exactly reacts with $14.0\,g$ of tin(IV) oxide. Give your answer to 3 significant figures.

(A_r values: C = 12.0, O = 16.0, Sn = 118.7)

The stoichiometry of a reaction

We can find the stoichiometry of a reaction if we know the amounts of each reactant that exactly react together and the amounts of each product formed.

For example, if we react $4.0\,g$ of hydrogen with $32.0\,g$ of oxygen we get $36.0\,g$ of water. (A_r values: H = 1.0, O = 16.0) hydrogen (H_2) + oxygen (O_2) $\longrightarrow$ water (H_2O)

$$\frac{4.0}{2 \times 1.0} \qquad \frac{32.0}{2 \times 16.0} \qquad \frac{36.0}{(2 \times 1.0) + 16.0}$$

$$= 2 \text{ mol} \qquad = 1 \text{ mol} \qquad = 2 \text{ mol}$$

This ratio is the ratio of stoichiometric numbers in the equation. So the equation is:

$$2H_2 + O_2 \longrightarrow 2H_2O$$

We can still deduce the stoichiometry of this reaction even if we do not know the mass of oxygen that reacted. The ratio of hydrogen to water is $1:1$. But there is only one atom of oxygen in a molecule of water – half the amount in an oxygen molecule. So the mole ratio of oxygen to water in the equation must be $1:2$.

QUESTION

6 56.2 g of silicon, Si, reacts exactly with 284.0 g of chlorine, Cl_2, to form 340.2 g of silicon(IV) chloride, $SiCl_4$. Use this information to calculate the stoichiometry of the reaction.

(A_r values: Cl = 35.5, Si = 28.1)

Significant figures

When we perform chemical calculations it is important that we give the answer to the number of significant figures that fits with the data provided. The examples show the number 526.84 rounded up to varying numbers of significant figures.

rounded to 4 significant figures = 526.8
rounded to 3 significant figures = 527
rounded to 2 significant figures = 530

When you are writing an answer to a calculation, the answer should be to the same number of significant figures as the least number of significant figures in the data.

WORKED EXAMPLE

5 How many moles of calcium oxide are there in 2.9 g of calcium oxide?

(A_r values: Ca = 40.1, O = 16.0)

If you divide 2.9 by 56.1, your calculator shows 0.051 693 …. The least number of significant figures in the data, however, is 2 (the mass is 2.9 g). So your answer should be expressed to 2 significant figures, as 0.052 mol.

WORKED EXAMPLE (CONTINUED)

Note 1 Zeros before a number are not significant figures. For example, 0.004 is only to 1 significant figure.

Note 2 After the decimal point, zeros after a number are significant figures. 0.0040 has 2 significant figures and 0.004 00 has 3 significant figures.

Note 3 If you are performing a calculation with several steps, do not round up in between steps. Round up at the end.

Percentage composition by mass

We can use the formula of a compound and relative atomic masses to calculate the percentage by mass of a particular element in a compound.

% by mass

$$= \frac{\text{atomic mass} \times \text{number of moles of particular element in a compound}}{\text{molar mass of compound}} \times 100$$

WORKED EXAMPLE

6 Calculate the percentage by mass of iron in iron(III) oxide, Fe_2O_3.

(A_r values: Fe = 55.8, O = 16.0)

$$\% \text{ mass of iron} = \frac{2 \times 55.8}{(2 \times 55.8) + (3 \times 16.0)} \times 100$$

$$= 69.9\%$$

Figure 1.10 This iron ore is impure Fe_2O_3. We can calculate the mass of iron that can be obtained from Fe_2O_3 by using molar masses.

QUESTION

7   Calculate the percentage by mass of carbon in ethanol, C_2H_5OH.

(A_r values: C = 12.0, H = 1.0, O = 16.0)

Empirical formulae

The **empirical formula** of a compound is the simplest whole number ratio of the elements present in one molecule or formula unit of the compound. The **molecular formula** of a compound shows the total number of atoms of each element present in a molecule.

Table 1.2 shows the empirical and molecular formulae for a number of compounds.

■   The formula for an ionic compound is always its empirical formula.

■   The empirical formula and molecular formula for simple inorganic molecules are often the same.

■   Organic molecules often have different empirical and molecular formulae.

Compound	Empirical formula	Molecular formula
water	H_2O	H_2O
hydrogen peroxide	HO	H_2O_2
sulfur dioxide	SO_2	SO_2
butane	C_2H_5	C_4H_{10}
cyclohexane	CH_2	C_6H_{12}

Table 1.2 Some empirical and molecular formulae.

QUESTION

8   Write the empirical formula for:

a   hydrazine, N_2H_4

b   octane, C_8H_{18}

c   benzene, C_6H_6

d   ammonia, NH_3

The empirical formula can be found by determining the mass of each element present in a sample of the compound. For some compounds this can be done by combustion. An organic compound must be very pure in order to calculate its empirical formula. Chemists often use gas chromatography to purify compounds before carrying out formula analysis.

WORKED EXAMPLES

7   Deduce the formula of magnesium oxide.

This can be found as follows:

■   burn a known mass of magnesium (0.486 g) in excess oxygen

■   record the mass of magnesium oxide formed (0.806 g)

■   calculate the mass of oxygen that has combined with the magnesium (0.806 – 0.486 g) = 0.320 g

■   calculate the mole ratio of magnesium to oxygen

■   (A_r values: Mg = 24.3, O = 16.0)

$$\text{moles of Mg} = \frac{0.486\,g}{24.3\,g\,mol^{-1}} = 0.0200\,mol$$

$$\text{moles of oxygen} = \frac{0.320\,g}{16.0\,g\,mol^{-1}} = 0.0200\,mol$$

The simplest ratio of magnesium : oxygen is 1 : 1. So the empirical formula of magnesium oxide is MgO.

8   When 1.55 g of phosphorus is completely combusted 3.55 g of an oxide of phosphorus is produced. Deduce the empirical formula of this oxide of phosphorus.

(A_r values: O = 16.0, P = 31.0)

		P	**O**
Step 1	note the mass of each element	1.55 g	3.55 – 1.55 = 2.00 g
Step 2	divide by atomic masses	$\frac{1.55\,g}{31.0\,g\,mol^{-1}}$ = 0.05 mol	$\frac{2.00\,g}{16.0\,g\,mol^{-11}}$ = 0.125 mol
Step 3	divide by the lowest figure	$\frac{0.05}{0.05} = 1$	$\frac{0.125}{0.05} = 2.5$
Step 4	if needed, obtain the lowest whole number ratio to get empirical formula		P_2O_5

An empirical formula can also be deduced from data that give the percentage composition by mass of the elements in a compound.

WORKED EXAMPLE

9 A compound of carbon and hydrogen contains 85.7% carbon and 14.3% hydrogen by mass. Deduce the empirical formula of this hydrocarbon.
(A_r values: C = 12.0, O = 16.0)

	C	**H**
Step 1 note the % by mass	85.7	14.3
Step 2 divide by A_r values	$\frac{85.7}{12.0} = 7.142$	$\frac{14.3}{1.0} = 14.3$
Step 3 divide by the lowest figure	$\frac{7.142}{7.142} = 1$	$\frac{14.3}{7.142} = 2$

Empirical formula is CH_2.

QUESTION

9 The composition by mass of a hydrocarbon is 10% hydrogen and 90% carbon. Deduce the empirical formula of this hydrocarbon.
(A_r values: C = 12.0, H = 1.0)

Molecular formulae

The molecular formula shows the actual number of each of the different atoms present in a molecule. The molecular formula is more useful than the empirical formula. We use the molecular formula to write balanced equations and to calculate molar masses. The molecular formula is always a multiple of the empirical formula. For example, the molecular formula of ethane, C_2H_6, is two times the empirical formula, CH_3.

In order to deduce the molecular formula we need to know:

- the relative formula mass of the compound
- the empirical formula.

WORKED EXAMPLE

10 A compound has the empirical formula CH_2Br. Its relative molecular mass is 187.8. Deduce the molecular formula of this compound.
(A_r values: Br = 79.9, C = 12.0, H = 1.0)

Step 1 find the empirical formula mass:
$12.0 + (2 \times 1.0) + 79.9 = 93.9$

WORKED EXAMPLE (CONTINUED)

Step 2 divide the relative molecular mass by the empirical formula mass: $\frac{187.8}{93.9} = 2$

Step 3 multiply the number of atoms in the empirical formula by the number in step 2:
$2 \times CH_2Br$, so molecular formula is $C_2H_4Br_2$.

QUESTION

10 The empirical formulae and molar masses of three compounds, A, B and C, are shown in the table below. Calculate the molecular formula of each of these compounds.
(A_r values: C = 12.0, Cl = 35.5, H = 1.0)

Compound	Empirical formula	M_r
A	C_3H_5	82
B	CCl_3	237
C	CH_2	112

Chemical formulae and chemical equations

Deducing the formula

The electronic structure of the individual elements in a compound determines the formula of a compound (see page 33). The formula of an ionic compound is determined by the charges on each of the ions present. The number of positive charges is balanced by the number of negative charges so that the total charge on the compound is zero. We can work out the formula for a compound if we know the charges on the ions. Figure 1.11 shows the charges on some simple ions related to the position of the elements in the Periodic Table. The form of the Periodic Table that we shall be using has 18 groups because the transition elements are numbered as Groups 3 to 12. So, aluminium is in Group 13 and chlorine is in Group 17.

For simple metal ions in Groups 1 and 2, the value of the positive charge is the same as the group number. For a simple metal ion in Group 13, the value of the positive charge is 3+. For a simple non-metal ion in Groups 15 to 17, the value of the negative charge is 18 minus the group

Group		H⁺						18
1	2		13	14	15	16	17	none
Li⁺	Be²⁺					O²⁻	F⁻	none
Na⁺	Mg²⁺		Al³⁺			S²⁻	Cl⁻	none
K⁺	Ca²⁺	transition elements	Ga³⁺				Br⁻	none
Rb⁺	Sr²⁺						I⁻	none

Figure 1.11 The charge on some simple ions is related to their position in the Periodic Table.

number. The charge on the ions of transition elements can vary. For example, iron forms two types of ions, Fe^{2+} and Fe^{3+} (Figure 1.12).

Figure 1.12 Iron(II) chloride (left) and iron(III) chloride (right). These two chlorides of iron both contain iron and chlorine, but they have different formulae.

Ions that contain more than one type of atom are called compound ions. Some common compound ions that you should learn are listed in Table 1.3. The formula for an ionic compound is obtained by balancing the charges of the ions.

Ion	Formula
ammonium	NH_4^+
carbonate	CO_3^{2-}
hydrogencarbonate	HCO_3^-
hydroxide	OH^-
nitrate	NO_3^-
phosphate	PO_4^{3-}
sulfate	SO_4^{2-}

Table 1.3 The formulae of some common compound ions.

WORKED EXAMPLES

11 Deduce the formula of magnesium chloride.

Ions present: Mg^{2+} and Cl^-.

For electrical neutrality, we need two Cl^- ions for every Mg^{2+} ion. $(2 \times 1-) + (1 \times 2+) = 0$

So the formula is $MgCl_2$.

12 Deduce the formula of aluminium oxide.

Ions present: Al^{3+} and O^{2-}.

For electrical neutrality, we need three O^{2-} ions for every two Al^{3+} ions. $(3 \times 2-) + (2 \times 3+) = 0$

So the formula is Al_2O_3.

The formula of a covalent compound is deduced from the number of electrons needed to achieve the stable electronic configuration of a noble gas (see page 49). In general, carbon atoms form four bonds with other atoms, hydrogen and halogen atoms form one bond and oxygen atoms form two bonds. So the formula of water, H_2O, follows these rules. The formula for methane is CH_4, with each carbon atom bonding with four hydrogen atoms. However, there are many exceptions to these rules.

Compounds containing a simple metal ion and non-metal ion are named by changing the end of the name of the non-metal element to -ide.

sodium + chlorine $\longrightarrow$ sodium chloride

zinc + sulfur $\longrightarrow$ zinc sulfide

Compound ions containing oxygen are usually called -ates. For example, the sulfate ion contains sulfur and oxygen, the phosphate ion contains phosphorus and oxygen.

QUESTION

11 a Write down the formula of each of the following compounds:

    i magnesium nitrate

    ii calcium sulfate

    iii sodium iodide

    iv hydrogen bromide

    v sodium sulfide

  b Name each of the following compounds:

    i Na_3PO_4 iii $AlCl_3$

    ii $(NH_4)_2SO_4$ iv $Ca(NO_3)_2$

11

Balancing chemical equations

When chemicals react, atoms cannot be either created or destroyed. So there must be the same number of each type of atom on the reactants side of a chemical equation as there are on the products side. A symbol equation is a shorthand way of describing a chemical reaction. It shows the number and type of the atoms in the reactants and the number and type of atoms in the products. If these are the same, we say the equation is balanced. Follow these examples to see how we balance an equation.

WORKED EXAMPLES

13 Balancing an equation

Step 1 Write down the formulae of all the reactants and products. For example:

$$H_2 \quad + \quad O_2 \quad \longrightarrow \quad H_2O$$

Step 2 Count the number of atoms of each reactant and product.

$$H_2 \quad + \quad O_2 \quad \longrightarrow \quad H_2O$$
$$2[H] \qquad 2[O] \qquad\qquad 2[H] + 1[O]$$

Step 3 Balance one of the atoms by placing a number in front of one of the reactants or products. In this case the oxygen atoms on the right-hand side need to be balanced, so that they are equal in number to those on the left-hand side. Remember that the number in front multiplies everything in the formula. For example, $2H_2O$ has 4 hydrogen atoms and 2 oxygen atoms.

$$H_2 \quad + \quad O_2 \quad \longrightarrow \quad 2H_2O$$
$$2[H] \qquad 2[O] \qquad\qquad 4[H] + 2[O]$$

Step 4 Keep balancing in this way, one type of atom at a time until all the atoms are balanced.

$$2H_2 \quad + \quad O_2 \quad \longrightarrow \quad 2H_2O$$
$$4[H] \qquad 2[O] \qquad\qquad 4[H] + 2[O]$$

Note that when you balance an equation you must not change the formulae of any of the reactants or products.

14 Write a balanced equation for the reaction of iron(III) oxide with carbon monoxide to form iron and carbon dioxide.

Step 1 formulae $\quad Fe_2O_3 + CO \longrightarrow Fe + CO_2$

Step 2 count the number of atoms $\quad Fe_2O_3 + CO \longrightarrow Fe + CO_2$

	2[Fe]+	1[C]+	1[Fe]	1[C]+
	3[O]	1[O]		2[O]

WORKED EXAMPLES (CONTINUED)

Step 3 balance the iron $\quad Fe_2O_3 + CO \longrightarrow 2Fe + CO_2$

	2[Fe]+	1[C]+	2[Fe] +	1[C]+
	3[O]	1[O]		2[O]

Step 4 balance the oxygen $\quad Fe_2O_3 + 3CO \longrightarrow 2Fe + 3CO_2$

	2[Fe]+	3[C]+	2[Fe] +	3[C]+
	3[O]	3[O]		6[O]

In step 4 the oxygen in the CO_2 comes from two places, the Fe_2O_3 and the CO. In order to balance the equation, the same number of oxygen atoms (3) must come from the iron oxide as come from the carbon monoxide.

QUESTION

12 Write balanced equations for the following reactions.

a Iron reacts with hydrochloric acid to form iron(II) chloride, $FeCl_2$, and hydrogen.

b Aluminium hydroxide, $Al(OH)_3$, decomposes on heating to form aluminium oxide, Al_2O_3, and water.

c Hexane, C_6H_{14}, burns in oxygen to form carbon dioxide and water.

Using state symbols

We sometimes find it useful to specify the physical states of the reactants and products in a chemical reaction. This is especially important where chemical equilibrium and rates of reaction are being discussed (see Chapter 8 and Chapter 9). We use the following **state symbols**:

- (s) solid
- (l) liquid
- (g) gas
- (aq) aqueous (a solution in water).

State symbols are written after the formula of each reactant and product. For example:

$$ZnCO_3(s) + H_2SO_4(aq) \longrightarrow ZnSO_4(aq) + H_2O(l) + CO_2(g)$$

QUESTION

13 Write balanced equations, including state symbols, for the following reactions.

a Solid calcium carbonate reacts with aqueous hydrochloric acid to form water, carbon dioxide and an aqueous solution of calcium chloride.

b An aqueous solution of zinc sulfate, $ZnSO_4$, reacts with an aqueous solution of sodium hydroxide. The products are a precipitate of zinc hydroxide, $Zn(OH)_2$, and an aqueous solution of sodium sulfate.

Figure 1.13 The reaction between calcium carbonate and hydrochloric acid. The equation for this reaction, with all the state symbols, is:

$$CaCO_3(s) + 2HCl(aq) \longrightarrow CaCl_2(aq) + CO_2(g) + H_2O(l)$$

Balancing ionic equations

When ionic compounds dissolve in water, the ions separate from each other. For example:

$$NaCl(s) + aq \longrightarrow Na^+(aq) + Cl^-(aq)$$

Ionic compounds include salts such as sodium bromide, magnesium sulfate and ammonium nitrate. Acids and alkalis also contain ions. For example $H^+(aq)$ and $Cl^-(aq)$ ions are present in hydrochloric acid and $Na^+(aq)$ and $OH^-(aq)$ ions are present in sodium hydroxide.

Many chemical reactions in aqueous solution involve ionic compounds. Only some of the ions in solution take part in these reactions.

The ions that play no part in the reaction are called spectator ions.

An ionic equation is simpler than a full chemical equation. It shows only the ions or other particles that are reacting. Spectator ions are omitted. Compare the full equation for the reaction of zinc with aqueous copper(II) sulfate with the ionic equation.

full chemical equation: $Zn(s) + CuSO_4(aq)$
$$\longrightarrow ZnSO_4(aq) + Cu(s)$$

with charges: $Zn(s) + Cu^{2+}SO_4{}^{2-}(aq)$
$$\longrightarrow Zn^{2+}SO_4{}^{2-}(aq) + Cu(s)$$

cancelling spectator ions: $Zn(s) + Cu^{2+}\cancel{SO_4{}^{2-}(aq)}$
$$\longrightarrow Zn^{2+}\cancel{SO_4{}^{2-}(aq)} + Cu(s)$$

ionic equation: $Zn(s) + Cu^{2+}(aq)$
$$\longrightarrow Zn^{2+}(aq) + Cu(s)$$

In the ionic equation you will notice that:

- there are no sulfate ions – these are the spectator ions as they have not changed
- both the charges and the atoms are balanced.

The next examples show how we can change a full equation into an ionic equation.

WORKED EXAMPLES

15 Writing an ionic equation

Step 1 Write down the full balanced equation.

$$Mg(s) + 2HCl(aq) \longrightarrow MgCl_2(aq) + H_2(g)$$

Step 2 Write down all the ions present. Any reactant or product that has a state symbol (s), (l) or (g) or is a molecule in solution such as chlorine, $Cl_2(aq)$, does not split into ions.

$$Mg(s) + 2H^+(aq) + 2Cl^-(aq)$$
$$\longrightarrow Mg^{2+}(aq) + 2Cl^-(aq) + H_2(g)$$

Step 3 Cancel the ions that appear on both sides of the equation (the spectator ions).

$$Mg(s) + 2H^+(aq) + \cancel{2Cl^-(aq)}$$
$$\longrightarrow Mg^{2+}(aq) + \cancel{2Cl^-(aq)} + H_2(g)$$

Step 4 Write down the equation omitting the spectator ions.

$$Mg(s) + 2H^+(aq) \longrightarrow Mg^{2+}(aq) + H_2(g)$$

16 Write the ionic equation for the reaction of aqueous chlorine with aqueous potassium bromide. The products are aqueous bromine and aqueous potassium chloride.

Step 1 The full balanced equation is:

$$Cl_2(aq) + 2KBr(aq) \longrightarrow Br_2(aq) + 2KCl(aq)$$

Step 2 The ions present are:

$$Cl_2(aq) + 2K^+(aq) + 2Br^-(aq)$$
$$\longrightarrow Br_2(aq) + 2K^+(aq) + 2Cl^-(aq)$$

Step 3 Cancel the spectator ions:

$$Cl_2(aq) + \cancel{2K^+(aq)} + 2Br^-(aq)$$
$$\longrightarrow Br_2(aq) + \cancel{2K^+(aq)} + 2Cl^-(aq)$$

Step 4 Write the final ionic equation:

$$Cl_2(aq) + 2Br^-(aq) \longrightarrow Br_2(aq) + 2Cl^-(aq)$$

13

14 Change these full equations to ionic equations.

   a $H_2SO_4(aq) + 2NaOH(aq) \longrightarrow 2H_2O(aq) + Na_2SO_4(aq)$

   b $Br_2(aq) + 2KI(aq) \longrightarrow 2KBr(aq) + I_2(aq)$

Chemists usually prefer to write ionic equations for precipitation reactions. A precipitation reaction is a reaction where two aqueous solutions react to form a solid – the precipitate. For these reactions the method of writing the ionic equation can be simplified. All you have to do is:

■ write the formula of the precipitate as the product

■ write the ions that go to make up the precipitate as the reactants.

WORKED EXAMPLE

17 An aqueous solution of iron(II) sulfate reacts with an aqueous solution of sodium hydroxide. A precipitate of iron(II) hydroxide is formed, together with an aqueous solution of sodium sulfate.

   ■ Write the full balanced equation:

   $FeSO_4(aq) + 2NaOH(aq) \longrightarrow Fe(OH)_2(s) + Na_2SO_4(aq)$

   ■ The ionic equation is:

   $Fe^{2+}(aq) + 2OH^-(aq) \longrightarrow Fe(OH)_2(s)$

QUESTION

15 Write ionic equations for these precipitation reactions.

   a $CuSO_4(aq) + 2NaOH(aq)$
   $\longrightarrow Cu(OH)_2(s) + Na_2SO_4(aq)$

   b $Pb(NO_3)_2(aq) + 2KI(aq) \longrightarrow PbI_2(s) + 2KNO_3(aq)$

Solutions and concentration

Calculating the concentration of a solution

The concentration of a solution is the amount of solute dissolved in a solvent to make $1\,dm^3$ (one cubic decimetre) of solution. The solvent is usually water. There are $1000\,cm^3$ in a cubic decimetre. When 1 mole of a compound is dissolved to make $1\,dm^3$ of solution the concentration is $1\,mol\,dm^{-3}$.

$$\text{concentration (mol\,dm}^{-3}) = \frac{\text{number of moles of solute (mol)}}{\text{volume of solution (dm}^3)}$$

We use the terms 'concentrated' and 'dilute' to refer to the relative amount of solute in the solution. A solution with a low concentration of solute is a dilute solution. If there is a high concentration of solute, the solution is concentrated.

When performing calculations involving concentrations in $mol\,dm^{-3}$ you need to:

■ change mass in grams to moles

■ change cm^3 to dm^3 (by dividing the number of cm^3 by 1000).

WORKED EXAMPLE

18 Calculate the concentration in $mol\,dm^{-3}$ of sodium hydroxide, NaOH, if $250\,cm^3$ of a solution contains $2.0\,g$ of sodium hydroxide.

   (M_r value: NaOH = 40.0)

   Step 1 Change grams to moles.

   $\dfrac{2.0}{40.0} = 0.050\,mol\,NaOH$

   Step 2 Change cm^3 to dm^3.

   $250\,cm^3 = \dfrac{250}{1000}\,dm^3 = 0.25\,dm^3$

   Step 3 Calculate concentration.

   $\dfrac{0.050\,(mol)}{0.25\,(dm^3)} = 0.20\,mol\,dm^{-3}$

Figure 1.14 The concentration of chlorine in the water in a swimming pool must be carefully controlled.

We often need to calculate the mass of a substance present in a solution of known concentration and volume. To do this we:

■ rearrange the concentration equation to:

number of moles (mol)
= concentration (mol dm^{-3}) × volume (dm^3)

■ multiply the moles of solute by its molar mass

mass of solute (g)
= number of moles (mol) × molar mass (g mol^{-1})

WORKED EXAMPLE

19 Calculate the mass of anhydrous copper(II) sulfate in 55 cm^3 of a 0.20 mol dm^{-3} solution of copper(II) sulfate. (A_r values: Cu = 63.5, O = 16.0, S = 32.1)

Step 1 Change cm^3 to dm^3.

$$= \frac{55}{1000} = 0.055 \, dm^3$$

Step 2 moles = concentration (mol dm^{-3})
× volume of solution (dm^3)

$$= 0.20 × 0.055 = 0.011 \, mol$$

Step 3 mass (g) = moles × M

$$= 0.011 × (63.5 + 32.1 + (4 × 16.0))$$

$$= 1.8 \, g \text{ (to 2 significant figures)}$$

QUESTION

16 a Calculate the concentration, in mol dm^{-3}, of the following solutions: (A_r values: C = 12.0, H = 1.0, Na = 23.0, O = 16.0)

   i a solution of sodium hydroxide, NaOH, containing 2.0 g of sodium hydroxide in 50 cm^3 of solution

   ii a solution of ethanoic acid, CH$_3$CO$_2$H, containing 12.0 g of ethanoic acid in 250 cm^3 of solution.

   b Calculate the number of moles of solute dissolved in each of the following:

   i 40 cm^3 of aqueous nitric acid of concentration 0.2 mol dm^{-3}

   ii 50 cm^3 of calcium hydroxide solution of concentration 0.01 mol dm^{-3}.

CARRYING OUT A TITRATION

A procedure called a titration is used to determine the amount of substance present in a solution of unknown concentration. There are several different kinds of titration. One of the commonest involves the exact neutralisation of an alkali by an acid (Figure 1.15).

If we want to determine the concentration of a solution of sodium hydroxide we use the following procedure.

■ Get some of acid of known concentration.

■ Fill a clean burette with the acid (after having washed the burette with a little of the acid).

■ Record the initial burette reading.

■ Measure a known volume of the alkali into a titration flask using a graduated (volumetric) pipette.

■ Add an indicator solution to the alkali in the flask.

■ Slowly add the acid from the burette to the flask, swirling the flask all the time until the indicator changes colour (the end-point).

■ Record the final burette reading. The final reading minus the initial reading is called the **titre**. This first titre is normally known as a 'rough' value.

■ Repeat this process, adding the acid drop by drop near the end-point.

■ Repeat again, until you have two titres that are no more than 0.10 cm^3 apart.

■ Take the average of these two titre values.

Your results should be recorded in a table, looking like this:

	rough	1	2	3
final burette reading / cm^3	37.60	38.65	36.40	34.75
initial burette reading / cm^3	2.40	4.00	1.40	0.00
titre / cm^3	35.20	34.65	35.00	34.75

CARRYING OUT A TITRATION (CONTINUED)

Figure 1.15 a A funnel is used to fill the burette with hydrochloric acid. **b** A graduated pipette is used to measure 25.0 cm³ of sodium hydroxide solution into a conical flask. **c** An indicator called litmus is added to the sodium hydroxide solution, which turns blue. **d** 12.5 cm³ of hydrochloric acid from the burette have been added to the 25.0 cm³ of alkali in the conical flask. The litmus has gone red, showing that this volume of acid was just enough to neutralise the alkali.

You should note:

- all burette readings are given to an accuracy of 0.05 cm³
- the units are shown like this '/ cm³'
- the two titres that are no more than 0.10 cm³ apart are 1 and 3, so they would be averaged
- the average titre is 34.70 cm³.

In every titration there are five important pieces of knowledge:

1 the balanced equation for the reaction
2 the volume of the solution in the burette (in the example above this is hydrochloric acid)
3 the concentration of the solution in the burette
4 the volume of the solution in the titration flask (in the example above this is sodium hydroxide)
5 the concentration of the solution in the titration flask.

If we know four of these five things, we can calculate the fifth. So in order to calculate the concentration of sodium hydroxide in the flask we need to know the first four of these points.

Calculating solution concentration by titration

A titration is often used to find the exact concentration of a solution. Worked example **20** shows the steps used to calculate the concentration of a solution of sodium hydroxide when it is neutralised by aqueous sulfuric acid of known concentration and volume.

WORKED EXAMPLE

20 $25.0\,cm^3$ of a solution of sodium hydroxide is exactly neutralised by $15.10\,cm^3$ of sulfuric acid of concentration $0.200\,mol\,dm^{-3}$.

$$2NaOH + H_2SO_4 \longrightarrow Na_2SO_4 + 2H_2O$$

Calculate the concentration, in $mol\,dm^{-3}$, of the sodium hydroxide solution.

Step 1 Calculate the moles of acid.

moles = concentration $(mol\,dm^{-3})$
$\qquad\qquad\qquad \times$ volume of solution (dm^3)

$0.200 \times \dfrac{15.10}{1000} = 0.003\,02\,mol\ H_2SO_4$

Step 2 Use the stoichiometry of the balanced equation to calculate the moles of NaOH.

moles of NaOH = moles of acid (from step 1) × 2

Step 3 Calculate the concentration of NaOH.

concentration $(mol\,dm^{-3})$
$\qquad = \dfrac{\text{number of moles of solute (mol)}}{\text{volume of solution } (dm^3)}$
$\qquad = \dfrac{0.00604}{0.0250}$
$\qquad = 0.242\,mol\,dm^{-3}$

Note 1 In the first step we use the reagent for which the concentration and volume are both known.

Note 2 In step 2, we multiply by 2 because the balanced equation shows that 2 mol of NaOH react with every 1 mol of H_2SO_4.

Note 3 In step 3, we divide by 0.0250 because we have changed cm^3 to dm^3 $\left(0.0250 = \dfrac{25.0}{1000}\right)$.

Note 4 The answer is given to 3 significant figures because the smallest number of significant figures in the data is 3.

QUESTION

17 a The equation for the reaction of strontium hydroxide with hydrochloric acid is shown below.

$$Sr(OH)_2 + 2HCl \longrightarrow SrCl_2 + 2H_2O$$

$25.0\,cm^3$ of a solution of strontium hydroxide was exactly neutralised by $15.00\,cm^3$ of $0.100\,mol\,dm^{-3}$ hydrochloric acid. Calculate the concentration, in $mol\,dm^{-3}$, of the strontium hydroxide solution.

b $20.0\,cm^3$ of a $0.400\,mol\,dm^{-3}$ solution of sodium hydroxide was exactly neutralised by $25.25\,cm^3$ of sulfuric acid. Calculate the concentration, in $mol\,dm^{-3}$, of the sulfuric acid. The equation for the reaction is:

$$H_2SO_4 + 2NaOH \longrightarrow Na_2SO_4 + 2H_2O$$

Deducing stoichiometry by titration

We can use titration results to find the stoichiometry of a reaction. In order to do this, we need to know the concentrations and the volumes of both the reactants. The example below shows how to determine the stoichiometry of the reaction between a metal hydroxide and an acid.

WORKED EXAMPLE

21 $25.0\,cm^3$ of a $0.0500\,mol\,dm^{-3}$ solution of a metal hydroxide was titrated against a solution of $0.200\,mol\,dm^{-3}$ hydrochloric acid. It required $12.50\,cm^3$ of hydrochloric acid to exactly neutralise the metal hydroxide. Deduce the stoichiometry of this reaction.

Step 1 Calculate the number of moles of each reagent.

moles of metal hydroxide
$\quad$ = concentration $(mol\,dm^{-3})$ × volume of solution (dm^3)
$\quad = 0.0500 \times \dfrac{25.0}{1000} = 1.25 \times 10^{-3}\,mol$

moles of hydrochloric acid
$\quad$ = concentration $(mol\,dm^{-3})$ × volume of solution (dm^3)
$\quad = 0.200 \times \dfrac{12.50}{1000} = 2.50 \times 10^{-3}\,mol$

Step 2 Deduce the simplest mole ratio of metal hydroxide to hydrochloric acid.

1.25×10^{-3} moles of hydroxide : 2.50×10^{-3} moles of acid

$\quad = 1$ hydroxide : 2 acid

WORKED EXAMPLE (CONTINUED)

Step 3 Write the equation.

$$M(OH)_2 + 2HCl \longrightarrow MCl_2 + 2H_2O$$

One mole of hydroxide ions neutralises one mole of hydrogen ions. As one mole of the metal hydroxide neutralises two moles of hydrochloric acid, the metal hydroxide must contain two hydroxide ions in each formula unit.

QUESTION

18 $20.0\,cm^3$ of a metal hydroxide of concentration $0.0600\,mol\,dm^{-3}$ was titrated with $0.100\,mol\,dm^{-3}$ hydrochloric acid. It required $24.00\,cm^3$ of the hydrochloric acid to exactly neutralise the metal hydroxide.

    a Calculate the number of moles of metal hydroxide used.

    b Calculate the number of moles of hydrochloric acid used.

    c What is the simplest mole ratio of metal hydroxide to hydrochloric acid?

    d Write a balanced equation for this reaction using your answers to parts **a**, **b** and **c** to help you. Use the symbol **M** for the metal.

Calculations involving gas volumes

Using the molar gas volume

In 1811 the Italian scientist Amedeo Avogadro suggested that equal volumes of all gases contain the same number of molecules. This is called Avogadro's hypothesis. This idea is approximately true as long as the pressure is not too high or the temperature too low. It is convenient to measure volumes of gases at room temperature (20 °C) and pressure (1 atmosphere). At room temperature and pressure (r.t.p.) one mole of any gas has a volume of $24.0\,dm^3$. So, $24.0\,dm^3$ of carbon dioxide and $24.0\,dm^3$ of hydrogen both contain one mole of gas molecules.

We can use the molar gas volume of $24.0\,dm^3$ at r.t.p. to find:

- the volume of a given mass or number of moles of gas
- the mass or number of moles of a given volume of gas.

WORKED EXAMPLES

22 Calculate the volume of 0.40 mol of nitrogen at r.t.p.

    (volume (in dm^3) = 24.0 × number of moles of gas

    volume   = 24.0 × 0.40

                  = $9.6\,dm^3$

23 Calculate the mass of methane, CH_4, present in $120\,cm^3$ of methane.

    (M_r value: methane = 16.0)

    $120\,cm^3$ is $0.120\,dm^3 \left(\dfrac{120}{1000} = 0.120 \right)$

    moles of methane $= \dfrac{\text{volume of methane (dm}^3)}{24.0}$

                       $= \dfrac{0.120}{24.0}$

                       $= 5 \times 10^{-3}\,mol$

    mass of methane $= 5 \times 10^{-3} \times 16.0$

                       $= 0.080\,g$ methane

QUESTION

19 **a** Calculate the volume, in dm^3, occupied by 26.4 g of carbon dioxide at r.t.p.

        (A_r values: C = 12.0, O = 16.0)

    b A flask of volume $120\,cm^3$ is filled with helium gas at r.t.p. Calculate the mass of helium present in the flask.

        (A_r value: He = 4.0)

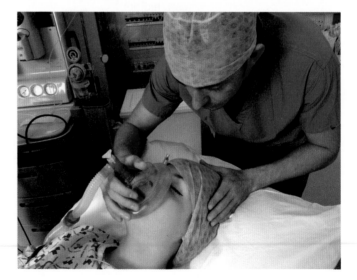

Figure 1.16 Anaesthetists have to know about gas volumes so that patients remain unconscious during major operations.

Gas volumes and stoichiometry

We can use the ratio of reacting volumes of gases to deduce the stoichiometry of a reaction. If we mix $20\,cm^3$ of hydrogen with $10\,cm^3$ of oxygen and explode the mixture, we will find that the gases have exactly reacted together and no hydrogen or oxygen remains. According to Avogadro's hypothesis, equal volumes of gases contain equal numbers of molecules and therefore equal numbers of moles of gases. So the mole ratio of hydrogen to oxygen is $2:1$. We can summarise this as:

$$hydrogen + oxygen \longrightarrow water$$
$$(H_2) \qquad (O_2) \qquad (H_2O)$$
$$20\,cm^3 \qquad 10\,cm^3$$

ratio of moles $\quad 2 \quad : \quad 1$

equation $\qquad 2H_2 \quad + \quad O_2 \longrightarrow 2H_2O$

We can extend this idea to experiments involving combustion data of hydrocarbons. The example below shows how the formula of propane and the stoichiometry of the equation can be deduced. Propane is a hydrocarbon – a compound of carbon and hydrogen only.

20 $50\,cm^3$ of a gaseous hydride of phosphorus, PH_n reacts with exactly $150\,cm^3$ of chlorine, Cl_2, to form liquid phosphorus trichloride and $150\,cm^3$ of hydrogen chloride gas, HCl.

    a How many moles of chlorine react with 1 mole of the gaseous hydride?

    b Deduce the formula of the phosphorus hydride.

    c Write a balanced equation for the reaction.

WORKED EXAMPLE

24 When $50\,cm^3$ of propane reacts exactly with $250\,cm^3$ of oxygen, $150\,cm^3$ of carbon dioxide is formed.

$$propane + oxygen \longrightarrow carbon\ dioxide + water$$
$$(O_2) \qquad\qquad (CO_2) \qquad (H_2O)$$
$$50\,cm^3 \quad 250\,cm^3 \qquad 150\,cm^3$$

ratio
of moles $\quad 1 \qquad 5 \qquad\qquad 3$

As 1 mole of propane produces 3 moles of carbon dioxide, there must be 3 moles of carbon atoms in one mole of propane.

$$C_3H_x + 5O_2 \longrightarrow 3CO_2 + yH_2O$$

The 5 moles of oxygen molecules are used to react with both the carbon and the hydrogen in the propane. 3 moles of these oxygen molecules have been used in forming carbon dioxide. So $5 - 3 = 2$ moles of oxygen molecules must be used in reacting with the hydrogen to form water. There are 4 moles of atoms in 2 moles of oxygen molecules. So there must be 4 moles of water formed.

$$C_3H_x + 5O_2 \longrightarrow 3CO_2 + 4H_2O$$

So there must be 8 hydrogen atoms in 1 molecule of propane.

$$C_3H_8 + 5O_2 \longrightarrow 3CO_2 + 4H_2O$$

Summary

- Relative atomic mass is the weighted average mass of naturally occurring atoms of an element on a scale where an atom of carbon-12 has a mass of exactly 12 units. Relative molecular mass, relative isotopic mass and relative formula mass are also based on the ^{12}C scale.

- The type and relative amount of each isotope in an element can be found by mass spectrometry.

- The relative atomic mass of an element can be calculated from its mass spectrum.

- One mole of a substance is the amount of substance that has the same number of particles as there are in exactly 12 g of carbon-12.

- The Avogadro constant is the number of a stated type of particle (atom, ion or molecule) in a mole of those particles.

- Empirical formulae show the simplest whole number ratio of atoms in a compound.

- Empirical formulae may be calculated using the mass of the elements present and their relative atomic masses or from combustion data.

- Molecular formulae show the total number of atoms of each element present in one molecule or one formula unit of the compound.

- The molecular formula may be calculated from the empirical formula if the relative molecular mass is known.

- The mole concept can be used to calculate:
  - reacting masses
  - volumes of gases
  - volumes and concentrations of solutions.

- The stoichiometry of a reaction can be obtained from calculations involving reacting masses, gas volumes, and volumes and concentrations of solutions.

End-of-chapter questions

1 a i   What do you understand by the term **relative atomic mass**?   [1]

   ii A sample of boron was found to have the following % composition by mass:

   $^{10}_{5}B$ (18.7%), $^{11}_{5}B$ (81.3%)

   Calculate a value for the relative atomic mass of boron. Give your answer to 3 significant figures.   [2]

   b   Boron ions, B^{3+}, can be formed by bombarding gaseous boron with high-energy electrons in a mass spectrometer. Deduce the number of electrons in one B^{3+} ion.   [1]

   c   Boron is present in compounds called borates.

   i   Use the A_r values below to calculate the relative molecular mass of iron(III) borate, $Fe(BO_2)_3$.
       (A_r values: Fe = 55.8, B = 10.8, O = 16.0)   [1]

   ii The accurate relative atomic mass of iron, Fe, is 55.8. Explain why the accurate relative atomic mass is not a whole number.   [1]

Total = 6

2 This question is about two transition metals, hafnium (Hf) and zirconium (Zr).

   a Hafnium forms a peroxide whose formula can be written as $HfO_3.2H_2O$. Use the A_r values below to calculate the relative molecular mass of hafnium peroxide.

      (A_r values: Hf = 178.5, H = 1.0, O = 16.0)   [1]

   b A particular isotope of hafnium has 72 protons and a nucleon number of 180. Write the isotopic symbol for this isotope, showing this information.   [1]

   c The mass spectrum of zirconium is shown below.

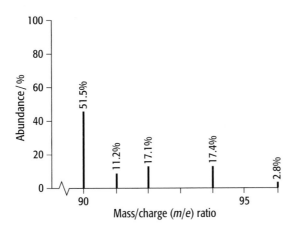

     i Use the information from this mass spectrum to calculate the relative atomic mass of zirconium. Give your answer to 3 significant figures.   [2]

     ii High-resolution mass spectra show accurate relative isotopic masses. What do you understand by the term **relative isotopic mass**?   [1]

                                                                  Total = 5

3 Solid sodium carbonate reacts with aqueous hydrochloric acid to form aqueous sodium chloride, carbon dioxide and water.

$$Na_2CO_3 + 2HCl \longrightarrow 2NaCl + CO_2 + H_2O$$

   a Rewrite this equation to include state symbols.   [1]

   b Calculate the number of moles of hydrochloric acid required to react exactly with 4.15 g of sodium carbonate.

      (A_r values: C = 12.0, Na = 23.0, O = 16.0)   [3]

   c Define the term **mole**.   [1]

   d An aqueous solution of 25.0 cm³ sodium carbonate of concentration 0.0200 mol dm⁻³ is titrated with hydrochloric acid. The volume of hydrochloric acid required to exactly react with the sodium carbonate is 12.50 cm³.

     i Calculate the number of moles of sodium carbonate present in the solution of sodium carbonate.   [1]

     ii Calculate the concentration of the hydrochloric acid.   [2]

   e How many moles of carbon dioxide are produced when 0.2 mol of sodium carbonate reacts with excess hydrochloric acid?   [1]

   f Calculate the volume of this number of moles of carbon dioxide at r.t.p. (1 mol of gas occupies 24 dm³ at r.t.p.)   [1]

                                                                  Total = 10

4 Hydrocarbons are compounds of carbon and hydrogen only. Hydrocarbon **Z** is composed of 80% carbon and 20% hydrogen.

   a Calculate the empirical formula of hydrocarbon **Z**.
      (A_r values: C = 12.0, H = 1.0) [3]

   b The molar mass of hydrocarbon **Z** is 30.0 g mol^{-1}. Deduce the molecular formula of this hydrocarbon. [1]

   c When 50 cm^3 of hydrocarbon **Y** is burnt, it reacts with exactly 300 cm^3 of oxygen to form 200 cm^3 of carbon dioxide. Water is also formed in the reaction. Deduce the equation for this reaction. Explain your reasoning. [4]

   d Propane has the molecular formula C_3H_8. Calculate the mass of 600 cm^3 of propane at r.t.p. (1 mol of gas occupies 24 dm^3 at r.t.p.)
      (A_r values: C = 12.0, H = 1.0) [2]

   Total = 10

5 When sodium reacts with titanium chloride ($TiCl_4$), sodium chloride (NaCl) and titanium (Ti) are produced.

   a Write the balanced symbol equation for the reaction. [2]

   b What mass of titanium is produced from 380 g of titanium chloride? Give your answer to 3 significant figures.
      (A_r values: Ti = 47.9, Cl = 35.5) [2]

   c What mass of titanium is produced using 46.0 g of sodium? Give your answer to 3 significant figures.
      (A_r values: Na = 23.0) [2]

   Total = 6

6 In this question give all answers to 3 significant figures.
   The reaction between NaOH and HCl can be written as:

   $$HCl + NaOH \longrightarrow NaCl + H_2O$$

   In such a reaction, 15.0 cm^3 of hydrochloric acid was neutralised by 20.0 cm^3 of 0.0500 mol dm^{-3} sodium hydroxide.

   a What was the volume in dm^3 of:
      i   the acid? [1]
      ii the alkali? [1]

   b Calculate the number of moles of alkali. [1]

   c Calculate the number of moles of acid and then its concentration. [2]

   Total = 5

7 Give all answers to 3 significant figures.
   Ammonium nitrate decomposes on heating to give nitrogen(I) oxide and water as follows:

   $$NH_4NO_3(s) \longrightarrow N_2O(g) + 2H_2O(l)$$

   a What is the formula mass of ammonium nitrate? [1]

   b How many moles of ammonium nitrate are present in 0.800 g of the solid? [2]

   c What volume of N_2O gas would be produced from this mass of ammonium nitrate? [2]

   Total = 5

8 Give all answers to 3 significant figures.
   a $1.20\,dm^3$ of hydrogen chloride gas was dissolved in $100\,cm^3$ of water.
       i   How many moles of hydrogen chloride gas are present?   [1]
       ii   What was the concentration of the hydrochloric acid formed?   [2]
   b $25.0\,cm^3$ of the acid was then titrated against sodium hydroxide of concentration $0.200\,mol\,dm^{-3}$
       to form NaCl and water:

   $$NaOH + HCl \longrightarrow H_2O + NaCl$$

       i   How many moles of acid were used?   [2]
       ii   Calculate the volume of sodium hydroxide used.   [2]

                                                                                          Total = 7

9 Give all answers to 3 significant figures.
   $4.80\,dm^3$ of chlorine gas was reacted with sodium hydroxide solution. The reaction taking place was
   as follows:

   $$Cl_2(g) + 2NaOH(aq) \longrightarrow NaCl(aq) + NaOCl(aq) + H_2O(l)$$

   a   How many moles of Cl_2 reacted?   [1]
   b   What mass of NaOCl was formed?   [2]
   c   If the concentration of the NaOH was $2.00\,mol\,dm^{-3}$, what volume of sodium hydroxide solution
       was required?   [2]
   d   Write an ionic equation for this reaction.   [1]

                                                                                          Total = 6

10 Calcium oxide reacts with hydrochloric acid according to the equation:

   $$CaO + 2HCl \longrightarrow CaCl_2 + H_2O$$

   a   What mass of calcium chloride is formed when $28.05\,g$ of calcium oxide reacts with excess
       hydrochloric acid?   [2]
   b   What mass of hydrochloric acid reacts with $28.05\,g$ of calcium oxide?   [2]
   c   What mass of water is produced?   [1]

                                                                                          Total = 5

11 When ammonia gas and hydrogen chloride gas mix together, they react to form a solid called ammonium
   chloride.
   a   Write a balanced equation for this reaction, including state symbols.   [2]
   b   Calculate the molar masses of ammonia, hydrogen chloride and ammonium chloride.   [3]
   c   What volumes of ammonia and hydrogen chloride gases must react at r.t.p. in order to produce $10.7\,g$ of
       ammonium chloride? (1 mol of gas occupies $24\,dm^3$ at r.t.p.)   [3]

                                                                                          Total = 8

23

Chapter 2:
Atomic structure

Learning outcomes

You should be able to:

- identify and describe protons, neutrons and electrons in terms of their relative charges and relative masses

- deduce the behaviour of beams of protons, neutrons and electrons in electric fields

- describe the distribution of mass and charges within an atom

- deduce the numbers of protons, neutrons and electrons present in both atoms and ions given proton and nucleon numbers and charge

- describe the contribution of protons and neutrons to atomic nuclei in terms of proton number and nucleon number

- distinguish between isotopes on the basis of different numbers of neutrons present

- recognise and use the symbolism $^x_y A$ for isotopes, where ^{x} is the nucleon number and $_y$ is the proton number.

Introduction

In order to explain how chemical substances behaved, scientists first had to understand what the substances themselves were made from. Over time, a model was developed in which all substances were composed of atoms of elements. Originally it was thought that atoms could not themselves be broken up into yet smaller parts, but now we understand the structure inside the atoms themselves, and the role of electrons, protons and neutrons. We can now design and make materials and objects almost at the atomic level.

Nanotechnology is the design and making of objects that may have a thickness of only a few thousand atoms or less. Groups of atoms can be moved around on special surfaces. In this way scientists hope to develop tiny machines that may help deliver medical drugs to exactly where they are needed in the body.

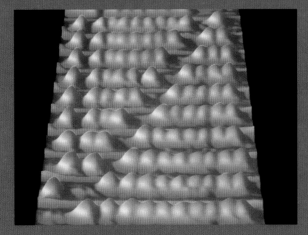

Figure 2.1 Each of the blue peaks in this image is an individual molecule. The molecules can be moved over a copper surface, making this a molecular abacus or counting device.

Elements and atoms

Every substance in our world is made up from chemical elements. These chemical elements cannot be broken down further into simpler substances by chemical means. A few elements, such as nitrogen and gold, are found on their own in nature, not combined with other elements. Most elements, however, are found in combination with other elements as compounds.

Every element has its own chemical symbol. The symbols are often derived from Latin or Greek words. Some examples are shown in Table 2.1.

Element	Symbol
carbon	C
lithium	Li (from Greek 'lithos')
iron	Fe (from Latin 'ferrum')
potassium	K (from Arabic 'al-qualyah' or from the Latin 'kalium')

Table 2.1 Some examples of chemical symbols.

Chemical elements contain only one type of atom. An atom is the smallest part of an element that can take part in a chemical change. Atoms are very small. The diameter of a hydrogen atom is approximately 10^{-10} m, so the mass of an atom must also be very small. A single hydrogen atom weighs only 1.67×10^{-27} kg.

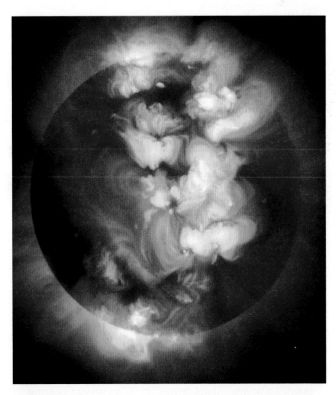

Figure 2.2 Our Sun is made largely of the elements hydrogen and helium. This is a composite image made using X-ray and solar optical telescopes.

Inside the atom
The structure of an atom

Every atom has nearly all of its mass concentrated in a tiny region in the centre of the atom called the nucleus. The nucleus is made up of particles called nucleons. There are two types of nucleon: **protons** and **neutrons**. Atoms of different elements have different numbers of protons.

Outside the nucleus, particles called **electrons** move around in regions of space called orbitals (see page 37). Chemists often find it convenient to use a model of the atom in which electrons move around the nucleus in electron shells. Each shell is a certain distance from the nucleus at its own particular energy level (see page 37). In a neutral atom, the number of electrons is equal to the number of protons. A simple model of a carbon atom is shown in Figure 2.3.

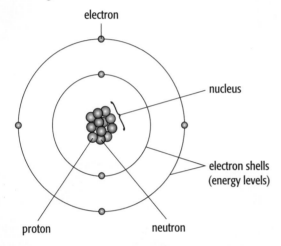

Figure 2.3 A model of a carbon atom. This model is not very accurate but it is useful for understanding what happens to the electrons during chemical reactions.

Atoms are tiny, but the nucleus of an atom is far tinier still. If the diameter of an atom were the size of a football stadium, the nucleus would only be the size of a pea. This means that most of the atom is empty space! Electrons are even smaller than protons and neutrons.

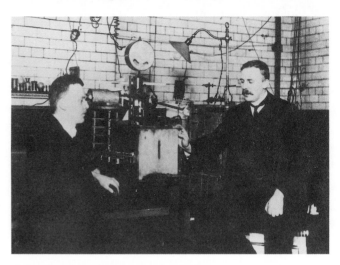

Figure 2.4 Ernest Rutherford (left) and Hans Geiger (right) using their alpha-particle apparatus. Interpretation of the results led to Rutherford proposing the nuclear model for atoms.

EXPERIMENTS WITH SUBATOMIC PARTICLES

We can deduce the electric charge of subatomic particles by showing how beams of electrons, protons and neutrons behave in electric fields. If we fire a beam of electrons past electrically charged plates, the electrons are deflected (bent) away from the negative plate and towards the positive plate (Figure 2.5a). This shows us that the electrons are negatively charged.

A cathode-ray tube (Figure 2.5b) can be used to produce beams of electrons. At one end of the tube

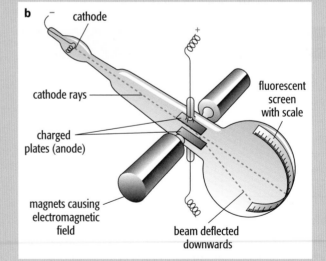

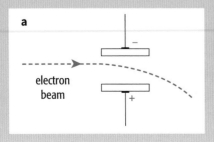

Figure 2.5 a The beam of electrons is deflected away from a negatively charged plate and towards a positively charged plate. **b** The electron beam in a cathode-ray tube is deflected (bent) by an electromagnetic field. The direction of the deflection shows us that the electron is negatively charged.

EXPERIMENTS WITH SUBATOMIC PARTICLES (CONTINUED)

is a metal wire (cathode), which is heated to a high temperature when a low voltage is applied to it. At the other end of the tube is a fluorescent screen, which glows when electrons hit it.

The electrons are given off from the heated wire and are attracted towards two metal plates, which are positively charged. As they pass through the metal plates the electrons form a beam. When the electron beam hits the screen a spot of light is produced. When an electric field is applied across this beam the electrons are deflected (bent). The fact that the electrons are so easily attracted to the positively charged anode and that they are easily deflected by an electric field shows us that:

- electrons have a negative charge
- electrons have a very small mass.

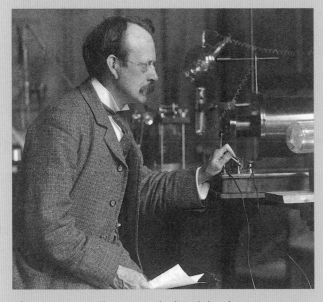

Figure 2.6 J. J. Thomson calculated the charge to mass ratio of electrons. He used results from experiments with electrons in cathode-ray tubes.

In recent years, experiments have been carried out with beams of electrons, protons and neutrons. The results of these experiments show that:

- a proton beam is deflected away from a positively charged plate; as like charges repel, the protons must have a positive charge (Figure 2.7)
- an electron beam is deflected towards a positively charged plate; as unlike charges attract, the electrons must have a negative charge
- a beam of neutrons is not deflected; this is because they are uncharged.

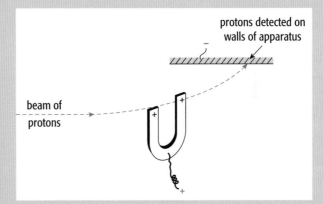

Figure 2.7 A beam of protons is deflected away from a positively charged area. This shows us that protons have a positive charge.

In these experiments, huge voltages have to be used to show the deflection of the proton beam. This contrasts with the very low voltages needed to show the deflection of an electron beam. These experiments show us that protons are much heavier than electrons. If we used the same voltage to deflect electrons and protons, the beam of electrons would have a far greater deflection than the beam of protons. This is because a proton is about 2000 times as heavy as an electron.

27

QUESTION

1 A beam of electrons is passing close to a highly negatively charged plate. When the electrons pass close to the plate, they are deflected (bent) away from the plate.

a What deflection would you expect, if any, when the experiment is repeated with beams of **i** protons and **ii** neutrons? Explain your answers.

b Which subatomic particle (electron, proton or neutron) would deviate the most? Explain your answer.

Masses and charges: a summary

Electrons, protons and neutrons have characteristic charges and masses. The values of these are too small to be very useful when discussing general chemical properties. For example, the charge on a single electron is -1.602×10^{-19} coulombs. We therefore compare their masses and charges by using their relative charges and masses. These are shown in Table 2.2.

Subatomic particle	Symbol	Relative mass	Relative charge
electron	e	$\frac{1}{1836}$	-1
neutron	n	1	0
proton	p	1	$+1$

Table 2.2 Comparing electrons, neutrons and protons.

Numbers of nucleons

Proton number and nucleon number

The number of protons in the nucleus of an atom is called the proton number (Z). It is also known as the atomic number. Every atom of the same element has the same number of protons in its nucleus. It is the proton number that makes an atom what it is. For example, an atom with a proton number of 11 must be an atom of the element sodium. The Periodic Table of elements is arranged in order of the proton numbers of the individual elements (see Appendix 1, page 473).

The nucleon number (A) is the number of protons plus neutrons in the nucleus of an atom. This is also known as the mass number.

How many neutrons?

We can use the nucleon number and proton number to find the number of neutrons in an atom. As:

nucleon number = number of protons + number of neutrons

Then:

number of neutrons = nucleon number − number of protons
$$= A - Z$$

For example, an atom of aluminium has a nucleon number of 27 and a proton number of 13. So an aluminium atom has 27 − 13 = 14 neutrons.

---

2 Use the information in the table to deduce the number of electrons and neutrons in a neutral atom of:
   a vanadium
   b strontium
   c phosphorus.

Atom	Nucleon number	Proton number
vanadium	51	23
strontium	84	38
phosphorus	31	15

Isotopes

All atoms of the same element have the same number of protons. However, they may have different numbers of neutrons. Atoms of the same element that have differing numbers of neutrons are called isotopes.

Isotopes are atoms of the same element with different nucleon (mass) numbers.

Isotopes of a particular element have the same chemical properties because they have the same number of electrons. They have slightly different physical properties, such as small differences in density.

We can write symbols for isotopes. We write the nucleon number at the top left of the chemical symbol and the proton number at the bottom left.

The symbol for the isotope of boron with 5 protons and 11 nucleons is written:

nucleon number $\longrightarrow$ $^{11}_{5}\text{B}$
proton number $\longrightarrow$

Hydrogen has three isotopes. The atomic structure and isotopic symbols for the three isotopes of hydrogen are shown in Figure 2.8.

When writing generally about isotopes, chemists also name them by omitting the proton number and placing the nucleon number after the name. For example, the isotopes of hydrogen can be called hydrogen-1, hydrogen-2 and hydrogen-3.

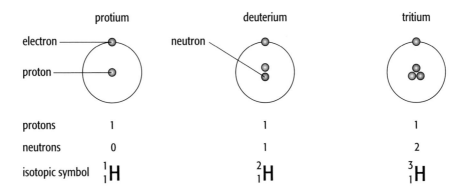

	protium	deuterium	tritium
protons	1	1	1
neutrons	0	1	2
isotopic symbol	$_1^1H$	$_1^2H$	$_1^3H$

Figure 2.8 The atomic structure and isotopic symbols for the three isotopes of hydrogen.

Isotopes can be radioactive or non-radioactive. Specific radioisotopes (radioactive isotopes) can be used to check for leaks in oil or gas pipelines and to check the thickness of paper. They are also used in medicine to treat some types of cancer and to check the activity of the thyroid gland in the throat.

QUESTION

3 Use the Periodic Table on page 473 to help you.
   Write isotopic symbols for the following neutral atoms:
   a bromine-81
   b calcium-44
   c iron-58
   d palladium-110.

How many protons, neutrons and electrons?

In a neutral atom the number of positively charged protons in the nucleus equals the number of negatively charged electrons outside the nucleus. When an atom gains or loses electrons, ions are formed, which are electrically charged. For example:

$$Cl \quad + \quad e^- \quad \longrightarrow \quad Cl^-$$

chlorine atom	1 electron gained	chloride ion
17 protons		17 protons
17 electrons		18 electrons

The chloride ion has a single negative charge because there are 17 protons (+) and 18 electrons (–).

$$Mg \quad \longrightarrow \quad Mg^{2+} \quad + \quad 2e^-$$

magnesium atom	magnesium ion	2 electrons removed
12 protons		12 protons
12 electrons		10 electrons

The magnesium ion has a charge of 2+ because it has 12 protons (+) but only 10 electrons (–).

The isotopic symbol for an ion derived from sulfur-33 is $_{16}^{33}S^{2-}$. This sulfide ion has 16 protons, 17 neutrons (because $33 - 16 = 17$) and 18 electrons (because $16 + 2 = 18$).

QUESTION

4 Deduce the number of electrons in each of these ions:
   a $_{19}^{40}K^+$
   b $_7^{15}N^{3-}$
   c $_8^{18}O^{2-}$
   d $_{31}^{71}Ga^{3+}$

29

Summary

- Every atom has an internal structure with a nucleus in the centre and the negatively charged electrons arranged in 'shells' outside the nucleus.

- Most of the mass of the atom is in the nucleus, which contains protons (positively charged) and neutrons (uncharged).

- Beams of protons and electrons are deflected by electric fields but neutrons are not.

- All atoms of the same element have the same number of protons. This is the proton number (Z), which is also called the atomic number.

- The nucleon number, which is also called the mass number (A), is the total number of protons and neutrons in an atom.

- The number of neutrons in an atom is found by subtracting the proton number from the nucleon number (A – Z).

- In a neutral atom, number of electrons = number of protons. When there are more protons than electrons, the atom becomes a positive ion. When there are more electrons than protons, a negatively charged ion is formed.

- Isotopes are atoms with the same atomic number but different nucleon numbers. They only differ in the number of neutrons they contain.

End-of-chapter questions

1   Boron is an element in Group 13 of the Periodic Table.

   a   Boron has two isotopes.
       What do you understand by the term **isotope**?   [1]

   b   State the number of **i** protons, **ii** neutrons and **iii** electrons in one neutral atom of the isotope $^{11}_{5}B$.   [3]

   c   State the relative masses and charges of:

       i   an electron   [2]

       ii   a neutron   [2]

       iii   a proton   [2]

                                 Total = 10

2   Zirconium, Zr, and hafnium, Hf, are metals.

   An isotope of zirconium has 40 protons and 91 nucleons.

   a   **i**   Write the isotopic symbol for this isotope of zirconium.   [1]

       ii   How many neutrons are present in one atom of this isotope?   [1]

   b   Hafnium ions, $^{180}_{72}Hf^{2+}$, are produced in a mass spectrometer.
       How many electrons are present in one of these hafnium ions?   [1]

c The subatomic particles present in zirconium and hafnium are electrons, neutrons and protons. A beam of protons is fired into an electric field produced by two charged plates, as shown in the diagram.

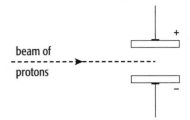

beam of protons

   i   Describe how the beam of protons behaves when it passes through the gap between the charged plates. Explain your answer. [2]
   ii Describe and explain what happens when a beam of neutrons passes through the gap between the charged plates. [2]

Total = 7

3 a Describe the structure of an atom, giving details of the subatomic particles present. [6]
  b Explain the terms **atomic number** and **nucleon number**. [2]
  c Copy and complete the table:

Neutral atom	Atomic number	Nucleon number	Numbers of each subatomic particle present
Mg	12	24	
Al	13	27	

[2]

  d Explain why atoms are neutral. [1]
  e An oxygen atom has 8 protons in its nucleus. Explain why it cannot have 9 protons. [1]
  f When calculating the relative mass of an atom, the electrons are not used in the calculation. Explain why not. [1]

Total = 13

4 The symbols below describe two isotopes of the element uranium.

$^{235}_{92}U$ $^{238}_{92}U$

  a State the meaning of the term **isotope**. [1]
  b i   In what ways are these two isotopes of uranium identical? [2]
     ii In what ways do they differ? [2]
  c In a mass spectrometer uranium atoms can be converted to uranium ions, U^{2+}.
    State the number of electrons present in one U^{2+} ion. [1]

Total = 6

5 The table below shows the two naturally occurring isotopes of chlorine.
  a Copy and complete the table.

	$^{35}_{17}Cl$	$^{37}_{17}Cl$
number of protons		
number of electrons		
number of neutrons		

[3]

  b The relative atomic mass of chlorine is 35.5. What does this tell you about the relative abundance of the two naturally occurring isotopes of chlorine? [2]
  c Magnesium chloride contains magnesium ions, Mg^{2+}, and chloride ions, Cl^-.
    i   Explain why a magnesium ion is positively charged. [1]
    ii Explain why a chloride ion has a single negative charge. [2]

Total = 8

31

Chapter 3:
Electrons in atoms

Learning outcomes

You should be able to:

- describe the number and relative energies of the s, p and d orbitals for the principal quantum numbers 1, 2 and 3 and also the 4s and 4p orbitals

- describe the shapes of s and p orbitals

- state the electronic configuration of atoms and ions given the proton number and charge, using the convention $1s^2 2s^2 2p^6$, etc.

- explain and use the term ionisation energy, and the factors influencing the ionisation energies of elements

- use ionisation energy data to:
  - explain the trends across a period and down a group of the Periodic Table
  - deduce the electronic configurations of elements

- interpret successive ionisation energy data of an element in terms of the position of that element within the Periodic Table.

Introduction

The arrangement of the electrons within each atom determines how that atom interacts with other atoms and with its surroundings. The electrons are organised into different levels of energy, and understanding the effects of this arrangement is key to understanding chemistry itself. We can also make use of these electron levels. For example, causing an electron to move between energy levels can cause energy to be emitted or absorbed. Sometimes, we can see this in the form of light.

Figure 3.1 Electrons moving between energy levels are the source of this light energy. Chemicals in the tubes are said to be 'chemiluminescent'.

Simple electronic structure

On page 26 we saw that electrons are arranged outside the nucleus in energy levels or quantum shells. These principal energy levels or principal quantum shells (symbol n) are numbered according to how far they are from the nucleus. The lowest energy level, $n = 1$, is closest to the nucleus, the energy level $n = 2$ is further out, and so on. The electrons in quantum shells further away from the nucleus have more energy and are held less tightly to the nucleus.

The arrangement of electrons in an atom is called its electronic structure or electronic configuration. The electronic configurations of lithium, carbon and neon are shown in Figure 3.2, together with a shorthand way of writing this structure.

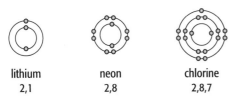

lithium	neon	chlorine
2,1	2,8	2,8,7

Figure 3.2 The simple electronic structures of lithium, neon and chlorine. The nuclei of the atoms are not shown.

Table 3.1 shows the number of electrons in each of the principal quantum shells (energy levels) for the first 11

elements in the Periodic Table. Each principal quantum shell can hold a maximum number of electrons:

- shell 1 – up to 2 electrons
- shell 2 – up to 8 electrons
- shell 3 – up to 18 electrons
- shell 4 – up to 32 electrons.

	Atomic number	Number of electrons in shell		
		$n = 1$	$n = 2$	$n = 3$
H	1	1		
He	2	2		
Li	3	2	1	
Be	4	2	2	
B	5	2	3	
C	6	2	4	
N	7	2	5	
O	8	2	6	
F	9	2	7	
Ne	10	2	8	
Na	11	2	8	1

Table 3.1 Simple electronic configurations of the first 11 elements in the Periodic Table.

QUESTION

1   Write the simple electronic configuration of the
    following atoms, showing the principal quantum shells
    only:

    a   sulfur; the atomic number of sulfur, $Z = 16$

    b   magnesium, $Z = 12$

    c   fluorine, $Z = 9$

    d   potassium, $Z = 19$

    e   carbon, $Z = 6$

Evidence for electronic structure

Ionisation energy, ΔH_i

By firing high-speed electrons at atoms, scientists can
work out how much energy has to be supplied to form an
ion by knocking out one electron from each atom.

The energy change that accompanies this process is
called the **ionisation energy**.

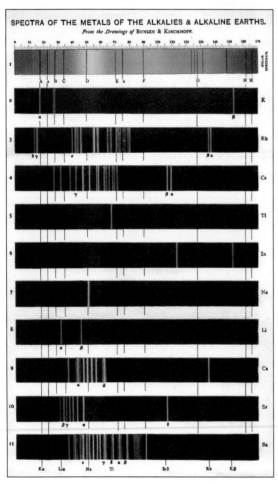

Figure 3.3 The frequencies of the lines in an atomic
emission spectrum can be used to calculate a value for the
ionisation energy.

The 1st ionisation energy of an element is the energy
needed to remove one electron from each atom in one
mole of atoms of the element in the gaseous state to form
one mole of gaseous 1+ ions.

Ionisation energies are measured under standard
conditions. The general symbol for ionisation energy is
ΔH_i. Its units are kJ mol^{-1}.

The symbol for the 1st ionisation energy is ΔH_{i1}. Using
calcium as an example:

1st ionisation energy: $Ca(g) \longrightarrow Ca^+(g) + e^-$

$\Delta H_{i1} = 590 \, kJ \, mol^{-1}$

If a second electron is removed from each ion in a mole of
gaseous 1+ ions, we call it the 2nd ionisation energy, ΔH_{i2}.
Again, using calcium as an example:

2nd ionisation energy: $Ca^+(g) \longrightarrow Ca^{2+}(g) + e^-$

$\Delta H_{i2} = 1150 \, kJ \, mol^{-1}$

Removal of a third electron from each ion in a mole of
gaseous 2+ ions is called the 3rd ionisation energy. Again,
using calcium as an example:

3rd ionisation energy: $Ca^{2+}(g) \longrightarrow Ca^{3+}(g) + e^-$

$\Delta H_{i3} = 4940 \, kJ \, mol^{-1}$

We can continue to remove electrons from an atom until
only the nucleus is left. We call this sequence of ionisation
energies, **successive ionisation energies**.

The successive ionisation energies for the first 11
elements in the Periodic Table are shown in Table 3.2.

The data in Table 3.2 shows us that:

- For each element, the successive ionisation energies
  increase. This is because the charge on the ion gets
  greater as each electron is removed. As each electron is
  removed there is a greater attractive force between the
  positively charged protons in the nucleus and the remaining
  negatively charged electrons. Therefore more energy is
  needed to overcome these attractive forces.

- There is a big difference between some successive
  ionisation energies. For nitrogen this occurs between
  the 5th and 6th ionisation energies. For sodium the first
  big difference occurs between the 1st and 2nd ionisation
  energies. These large changes indicate that for the second
  of these two ionisation energies the electron being removed
  is from a principal quantum shell closer to the nucleus.

For example, for the 5th ionisation energy of nitrogen,
the electron being removed is from the 2nd principal
quantum shell. For the 6th ionisation energy of nitrogen,
the electron being removed is from the 1st principal
quantum shell.

Element		Electrons removed										
		1	2	3	4	5	6	7	8	9	10	11
1	H	1310										
2	He	2370	5250									
3	Li	519	7300	11800								
4	Be	900	1760	14850	21000							
5	B	799	2420	3660	25000	32800						
6	C	1090	2350	4620	6220	37800	47300					
7	N	1400	2860	4580	7480	9450	53300	64400				
8	O	1310	3390	5320	7450	11000	13300	71300	84100			
9	F	1680	3370	6040	8410	11000	15200	17900	92000	106000		
10	Ne	2080	3950	6150	9290	12200	15200	20000	23000	117000	131400	
11	Na	494	4560	6940	9540	13400	16600	20100	25500	28900	141000	158700

Table 3.2 Successive ionisation energies for the first 11 elements in the Periodic Table.

QUESTION

2 **a** Write equations that describe:
   i the 1st ionisation energy of calcium
   ii the 3rd ionisation energy of potassium
   iii the 2nd ionisation energy of lithium
   iv the 5th ionisation energy of sulfur.

b The 2nd ionisation energy of nitrogen is 2860 kJ mol^{-1}. The 3rd ionisation energy of nitrogen is 4590 kJ mol^{-1}. Explain why the 3rd ionisation energy is higher.

Three factors that influence ionisation energies

1 The size of the nuclear charge

As the atomic number (number of protons) increases, the positive nuclear charge increases. The bigger the positive charge, the greater the attractive force between the nucleus and the electrons. So, more energy is needed to overcome these attractive forces if an electron is to be removed.

■ In general, ionisation energy increases as the proton number increases.

2 Distance of outer electrons from the nucleus

The force of attraction between positive and negative charges decreases rapidly as the distance between them increases. So, electrons in shells further away from the nucleus are less attracted to the nucleus than those closer to the nucleus.

■ The further the outer electron shell is from the nucleus, the lower the ionisation energy.

3 Shielding effect of inner electrons

As all electrons are negatively charged, they repel each other. Electrons in full inner shells repel electrons in outer shells. Full inner shells of electrons prevent the full nuclear charge being felt by the outer electrons. This is called shielding. The greater the shielding of outer electrons by the inner electron shells, the lower the attractive forces between the nucleus and the outer electrons.

■ The ionisation energy is lower as the number of full electron shells between the outer electrons and the nucleus increases.

Interpreting successive ionisation energies

Figure 3.4 shows a graph of successive ionisation energies against the number of electrons removed for sodium. A logarithmic scale (to the base 10) is used because the values of successive ionisation energies have such a large range.

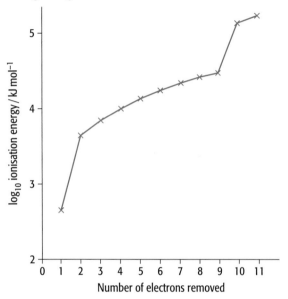

Figure 3.4 Graph of logarithm ($\log_{10}$) of ionisation energy of sodium against the number of electrons removed.

We can deduce the following about sodium from Figure 3.4:

- The first electron removed has a low 1st ionisation energy, when compared with the rest of the data. It is very easily removed from the atom. It is therefore likely to be a long way from the nucleus and well shielded by inner electron shells.
- The second electron is much more difficult to remove than the first electron. There is a big jump in the value of the ionisation energy. This suggests that the second electron is in a shell closer to the nucleus than the first electron. Taken together, the 1st and 2nd ionisation energies suggest that sodium has one electron in its outer shell.
- From the second to the ninth electrons removed there is only a gradual change in successive ionisation energies. This suggests that all these eight electrons are in the same shell.
- The 10th and 11th electrons have extremely high ionisation energies, when compared with the rest of the data. This suggests that they are very close to the nucleus. There must be a very great force of attraction between the nucleus and these electrons and there are no inner electrons to shield them. The large increase in ionisation energy between the 9th and 10th electrons confirms that the 10th electron is in a shell closer to the nucleus than the 9th electron.

Figure 3.5 shows this arrangement of electrons.

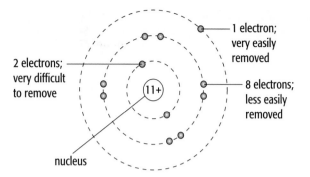

Figure 3.5 The arrangement of electrons in an atom of sodium can be deduced from the values of successive ionisation energies.

QUESTION

3 a The successive ionisation energies of boron are shown in Table 3.3.

Ionisation	1st	2nd	3rd	4th	5th
Ionisation energy / kJ mol^{-1}	799	2 420	3 660	25 000	32 800

Table 3.3 Successive ionisation energies of boron.

    i Why is there a large increase between the third and fourth ionisation energies?

    ii Explain how these figures confirm that the electronic structure of boron is 2, 3.

b For the element aluminium ($Z = 13$), draw a sketch graph to predict the $\log_{10}$ of the successive ionisation energies (y-axis) against the number of electrons removed (x-axis).

We can use successive ionisation energies in this way to:

- predict or confirm the simple electronic configuration of elements
- confirm the number of electrons in the outer shell of an element and hence the group to which the element belongs.

WORKED EXAMPLE

1 The successive ionisation energies, ΔH_i, of an element X are shown in Table 3.4. Which group in the Periodic Table does X belong to?

We look for a large jump in the value of the ionisation energy. This occurs between the removal of the 6th and 7th electrons. So, six electrons have been removed comparatively easily. The removal of the 7th electron requires about three times the energy required to remove the 6th electron. So, there must be six electrons in the outer shell of X. So, element X must be in Group 16 of the Periodic Table.

	Number of electrons removed									
	1	**2**	**3**	**4**	**5**	**6**	**7**	**8**	**9**	**10**
ΔH_i / kJ mol^{-1}	1000	2260	3390	4540	7010	8500	27100	31670	36580	43140

Table 3.4 The successive ionisation energies of an element X. For Worked example 1.

QUESTION

4 **a** The first six ionisation energies of an element are 1090, 2350, 4610, 6220, 37800 and 47300 kJ mol^{-1}. Which group in the Periodic Table does this element belong to? Explain your decision.

  b Draw a sketch graph to show the log$_{10}$ values of the first four successive ionisation energies of a Group 2 element.

Subshells and atomic orbitals

Quantum subshells

The principal quantum shells, apart from the first, are split into subshells (sublevels). Each principal quantum shell contains a different number of subshells. The subshells are distinguished by the letters s, p or d. There are also f subshells for elements with more than 57 electrons. Figure 3.6 shows the subshells for the first four principal quantum levels. In any principal quantum shell, the energy of the electrons in the subshells increases in the order s < p < d.

The maximum number of electrons that are allowed in each subshell is: s = 2 electrons, p = 6 electrons, d = 10 electrons.

- The first principal quantum level, $n = 1$, can hold a maximum of 2 electrons in an s subshell.
- The second principal quantum level, $n = 2$, can hold a maximum of 8 electrons: 2 electrons in the s subshell and 6 electrons in the p subshell.
- The third principal quantum level, $n = 3$, can hold a maximum of 18 electrons: 2 electrons in the s subshell, 6 electrons in the p subshell and 10 electrons in the d subshell.

You will also notice from Figure 3.6 that the order of the subshells in terms of increasing energy does not follow a regular pattern of s then p then d after the element argon. The order of subshells after argon appears to overlap. The next element after argon is potassium. Potassium's outer electron is in the 4s, not in the 3d, subshell. The first element with an electron in the 3d subshell is element 21, scandium.

When high-speed electrons hit gas particles at low pressure, coloured lines are seen through an instrument called a spectroscope. The letters s, p and d come from the terms used to describe these lines: s for 'sharp', p for 'principal' and 'd for 'diffuse'.

Atomic orbitals

Each subshell contains one or more atomic orbitals.

> An atomic orbital is a region of space around the nucleus of an atom that can be occupied by one or two electrons.

As each orbital can only hold a maximum of two electrons, the number of orbitals in each subshell must be:

  s – one orbital
  p – three orbitals
  d – five orbitals.

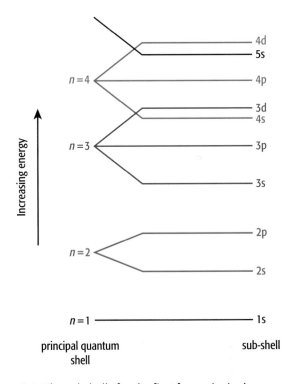

Figure 3.6 The subshells for the first four principal quantum shells.

37

Shapes of the orbitals

Each orbital has a three-dimensional shape. Within this shape there is a high probability of finding the electron or electrons in the orbital. Figure 3.7 shows how we represent the s and p orbitals.

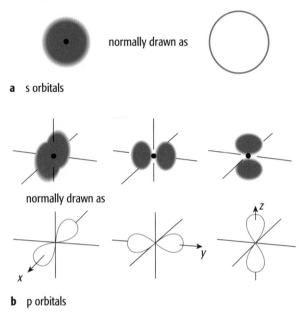

normally drawn as

a   s orbitals

normally drawn as

b   p orbitals

Figure 3.7 Representations of orbitals (the position of the nucleus is shown by the black dot): **a** s orbitals are spherical; **b** p orbitals, p_x, p_y and p_z, have 'lobes' along the x, y and z axes.

An s orbital has a spherical shape. The 2s orbital in the second principal quantum shell has the same shape as the 1s orbital in the first quantum shell. They are both spherical, but electrons in the 2s orbital have more energy than electrons in the 1s orbital. There are three 2p orbitals in the second quantum shell. Each of these has the same shape. The shape is like an hourglass with two 'lobes'. The three sets of 'lobes' are arranged at right angles to each other along the x, y and z axes. Hence the three 2p orbitals are named $2p_x$, $2p_y$ and $2p_z$. The three 2p orbitals have the same energy as each other. There are also three 3p orbitals in the third quantum shell. Their shapes are similar to the shapes of the 2p orbitals.

The d orbitals are more complex in shape and arrangement in space. In 1925 Louis de Broglie suggested that electrons behaved like waves. This led to the idea of electron probability clouds. The electron probability cloud for one type of d orbital is very strange – it is like a modified p orbital with a ring around the middle (Figure 3.8). You will not need to know the d-orbital shapes at AS level, but you will for A level when studying the transition elements (see Chapter 24).

Figure 3.8 The shape of a dz^2 orbital.

Filling the shells and orbitals

The most stable electronic configuration (electronic structure) of an atom is the one that has the lowest amount of energy. The order in which the subshells are filled depends on their relative energy. The subshell with the lowest energy, the 1s, is therefore filled first, followed by those that are successively higher in energy. As we noted in Figure 3.6, the order of the subshells in terms of increasing energy does not follow a regular pattern of s then p then d after argon, where the 3p subshell is full. Figure 3.9 shows the order of filling the subshells.

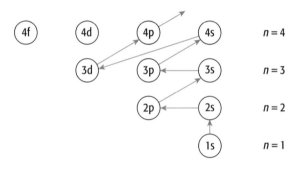

Figure 3.9 Diagram to show the order in which orbitals are filled up to shell $n = 4$.

Electronic configurations

Representing electronic configurations

A detailed way of writing the electronic configuration of an atom that includes information about the number of electrons in each subshell is shown below for hydrogen.

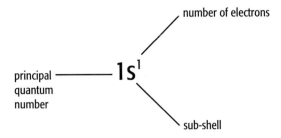

- Helium has two electrons. Both electrons can go into the 1s orbital, as this can hold a maximum of two electrons. So, the electronic structure of helium is $1s^2$.
- Lithium has three electrons. The 1s orbital can only hold a maximum of two electrons so the third electron must go into the next highest subshell, the 2s. So, the electronic structure of lithium is $1s^2 2s^1$.

Electrons are added one by one for successive elements, filling each subshell in order of increasing energy. The electronic configurations of the first 18 elements are shown in Table 3.5.

A question about this type of detailed notation will often be stated like this: 'Use $1s^2$ notation to give the electronic configuration …'

QUESTION

6 Use $1s^2$ notation to give the electronic configurations of the atoms with the following atomic numbers:

   a 16

   b 9

   c 20

Proton number	Symbol	Electronic configuration
1	H	$1s^1$
2	He	$1s^2$
3	Li	$1s^2 2s^1$
4	Be	$1s^2 2s^2$
5	B	$1s^2 2s^2 2p^1$
6	C	$1s^2 2s^2 2p^2$
7	N	$1s^2 2s^2 2p^3$
8	O	$1s^2 2s^2 2p^4$
9	F	$1s^2 2s^2 2p^5$
10	Ne	$1s^2 2s^2 2p^6$
11	Na	$1s^2 2s^2 2p^6 3s^1$
12	Mg	$1s^2 2s^2 2p^6 3s^2$
13	Al	$1s^2 2s^2 2p^6 3s^2 3p^1$
14	Si	$1s^2 2s^2 2p^6 3s^2 3p^2$
15	P	$1s^2 2s^2 2p^6 3s^2 3p^3$
16	S	$1s^2 2s^2 2p^6 3s^2 3p^4$
17	Cl	$1s^2 2s^2 2p^6 3s^2 3p^5$
18	Ar	$1s^2 2s^2 2p^6 3s^2 3p^6$

Table 3.5 Electronic configurations for the first 18 elements in the Periodic Table.

The electronic configurations of some of the elements after argon are shown in Table 3.6. In this table part of the electronic configuration of each element is represented by [Ar]. This 'noble gas core' represents the electronic configuration of argon: $1s^2 2s^2 2p^6 3s^2 3p^6$. This method is a shorthand way of writing electronic structures of atoms with many electrons. However, in an exam you should be prepared to write out the full electronic configuration. You should note the following:

- **Electronic configuration of potassium**
  Potassium has the electronic structure $1s^2 2s^2 2p^6 3s^2 3p^6 4s^1$. The outer electron goes into the 4s subshell rather than the 3d subshell because the 4s is below the 3d in terms of its energy.

- **Filling the 3d subshell**
  After calcium, a new subshell becomes occupied. The next electron goes into a 3d subshell rather than a 4p

subshell. So scandium has the electronic configuration [Ar] $3d^1 4s^2$. This is because electrons occupy the orbitals with the lowest energy – the 3d subshell is just above the 4s subshell but below the 4p subshell. This begins a pattern of filling the 3d subshell ending with zinc. Zinc has the electronic configuration [Ar] $3d^{10} 4s^2$.

- **Chromium and copper**
  The electronic configurations of chromium and copper do not follow the expected pattern. Chromium has the electronic configuration [Ar] $3d^5 4s^1$ (rather than the expected [Ar] $3d^4 4s^2$). Copper has the electronic configuration [Ar] $3d^{10} 4s^1$ (rather than the expected [Ar] $3d^9 4s^2$). You will have to learn that these two elements are exceptions to the pattern.

- **Gallium to krypton**
  The electrons add to the 4p subshell because this is the next highest energy level above the 3d.

Proton number	Name (Symbol)	Electronic configuration
19	potassium (K)	$[Ar]\,4s^1$
20	calcium (Ca)	$[Ar]\,4s^2$
21	scandium (Sc)	$[Ar]\,3d^1\,4s^2$
24	chromium (Cr)	$[Ar]\,3d^5\,4s^1$
25	manganese (Mn)	$[Ar]\,3d^5\,4s^2$
29	copper (Cu)	$[Ar]\,3d^{10}\,4s^1$
30	zinc (Zn)	$[Ar]\,3d^{10}\,4s^2$
31	gallium (Ga)	$[Ar]\,3d^{10}\,4s^2\,4p^1$
35	bromine (Br)	$[Ar]\,3d^{10}\,4s^2\,4p^5$
36	krypton (Kr)	$[Ar]\,3d^{10}\,4s^2\,4p^6$

Table 3.6 Electronic configurations for some of the elements 19 to 36, where [Ar] is the electronic structure of argon $1s^2\,2s^2\,2p^6\,3s^2\,3p^6$.

QUESTION

7 Use $1s^2$ notation to give the electronic configurations for the following elements:

    a vanadium ($Z = 23$)

    b copper ($Z = 29$)

    c selenium ($Z = 34$)

Orbitals and the Periodic Table

The arrangement of elements in the Periodic Table reflects the electronic structure of the elements. The Periodic Table can be split into blocks of elements (Figure 3.10).

- Elements in Groups 1 and 2 have outer electrons in an s subshell.

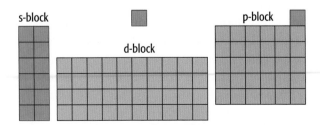

Figure 3.10 Some of the blocks of elements in the Periodic Table.

- Elements in Groups 3 to 18 (apart from He) have outer electrons in a p subshell.
- Elements that add electrons to the d subshells are called the d-block elements. Most of these are transition elements.

QUESTION

8 **a** An element has the electronic configuration $1s^2\,2s^2\,2p^6\,3s^2\,3p^6\,3d^{10}\,4s^2\,4p^6\,4d^{10}\,5s^2\,5p^5$.

    i Which block in the Periodic Table does this element belong to?

    ii Which group does it belong to?

    iii Identify this element.

  b Which block in the Periodic Table does the element with the electronic configuration $1s^2\,2s^2\,2p^6\,3s^2\,3p^6\,3d^5\,4s^1$ belong to?

Filling the orbitals

A useful way of representing electronic configurations is a diagram that places electrons in boxes (Figure 3.11).

- Each box represents an atomic orbital.
- The boxes (orbitals) can be arranged in order of increasing energy from bottom to top.
- An electron is represented by an arrow.
- The direction of the arrow represents the 'spin' of the electron. (We imagine an electron rotating around its own axis either in a clockwise or anticlockwise direction.)
- When there are two electrons in an orbital, the 'spins' of the electrons are opposite, so the two arrows in this box point in opposite directions.

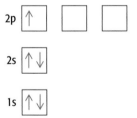

Figure 3.11 The electronic configuration of boron in box form.

Electrons in the same region of space repel each other because they have the same charge. So wherever possible, electrons will occupy separate orbitals in the same subshell to minimise this repulsion. These electrons have their 'spin' in the same direction. Electrons are only paired when there are no more empty orbitals available within a subshell. The spins are then opposite to minimise repulsion. Figure 3.12 shows the electronic structures of carbon, nitrogen and oxygen to illustrate these points.

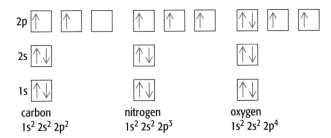

Figure 3.12 When adding electrons to a particular subshell, the electrons are only paired when no more empty orbitals are available.

Electronic configuration of ions

Positive ions are formed when electrons are removed from atoms. The sodium ion, Na^+ (proton number = 11), has 10 electrons. So, its electronic configuration is $1s^2 2s^2 2p^6$. Note that this is the same as the electronic configuration of neon, the element with 10 electrons in each atom.

Negative ions are formed when atoms gain electrons. The sulfide ion, S^{2-} (proton number = 16), has 18 electrons. Its electronic configuration is $1s^2 2s^2 2p^6 3s^2 3p^6$, which is the same as argon, the element with 18 electrons in each atom.

Note that, in general, electrons in the outer subshell are removed when metal ions form their positive ions. However, the d-block elements behave slightly differently. Reading across the Periodic Table from potassium to zinc, the 4s subshell fills before the 3d subshell. But when atoms of a d-block element lose electrons to form ions, the 4s electrons are lost first.

For example:

Ti atom: $1s^2 2s^2 2p^6 3s^2 3p^6 3d^2 4s^2$
$\longrightarrow$ Ti^{2+} ion: $1s^2 2s^2 2p^6 3s^2 3p^6 3d^2$

Cr atom: $1s^2 2s^2 2p^6 3s^2 3p^6 3d^5 4s^1$
$\longrightarrow$ Cr^{3+} ion: $1s^2 2s^2 2p^6 3s^2 3p^6 3d^3$

QUESTION

9 Write electronic configurations for the following ions:

a Al^{3+} ($Z = 13$)   d Cu^{2+} ($Z = 29$)

b O^{2-} ($Z = 8$)   e Cu^+ ($Z = 29$)

c Fe^{3+} ($Z = 26$)

Patterns in ionisation energies in the Periodic Table

Patterns across a period

Figure 3.13 shows how the first ionisation energy, ΔH_{i1}, changes across the first two periods. We can explain the form of the graph mainly by referring to the factors that influence ionisation energies (see page 35).

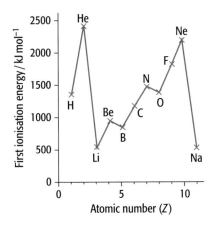

Figure 3.13 A graph of the first ionisation energies of the elements hydrogen to sodium plotted against atomic number.

1 There is a general increase in ΔH_{i1} across a period. This applies to Period 1 (hydrogen and helium), Period 2 (lithium to neon) and also to other periods. As you go across a period the nuclear charge increases. But the electron removed comes from the same shell. So, the force of attraction between the positive nucleus and the outer negative electrons increases across the period because:

i the nuclear charge increases

ii the distance between the nucleus and the outer electron remains reasonably constant

iii the shielding by inner shells remains reasonably constant.

2 There is a rapid decrease in ionisation energy between the last element in one period and the first element in the next period. The ΔH_{i1} for lithium is much smaller than the ΔH_{i1} for helium. Helium has two electrons. These are in the first quantum shell. But lithium has three electrons. The third electron must go into the next quantum shell further away from the nucleus. So, the force of attraction between the positive nucleus and the outer negative electrons decreases because:

i   the distance between the nucleus and the outer electron increases

ii   the shielding by inner shells increases

iii   these two factors outweigh the increased nuclear charge.

3   There is a slight decrease in ΔH_{i1} between beryllium and boron. Although boron has one more proton than beryllium, there is a slight decrease in ΔH_{i1} on removal of the outer electron. Beryllium has the electronic structure $1s^2 2s^2$ and boron has the electronic structure $1s^2 2s^2 2p^1$. The fifth electron in boron must be in the 2p subshell, which is slightly further away from the nucleus than the 2s subshell. There is less attraction between the fifth electron in boron and the nucleus because:

i   the distance between the nucleus and the outer electron increases slightly

ii   the shielding by inner shells increases slightly

iii   these two factors outweigh the increased nuclear charge.

4   There is a slight decrease in ΔH_{i1} between nitrogen and oxygen. Oxygen has one more proton than nitrogen and the electron removed is in the same 2p subshell. So, you might think that ΔH_{i1} would increase. However, the spin-pairing of the electrons plays a part here. If you look back at Figure 3.12, you will see that the electron removed from the nitrogen is from an orbital that contains an unpaired electron. The electron removed from the oxygen is from the orbital that contains a pair of electrons. The extra repulsion between the pair of electrons in this orbital results in less energy being needed to remove an electron. So, ΔH_{i1} for oxygen is lower, because of spin-pair repulsion.

These patterns repeat themselves across the third period. However, the presence of the d-block elements in Period 4 disrupts the pattern, as d-block elements have first ionisation energies that are relatively similar and fairly high.

Patterns down a group

The first ionisation energy decreases as you go down a group in the Periodic Table. For example, in Group 1 the values of ΔH_{i1} are:

- Li = 519 kJ mol^{-1}
- Na = 494 kJ mol^{-1}
- K = 418 kJ mol^{-1}
- Rb = 403 kJ mol^{-1}

As you go down the group, the outer electron removed is from the same type of orbital but from a successively higher principal quantum level – 2s from lithium, 3s for sodium and 4s for potassium. Although the nuclear charge is increasing down the group there is less attraction between the outer electron and the nucleus because:

1   the distance between the nucleus and the outer electron increases

2   the shielding by complete inner shells increases

3   these two factors outweigh the increased nuclear charge.

QUESTION

10 a   The first ionisation energies of four consecutive elements in the Periodic Table are:

sodium = 494 kJ mol^{-1}

magnesium = 736 kJ mol^{-1}

aluminium = 577 kJ mol^{-1}

silicon = 786 kJ mol^{-1}

   i   Explain the general increase in ionisation energies from sodium to silicon.

   ii   Explain why aluminium has a lower first ionisation energy than magnesium.

b   The first ionisation energy of fluorine is 1680 kJ mol^{-1} whereas the first ionisation energy of iodine is 1010 kJ mol^{-1}. Explain why fluorine has a higher first ionisation energy than iodine despite it having a smaller nuclear charge.

Summary

- Electrons in an atom can exist only in certain energy levels (shells) outside the nucleus.

- The main energy levels (shells) are given principal quantum numbers n = 1, 2, 3, 4, etc. The lowest energy level (n = 1) is closest to the nucleus.

- The shells may be divided into subshells known as s, p and d subshells, which can hold a maximum of 2, 6 and 10 electrons, respectively.

- The region of space in which an electron is likely to be found is called an orbital. Each subshell has a number of orbitals which can each hold a maximum of two electrons. Subshells s, p and d have 1, 3 and 5 orbitals, respectively.

- The s orbitals are spherical in shape. The p orbitals have two 'lobes'.

- When two electrons are present in an orbital they spin in opposite directions and are said to be paired.

- The electronic configuration of atoms is found by adding electrons to each orbital starting from those in the lowest energy level.

- When electrons are added to orbitals in the same subshell they go into separate orbitals if possible. Electrons pair up where this is not possible.

- The 1st ionisation energy of an element is the energy needed to remove one electron from each atom in one mole of atoms of the element in the gaseous state (to form gaseous 1+ ions).

- The ionisation energies needed to remove the first, second, third, fourth, etc., electrons from each atom or ion in a mole of gaseous atoms are called successive ionisation energies.

- The magnitude of the ionisation energy depends on these four factors:
  - the distance of the electron from the nucleus
  - the number of positive charges in the nucleus
  - the degree of shielding of outer electrons by inner electron shells
  - spin-pair repulsion.

- The trends in 1st ionisation energy of the elements across a period and down a group can be explained using the four factors above.

- Values of successive ionisation energies of atoms provide evidence for their electronic configuration.

End-of-chapter questions

1 The sketch graph shows the 13 successive ionisation energies of aluminium.

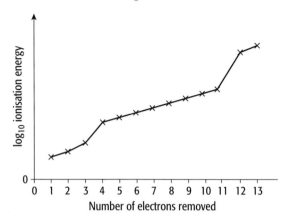

a Define the term **1st ionisation energy**. [3]

b How does the graph provide evidence for the existence of three electron shells in an aluminium atom? [6]

c Write an equation, including state symbols, to represent the 2nd ionisation energy of aluminium. [2]

d Write the electronic configuration of an aluminium ion, Al^{3+}, using $1s^2$ notation. [1]

Total = 12

2 The table below shows the 1st ionisation energies, ΔH_{i1}, in $kJ\,mol^{-1}$, of the elements in Period 3 of the Periodic Table.

Element	Na	Mg	Al	Si	P	S	Cl	Ar
ΔH_{i1}	494	736	577	786	1060	1000	1260	1520

a Explain why there is a general increase in the value of ΔH_{i1} across the period. [4]

b Explain why aluminium has a lower value of ΔH_{i1} than magnesium. [4]

c Write the electronic configuration for argon ($Z = 18$) using $1s^2$ notation. [1]

d Copy and complete the diagram below for the 15 electrons in phosphorus by

  i adding labels for the other subshells [1]

  ii showing how the electrons are arranged. [3]

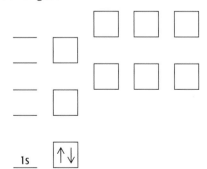

e Predict a value for the 1st ionisation energy for potassium, which has one more proton than argon. [1]

Total = 14

3 **a** What do you understand by the term **atomic orbital**? [1]

   b Draw diagrams to show the shape of:

      i an s orbital [1]

      ii a p orbital. [1]

   c Element X has the electronic configuration $1s^2 2s^2 2p^6 3s^2 3p^6 3d^8 4s^2$.

      i Which block in the Periodic Table does element X belong to? [1]

      ii State the maximum number of electrons in a d subshell. [1]

      iii Element X forms an ion of type X^{2+}.

         Write the full electronic configuration for this ion using $1s^2$ notation. [1]

      iv Write the symbol for the subshell that begins to fill after the 3d and 4s are completely full. [1]

Total = 7

4 The 1st ionisation energies of several elements with consecutive atomic numbers are shown in the graph below. The letters are not the symbols of the elements.

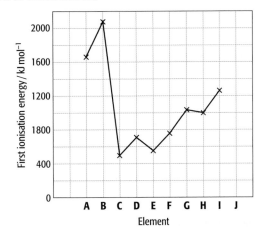

a Which of the elements **A** to **I** belong to Group 1 in the Periodic Table? Explain your answer. [3]

b Which of the elements **A** to **I** could have the electronic configuration $1s^2 2s^2 2p^6 3s^2$? [1]

c Explain the rise in 1st ionisation energy between element **E** and element **G**. [4]

d Estimate the 1st ionisation energy of element **J**. [2]

e The successive ionisation energies of element **A** are shown in the sketch graph.

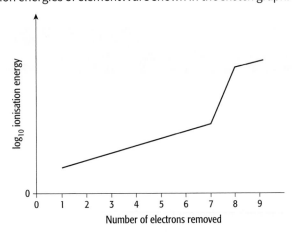

   What information does this graph give about how the electrons are arranged in shells for element **A**? [3]

Total = 13

5   a   Define the following:
       i   1st ionisation energy   [3]
       ii 3rd ionisation energy.   [3]
    b   Give the equations representing:
       i   the 1st ionisation energy of magnesium   [2]
       ii the 3rd ionisation energy of magnesium.   [2]
    c   Which ionisation energies are represented by the equations below?
       i $Mg^{3+}(g) \longrightarrow Mg^{4+}(g) + e^-$ [1]
       ii $Al^{5+}(g) \longrightarrow Al^{6+}(g) + e^-$ [1]

                                                                              Total = 12

6   The graph shows a sketch of $\log_{10}$ ionisation energy against number of electrons removed for magnesium.
    Use this sketch graph to answer the following questions.

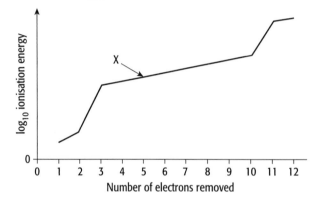

    a   Explain why the first two electrons are relatively easy to remove.   [3]
    b   Why is there a sharp rise in ionisation energy when the third electron is removed? [3]
    c   What information does the graph give about the electron arrangement of magnesium? [3]
    d   Give the equation for the ionisation energy marked X (the 5th ionisation energy). [2]

                                                                              Total = 11

7   a   The table shows the first five ionisation energies for five elements (**A** to **E**). For each one state which
        group the element belongs to.   [5]

Element	Ionisation energy / kJ mol^{-1}				
	1st	**2nd**	**3rd**	**4th**	**5th**
A	786.5	1577.1	3231.6	4355.5	16091
B	598.8	1145.4	4912	6491	8153
C	496	4562	6910	9543	13354
D	1087	2353	4621	6223	37831
E	578	1817	2744	11577	14842

    b   Explain your reasoning behind your answer for element **E**.   [1]
    c   Draw a sketch graph to show how $\log_{10}$ ionisation energy for phosphorus (atomic number 15) varies
        when plotted against number of electrons removed.   [6]

                                                                              Total = 12

8 a Define the term 1st ionisation energy. [3]

   b Draw a sketch graph to show how $\log_{10}$ ionisation energy for chlorine (atomic number 17) varies when plotted against number of electrons removed. [6]

   c Explain the shape of the graph you have drawn. [6]

Total = 15

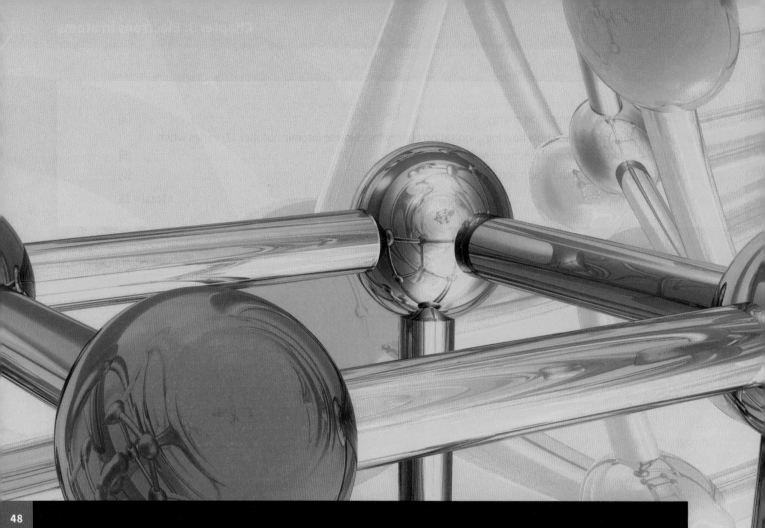

Chapter 4:
Chemical bonding

Learning outcomes

You should be able to:

- describe different types of bonding using 'dot-and-cross' diagrams, including:
  - ionic bonding
  - covalent bonding
  - co-ordinate (dative covalent) bonding
- explain the shapes of, and bond angles in, molecules by using the qualitative model of electron-pair repulsion (including lone pairs) using as simple examples: BF_3 (trigonal), CO_2 (linear), CH_4 (tetrahedral), NH_3 (pyramidal), H_2 (non-linear), SF_6 (octahedral) and PF_5 (trigonal bipyramidal)
- describe covalent bonding in terms of orbital overlap, giving σ and π bonds, including the concept of hybridisation to form sp, sp^2 and sp^3 orbitals

- explain the shape of, and bond angles in, ethane and ethene, and use this knowledge to predict the shapes of, and bond angles in, similar molecules
- explain the terms **bond energy**, **bond length** and **bond polarity** and use them to compare the reactivities of covalent bonds
- describe intermolecular forces based on permanent and induced dipoles, hydrogen bonding and metallic bonding
- describe, interpret and predict the effect of different types of bonding on the physical properties of substances
- deduce the type of bonding present from given information.

Introduction

In Chapter 3 we looked at the electronic configurations of individual atoms. We can use these electronic configurations to help us understand what happens when atoms combine to form compounds. The atoms in compounds are held together by different types of chemical bonding. Understanding what bonding is, and how bonds can be formed or broken, gives us the ability to extract resources from the Earth and make new compounds.

Figure 4.1 This sodium chloride (salt) has been extracted from the ground. Sodium chloride is an ionic compound.

Types of chemical bonding

Ionic bonding is the electrostatic attraction between positive and negative ions in an ionic crystal lattice. Covalent bonds are formed when the outer electrons of two atoms are shared. The ionic or covalent bonds formed are usually very strong – it takes a lot of energy to break them. There is also a third form of strong bonding: metallic bonding.

Although the atoms within molecules are kept together by strong covalent bonds, the forces between molecules are weak. We call these weak forces intermolecular forces.

There are several types of intermolecular force:

- van der Waals' forces (also called 'dispersion forces' and 'temporary dipole–induced dipole forces')
- permanent dipole–dipole forces
- hydrogen bonds.

An understanding of these different types of chemical bonding and an understanding of intermolecular forces helps us to explain the structure and physical properties of elements and compounds.

Ionic bonding

How are ions formed?

One way of forming ions is for atoms to gain or lose one or more electrons.

- Positive ions are formed when an atom loses one or more electrons. Metal atoms usually lose electrons and form positive ions.
- Negative ions are formed when an atom gains one or more electrons. Non-metal atoms usually gain electrons and form negative ions.

The charge on the ion depends on the number of electrons lost or gained (see page 41).

When metals combine with non-metals, the electrons in the outer shell of the metal atoms are transferred to the non-metal atoms. Each non-metal atom usually gains enough electrons to fill its outer shell. As a result of this, the metal and non-metal atoms usually end up with outer electron shells that are complete – they have an electronic configuration of a noble gas.

In Figure 4.2 we can see that:

- the sodium ion has the electronic structure $[2,8]^+$, the same as that of neon
- the chloride ion has the electronic structure $[2,8,8]^-$, the same as that of argon.

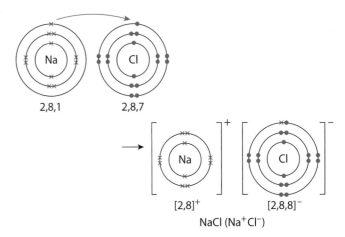

Figure 4.2 The formation of a sodium ion and chloride ion by electron transfer.

49

Figure 4.3 These crystals of salt are made up of millions of sodium ions and chloride ions.

The strong force of attraction between the positive and negative ions in the ionic crystal lattice results in an **ionic bond**. An ionic bond is sometimes called an **electrovalent bond**. In an ionic structure, the ions are arranged in a regular repeating pattern (see Chapter 5). As a result of this, the force between one ion and the ions of opposite charge that surround it is very great. In other words, ionic bonding is very strong.

Dot-and-cross diagrams

You will notice that in Figure 4.2 we used dots and crosses to show the electronic configuration of the chloride and sodium ions. This helps us keep track of where the electrons have come from. It does not mean that the electron transferred is any different from the others. Diagrams like this are called dot-and-cross diagrams.

When drawing a dot-and-cross diagram for an ionic compound it is usually acceptable to draw the outer electron shell of the metal ion without any electrons. This is because it has transferred these electrons to the negative ion. Figure 4.4 shows the outer shell dot-and-cross diagram for sodium chloride.

A dot-and-cross diagram shows:

- the outer electron shells only
- that the charge of the ion is spread evenly, by using square brackets
- the charge on each ion, written at the top right-hand corner of the square brackets.

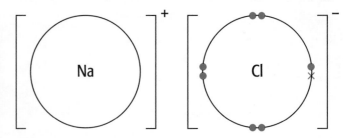

Figure 4.4 Dot-and-cross diagram for sodium chloride.

Some examples of dot-and-cross diagrams

Magnesium oxide

When magnesium reacts with oxygen to form magnesium oxide, the two electrons in the outer shell of each magnesium atom are transferred to the incompletely filled orbitals of an oxygen atom. By losing two electrons, each magnesium atom achieves the electronic configuration [2,8] (Figure 4.5). By gaining two electrons, each oxygen atom achieves the electronic configuration [2,8]. [2,8] is the electronic configuration of neon; it is a 'noble-gas configuration'.

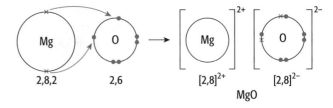

Figure 4.5 Dot-and-cross diagram for magnesium oxide.

Calcium chloride

Each calcium atom has two electrons in its outer shell, and these can be transferred to two chlorine atoms. By losing two electrons, each calcium atom achieves the electronic configuration [2,8,8] (Figure 4.6). The two chlorine atoms each gain one electron to achieve the electronic configuration [2,8,8]. [2,8,8] is the electronic configuration of argon; it is a 'noble-gas configuration'.

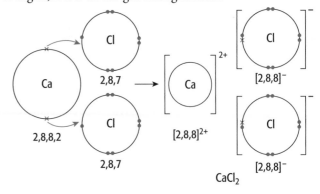

Figure 4.6 Dot-and-cross diagram for calcium chloride.

50

QUESTION

1 Draw dot-and-cross diagrams for the ions in the following ionic compounds. Show only the outer electron shells.

   a Potassium chloride, KCl

   b Sodium oxide, Na_2O

   c Calcium oxide, CaO

   d Magnesium chloride, $MgCl_2$

Covalent bonding

Single covalent bonds

When two non-metal atoms combine, they share one, or more, pairs of electrons. A shared pair of electrons is called a single covalent bond, or a bond pair. A single covalent bond is represented by a single line between the atoms: for example, Cl—Cl.

Figure 4.7 a Bromine and **b** iodine are elements. They both have simple covalent molecules.

You can see that when chlorine atoms combine not all the electrons are used in bonding. The pairs of outer-shell electrons not used in bonding are called lone pairs. Each atom in a chlorine molecule has three lone pairs of electrons and shares one bonding pair of electrons (Figure 4.8).

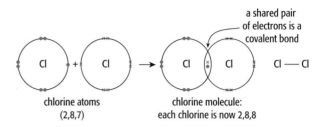

chlorine atoms
(2,8,7)

chlorine molecule:
each chlorine is now 2,8,8

Figure 4.8 Atoms of chlorine share electrons to form a single covalent bond.

When drawing the arrangement of electrons in a molecule we:

- use a 'dot' for electrons from one of the atoms and a 'cross' for the electrons from the other atom
- if there are more than two types of atom we can use additional symbols such as a small circle or a small triangle
- we draw the outer electrons in pairs, to emphasise the number of bond pairs and the number of lone pairs.

Some examples of dot-and-cross diagrams for simple covalently bonded molecules are shown in Figure 4.9.

There are some cases in which the electrons around a central atom may not have a noble gas configuration. For example:

- boron trifluoride, BF_3, has only six electrons around the boron atom; we say that the boron atom is 'electron deficient'
- sulfur hexafluoride, SF_6, has twelve electrons around the central sulfur atom; we say that the sulfur atom has an 'expanded octet' (Figure 4.10).

a Hydrogen

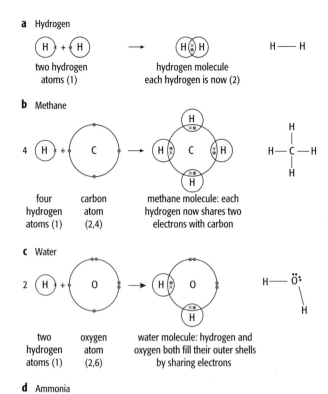

b Methane

c Water

d Ammonia

e Hydrogen chloride

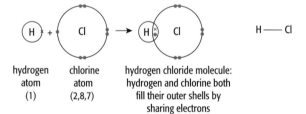

Figure 4.9 Dot-and-cross diagrams for some covalent compounds: **a** hydrogen, H_2, **b** methane, CH_4, **c** water, H_2O, **d** ammonia, NH_3, and **e** hydrogen chloride, HCl.

a Boron trifluoride

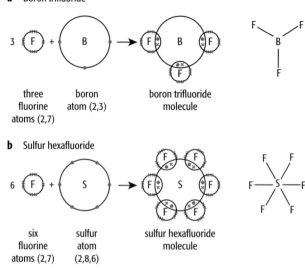

b Sulfur hexafluoride

Figure 4.10 Dot-and-cross diagrams for **a** boron trifluoride, BF_3, and **b** sulfur hexafluoride, SF_6.

QUESTION

2 Draw dot-and-cross diagrams for the following covalently bonded molecules. Show only the outer electron shells. Note that in part **d** the beryllium atom is electron deficient and in part **e** the phosphorus atom has an expanded octet.

   a Tetrachloromethane, CCl_4

   b Phosphorus(III) chloride

   c Bromine, Br_2

   d Beryllium chloride, $BeCl_2$

   e Phosphorus(V) chloride, PCl_5

Multiple covalent bonds

Some atoms can bond together by sharing two pairs of electrons. We call this a **double covalent bond**. A double covalent bond is represented by a double line between the atoms: for example, O=O. The dot-and-cross diagrams for oxygen, carbon dioxide and ethene, all of which have double covalent bonds, are shown in Figure 4.11.

■ In order to form an oxygen molecule, each oxygen atom needs to gain two electrons to complete its outer shell. So two pairs of electrons are shared and two covalent bonds are formed.

■ For carbon dioxide, each oxygen atom needs to gain two electrons as before. But the carbon atom needs to gain four electrons to complete its outer shell. So two oxygen atoms each form two bonds with carbon, so that the carbon atom has eight electrons around it.

a Oxygen

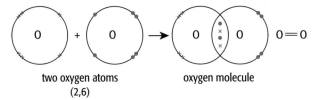

two oxygen atoms
(2,6)

oxygen molecule

b Carbon dioxide

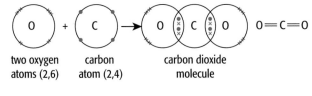

two oxygen
atoms (2,6)

carbon
atom (2,4)

carbon dioxide
molecule

c Ethene

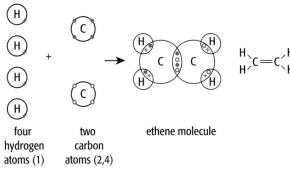

four
hydrogen
atoms (1)

two
carbon
atoms (2,4)

ethene molecule

Figure 4.11 Dot-and-cross diagrams for **a** oxygen, O_2, **b** carbon dioxide, CO_2, and **c** ethene, C_2H_4.

- In ethene, two hydrogen atoms share a pair of electrons with each carbon atom. This leaves each carbon atom with two outer shell electrons for bonding with each other. A double bond is formed.

Atoms can also bond together by sharing three pairs of electrons. We call this a **triple covalent bond**. Figure 4.12 shows a dot-and-cross diagram for the triple-bonded nitrogen molecule.

In order to form a nitrogen molecule, each nitrogen atom needs to gain three electrons to complete its outer shell. So three pairs of electrons are shared and three covalent bonds are formed.

Nitrogen

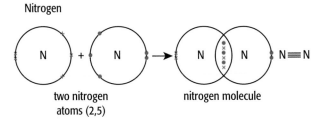

two nitrogen
atoms (2,5)

nitrogen molecule

Figure 4.12 Dot-and-cross diagram for a nitrogen molecule, N_2.

3   Draw dot-and-cross diagrams for the following covalently bonded molecules; show only the outer electron shells:

   a   ethene, $CH_2{=}CH_2$

   b   carbon disulfide, CS_2.

Co-ordinate bonding (dative covalent bonding)

A co-ordinate bond (or dative covalent bond) is formed when one atom provides both the electrons needed for a covalent bond.

For dative covalent bonding we need:

- one atom having a lone pair of electrons
- a second atom having an unfilled orbital to accept the lone pair; in other words, an electron-deficient compound.

An example of this is the ammonium ion, NH_4^+, formed when ammonia combines with a hydrogen ion, H^+. The hydrogen ion is electron deficient; it has space for two electrons in its shell. The nitrogen atom in the ammonia molecule has a lone pair of electrons. The lone pair on the nitrogen atom provides both electrons for the bond (Figure 4.13).

In a displayed formula (which shows all atoms and bonds), a co-ordinate bond is represented by an arrow. The head of the arrow points away from the lone pair that forms the bond.

Another molecule that has co-ordinate bonds is aluminium chloride. At high temperatures aluminium chloride exists as molecules with the formula $AlCl_3$. This molecule is electron deficient; it still needs two electrons to complete the outer shell of the aluminium atom. At lower

53

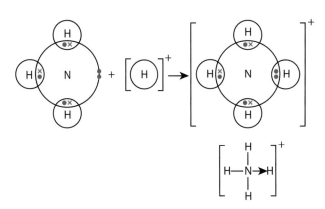

Figure 4.13 The formation of a co-ordinate bond in the ammonium ion.

temperatures two molecules of $AlCl_3$ combine to form a molecule with the formula Al_2Cl_6. The $AlCl_3$ molecules are able to combine because lone pairs of electrons on two of the chlorine atoms form co-ordinate bonds with the aluminium atoms, as shown in Figure 4.14.

Bond length and bond energy

In general, double bonds are shorter than single bonds. This is because double bonds have a greater quantity of negative charge between the two atomic nuclei. The greater force of attraction between the electrons and the nuclei pulls the atoms closer together. This results in a stronger bond. We measure the strength of a bond by its **bond energy**. This is the energy needed to break one mole of a given bond in a gaseous molecule (see also Chapter 6). Table 4.1 shows some values of bond lengths and bond energies.

Bond	Bond energy / kJ mol^{-1}	Bond length / nm
C—C	350	0.154
C=C	610	0.134
C—O	360	0.143
C=O	740	0.116

Table 4.1 Examples of values for bond energies and bond lengths.

Bond strength can influence the reactivity of a compound. The molecules in liquids and gases are in random motion so they are constantly colliding with each other. A reaction only happens between molecules when a collision occurs with enough energy to break bonds in either or both molecules. Nitrogen is unreactive because it has a triple bond, $N \equiv N$. It takes a lot of energy to break the nitrogen atoms apart; the bond energy required is 994 kJ mol^{-1}. Oxygen is much more reactive. Although it has a double bond, it only takes 496 kJ to break a mole of $O = O$ bonds. However, bond strength is only one factor that influences the reactivity of a molecule. The polarity of the bond (see page 61) and whether the bond is a σ bond (sigma bond) or a π bond (pi bond) (see page 57) both play a large part in determining chemical reactivity.

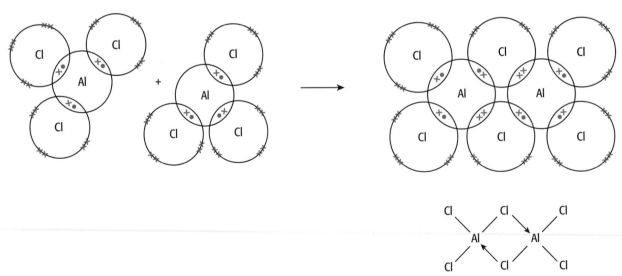

Figure 4.14 A dot-and-cross diagram for an aluminium chloride molecule, Al_2Cl_6.

QUESTION

5   The table lists bond lengths and bond energies of some hydrogen halides.

Hydrogen halide	Bond length / nm	Bond energy / kJ mol^{-1}
HCl	0.127	431
HBr	0.141	366
HI	0.161	299

a   What is the relationship between the bond length and the bond energy for these hydrogen halides?

b   Suggest why the bond energy values decrease in the order HCl > HBr > HI.

c   Suggest a value for the bond length in hydrogen fluoride, HF.

Shapes of molecules

Electron-pair repulsion theory

Because all electrons have the same (negative) charge, they repel each other when they are close together. So, a pair of electrons in the bonds surrounding the central atom in a molecule will repel other electron pairs. This repulsion forces the pairs of electrons apart until the repulsive forces are minimised.

The shape and bond angles of a covalently bonded molecule depend on:

■   the number of pairs of electrons around each atom
■   whether these pairs are lone pairs or bonding pairs.

Lone pairs of electrons have a more concentrated electron charge cloud than bonding pairs of electrons. Their cloud charges are wider and slightly closer to the nucleus of the central atom. This results in a different amount of repulsion between different types of electron pairs. The order of repulsion is lone pair–lone pair (most repulsion) > lone pair–bond pair > bond pair–bond pair (least repulsion).

Figure 4.15 shows the repulsions between lone pairs (pink) and bonding pairs (white) in a water molecule.

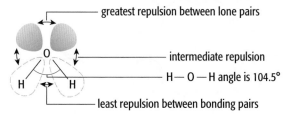

Figure 4.15   Repulsion between lone and bonding electron pairs in water.

Working out the shapes of molecules

The differences in electron-pair repulsion determine the shape and bond angles in a molecule. Figure 4.16 compares the shapes and bond angles of methane, ammonia and water. Space-filling models of these molecules are shown in Figure 4.17. Each of these molecules has four pairs of electrons surrounding the central atom. Note that in drawing three-dimensional diagrams, the triangular 'wedge' is the bond coming towards you and the dashed black line is the bond going away from you.

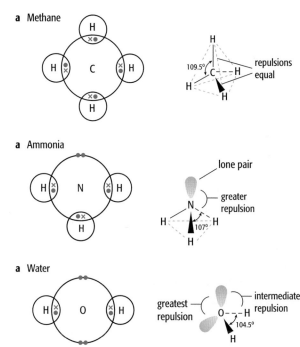

Figure 4.16   The bond angles in **a** methane, **b** ammonia and **c** water depend on the type of electron-pair repulsion.

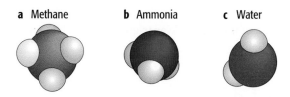

Figure 4.17   Shapes of molecules. These space-filling models show the molecular shapes of **a** methane, CH_4, **b** ammonia, NH_3, and **c** water, H_2O.

■   Methane has four bonding pairs of electrons surrounding the central carbon atom. The equal repulsive forces of each bonding pair of electrons results in a tetrahedral structure with all H—C—H bond angles being 109.5°.

In ammonia and water, the tetrahedral arrangement of the electron pairs around the central atom becomes distorted.

55

- Ammonia has three bonding pairs of electrons and one lone pair. As lone pair–bond pair repulsion is greater than bond pair–bond pair repulsion, the bonding pairs of electrons are pushed closer together. This gives the ammonia molecule a triangular pyramidal shape. The H—N—H bond angle is about 107°.
- Water has two bonding pairs of electrons and two lone pairs. The greatest electron pair repulsion is between the two lone pairs. This results in the bonds being pushed even closer together. The shape of the water molecule is a non-linear V shape. The H—O—H bond angle is 104.5°.

QUESTION

6 a Predict the shapes of the following molecules, which you drew in question 2 on page 52:

    i tetrachloromethane, CCl_4

    ii beryllium chloride, $BeCl_2$

    iii phosphorus(III) chloride.

b Draw dot-and-cross diagrams for the following molecules and then predict their shapes:

    i hydrogen sulfide, H_2S

    ii phosphine, PH_3.

More molecular shapes

We can work out the shapes of other molecules by following the rules for electron-pair repulsion.

Boron trifluoride

Boron trifluoride is an electron-deficient molecule. It has only six electrons in its outer shell. The three bonding pairs of electrons repel each other equally, so the F—B—F bond angles are 120° (Figure 4.18). We describe the shape of the molecule as trigonal planar. 'Trigonal' means 'having three angles'.

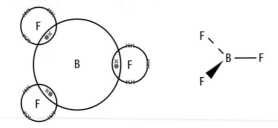

Figure 4.18 Boron trifluoride.

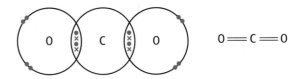

Figure 4.19 Carbon dioxide.

Carbon dioxide

Carbon dioxide has two carbon–oxygen double bonds and no lone pairs. The four electrons in each double bond repel other electrons in a similar way to the two electrons in a single bond (Figure 4.19). So, the O—C—O bond angle is 180°. We describe the shape of the carbon dioxide molecule as linear.

Phosphorus pentafluoride

Phosphorus pentafluoride has five bonding pairs of electrons and no lone pairs. The repulsion between the electron pairs results in the most stable structure being a trigonal bipyramid (Figure 4.20). Three of the fluorine atoms lie in the same plane as the phosphorus atom. The bond angles FPF within this plane are 120°. Two of the fluorine atoms lie above and below this plane at 90° to it.

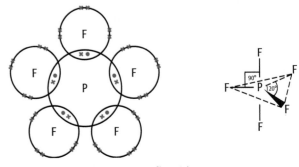

Figure 4.20 Phosphorus pentafluoride.

Sulfur hexafluoride

Sulfur hexafluoride has six bonding pairs of electrons and no lone pairs. The equal repulsion between the electron pairs results in the structure shown in Figure 4.21. All F—S—F bond angles are 90°. We describe the shape as octahedral.

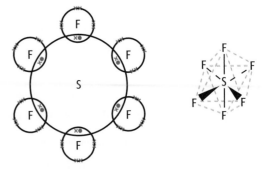

Figure 4.21 Sulfur hexafluoride.

QUESTION

7 a Draw a dot-and-cross diagram for a molecule of selenium hexafluoride, SeF_6. A single selenium atom has six electrons in its outer shell.

   b Predict the shape of selenium hexafluoride.

   c Draw the shape of the phosphorus(V) chloride molecule that you drew as a dot-and-cross diagram in question 2 on page 52.

σ bonds and π bonds

A single covalent bond is formed when two non-metal atoms combine. Each atom that combines has an atomic orbital containing a single unpaired electron. In the formation of a covalent bond the atomic orbitals overlap so that a combined orbital is formed, containing two electrons. We call this combined orbital a molecular orbital. The amount of overlap of the atomic orbitals determines the strength of the bond: the greater the overlap, the stronger the bond. Figure 4.22 shows how the s atomic orbitals of two hydrogen atoms overlap to form a covalent bond.

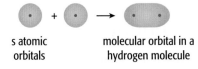

Figure 4.22 Two 1s atomic orbitals in hydrogen overlap to form a covalent bond.

The p atomic orbitals can also overlap linearly (end-on) to form covalent bonds. When p orbitals are involved in forming single bonds, they become modified to include some s orbital character. The orbital is slightly altered in shape to make one of the lobes of the p orbital bigger. The process of mixing atomic orbitals (for example one s orbital and three p orbitals) in this way is called

hybridisation. The hybrids are called sp^3 hybrids. In sp^3 hybrids, each orbital has $\frac{1}{4}$ s character and $\frac{3}{4}$ p character. When one s orbital and two p orbitals are hybridised, the hybrids are called sp^2 hybrids. When one s orbital and one p orbital are hybridised, the hybrids are called sp orbitals. When hybridised orbitals overlap linearly (end-on) we call the bond a σ bond (sigma bond). Figure 4.23 shows the formation of σ bonds.

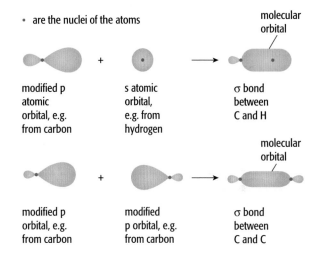

Figure 4.23 Bonds are formed by the linear (end-on) overlap of atomic orbitals.

The electron density of each σ bond is symmetrical about a line joining the nuclei of the atoms forming the bond.

Bonds formed by the sideways overlap of p orbitals are called π bonds (pi bonds). A π bond is not symmetrical about the axes joining the nuclei of the atoms forming the bond. Figure 4.24 shows how a π bond is formed from two p orbitals overlapping sideways.

We often draw a single π bond as two electron clouds, one arising from each lobe of the p orbitals. You must remember, though, that the two clouds of electrons in a π bond represent one bond consisting of a total of two electrons.

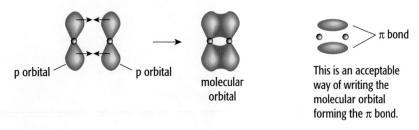

Figure 4.24 π bonds are formed by the sideways overlap of atomic orbitals.

The shape of some organic molecules

We can explain the shapes of molecules in terms of the patterns of electron density found in σ bonds and π bonds.

Ethane

The displayed formula for ethane is:

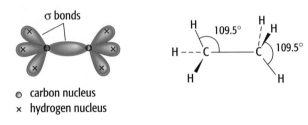

All the bonds in ethane are formed by linear overlap of atomic orbitals. They are all σ bonds.

Figure 4.25 shows the electron density distribution in ethane formed by these σ bonds. All the areas of electron density repel each other equally. This makes the HCH bond angles all the same (109.5°).

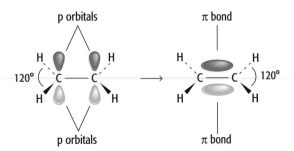

○ carbon nucleus
× hydrogen nucleus

Figure 4.25 The electron density distribution in ethane.

Ethene

The displayed formula for ethene is

Each carbon atom in ethene uses three of its four outer electrons to form σ bonds. Two σ bonds are formed with the hydrogen atoms and one σ bond is formed with the other carbon atom.

The fourth electron from each carbon atom occupies a p orbital, which overlaps sideways with a similar p orbital on the other carbon atom. This forms a π bond. Figure 4.26 shows how this occurs.

Figure 4.26 Overlap of p orbitals to produce a π bond in ethene.

The electron density distribution of both the σ and π bonds in ethene is shown in Figure 4.27.

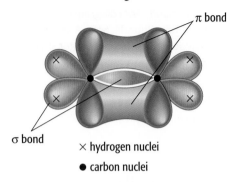

σ bond
× hydrogen nuclei
● carbon nuclei

Figure 4.27 The electron density distribution in ethene.

Ethene is a planar molecule because this ensures the maximum overlap of the p orbitals that form the π bond. You will notice that the electron clouds that make up the π bond lie above and below the plane of the carbon and hydrogen nuclei. We would expect the H—C—H bond angle in ethene to be about 120° because the three areas of electron density of the σ bonds are equally distributed. However, because of the position of the π bond, this bond angle is actually 117°. This minimises the repulsive forces.

Metallic bonding

What is a metallic bond?

Figure 4.28 Metals, clockwise from top left: sodium, gold, mercury, magnesium and copper.

In a metal, the atoms are packed closely together in a regular arrangement called a lattice. Metal atoms in a lattice tend to lose their outer shell electrons and become positive ions. The outer shell electrons occupy new energy levels and are free to move throughout the metal lattice. We call these electrons delocalised electrons (mobile electrons). Delocalised electrons are electrons that are not associated with any one particular atom or bond.

Metallic bonding is strong. This is because the ions are held together by the strong electrostatic attraction between their positive charges and the negative charges of the delocalised electrons (Figure 4.29). This electrostatic attraction acts in all directions. The strength of metallic bonding increases with:

- increasing positive charge on the ions in the metal lattice
- decreasing size of metal ions in the lattice
- increasing number of mobile electrons per atom.

Metallic bonding and the properties of metals

We can use our model of metallic bonding to explain many of the properties of metals.

Most metals have high melting points and high boiling points

It takes a lot of energy to weaken the strong attractive forces between the metal ions and the delocalised electrons. These attractive forces can only be overcome at high temperatures. However, mercury is a liquid at room temperature (Figure 4.30). This is because some of the electrons in a mercury atom are bound more tightly than usual to the nucleus, weakening the metallic bonds between atoms.

Figure 4.30 Mercury is a liquid at room temperature.

Metals conduct electricity

When a voltage is applied to a piece of metal, an electric current flows in it because the delocalised electrons (mobile electrons) are free to move. Metallic bonding is the only type of bonding that allows us to predict reliably that a solid will conduct electricity. Covalent solids cannot conduct electricity because none of their electrons are free to move, although graphite is an exception to this. Ionic solids cannot conduct because neither their electrons nor their ions are free to move.

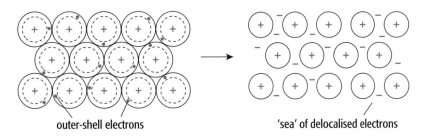

outer-shell electrons · 'sea' of delocalised electrons

Figure 4.29 Metallic bonding: there are strong attractive forces between the positively charged ions and the delocalised electrons.

QUESTION

8 Answer the following, giving a full explanation in terms of metallic bonding.

  a Explain why aluminium has a higher melting point than sodium.

  b The thermal conductivity of stainless steel is $82 \, W \, m^{-1} \, K^{-1}$. The thermal conductivity of copper is $400 \, W \, m^{-1} \, K^{-1}$. Why do some stainless steel saucepans have a copper base?

  c Why does aluminium conduct electricity better than sodium?

Metals conduct heat

The conduction of heat is partly due to the movement of the delocalised electrons and partly due to the vibrations passed on from one metal ion to the next.

Intermolecular forces

The forces within molecules due to covalent bonding are strong. However, the forces between molecules are much weaker. We call these forces **intermolecular forces**.

There are three types of intermolecular force:

- van der Waals' forces (which are also called dispersion forces and temporary dipole–induced dipole forces)
- permanent dipole–dipole forces
- hydrogen bonding.

Table 4.2 compares the relative strength of these intermolecular forces and other bonds.

Type of bond	Bond strength / kJ mol^{-1}
ionic bonding in sodium chloride	760
O—H covalent bond in water	464
hydrogen bonding	20–50
permanent dipole–dipole force	5–20
van der Waals' forces	1–20

Table 4.2 Strengths of different types of bond and intermolecular force.

In order to understand how intermolecular forces work, we first have to know about electronegativity and bond polarity.

Figure 4.31 The intermolecular forces in water allow some insects to skate over its surface.

Electronegativity

Electronegativity is the ability of a particular atom, which is covalently bonded to another atom, to attract the bond pair of electrons towards itself.

The greater the value of the electronegativity, the greater the power of an atom to attract the electrons in a covalent bond towards itself. For Groups 1 to 17 the pattern of electronegativity is:

- electronegativity increases across a period from Group 1 to Group 17
- electronegativity increases up each group.

This means that fluorine is the most electronegative element.

For the most electronegative elements, the order of electronegativity is:

increasing electronegativity

$$Br < Cl < N < O < F$$

Carbon and hydrogen have electronegativities that are lower than those of most other non-metallic elements.

Polarity in molecules

When the electronegativity values of the two atoms forming a covalent bond are the same, the pair of electrons is equally shared. We say that the covalent bond is **non-polar**. For example, hydrogen (H_2), chlorine (Cl_2) and bromine (Br_2) are non-polar molecules.

When a covalent bond is formed between two atoms having different electronegativity values, the more electronegative atom attracts the pair of electrons in the bond towards it.

As a result:

- the centre of positive charge does not coincide with the centre of negative charge
- we say that the electron distribution is asymmetric
- the two atoms are partially charged
- we show
  - the less electronegative atom with the partial charge $\delta+$ ('delta positive')
  - the more electronegative atom with the partial charge $\delta-$ ('delta negative')
- we say that the bond is polar (or that it has a dipole).

Figure 4.32 shows the polar bond in a hydrogen chloride molecule.

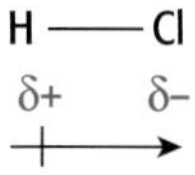

$$H \underset{\delta+}{\longrightarrow} Cl$$
$$\delta-$$

Figure 4.32 Hydrogen chloride is a polar molecule.

As the difference in electronegativity values of the atoms in a covalent bond increases, the bond becomes more polar. The degree of polarity of a molecule is measured as a dipole moment. The direction of the dipole is shown by the sign $\longmapsto$. The arrow points to the partially negatively charged end of the dipole.

In molecules containing more than two atoms, we have to take into account:

- the polarity of each bond
- the arrangement of the bonds in the molecule.

Trichloromethane, $CHCl_3$, is a polar molecule. The three C—Cl dipoles point in a similar direction. Their combined effect is not cancelled out by the polarity of the C—H bond. This is because the C—H bond is virtually non-polar. The electron distribution is asymmetric. The molecule is polar, with the negative end towards the chlorine atoms. This is shown in Figure 4.33a.

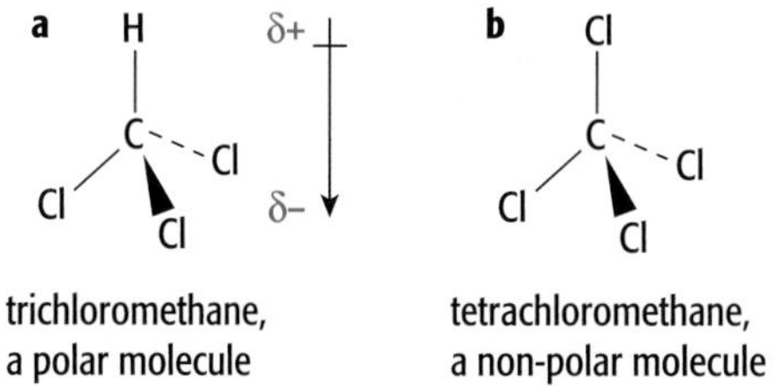

Figure 4.33 The polarity of **a** trichloromethane and **b** tetrachloromethane.

Some molecules contain polar bonds but have no overall polarity. This is because the polar bonds in these molecules are arranged in such a fashion that the dipole moments cancel each other out. An example is tetrachloromethane, CCl_4 (Figure 4.33b). Tetrachloromethane has four polar C—Cl bonds pointing towards the four corners of a tetrahedron. The dipoles in each bond cancel each other. So, tetrachloromethane is non-polar.

The charge distribution in molecules and ions can be determined by a method called X-ray spectroscopy. One method involves firing X-rays at molecules and measuring the energy of the electrons given off. Using this method, scientists have found that in a sulfate ion, the sulfur atom has a charge of +1.12 units and the four oxygen atoms each have a charge of –0.78 units.

QUESTION

9 Are the following molecules polar or non-polar? In each case give a reason for your answer.

(Electronegativity values: F = 4.0, Cl = 3.0, Br = 2.8, S = 2.5, C = 2.5, H = 2.1)

a Chlorine, Cl_2

b Hydrogen fluoride, HF

c The V-shaped molecule, sulfur dichloride, SCl_2

d The tetrahedral molecule, chloromethane, CH_3Cl

e The tetrahedral molecule tetrabromomethane, CBr_4.

Polarity and chemical reactivity

Bond polarity influences chemical reactivity. For example, both nitrogen, N≡N, and carbon monoxide, C≡O, have triple bonds requiring a similar amount of energy to break them. Nitrogen is a non-polar molecule and is fairly unreactive. But carbon monoxide is a polar molecule, and this explains its reactivity with oxygen and its use as a reducing agent. Many chemical reactions are started by a reagent attacking one of the electrically charged ends of a polar molecule. For example, chloroethane, C_2H_5Cl, is far more reactive than ethane, C_2H_6. This is because reagents such as OH^- ions can attack the delta-positive carbon atom of the polarised C—Cl bond (see also page 220).

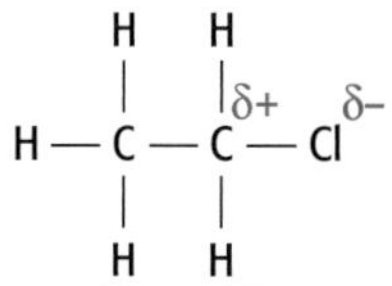

Such an attack is not possible with ethane because the C—H bond is virtually non-polar. This helps to explain why alkanes, such as ethane, are not very reactive.

van der Waals' forces

Noble gases such as neon and argon exist as isolated atoms. Noble gases can be liquefied, but at very low temperatures, so there must be very weak forces of attraction between their atoms. These weak forces keep the atoms together in the liquid state.

Bromine is a non-polar molecule that is liquid at room temperature. The weak forces of attraction are keeping the bromine molecules together at room temperature. These very weak forces of attraction are called van der Waals' forces. Van der Waals' forces exist between all atoms or molecules. So, how do van der Waals' forces arise?

The electron charge clouds in a non-polar molecule (or atom) are constantly moving. It often happens that more of the charge cloud is on one side of the molecule than the other. This means that one end of the molecule has, for a short moment, more negative charge than the other. A temporary dipole is set up. This dipole can set up (induce) a dipole on neighbouring molecules. As a result of this, there are forces of attraction between the δ+ end of the dipole in one molecule and the δ– end of the dipole in a neighbouring molecule (Figure 4.34). These dipoles are always temporary because the electrons clouds are always moving. Van der Waals' forces are sometimes called temporary dipole–induced dipole forces.

Van der Waals' forces increase with

- increasing number of electrons (and protons) in the molecule
- increasing the number of contact points between the molecules – contact points are places where the molecules come close together.

Differences in the size of the van der Waals' forces can be used to explain the trend in the enthalpy change of vaporisation and boiling points of the noble gases. Figure 4.35 shows how these vary with the number of electrons present. (The enthalpy change of vaporisation is the energy required to convert a mole of liquid into a mole of gas.)

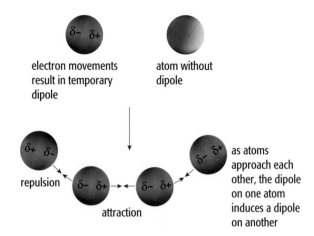

Figure 4.34 How van der Waals' forces arise.

You can see that both the enthalpy change of vaporisation and the boiling points of the noble gases increase as the number of electrons increases. This is because the van der Waals' forces between the atoms are increased with an increasing number of electrons. So, more energy is needed to change the liquid into vapour and the boiling point is higher.

The effect of increasing the number of contact points can be seen by comparing the boiling points of pentane (boiling point 36 °C) and 2,2-dimethylpropane (boiling point 10 °C) (Figure 4.36). These compounds have equal numbers of electrons in their molecules.

The molecules in pentane can line up beside each other so there are a large number of contact points. The van der Waals' forces are higher, so the boiling point is higher. The molecules of 2,2-dimethylpropane are more compact. The surface area available for coming into contact with neighbouring molecules is smaller. The van der Waals' forces are relatively lower, so the boiling point is lower.

The van der Waals' forces between individual atoms are very small. However, the total van der Waals' forces between very long non-polar molecules such as poly(ethene) molecules (see page 211) can be much larger. That is why poly(ethene) is a solid at room temperature.

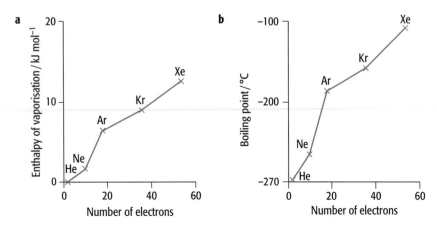

Figure 4.35 a Enthalpy changes of vaporisation and **b** boiling points of the noble gases plotted against the number of electrons present.

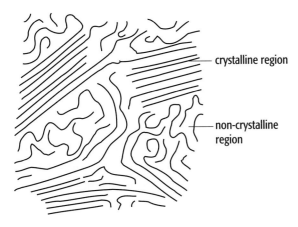

pentane,
boiling point 36 °C

2,2-dimethylpropane,
boiling point 10 °C

Figure 4.36 The difference in boiling points of pentane and 2,2-dimethylpropane can be explained by the strength of the van der Waals' forces.

Two types of poly(ethene) are low-density poly(ethene), LDPE, and high-density poly(ethene), HDPE. Both have crystalline and non-crystalline regions in them (Figure 4.37).

crystalline region

non-crystalline region

Figure 4.37 Crystalline and non-crystalline regions in poly(ethene).

HDPE has more crystalline regions where the molecules are closer together than LDPE. The total van der Waals' forces are greater, so HDPE is the stronger of the two.

QUESTION

10 a The boiling points of the halogens are:

fluorine	–188 °C	chlorine	–35 °C
bromine	+59 °C	iodine	+184 °C

    i Describe the trend in these boiling points going down Group 17.

    ii Explain the trend in these boiling points.

b The table lists the formulae and boiling points of some alkanes. Explain this trend.

Alkane	Structural formula	Boiling point / °C
methane	CH_4	–164
ethane	CH_3CH_3	–88
propane	$CH_3CH_2CH_3$	–42
butane	$CH_3CH_2CH_2CH_3$	0

Permanent dipole–dipole forces

In some molecules, the dipole is permanent. Molecules with a permanent dipole are called polar molecules. A fine jet of polar molecules will be attracted towards an electrically charged plastic rod or comb. (The rod can be charged by rubbing it with a woollen cloth.) Figure 4.38 shows the result of this experiment.

The molecules are always attracted to the charged rod, whether it is positively or negatively charged. This is because the molecules have both negatively and positively charged ends.

The forces between two molecules having permanent dipoles are called **permanent dipole–dipole forces**. The attractive force between the δ+ charge on one molecule and the δ– charge on a neighbouring molecule causes a weak attractive force between the molecules (Figure 4.39).

63

Figure 4.38 The deflection of water by an electrically charged nylon comb.

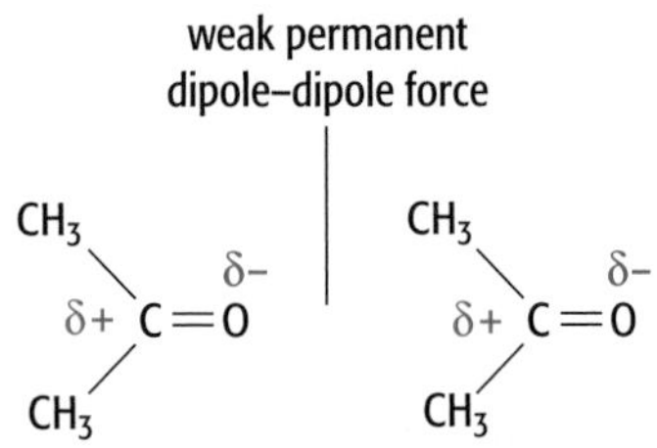

Figure 4.39 Dipole–dipole forces in propanone.

For small molecules with the same number of electrons, permanent dipole–dipole forces are often stronger than van der Waals' forces. For example, propanone (CH_3COCH_3, $M_r = 58$) has a higher boiling point than butane ($CH_3CH_2CH_2CH_3$, $M_r = 58$) (Figure 4.40). This means that more energy is needed to break the intermolecular forces between propanone molecules than between butane molecules.

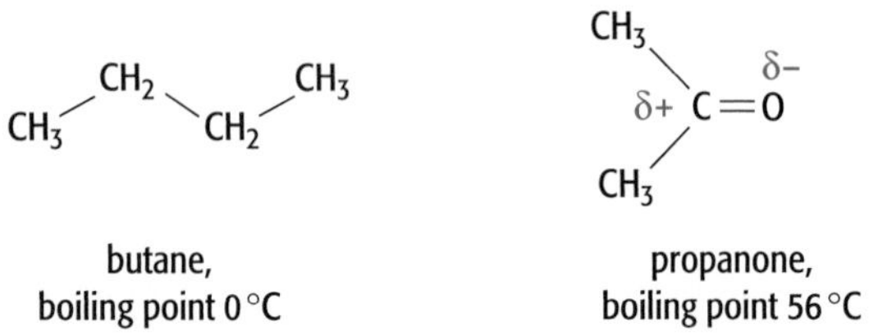

Figure 4.40 The difference in the boiling points of propanone and butane can be explained by the different types of intermolecular force between the molecules.

The permanent dipole–dipole forces between propanone molecules are strong enough to make this substance a liquid at room temperature. There are only van der Waals' forces between butane molecules. These forces are comparatively weak, so butane is a gas at room temperature.

QUESTION

11 Bromine, Br_2, and iodine monochloride, ICl, have the same number of electrons. But the boiling point of iodine monochloride is nearly 40 °C higher than the boiling point of bromine. Explain this difference.

Hydrogen bonding

Hydrogen bonding is the strongest type of intermolecular force. For hydrogen bonding to occur between two molecules we need:

- one molecule having a hydrogen atom covalently bonded to F, O or N (the three most electronegative atoms)
- a second molecule having a F, O or N atom with an available lone pair of electrons.

When a hydrogen atom is covalently bonded to a very electronegative atom, the bond is very highly polarised. The $\delta+$ charge on the hydrogen atom is high enough for a bond to be formed with a lone pair of electrons on the F, O or N atom of a neighbouring molecule (Figure 4.41). The force of attraction is about one-tenth of the strength of a normal covalent bond. For maximum bond strength, the angle between the covalent bond to the hydrogen atom and the hydrogen bond is usually 180°.

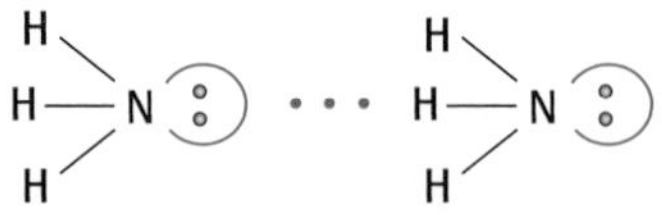

Figure 4.41 Hydrogen bonding between two ammonia molecules. A hydrogen bond is represented by a line of dots.

The average number of hydrogen bonds formed per molecule depends on:

- the number of hydrogen atoms attached to F, O or N in the molecule
- the number of lone pairs present on the F, O or N.

Water has two hydrogen atoms and two lone pairs per molecule (Figure 4.42). So water is extensively hydrogen bonded with other water molecules. It has an average of two hydrogen bonds per molecule.

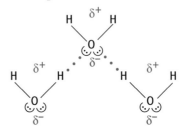

Figure 4.42 Water can form, on average, two hydrogen bonds per molecule.

Ammonia is less extensively hydrogen bonded than water (see Figure 4.41). It can form, on average, only one hydrogen bond per molecule. Although each ammonia molecule has three hydrogen atoms attached to the nitrogen atom, it has only one lone pair of electrons that can be involved in hydrogen bond formation.

QUESTION

12 Draw diagrams to show hydrogen bonding between the following molecules:

a ethanol, C_2H_5OH, and water

b ammonia and water

c two hydrogen fluoride molecules.

How does hydrogen bonding affect boiling point?

Some compounds may have higher boiling points than expected. This can be due to hydrogen bonding. Figure 4.43 shows a graph of the boiling points of the hydrogen halides, HF, HCl, HBr and HI, plotted against the position of the halogen in the Periodic Table.

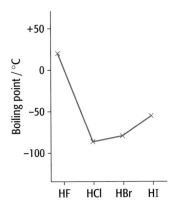

Figure 4.43 The boiling points of the hydrogen halides.

The rise in boiling point from HCl to HI is due to the increasing number of electrons in the halogen atoms as we go down the group. This leads to increased van der Waals' forces as the molecules get bigger. If hydrogen fluoride only had van der Waals' forces between its molecules, we would expect its boiling point to be about –90 °C. However, the boiling point of hydrogen fluoride is 20 °C, which is much higher. This is because of the stronger intermolecular forces of hydrogen bonding between the HF molecules.

QUESTION

13 The table lists the boiling points of some Group 15 hydrides.

Hydride	Boiling point / °C
ammonia, NH_3	–33
phosphine, PH_3	–88
arsine, AsH_3	–55
stibine, SbH_3	–17

a Explain the trend in the boiling points from phosphine to stibine.

b Explain why the boiling point of ammonia does not follow this trend.

The peculiar properties of water

1 Enthalpy change of vaporisation and boiling point

Water has a much higher enthalpy change of vaporisation and boiling point than expected.

This is due to its extensive hydrogen bonding. Figure 4.44 shows the enthalpy changes of vaporisation of water and other Group 16 hydrides.

The rise in enthalpy change of vaporisation from H_2S to H_2Te is due to the increasing number of electrons in the Group 16 atoms as we go down the group. This leads to increased van der Waals' forces as the molecules get bigger. If water only had van der Waals' forces between its molecules, we would expect its enthalpy change to be about 17 kJ mol^{-1}. But the enthalpy change of vaporisation of water is much higher. This is because water is extensively hydrogen bonded. The boiling point of water is also much higher than predicted by the trend in boiling points for the other Group 16 hydrides. This also indicates that much more energy is required to break the bonds between water molecules compared with other hydrides of Group 16 elements.

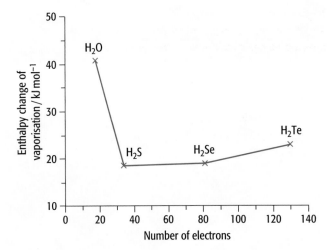

Figure 4.44 Enthalpy changes of vaporisation for Group 16 hydrides plotted against number of electrons present.

2 Surface tension and viscosity

Water has a high surface tension and high viscosity.

Hydrogen bonding reduces the ability of water molecules to slide over each other, so the viscosity of water is high. The hydrogen bonds in water also exert a significant downward force at the surface of the liquid. This causes the surface tension of water to be higher than for most liquids.

3 Ice is less dense than water

Most solids are denser than their liquids. This is because the molecules are more closely packed in the solid state. But this is not true of water. In ice, there is a three-dimensional hydrogen-bonded network of water molecules. This produces a rigid lattice in which each oxygen atom is surrounded by a tetrahedron of hydrogen atoms. This 'more open' arrangement, due to the relatively long hydrogen bonds, allows the water molecules to be slightly further apart than in the liquid (Figure 4.46). So the density of ice is less than that of liquid water.

Figure 4.45 Ice floats on water.

Figure 4.46 A model of ice. Oxygen atoms are red, hydrogen atoms are white, hydrogen bonds are lilac. This hydrogen-bonded arrangement makes ice less dense than water.

Bonding and physical properties

The type of bonding between atoms, ions or molecules influences the physical properties of a substance.

Physical state at room temperature and pressure

Ionic compounds

Ionic compounds are solids at room temperature and pressure. This is because:

- there are strong electrostatic forces (ionic bonds) holding the positive and negative ions together
- the ions are regularly arranged in a lattice (see Chapter 5), with the oppositely charged ions close to each other.

Ionic compounds have high melting points, high boiling points and high enthalpy changes of vaporisation. It takes a lot of energy to overcome the strong electrostatic attractive forces.

Metals

Metals, apart from mercury, are solids. Most metals have high melting points, high boiling points and high enthalpy changes of vaporisation. This is because it takes a lot of energy to overcome the strong attractive forces between the positive ions and the 'sea' of delocalised electrons.

Covalent compounds

Covalently bonded substances with a simple molecular structure, for example water and ammonia, are usually liquids or gases. This is because the forces between the molecules are weak. It does not take much energy to overcome these intermolecular forces, so these substances have low melting points, low boiling points and low enthalpy changes of vaporisation compared with ionic compounds. Some substances that have covalently bonded molecules may be solids at room temperature, for example iodine and poly(ethene). These are usually molecules where the van der Waals' forces are considerable. However, the melting points of these substances are still fairly low compared with ionic compounds or most metals.

Solubility

Ionic compounds

Most ionic compounds are soluble in water. This is because water molecules are polar and they are attracted to the ions on the surface of the ionic solid. These attractions are called ion–dipole attractions (see page 265). These attractions replace the electrostatic forces between the ions and the ions go into solution.

Metals

Metals do not dissolve in water. However, some metals, for example sodium and calcium, react with water.

Covalent compounds

Covalently bonded substances with a simple molecular structure fall into two groups.

- Those that are insoluble in water. Most covalently bonded molecules are non-polar. Water molecules are not attracted to them so they are insoluble. An example is iodine.
- Those that are soluble in water. Small molecules that can form hydrogen bonds with water are generally soluble. An example is ethanol, C_2H_5OH.

Some covalently bonded substances react with water rather than dissolving in it. For example, hydrogen chloride reacts with water to form hydrogen ions and chloride ions, and the ions are soluble. Silicon chloride reacts with water to form hydrogen ions, chloride ions and silicon dioxide. This reaction is called a hydrolysis reaction.

Electrical conductivity

Ionic compounds

Ionic compounds do not conduct electricity when in the solid state. This is because the ions are fixed in the lattice and can only vibrate around a fixed point. When molten, an ionic compound conducts electricity because the ions are mobile.

Metals

Metals conduct electricity both when solid and when molten. This is because the delocalised electrons are mobile.

Covalent compounds

Covalently bonded substances with a simple molecular structure do not conduct electricity. This is because they have neither ions nor electrons that are mobile.

QUESTION

14 Explain the following differences in terms of the type of bonding present.

  a Aluminium oxide has a melting point of 2980 °C but aluminium chloride changes to a vapour at 178 °C.

  b Magnesium chloride conducts electricity when molten but not when solid.

  c Iron conducts electricity when solid but the ionic solid iron(II) chloride does not conduct when solid.

  d Sodium sulfate dissolves in water but sulfur does not.

  e Propanol, $CH_3CH_2CH_2OH$, is soluble in water but propane, $CH_3CH_2CH_3$, is not.

  f A solution of hydrogen chloride in water conducts electricity.

Summary

- Ions are formed when atoms gain or lose electrons.

- Ionic (electrovalent) bonding involves an attractive force between positively and negatively charged ions in an ionic lattice.

- A covalent bond is formed when atoms share a pair of electrons.

- When atoms form covalent or ionic bonds each atom or ion has a full outer electron shell of electrons. (Some covalent compounds may be electron deficient or have an 'expanded octet'.)

- Dot-and-cross diagrams can be drawn to show the arrangement of electrons in ionic and covalent compounds.

- In dative covalent bonding one atom provides both electrons in the formation of the covalent bond.

- The shapes and bond angles in molecules can be predicted using the idea that lone pairs of electrons repel other lone pairs more than bond pair electrons, and that bond pair to bond pair repulsion is least.

- σ bonds (sigma bonds) are formed by end-on overlap of atomic orbitals, whereas π bonds (pi bonds) are formed by sideways overlap of p-type atomic orbitals.

- Three types of relatively weak intermolecular forces are hydrogen bonding, permanent dipole–dipole forces and van der Waals' forces.

- Electronegativity differences can be used to predict the type of weak intermolecular forces between molecules.
- Hydrogen bonding occurs between molecules that have a hydrogen atom covalently bonded to an atom of a very electronegative element (fluorine, oxygen or nitrogen).
- The reactivities of covalent bonds can be explained in terms of bond energy, bond length and bond polarity.
- Intermolecular forces are based on either permanent dipoles, as in $CHCl_3(l)$, or temporary induced dipoles (van der Waals' forces), as in $Br_2(l)$.

- Metallic bonding can be explained in terms of a lattice of positive ions surrounded by mobile electrons.
- The physical properties of substances may be predicted from the type of bonding present.
- Substances with ionic bonding have high melting and boiling points, whereas simple molecules with covalent bonding have low melting points.
- The presence of hydrogen bonding in a molecule influences its melting point and boiling point.

End-of-chapter questions

1 The table shows the atomic number and boiling points of some noble gases.

Gas	helium	neon	argon	krypton	xenon
Atomic number	2	10	18	36	54
Boiling point / °C	−253	−246	−186	−152	−107

    a   Use ideas about forces between atoms to explain this trend in boiling points.   [2]

    b   Xenon forms a number of covalently bonded compounds with fluorine.

        i   What do you understand by the term **covalent bond**?   [1]

        ii   Draw a dot-and-cross diagram for xenon tetrafluoride, XeF_4.   [1]

        iii Suggest a shape for XeF_4. Explain why you chose this shape.   [3]

    c   The structure of xenon trioxide is shown below.

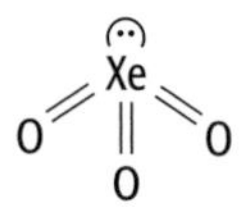

        i   By referring to electron pairs, explain why xenon trioxide has this shape.   [2]

        ii   Draw the structure of xenon trioxide to show the partial charges on the atoms and the direction of the dipole in the molecule.   [2]

                                                           Total = 11

2 Aluminium chloride, $AlCl_3$, and ammonia, NH_3, are both covalent molecules.

    a **i** Draw a diagram of an ammonia molecule, showing its shape. Show any lone pairs of electrons.   [3]

        ii State the bond angle 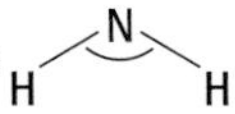   in the ammonia molecule.   [1]

    b Explain why ammonia is a polar molecule.   [2]

    c An ammonia molecule and an aluminium chloride molecule can join together by forming a co-ordinate bond.

        i Explain how a co-ordinate bond is formed.   [1]

        ii Draw a dot-and-cross diagram to show the bonding in the compound formed between ammonia and aluminium chloride, H_3NAlCl_3.

           (Use a ● for a nitrogen electron, a ○ for an aluminium electron and an ✕ for the hydrogen and chlorine electrons.)   [3]

    d Aluminium chloride molecules join together to form a compound with the formula Al_2Cl_6.

        Draw a displayed formula (showing all atoms and bonds) to show the bonding in one Al_2Cl_6 molecule. Show the dative covalent bonds by arrows.   [2]

                                                                                   Total = 12

3 Electronegativity values can be used to predict the polarity of bonds.

    a Explain the term **electronegativity**.   [2]

    b The electronegativity values for some atoms are given below:

        H = 2.1, C = 2.5, F = 4.0, Cl = 3.0, I = 2.5

        Use these values to predict the polarity of each of the following bonds by copying the bonded atoms shown below and adding δ+ or δ− above each atom.

        i H—I

        ii F—I

        iii C—Cl   [2]

    c The shape of iodine trichloride, ICl_3, is shown below.

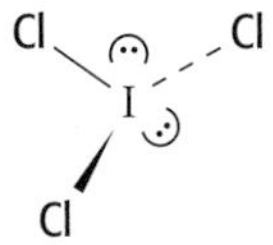

        i Describe the shape of this molecule.   [2]

        ii Explain why the ICl_3 molecule has this shape.   [2]

        iii Suggest a value for the Cl—I—Cl bond angle.   [1]

    d The boiling points of the hydrogen halides are shown in the table.

Hydrogen halide	HF	HCl	HBr	HI
Boiling point / °C	+20	−85	−67	−35

        i Explain the trend in boiling points from HCl to HI.   [2]

        ii Explain why the boiling point of HF is so much higher than the boiling point of HCl.   [3]

    e Tetrachloromethane, CCl_4, is a non-polar molecule.

        i Draw a diagram to show the shape of this molecule.   [2]

        ii Explain why this molecule is non-polar.   [1]

                                                                                   Total = 17

4 The diagram below shows part of a giant metallic structure.

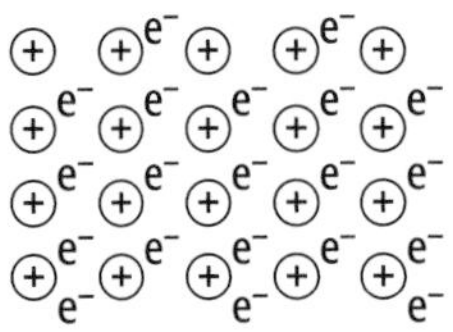

a Use this diagram to explain the main features of metallic bonding. [3]

b Explain why metals are good conductors of electricity. [2]

c Explain why, in general, metals have high melting points. [2]

d Suggest why potassium is a better conductor of electricity than lithium. [4]

Total = 11

5 Methane, CH_4, is a gas at room temperature.

a Explain why methane is a gas at room temperature. [2]

b Draw a diagram to show the shape of a molecule of methane. On your diagram show a value for

the $\overset{C}{\underset{H \quad H}{\diagup \diagdown}}$ bond angle. [3]

c Perfumes often contain molecules that have simple molecular structures. Explain why. [2]

d When a negatively charged rod is held next to a stream of propanone, CH_3COCH_3, the stream of propanone is attracted to the rod.

Draw the full structure of a molecule of propanone and use your diagram to explain why the stream of propanone is attracted to the rod. [3]

Total = 10

6 Sodium iodide and magnesium oxide are ionic compounds. Iodine and oxygen are covalent molecules.

a Draw dot-and-cross diagrams for:

  i magnesium oxide

  ii oxygen. [2]

b How do sodium iodide and iodine differ in their solubility in water? Explain your answer. [3]

c Explain why molten sodium iodide conducts electricity but molten iodine does not. [2]

d The boiling point of sodium iodide is 1304 °C. The boiling point of iodine is 184 °C. Explain this difference. [5]

Total = 12

7 Hydrogen sulfide, H_2S, is a covalent compound.

a Draw a dot-and-cross diagram for hydrogen sulfide. [2]

b Draw a diagram of a hydrogen sulfide molecule to show its shape. Show on your diagram:

  i the value of the $\overset{S}{\underset{H \quad H}{\diagup \diagdown}}$ bond angle

  ii the partial charges on each atom as δ+ or δ–

  iii an arrow showing the exact direction of the dipole in the molecule as a whole. [4]

c Oxygen, O, sulfur, S, and selenium, Se, are in the same group in the Periodic Table.

  i Explain why hydrogen selenide, H_2Se, has a higher boiling point than hydrogen sulfide, H_2S. [2]

  ii Explain why the boiling point of water is so much higher than the boiling point of hydrogen sulfide. [5]

Total = 13

8   The table shows the type of bonding in a number of elements and compounds.

Element or compound	Type of bonding
Fe, Na	metallic
NaCl, MgCl$_2$	ionic
CO$_2$, Br$_2$	covalent within the molecules

a   Draw a labelled diagram to show metallic bonding.   [2]
b   Explain why magnesium chloride has a high melting point but bromine has a low melting point.   [5]
c   Explain why solid sodium conducts electricity but solid sodium chloride does not conduct electricity. [2]
d   i   Draw a dot-and-cross diagram for carbon dioxide.   [1]
    ii   Describe the shape of the carbon dioxide molecule.   [1]
    iii Explain why a carbon dioxide molecule has this shape.   [2]
e   Bromine is a liquid at room temperature. Weak van der Waals' forces hold the bromine molecules
    together. Describe how van der Waals' forces arise.   [5]

Total = 18

9   Water is extensively hydrogen bonded. This gives it anomalous (peculiar) properties.
a   Explain why ice is less dense than liquid water.   [3]
b   State two other anomalous properties of water.   [2]
c   Propanone has the structure shown below.

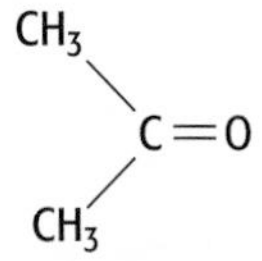

When propanone dissolves in water, it forms a hydrogen bond with water.
    i   What features must water and propanone molecules posses in order to form a hydrogen bond?   [2]
    ii   Draw a diagram to show a propanone molecule and a water molecule forming a hydrogen bond.   [2]
d   Propanone has a double bond. One of the bonds is a σ bond (sigma bond). The other is a π bond (pi bond).
    i   Explain the difference between a σ bond and a π bond in terms of how they are formed.   [3]
    ii   Copy the diagram, then complete it to show the shapes of the electron clouds in the σ bond and the
         π bond between the carbon atoms in ethene. Label your diagram.   [3]

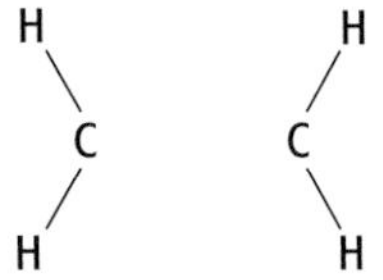

Total = 15

Chapter 5:
States of matter

Learning outcomes

You should be able to:

- state the basic assumptions of the kinetic theory as applied to an ideal gas
- explain qualitatively in terms of intermolecular forces and molecular size:
  - the conditions necessary for a gas to approach ideal behaviour
  - the limitations of ideality at very high pressures and very low temperatures
- state and use the general gas equation $pV = nRT$ in calculations, including the determination of M_r
- describe, using a kinetic-molecular model, the liquid state, melting, vaporisation and vapour pressure

- describe in simple terms the lattice structures of crystalline solids, including those that are ionic, simple molecular (as in iodine and the fullerene allotropes of carbon), giant molecular (as in silicon(IV) oxide and the graphite, diamond and graphene allotropes of carbon), hydrogen bonded or metallic
- discuss the finite nature of materials as a resource and the importance of recycling processes
- outline the importance of hydrogen bonding to the physical properties of substances, including ice and water
- suggest from quoted physical data the type of structure and bonding present in a substance.

Introduction

In the last chapter we looked at the types of forces that keep the particles in solids and liquids together and make it possible to liquefy gases. In this chapter, we shall also consider how the closeness and motion of the particles influences the properties of these three states of matter (Figure 5.1).

Figure 5.1 The three states of water are ice, water and steam. The 'steam' we see from the kettle is condensed droplets of water. The real gaseous water is in the area between this condensation and the spout of the kettle. We can't see it because it is colourless.

States of matter

Gases have no fixed shape or volume. Gas particles:

- are far apart, therefore gases can be compressed
- are randomly arranged
- can move freely from place to place, in all directions.

Liquids take the shape of the container they occupy. Liquid particles:

- are close together, so liquids have a fixed volume and can only be compressed slightly
- are arranged fairly randomly
- have limited movement from place to place, in all directions.

Solids have a fixed shape and volume. Solid particles:

- are touching each other, so solids cannot be compressed
- are usually in a regular arrangement
- cannot change positions with each other – they can only vibrate.

> **QUESTION**
>
> 1 Describe the changes that occur in the closeness and motion of the particles when:
>   a a solid changes to a liquid
>   b a liquid changes to a gas.

The state of a substance at room temperature and pressure depends on its structure and bonding. Five types of structure are found in elements and compounds:

- simple atomic, e.g. argon
- simple molecular, e.g. carbon dioxide
- giant ionic, e.g. sodium chloride
- giant metallic, e.g. iron
- giant molecular, e.g. silicon(IV) oxide.

The simple atomic structures found in the noble gases generally have similar physical properties to simple molecular gases.

The gaseous state
The kinetic theory of gases

The idea that molecules in gases are in constant movement is called the **kinetic theory of gases**. This theory makes certain assumptions:

- the gas molecules move rapidly and randomly
- the distance between the gas molecules is much greater than the diameter of the molecules so the volume of the molecules is negligible
- there are no forces of attraction or repulsion between the molecules
- all collisions between particles are elastic – this means no kinetic energy is lost in collisions (kinetic energy is the energy associated with moving particles)

73

■ the temperature of the gas is related to the average kinetic energy of the molecules.

A theoretical gas that fits this description is called an **ideal gas**. In reality, the gases we encounter don't fit this description exactly, although they may come very close. The gases we encounter are called **real gases**.

Noble gases with small atoms, such as helium and neon, approach ideal gas behaviour. This is because the intermolecular forces are so small.

> **QUESTION**
>
> 2 Explain why the intermolecular forces in a sample of helium and neon are very small.

Ideal gases

The volume that a gas occupies depends on:

■ its pressure; we measure pressure in pascals, Pa
■ its temperature; we measure temperatures of gases in kelvin, K.

The kelvin temperature equals the Celsius temperature plus 273. For example, $100\,°C$ is $100 + 273 = 373\,K$.

> **QUESTION**
>
> 3 a Convert the following temperatures into the kelvin temperature:
>
>   i $245\,°C$
>
>   ii $-45\,°C$
>
>   b How many pascals are there in $15\,kPa$?

Gases in a container exert a pressure. This is because the gas molecules are constantly hitting the walls of the container. If we decrease the volume of a gas (at constant temperature) the molecules are squashed closer together and hit the walls of the container more often. So the pressure of the gas increases (Figure 5.2a). A graph of volume of gas plotted against 1/pressure gives a proportional relationship (as shown by the straight line in Figure 5.2b). We say that the volume is inversely proportional to the pressure.

When a gas is heated at constant pressure its volume increases (Figure 5.3a). This is because the particles move faster and hit the walls of the container with greater force. If the pressure is to be constant the molecules must get further apart. The volume of a gas at constant pressure is proportional to its temperature measured in kelvin (Figure 5.3b).

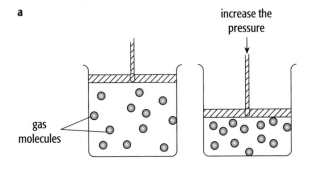
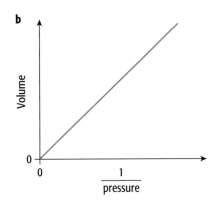

Figure 5.2 a As the volume of a gas decreases, its pressure increases due to the increased frequency of the gas molecules hitting the walls of the container. **b** For an ideal gas a plot of the volume of gas against 1/pressure shows a proportional relationship.

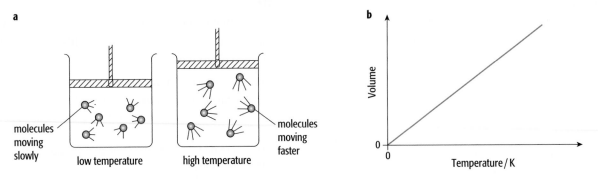

Figure 5.3 a As the temperature increases, the volume of a gas increases. Molecules hit the walls with increased force. **b** For an ideal gas, the volume of a gas is proportional to its kelvin temperature.

An ideal gas will have a volume that varies exactly in proportion to its temperature and exactly in inverse proportion to its pressure.

> **QUESTION**
>
> 4   Some chemical reactions involving gases are performed in sealed glass tubes that do not melt at high temperatures. The tubes have thin walls and can easily break. Use the kinetic theory of gases to explain why the tubes should not be heated to high temperatures.

Limitations of the ideal gas laws

Scientists have taken accurate measurements to show how the volumes of gases change with temperature and pressure. These show us that gases do not always behave exactly as we expect an ideal gas to behave. This is because real gases do not always obey the kinetic theory in two ways:

- there is not zero attraction between the molecules
- we cannot ignore the volume of the molecules themselves.

These differences are especially noticeable at very high pressures and very low temperatures. Under these conditions:

- the molecules are close to each other
- the volume of the molecules is not negligible compared with the volume of the container
- there are van der Waals' or dipole–dipole forces of attraction between the molecules
- attractive forces pull the molecules towards each other and away from the walls of the container
- the pressure is lower than expected for an ideal gas
- the effective volume of the gas is smaller than expected for an ideal gas.

> **QUESTION**
>
> 5   **a**   What is meant by the term **ideal gas**?
>
>   **b**   Under what conditions do real gases differ from ideal gases? Give reasons for your answer.

The general gas equation

For an ideal gas, we can combine the laws about how the volume of a gas depends on temperature and pressure. We also know from page 18 that the volume of a gas is proportional to the number of moles present. Putting all these together, gives us the general gas equation:

$pV = nRT$

    p is the pressure in pascals, Pa

    V is the volume of gas in cubic metres, m^3

    ($1\,m^3 = 1000\,dm^3$)

    n is the number of moles of gas $\left(n = \dfrac{m}{M_r}\right)$

    R is the gas constant, which has a value of $8.31\,J\,K^{-1}\,mol^{-1}$

    T is the temperature in kelvin, K.

Calculations using the general gas equation

If we know any four of the five physical quantities in the general gas equation, we can calculate the fifth.

> **WORKED EXAMPLES**
>
> 1   Calculate the volume occupied by 0.500 mol of carbon dioxide at a pressure of 150 kPa and a temperature of 19 °C.
>
>   ($R = 8.31\,J\,K^{-1}\,mol^{-1}$)
>
> **Step 1**   Change pressure and temperature to their correct units:
>
>   150 kPa = 150 000 Pa; 19 °C = 19 + 273 = 292 K
>
> **Step 2**   Rearrange the general gas equation to the form you require:
>
> $pV = nRT$ so $V = \dfrac{nRT}{p}$
>
> **Step 3**   Substitute the figures:
>
> $V = \dfrac{nRT}{p}$
>
> $= \dfrac{0.500 \times 8.31 \times 292}{150\,000}$
>
> $= 8.09 \times 10^{-3}\,m^3$
>
> $= 8.09\,dm^3$
>
> 2   A flask of volume 5.00 dm^3 contained 4.00 g of oxygen. Calculate the pressure exerted by the gas at a temperature of 127 °C.
>
>   ($R = 8.31\,J\,K^{-1}\,mol^{-1}$; M_r oxygen = 32.0)
>
> **Step 1**   Change temperature and volume to their correct units and calculate the number of moles of oxygen.
>
>   127 °C = 127 + 273 = 400 K
>
> $5\,dm^3 = \dfrac{5.00}{1000}\,m^3 = 5.00 \times 10^{-3}\,m^3$
>
> $n = \dfrac{m}{M_r}$
>
> $= \dfrac{4.00}{32.0}$
>
> $= 0.125\,mol$

WORKED EXAMPLES (CONTINUED)

Step 2 Rearrange the general gas equation to the form you require:

$$pV = nRT \quad \text{so} \quad p = \frac{nRT}{V}$$

Step 3 Substitute the figures:

$$p = \frac{nRT}{V}$$

$$p = \frac{0.125 \times 8.31 \times 400}{5 \times 10^{-3}}$$

$$p = 8.31 \times 10^4 \, \text{Pa}$$

QUESTION

6 **a** Calculate the volume occupied by 272 g of methane at a pressure of 250 kPa and a temperature of 54 °C.

($R = 8.31 \, \text{J K}^{-1} \text{mol}^{-1}$; M_r methane = 16.0)

b The pressure exerted by 0.25 mol of carbon monoxide in a 10 dm³ flask is 120 kPa. Calculate the temperature in the flask in kelvin.

Calculating relative molecular masses

An accurate method of finding the relative molecular mass of a substance is to use a mass spectrometer (see Chapter 1). A less accurate method, but one that is suitable for a school laboratory, is to use the general gas equation to find the mass of gas in a large flask. As the number of moles is the mass of a substance divided by its relative molecular mass, we can find the relative molecular mass of a gas by simply substituting in the general gas equation. Although weighing gases is a difficult process because they are so light and the buoyancy of the air has to be taken into account, the method can give reasonable results.

WORKED EXAMPLES

3 A flask of volume 2.0 dm³ was found to contain 5.28 g of a gas. The pressure in the flask was 200 kPa and the temperature was 20 °C. Calculate the relative molecular mass of the gas.

($R = 8.31 \, \text{J K}^{-1} \text{mol}^{-1}$)

Step 1 Change pressure, temperature and volume to their correct units and calculate the number of moles of oxygen.

$$200 \, \text{kPa} = 2.00 \times 10^5 \, \text{Pa}$$

$$20 \, °\text{C} = 20 + 273 = 293 \, \text{K}$$

$$200 \, \text{dm}^3 = \frac{2.00}{1000} \, \text{m}^3 = 2.00 \times 10^{-3} \, \text{m}^3$$

Step 2 Rearrange the general gas equation to the form you require:

$$pV = nRT \text{ and } n = \frac{m}{M_r}, \text{ so } pV = \frac{m}{M_r} RT,$$

which gives $M_r = \frac{mRT}{pV}$

Step 3 Substitute the figures:

$$M_r = \frac{mRT}{pV}$$

$$= \frac{5.28 \times 8.31 \times 293}{(2.00 \times 10^5) \times (2.0 \times 10^{-3})}$$

$$= 32.14$$

$$= 32 \, \text{g mol}^{-1}$$

This method can also be applied to find the relative molecular mass of a volatile liquid. The volatile liquid is injected into a gas syringe placed in a syringe oven (Figure 5.4). The liquid vaporises and the volume of the vapour is recorded.

The procedure is:

1 put a gas syringe in the syringe oven and leave until the temperature is constant

2 record the volume of air in the gas syringe

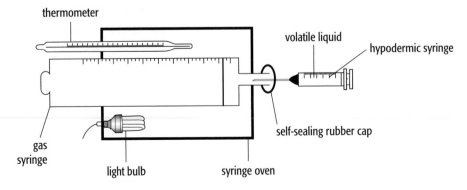

Figure 5.4 The relative molecular mass of a volatile liquid can be found using a syringe oven.

3 fill a hypodermic syringe with the volatile liquid and find its total mass

4 inject a little of the liquid into the gas syringe then find the total mass of the hypodermic syringe again

5 allow the liquid to vaporise in the gas syringe

6 record the final volume of vapour + air in the gas syringe

7 record the atmospheric temperature and pressure.

The calculation is carried out in the same way as Worked example 3.

The volume of vapour produced is:

final gas syringe volume – initial gas syringe volume

The mass used in the calculation is:

initial mass of hypodermic syringe + liquid
– final mass of hypodermic syringe + liquid

QUESTION

7 When 0.08 g of liquid X was vaporised at 100 °C, 23 cm³ of vapour was formed. The atmospheric pressure was 1.02×10^5 Pa. Calculate the relative molecular mass of liquid X.

($R = 8.31$ J K⁻¹ mol⁻¹)

The liquid state

The behaviour of liquids

When we heat a solid:

■ the energy transferred to the solid makes the particles vibrate more vigorously

■ the forces of attraction between the particles weaken

■ the solid changes to a liquid when its temperature is sufficiently high.

We call this change of state melting.

For ionic compounds, a high temperature is needed because ionic bonding is very strong. For molecular solids, a lower temperature is needed, just enough to overcome the weak intermolecular forces between the particles.

The particles in a liquid are still close to each other but they have enough kinetic energy to keep sliding past each other in a fairly random way. They do not move freely as gas particles do. For brief periods, the particles in liquids are arranged in a slightly ordered way. But this order is always being broken up when the particles gain kinetic energy from neighbouring particles.

When we cool a liquid, the particles:

■ lose kinetic energy so they do not move around so readily

■ experience increasing forces of attraction

■ stop sliding past each other when the temperature is sufficiently low; the liquid solidifies.

We call this change of state freezing.

Vaporisation and vapour pressure

When we heat a liquid:

■ the energy transferred to the liquid makes the particles move faster

■ the forces of attraction between the particles weaken

■ the particles with most energy are the first to escape from the forces holding them together in the liquid

■ the liquid evaporates – this happens at a temperature below the boiling point

■ the forces weaken enough for all the particles to become completely free from each other; they move fast and randomly and they spread out

■ the liquid boils; this happens at the boiling point.

This change from the liquid state to the gas state is called vaporisation. The energy required to change one mole of liquid to one mole of gas is called the enthalpy change of vaporisation.

When we cool a vapour, the particles:

■ lose kinetic energy so the molecules move around less quickly

■ experience increasing forces of attraction

■ move more slowly and become closer together when the temperature is sufficiently low; the gas liquefies.

We call this change of state condensation.

These changes in state are reversible. Water can be boiled to form steam, and steam can be condensed to form liquid water. These changes involve opposite energy transfers. For example: energy has to be transferred to water to boil it to form steam. But when steam condenses to form water, energy is transferred from the steam.

If we put some water in an open beaker, it evaporates until none is left. But what happens when we allow water to evaporate in a closed container?

At first, water molecules escape from the surface of the liquid to become vapour (Figure 5.5a). As more and more molecules escape, the molecules in the vapour become closer together. Eventually the molecules with lower kinetic energy will not be able to overcome the attractive forces of neighbouring molecules. The vapour begins to condense. So some water molecules return to the liquid (Figure 5.5b). Eventually, water molecules return to the liquid at the same rate as water molecules escape to the vapour. A position of equilibrium is reached (Figure 5.5c; see Chapter 8).

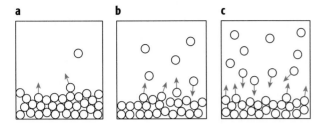

Figure 5.5 a Water molecules move from liquid to vapour. **b** As more molecules move from liquid to vapour, some begin to move back to the liquid. **c** An equilibrium is reached with molecules going from liquid to vapour at the same rate as from vapour to liquid.

At equilibrium the concentration of water molecules in the vapour remains constant.

$$\text{water molecules in liquid} \underset{\text{equal rate of movement}}{\rightleftharpoons} \text{water molecules in vapour}$$

In this situation the pressure exerted by a vapour in equilibrium with its liquid is called its **vapour pressure**. The vapour pressure is caused by the gas particles hitting the walls of the container. Vapour pressure will increase when the temperature increases because:

- the gas particles have more kinetic energy
- the gas particles move faster, so are able to overcome intermolecular forces of attraction more easily.

The temperature at which the vapour pressure is equal to the atmospheric pressure is the **boiling point** of the liquid.

> **QUESTION**
>
> 8 Bromine is a reddish-brown liquid. Some liquid bromine is placed in a closed jar. The bromine starts to evaporate. The colour of the vapour above the liquid bromine becomes darker and darker. After a time the bromine vapour does not get any darker.
>
> Use ideas about moving particles to explain these observations.

The solid state

Many ionic, metallic and covalent compounds are crystalline. The regular structure of crystals is due to the regular packing of the particles within the crystal. We call this regularly repeating arrangement of ions, atoms or molecules a crystal **lattice**.

Ionic lattices

Ionic lattices have a three-dimensional arrangement of alternating positive and negative ions. Compounds with ionic lattices are sometimes called giant ionic structures.

The type of lattice formed depends on the relative sizes of the ions present. The ionic lattices for sodium chloride and magnesium oxide are cubic. In sodium chloride, each sodium ion is surrounded by six oppositely charged chloride ions. The chloride ions are much larger than the sodium ions. The sodium ions fit into the spaces between the chloride ions so that they are as close as possible to them (Figure 5.6).

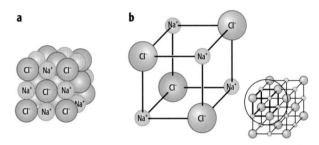

Figure 5.6 The arrangement of the ions in sodium chloride: **a** the actual packing of the ions; **b** an 'exploded' view so that you can see the arrangement of the ions clearly.

Magnesium oxide has the same lattice structure as sodium chloride. Magnesium ions replace sodium ions and the oxide ions replace the chloride ions.

The properties of ionic compounds reflect their structure as well as their bonding.

- They are hard. It takes a lot of energy to scratch the surface because of the strong attractive forces keeping the ions together.
- They are brittle. Ionic crystals may split apart when hit in the same direction as the layers of ions. The layers of ions may be displaced by the force of the blow so that ions with the same charge come together. The repulsions between thousands of ions in the layers, all with the same charge, cause the crystal to split along these cleavage planes.
- They have high melting points and high boiling points because the attraction between the large numbers of oppositely charged ions in the lattice acts in all directions and bonds them strongly together. The melting points and boiling points increase with the charge density on the ions. So magnesium oxide, $Mg^{2+}O^{2-}$, has a higher melting point (2852 °C) than sodium chloride, Na^+Cl^- (801 °C). This is because there is a greater electrostatic attraction between doubly charged ions than singly charged ions of similar size.
- Many of them are soluble in water (see page 265).
- They only conduct electricity when molten or in solution (see page 67).

Figure 5.7 Sapphires sparkle in the light when polished. They are cut by exerting a force on the cleavage planes between layers of ions in the crystal.

Metallic lattices

In Chapter 4, we learnt that a metallic lattice consists of ions surrounded by a sea of electrons. The ions are often packed in hexagonal layers or in a cubic arrangement. When a force is applied, the layers can slide over each other. But in a metallic bond, the attractive forces between the metal ions and the delocalised electrons act in all directions. So when the layers slide, new metallic bonds are easily re-formed between ions in new lattice positions and the delocalised electrons (Figure 5.8). The delocalised electrons continue to hold the ions in the lattice together. The metal now has a different shape. This explains why metals are malleable (they can be hammered into different shapes) and ductile (they can be drawn into wires). The high tensile strength and hardness of most metals is also due to the strong attractive forces between the metal ions and the delocalised electrons.

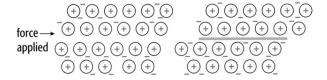

Figure 5.8 When a force is applied to a metallic structure, the layers slide over each other and re-form in new lattice positions.

Figure 5.9 You can clearly see the metal crystals or 'grains' in this metal plate.

Alloys and their properties

An **alloy** is a mixture of two or more metals or a metal with a non-metal. The metal added to create the alloy becomes part of the crystal lattice of the other metal.

Brass is an alloy of copper (70%) with zinc (30%). It is stronger than copper but still malleable. For these reasons it is used for musical instruments, ornaments and household items such as door handles.

But why is brass stronger than pure copper?

Zinc ions are larger than copper ions. The presence of different-sized metal ions makes the arrangement of the lattice less regular. This stops the layers of ions from sliding over each other so easily when a force is applied (Figure 5.10).

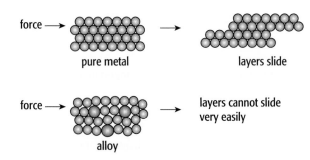

Figure 5.10 The layers of ions in an alloy slide less easily than in a pure metal because the structure of the lattice is less regular.

Pure aluminium is soft, ductile and has high electrical and thermal conductivity. Because of its low strength, pure aluminium is of little use in engineering. But its strength can be increased by addition of other elements such as copper, magnesium, silicon and manganese. Many alloys of aluminium are lightweight, strong and resistant to corrosion. These are used for the bodies of aircraft, for the

79

cylinder blocks of car engines and for bicycle frames, all situations where low density combined with strength and corrosion resistance is important.

Bronze is an alloy of copper and tin. A 33-metre high bronze statue was built near the harbour in Rhodes (Greece) over 2000 years ago. The statue fell down after an earthquake and was eventually bought by a Syrian merchant. The bronze was recycled to make useful implements.

QUESTION

9 Explain the following:

   a why are most metals strong, but ionic solids are brittle?

   b why is an alloy of copper and tin stronger than either copper or tin alone?

Simple molecular lattices

Substances with a simple molecular structure, such as iodine, can also form crystals (Figure 5.11). This reflects the regular packing of the molecules in a lattice structure.

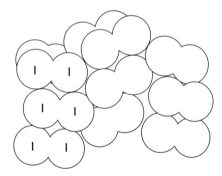

Figure 5.11 Iodine molecules are arranged in a lattice structure.

Ice also forms a crystalline lattice. Ice and water have peculiar properties because of hydrogen bonding (see page 66).

The distance between the nuclei of neighbouring iodine molecules is greater than the distance between the nuclei within the iodine molecule. This is because the forces between the molecules are weak van der Waals' forces whereas the forces between the atoms within the molecule are strong covalent bonds. Very little energy is needed to overcome the weak van der Waals' forces between the molecules. The lattice is easily broken down when iodine crystals are heated; iodine has a low melting point.

QUESTION

10 The table shows some properties of four elements. Use the data to answer the following questions. (Assume that steel has similar properties to iron.)

Element	Density / g cm^{-3}	Tensile strength / 10^{10} Pa	Electrical conductivity / 10^8 S m^{-1}
aluminium	2.70	7.0	0.38
iron	7.86	21.1	0.10
copper	8.92	13.0	0.59
sulfur	2.07	breaks easily	1×10^{-23}

   a Why is aluminium with a steel core used for overhead electricity cables in preference to copper?

   b Suggest why many car engine blocks are made from aluminium alloys rather than from steel.

   c Explain the differences in tensile strength and electrical conductivity of iron and sulfur.

Giant molecular structures

Some covalently bonded structures have a three-dimensional network of covalent bonds throughout the whole structure. We call these structures **giant molecular structures** or giant covalent structures. They have high melting and boiling points because of the large number of strong covalent bonds linking the whole structure. Both elements, such as carbon (graphite and diamond), and compounds, such as silicon dioxide, can be giant molecular structures. Carbon and graphite are different forms of the same element. Different crystalline or molecular forms of the same element are called **allotropes**.

Graphite

In graphite, the carbon atoms are arranged in planar layers. Within the layers, the carbon atoms are arranged in hexagons. Each carbon atom is joined to three other carbon atoms by strong covalent bonds (Figure 5.12). The fourth electron of each carbon atom occupies a p orbital. These p orbitals on every carbon atom in each planar layer overlap sideways. A cloud of delocalised electrons is formed above and below the plane of the carbon rings. These electron clouds join up to form extended delocalised rings of electrons.

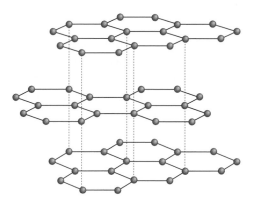

Figure 5.12 The structure of graphite.

The layers of carbon atoms are kept next to each other by weak van der Waals' forces.

The properties of graphite are related to its structure.

■ High melting and boiling points: there is strong covalent bonding throughout the layers of carbon atoms. A lot of energy is needed to overcome these strong bonds.

■ Softness: graphite is easily scratched. The forces between the layers of carbon atoms are weak. The layers of graphite can slide over each other when a force is applied. The layers readily flake off. This 'flakiness' is why graphite is used in pencil 'leads' and feels slippery.

■ Good conductor of electricity: when a voltage is applied, the delocalised electrons (mobile electrons) can move along the layers.

Diamond

In diamond, each carbon atom forms four covalent bonds with other carbon atoms (Figure 5.13). The carbon atoms are tetrahedrally arranged around each other. The network of carbon atoms extends almost unbroken throughout the whole structure. The regular arrangement of the atoms gives diamond a crystalline structure.

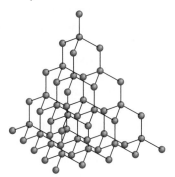

Figure 5.13 The structure of diamond.

The properties of diamond are related to its structure.

■ High melting and boiling points: there is strong covalent bonding throughout the whole structure. A lot of energy is needed to break these strong bonds and separate the atoms.

■ Hardness: diamond cannot be scratched easily because it is difficult to break the three-dimensional network of strong covalent bonds.

■ Does not conduct electricity or heat: each of the four outer electrons on every carbon atom is involved in covalent bonding. This means that there are no free electrons available to carry the electric current.

Most of the diamonds used around the world have been mined from the Earth's crust. However, artificial diamonds can be made by heating other forms of carbon under high pressure. Artificial diamonds are too small to be used for jewellery but they can be used for drill tips.

Silicon(IV) oxide

There are several forms of silicon(IV) oxide. The silicon(IV) oxide found in the mineral quartz (Figure 5.14) has a structure similar to diamond (Figure 5.15).

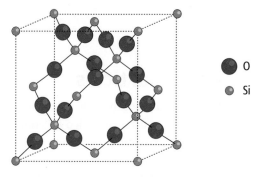

Figure 5.14 The shape of these quartz crystals reflects the regular arrangement of the silicon and oxygen atoms.

81

● O
○ Si

Figure 5.15 The structure of silicon(IV) oxide.

Each silicon atom is bonded to four oxygen atoms but each oxygen atom is bonded to only two silicon atoms. So the formula for silicon(IV) oxide is SiO_2. Silicon dioxide has properties similar to that of diamond. It forms hard, colourless crystals with high melting and boiling points and it does not conduct electricity.

Sand is largely silicon(IV)oxide.

QUESTIONS

11 Explain the following properties of silicon(IV) oxide by referring to its structure and bonding.

   a It has a high melting point.

   b It does not conduct electricity.

   c It is a crystalline solid.

   d It is hard.

12 Copy and complete the table below to compare the properties of giant ionic, giant molecular, giant metallic and simple molecular structures.

	Giant ionic	Giant molecular	Metallic	Simple molecular
Two examples				
Particles present				
Forces keeping particles together				
Physical state at room temperature				
Melting points and boiling points				
Hardness				
Electrical conductivity				
Solubility in water				

Carbon nanoparticles

Graphite and diamond are not the only allotropes of carbon. In recent years, substances called fullerenes have been made. The structure of many fullerenes is based on rings of carbon atoms, as is the structure of graphite. But many fullerenes exhibit properties unlike those of graphite. The individual particles in fullerenes may have one of their dimensions between 0.1 and 100 nanometres (1 nanometre = 10^{-9} m). Particles of this size are called nanoparticles. Another form of carbon, graphene, can be regarded as a single layer of graphite.

Fullerenes

Fullerenes are allotropes of carbon in the form of hollow spheres or tubes. They are similar in structure to graphite, in that each carbon atom is bonded to three other carbon atoms. They contain rings of carbon atoms arranged in hexagons and in addition many contain rings of carbon atoms arranged in pentagons. The first fullerene discovered was called **buckminsterfullerene**, C_{60} (Figure 5.16). The C_{60} molecule has the shape of a football (soccer ball). The carbon atoms are arranged at the corners of 20 hexagons and 12 pentagons. The bonds where two hexagons join are shorter than the bonds between the hexagons and the pentagons. As in graphite, some of the electrons in C_{60} are delocalised, but to a lesser extent than in graphite. Since the discovery of the C_{60} molecule, many types of buckminsterfullerene have been discovered. Some are ball-shaped molecules that are multiples of C_{60}, e.g. C_{120}. Other fullerene molecules include C_{20}, C_{70} and C_{72}.

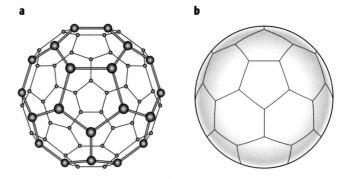

a   b

Figure 5.16 The shape of a buckminsterfullerene molecule, C_{60}, **a** is similar to that of a football **b**.

The properties of buckminsterfullerene are significantly different from those of graphite and diamond.

■ It has a relatively low sublimation point: it turns directly from the solid to the vapour state when heated to about 600 °C. (Graphite only turns from the solid to the vapour state at about 3700 °C). This is because there are weak van der Waal's forces between each buckminsterfullerene molecule and no continuous layered giant structure as in graphite.

■ It is relatively soft because it does not require much energy to overcome the weak intermolecular forces.

■ It is a poor conductor of electricity compared with graphite because the extent of electron delocalisation is lower.

■ It is slightly soluble in solvents such as carbon disulphide and methylbenzene. Neither diamond nor graphite is soluble in common solvents.

■ It is more reactive compared with graphite or diamond. Buckminsterfullerene reacts with hydrogen, fluorine, chlorine, bromine and oxygen. This is due to the relatively high electron density in certain parts of the molecule (see electrophilic addition on page 209).

A second type of fullerene is a class of molecules described as **nanotubes**. Nanotubes are fullerenes of hexagonally arranged carbon atoms like a single layer of graphite bent into the form of a cylinder (Figure 5.17). The first nanotubes to be made were one layer of carbon atoms in thickness. More recently nanotubes have behave been made with thicker walls with several tubes inside one another. Although the diameter of a nanotube is very small, it can be made relatively long. The length of the nanotube cylinder can be a million times greater than its diameter.

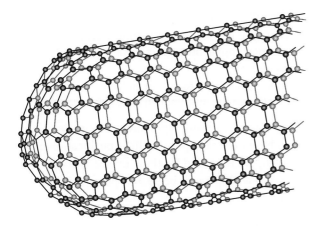

Figure 5.17 Part of the structure of a nanotube. The ends of the cylinder are often closed.

Nanotubes have characteristic properties:

- They have high electrical conductivity along the long axis of the cylinder. This is because, like graphite, some of the electrons are delocalised and are able to move along the cylinder when a voltage is applied.
- They have a very high tensile strength when a force is applied along the long axis of the cylinder. They can be up to 100 times stronger than steel of the same thickness.
- They have very high melting points (typically about 3500 °C). This is because there is strong covalent bonding throughout the structure.

Fullerenes have a large range of potential uses. Reactive groups can be attached to their surfaces and metal complexes (see page 371) can also be formed. Small molecules or atoms can be trapped in the cage of buckminsterfullerenes. Possible medical uses include delivering drugs to specific places in the body. Nanotubes are used in tiny electrical circuits as 'wires' and as electrodes in paper-thin batteries. They can be incorporated into clothing and sports equipment for added strength. They have also been used in the treatment of certain types of cancer.

Graphene

Graphene is a single isolated layer of graphite (Figure 5.18). The hexagonally arranged sheet of carbon atoms is not completely rigid and it can be distorted.

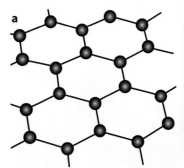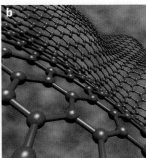

Figure 5.18 a Part of a graphene sheet. **b** 'Waves' in a sheet of graphene.

Graphene has some of the properties of graphite, but they are more exaggerated. For example:

- Graphene is the most chemically reactive form of carbon. Single sheets of graphene burn at very low temperatures and are much more reactive than graphite.
- Graphene is extremely strong for its mass.
- For a given amount of material, graphene conducts electricity and heat much better than graphite.

It has been said that 'a one square metre hammock made of graphene could support a 4 kg cat but would weigh only as much as the cat's whisker'. Potential applications of graphene include use in tiny electrical circuits and for tiny transistors, touchscreens, solar cells and other energy storage devices.

> **QUESTION**
>
> 13 Suggest, using ideas of structure and bonding, why:
>
>   **a** buckminsterfullerene, C_{60}, is converted from a solid to a gas at a relatively low temperature
>
>   **b** graphene is a good conductor of electricity
>
>   **c** nanotubes conduct electricity better along the long axis of the tube than across the tube
>
>   **d** buckminsterfullerene, C_{60}, is relatively soft.

Conserving materials
Why conserve materials?

There is only a limited supply of metal ores in the Earth. If we use them all up, they cannot be replaced. The things we make from metals and other materials from the

Earth's crust are often thrown away. This leads to huge waste dumps and landfill sites scarring the landscape and problems with litter. Extracting metals from their ores requires a lot of energy. Energy resources are also limited and we need to conserve these as well. One way to help conserve materials and energy is to recycle metals (Figure 5.19).

Figure 5.19 Remember to recycle your cans. As well as aluminium cans, we can also save energy and resources by recycling steel cans.

Recycling materials

Large amounts of energy are needed to extract and purify metals. It is often cheaper to collect used metals and recycle them rather than extract them from their ores.

Recycling has several advantages:

■ it saves energy (this helps tackle global warming, as we burn less fossil fuel)
■ it conserves supplies of the ore

■ landfill sites do not get filled up as fast and there is less waste
■ it is cheaper than extracting the metal from the ore.

It is not always easy to recycle metals. They have to be collected and sorted and then transported to the recycling plant. This takes energy and money. It may be difficult to separate individual metals. For example 'tin' cans are made from steel coated with tin. The two metals have to be separated before they can be used again. Two metals that can be recycled easily are copper and aluminium.

Copper

Most copper ores remaining in the Earth contain less than 1% copper. Recycling copper is important because:

■ less energy is needed to recycle copper than is needed to transport copper ore to the smelting plant and extract copper from it
■ less energy is needed to extract and refine the recycled copper so that it is pure enough to be electrolysed.

The copper used for water pipes and cooking utensils does not have to be very pure, so little purification of recycled copper is needed for these uses. The copper used for electrical wiring has to be 99.99% pure. This has to be purified by electrolysis.

Aluminium

Purifying and remoulding aluminium is much cheaper than extracting aluminium from bauxite ore. Savings are made because:

■ it is not necessary to extract the aluminium ore from the ground or to transport it to the smelting plant; these processes require energy
■ the treatment of bauxite to make pure aluminium oxide for electrolysis does not need to be carried out
■ the aluminium scrap needs less energy to melt it, compared with melting aluminium oxide
■ the expensive electrolysis of aluminium oxide does not need to be carried out .

There is a 95% saving in energy if we recycle aluminium rather than extract it from its ore.

Summary

- The kinetic theory of gases states that gas particles are always in constant random motion at a variety of speeds.

- The volume of a gas increases when the temperature increases and decreases when the pressure increases.

- The volume of a gas under different conditions of temperature and pressure can be calculated using the ideal gas equation $pV = nRT$.

- The ideal gas equation can be used to determine the relative molecular mass of simple molecules.

- Gases do not obey the ideal gas equation at low temperatures and high pressures.

- The kinetic-molecular model can be used to describe the states of matter in terms of proximity and motion of the particles, and to describe changes of state and vapour pressure.

- Ionic compounds such as sodium chloride and magnesium oxide form a giant three-dimensional lattice structure containing ions in a regularly repeating pattern.

- The strong ionic forces acting in all directions between the ions in the lattice cause ionic substances to have high melting and boiling points.

- Simple molecular solids with low melting points such as iodine have a regular arrangement of molecules; they are crystalline. There are weak intermolecular forces between the molecules.

- Giant covalent (giant molecular) structures such as diamond have a large number of covalent bonds arranged in a regularly repeating pattern.

- Fullerenes are allotropes of carbon in the shape of hollow spheres (buckminsterfullerene) or tubes (nanotubes).

- Graphene is composed of a single flat sheet of hexagonally-arranged carbon atoms.

- The strong covalent bonds between the atoms in giant molecular structures cause these substances to have high melting and boiling points.

- In metals, the atoms are closely packed in a giant lattice in which the outer electrons are free to move.

- Metals such as aluminium and copper and their alloys have a variety of uses, which can be related to their physical properties, e.g. density, malleability, conductivity, hardness.

- Physical data can be used to suggest the type of structure and bonding present in a substance.

- Recycling plays an important part in conserving finite resources such as metals.

End-of-chapter questions

1 Four types of structure are:
   giant molecular
   giant ionic
   giant metallic
   simple molecular

   a Give two examples of a giant ionic structure and two examples of a simple molecular structure. [4]

   b Explain why substances with giant ionic structures are often brittle but metallic structures are malleable. [6]

   c Explain why giant molecular structures have higher melting points than simple molecular structures. [6]

   d Diamond and graphite are two forms of carbon with giant molecular structures. Explain why graphite conducts electricity but diamond does not. [5]

   Total = 21

2 The structures of carbon dioxide and silicon dioxide are shown in the diagram below.

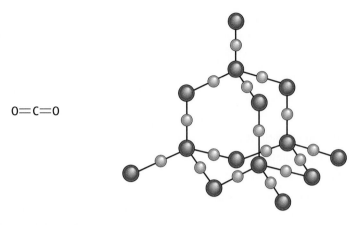

$O=C=O$

Use your knowledge of structure and bonding to explain the following:

a   carbon dioxide is a gas at room temperature [3]

b   silicon(IV) oxide is a solid with a high melting point [3]

c   neither carbon dioxide nor silicon(IV) oxide conducts electricity. [2]

Total = 8

3 This question is about gases.

a   What do you understand by the term **ideal gas**? [1]

b   Under what conditions does a gas not behave ideally? Explain your answer for one of these conditions. [4]

c   Helium is a noble gas. It exists as single atoms. Explain why:

  i   helium has a very low boiling point [2]

  ii   helium does not conduct electricity. [1]

d   A weather balloon contains 0.500 kg of helium. Calculate the volume of the gas in the balloon at a pressure of 0.500×10^5 Pa and a temperature of –20.0 °C.

  ($R = 8.31$ J K^{-1} mol^{-1}; A_r He = 4.0) [5]

Total = 13

4 Water and bromine are both simple molecular substances.

a   Both water and bromine form a lattice structure in the solid state. What do you understand by the term **lattice**? [2]

b   The boiling point of water is 100 °C. The boiling point of bromine is 59 °C. Explain the reason for this difference in terms of intermolecular forces. [4]

c   Use ideas about the kinetic theory to explain what happens when liquid bromine evaporates to form bromine vapour. [4]

d   Some liquid bromine is allowed to evaporate in a closed glass jar until no further change is seen in the colour of the bromine vapour. Under these conditions the vapour pressure is constant.

  i   What do you understand by the term **vapour pressure**? [1]

  ii   Explain why the vapour pressure remains constant in the jar. [2]

e   When 0.20 g of a liquid, **Y**, with a simple molecular structure was evaporated it produced 80 cm^3 of vapour. The temperature was 98 °C and the pressure 1.1×10^5 Pa. Calculate the relative molecular mass of **Y**.

  ($R = 8.31$ J K^{-1} mol^{-1}) [5]

Total = 18

5 The table gives data on the physical properties of five substances, **A** to **E**.

   a Copy the table and fill in the gaps. [7]

| Substance | Melting point | Electrical conductivity | | Type of structure |
		as a solid	as a liquid	
A	high	poor	good	i
B	low	ii	iii	iv
C	high	poor	poor	v
D	high	good	vi	giant metallic
E	high	poor	vii	giant covalent

   b Explain the melting point and electrical conductivity of substance **A**. [6]

   c Explain the melting point and electrical conductivity of substance **B**. [5]

Total = 18

6 The uses of metals are often related to their properties.

   a Describe the structure of a typical metal. [2]

   b Explain why metals are malleable. [4]

   c Use the information in the table below to answer the questions that follow.

Element	Density / $g\,cm^{-3}$	Tensile strength / $10^{10}\,Pa$	Electrical conductivity / $10^{8}\,S\,m^{-1}$
aluminium	2.70	7.0	0.38
copper	8.92	13.0	0.59
steel	7.86	21.1	0.10

     i Why is aluminium more suitable than steel for building aeroplane bodies? [1]

     ii Explain why overhead electricity cables are made from aluminium with a steel core rather than just from copper. [5]

   d The effect of alloying copper with zinc on the strength of the alloy is shown in the table below.

% copper	% zinc	Tensile strength / $10^{8}\,Pa$
100	0	2.3
80	20	3.0
60	40	3.6
0	100	1.4

     i Describe and explain the change in tensile strength as the percentage of zinc increases from 0% to 40%. [5]

     ii State the name of the alloy of copper with zinc. [1]

   e Many metals, such aluminium, can be recycled. Give three reasons why about 90% of aluminium is made by recycling rather than extracting it from its ore. [3]

Total = 21

87

7   The diagram shows the structures of graphite and diamond.

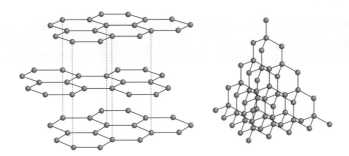

Use the diagrams and your knowledge of structure and bonding to answer the following questions.

a   Explain why both diamond and graphite have high melting points.   [2]

b   i   Why is graphite used in making handles for tennis racquets?   [3]

    ii Explain why graphite is used in pencil 'leads' for writing.   [4]

c   Explain why diamond is used on the tips of high-speed drills.   [5]

Total = 14

8   Crystals of sodium chloride have a lattice structure.

a   Describe a sodium chloride lattice.   [3]

b   Explain the following properties of sodium chloride.

    i   Sodium chloride has a high melting point.   [3]

    ii   Sodium chloride conducts electricity when molten but not when solid.   [3]

    iii Sodium chloride is hard but brittle.   [5]

Total = 14

9   The diagram shows some allotropes of carbon.

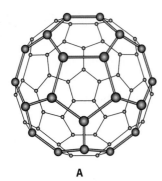 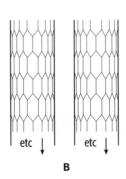 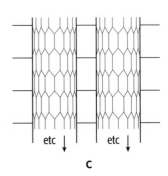

a   Give the name of allotrope **A**, which has the formula C_{60}.   [1]

b   Explain in terms of structure and bonding why structure **A** is gaseous at 800 °C but diamond is not.   [6]

c   Structure **B** shows an allotrope of carbon in the form of tubes.

    i   Give the name of this allotrope of carbon.   [1]

    ii Describe the similarities and differences between structure **B** and graphite.   [4]

d   Structure **C** is stronger than structure **B** when a force is applied in the same direction as the long axis of the tube.
    Explain why structure **C** is stronger.   [5]

Total = 17

Chapter 6:
Enthalpy changes

Learning outcomes

You should be able to:

- explain that some chemical reactions are accompanied by exothermic or endothermic energy changes, mainly in the form of heat energy, and that energy changes can be exothermic or endothermic

- explain and use the terms **enthalpy change of reaction** and **standard conditions** with reference to enthalpy changes of: formation, combustion, hydration, solution, neutralisation and atomisation

- explain and use the term **bond energy**

- calculate enthalpy changes from experimental results, including the use of the relationship: enthalpy change, $\Delta H = -mc\Delta T$

- apply Hess's law to construct simple energy cycles and carry out calculations, in particular:
  - determining enthalpy changes that cannot be found by direct experiment
  - calculating average bond energies

- construct and interpret a reaction pathway diagram in terms of the enthalpy change of reaction and the activation energy.

Introduction

When chemical reactions take place there is an energy change. Energy can take many forms, including heat, light, sound and electrical energy. The chemical energy in the atoms and bonds of a substance is also very important. One of the most obvious energy transfers in chemical reactions is the transfer of heat (Figure 6.1). A car engine gets hot when the energy is transferred from the burning fuel. Fireworks release a lot of energy as heat (as well as light and sound) when they explode. Our bodies keep warm because of the continuous oxidation of the food we eat.

Figure 6.1 The chemical reactions in this fire are releasing large quantities of energy.

What are enthalpy changes?

Exothermic or endothermic?

Chemical reactions that release energy to the surroundings are described as exothermic. In an exothermic reaction the temperature of the surroundings increases. For example, when magnesium reacts with sulfuric acid in a test tube, the energy released is transferred to the surroundings and the temperature of the reaction mixture in the tube increases.

$$Mg(s) + H_2SO_4(aq) \longrightarrow MgSO_4(aq) + H_2(g) \quad \text{(energy released)}$$

The surroundings include:

- the solvent (in this case water)
- the air around the test tube
- the test tube itself
- anything dipping into the test tube (e.g. a thermometer).

Other examples of exothermic reactions include:

- the combustion of fuels
- the oxidation of carbohydrates in the bodies of animals and plants (respiration)
- the reaction of water with quicklime (calcium oxide) (see page 166).

Chemical reactions that absorb energy from the surroundings are described as endothermic. In an endothermic reaction the temperature of the surroundings decreases (Figure 6.2). For example, when sodium hydrogencarbonate reacts with an aqueous solution of citric acid in a test tube the temperature of the reaction mixture in the tube decreases. The citric acid and sodium hydrogencarbonate are absorbing the heat energy from the solvent, the test tube and the air.

Other examples of endothermic reactions include:

- the decomposition of limestone by heating (all thermal decomposition reactions are endothermic)
- photosynthesis (in which the energy is supplied by sunlight)
- dissolving certain ammonium salts in water

$$NH_4Cl(s) + aq \longrightarrow NH_4^+(aq) + Cl^-(aq)$$

ammonium chloride   water   ammonium ions   chloride ions

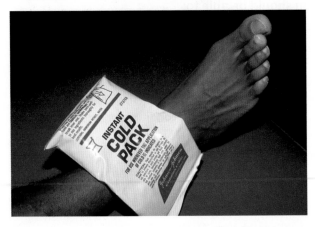

Figure 6.2 Using a cooling pack to treat a sports injury. When the pack is kneaded, water and ammonium chloride crystals mix. As the crystals dissolve, energy is transferred from the surroundings, cooling the injury.

1 Classify each process as exothermic or endothermic:

   a   the burning of magnesium in air

   b   the crystallisation of copper(II) sulfate from a saturated solution

   c   the thermal decomposition of magnesium nitrate

   d   the fermentation of glucose by yeast

   e   the evaporation of sea water.

Enthalpy changes and enthalpy profile diagrams

We call the energy exchange between a chemical reaction and its surroundings at constant pressure the **enthalpy change**. Enthalpy is the total energy associated with the materials that react. The symbol for enthalpy is H. We cannot measure enthalpy, but we can measure an enthalpy change when heat energy is exchanged with the surroundings. We can write this as:

$$\underset{\substack{\text{enthalpy} \\ \text{change}}}{\Delta H} = \underset{\substack{\text{enthalpy of} \\ \text{products}}}{H_{\text{products}}} - \underset{\substack{\text{enthalpy of} \\ \text{reactants}}}{H_{\text{reactants}}}$$

The symbol Δ is the upper case Greek letter 'delta'. This symbol is often used to mean a change in a quantity. For example, ΔT means a change in temperature and ΔH means the enthalpy change.

The units of enthalpy change are kilojoules per mole ($kJ\,mol^{-1}$).

We can draw **enthalpy profile diagrams** (also known as reaction pathway diagrams) to show enthalpy changes. The enthalpy of the reactants and products is shown on the y-axis. The x-axis shows the reaction pathway, with reactants on the left and products on the right. For an exothermic reaction, energy is released to the surroundings. So the enthalpy of the reactants must be greater than the enthalpy of the products. We can see from the enthalpy profile diagram for the combustion of methane (Figure 6.3) that $H_{\text{products}} - H_{\text{reactants}}$ is negative.

We can include this information in the equation for the reaction:

$$CH_4(g) + 2O_2(g) \longrightarrow CO_2(g) + 2H_2O(l)$$
$$\Delta H = -890.3\,kJ\,mol^{-1}$$

The negative sign shows that the reaction is exothermic.

For an endothermic reaction, energy is absorbed from the surroundings by the chemicals in the reaction. So

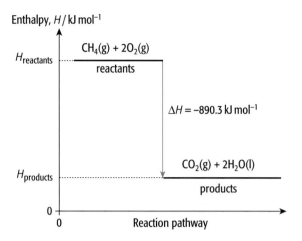

Figure 6.3 Enthalpy profile diagram for the combustion of methane.

the enthalpy of the products must be greater than the enthalpy of the reactants. We can see from the enthalpy profile diagram for the thermal decomposition of calcium carbonate (Figure 6.4) that $H_{\text{products}} - H_{\text{reactants}}$ is positive.

$$CaCO_3(s) \longrightarrow CaO(s) + CO_2(g) \qquad \Delta H = +572\,kJ\,mol^{-1}$$

The positive sign shows that the reaction is endothermic.

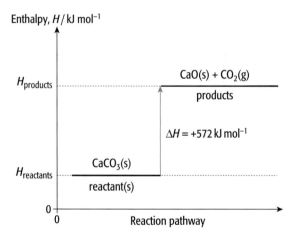

Figure 6.4 Enthalpy profile diagram for the decomposition of calcium carbonate.

2 Draw enthalpy profile diagrams for:

   a   the combustion of sulfur to form sulfur dioxide

   b   the endothermic reaction

$$H_2O(g) + C(s) \longrightarrow H_2(g) + CO(g)$$

91

Standard enthalpy changes

Standard conditions

To make any comparison of enthalpy changes a fair comparison, we must use the same conditions. These are called standard conditions:

- a pressure of 10^5 Pa (10^5 Pa is 100 kPa, approximately normal atmospheric pressure)
- a temperature of 298 K (25 °C) (add 273 to the Celsius temperature to convert a temperature into kelvin)
- each substance involved in the reaction is in its normal physical state (solid, liquid or gas) at 10^5 Pa and 298 K.

The symbol $\ominus$ indicates that the enthalpy change refers to a reaction carried out under standard conditions.

The information in the equation:

$$CH_4(g) + 2O_2(g) \longrightarrow CO_2(g) + 2H_2O(l)$$
$$\Delta H^{\ominus} = -890.3 \text{ kJ mol}^{-1}$$

shows us that when one mole of methane gas reacts with two moles of oxygen gas to form one mole of carbon dioxide gas and two moles of water in the liquid state the standard enthalpy change is -890.3 kJ mol^{-1}.

A variety of enthalpy changes

We can describe enthalpy changes according to the type of chemical reaction taking place. For example:

- enthalpy change of formation
- enthalpy change of combustion
- enthalpy change of neutralisation
- enthalpy change of solution
- enthalpy change of atomisation
- enthalpy change of hydration.

In more general cases we can use the term:

- enthalpy change of reaction.

Standard enthalpy change of reaction, $\Delta H^{\ominus}_r$

The standard enthalpy change of reaction is the enthalpy change when the amounts of reactants shown in the equation react to give products under standard conditions. The reactants and products must be in their standard states.

The symbol for standard enthalpy change of reaction is $\Delta H^{\ominus}_r$. Enthalpy changes of reaction can be exothermic or endothermic.

The equation that describes the reaction must be given. For example, the equation:

$$H_2(g) + \tfrac{1}{2}O_2(g) \longrightarrow H_2O(l) \quad \Delta H^{\ominus}_r = -286 \text{ kJ mol}^{-1}$$

shows us the enthalpy change when one mole of water is formed from hydrogen and oxygen. In this case 286 kJ of energy are released.

However, if we write the equation as

$$2H_2(g) + O_2(g) \longrightarrow 2H_2O(l) \quad \Delta H^{\ominus}_r = -572 \text{ kJ mol}^{-1}$$

two moles of water are formed from hydrogen and oxygen. In this case 572 kJ of energy are released.

Standard enthalpy change of formation, $\Delta H^{\ominus}_f$

The standard enthalpy change of formation is the enthalpy change when one mole of a compound is formed from its elements under standard conditions. The reactants and products must be in their standard states.

The symbol for standard enthalpy change of formation is $\Delta H^{\ominus}_f$. Enthalpy changes of formation can be exothermic or endothermic. We write the formula of the compound in square brackets after $\Delta H^{\ominus}_f$ to help us when we do calculations involving enthalpy changes. Examples are:

$$2Fe(s) + 1\tfrac{1}{2}O_2(g) \longrightarrow Fe_2O_3(s)$$

$$\Delta H^{\ominus}_f [Fe_2O_3(s)] = -824.2 \text{ kJ mol}^{-1}$$

$$C(\text{graphite}) + 2S(s) \longrightarrow CS_2(l)$$

$$\Delta H^{\ominus}_f [CS_2(l)] = +98.7 \text{ kJ mol}^{-1}$$

Note that the state symbol for carbon is shown as 'graphite'. This is because there are several forms of carbon but the most stable is graphite and we choose the most stable form when writing equations where enthalpy changes are shown.

By definition, the standard enthalpy change of formation of any element in its standard state is zero.

Standard enthalpy change of combustion, $\Delta H^{\ominus}_c$

The standard enthalpy change of combustion is the enthalpy change when one mole of a substance is burnt in excess oxygen under standard conditions. The reactants and products must be in their standard states.

The symbol for standard enthalpy change of combustion is $\Delta H_c^\ominus$. Enthalpy changes of combustion are always exothermic. The substances combusted can be either elements or compounds.

$$S(s) + O_2(g) \longrightarrow SO_2(g)$$

$$\Delta H_c^\ominus\,[S(s)] = -296.8\,\text{kJ}\,\text{mol}^{-1}$$

$$CH_4(g) + 2O_2(g) \longrightarrow CO_2(g) + 2H_2O(l)$$

$$\Delta H_c^\ominus\,[CH_4(g)] = -890.3\,\text{kJ}\,\text{mol}^{-1}$$

Note that the first equation can be considered as either the enthalpy change of combustion of sulfur or the enthalpy change of formation of sulfur dioxide.

QUESTION

3 Classify each of the following reactions as $\Delta H_r^\ominus$, $\Delta H_f^\ominus$ or $\Delta H_c^\ominus$:

a $MgCO_3(s) \longrightarrow MgO(s) + CO_2(g)$

b $C(\text{graphite}) + O_2(g) \longrightarrow CO_2(g)$

c $HCl(g) + NH_3(g) \longrightarrow NH_4Cl(s)$

d $H_2(g) + \frac{1}{2}O_2(g) \longrightarrow H_2O(l)$

Standard enthalpy change of neutralisation, $\Delta H_n^\ominus$

The standard enthalpy change of neutralisation ($\Delta H_n^\ominus$) is the enthalpy change when one mole of water is formed by the reaction of an acid with an alkali under standard conditions.

For example:

$$HCl(aq) + NaOH(aq) \longrightarrow NaCl(aq) + H_2O(l)$$

$$\Delta H_n^\ominus = -57.1\,\text{kJ}\,\text{mol}^{-1}$$

For any acid–alkali reaction the ionic equation is:

$$H^+(aq) + OH^-(aq) \longrightarrow H_2O(l)$$

The other ions in solution (Cl^- and Na^+) are spectator ions and take no part in the reaction (see page 13).

Standard enthalpy change of solution, $\Delta H_{sol}^\ominus$

The standard enthalpy change of solution ($\Delta H_{sol}^\ominus$) is the enthalpy change when one mole of solute is dissolved in a solvent to form an infinitely dilute solution under standard conditions.

An infinitely dilute solution is one that does not produce any further enthalpy change when more solvent is added. An example is the addition of a small amount of solid sodium hydroxide to a large amount of water.

$$NaOH(s) + aq \longrightarrow NaOH(aq)$$

We use known amounts of solute and solvent with the solvent in excess to make sure that all the solute dissolves.

Standard enthalpy change of atomisation, $\Delta H_{at}^\ominus$

The standard enthalpy change of atomisation, $\Delta H_{at}^\ominus$, is the enthalpy change when one mole of gaseous atoms is formed from its element under standard conditions.

The standard enthalpy change of atomisation of hydrogen relates to the equation:

$$\tfrac{1}{2}H_2(g) \longrightarrow H(g) \qquad \Delta H_{at}^\ominus\left[\tfrac{1}{2}H_2(g)\right] = +218\,\text{kJ}\,\text{mol}^{-1}$$

Standard enthalpy change of hydration of an anhydrous salt

The standard enthalpy change of hydration of an anhydrous salt is the enthalpy change when one mole of a hydrated salt is formed from one mole of the anhydrous salt under standard conditions.

For example:

$$Na_2S_2O_3(s) + 5H_2O(l) \longrightarrow Na_2S_2O_3.5H_2O(s)$$

$$\Delta H^\ominus = -55.0\,\text{kJ}\,\text{mol}^{-1}$$

This should not be confused with the standard enthalpy change of hydration of gaseous ions to form aqueous ions (see page 265 for this material, which is not required for AS level).

Measuring enthalpy changes

We can measure the enthalpy change of some reactions by different techniques. These are outlined in the 'Measuring enthalpy changes' box.

MEASURING ENTHALPY CHANGES

Calorimetry

We can measure the enthalpy change of some reactions by a technique called calorimetry. The apparatus used is called a calorimeter. A simple calorimeter can be a polystyrene drinking cup (Figure 6.5), a vacuum flask or a metal can.

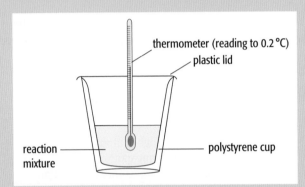

thermometer (reading to 0.2 °C)

plastic lid

reaction mixture

polystyrene cup

Figure 6.5 A polystyrene cup can act as a calorimeter for finding some enthalpy changes.

When carrying out experiments in calorimeters we use known amounts of reactants and known volumes of liquids. We also measure the temperature change of the liquid in the calorimeter as the reaction occurs. The thermometer should be accurate to 0.1 or 0.2 °C.

Calorimetry relies on the fact that it takes 4.18 J of energy to increase the temperature of 1 g of water by 1 °C. The energy required to raise the temperature of 1 g of a liquid by 1 °C is called the specific heat capacity, c, of the liquid. So, the specific heat capacity of water is $4.18\,J\,g^{-1}\,°C^{-1}$.

The energy transferred as heat (the enthalpy change) is given by the relationship:

$$\Delta H = -mc\Delta T$$

where:

ΔH is the enthalpy change, in J
m is the mass of water, in g
c is the specific heat capacity, in $J\,g^{-1}\,°C^{-1}$
ΔT is the temperature change, in °C

As 1 cm³ of water weighs 1 g, we can substitute volume of water in cm³ of water for mass of water in g in the equation. Aqueous solutions of acids, alkalis and salts are assumed to be largely water.

With solutions we make the assumptions that:

- 1 cm³ of solution has a mass of 1 g
- the solution has the same specific heat capacity as water.

Note: A rise in temperature is given a positive sign. So the value of ΔH is negative for an exothermic reaction. A fall in temperature is given a negative sign. So the value of ΔH is positive for an endothermic reaction.

The enthalpy change of neutralisation by experiment

We can find the enthalpy change of neutralisation of sodium hydroxide with hydrochloric acid by mixing equal volumes of known equimolar concentrations of acid and alkali together in a polystyrene cup. A typical procedure for the reaction above is as follows.

1 Place 50 cm³ of 1.0 mol dm⁻³ hydrochloric acid in the cup and record its temperature.
2 Add 50 cm³ of 1.0 mol dm⁻³ sodium hydroxide (at the same temperature) to the acid in the cup.
3 Stir the reaction mixture with the thermometer and record the highest temperature.

In this experiment most of the heat is transferred to the solution, as the polystyrene cup is a good insulator. Cooling of the warm solution is not a great problem: the reaction is rapid so the maximum temperature is reached before much cooling of the warm solution has occurred. However, there are still heat losses to the air and to the thermometer, which make the result less exothermic than the data book value of −57.1 kJ mol⁻¹.

Results and calculation

mass of solution	= 100 g (50 cm³ of acid plus 50 cm³ of alkali and assuming that 1.0 cm³ of solution has a mass of 1.0 g)

MEASURING ENTHALPY CHANGES (CONTINUED)

specific heat capacity $= 4.18\,J\,g^{-1}\,°C^{-1}$ (assuming that the heat capacity of the solution is the same as the heat capacity of water)

starting temperature of reactant solutions $= 21.3\,°C$

final temperature of product solution $= 27.8\,°C$

temperature rise $= +6.5\,°C$

use the relationship $\Delta H = -mc\Delta T$

heat energy released $= -100 \times 4.18 \times 6.5 = -2717\,J$

At the start, the reaction mixture contained $50\,cm^3$ of $1.0\,mol\,dm^{-3}$ hydrochloric acid and $50\,cm^3$ of $1.0\,mol\,dm^{-3}$ sodium hydroxide. The number of moles of each (and of the water formed) is calculated using

$$\frac{\text{concentration} \times \text{volume (in cm}^3)}{1000} = \frac{1.0 \times 50}{1000} = 0.050\ \text{moles}$$

So 2717 J of energy was released by 0.050 moles of acid.

Therefore for one mole of acid (forming one mole of water) the energy released was

$$\frac{2717}{0.050} = -54\,340\,J\,mol^{-1}$$
$$= -54\,kJ\,mol^{-1} \text{ (to 2 significant figures).}$$

The negative sign shows that the reaction is exothermic.

Enthalpy change of solution by experiment

The enthalpy change of solution of sodium hydroxide can be found using a polystyrene cup as a calorimeter. We use known amounts of solute and solvent with the solvent in excess to make sure that all the solute dissolves.

The procedure is:

1 Weigh an empty polystyrene cup.
2 Pour $100\,cm^3$ of water into the cup and weigh the cup and water.
3 Record the steady temperature of the water with a thermometer reading to at least the nearest $0.2\,°C$.
4 Add a few pellets of sodium hydroxide (corrosive!) which have been stored under dry conditions.
5 Keep the mixture stirred continuously with a thermometer and record the temperature at fixed intervals, e.g. every 20 seconds.
6 Keep recording the temperature for 5 minutes after the maximum temperature has been reached.

7 Weigh the cup and its contents to calculate the mass of sodium hydroxide which dissolved.

Results and calculations

mass of polystyrene cup	$= 23.00\,g$
mass of polystyrene cup + water	$= 123.45\,g$
mass of water	$= 100.45\,g$
mass of cup + water + sodium hydroxide	$= 124.95\,g$
mass of sodium hydroxide that dissolved	$= 1.50\,g$
initial temperature of water	$= 18.0\,°C$
final temperature of water	$= 21.6\,°C$
temperature rise	$= +3.6\,°C$

From the results, 1.50 g of sodium hydroxide dissolved in $100.45\,cm^3$ (100.45 g) of water and produced a temperature change of $+3.6\,°C$.

$$\begin{aligned}
\text{enthalpy change (in J)} &= -\left(\text{mass of water (in g)} \times \text{specific heat capacity (in } J\,g^{-1}\,°C^{-1}) \times \text{temperature change (in } °C)\right)\\
&= -(100.45 \times 4.18 \times 3.6)\\
&= -1511.57\,J = -1.5\,kJ \text{ (to 2 significant figures)}
\end{aligned}$$

The enthalpy change for 1.5 g sodium hydroxide is $-1.5\,kJ$.

The enthalpy change for 1.0 mole of sodium hydroxide ($M_r = 40\,g\,mol^{-1}$)

is $-\dfrac{40}{1.5} \times 1.5\,kJ = -40\,kJ$

$\Delta H_{sol}^{\ominus} = -40\,kJ\,mol^{-1}$

In this experiment we are assuming that the specific heat capacity of the solution is the same as the specific heat capacity of water. The heat losses in this experiment, however, are likely to be considerable because the sodium hydroxide takes some time to dissolve. This means that the reaction mixture has a longer period of cooling.

Finding the enthalpy change of combustion

Experiment: the enthalpy change of combustion of propan-1-ol

We can find the enthalpy change of combustion by burning a known mass of substance and using the heat released to raise the temperature of a known mass of water. The apparatus used for this consists of a spirit burner and a metal calorimeter (Figure 6.6).

95

MEASURING ENTHALPY CHANGES (CONTINUED)

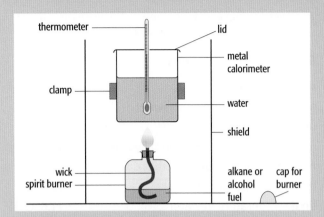

Figure 6.6 A simple apparatus used to find the enthalpy change of combustion of fuels.

The procedure is:

1 Weigh the spirit burner containing propan-1-ol. The cap on the burner must be kept on when the burner is not lit to avoid evaporation of the fuel.

2 Pour 100 cm³ (100 g) of water into the calorimeter. For greater accuracy this should be weighed out.

3 Stir the water and record its temperature with a thermometer reading to at least the nearest 0.1 °C.

4 Place the spirit burner beneath the calorimeter, remove the cap and light the wick. The length of the wick should have been previously adjusted so that the material of the wick does not burn and the flame just touches the bottom of the calorimeter.

5 Keep stirring the water with the thermometer until there is a temperature rise of about 10 °C. Record this temperature.

6 Remove the spirit burner, place the cap on it and reweigh it.

Results and calculations

To find the standard enthalpy change of combustion we need to know:

- the mass of fuel burnt
- the temperature rise of the water
- the mass of the water
- the relative molecular mass of the fuel (propan-1-ol).

mass of water in calorimeter	= 100 g
mass of spirit burner and propan-1-ol at start	= 86.27 g
mass of spirit burner and propan-1-ol at end	= 86.06 g
mass of propan-1-ol burnt	= 0.21 g
initial temperature of water	= 30.9 °C
final temperature of water	= 20.2 °C
temperature change of the water	= +10.7 °C

Using the relationship $\Delta H = -mc\Delta T$ (mass of water × specific heat capacity of water × temperature change)

energy released by burning 0.21 g propanol
$$= -(100 \times 4.18 \times 10.7) = -4472.6 \text{ J}$$

the mass of 1 mole of propan-1-ol, C_3H_7OH, is 60 g

so for 60 g propan-1-ol the energy released is

$$-4472.6 \times \frac{60}{0.21} = -1\,277\,885.7 \text{ J mol}^{-1} = -1300 \text{ kJ mol}^{-1}$$

(to 2 significant figures)

This is much less than the data book value of -2021 kJ mol^{-1}, mainly due to heat losses to the surroundings.

QUESTIONS

4 a Calculate the energy transferred when the temperature of 75 cm³ of water rises from 23 °C to 54 °C.

   b When 8 g of sodium chloride is dissolved in 40 cm³ of water the temperature falls from 22 °C to 20.5 °C. Calculate the energy absorbed by the solution when sodium chloride dissolves.

   c A student added 50 cm³ of sodium hydroxide to 50 cm³ of hydrochloric acid. Both solutions were at 18 °C to start with. When the solutions were mixed a reaction occurred. The temperature rose to 33 °C. Calculate the energy released in this reaction.

5 Explain why the enthalpy change of neutralisation of one mole of sulfuric acid, H_2SO_4, is not the standard enthalpy change of neutralisation.

6 A student added 10 g (0.25 mol) of sodium hydroxide to 40 cm³ of water to make a concentrated solution. All the sodium hydroxide dissolved. He measured the maximum temperature rise. He suggested that these results would give an accurate value for the standard enthalpy change of solution. Give two reasons why he is incorrect.

7 A student calculated the standard enthalpy change of combustion of ethanol $\Delta H^{\ominus}_c$ [C_2H_5OH] by calorimetry as -870 kJ mol^{-1}. The data book value is -1367 kJ mol^{-1}. Explain the difference between these values.

Hess's law

Conserving energy

The Law of Conservation of Energy states that 'energy cannot be created or destroyed'. This is called the First Law of Thermodynamics.

This law also applies to chemical reactions. The total energy of the chemicals and their surroundings must remain constant. In 1840 Germain Hess applied the Law of Conservation of Energy to enthalpy changes.

> **Hess's law** states that 'the total enthalpy change in a chemical reaction is independent of the route by which the chemical reaction takes place as long as the initial and final conditions are the same'.

Enthalpy cycles

We can illustrate Hess's law by drawing enthalpy cycles (Hess cycles). In Figure 6.7, the reactants A and B combine directly to form C. This is the direct route.

Two indirect routes are also shown. One other way of changing A + B to C is to convert A + B into different substances F + G (intermediates), which then combine to form C.

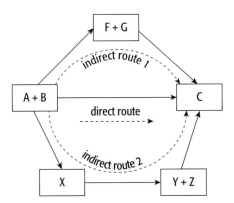

Figure 6.7 The enthalpy change is the same no matter which route is followed.

Hess's law tells us that the enthalpy change of reaction for the direct route is the same as for the indirect route. It does not matter how many steps there are in the indirect route. We can still use Hess's law.

We can use Hess's law to calculate enthalpy changes that cannot be found by experiments using calorimetry. For example, the enthalpy change of formation of propane cannot be found by direct experiment because hydrogen does not react with carbon under standard conditions.

Enthalpy change of reaction from enthalpy changes of formation

We can calculate the enthalpy change of reaction by using the type of enthalpy cycle shown in Figure 6.8.

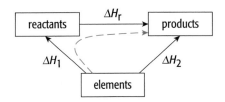

Figure 6.8 An enthalpy cycle for calculating an enthalpy change of reaction. The dashed line shows the indirect (two-step) route.

We use the enthalpy changes of formation of the reactants and products to calculate the enthalpy change of the reaction. We take note of the directions of the arrows to find the one-stage (direct) and two-stage (indirect) routes. When we use Hess's law we see that:

$$\underset{\text{direct route}}{\Delta H_2} = \underset{\text{indirect route}}{\Delta H_1 + \Delta H_r}$$

So $\Delta H_r = \Delta H_2 - \Delta H_1$

To calculate the enthalpy change of reaction using this type of enthalpy cycle we use the following procedure:

- write the balanced equation at the top
- draw the cycle with elements at the bottom
- draw in all arrows, making sure they go in the correct directions
- apply Hess's law, taking into account the number of moles of each reactant and product.

If there are 3 moles of a product, e.g. $3CO_2(g)$, we must multiply the enthalpy change of formation by 3. Also remember that the standard enthalpy change of formation of an element in its standard state is zero.

> **WORKED EXAMPLE**
>
> 1 Calculate the standard enthalpy change for the reaction:
>
> $$2NaHCO_3(s) \longrightarrow Na_2CO_3(s) + CO_2(g) + H_2O(l)$$
>
> The relevant enthalpy changes of formation are:
> $\Delta H_f^{\ominus} [NaHCO_3(s)] = -950.8 \, kJ \, mol^{-1}$
> $\Delta H_f^{\ominus} [Na_2CO_3(s)] = -1130.7 \, kJ \, mol^{-1}$
> $\Delta H_f^{\ominus} [CO_2(g)] = -393.5 \, kJ \, mol^{-1}$
> $\Delta H_f^{\ominus} [H_2O(l)] = -285.8 \, kJ \, mol^{-1}$

WORKED EXAMPLE (CONTINUED)

The enthalpy cycle is shown in Figure 6.9.

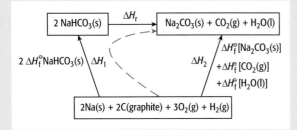

Figure 6.9 The enthalpy cycle for the decomposition of sodium hydrogencarbonate. The dashed line shows the two-step route.

Using Hess's law:

$$\Delta H_2 = \Delta H_1 + \Delta H_r$$

$$\Delta H_f^{\ominus}[Na_2CO_3(s)] + \Delta H_f^{\ominus}[CO_2(g)] + \Delta H_f^{\ominus}[H_2O(l)]$$
$$= 2\Delta H_f^{\ominus}[NaHCO_3(s)] + \Delta H_r^{\ominus}$$

$(-1130.7) + (-393.5) + (-285.8) = 2(-950.8) + \Delta H_r$

$-1810.0 = -1901.6 + \Delta H_r$

So $\Delta H_r^{\ominus} = (-1810.0) - (-1901.6)$

$= +91.6\,kJ\,mol^{-1}$ (for the equation shown)

Note:

i the value for $\Delta H_f^{\ominus}[NaHCO_3(s)]$ is multiplied by 2 because 2 moles of $NaHCO_3$ appear in the equation

ii the values for $\Delta H_f^{\ominus}[Na_2CO_3(s)]$, $\Delta H_f^{\ominus}[CO_2(g)]$ and $\Delta H_f^{\ominus}[H_2O(l)]$ are added together to give ΔH_2. Take care to account for the fact that some values may be positive and some negative.

QUESTION

8 a Draw an enthalpy cycle to calculate $\Delta H_r^{\ominus}$ for the reaction

$$2Al(s) + Fe_2O_3(s) \longrightarrow 2Fe(s) + Al_2O_3(s)$$

b Calculate $\Delta H_r^{\ominus}$ using the following information:

$\Delta H_f^{\ominus}[Fe_2O_3(s)] = -824.2\,kJ\,mol^{-1}$

$\Delta H_f^{\ominus}[Al_2O_3(s)] = -1675.7\,kJ\,mol^{-1}$

Enthalpy change of formation from enthalpy changes of combustion

We can calculate the enthalpy change of formation of many compounds by using the type of enthalpy cycle shown in Figure 6.10.

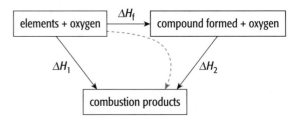

Figure 6.10 An enthalpy cycle for calculating an enthalpy change of formation from enthalpy changes of combustion. The dashed line shows the two-step route.

We use the enthalpy changes of combustion of the reactants and products to calculate the enthalpy change of formation. When we take note of the direction of the arrows to find the one-stage (direct) and two-stage (indirect) routes and use Hess's law we see that:

$$\underset{\text{direct route}}{\Delta H_1} = \underset{\text{indirect route}}{\Delta H_f + \Delta H_2}$$

So $\Delta H_f = \Delta H_1 - \Delta H_2$

To calculate the enthalpy change of formation using this type of cycle:

- write the equation for enthalpy change of formation at the top; add oxygen on both sides of the equation to balance the combustion reactions
- draw the cycle with the combustion products at the bottom
- draw in all arrows, making sure they go in the correct directions
- apply Hess's law, taking into account the number of moles of each reactant and product.

WORKED EXAMPLE

2 Calculate the standard enthalpy change of formation of ethane, C_2H_6.

The relevant enthalpy changes of combustion are:

$$C(graphite) + O_2(g) \longrightarrow CO_2(g)$$
$$\Delta H_c^{\ominus}[C(graphite)] = -393.5\,kJ\,mol^{-1}$$

$$H_2(g) + \tfrac{1}{2}O_2(g) \longrightarrow H_2O(l)$$
$$\Delta H_c^{\ominus}[H_2(g)] = -285.8\,kJ\,mol^{-1}$$

WORKED EXAMPLE (CONTINUED)

$$C_2H_6(g) + 3\tfrac{1}{2}O_2(g) \longrightarrow 2CO_2(g) + 3H_2O(l)$$
$$\Delta H_c^{\ominus}[C_2H_6(g)] = -1559.7\,\text{kJ mol}^{-1}$$

The enthalpy cycle is shown in Figure 6.11.

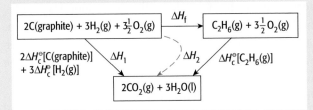

Figure 6.11 The enthalpy cycle to find the enthalpy change of formation of ethane using enthalpy changes of combustion. The dashed line shows the two-step route.

Using Hess's law:

$$\begin{aligned}
\Delta H_1 &= \Delta H_f + \Delta H_2 \\
2(-393.5) + 3(-285.8) &= \Delta H_f + (-1559.7) \\
-1644.4 &= \Delta H_f + (-1559.7)
\end{aligned}$$

So $\Delta H_f = -1644.4 - (-1559.7) = -84.7\,\text{kJ mol}^{-1}$

QUESTION

9 a Draw an enthalpy cycle to calculate the enthalpy change of formation of ethanol, C_2H_5OH, using enthalpy changes of combustion.

  b Calculate a value for $\Delta H_f^{\ominus}[C_2H_5OH(l)]$ using the following data:

$$\Delta H_c^{\ominus}[C(graphite)] = -393.5\,\text{kJ mol}^{-1}$$
$$\Delta H_c^{\ominus}[H_2(g)] = -285.8\,\text{kJ mol}^{-1}$$
$$\Delta H_c^{\ominus}[C_2H_5OH(l)] = -1367.3\,\text{kJ mol}^{-1}$$

Calculating the enthalpy change of hydration of an anhydrous salt

Hydrated salts such as hydrated copper(II) sulfate, $CuSO_4.5H_2O$, contain water molecules surrounding their ions. It is very difficult to measure the enthalpy change when an anhydrous salt such as anhydrous sodium thiosulfate becomes hydrated.

$$Na_2S_2O_3(s) + 5H_2O(l) \longrightarrow Na_2S_2O_3.5H_2O(s)$$

We can, however, use an enthalpy cycle to calculate this. We use the standard enthalpy changes of solution to complete the enthalpy cycle (Figure 6.12).

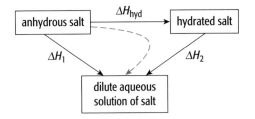

Figure 6.12 An enthalpy cycle to calculate the enthalpy change of hydration of an anhydrous salt. The dashed line shows the two-step route.

The enthalpy cycle for calculating the enthalpy of hydration of anhydrous sodium thiosulfate is shown in Figure 6.13.

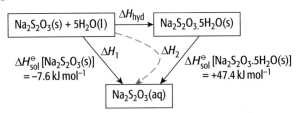

Figure 6.13 An enthalpy cycle to calculate the enthalpy change when anhydrous sodium thiosulfate is hydrated. The dashed line shows the two-step route.

Using Hess's law:

$$\begin{aligned}
\Delta H_1 &= \Delta H_{hyd} + \Delta H_2 \\
(-7.6) &= \Delta H_{hyd} + (+47.4)
\end{aligned}$$

So $\Delta H_{hyd} = (-7.6) - (+47.4) = -55.0\,\text{kJ mol}^{-1}$

QUESTION

10 Suggest why it is difficult to measure the enthalpy change directly when an anhydrous salt is converted to a hydrated salt.

Bond energies and enthalpy changes

Bond breaking and bond making

Enthalpy changes are due to the breaking and forming of bonds. Breaking bonds requires energy. The energy is needed to overcome the attractive forces joining the atoms together. Energy is released when new bonds are formed. Bond breaking is endothermic and bond forming is exothermic.

In a chemical reaction:

■ if the energy needed to break bonds is less than the energy released when new bonds are formed, the reaction will release energy and is exothermic.

■ if the energy needed to break bonds is more than the energy released when new bonds are formed, the reaction will absorb energy and is endothermic.

We can draw enthalpy level (reaction pathway) diagrams to show these changes (Figure 6.14). In reality, not all the bonds in a compound are broken and then re-formed during a reaction. In most reactions only some of the bonds in the reactants are broken and then new bonds are formed in a specific sequence. The minimum energy required to break certain bonds in a compound to get a reaction to start is called the activation energy (see page 141).

Bond energy

The amount of energy needed to break a specific covalent bond is called the bond dissociation energy. We sometimes call this the bond energy or bond enthalpy. The symbol for bond energy is E. We put the type of bond broken in brackets after the symbol. So $E(C—H)$ refers to the bond energy of a mole of single bonds between carbon and hydrogen atoms.

The bond energy for double and triple bonds refers to a mole of double or triple bonds. Two examples of equations relating to bond energies are:

$$Br_2(g) \longrightarrow 2Br(g) \qquad E(Br—Br) = +193\,kJ\,mol^{-1}$$

$$O{=}O(g) \longrightarrow 2O(g) \qquad E(O{=}O) = +498\,kJ\,mol^{-1}$$

The values of bond energies are always positive because they refer to bonds being broken.

When new bonds are formed the amount of energy released is the same as the amount of energy absorbed when the same type of bond is broken. So, for the formation of oxygen molecules from oxygen atoms:

$$2O(g) \longrightarrow O_2(g) \qquad E(O{=}O) = -498\,kJ\,mol^{-1}$$

Average bond energy

Bond energy is affected by other atoms in the molecule. The O—H bond in water has a slightly different bond energy value to the O—H bond in ethanol; in ethanol the oxygen is connected to a carbon atom rather than another hydrogen atom. The O—H bond is in a different environment. Identical bonds in molecules with two (or more) types of bond have different bond energies when we measure them. It takes more energy to break the first O—H bond in water than to break the second. For these reasons we use average bond energies taken from a number of bonds of the same type but in different environments.

We cannot usually find the value of bond energies directly so we have to use an enthalpy cycle. The average bond energy of the C—H bond in methane can be found using the enthalpy changes of atomisation of carbon and hydrogen and the enthalpy change of combustion or formation of methane.

The enthalpy cycle for calculating the average C—H bond energy is shown in Figure 6.15. Using the enthalpy cycle shown in Figure 6.15, the average C—H bond energy can be found by dividing the value of ΔH on the diagram by four (because there are four C—H bonds in a molecule of methane).

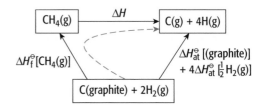

Figure 6.15 An enthalpy cycle to find the average bond energy of the C—H bond. The dashed line shows the two-step route.

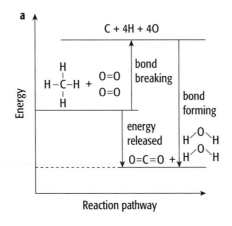

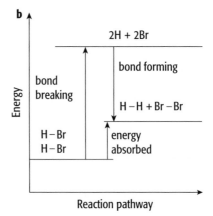

Figure 6.14 a An energy level diagram showing bond breaking and bond forming for the combustion of methane (exothermic).
b An energy level diagram showing bond breaking and bond forming for the decomposition of hydrogen bromide (endothermic).

11 Use the information in Figure 6.15 and the information below to show that the average bond energy of the C—H bond is 415.9 kJ mol^{-1}.

$\Delta H^{\ominus}_f [CH_4] = -74.8$ kJ mol^{-1}

$\Delta H^{\ominus}_{at} [\frac{1}{2}H_2] = +218$ kJ mol^{-1}

$\Delta H^{\ominus}_{at} [C(graphite)] = +716.7$ kJ mol^{-1}

Calculating enthalpy changes using bond energies

We can use bond enthalpies to calculate the enthalpy change of a reaction that we cannot measure directly. For example, the reaction for the Haber process (see page 129):

$$N_2(g) + 3H_2(g) \rightleftharpoons 2NH_3(g)$$

The enthalpy cycle for this reaction is shown in Figure 6.16. The relevant bond energies are:

$E(N\equiv N) = 945$ kJ mol^{-1}

$E(H-H) = 436$ kJ mol^{-1}

$E(N-H) = 391$ kJ mol^{-1}

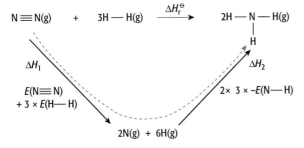

Figure 6.16 The enthalpy cycle for ammonia synthesis. The dashed line shows the two-step route.

It is often easier to set out the calculation as a balance sheet, as shown below.

Bonds broken ΔH_1 (kJ)	Bonds formed ΔH_2 (kJ)
$1 \times N\equiv N = 1 \times 945 = 945$ $3 \times H-H = 3 \times 436 = 1308$	$6 \times N-H = 6 \times 391$
total $= +2253$	total $= -2346$

Note in these calculations that:

- one triple bond in nitrogen is broken
- three single bonds in hydrogen are broken
- six single N—H bonds in hydrogen are formed (because each of the two ammonia molecules has three N—H bonds)
- values for bond breaking are positive, as these are endothermic, and values for bond forming are negative, as these are exothermic.

From the enthalpy cycle in Figure 6.16:

$\Delta H_r = \Delta H_1 + \Delta H_2$

$\Delta H_r = $ enthalpy change for bonds broken
$\qquad\qquad + $ enthalpy change for bonds formed

$\Delta H_r = 2253 + (-2346) = -93$ kJ mol^{-1}

12 The equation for the combustion of ethanol is:

$$C_2H_5OH(l) + 3O_2(g) \longrightarrow 2CO_2(g) + 3H_2O(l)$$

a Rewrite this equation to show all the bonds in the reactants and products.

b Use the following bond energies (in kJ mol^{-1}) to calculate a value for the standard enthalpy change of this reaction:

$E(C-C) = +347$
$E(C-H) = +410$
$E(C-O) = +336$
$E(O=O) = +496$
$E(C=O) = +805$
$E(O-H) = +465$

c The standard enthalpy change of combustion of ethanol is -1367.3 kJ mol^{-1}. Suggest why this value differs from the value obtained using bond energies.

Summary

- When a chemical reaction occurs, energy is transferred to or from the surroundings.

- In an exothermic reaction, heat is given out to the surroundings so the products have less energy than the reactants. In an endothermic reaction, heat is absorbed from the surroundings so the products have more energy than the reactants.

- Energy changes in chemical reactions that lead to heating or cooling are called enthalpy changes (ΔH).

- Exothermic enthalpy changes are shown as negative values (−).

- Endothermic enthalpy changes are shown as positive values (+).

- Standard enthalpy changes are compared under standard conditions of pressure, 10^5 Pa (100 kPa), and temperature, 298 K (25 °C).

- Enthalpy changes can be calculated experimentally using the relationship:

  enthalpy change = −mass of liquid × specific heat capacity × temperature change
  $\Delta H = -mc\Delta T$

- The standard enthalpy change of formation ($\Delta H_f^{\ominus}$) is the enthalpy change when one mole of a compound is formed from its elements under standard conditions.

- The standard enthalpy change of combustion ($\Delta H_c^{\ominus}$) is the enthalpy change when one mole of a substance is burnt in excess oxygen under standard conditions.

- The standard enthalpy change of atomisation ($\Delta H_{at}^{\ominus}$) is the enthalpy change when one mole of gaseous atoms is formed from the element in its standard state under standard conditions.

- The standard enthalpy changes of hydration and solution can be defined in terms of one mole of a specified compound reacting completely.

- The standard enthalpy change of neutralisation can be defined in terms of one mole of water formed when hydrogen ions and hydroxide ions react.

- Hess's law states that 'the total enthalpy change for a chemical reaction is independent of the route by which the reaction takes place'.

- Hess's law can be used to calculate enthalpy changes for reactions that do not occur directly or cannot be found by experiment.

- Hess's law can be used to calculate the enthalpy change of a reaction using the enthalpy changes of formation of the reactants and products.

- Hess's law can be used to calculate the enthalpy change of formation of a compound using the enthalpy changes of combustion of the reactants and products.

- Bond breaking is endothermic; bond making is exothermic.

- Bond energy is a measure of the energy needed to break a covalent bond.

- Average bond energies are often used because the strength of a bond between two particular types of atom is slightly different in different compounds.

- Hess's law can be used to calculate the enthalpy change of a reaction using the average bond energies of the reactants and products.

End-of-chapter questions

1 Copper(II) nitrate decomposes on heating. The reaction is endothermic.

$$2Cu(NO_3)_2(s) \longrightarrow 2CuO(s) + 4NO_2(g) + O_2(g)$$

  a Draw an enthalpy level diagram (reaction profile diagram) for this reaction. [3]

  b Draw an enthalpy cycle diagram to calculate the standard enthalpy change for this reaction, using enthalpy changes of formation. [3]

  c Calculate the enthalpy change for this reaction using the following enthalpy changes of formation.

    $\Delta H_f^{\ominus} [Cu(NO_3)_2(s)] = -302.9 \, kJ \, mol^{-1}$

    $\Delta H_f^{\ominus} [CuO(s)] = -157.3 \, kJ \, mol^{-1}$

    $\Delta H_f^{\ominus} [NO_2(g)] = +33.2 \, kJ \, mol^{-1}$ [3]

  d Copper(II) sulfate is soluble in water. A student dissolved 25.0 g of copper(II) sulfate in 100 cm^3 of water in a polystyrene beaker stirring all the time. The temperature of the water fell by 2.9 °C.

    i Calculate the enthalpy change of solution of copper(II) sulfate. (specific heat capacity of water = 4.18 J g^{-1} °C^{-1}; relative molecular mass of copper(II) sulfate = 249.7 g mol^{-1}) [3]

    ii Suggest one source of error in this experiment and explain how the error affects the results. [2]

                                       Total = 14

2 Propanone is a liquid. It has the structure

$$\begin{array}{ccccc} & H & O & H & \\ & | & \| & | & \\ H - & C - & C - & C & - H \\ & | & & | & \\ & H & & H & \end{array}$$

The equation for the complete combustion of propanone is:

$$CH_3COCH_3(l) + 4O_2(g) \longrightarrow 3CO_2(g) + 3H_2O(l)$$

  a Use the following bond energies (in kJ mol^{-1}) to calculate a value for the standard enthalpy change of this reaction:

    $E(C-C) = +347$

    $E(C-H) = +413$

    $E(O=O) = +496$

    $E(C=O) = +805$

    $E(O-H) = +465$ [4]

  b Suggest why it would be more accurate to use bond energies that are not average bond energies in this calculation. [2]

  c The standard enthalpy change of combustion of propanone is −1816.5 kJ mol^{-1}. Suggest why this value differs from the value obtained using bond energies. [2]

  d The standard enthalpy change of formation of propanone is −248 kJ mol^{-1}.

    i Define the term **standard enthalpy change of formation**. [3]

    ii Write the equation that describes the standard enthalpy change of formation of propanone. [2]

    iii Explain why the enthalpy change of formation of propanone cannot be found by a single experiment. [1]

                                        Total = 14

3    $240\,cm^3$ of ethane (C_2H_6) was burnt in a controlled way and found to raise the temperature of $100\,cm^3$ of water by $33.5\,°C$. (specific heat capacity of water $= 4.18\,J\,g^{-1}\,K^{-1}$; 1 mol of gas molecules occupies $24.0\,dm^3$ at r.t.p.)

     a   How many moles of ethane were burnt?   [1]

     b   Calculate the heat change for the experiment.   [2]

     c   Calculate the molar enthalpy change of combustion for ethane, as measured by this experiment.   [2]

     d   Use the values below to calculate the standard molar enthalpy change for the complete combustion of ethane.

       $\Delta H_f^{\ominus}[CO_2] = -394\,kJ\,mol^{-1}$

       $\Delta H_f^{\ominus}[H_2O] = -286\,kJ\,mol^{-1}$

       $\Delta H_f^{\ominus}[C_2H_6] = -85\,kJ\,mol^{-1}$ [4]

     e   Give possible reasons for the discrepancy between the two results.   [2]

                                             Total = 11

4   **a**   Define **standard enthalpy change of combustion**.   [3]

     b   When red phosphorus burns in oxygen the enthalpy change is $-2967\,kJ\,mol^{-1}$. For white phosphorus the enthalpy change is $-2984\,kJ\,mol^{-1}$. For both forms of phosphorus the reaction taking place is:

       $P_4(s) + 5O_2(g) \longrightarrow P_4O_{10}(s)$

       i   Use this information to calculate the enthalpy change for the transformation: $P_4(white) \longrightarrow P_4(red)$ [5]

       ii   Represent these changes on an enthalpy profile diagram.   [3]

                                             Total = 11

5   **a**   Define **standard enthalpy change of formation**.   [3]

     b   Calculate the standard enthalpy change of formation of methane from the following standard enthalpy changes of combustion:

       carbon $= -394\,kJ\,mol^{-1}$

       hydrogen $= -286\,kJ\,mol^{-1}$

       methane $= -891\,kJ\,mol^{-1}$ [4]

     c   Calculate the standard enthalpy change of combustion of methane using the following bond energies:

       $E(C-H) = +412\,kJ\,mol^{-1}$

       $E(O-O) = +496\,kJ\,mol^{-1}$

       $E(C=O) = +805\,kJ\,mol^{-1}$

       $E(O-H) = +463\,kJ\,mol^{-1}$ [4]

                                             Total = 11

6   **a**   Define **average bond enthalpy**.   [2]

     b   Use the average bond enthalpies that follow to calculate a value for the enthalpy change for the reaction:

       $H_2 + I_2 \longrightarrow 2HI$

       $E(H-H) = +436\,kJ\,mol^{-1}$

       $E(I-I) = +151\,kJ\,mol^{-1}$

       $E(H-I) = +299\,kJ\,mol^{-1}$ [3]

     c   Represent these changes on an enthalpy profile diagram.   [3]

                                             Total = 8

7 **a** Define **enthalpy change of solution**. [3]

b Given the enthalpy changes ΔH_1 and ΔH_2 below, construct a Hess's cycle that will enable you to find the enthalpy change, ΔH_r, for the reaction:

$MgCl_2(s) + 6H_2O(l) \longrightarrow MgCl_2.6H_2O(s) \quad \Delta H_r$
$MgCl_2(s) + aq \longrightarrow MgCl_2(aq) \quad \Delta H_1$
$MgCl_2.6H_2O(s) + aq \longrightarrow MgCl_2(aq) \quad \Delta H_2$ [4]

Total = 7

8 **a** Define **standard enthalpy change of reaction**. [3]

b Given the enthalpy changes ΔH_1 and ΔH_2 below, construct a Hess's cycle that will enable you to find the enthalpy change, ΔH_r, for the reaction:

$MgCO_3(s) \longrightarrow MgO(s) + CO_2(g) \quad\quad\quad \Delta H_r$
$MgCO_3(s) + 2HCl(aq) \longrightarrow MgCl_2(aq) + CO_2(g) + H_2O(l) \quad \Delta H_1$
$MgO(s) + 2HCl(aq) \longrightarrow H_2O(l) + MgCl_2(aq) \quad\quad \Delta H_2$ [4]

Total = 7

9 In an experiment, a spirit burner is used to heat $250\,cm^3$ of water by burning methanol (CH_3OH).
(A_r values: C = 12.0, H = 1.0, O = 16.0; specific heat capacity of water = $4.18\,J\,g^{-1}\,°C^{-1}$)

Results:
starting temperature of water = 20.0 °C
starting mass of burner + fuel = 248.8 g
final temperature of water = 43.0 °C
final mass of burner + fuel = 245.9 g

a How many joules of heat energy went into the water? [2]
b How many moles of fuel were burnt? [2]
c Calculate an experimental value for the enthalpy change of combustion of methanol from these results. [2]
d Suggest three reasons why your answer is much smaller than the accepted standard enthalpy of combustion of methanol. [3]

Total = 9

Chapter 7:
Redox reactions

Learning outcomes

You should be able to:

- calculate oxidation numbers of elements in compounds and ions
- describe and explain redox processes in terms of electron transfer and changes in oxidation number
- use changes in oxidation numbers to help balance chemical equations.

Introduction

Some types of reactions can cost a lot of money due to the damage they cause. Rusting is an oxidation reaction that destroys about 20% of iron and steel every year. Rust is hydrated iron(III) oxide. This forms when iron reacts with oxygen in the presence of water. Another costly example of oxidation is the reaction between hydrogen and oxygen that is used to propel some types of rockets into space. In this reaction, the hydrogen is oxidised – but the oxygen is also reduced. In fact, oxidation and reduction always take place together, in what we call redox reactions.

Figure 7.1 A redox reaction is taking place when the fuel in the Space Shuttle's rockets burns.

What is a redox reaction?

A simple definition of **oxidation** is gain of oxygen by an element. For example, when magnesium reacts with oxygen, the magnesium combines with oxygen to form magnesium oxide. Magnesium has been oxidised.

$$2Mg(s) + O_2(g) \longrightarrow 2MgO(s)$$

A simple definition of **reduction** is loss of oxygen. When copper(II) oxide reacts with hydrogen, this is the equation for the reaction:

$$CuO(s) + H_2(g) \longrightarrow Cu(s) + H_2O(l)$$

Copper(II) oxide loses its oxygen. Copper(II) oxide has been reduced.

But if we look carefully at the copper oxide/hydrogen equation, we can see that oxidation is also taking place. The hydrogen is gaining oxygen to form water. The hydrogen has been oxidised. We can see that reduction and oxidation have taken place together.

Oxidation and reduction always take place together. We call the reactions in which this happens **redox reactions**. Redox reactions are very important. For example, one redox reaction – photosynthesis – provides food for the entire planet, and another one – respiration – keeps you alive. Both are redox reactions.

We can also define reduction as addition of hydrogen to a compound and oxidation as removal of hydrogen from a compound. This is often seen in the reaction of organic compounds (see page 237).

There are two other ways of finding out whether or not a substance has been oxidised or reduced during a chemical reaction:

- electron transfer
- changes in oxidation number.

> **QUESTION**
>
> 1 a In each of the following equations, state which reactant has been oxidised:
>
> i $PbO + H_2 \longrightarrow Pb + H_2O$
>
> ii $CO + Ag_2O \longrightarrow 2Ag + CO_2$
>
> iii $2Mg + CO_2 \longrightarrow 2MgO + C$
>
> b In each of the following equations, state which reactant has been reduced:
>
> i $5CO + I_2O_5 \longrightarrow 5CO_2 + I_2$
>
> ii $2H_2S + SO_2 \longrightarrow 3S + 2H_2O$
>
> iii $CH_2{=}CH_2 + H_2 \longrightarrow CH_3CH_3$

Redox and electron transfer

Half-equations

We can extend our definition of redox to include reactions involving ions.

> **O**xidation **I**s **L**oss of electrons.
> **R**eduction **I**s **G**ain of electrons.
> The initial letters shown in bold spell **OIL RIG**. This may help you to remember these two definitions!

Sodium reacts with chlorine to form the ionic compound sodium chloride.

$$2Na(s) + Cl_2(g) \longrightarrow 2NaCl(s)$$

We can divide this reaction into two separate equations, one showing oxidation and the other showing reduction. We call these half-equations.

When sodium reacts with chlorine:

- Each sodium atom loses one electron from its outer shell. Oxidation is loss of electrons (OIL). The sodium atoms have been oxidised.

$$Na \longrightarrow Na^+ + e^-$$

This half-equation shows that sodium is oxidised.

It is also acceptable to write this half-equation as:

$$Na - e^- \longrightarrow Na^+$$

- Each chlorine atom gains one electron to complete its outer shell. Reduction is gain of electrons (RIG). The chlorine atoms have been reduced.

$$Cl_2 + 2e^- \longrightarrow 2Cl^-$$

This is a half-equation showing chlorine being reduced. There are two chlorine atoms in a chlorine molecule, so two electrons are gained.

In another example iron reacts with copper(II) ions, Cu^{2+}, in solution to form iron(II) ions, Fe^{2+}, and copper.

$$Fe(s) + Cu^{2+}(aq) \longrightarrow Fe^{2+}(aq) + Cu(s)$$

- Each iron atom loses two electrons to form an Fe^{2+} ion. The iron atoms have been oxidised.

$$Fe \longrightarrow Fe^{2+} + 2e^-$$

It is also acceptable to write this half-equation as:

$$Fe - 2e^- \longrightarrow Fe^{2+}$$

- Each copper(II) ion gains two electrons. The copper ions have been reduced.

$$Cu^{2+} + 2e^- \longrightarrow Cu$$

Balancing half-equations

We can construct a balanced ionic equation from two half-equations by balancing the numbers of electrons lost and gained and then adding the two half-equations together. The numbers of electrons lost and gained in a redox reaction must be equal.

> **WORKED EXAMPLES**
>
> 1 Construct the balanced ionic equation for the reaction between nickel and iron(III) ions, Fe^{3+}, from the half-equations:
>
> $$Ni(s) \longrightarrow Ni^{2+}(aq) + 2e^-$$
> $$Fe^{3+}(aq) + e^- \longrightarrow Fe^{2+}(aq)$$
>
> - Each Ni atom loses two electrons when it is oxidised. Each Fe^{3+} ion gains one electron when it is reduced.
> - So two Fe^{3+} ions are needed to gain the two electrons lost when each Ni^{2+} ion is formed
>
> $$2Fe^{3+}(aq) + 2e^- \longrightarrow 2Fe^{2+}(aq)$$
> $$Ni(s) \longrightarrow Ni^{2+}(aq) + 2e^-$$
>
> - The balanced ionic equation is:
>
> $$Ni(s) + 2Fe^{3+}(aq) \longrightarrow Ni^{2+}(aq) + 2Fe^{2+}(aq)$$
>
> Note how the electrons have cancelled out.
>
> 2 Construct the balanced ionic equation for the reaction of iodide ions (I^-) with manganate(VII) ions (MnO_4^-) in the presence of hydrogen ions (H^+). Use the following two half-equations to help you:
>
> **i** $\quad 2I^-(aq) \longrightarrow I_2(aq) + 2e^-$
>
> **ii** $\quad MnO_4^-(aq) + 8H^+(aq) + 5e^- \longrightarrow Mn^{2+}(aq) + 4H_2O(l)$
>
> - When two iodide ions are oxidised, they lose two electrons. Each MnO_4^- ion gains five electrons when it is reduced.
> - So we must multiply equation **i** by 5 and equation **ii** by 2 to balance the number of electrons:
>
> $$10I^-(aq) \longrightarrow 5I_2(aq) + 10e^-$$
> $$2MnO_4^-(aq) + 16H^+(aq) + 10e^- \longrightarrow 2Mn^{2+}(aq) + 8H_2O(l)$$
>
> - The balanced ionic equation is:
>
> $$2MnO_4^-(aq) + 10I^-(aq) + 16H^+(aq)$$
> $$\longrightarrow 2Mn^{2+}(aq) + 5I_2(aq) + 8H_2O$$

2 **a** Write two half-equations for the following reactions. For each half-equation state whether oxidation or reduction is occurring.

  i $Cl_2 + 2I^- \longrightarrow I_2 + 2Cl^-$

  ii $2Mg + O_2 \longrightarrow 2MgO$

  iii $4Fe + 3O_2 \longrightarrow 2Fe_2O_3$

  b Zinc metal reacts with IO_3^- ions in acidic solution. Construct a balanced ionic equation for this reaction, using the two half-equations below:

  $2IO_3^- + 12H^+ + 10e^- \longrightarrow I_2 + 6H_2O$

  $Zn \longrightarrow Zn^{2+} + 2e^-$

Oxidation numbers

What are oxidation numbers?

We can extend our definition of redox even further to include oxidation and reduction in reactions involving covalent compounds. We do this by using oxidation numbers (oxidation numbers are also called oxidation states). An oxidation number is a number given to each atom or ion in a compound that shows us its degree of oxidation. Oxidation numbers can be positive, negative or zero. The + or – sign must always be included. Higher positive oxidation numbers mean that an atom or ion is more oxidised. Higher negative oxidation numbers mean that an atom or ion is more reduced.

Oxidation number rules

We can deduce the oxidation number of any atom or ion by using oxidation number rules. It is important to note that an oxidation number refers to a single atom in a compound.

1 The oxidation number of any uncombined element is zero. For example, the oxidation number of each atom in S_8, Cl_2 and Zn is zero.

2 In compounds many atoms or ions have fixed oxidation numbers

  – Group 1 elements are always +1
  – Group 2 elements are always +2
  – fluorine is always –1
  – hydrogen is +1 (except in metal hydrides such as NaH, where it is –1)
  – oxygen is –2 (except in peroxides, where it is –1, and in F_2O, where it is +2).

3 The oxidation number of an element in a monatomic ion is always the same as the charge. For example, Cl^- is –1, Al^{3+} is +3.

4 The sum of the oxidation numbers in a compound is zero.

5 The sum of the oxidation numbers in an ion is equal to the charge on the ion.

6 In either a compound or an ion, the more electronegative element is given the negative oxidation number.

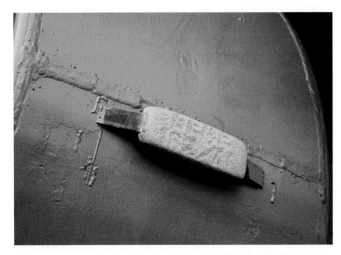

Figure 7.2 This is part of a ship's hull. It is made of iron protected by bars of magnesium metal. The magnesium atoms (oxidation number = 0) are oxidised to Mg^{2+} ions (oxidation number = +2) in preference to iron atoms changing to Fe^{3+}. This is called sacrificial protection.

Applying the oxidation number rules

In the following examples we shall use 'ox. no.' as an abbreviation for oxidation number.

Compounds of a metal with a non-metal

The metal always has the positive ox. no. and the non-metal has the negative ox. no. For example in sodium oxide, Na_2O, Na = +1 and O = –2.

If we do not know the ox. no. of one of the atoms, we can often work it out using the invariable ox. nos. in rule 2. For example in sodium sulfide:

■ ox. no. of each Na atom = +1
■ for two sodium atoms = +2
■ Na_2S has no overall charge, so the total ox. no. is zero (rule 4)
■ ox. no. of S = –2.

Compounds of a non-metal with a non-metal

In compounds containing two different non-metals, the sign of the ox. no. depends on the electronegativity of each atom (see page 157). The most electronegative element is given the negative sign (rule 6).

Sulfur dioxide, SO_2

- ox. no. of each O atom = –2
- for two oxygen atoms = 2 × (–2) = –4
- SO_2 has no charge, so the total ox. no. is zero (rule 4)
- ox. no. of S = +4

Iodine trichloride, ICl_3

- chlorine is more electronegative than iodine, so chlorine is – and iodine is +
- ox. no. of each Cl atom = –1
- for three chlorine atoms = 3 × (–1) = –3
- ICl_3 has no charge, so the total ox. no. is zero (rule 4)
- ox. no. of I = +3

Hydrazine, N_2H_4

- nitrogen is more electronegative than hydrogen, so nitrogen is – and hydrogen is +
- ox. no. of each H atom = +1 (rule 2)
- for four hydrogen atoms = 4 × (+1) = +4
- N_2H_4 has no charge, so the total ox. no. is zero (rule 4)
- ox. no. of two N atoms = –4
- ox. no. of each N atom = –2

Compound ions

Compound ions are ions with two or more different atoms. Examples are the sulfate ion, SO_4^{2-}, and the nitrate ion, NO_3^-. We use rule 5 to work out the ox. no. that we do not know.

Nitrate ion, NO_3^-

- ox. no. of each O atom = –2
- for three oxygen atoms = 3 × (–2) = –6
- NO_3^- has a charge of 1–, so the total ox. no. of N and O atoms is –1 (rule 5)
- ox. no. of the nitrogen atom plus ox. no. of the three oxygen atoms (–6) = –1
- ox. no. of N = +5

> ### QUESTION
>
> 3 State the ox. no. of the bold atoms in these compounds or ions:
>
> a **P**$_2$O$_5$ e **N**H$_3$
> b **S**O$_4^{2-}$ f **Cl**O$_2^-$
> c H$_2$**S**   g Ca**C**O$_3$
> d **Al**$_2$Cl$_6$

Redox and oxidation number

We can define oxidation and reduction in terms of the oxidation number changes of particular atoms during a reaction.

> Oxidation is an increase of oxidation number.
> Reduction is a decrease in oxidation number.

For example, when tin reacts with nitric acid, the oxidation numbers of each atom of tin and nitrogen change as shown below.

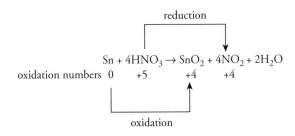

$$Sn + 4HNO_3 \rightarrow SnO_2 + 4NO_2 + 2H_2O$$
oxidation numbers 0   +5   +4   +4

Figure 7.3 Copper reacts with silver nitrate to form silver and copper(II) nitrate. The ox. no. of each copper atom has increased by two. The ox. no. of each silver ion decreases by one.

Each tin atom (Sn) has increased in ox. no. by +4: tin has been oxidised. Each nitrogen atom has decreased in ox. no. by –1: nitrogen has been reduced. The ox. no. of each oxygen atom is unchanged at –2. The ox. no. of each hydrogen atom is unchanged at +1. Oxygen and hydrogen are neither oxidised nor reduced.

In this reaction nitric acid is acting as an **oxidising agent**:

- oxidising agents increase the ox. no. of another atom
- an atom in the oxidising agent decreases in ox. no.
- the oxidising agent is the substance which gets reduced – it gains electrons.

In this reaction tin is acting as a **reducing agent**:

- reducing agents decrease the ox. no. of another atom
- an atom in the reducing agent increases in ox. no.
- the reducing agent is the substance that gets oxidised – it loses electrons.

QUESTION

4 a Deduce the change in ox. no. for the bold atoms or ions in each of the following equations. In each case, state whether oxidation or reduction has taken place.

   i $2I^- + \mathbf{Br_2} \longrightarrow I_2 + 2\mathbf{Br^-}$

   ii $\mathbf{(NH_4)_2Cr_2O_7} \longrightarrow \mathbf{N_2} + 4H_2O + \mathbf{Cr_2O_3}$

   iii $\mathbf{As_2O_3} + 2\mathbf{I_2} + 2H_2O \longrightarrow \mathbf{As_2O_5} + 2H^+ + 4\mathbf{I^-}$

   iv $2K\mathbf{MnO_4} + 16HCl$

                $\longrightarrow 2\mathbf{MnCl_2} + 2KCl + 5\mathbf{Cl_2} + 8H_2O$

b Identify the reducing agent in each of the equations above.

Naming compounds

We sometimes use Roman numbers, in brackets, to name compounds. We use these systematic names to distinguish different compounds made of the same elements. For example, there are two types of iron chloride. We show the difference by naming them iron(II) chloride and iron(III) chloride. The numbers in brackets are the oxidation numbers of the iron.

- In iron(II) chloride, the ox. no. of the iron is +2. The compound contains Fe^{2+} ions. The formula is $FeCl_2$.
- In iron(III) chloride, the ox. no. of the iron is +3. The compound contains Fe^{3+} ions. The formula is $FeCl_3$.

We can also use oxidation numbers to distinguish between non-metal atoms in molecules and ions.

Oxides of nitrogen

There are several oxides of nitrogen, including N_2O, NO and NO_2. We distinguish between these according to the ox. no. of the nitrogen atom. (The ox. no. of oxygen is generally –2.)

- The ox. no. of N in N_2O is +1. So this compound is nitrogen(I) oxide.
- The ox. no. of N in NO is +2. So this compound is nitrogen(II) oxide.
- The ox. no. of N in NO_2 is +4. So this compound is nitrogen(IV) oxide.

Nitrate ions

Sodium, nitrogen and oxygen can form two different compounds $Na^+NO_2^-$ and $Na^+NO_3^-$ (Figure 7.4). The ox. no. of sodium is +1 and the ox. no. of oxygen is –2. So it is the ox. no. of nitrogen that varies.

- The ox. no. of N in the NO_2^- ion is +3. So $NaNO_2$ is sodium nitrate(III).
- The ox. no. of N in the NO_3^- ion is +5. So $NaNO_3$ is sodium nitrate(V).

Note that the ox. no. comes after the ion it refers to.

Ions containing oxygen and one other element have the ending -ate (but hydroxide ions, OH^-, are an exception to this rule). For example, ions containing chlorine and oxygen are chlorates and ions containing sulfur and oxygen are sulfates.

The names of inorganic acids containing oxygen end in –ic. The Roman number goes directly after the ion that contains the oxygen and another element.

- H_3PO_3 is phosphoric(III) acid because the ox. no. of phosphorus is +3.
- $HClO_4$ is chloric(VII) acid because the ox. no. of chlorine is +7.

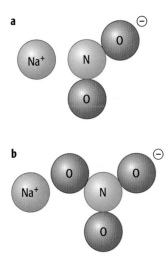

Figure 7.4 a One formula unit of 'sodium nitrate(III)' and **b** one formula unit of 'sodium nitrate(V)'.

Salts of the common acids are usually named without including the ox. no. of the non-metal ion. For example, $Mg(NO_3)_2$ is magnesium nitrate not magnesium nitrate(V) and K_2SO_4 is potassium sulfate not potassium sulfate(VI). Note also that we do not state the ox. no. of the metal if it has only one oxidation state.

QUESTION

5   Give the full systematic names of the following:

   a Na_2SO_3 **e** $FeSO_4$
   b Na_2SO_4 **f** Cu_2O
   c $Fe(NO_3)_2$ **g** H_2SO_3
   d $Fe(NO_3)_3$ **h** Mn_2O_7

From name to formula

You can work out the formula of a compound from its name.

WORKED EXAMPLE

3   Each formula unit of sodium chlorate(V) contains one sodium ion. What is the formula of sodium chlorate(V)?

   We know that:

   ▪ sodium has an ox. no. of +1
   ▪ oxygen has an ox. no. of –2
   ▪ the ox. no. of chlorine is +5
   ▪ the chlorate(V) ion has a charge of 1– (to balance the 1+ charge of the sodium).

   We can work out the formula of the chlorate(V) ion from the oxidation numbers of oxygen and chlorine (let n be the number of oxygen atoms):

   ox. no.(Cl) + ox. no.(O) = –1
   +5 $n \times (-2)$ = –1
                               n = 3

   So the chlorate(V) ion is ClO_3^- and sodium chlorate(V) is $NaClO_3$.

QUESTION

6   Give the formulae of:

   a sodium chlorate(I)
   b iron(III) oxide
   c potassium nitrate(III)
   d phosphorus(III) chloride.

Balancing chemical equations using oxidation numbers

We can use oxidation numbers to balance equations involving redox reactions. This method is especially useful where compound ions such as nitrate(V) or manganate(VII) are involved.

WORKED EXAMPLES

4   Copper(II) oxide (CuO) reacts with ammonia (NH_3) to form copper, nitrogen (N_2) and water.

   Step 1 Write the unbalanced equation and identify the atoms which change in ox. no. (shown here in red).

   $$CuO + NH_3 \longrightarrow Cu + N_2 + H_2O$$
   $$+2\ -2\ \ -3\ +10\ \ \ \ 0\ \ \ \ +1\ -2$$

   Step 2 Deduce the ox. no. changes.

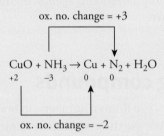

   Step 3 Balance the ox. no. changes.

   ox. no. change = $2 \times (+3) = +6$

   $$3CuO + 2NH_3 \rightarrow 3Cu + N_2 + H_2O$$
   $$3 \times (+2)\ \ 2 \times (-3)\ \ \ \ 0\ \ \ \ 0$$

   ox. no. change = $3 \times (-2) = -6$

   The change in ox. nos. are –2 for the copper and +3 for the nitrogen. To balance the ox. no. changes, we need to multiply the copper by 3 and the nitrogen in the ammonia by 2. The total ox. no. changes are then balanced (–6 and +6). Note that we do not multiply the N_2 by 2 because there are already two atoms of nitrogen present. Once these ratios have been fixed you must not change them.

   Step 4 Balance the atoms.

   There are six hydrogen atoms in the $2NH_3$ on the left. These are balanced with six on the right (as $3H_2O$). This also balances the number of oxygen atoms. The final equation is

   $$3CuO + 2NH_3 \longrightarrow 3Cu + N_2 + 3H_2O$$

WORKED EXAMPLES (CONTINUED)

5 Manganate(VII) ions (MnO_4^-) react with Fe^{2+} ions in the presence of acid (H^+) to form Mn^{2+} ions, Fe^{3+} ions and water.

Step 1 Write the unbalanced equation and identify the atoms that change in ox. no.

$$MnO_4^- + Fe^{2+} + H^+ \longrightarrow Mn^{2+} + Fe^{3+} + H_2O$$
$$\scriptstyle +7\ -2 \qquad +2 \qquad +1 \qquad\qquad +2 \qquad +3 \qquad +1\ -2$$

Step 2 Deduce the ox. no. changes.

ox. no. change = −5

$$MnO_4^- + Fe^{2+} + H^+ \rightarrow Mn^{2+} + Fe^{3+} + H_2O$$
$$\scriptstyle +7 \qquad +2 \qquad\qquad +2 \qquad +3$$

ox. no. change = +1

Step 3 Balance the ox. no. changes.

ox. no. change = $1 \times (-5) = -5$

$$MnO_4^- + 5Fe^{2+} + H^+ \rightarrow Mn^{2+} + 5Fe^{3+} + H_2O$$
$$\scriptstyle +7 \qquad +2 \qquad\qquad +2 \qquad +3$$

ox. no. change = $5 \times (+1) = +5$

Step 4 Balance the charges.

Initially ignore the hydrogen ions, as these will be used to balance the charges.

- The total charge on the other reactants is:
  (1−)(from MnO_4^-) + (5 × 2+)(from $5Fe^{2+}$) = 9+

- The total charge on the products is:
  (2+)(from Mn^{2+}) + (5 × 3+)(from $5Fe^{3+}$) = 17+

- To balance the charges we need 8 H^+ ions on the left.
  $$MnO_4^- + 5Fe^{2+} + 8H^+ \longrightarrow Mn^{2+} + 5Fe^{3+} + H_2O$$

Step 5 Balance the hydrogen atoms in the water.

$$MnO_4^- + 5Fe^{2+} + 8H^+ \longrightarrow Mn^{2+} + 5Fe^{3+} + 4H_2O$$

QUESTION

7 Use the oxidation number method to balance these equations.

a $H_2SO_4 + HI \longrightarrow S + I_2 + H_2O$

b $HBr + H_2SO_4 \longrightarrow Br_2 + SO_2 + H_2O$

c $V^{3+} + I_2 + H_2O \longrightarrow VO^{2+} + I^- + H^+$

Summary

- Redox reactions can be explained in terms of:
  - increase in oxidation number (oxidation state), which is oxidation
  - decrease in oxidation number, which is reduction.
- Oxidation numbers can be used to balance equations.
- Redox reactions can be explained in terms of electron loss (oxidation) or electron gain (reduction).

End-of-chapter questions

1 In the industrial production of nitric acid the following changes take place to the nitrogen.

$$N_2 \xrightarrow{\text{stage 1}} NH_3 \xrightarrow{\text{stage 2}} NO \xrightarrow{\text{stage 3}} NO_2 \xrightarrow{\text{stage 4}} HNO_3$$

a Give the oxidation number of the nitrogen atom in each molecule. [5]

b For each stage, state whether oxidation or reduction has taken place. In each case explain your answer. [2]

c Give the full systematic name for NO_2. [1]

d Nitric acid, HNO_3, reacts with red phosphorus.

$$P + 5HNO_3 \longrightarrow H_3PO_4 + 5NO_2 + H_2O$$

By referring to oxidation number changes, explain why this is a redox reaction. [5]

e Explain why nitric acid can be described as an oxidising agent in this reaction. [1]

Total = 14

2 Calcium reacts with cold water to form calcium hydroxide, $Ca(OH)_2$, and hydrogen, H_2.

a State the oxidation number of calcium in:

  i calcium metal [1]

  ii calcium hydroxide. [1]

b State the oxidation number of hydrogen in:

  i water [1]

  ii hydrogen gas. [1]

c Write two half-equations for the reaction between water and calcium hydroxide to show:

  i the change from calcium to calcium ions [1]

  ii the change from water to hydroxide ions and hydrogen. [1]

d In which one of the half-equations in part c is a reduction occurring? Give a reason for your answer. [1]

e Write a balanced equation for the reaction of calcium with water. [1]

f Explain the role played by water in this reaction. [1]

Total = 9

3 The unbalanced equation for the reaction of sulfur dioxide with bromine is shown below.

$$SO_2 + Br_2 + H_2O \longrightarrow SO_4^{2-} + Br^- + H^+$$

a State the oxidation number of sulfur in:

  i SO_2 [1]

  ii SO_4^{2-} [1]

b State the oxidation number of bromine in:

  i Br_2 [1]

  ii Br^- [1]

c Identify the reducing agent in this reaction. Give a reason for your answer. [1]

d State the change in oxidation number for:

  i each S atom [1]

  ii each bromine atom. [1]

e Construct a balanced equation for this reaction. [2]

Total = 9

4 Aluminium reacts with hydrochloric acid to form aluminium chloride, $AlCl_3$, and hydrogen. This is a redox reaction.

    a Explain in term of electrons, what is meant by a **redox reaction**.   [3]

    b **i** Write a half-equation to show aluminium changing to aluminium ions.   [1]

       ii Write a second half-equation to show what happens to the hydrogen ions from the acid.   [1]

       iii What is the change in oxidation number when a hydrogen ion turns into a hydrogen atom?   [1]

    c Construct a balanced ionic equation for the reaction between aluminium atoms and hydrogen ions.   [1]

                                                                              Total = 7

5 Iodine, I_2, reacts with thiosulfate ions, $S_2O_3^{2-}$ to form iodide ions, I^-, and tetrathionate ions, $S_4O_6^{2-}$.

$$I_2 + 2S_2O_3^{2-} \longrightarrow 2I^- + S_4O_6^{2-}$$

    a State the oxidation number of each sulfur atom in:

       i a $S_2O_3^{2-}$ ion   [1]

       ii a $S_4O_6^{2-}$ ion.   [1]

    b Explain in terms of electron transfer why the conversion of iodine to iodide ions is a reduction reaction.   [1]

    c When a salt containing iodide ions is warmed with concentrated sulfuric acid and MnO_2, iodine is evolved.

$$2I^- + MnO_2 + 6H^+ + 2SO_4^{2-} \longrightarrow I_2 + Mn^{2+} + 2HSO_4^- + 2H_2O$$

       i State the systematic name for MnO_2.   [1]

       ii What is the oxidation number of S in the SO_4^{2-} ion?   [1]

       iii Which reactant gets oxidised in this reaction? Explain your answer by using oxidation numbers.   [1]

       iv Which substance is the oxidising agent? Explain your answer.   [1]

                                                                              Total = 7

115

6 The compound $KBrO_3$ decomposes when heated.

$$2KBrO_3 \longrightarrow 2KBr + 3O_2$$

    a State the oxidation numbers of bromine in:

       i $KBrO_3$ [1]

       ii KBr.   [1]

    b Explain using oxidation numbers why this reaction is a redox reaction.   [3]

    c State the systematic name of $KBrO_3$.   [1]

    d When $KBrO_3$ reacts with hydrazine, N_2H_4, nitrogen gas is evolved.

$$2KBrO_3 + 3N_2H_4 \longrightarrow 2KBr + 3N_2 + 6H_2O$$

       i What is the oxidation number change of the bromine atom when $KBrO_3$ is converted to KBr?   [1]

       ii What is the oxidation number change for each nitrogen atom when N_2H_4 is converted to N_2?   [2]

       iii Use your answers to **i** and **ii** to explain why 2 moles of $KBrO_3$ react with 3 moles of N_2H_4.   [3]

                                                                              Total = 12

Chapter 8:
Equilibrium

Learning outcomes

You should be able to:

- explain what is meant by a **reversible reaction** and **dynamic equilibrium**
- state Le Chatelier's principle and apply it to deduce qualitatively the effect of changes in temperature, concentration or pressure on a system at equilibrium
- state whether changes in temperature, concentration or pressure or the presence of a catalyst affect the value of the equilibrium constant for a reaction
- deduce expressions for equilibrium constants in terms of concentrations, K_c, and partial pressure, K_p

- calculate:
  - the value of equilibrium constants in terms of concentrations or partial pressures
  - the quantities of substances present at equilibrium
- describe and explain the conditions used in the Haber process and the Contact process
- show understanding of, and use, the Brønsted–Lowry theory of acids and bases
- explain qualitatively the differences in behaviour between strong and weak acids and bases and the pH values of their aqueous solutions in terms of the extent of dissociation.

Introduction

Many chemical reactions go to completion. For example, when magnesium reacts with excess hydrochloric acid, the reaction stops when all the magnesium has been used up. The products cannot be converted back to the reactants. This reaction is irreversible.

However, some reactions can be reversed. There is the forward reaction, where reactants are converted into products, and the reverse reaction, where the products are converted back into the reactants. When the rates of the forward and reverse reactions balance, we say the reversible reaction is in equilibrium. It may help to think of other situations in which forces or processes are in equilibrium (Figure 8.1).

Figure 8.1 Both the moving belt and runner are moving. When the movement of the belt balances the movement of the runner, they are in equilibrium.

Reversible reactions and equilibrium

Reversible reactions

Some reactions can be reversed. For example, when blue, hydrated copper(II) sulfate is heated, it loses its water of crystallisation and changes to white, anhydrous copper(II) sulfate.

$$CuSO_4.5H_2O(s) \longrightarrow CuSO_4(s) + 5H_2O(l)$$

hydrated copper(II)   anhydrous
sulfate   copper(II) sulfate

This is called the forward reaction.

When water is added to anhydrous copper(II) sulfate, the reaction is reversed.

$$CuSO_4(s) + 5H_2O(l) \longrightarrow CuSO_4.5H_2O(s)$$

This is called the backward (or reverse) reaction.

We can show these two reactions in the same equation by using two arrows.

$$CuSO_4.5H_2O(s) \rightleftharpoons CuSO_4(s) + 5H_2O(l)$$

Figure 8.2 Hydrated copper(II) sulfate (left) and anhydrous copper(II) sulfate (right).

A reaction in which the products can react to re-form the original reactants is called a **reversible reaction**. In this case heating and adding water are not being carried out at the same time. However, there is a type of chemical reaction in which the forward reaction and the backward reaction take place at the same time.

In many chemical reactions the reactants are not used up completely. Some products are formed but the maximum theoretical yield is not obtained. A mixture of products and reactants is formed. The products react together to re-form reactants at the same time as the reactants are forming products. This type of reversible reaction is called an **equilibrium** reaction. We show that equilibrium reactions are reversible by the sign $\rightleftharpoons$.

For example, consider the reaction between hydrogen and iodine carried out in a sealed glass tube at 400 °C:

$$H_2(g) + I_2(g) \rightleftharpoons 2HI(g)$$

Molecules of hydrogen iodide are breaking down to hydrogen and iodine at the same rate as hydrogen and iodine molecules are reacting together to form hydrogen iodide.

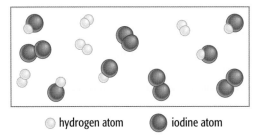

◯ hydrogen atom   ⬤ iodine atom

Figure 8.3 A snapshot of the dynamic equilibrium between hydrogen gas, iodine gas and hydrogen iodide gas.

When fizzy drinks are made, carbon dioxide gas is dissolved in the drink under pressure. When you take the lid off a bottle of fizzy drink, bubbles of carbon dioxide suddenly appear. When you put the lid back on, the bubbles stop. This is because of the equilibrium

$$CO_2(g) \rightleftharpoons CO_2(aq)$$

The forward reaction happens during manufacture and the backward reaction happens on opening.

Characteristics of equilibrium

An equilibrium reaction has four particular features under constant conditions:

- it is dynamic
- the forward and reverse reactions occur at the same rate
- the concentrations of reactants and products remain constant at equilibrium
- it requires a closed system.

1 It is dynamic

The phrase **dynamic equilibrium** means that the molecules or ions of reactants and products are continuously reacting. Reactants are continuously being changed to products and products are continuously being changed back to reactants.

2 The forward and backward reactions occur at the same rate

At equilibrium the rate of the forward reaction equals the rate of the backward reaction. Molecules or ions of reactants are becoming products, and those in the products are becoming reactants, at the same rate.

3 The concentrations of reactants and products remain constant at equilibrium

The concentrations remain constant because, at equilibrium, the rates of the forward and backward reactions are equal. The equilibrium can be approached from two directions. For example, in the reaction

$$H_2(g) + I_2(g) \rightleftharpoons 2HI(g)$$

We can start by either:

- using a mixture of colourless hydrogen gas and purple iodine vapour, or
- using only colourless hydrogen iodide gas.

Figure 8.4 shows what happens when 5.00 mol of hydrogen molecules and 5.00 mol of iodine molecules react at 500 K in a vessel of volume 1 dm³. As time passes, the purple colour of the iodine vapour fades until equilibrium is reached. At equilibrium the mixture contains 0.68 mol of iodine, 0.68 mol of hydrogen and 8.64 mol of hydrogen iodide.

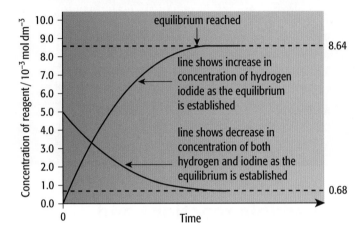

Figure 8.4 The changes in the concentrations of reagents as 5.00 mol of each of hydrogen and iodine react to form an equilibrium mixture with hydrogen iodide in a vessel of volume 1 dm³.

Figure 8.5 shows that the same equilibrium can be achieved when 10.00 mol of hydrogen iodide molecules decompose to iodine and hydrogen iodide. You can see that the same equilibrium concentrations of all three molecules are achieved.

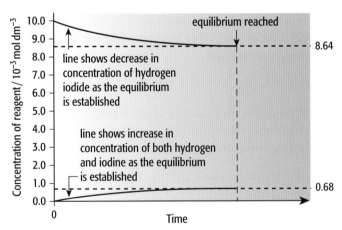

Figure 8.5 The changes in the concentrations of reagents as 10.00 mol of hydrogen iodide react to form an equilibrium mixture with hydrogen and iodine gases in a vessel of 1 m³.

1   These questions relate to the information in Figure 8.5.

   a   Why are the concentrations of iodine and hydrogen at equilibrium the same?

   b   Describe how the depth of colour of the reaction mixture changes as time progresses.

   c   Explain why there must be 8.64 mol of hydrogen iodide molecules in the equilibrium mixture if 0.68 mol of iodine are present.

4 Equilibrium requires a closed system

A closed system is one in which none of the reactants or products escapes from the reaction mixture. In an open system some matter is lost to the surroundings. Figure 8.6 shows the difference between a closed system and an open system when calcium carbonate is heated at a high temperature in a strong container.

   Many chemical reactions can be studied without placing them in closed containers. They can reach equilibrium in open flasks if the reaction takes place entirely in solution and no gas is lost.

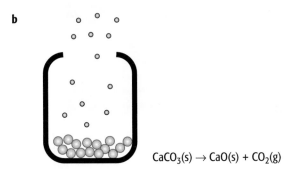

a

$CaCO_3(s) \rightleftharpoons CaO(s) + CO_2(g)$
   ○ $CaCO_3(s)$ ○ $CaO(s)$ ∘ $CO_2(g)$

b

$CaCO_3(s) \rightarrow CaO(s) + CO_2(g)$

Figure 8.6 a A closed system. No carbon dioxide escapes. The calcium carbonate is in equilibrium with calcium oxide and carbon dioxide. **b** An open system. The calcium carbonate is continually decomposing as the carbon dioxide is lost. The reaction eventually goes to completion.

2   A beaker contains saturated aqueous sodium chloride solution in contact with undissolved solid sodium chloride. Sodium ions and chloride ions are constantly moving from solid to solution and from solution to solid.

   a   i   Explain why this is a closed system.

      ii   Explain why the concentration of the saturated sodium chloride solution does not change, even though ions are still moving into the solution from the solid.

   b   Bromine is a reddish-brown liquid that vaporises at room temperature. Some liquid bromine is put in a closed jar. The colour of the bromine vapour above the liquid gets darker and darker until the depth of colour remains constant. Bromine liquid still remains in the jar. Explain what is happening in terms of changes in concentration of the bromine molecules in the vapour.

Changing the position of equilibrium

Position of equilibrium

The position of equilibrium refers to the relative amounts of products and reactants present in an equilibrium mixture.

■   If a system in equilibrium is disturbed (e.g. by a change in temperature) and the concentration of products is increased relative to the reactants, we say that the position of equilibrium has shifted to the right.

■   If the concentration of products is decreased relative to the reactants, we say that the position of equilibrium has shifted to the left.

Le Chatelier's principle

Changes in both concentration and temperature affect the position of equilibrium. When any of the reactants or products are gases, changes in pressure may also affect the position of equilibrium. French chemist Henri Le Chatelier (1850–1936) observed how these factors affect the position of equilibrium. He put forward a general rule, known as Le Chatelier's principle:

If one or more factors that affect an equilibrium is changed, the position of equilibrium shifts in the direction that reduces (opposes) the change.

We can predict the effect of changing concentration and pressure by referring to the stoichiometric equation for the reaction. We can predict the effect of changing the temperature by referring to the enthalpy change of the reaction.

How does change in concentration affect the position of equilibrium?

When the concentration of one or more of the reactants is increased:

- the system is no longer in equilibrium
- the position of equilibrium moves to the right to reduce the effect of the increase in concentration of reactant
- more products are formed until equilibrium is restored.

When the concentration of one or more of the products is increased:

- the system is no longer in equilibrium
- the position of equilibrium moves to the left to reduce the effect of the increase in concentration of product
- more reactants are formed until equilibrium is restored.

For example, look at the reaction:

$$CH_3COOH(l) + C_2H_5OH(l) \rightleftharpoons CH_3COOC_2H_5(l) + H_2O(l)$$

ethanoic acid   ethanol   ethyl ethanoate   water

What happens when we add more ethanol?

- The concentration of ethanol is increased.
- According to Le Chatelier's principle, some of the ethanol must be removed to reduce the concentration of the added ethanol.
- The position of equilibrium shifts to the right.
- More ethanol reacts with ethanoic acid and more ethyl ethanoate and water are formed.

What happens when we add more water?

- The concentration of water is increased.
- According to Le Chatelier's principle, some of the water must be removed to reduce the concentration of the added water.
- The position of equilibrium shifts to the left.
- So more water reacts with ethyl ethanoate and more ethanoic acid and ethanol are formed.

What happens when we remove some water?

- The concentration of water is decreased.
- According to Le Chatelier's principle, some water must be added to increase its concentration.
- The position of equilibrium shifts to the right.
- So more ethanoic acid reacts with ethanol and more water and ethyl ethanoate are formed.

QUESTION

3 a Use this reaction:

$$CH_3COOH(l) + C_2H_5OH(l) \rightleftharpoons CH_3COOC_2H_5(l) + H_2O(l)$$

Explain what happens to the position of equilibrium when:

  i   more $CH_3COOC_2H_5(l)$ is added

  ii   some $C_2H_5OH(l)$ is removed.

b Use this reaction:

$$Ce^{4+}(aq) + Fe^{2+}(aq) \rightleftharpoons Ce^{3+}(aq) + Fe^{3+}(aq)$$

Explain what happens to the position of equilibrium when:

  i   the concentration of $Fe^{2+}(aq)$ ions is increased

  ii   water is added to the equilibrium mixture.

Figure 8.7 Stalactites and stalagmites are formed as a result of water passing through rocks containing calcium carbonate. The solution running through these rocks contains water, dissolved carbon dioxide and calcium hydrogencarbonate:

$$CaCO_3(s) + H_2O(l) + CO_2(aq) \rightleftharpoons Ca(HCO_3)_2(aq)$$

When droplets of this mixture are formed on the roof of the cave, some of the carbon dioxide in the droplets escapes into the air. The position of equilibrium shifts to the left and calcium carbonate is deposited.

The effect of pressure on the position of equilibrium

Change in pressure only affects reactions where gases are reactants or products. The molecules or ions in solids and liquids are packed closely together and cannot be compressed very easily. In gases, the molecules are far apart (Figure 8.8).

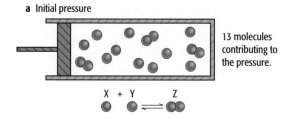

a Initial pressure

13 molecules contributing to the pressure.

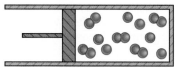

b Pressure is increased

More molecules of Z are formed, reducing the total number of molecules from 13 to 11.

Figure 8.9 An increase in pressure in this case causes the equilibrium to shift to the right, to produce more molecules of Z than before, but fewer molecules in the reaction vessel overall.

For example, consider the reaction:

$$2SO_2(g) + O_2(g) \rightleftharpoons 2SO_3(g)$$

There are three moles of gas molecules on the left of the equation and two on the right.
What happens when we increase the pressure?

- The molecules are closer together, because the pressure is higher.
- According to Le Chatelier's principle, the reaction must shift in the direction that reduces the number of molecules of gas.
- The position of equilibrium shifts to the right.
- So more SO_2 reacts with O_2 to form SO_3.

What happens when we decrease the pressure?

- The molecules are further apart, because the pressure is lower.
- According to Le Chatelier's principle, the reaction must shift in the direction that increases the number of molecules of gas.
- The position of equilibrium shifts to the left.
- So more SO_2 and O_2 molecules are formed by the decomposition of SO_3 molecules.

Table 8.1 summarises the effect of changes in pressure on two other gas reactions.
Note that:

- if there are equal numbers of molecules of gas on each side of the equation, the position of equilibrium is not affected by a change in pressure
- in a reaction involving gases and solids (or liquids), it is only the molecules of gases that count when determining how pressure affects the position of equilibrium.

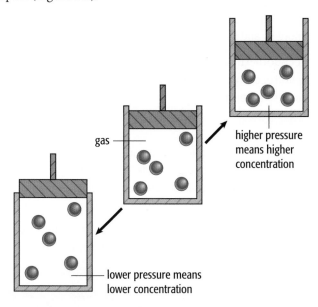

gas

higher pressure means higher concentration

lower pressure means lower concentration

Figure 8.8 Pressure has a considerable effect on the concentration of gases.

The pressure of a gas is caused by the molecules hitting the walls of the container. Each molecule in a mixture of gases contributes towards the total pressure. So, at constant temperature, the more gas molecules there are in a given volume, the higher the pressure.

Figure 8.9 shows what happens when we increase the pressure on the reaction represented by:

$$X(g) + Y(g) \rightleftharpoons Z(g)$$

1 mol   1 mol   1 mol

In this reaction there are two moles of gas on the left and one on the right. When the pressure is increased at constant temperature:

- the molecules are closer together, because the pressure has increased
- the position of equilibrium shifts to minimise this increase
- it shifts in the direction of fewer gas molecules (in the direction that opposes the increase in pressure)
- more product, Z, is formed from X and Y until equilibrium is re-established.

121

Change in pressure	Fewer molecules of gas on right $N_2(g) + 3H_2(g) \rightleftharpoons 2NH_3(g)$	More molecules of gas on right $N_2O_4(g) \rightleftharpoons 2NO_2$
pressure increase	equilibrium position shifts towards products: more NH_3 forms	equilibrium position shifts towards reactants: more N_2O_4 forms
pressure decrease	equilibrium position shifts towards reactants: more N_2 and H_2 form	equilibrium position shifts towards products: more NO_2 forms

Table 8.1 The effect of changes in pressure on gas reactions.

QUESTION

4   a   Predict the effect of increasing the pressure on the following reactions:

   i $N_2O_4(g) \rightleftharpoons 2NO_2(g)$

   ii $CaCO_3(s) \rightleftharpoons CaO(s) + CO_2(g)$

   b   Predict the effect of decreasing the pressure on the reaction:

   $2NO_2(g) \rightleftharpoons 2NO(g) + O_2(g)$

The effect of temperature on the position of equilibrium

The decomposition of hydrogen iodide is an endothermic reaction.

$$2HI \rightleftharpoons H_2 + I_2 \qquad \Delta H_r = +9.6\,kJ\,mol^{-1}$$

The effect of temperature on the equilibrium concentration of hydrogen iodide and hydrogen at equilibrium for the forward reaction is shown in Table 8.2.

Temperature / °C	Equilibrium concentration of HI / mol dm^{-3}	Equilibrium concentration of H$_2$ (or I$_2$) / mol dm^{-3}
25	0.934	0.033
230	0.864	0.068
430	0.786	0.107
490	0.773	0.114

Table 8.2 Effect of temperature on the decomposition of hydrogen iodide.

You can see from Table 8.2 that, as the temperature increases, the concentration of product increases. The

position of equilibrium shifts to the right. We can explain this using Le Chatelier's principle:

■ an increase in temperature increases the energy of the surroundings

■ according to Le Chatelier's principle, the reaction will go in the direction that opposes the increase in energy

■ so the reaction will go in the direction in which energy is absorbed, which is the endothermic reaction

■ the position of equilibrium shifts to the right, producing more H_2 and I_2.

If an endothermic reaction is favoured by an increase in temperature, an exothermic reaction must be favoured by a decrease in temperature:

■ a decrease in temperature decreases the energy of the surroundings

■ according to Le Chatelier's principle, the reaction will go in the direction that opposes the decrease in energy

■ so the reaction will go in the direction in which energy is released, which is the exothermic reaction.

Table 8.3 summarises the effect of temperature changes on the position of equilibrium for endothermic and exothermic reactions.

Temperature change	Endothermic reaction $2HI \rightleftharpoons H_2 + I_2$	Exothermic reaction $2SO_2(g) + O_2(g) \rightleftharpoons 2SO_3(g)$
Temperature increase	position of equilibrium shifts towards products: more H_2 and I_2 formed	position of equilibrium shifts towards reactants: more SO_2 and O_2 formed
Temperature decrease	position of equilibrium shifts towards reactant: more HI formed	position of equilibrium shifts towards product: more SO_3 formed

Table 8.3 Effect of temperature on endothermic and exothermic reactions.

QUESTION

5   a   Predict the effect of increasing the temperature on the reaction:

   $H_2(g) + CO_2(g) \rightleftharpoons H_2O(g) + CO(g)$

   $\Delta H_r = +41.2\,kJ\,mol^{-1}$

   b   In the reaction

   $Ag_2CO_3(s) \rightleftharpoons Ag_2O(s) + CO_2(g)$

   increasing the temperature increases the amount of carbon dioxide formed at constant pressure. Is this reaction exothermic or endothermic? Explain your answer.

Do catalysts have any effect on the position of equilibrium?

A catalyst is a substance that increases the rate of a chemical reaction. Catalysts speed up the time taken to reach equilibrium, but they have no effect on the position of equilibrium once this is reached. This is because they increase the rate of the forward and reverse reactions equally.

Equilibrium expressions and the equilibrium constant, K_c

Equilibrium expressions

When hydrogen reacts with iodine in a closed tube at 500 K, the following equilibrium is set up:

$$H_2 + I_2 \rightleftharpoons 2HI$$

Table 8.4 shows the relationship between the equilibrium concentrations of H_2, I_2 and HI. The square brackets in the last column refer to the concentration, in $mol\,dm^{-3}$, of the substance inside the brackets. The results are obtained as follows:

- several tubes are set up with different starting concentrations of hydrogen and iodine
- the contents of the tubes are allowed to reach equilibrium at 500 K
- the concentrations of hydrogen, iodine and hydrogen iodide at equilibrium are determined.

The last column in Table 8.4 shows the number we get by arranging the concentrations of H_2, I_2 and HI in a particular way. We get this expression by taking the square of the concentration of hydrogen iodide and dividing it by the concentrations of hydrogen and iodine at equilibrium. So for the first line of data in Table 8.4:

$$\frac{[HI]^2}{[H_2]\,[I_2]} = \frac{(8.64 \times 10^{-3})^2}{(0.68 \times 10^{-3})(0.68 \times 10^{-3})}$$
$$= 161$$

You can see that this expression gives an approximately constant value close to about 160 whatever the starting concentrations of H_2, I_2 and HI.

We call this constant the equilibrium constant, K_c. The subscript 'c' refers to the fact that concentrations have been used in the calculations.

There is a simple relationship that links K_c to the equilibrium concentrations of reactants and products and the stoichiometry of the equation. This is called an equilibrium expression.

For a general reaction:

$$mA + nB \rightleftharpoons pC + qD$$

(where m, n, p and q are the number of moles in the equation)

concentration of product D

$$K_c = \frac{[C]^p\,[D]^q}{[A]^m\,[B]^n} \begin{array}{l} \leftarrow \text{number of moles of product D} \\ \leftarrow \text{number of moles of reactant B} \end{array}$$

concentration of reactant B

> **WORKED EXAMPLES**
>
> 1 Write an expression for K_c:
> $$N_2(g) + 3H_2(g) \rightleftharpoons 2NH_3(g)$$
> $$K_c = \frac{[NH_3]^2}{[N_2]\,[H_2]^3}$$
>
> 2 Write an expression for K_c:
> $$2SO_2(g) + O_2(g) \rightleftharpoons 2SO_3(g)$$
> $$K_c = \frac{[SO_3]^2}{[SO_2]^2\,[O_2]}$$

123

Concentration of H_2 at equilibrium / $mol\,dm^{-3}$	Concentration of I_2 at equilibrium / $mol\,dm^{-3}$	Concentration of HI at equilibrium / $mol\,dm^{-3}$	$\dfrac{[HI]^2}{[H_2]\,[I_2]}$
0.68×10^{-3}	0.68×10^{-3}	8.64×10^{-3}	161
0.50×10^{-3}	0.50×10^{-3}	6.30×10^{-3}	159
1.10×10^{-3}	2.00×10^{-3}	18.8×10^{-3}	161
2.50×10^{-3}	0.65×10^{-3}	16.1×10^{-3}	160

Table 8.4 The relationship between the equilibrium concentrations of H_2, I_2 and HI in the reaction $H_2 + I_2 \rightleftharpoons 2HI$.

In equilibrium expressions involving a solid, we ignore the solid. This is because its concentration remains constant, however much solid is present. For example:

$$Ag^+(aq) + Fe^{2+}(aq) \rightleftharpoons Ag(s) + Fe^{3+}(aq)$$

The equilibrium expression for this reaction is:

$$K_c = \frac{[Fe^{3+}(aq)]}{[Ag^+(aq)][Fe^{2+}(aq)]}$$

What are the units of K_c?

In the equilibrium expression each figure within a square bracket represents the concentration in $mol\,dm^{-3}$. The units of K_c therefore depend on the form of the equilibrium expression.

WORKED EXAMPLES

3 State the units of K_c for the reaction:

$$H_2 + I_2 \rightleftharpoons 2HI$$

$$K_c = \frac{[HI]^2}{[H_2][I_2]}$$

Units of $K_c = \dfrac{(mol\,dm^{-3}) \times (mol\,dm^{-3})}{(mol\,dm^{-3}) \times (mol\,dm^{-3})}$

The units of $mol\,dm^{-3}$ cancel, so K_c has no units.

4 State the units of K_c for the reaction:

$$2SO_2(g) + O_2(g) \rightleftharpoons 2SO_3(g)$$

Units of $K_c = \dfrac{(mol\,dm^{-3}) \times (mol\,dm^{-3})}{(mol\,dm^{-3}) \times (mol\,dm^{-3}) \times (mol\,dm^{-3})}$

$$= \frac{1}{(mol\,dm^{-3})} = dm^3\,mol^{-1}$$

QUESTION

6 Write equilibrium expressions for the following reactions and state the units of K_c.
  a $CO(g) + 2H_2(g) \rightleftharpoons CH_3OH(g)$
  b $4HCl(g) + O_2(g) \rightleftharpoons 2H_2O(g) + 2Cl_2(g)$

Some examples of equilibrium calculations

WORKED EXAMPLES

5 In this calculation we are given the number of moles of each of the reactants and products at equilibrium together with the volume of the reaction mixture.

Ethanol reacts with ethanoic acid to form ethyl ethanoate and water.

$$CH_3COOH(l) + C_2H_5OH(l) \rightleftharpoons CH_3COOC_2H_5(l) + H_2O(l)$$
ethanoic acid　　ethanol　　ethyl ethanoate　　water

$500\,cm^3$ of the reaction mixture at equilibrium contained 0.235 mol of ethanoic acid and 0.0350 mol of ethanol together with 0.182 mol of ethyl ethanoate and 0.182 mol of water. Use this data to calculate a value of K_c for this reaction.

Step 1 Write out the balanced chemical equation with the concentrations beneath each substance.

$$CH_3COOH(l) + C_2H_5OH(l)$$
$\frac{0.235 \times 1000}{500}$　　$\frac{0.035 \times 1000}{500}$

$0.470\,mol\,dm^{-3}$　　$0.070\,mol\,dm^{-3}$

$$\rightleftharpoons CH_3COOC_2H_5(l) + H_2O(l)$$
$\frac{0.182 \times 1000}{500}$　　$\frac{0.182 \times 1000}{500}$

$0.364\,mol\,dm^{-3}$　　$0.364\,mol\,dm^{-3}$

Step 2 Write the equilibrium constant for this reaction in terms of concentrations.

$$K_c = \frac{[CH_3COOC_2H_5][H_2O]}{[CH_3COOH][C_2H_5OH]}$$

Step 3 Substitute the equilibrium concentrations into the expression

$$K_c = \frac{(0.364) \times (0.364)}{(0.470) \times (0.070)} = 4.03$$

(to 3 significant figures)

Step 4 Add the correct units by referring back to the equilibrium expression:

$$\frac{(mol\,dm^{-3}) \times (mol\,dm^{-3})}{(mol\,dm^{-3}) \times (mol\,dm^{-3})}$$

The units of $mol\,dm^{-3}$ cancel, so K_c has no units. Therefore $K_c = 4.03$.

Note: if there are equal numbers of moles on the top and bottom of the equilibrium expression, you can use moles rather than concentration in $mol\,dm^{-3}$ in the calculation. In all other cases, if volumes are given, the concentrations must be calculated before they are substituted into the equilibrium expression.

WORKED EXAMPLES (CONTINUED)

6 In this example we are only given the initial concentrations of the reactants and the equilibrium concentration of the product.

Propanone reacts with hydrogen cyanide as follows:

$$CH_3COCH_3 + HCN \rightleftharpoons CH_3C(OH)(CN)CH_3$$

propanone   hydrogen cyanide   product

A mixture of $0.0500\,mol\,dm^{-3}$ propanone and $0.0500\,mol\,dm^{-3}$ hydrogen cyanide is left to reach equilibrium at room temperature. At equilibrium the concentration of the product is $0.0233\,mol\,dm^{-3}$. Calculate K_c for this reaction.

Step 1 Write out the balanced chemical equation with all the data underneath:

$$CH_3COCH_3 + HCN \rightleftharpoons CH_3C(OH)(CN)CH_3$$

initial conc.	0.0500 $mol\,dm^{-3}$	0.0500 $mol\,dm^{-3}$	0
Conc. at equilibrium	to be calculated	to be calculated	0.0233 $mol\,dm^{-3}$

Step 2 Calculate the equilibrium concentrations of the reactants.

The chemical equation shows that for every mole of product formed, 1 mole of CH_3COCH_3 and 1 mole of HCN are consumed. So the equilibrium concentrations are as follows:

CH_3COCH_3; $0.0500 - 0.0233 = 0.0267\,mol\,dm^{-3}$

HCN; $0.0500 - 0.0233 = 0.0267\,mol\,dm^{-3}$

Step 3 Write the equilibrium constant for this reaction in terms of concentrations:

$$K_c = \frac{[CH_3C(OH)(CN)CH_3]}{[CH_3COCH_3]\,[HCN]}$$

Step 4 Substitute the equilibrium concentrations into the expression

$$K_c = \frac{(0.0233)}{(0.0267) \times (0.0267)} = 32.7$$

(to 3 significant figures)

Step 5 Add the correct units by referring back to the equilibrium expression.

$$\frac{(\cancel{mol\,dm^{-3}})}{(\cancel{mol\,dm^{-3}})(mol\,dm^{-3})} = \frac{1}{mol\,dm^{-3}} = dm^3\,mol^{-1}$$

So $K_c = 32.7\,dm^3\,mol^{-1}$

WORKED EXAMPLES (CONTINUED)

7 In this example we are given the initial and equilibrium concentrations of the reactants but not the products.

Ethyl ethanoate is hydrolysed by water:

$$CH_3COOC_2H_5 + H_2O \rightleftharpoons CH_3COOH + C_2H_5OH$$

ethyl ethanoate   water   ethanoic acid   ethanol

$0.1000\,mol$ of ethyl ethanoate are added to $0.1000\,mol$ of water. A little acid catalyst is added and the mixture made up to $1\,dm^3$ with an inert solvent. At equilibrium $0.0654\,mol$ of water are present. Calculate K_c for this reaction.

Step 1 Write out the balanced chemical equation with all the data underneath.

$$CH_3COOC_2H_5 + H_2O \rightleftharpoons$$
$$CH_3COOH + C_2H_5OH$$

initial conc.	0.1000 $mol\,dm^{-3}$	0.1000 $mol\,dm^{-3}$	0	0
conc. at equilibrium		0.0654 $mol\,dm^{-3}$		

Step 2 Calculate the unknown concentrations:

– the chemical equation shows that 1 mole of $CH_3COOC_2H_5$ reacts with 1 mole water, so the equilibrium concentration of $CH_3COOC_2H_5$ is also $0.0654\,mol\,dm^{-3}$ (as we started with the same initial concentrations of ethyl ethanoate and water)

– the amount of water used in forming the products is $(0.1000 - 0.0654) = 0.0346\,mol\,dm^{-3}$.

The chemical equation shows that 1 mole of water formed 1 mole of ethanoic acid and 1 mole of ethanol. So the concentrations of both the products at equilibrium is $0.0346\,mol\,dm^{-3}$

$$CH_3COOC_2H_5 + H_2O \rightleftharpoons$$
$$CH_3COOH + C_2H_5OH$$

conc. at equilibrium $mol\,dm^{-3}$	0.0654	0.0654	0.0346	0.0346

Step 3 Write the equilibrium constant for this reaction in terms of concentrations:

$$K_c = \frac{[CH_3COOH]\,[C_2H_5OH]}{[CH_3COOC_2H_5]\,[H_2O]}$$

Step 4 Substitute the equilibrium concentrations into the expression:

$$K_c = \frac{(0.0346) \times (0.0346)}{(0.0645) \times (0.0645)} = 0.280$$

(to 3 significant figures)

WORKED EXAMPLES (CONTINUED)

Step 5 Add the correct units by referring back to the equilibrium expression.

$$\frac{(\text{mol dm}^{-3}) \times (\text{mol dm}^{-3})}{(\text{mol dm}^{-3}) \times (\text{mol dm}^{-3})}$$

The units of mol dm^{-3} cancel, so K_c has no units. Therefore $K_c = 0.280$.

QUESTION

7 Calculate the value of K_c for the following reaction using the information below:

$H_2(g) + CO_2(g) \rightleftharpoons H_2O(g) + CO(g)$

initial concentration of $H_2(g) = 10.00\,\text{mol dm}^{-3}$.

initial concentration of $CO_2(g) = 10.00\,\text{mol dm}^{-3}$.

equilibrium concentration of $CO(g) = 9.47\,\text{mol dm}^{-3}$.

K_c and concentration changes

If all other conditions remain constant, the value of K_c does not change when the concentration of reactants or products is altered.

Take the example of the decomposition of hydrogen iodide.

$2HI \rightleftharpoons H_2 + I_2$

The equilibrium constant at 500 K for this reaction is 6.25×10^{-3}.

$$K_c = \frac{[H_2][I_2]}{[HI]^2} = 6.25 \times 10^{-3}$$

When more hydrogen iodide is added to the equilibrium mixture, the equilibrium is disturbed.

- The ratio of concentrations of products to reactants in the equilibrium expression decreases.
- To restore equilibrium, both $[H_2]$ and $[I_2]$ increase and $[HI]$ decreases.
- Equilibrium is restored when the values of the concentrations in the equilibrium expression are such that the value of K_c is once again 6.25×10^{-3}.

K_c and pressure changes

Where there are different numbers of gas molecules on each side of a chemical equation, a change in pressure

alters the position of equilibrium. It is shifted in the direction that results in fewer gas molecules being formed. However, if all other conditions remain constant, the value of K_c does not change when the pressure is altered.

K_c and temperature changes

We have seen on page 122 that for an endothermic reaction, an increase in temperature shifts the reaction in the direction of more products.

So for the endothermic reaction $2HI \rightleftharpoons H_2 + I_2$:

- the concentrations of H_2 and I_2 increase as the temperature increases
- the concentration of HI falls as the temperature increases.

Look at how these changes affect the equilibrium expression:

$$K_c = \frac{[H_2][I_2]}{[HI]^2}$$

We see that the equilibrium constant must increase with increasing temperature. This is because $[H_2]$ and $[I_2]$ are increasing and $[HI]$ is decreasing. Table 8.5 shows how the value of K_c for this reaction changes with temperature.

Temperature / K	K_c (no units)
300	1.26×10^{-3}
500	6.25×10^{-3}
1000	18.5×10^{-3}

Table 8.5 Variation of K_c for the reaction $2HI \rightleftharpoons H_2 + I_2$ with temperature.

For an exothermic reaction, an increase in temperature shifts the reaction in favour of more reactants.

Now look at the exothermic reaction:

$2SO_2 + O_2 \rightleftharpoons 2SO_3$

- The concentrations of SO_2 and O_2 increase as the temperature increases.
- The concentration of SO_3 falls as the temperature increases.

How do these changes affect the equilibrium expression?

$$K_c = \frac{[SO_3]^2}{[SO_2]^2[O_2]}$$

We see that the equilibrium constant must decrease with increasing temperature. This is because $[SO_2]$ and $[O_2]$ are increasing and $[SO_3]$ is decreasing.

127

8 a Deduce the effect of increase in temperature on the value of K_c for the reaction:

$$2NO_2(g) + O_2(g) \rightleftharpoons 2NO(g)$$

$\Delta H_r = -115\,kJ\,mol^{-1}$

b Explain why increasing the concentration of oxygen in this reaction does not affect the value of K_c.

9 The reaction below was carried out at a pressure of $10.00 \times 10^4\,Pa$ and at constant temperature.

$$N_2(g) + O_2(g) \rightleftharpoons 2NO(g)$$

The partial pressures of nitrogen and oxygen are both $4.85 \times 10^4\,Pa$.

Calculate the partial pressure of the nitrogen(II) oxide, NO(g), at equilibrium.

Equilibria in gas reactions: the equilibrium constant, K_p

Partial pressure

For reactions involving mixtures of gases, it is easier to measure the pressure than to measure concentrations. The total pressure in a mixture of gases is due to each molecule bombarding the walls of the container. At constant temperature, each gas in the mixture contributes to the total pressure in proportion to the number of moles present (Figure 8.10). The pressure exerted by any one gas in the mixture is called its **partial pressure**.

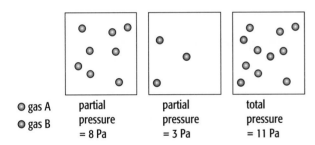

gas A	partial	partial	total
gas B	pressure	pressure	pressure
	= 8 Pa	= 3 Pa	= 11 Pa

the volumes of the containers are the same

Figure 8.10 Each gas in this mixture contributes to the pressure in proportion to the number of moles present.

The total pressure of a gas equals the sum of the partial pressures of the individual gases.

$$p_{total} = p_A + p_B + p_C \dots$$

where p_A, p_B, p_C are the partial pressures of the individual gases in the mixture.

Equilibrium expressions involving partial pressures

We write equilibrium expressions in terms of partial pressures in a similar way to equilibrium expressions in terms of concentrations. But there are some differences:

■ we use p for partial pressure
■ the reactants and products are written as subscripts after the p
■ the number of moles of particular reactants or products is written as a power after the p
■ square brackets are not used
■ we give the equilibrium constant the symbol K_p (the equilibrium constant in terms of partial pressures).

For example, the equilibrium expression for the reaction:

$$N_2(g) + 3H_2(g) \rightleftharpoons 2NH_3(g)$$

is written as $K_p = \dfrac{p^2_{NH_3}}{p_{N_2} \times p^3_{H_2}}$

What are the units of K_p?

The units of pressure are pascals, Pa. The units of K_p depend on the form of the equilibrium expression.

8 For the reaction:

$$N_2O_4(g) \rightleftharpoons 2NO_2(g)$$

The equilibrium expression is:

$$K_p = \frac{p^2_{NO_2}}{p_{N_2O_4}}$$

The units are $\dfrac{Pa \times Pa}{Pa} = Pa$

WORKED EXAMPLES (CONTINUED)

9 For the reaction:

$$2SO_2(g) + O_2(g) \rightleftharpoons 2SO_3(g)$$

The equilibrium expression is:

$$K_p = \frac{P_{SO_3}^2}{P_{SO_2}^2 \times P_{O_2}}$$

The units are $\dfrac{\text{Pa} \times \text{Pa}}{\text{Pa} \times \text{Pa} \times \text{Pa}} = \dfrac{1}{\text{Pa}} = \text{Pa}^{-1}$

Although the standard unit of pressure is the pascal, many chemists in industry use the atmosphere as the unit of pressure. 1 atmosphere = 1.01×10^5 Pa. Using 'atmospheres' as units simplifies calculations because the numbers used are not as large.

QUESTION

10 Deduce the units of K_p for the following reactions:

   a $PCl_5(g) \rightleftharpoons PCl_3(g) + Cl_2(g)$

   b $N_2(g) + 3H_2(g) \rightleftharpoons 2NH_3(g)$

   c $3Fe(s) + 4H_2O(g) \rightleftharpoons Fe_3O_4(s) + 4H_2(g)$

Calculations using partial pressures

WORKED EXAMPLES

10 In this example we are given the partial pressure of each gas in the mixture.

In the reaction

$$2SO_2(g) + O_2(g) \rightleftharpoons 2SO_3(g)$$

the equilibrium partial pressures at constant temperature are $SO_2 = 1.0 \times 10^6$ Pa, $O_2 = 7.0 \times 10^6$ Pa, $SO_3 = 8.0 \times 10^6$ Pa. Calculate the value of K_p for this reaction.

Step 1 Write the equilibrium expression for the reaction in terms of partial pressures.

$$K_p = \frac{P_{SO_3}^2}{P_{SO_2}^2 \times P_{O_2}}$$

Step 2 Substitute the equilibrium concentrations into the expression.

$$K_p = \frac{(8.0 \times 10^6)^2}{(1.0 \times 10^6)^2 \times 7.0 \times 10^6} = 9.1 \times 10^{-6}\,\text{Pa}^{-1}$$

WORKED EXAMPLES (CONTINUED)

Step 3 Add the correct units.

The units are $\dfrac{\text{Pa} \times \text{Pa}}{\text{Pa} \times \text{Pa} \times \text{Pa}} = \dfrac{1}{\text{Pa}} = \text{Pa}^{-1}$

$K_p = 9.1 \times 10^{-6}\,\text{Pa}^{-1}$

11 In this calculation we are given the partial pressure of two of the three gases in the mixture as well as the total pressure.

Nitrogen reacts with hydrogen to form ammonia.

$$N_2(g) + 3H_2(g) \rightleftharpoons 2NH_3(g)$$

The pressure exerted by this mixture of hydrogen, nitrogen and ammonia at constant temperature is 2.000×10^7 Pa. Under these conditions, the partial pressure of nitrogen is 1.490×10^7 Pa and the partial pressure of hydrogen is 0.400×10^7 Pa. Calculate the value of K_p for this reaction.

Step 1 Calculate the partial pressure of ammonia.

We know that the total pressure is the sum of the partial pressures.

$$P_{total} = P_{N_2} + P_{H_2} + P_{NH_3}$$

$$2.000 \times 10^7 = (1.490 \times 10^7) + (0.400 \times 10^7) + P_{NH_3}$$

So partial pressure of $NH_3 = 0.110 \times 10^7$ Pa

Step 2 Write the equilibrium expression for the reaction in terms of partial pressures.

$$K_p = \frac{P_{NH_3}^2}{P_{N_2} \times P_{H_2}^3}$$

Step 3 Substitute the equilibrium concentrations into the expression.

$$K_p = \frac{(0.110 \times 10^7)^2}{(1.490 \times 10^7) \times (0.400 \times 10^7)^3}$$

Step 4 Add the correct units.

The units are $\dfrac{\text{Pa} \times \text{Pa}}{\text{Pa} \times \text{Pa} \times \text{Pa} \times \text{Pa}} = \dfrac{1}{\text{Pa}^2} = \text{Pa}^{-2}$

$K_p = 1.27 \times 10^{-15}\,\text{Pa}^{-2}$

11 The information below gives the data for the reaction of hydrogen with iodine at 500 °C.

$$H_2(g) + I_2(g) \rightleftharpoons 2HI(g)$$

The table shows the initial partial pressures and the partial pressures at equilibrium of hydrogen, iodine and hydrogen iodide. The total pressure was constant throughout the experiment.

	Partial pressures / Pa		
	Hydrogen	Iodine	Hydrogen iodide
Initially	7.27×10^6	4.22×10^6	0
At equilibrium	3.41×10^6		7.72×10^6

a Deduce the partial pressure of the iodine at equilibrium.

b Calculate the value of K_p for this reaction, including the units.

Equilibria and the chemical industry

An understanding of equilibrium is important in the chemical industry. Equilibrium reactions are involved in some of the stages in the large-scale production of ammonia, sulfuric acid and many other chemicals.

Equilibrium and ammonia production

The synthesis of ammonia is carried out by the Haber process. The equilibrium reaction involved is:

$$N_2(g) + 3H_2(g) \rightleftharpoons 2NH_3(g) \qquad \Delta H_r = -92\,kJ\,mol^{-1}$$

We can use Le Chatelier's principle to show how to get the best yield of ammonia. At high temperatures, when the reaction is faster, the position of equilibrium is to the left because the reaction is exothermic (ΔH is negative).

■ What happens if we increase the pressure?
  – When we increase the pressure, the reaction goes in the direction that results in fewer molecules of gas being formed.
  – The equilibrium shifts in the direction that reduces the pressure.
  – In this case there are four molecules of gas on the left-hand side and two on the right-hand side. So the equilibrium shifts towards the right.
  – The yield of ammonia increases.

■ What happens if we decrease the temperature?
  – A decrease in temperature decreases the energy of the surroundings.
  – The reaction will go in the direction in which energy is released.
  – Energy is released in the exothermic reaction, in which the position of equilibrium favours ammonia production.
  – This shifts the position of equilibrium to the right. The value of K_p increases.

■ What happens if we remove ammonia by condensing it to a liquid? We can do this because ammonia has a much higher boiling point than hydrogen and nitrogen.
  – The position of equilibrium shifts to the right to replace the ammonia that has been removed.
  – More ammonia is formed from hydrogen and nitrogen to keep the value of K_p constant.

Equilibrium and the production of sulfuric acid

The synthesis of sulfuric acid is carried out by the Contact process. The main equilibrium reaction involved is:

$$2SO_2(g) + O_2(g) \rightleftharpoons 2SO_3(g) \qquad \Delta H_r = -197\,kJ\,mol^{-1}$$

We can use Le Chatelier's principle to show how to get the best yield of sulfur trioxide.

■ What happens when we increase the pressure?
  – When we increase the pressure, the reaction goes in the direction that results in fewer molecules of gas being formed, to reduce the pressure.
  – There are three molecules of gas on the left-hand side and two on the right-hand side, so the equilibrium shifts towards the right.

However, in practice, the reaction is carried out at just above atmospheric pressure. This is because the value of K_p is very high. The position of equilibrium is far over to the right even at atmospheric pressure. Very high pressure is unnecessary, and is not used as it is expensive.

■ What happens if we decrease the temperature?
  – Decreasing the temperature shifts the position of equilibrium to the right.
  – A decrease in temperature decreases the energy of the surroundings so the reaction will go in the direction in which energy is released.
  – This is the exothermic reaction, in which the position of equilibrium favours SO_3 production. The value of K_p increases.

SO$_3$ is removed by absorbing it in 98% sulfuric acid. Although the SO$_3$ is absorbed in a continuous process, this does not affect the equilibrium significantly because the position of equilibrium is already far over to the right.

QUESTION

12 The Haber process for the synthesis of ammonia may operate at a temperature of 450 °C and pressure of 1.50 × 10^7 Pa using an iron catalyst.

$$N_2(g) + 3H_2(g) \rightleftharpoons 2NH_3(g)$$

$\Delta H_r = -92 \, kJ \, mol^{-1}$

a Suggest why the temperature of more than 450 °C is not used even though the rate of reaction would be faster.

b Suggest why the reaction is carried out at a high pressure rather than at normal atmospheric pressure. Explain your answer.

c Explain why the removal of ammonia as soon as it is formed is an important part of this industrial process.

d When the ammonia has been removed, why doesn't it decompose back to nitrogen and hydrogen?

Acid–base equilibria

Some simple definitions of acids and bases

A very simple definition of an **acid** is that it is a substance which neutralises a base. A salt and water are formed.

$$\underset{\text{acid}}{2HCl(aq)} + \underset{\text{base}}{CaO(s)} \longrightarrow CaCl_2(aq) + H_2O(l)$$

The equation above also shows us a very simple definition of a base. A **base** is a substance that neutralises an acid.

If we look at the formulae for a number of acids in Table 8.6, we see that they all contain hydrogen atoms. When the acid dissolves in water, it ionises and forms hydrogen ions. Note that in organic acids such as carboxylic acids (see page 231) only some of the hydrogen atoms are capable of forming ions.

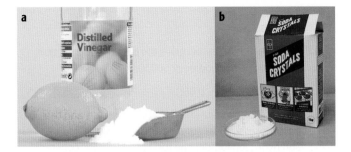

Figure 8.11 a The sour taste of lemons is due to citric acid and that of vinegar is due to ethanoic acid. **b** Washing soda is a base used to soften water prior to washing clothes. A solution of washing soda feels soapy.

Name of acid	Formula	Ions formed in water
hydrochloric acid	HCl	$H^+ + Cl^-$
nitric acid	HNO_3	$H^+ + NO_3^-$
sulfuric acid	H_2SO_4	$2H^+ + SO_4^{2-}$
ethanoic acid	CH_3COOH	$CH_3COO^- + H^+$
benzoic acid	C_6H_5COOH	$C_6H_5COO^- + H^+$

Table 8.6 Formulae and ions of some common acids.

A better definition of an acid is a substance that releases hydrogen ions when it dissolves in water. For example:

$$HCl(g) + aq \longrightarrow H^+(aq) + Cl^-(aq)$$

The formulae for a number of bases are given in Table 8.7. Many metal oxides or hydroxides are bases. Some bases dissolve in water to form hydroxide ions in solution. A base that is soluble in water is called an **alkali**. For example:

$$NaOH(g) + aq \longrightarrow Na^+(aq) + OH^-(aq)$$

Some alkalis are formed by the reaction of a base with water. When ammonia gas dissolves in water, some of the ammonia molecules react with water molecules. Hydroxide ions are released in this reaction.

$$NH_3(g) + H_2O(l) \longrightarrow NH_4^+(aq) + OH^-(aq)$$

Aqueous ammonia is therefore an alkali. We can also see from the equation above that the ammonia has accepted a hydrogen ion to become NH$_4^+$. So a wider definition of a base is a substance that accepts hydrogen ions.

Name of base	Formula
calcium oxide	CaO
copper(II) oxide	CuO
sodium hydroxide	NaOH
calcium hydroxide	Ca(OH)$_2$
ammonia	NH$_3$

Table 8.7 The formulae of some common bases.

QUESTION

13 a Write an equation to show potassium hydroxide dissolving in water.

b Write an equation for liquid nitric acid dissolving in water.

c Write ionic equations for:

i the reaction in aqueous solution between sodium hydroxide and nitric acid

ii the reaction in aqueous solution between potassium hydroxide and hydrochloric acid.

The Brønsted–Lowry theory of acids and bases

The definitions of acids and bases given above are limited to reactions taking place in water. In 1923 the Danish chemist J. Brønsted and the English chemist T. Lowry suggested a more general definition of acids and bases. This definition is based on the idea that in an acid–base reaction, a proton is transferred from an acid to a base (a proton is a hydrogen ion, H$^+$).

> A Brønsted–Lowry acid is a proton donor.
> A Brønsted–Lowry base is a proton acceptor.

When hydrochloric acid is formed, hydrogen chloride gas dissolves in water and reacts to form hydroxonium ions, H$_3$O$^+$, and chloride ions (Figure 8.12). You can see that the water is involved in the reaction.

$$HCl(g) + H_2O(l) \longrightarrow H_3O^+(aq) + Cl^-(aq)$$

Hydrochloric acid is an acid because it donates a proton to water. This means that water is acting as a Brønsted–Lowry base. The water is accepting a proton.

$$\overset{\text{H+ donated}}{\underset{\underset{\text{acid}}{}}{HCl(g)} + \underset{\text{base}}{H_2O(l)}} \longrightarrow H_3O^+(aq) + Cl^-(aq)$$

Water can also act as an acid. When ammonia reacts with water, it accepts a proton from the water and becomes an NH$_4$$^+$ ion (Figure 8.13).

$$\underset{\text{base}}{NH_3(g)} + \underset{\text{acid}}{H_2O(l)} \rightleftharpoons NH_4^+(aq) + OH^-(aq)$$

Substances like water, which can act as either acids or bases, are described as **amphoteric**.

131

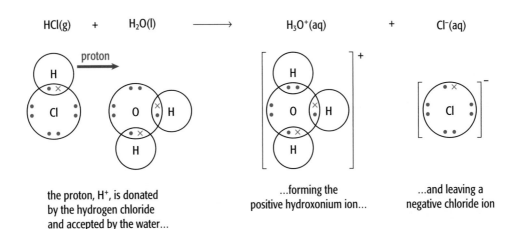

Figure 8.12 An acid is a proton donor. Hydrogen chloride is the acid in this reaction. A base is a proton acceptor. Water is the base in this reaction. Remember that a proton is a hydrogen ion, H$^+$.

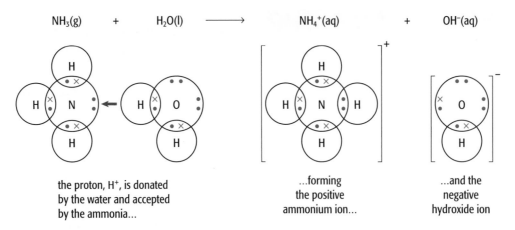

$$NH_3(g) + H_2O(l) \longrightarrow NH_4^+(aq) + OH^-(aq)$$

the proton, H^+, is donated by the water and accepted by the ammonia...

...forming the positive ammonium ion...

...and the negative hydroxide ion

Figure 8.13 Water is the proton donor (it is the acid); ammonia is the proton acceptor (it is the base).

Brønsted–Lowry acids and bases do not have to involve aqueous solutions. For example, when chloric(VII) acid ($HClO_4$) reacts with ethanoic acid (CH_3COOH) in an inert solvent, the following equilibrium is set up:

H+ donated

$$HClO_4 + CH_3COOH \rightleftharpoons ClO_4^- + CH_3COOH_2^+$$
acid   base

In this reaction $HClO_4$ is the acid because it is donating a proton to CH_3COOH. CH_3COOH is the base because it is a proton acceptor.

When an acid or base reacts with water, an equilibrium mixture is formed. For acids such as hydrochloric acid, the position of equilibrium is almost entirely in favour of the products. But for ammonia the position of equilibrium favours the reactants. The equations can be written to show this. For example:

$$HCl(g) + aq \longrightarrow H^+(aq) + Cl^-(aq)$$

A forward arrow is used as this reaction goes to completion.

$$NH_3(g) + H_2O(l) \rightleftharpoons NH_4^+(aq) + OH^-(aq)$$

An equilibrium arrow is used as this reaction does not go to completion.

QUESTION

14 Identify which reactants are acids and which are bases in the following reactions:

  a $NH_4^+ + H_2O \rightleftharpoons NH_3 + H_3O^+$

  b $HCOOH + HClO_2 \rightleftharpoons HCOOH_2^+ + ClO_2^-$

Conjugate acids and conjugate bases

In a reaction at equilibrium, products are being converted to reactants at the same rate as reactants are being converted to products. The reverse reaction can also be considered in terms of the **Brønsted–Lowry theory** of acids and bases.

Consider the reaction:

$$NH_3(g) + H_2O(l) \rightleftharpoons NH_4^+(aq) + OH^-(aq)$$

In the reverse reaction, the NH_4^+ ion donates a proton to the OH^- ion. So NH_4^+ is acting as an acid and OH^- is acting as a base.

H+ donated

$$NH_3(g) + H_2O(l) \rightleftharpoons NH_4^+(aq) + OH^-(aq)$$
acid   base

If a reactant is linked to a product by the transfer of a proton we call this pair a **conjugate pair**. Consider the following reaction:

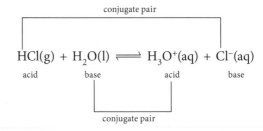

conjugate pair

$$HCl(g) + H_2O(l) \rightleftharpoons H_3O^+(aq) + Cl^-(aq)$$
acid   base   acid   base

conjugate pair

Looking at the forward reaction:

- Cl^- is the conjugate base of the acid HCl
- H_3O^+ is the conjugate acid of the base H_2O.

Looking at the reverse reaction:

- HCl is the conjugate acid of the base Cl^-
- H_2O is the conjugate base of the acid H_3O^+.

In a conjugate pair, the acid has one proton more.

The conjugate pairs for the equilibrium between ammonia and water to form ammonium ions and hydroxide ions are:

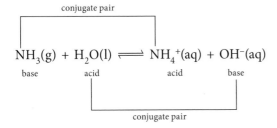

conjugate pair

$$NH_3(g) + H_2O(l) \rightleftharpoons NH_4^+(aq) + OH^-(aq)$$

base   acid   acid   base

conjugate pair

The idea of conjugate acids and bases is sometimes called the acid–1 base–1, acid–2 base–2 concept.

QUESTION

15 a Identify the acid and the base on the right-hand side of these equilibria.

   i $HClO_2 + HCOOH \rightleftharpoons ClO_2^- + HCOOH_2^+$

   ii $H_2S + H_2O \rightleftharpoons HS^- + H_3O^+$

b Identify the acid on the right-hand side of this equation which is conjugate with the base on the left-hand side.

   $CH_3NH_2 + H_2O \rightleftharpoons CH_3NH_3^+ + OH^-$

Figure 8.14 Many foods have high quantities of sugar in them. The sugar is converted to acid by bacteria in your mouth. This acid can attack the enamel on your teeth. By chewing sugar-free gum, more saliva is produced. Saliva is slightly alkaline. It neutralises the acid.

Strong and weak acids and bases

Strong acids

When hydrogen chloride dissolves in water to form a solution of concentration $0.1 \, mol \, dm^{-3}$, it ionises almost completely. We say that the acid is almost completely **dissociated**.

$$HCl(g) + H_2O(l) \longrightarrow H_3O^+(l) \, (aq) + Cl^-(aq)$$

The position of equilibrium is so far over to the right that we can show this as an irreversible reaction. The pH of this solution is pH 1. The pH of a solution depends on the concentration of hydroxonium ions, H_3O^+. The higher the concentration of hydroxonium ions, the lower the pH. The low pH shows that there is a high concentration of hydroxonium ions in solution.

> Acids that dissociate almost completely in solution are called **strong acids**.

The mineral acids, hydrochloric acid, sulfuric acid and nitric acid, are all strong acids.

Weak acids

When ethanoic acid dissolves in water to form a solution of concentration $0.1 \, mol \, dm^{-3}$, it is only slightly ionised. There are many more molecules of ethanoic acid in solution than ethanoate ions and hydroxonium ions. We say that the acid is partially dissociated.

$$CH_3COOH(l) + H_2O(l) \rightleftharpoons CH_3COO^-(aq) + H_3O^+(aq)$$

ethanoic acid   ethanoate ion   hydroxonium ion

The position of equilibrium is well over to the left. The pH of this solution is pH 2.9. The pH is much higher compared with a solution of hydrochloric acid of the same concentration. This is because the concentration of hydroxonium ions in solution is far lower.

> Acids that are only partially dissociated in solution are called **weak acids**.

Weak acids include most organic acids, hydrocyanic acid (HCN), hydrogen sulfide and 'carbonic acid'.

Although we sometimes talk about the weak acid, carbonic acid, you will never see a bottle of it. The acid is really an equilibrium mixture of carbon dioxide dissolved in water. The following equilibrium is set up:

$$CO_2(g) + H_2O(l) \rightleftharpoons HCO_3^-(aq) + H^+(aq)$$

The amount of CO_2 that forms undissociated carbonic acid, H_2CO_3, is very small as H_2CO_3 ionises readily.

Strong bases

When sodium hydroxide dissolves in water to form a solution of concentration 0.1 mol dm^{-3}, it ionises completely.

$$NaOH(s) + aq \longrightarrow Na^+(aq) + OH^-(aq)$$

The position of equilibrium is far over to the right. The solution formed is highly alkaline due to the high concentration of hydroxide ions present. The pH of this solution is pH 13.

> Bases that dissociate almost completely in solution are called **strong bases**.

The Group 1 metal hydroxides are strong bases.

Weak bases

When ammonia dissolves and reacts in water to form a solution of concentration 0.1 mol dm^{-3}, it is only slightly ionised. There are many more molecules of ammonia in solution than ammonium ions and hydroxide ions.

$$NH_3(g) + H_2O(l) \rightleftharpoons NH_4^+(aq) + OH^-(aq)$$

The position of equilibrium is well over to the left. The pH of this solution is pH 11.1. The pH is much lower compared with a solution of sodium hydroxide of the same concentration. This is because the concentration of hydroxide ions in solution is far lower.

> Bases which dissociate to only a small extent in solution are called **weak bases**.

Ammonia, amines (see page 220) and some hydroxides of transition metals are weak bases.

Table 8.8 compares the pH values of some typical strong and weak acids and bases.

QUESTIONS

16 Nitric acid is a strong acid but chloric(I) acid, HClO, is a weak acid.

   a   Explain the difference between a strong and a weak acid.

   b   Write equations showing the ionisation of each of these acids in water.

   c   Suggest relative pH values for 0.1 mol dm^{-3} aqueous solutions of:

         i   chloric(I) acid

         ii   nitric acid.

   d   Hydrazine, N_2H_4, is a weak base.

         i   Write a chemical equation to show the equilibrium reaction of hydrazine with water.

         ii   State the relative concentrations (high or low) of the N_2H_4 molecules and the products.

17 a   The pH of a solution depends on the hydrogen ion (hydroxonium ion) concentration. Which concentration of ethanoic acid in Table 8.8 has the highest concentration of hydrogen ions in solution?

   b   Which acid or alkali in Table 8.8 has the highest concentration of hydroxide ions?

   c   Explain why a solution of 0.1 mol dm^{-3} ethanoic acid has a lower electrical conductivity than a solution of 0.1 mol dm^{-3} hydrochloric acid.

   d   Both hydrochloric acid and ethanoic acid react with magnesium. The rate of reaction of 1.0 mol dm^{-3} hydrochloric acid with magnesium is much faster than the rate of reaction of 1.0 mol dm^{-3} ethanoic acid. Explain why.

Acid or base	pH of 1.0 mol dm^{-3} solution	pH of 0.1 mol dm^{-3} solution	pH of 0.01 mol dm^{-3} solution
hydrochloric acid (strong acid)	0	1	2
ethanoic acid (weak acid)	2.4	2.9	3.4
sodium hydroxide (strong base)	14	13	12
ammonia (weak base)	11.6	11.1	10.6

Table 8.8 pH values of some typical strong and weak acids and bases.

Summary

- A reversible reaction is one in which the products can be changed back to reactants.

- Chemical equilibrium is dynamic because the backward and forward reactions are both occurring at the same time.

- A chemical equilibrium is reached when the rates of the forward and reverse reactions are equal.

- Le Chatelier's principle states that when the conditions in a chemical equilibrium change, the position of equilibrium shifts to oppose the change.

- Changes in temperature, pressure and concentration of reactants and products affect the position of equilibrium.

- For an equilibrium reaction, there is a relationship between the concentrations of the reactants and products which is given by the equilibrium constant K.

- Equilibrium constants in terms of concentrations, K_c, and partial pressure, K_p, can be deduced from appropriate data.

- The quantities of reactants and products present at equilibrium can be calculated from the equilibrium expression and a value of K_c (or K_p), given appropriate data.

- A change in temperature affects the value of the equilibrium constant for a reaction but changes in concentration, pressure or the presence of a catalyst do not affect the value of the equilibrium constant.

- The conditions used in the Haber process and the Contact process are chosen so that a good yield of product is made.

- The Brønsted–Lowry theory of acids and bases states that acids are proton donors and bases are proton acceptors.

- Strong acids and bases are completely ionised in aqueous solution whereas weak acids and bases are only slightly ionised.

- Strong and weak acids and bases can be distinguished by the pH values of their aqueous solutions.

135

End-of-chapter questions

1 The reaction

$$2SO_2(g) + O_2(g) \rightleftharpoons 2SO_3(g)$$

reaches dynamic equilibrium in a closed vessel. The forward reaction is exothermic. The reaction is catalysed by V_2O_5.

a Explain the term **dynamic equilibrium**. [2]

b What will happen to the position of equilibrium when:
 i some sulfur trioxide, SO_3, is removed from the vessel? [1]
 ii the pressure in the vessel is lowered? [1]
 iii more V_2O_5 is added? [1]
 iv the temperature of the vessel is increased? [1]

c State Le Chatelier's principle. [2]

d Use Le Chatelier's principle to explain what will happen to the position of equilibrium in the reaction

$$H_2(g) + CO_2(g) \rightleftharpoons H_2O(g) + CO(g)$$

when the concentration of hydrogen is increased. [5]

Total = 13

2 Hydrogen, iodine and hydrogen iodide are in equilibrium in a sealed tube at constant temperature. The equation for the reaction is:

$$H_2 + I_2 \rightleftharpoons 2HI(g) \qquad \Delta H_r = -96\,kJ\,mol^{-1}$$

The partial pressures of each gas are shown in the table below.

Gas	Partial pressure / Pa
H_2	2.330×10^6
I_2	0.925×10^6
HI	10.200×10^6

a Explain the meaning of the term **partial pressure**. [2]

b Calculate the total pressure of the three gases in this mixture. [1]

c Write an equilibrium expression for this reaction in terms of partial pressures. [1]

d Calculate a value for K_p for this reaction, including the units. [1]

e Use Le Chatelier's principle to explain what happens to the position of equilibrium in this reaction when:

  i the temperature is increased [5]

  ii some iodine is removed. [5]

Total = 15

3 The equilibrium between three substances, **A**, **B** and **C** is shown below.

$$A(g) + B(g) \rightleftharpoons C(g)$$

Initially there were 0.1 mol of **A** and 0.2 mol of **B** in the reaction mixture. **A** and **B** reacted together to produce an equilibrium mixture containing 0.04 mol of **C**. The total volume of the mixture was 2.00 dm³.

a Calculate the number of moles of **A** and **B** at equilibrium. [2]

b Calculate the concentrations of **A**, **B** and **C** at equilibrium. [3]

c i Write the equilibrium expression for K_c. [1]

  ii Calculate the value of K_c and give the units. [2]

Total = 8

4 Gaseous hydrogen and gaseous iodine react together to form hydrogen iodide.

$H_2 + I_2 \rightleftharpoons 2HI$

a The graph shows how the amount of hydrogen iodide varies with time in a $1.00\,dm^3$ container. The initial amounts of hydrogen and iodine were $1.00\,mol\ H_2$ and $1.00\,mol\ I_2$.

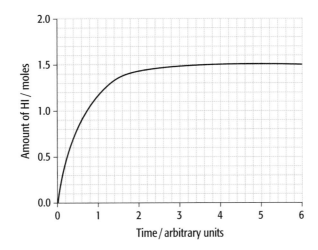

Draw a similar graph to show how the number of moles of hydrogen varies with time. [5]

b Calculate the number of moles of iodine present at equilibrium. [1]

c i Write the equilibrium expression for K_c for the reaction between gaseous hydrogen and iodine. [1]

ii Calculate the value of K_c and give the units. [2]

Total = 9

5 a Describe three characteristic features of chemical equilibrium. [3]

b When 1 mol of N_2O_4 gas is allowed to come to equilibrium with NO_2 gas under standard conditions, only 20% of the N_2O_4 is converted to NO_2.

$N_2O_4 \rightleftharpoons 2NO_2$ $\qquad \Delta H_r = +58\,kJ\,mol^{-1}$

i Give the equilibrium expression for this reaction. [1]

ii Calculate the value of K_c for the reaction. Assume that the volume of the reaction mixture is $1\,dm^3$. [4]

c Explain the effect on K_c of an increase in:

i pressure [2]

ii temperature. [2]

Total = 12

6 This question is about the following reaction:

$CH_3COOH(l) + C_2H_5OH(l) \rightleftharpoons CH_3COOC_2H_5(l) + H_2O(l)$

  ethanoic acid   ethanol   ethyl ethanoate   water

9.20 g of ethanol are mixed with 12.00 g of ethanoic acid in an inert solvent. The total volume of solution is $250\,cm^3$. The mixture is left to equilibrate for several days. At equilibrium 70% of the reactants are converted to products.

a What is the concentration of each reactant at the start? [2]

b What is the concentration of each reactant at equilibrium? [2]

c   What is the concentration of each product at equilibrium? [2]

d   i   Write the equilibrium expression for this reaction. [1]

ii   Calculate the value of K_c for the reaction. [1]

iii   Explain why there are no units for K_c for this reaction. [1]

e   What will happen to the numerical value of K_c if 100 cm^3 of water is added to the equilibrium mixture? [1]

f   What will happen to the yield of ethyl ethanoate if 100 cm^3 of water is added to the equilibrium mixture? Explain your answer. [2]

Total = 12

7   a   Hydrogen chloride and ammonia both ionise in water:

$$HCl + H_2O \rightleftharpoons H_3O^+ + Cl^- \qquad \text{equation 1}$$

$$NH_3 + H_2O \rightleftharpoons NH_4^+ + OH^- \qquad \text{equation 2}$$

i   State the name of the ion H_3O^+. [1]

ii   Identify the acid and the base on the left-hand side of each equation. [2]

iii   By referring to equation 1 and equation 2, explain why water is described as being **amphoteric**. [5]

b   When dissolved in an organic solvent, hydrogen chloride reacts with hydrogen iodide as follows:

$$HCl + HI \rightleftharpoons H_2Cl^+ + I^-$$

i   Use the Brønsted–Lowry theory of acids and bases to explain which reactant is the acid and which reactant is the base. [2]

ii   Identify which of the products is the conjugate acid and which is the conjugate base of the substances you have identified in part **b i**. [1]

c   Hydrochloric acid is a strong acid but ethanoic acid, CH_3COOH, is a weak acid.

i   Explain the difference between a strong acid and a weak acid. [2]

ii   Suggest a value of the pH for a 0.1 mol dm^{-3} solution of ethanoic acid in water. [1]

iii   Write a chemical equation to show the reaction when ethanoic acid donates a proton to water. [2]

Total = 16

8   This question is about the reaction:

$$N_2(g) + 3H_2(g) \rightleftharpoons 2NH_3(g) \qquad \Delta H_r = -92 \text{ kJ mol}^{-1}$$

120.0 mol of hydrogen gas are mixed with 40.0 mol of nitrogen gas then pressurised. The mixture of gases is passed at constant pressure over an iron catalyst at 450 °C until the mixture reaches equilibrium. The total volume of the mixture is 1.0 dm^3. 20% of the reactants are converted to ammonia.

a   How many moles of nitrogen and hydrogen remain at equilibrium? [2]

b   How many moles of ammonia are formed? [1]

c   Write an equilibrium expression for K_c. [1]

d   Calculate a value for K_c, including units. [2]

e   What will happen to the numerical value of K_c when the pressure is raised? [1]

f   What will happen to the numerical value of K_c when the temperature is raised? [1]

Total = 8

9 Ethanol can be manufactured by reacting ethene, C_2H_4, with steam.

$$C_2H_4(g) + H_2O(g) \rightleftharpoons C_2H_5OH(g)$$

a Write the equilibrium expression in terms of partial pressures, K_p, for this reaction. [1]

b State the units of K_p for this reaction. [1]

c The reaction is at equilibrium at 290 °C and 7.00×10^6 Pa pressure. Under these conditions the partial pressure of ethene is 1.50×10^6 Pa and the partial pressure of steam is 4.20×10^6 Pa.

   i Calculate the partial pressure of ethanol. [1]

   ii Calculate the value of the equilibrium constant, K_p, under these conditions. [1]

d The reaction is carried out in a closed system. Explain the meaning of the term **closed system**. [1]

e Use Le Chatelier's principle to explain what will happen to the position of equilibrium in this reaction when the pressure is increased. [3]

f The results in the table below show the effect of temperature on the percentage of ethene converted to ethanol at constant pressure. Use this information to deduce the sign of the enthalpy change for this reaction. Explain your answer.

Temperature / °C	% of ethene converted
260	40
290	38
320	36

[4]

Total = 12

139

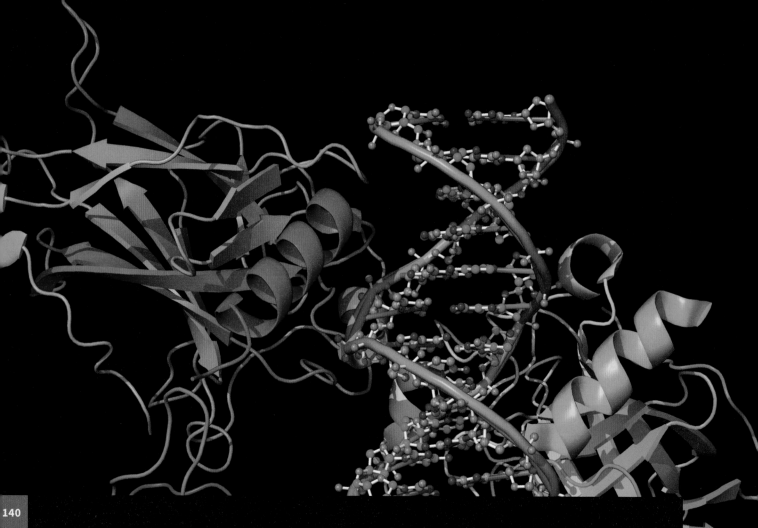

Chapter 9:
Rates of reaction

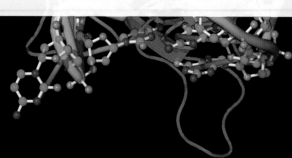

Learning outcomes

You should be able to:

- explain and use the terms
  - rate of reaction
  - activation energy, including reference to the Boltzmann distribution
  - catalysis
- explain qualitatively how the following affect the rate of a chemical reaction:
  - concentration (in terms of collision frequency)
  - temperature (in terms of both the Boltzmann distribution and collision frequency)
  - catalysts (in terms of changing a reaction's mechanism, lowering the activation energy and the Boltzmann distribution)
- explain that catalysts can be homogeneous or heterogeneous and describe enzymes as biological catalysts (proteins) that may have specificity.

Introduction

Some chemical reactions are very fast (they have a high rate of reaction) and others are much slower. Chemists study rates of reaction to control reactions in industrial processes and make useful products efficiently and safely.

Figure 9.1 a The reactions needed to produce firework explosions need to take place in a fraction of a second. **b** Corrosion of some metals, such as the rusting of iron, is a much slower reaction.

Reaction kinetics

Reaction kinetics is the study of the rates of chemical reactions. The data gathered from rate experiments can give us an insight into how reactions take place. We can then make deductions about the mechanism of a reaction.

The **rate of a reaction** can be defined as follows:

$$\text{rate} = \frac{\text{change in amount of reactants or products}}{\text{time}}$$

The balanced chemical equation gives us no information about the rate of a reaction. Experiments are needed to measure the rate at which reactants are used up or products are formed. For example, if a reaction gives off a gas, we can measure the volume of gas released in the course of the reaction at regular time intervals (Figure 9.2).

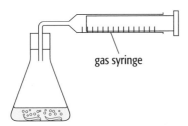

gas syringe

Figure 9.2 Measuring the volume of gas given off over time enables us to calculate the rate of reaction in cm^3 of gas per second.

Collision theory

141

When we explain the effects of concentration, temperature, surface area and catalysts on rates of reaction, we use the **collision theory**. Collision theory states that in order to react with each other, particles must collide in the correct orientation and with sufficient energy. The particles might be atoms, ions or molecules.

When reactant particles collide they may simply bounce off each other, without changing. This is called an unsuccessful collision. An unsuccessful collision will take place if the colliding particles do not have enough energy to react. If the reactant particles do have enough energy to react, they may change into product particles when they collide. This is called a successful (or effective) collision (Figure 9.3).

The minimum energy that colliding particles must possess for a successful collision to take place is called the **activation energy** of that particular reaction.

The activation energy for an exothermic reaction and an endothermic reaction can be shown on enthalpy profile diagrams, as shown in Figures 9.4 and 9.5.

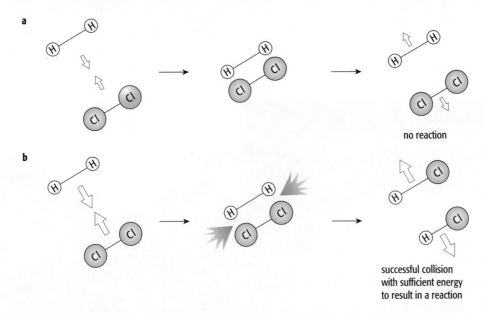

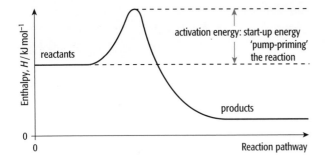

Figure 9.3 **a** Unsuccessful and **b** successful (or effective) collisions.

Figure 9.4 The activation energy in an exothermic reaction.

Figure 9.5 The activation energy in an endothermic reaction.

According to the collision theory, a reaction will speed up if:

- the frequency of collisions increases
- the proportion of particles with energy greater than the activation energy increases.

A **catalyst** is a substance that increases the rate of a reaction but remains chemically unchanged itself at the end of the reaction. A catalyst does this by making it possible for the particles to react by an alternative mechanism. This alternative mechanism has a lower activation energy (see Figure 9.6). You can read more about catalysts on page 144.

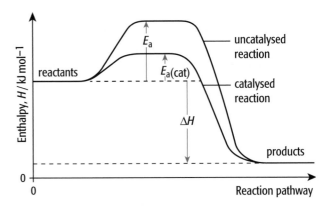

Figure 9.6 The effect of a catalyst on the activation energy in an exothermic reaction.

142

The effect of concentration on rate of reaction

In chemistry we usually measure the concentration of solutions in moles per decimetre cubed: $mol\,dm^{-3}$. The more concentrated a solution, the greater the number of particles of solute dissolved in a given volume of solvent. In reactions involving solutions, more concentrated reactants have a faster rate of reaction. This is because the random motion of the particles in solution results in more frequent collisions between reacting particles. This is shown in Figure 9.7.

The effect of pressure in reactions involving gases is similar to the effect of concentration in solutions. As we increase the pressure of reacting gases, there are more gas molecules in a given volume. This results in more collisions in any given time, and a faster rate of reaction.

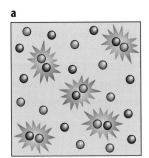
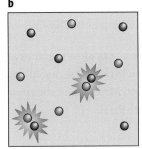

Figure 9.7 The particles in box **a** are closer together than those in box **b**. There are more particles in the same volume, so the chances and frequency of collisions between reacting particles are increased. Therefore, the rate of reaction is greater in box **a** than in box **b**.

The effect of temperature on rate of reaction

To fully understand rates of reaction, we need to look more closely at the energy possessed by the reactant particles. In a sample of any substance, at a given temperature, the particles will not all possess the same amount of energy as each other. A few particles will have a relatively small amount of energy. A few particles will have a relatively large amount of energy. Most particles will have an amount of energy somewhere in between. The distribution of energies at a given temperature can be shown on a graph (see Figure 9.8). This is called the **Boltzmann distribution**.

In Figure 9.8, the activation energy, E_a, is labelled. We have seen that the activation energy is defined as the minimum energy required for colliding particles to react. When we raise the temperature of a reaction mixture, the average kinetic (movement) energy of the particles increases. Particles in solution and in gases will move around more quickly at a higher temperature, resulting in more frequent collisions. However, experiments show us that the effect of temperature on rate of reaction cannot be totally explained by more frequent collisions. The key factor is that the proportion of successful collisions

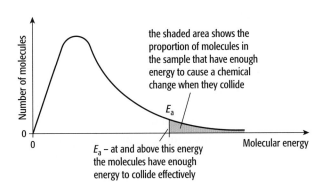

Figure 9.8 The Boltzmann distribution of molecular energies, showing the activation energy.

143

increases greatly as we increase the temperature. The distribution of molecular energies changes as we raise the temperature, as shown in Figure 9.9. The curve showing the Boltzmann distribution at the higher temperature flattens and the peak shifts to the right.

The area under the curve represents the number of particles. The shaded area shows the number of particles with energy greater than the activation energy, E_a. For a 10 °C rise in temperature this area under the curve approximately doubles, as does the rate of many reactions.

Therefore, increasing the temperature increases the rate of reaction because:

- the increased energy results in particles moving around more quickly, which increases the frequency of collisions
- the proportion of successful collisions (i.e. those that result in a reaction) increases because the proportion of particles exceeding the activation energy increases. This is the more important factor.

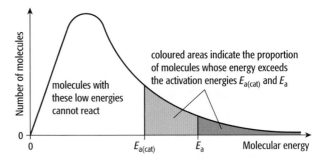

Figure 9.10 The Boltzmann distribution of molecular energies, showing the change in activation energy with and without a catalyst.

in the reaction mixture have sufficient energy to react. The shaded area under the curve represents the numbers of molecules that have energy greater than the activation energy of the reaction. The total shaded area (including both the light and dark shading) under the curve shows the number of particles with energy greater than the activation energy with the catalyst present ($E_{a(cat)}$). This area is much larger than the dark shaded area for the reaction without a catalyst. Therefore the rate at which effective collisions occur, and so the rate of the catalysed reaction, is greatly increased compared with the rate of the uncatalysed reaction.

Homogeneous and heterogeneous catalysts

When a catalyst and the reactants in a catalysed reaction are in the same phase, the catalyst is described as a homogeneous catalyst. For example, a catalyst can be described as homogeneous if it is dissolved in water and the reactants are also present as an aqueous solution.

If the catalyst is in a different phase to the reactants, the catalyst is described as a heterogeneous catalyst. You have probably met an example of heterogeneous catalysis when making oxygen gas. The reaction commonly used in the laboratory is the decomposition of hydrogen peroxide solution:

$$2H_2O_2(aq) \longrightarrow 2H_2O(l) + O_2(g) \quad \textit{slow reaction}$$

This is a very slow reaction at room temperature. However, when a little of the insoluble solid manganese(IV) oxide powder, $MnO_2(s)$, is added, oxygen is given off quickly (Figure 9.11).

$$2H_2O_2(aq) \xrightarrow{MnO_2(s)} 2H_2O(l) + O_2(g) \textit{ fast reaction}$$

At the end of the reaction, when no more gas is being released, the solid catalyst can be recovered by filtering off the water and drying the black powder of manganese(IV) oxide.

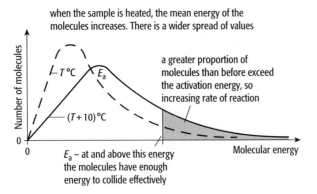

Figure 9.9 The Boltzmann distribution of molecular energies at temperatures T °C and $(T + 10)$ °C, showing the activation energy.

> **QUESTION**
>
> **3 a** What is the Boltzmann distribution?
>
> **b** Explain why a 10 °C rise in temperature can approximately double the rate of a reaction.

Catalysis

In Figure 9.6 we saw how a catalyst works by providing an alternative mechanism (or reaction pathway) with a lower activation energy. We can show this on a Boltzmann distribution (see Figure 9.10).

Note that the presence of a catalyst does not affect the shape of the Boltzmann distribution. However, by providing a lower activation energy, a greater proportion of molecules

Figure 9.11 a A solution of hydrogen peroxide at room temperature. **b** The solution of hydrogen peroxide with a little manganese(IV) oxide added.

Many heterogeneous catalysts are solids that catalyse gaseous reactants. The reactions take place on the surface of the solid catalyst. There are many examples in industry, including the iron catalyst used in the manufacture of ammonia from nitrogen gas and hydrogen gas, and the nickel catalyst used when adding hydrogen gas to vegetable oils to make margarine.

Enzymes

Enzymes are biological catalysts. They are large protein molecules which enable the biochemical reactions that happen in living things to take place very quickly at relatively low temperatures. Most enzyme-catalysed reactions happen in solution and are examples of homogeneous catalysis.

In common with inorganic catalysts, enzymes:

■ speed up a reaction without being used up
■ provide an alternative reaction pathway with a lower activation energy (Figure 9.12).

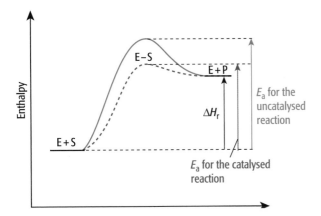

Figure 9.12 The energy profile for an enzyme-catalysed endothermic reaction, compared with the same reaction without a catalyst. As for inorganic catalysts, the enzyme provides a different reaction pathway with a lower activation energy (E_a) but the overall enthalpy change (ΔH_r) is unaffected.

However, enzyme catalysis has some specific features:

■ enzymes are more efficient than inorganic catalysts; the reaction rate is often increased by a factor of 10^6 to 10^{12}
■ enzymes are very specific; they usually only catalyse one particular reaction
■ as a consequence of this specificity, enzymes do not produce byproducts
■ enzymes work under very mild conditions; for example 35°C, pH 7, atmospheric pressure
■ the amount of enzyme present in a cell can be regulated according to need.

The specific substance that fits onto the surface of the enzyme molecule and is converted to product(s) is called a **substrate**. For example: the enzyme urease catalyses the reaction:

$$(NH_2)_2CO + H_2O \longrightarrow 2NH_3 + CO_2$$
$$\text{urea}$$

Urea is the substrate in this reaction, because it fits onto the surface of the enzyme molecule. Water reacts with the urea, but only when the urea is bound to the enzyme molecule.

> **QUESTION**
>
> 4 a i Explain whether the reaction below is an example of heterogeneous or homogeneous catalysis:
>
> $$2SO_2(g) + O_2(g) \overset{V_2O_5(s)}{\rightleftharpoons} 2SO_3(g)$$
>
> ii Explain how a catalyst increases the rate of reaction in terms of activation energy and the distribution of molecular energies in a sample of reactants.
>
> b Enzymes are used in the biotechnology industry. They are far more efficient than traditional catalysts used in industrial processes. What would be the benefits of using enzymes instead of traditional catalysts in the industrial production of a chemical?
>
> c Draw an energy profile diagram to show a typical uncatalysed reaction and an enzyme-catalysed reaction. On your diagram show:
>
> i the activation energy for the catalysed and uncatalysed reactions
>
> ii the enzyme, substrate and product and enzyme–substrate intermediate.

Summary

- Reaction kinetics is the study of the rates of chemical reactions.

- Factors that affect the rate of a chemical reaction are:
  - surface area
  - concentration (or pressure of gases)
  - temperature
  - catalysts.

- The activation energy of a reaction is the minimum energy required by colliding particles for a reaction to occur. Enthalpy profile diagrams show how the activation energy provides a barrier to reaction.

- At higher concentration (or pressure), more frequent collisions occur between reactant molecules. This increases reaction rate.

- At higher temperature, molecules have more kinetic energy, so a higher percentage of successful collisions occur between reactant molecules.

- The Boltzmann distribution represents the numbers of molecules in a sample with particular energies. The change in the Boltzmann distribution as temperature is increased shows how more molecules have energy greater than the activation energy. This in turn leads to an increase in reaction rate.

- A catalyst increases the rate of a reaction by providing an alternative reaction pathway with a lower activation energy. More molecules have sufficient energy to react, so the rate of reaction is increased.

- In homogeneous catalysis the reactants and catalyst are in the same phase (e.g. all in aqueous solution), whereas in heterogeneous catalysis the reactants and catalyst are in different phases (e.g. the reactants are gases and the catalyst is a solid).

- Enzymes are biological (protein) catalysts that provide an alternative reaction pathway of lower activation energy. Each enzyme reacts with a substrate (a specific molecule or class of molecules) and converts it into product(s).

End-of-chapter questions

1   a   Explain why gases react together faster at higher pressure.   [2]
    b   Explain why reactants in solution react faster at higher concentration.   [1]
    c   Explain why finely divided solids react more quickly than solid lumps.   [2]
    d   Explain why raising the temperature increases the rate of reaction.   [4]

                                                                                                                  Total = 9

2   a   Sketch a graph to show the Boltzmann distribution of molecular energies. Label the axes.   [4]
    b   What is meant by activation energy?   [2]
    c   Shade an area on the graph to show the number of molecules capable of reacting.   [2]
    d   Mark on your graph a possible activation energy for the same reaction in the presence of a catalyst.   [1]
    e   Shade an area on the graph to show the additional number of molecules capable of reacting because
        of the presence of a catalyst.   [1]
    f   Draw a second curve on your graph to show the Boltzmann distribution of molecular energies at a
        slightly higher temperature.   [2]

                                                                                                                 Total = 12

3   The Haber process is used in industry to convert nitrogen and hydrogen to ammonia. The formation of ammonia
    gas is exothermic.
    a   Sketch the enthalpy profile for the Haber process in the absence of a catalyst.   [1]
    b   On the same diagram, sketch the enthalpy profile for the Haber process in the presence of a catalyst.   [1]
    c   Label the activation energy on one of the profiles.   [1]

                                                                                                             Total = 3

4   The activation energy for the uncatalysed decomposition of ammonia to its elements is $+335\,kJ\,mol^{-1}$.
    a   Write the equation for this reaction, including state symbols.   [3]
    b   The enthalpy of reaction for this decomposition is $+92\,kJ\,mol^{-1}$. Calculate the activation energy for the
        uncatalysed formation of ammonia from nitrogen and hydrogen.   [3]
    c   If tungsten is used as a catalyst, the activation energy changes. Explain how it will change.   [1]

                                                                                                             Total = 7

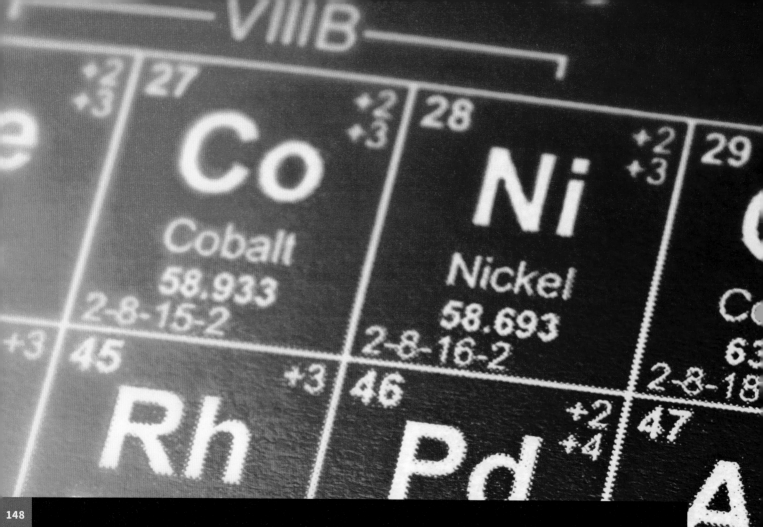

Chapter 10:
Periodicity

Learning outcomes

For the third period (sodium to argon), you should be able to:

- describe and explain qualitatively, and indicate the periodicity in, the variations in atomic radius, ionic radius, first ionisation energy, melting point and electrical conductivity of the elements

- explain the properties of ceramics

- describe the reactions, if any, of the elements with oxygen and chlorine (as well as sodium and magnesium with water)

- state and explain the variation in oxidation number of the oxides (sodium to sulfur only) and chlorides (sodium to phosphorus only)

- describe and explain the acid/base behaviour of oxides and hydroxides (including amphoteric behaviour), and the reactions of the oxides and chlorides with water

- suggest the types of chemical bonding and structure present in chlorides and oxides from their properties

- predict the characteristic properties of an element in a given group and deduce the properties, position in the Periodic Table, and identity of unknown elements from given information

Introduction

The Periodic Table was devised in 1869 by Russian chemist Dmitri Mendeleev.

He organised the elements known at that time in order of their atomic mass, arranging elements with similar properties into vertical columns. He left gaps where the pattern broke down, arguing that these spaces would eventually be filled by as-yet-undiscovered elements. For example, he left a space below silicon, and he made predictions of how the 'new' element would behave when it was discovered. He also changed the atomic mass order in places where similar elements did not quite line up in columns. These apparent inconsistencies resulted in some of his fellow chemists doubting the relevance of his table, but they were convinced following the discovery of germanium in 1886. Germanium closely matched the properties that Mendeleev had predicted for the 'new' element below silicon, using his Periodic Table.

Figure 10.1 a Dmitri Mendeleev (1834–1907). **b** This version of Mendeleev's Periodic Table is on the building in St Petersburg where he worked.

Structure of the Periodic Table

We now know that the chemical elements are arranged in the Periodic Table in order of atomic number, not atomic masses as first thought. This explains why Mendeleev had to re-order some elements in his table (which was developed before scientists knew about the structure of the atom). The modern Periodic Table is shown in Figure 10.2 on page 150. There are 18 groups (vertical columns) in the Periodic Table. The rows across the table are called periods. In this chapter we will be looking for patterns going across the third period, from sodium (Na) to argon (Ar). The patterns seen across Period 3 are seen across other periods, too. This recurrence of the same pattern is called **periodicity**.

QUESTION

1   Look at the Periodic Table in Figure 10.2.
    a Which element is found in Period 4, Group 17?
    b The relative atomic masses of tellurium (Te) and iodine (I) are 128 and 127, respectively. Why did this present a problem to Mendeleev when he was constructing his Periodic Table?
    c Why are the elements in Groups 1 and 2 known as s-block elements, whereas those in Group 17 are p-block elements?

Periodicity of physical properties

1 Periodic patterns of atomic radii

We can compare the size of different atoms using their atomic radii. The data for these measurements can come from an element's single covalent radius (Figure 10.3).

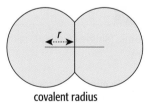

covalent radius

Figure 10.3 The distance between the two nuclei of the same type of atom can be determined and then divided by two to arrive at the atomic (single covalent) radius.

There are other measures of atomic radii, such as metallic radii and van der Waals' radii. However, covalent radii can be obtained for most elements, so these provide the best data for comparison purposes across a period.

The values of the atomic radii of the elements in Period 3 are given in Table 10.1. We can see the pattern across the period more clearly on a graph (Figure 10.4).

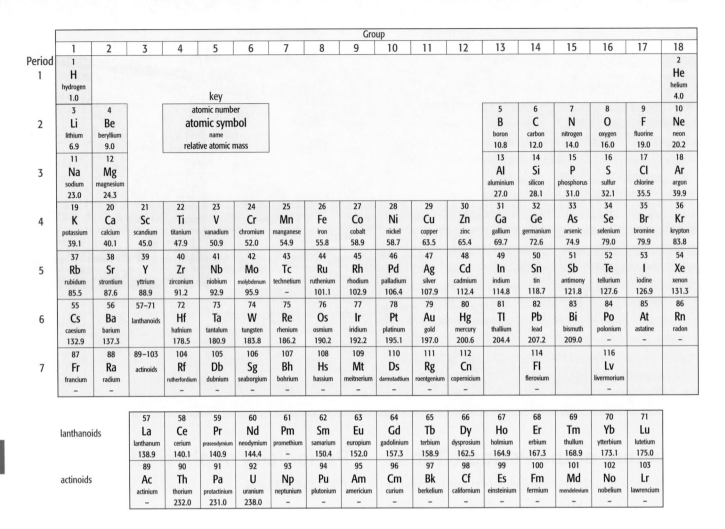

Figure 10.2 The Periodic Table of the elements. A larger version of the Periodic Table can be found in Appendix 1, page 473.

Period 3 element	sodium (Na)	magnesium (Mg)	aluminium (Al)	silicon (Si)	phosphorus (P)	sulfur (S)	chlorine (Cl)	argon (Ar)
Atomic radius / nm	0.157	0.136	0.125	0.117	0.110	0.104	0.099	–

Table 10.1 The atomic (single covalent) radii of Period 3 elements (no data are available for argon). The units are nanometres, where $1 \, nm = 10^{-9} \, m$.

The atoms of the noble gases in Group 18, such as argon in Period 3, do not have a covalent radius, as they do not form bonds with each other. Their atomic radii can be determined from their van der Waals' radius. This is found from the distance between the nuclei of two neighbouring, touching atoms, which are not chemically bonded together. This distance is divided by two to give the van der Waals' radius. This figure will be higher than the single covalent radius of any given element, as there is no overlap of electron clouds involved in the van der Waals' radius (see Figure 10.3).

As shown in Figure 10.4, the atomic radius decreases across Period 3. The same pattern is also found in other periods. Across a period, the number of protons (and hence the nuclear

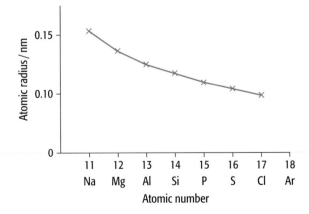

Figure 10.4 Plotting the atomic radii (single covalent radii) against atomic number for the elements in Period 3 (argon not included).

charge), and the number of electrons, increases by one with each successive element. The extra electron added to the atoms of each successive element occupies the same principal quantum shell (energy level). This means that the shielding effect remains roughly constant (see page 35). So the greater attractive force exerted by the increasing positive nuclear charge on the outer (valence) shell electrons pulls them in closer to the nucleus. Hence the atomic radius decreases across the period.

2 Periodic patterns of ionic radii

From your work in Chapter 4, you will know that the atoms of metallic elements produce positively charged ions (called cations), such as Na^+. By contrast, the atoms of non-metallic elements form negatively charged ions (called anions), such as Cl^-. What pattern in ionic radii do we see going across Period 3? The data are shown in Table 10.2 and are displayed graphically in Figure 10.5.

The positively charged ions have effectively lost their outer shell of electrons (the third principal quantum shell or energy level) from their original atoms. Hence the cations are much smaller than their atoms. To add to this effect, there is also less shielding of the outer electrons in these cations compared with their original atoms.

Going across the period, from Na^+ to Si^{4+}, the ions get smaller for reasons similar to those for the decreasing

atomic radii across a period. The increasing nuclear charge attracts the outermost (valence-shell) electrons in the second principal quantum shell (energy level) closer to the nucleus with increasing atomic number.

The negatively charged ions are larger than their original atoms. This is because each atom will have gained one or more extra electrons into their third principal quantum shell, increasing the repulsion between its electrons, whereas the nuclear charge remains constant. This increases the size of any anion compared with its atom.

The anions decrease in size, going from P^{3-} to Cl^-, as the nuclear charge increases across the period.

QUESTION

2 Look at the elements in Period 2 of the Periodic Table on page 473. Using your knowledge of Period 3 elements, predict and explain the relative sizes of:

   a   the atomic radii of lithium and fluorine

   b   a lithium atom and its ion, Li^+

   c   an oxygen atom and its ion, O^{2-}

   d   a nitride ion, N^{3-}, and a fluoride ion, F^-.

---

3 Periodic patterns of melting points and electrical conductivity

Physical properties, such as the melting point and electrical conductivity of the elements, also show trends across a period. Again, using Period 3 as an example, we can show the data in tables and on graphs (see Tables 10.3 and 10.4 and the graph in Figure 10.6).

The electrical conductivity increases across the metals of Period 3 from sodium (Group 1) to aluminium (Group 13). The electrical conductivity then drops dramatically to silicon, which is described as a semiconductor, and falls even further to the non-metallic insulators phosphorus and sulfur.

To explain the trend in melting points and electrical conductivity across a period, we have to consider the bonding and structure of the elements (see Table 10.5).

Sodium, magnesium and aluminium, at the start of Period 3, are all metallic elements. As you saw on page 59,

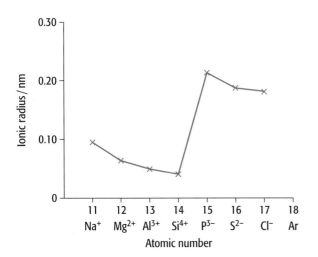

Figure 10.5 Plotting the ionic radii against atomic number for the elements in Period 3 (argon not included).

Ions of Period 3 elements	Na^+	Mg^{2+}	Al^{3+}	Si^{4+}	P^{3-}	S^{2-}	Cl^-	Ar
Ionic radius / nm	0.095	0.065	0.050	0.041	0.212	0.184	0.181	–

Table 10.2 The ionic radii of Period 3 elements (no data are available for argon).

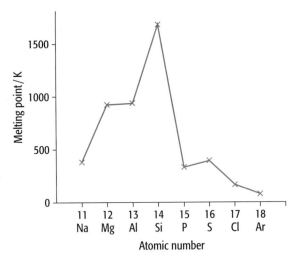

Figure 10.6 Plotting the melting point against atomic number for the elements in Period 3.

their metallic bonding can be described as positive ions arranged in a giant lattice held together by a 'sea' of delocalised electrons. The delocalised electrons are those from the outermost (valence) shell. These delocalised electrons are free to move around within the structure of the metal. When a potential difference is applied the delocalised electrons drift through the metal towards the positive terminal. Both the melting point and the electrical conductivity increase from sodium to magnesium to aluminium. This can be explained by the number of electrons each metal donates into the 'sea' of delocalised electrons and the increasing charge on the metal ions in the giant metallic lattice. Each sodium atom donates just one electron, forming Na^+ ions in the lattice, whereas

each aluminium atom donates three electrons, forming Al^{3+} ions. This makes the metallic bonding in aluminium stronger, as the electrostatic forces of attraction between its 3+ ions and the larger number of negatively charged delocalised electrons holding the giant structure together are stronger. There are also more delocalised electrons available to drift through the structure when aluminium metal conducts an electric current, making aluminium a better electrical conductor than sodium.

The element in the centre of Period 3, silicon, has the highest melting point because of its giant molecular structure (also called a giant covalent structure). Every silicon atom is held to its neighbouring silicon atoms by strong covalent bonds. However, its electrical conductivity is much lower than the metals at the start of the period because there are no delocalised electrons free to move around within its structure. Silicon is classed as a semimetal, or metalloid.

The elements to the right of silicon are all non-metallic elements. They exist as relatively small molecules. Sulfur exists as S_8 molecules, phosphorus as P_4 molecules and chlorine as Cl_2 molecules. Although the covalent bonds within each molecule are strong, there are only relatively weak van der Waals' forces between their molecules (see page 62). Therefore, it does not take much energy to break these weak intermolecular forces and melt the elements. At room temperature, phosphorus and sulfur are solids with low melting points and chlorine is a gas.

Argon gas exists as single atoms with very weak van der Waals' forces between these atoms.

Period 3 element	sodium (Na)	magnesium (Mg)	aluminium (Al)	silicon (Si)	phosphorus (P)	sulfur (S)	chlorine (Cl)	argon (Ar)
Melting point / K	371	923	932	1683	317	392	172	84

Table 10.3 The melting points of Period 3 elements (measured in kelvin, K, where $0\,°C = 273\,K$).

Period 3 element	sodium (Na)	magnesium (Mg)	aluminium (Al)	silicon (Si)	phosphorus (P)	sulfur (S)	chlorine (Cl)	argon (Ar)
Melting point / K	0.218	0.224	0.382	2×10^{-10}	10^{-17}	10^{-23}	–	–

Table 10.4 The electrical conductivity of Period 3 elements (measured in siemens per metre, $S\,m^{-1}$, where siemens are proportional to the ease with which electrons can pass through a material).

Period 3 element	sodium (Na)	magnesium (Mg)	aluminium (Al)	silicon (Si)	phosphorus (P)	sulfur (S)	chlorine (Cl)	argon (Ar)
Bonding	metallic	metallic	metallic	covalent	covalent	covalent	covalent	–
Structure	giant metallic	giant metallic	giant metallic	giant molecular	simple molecular	simple molecular	simple molecular	simple molecular

Table 10.5 The bonding and structures of Period 3 elements.

QUESTION

3 **a** Why does sulfur have a lower melting point than silicon?

   b Why does sulfur have a higher melting point than chlorine?

   c Why is magnesium a better electrical conductor than:

      i phosphorus?

      ii sodium?

4 Periodic patterns of first ionisation energies

You have looked at the pattern in first ionisation energies for the first two periods on page 41. In Period 3 the pattern is the same as in Period 2. This is shown by the data in Table 10.6 and the graph in Figure 10.7.

Period 3 element	First ionisation energy / kJ mol^{-1}
sodium (Na)	494
magnesium (Mg)	736
aluminium (Al)	577
silicon (Si)	786
phosphorus (P)	1060
sulfur (S)	1000
chlorine (Cl)	1260
argon (Ar)	1520

Table 10.6 The first ionisation energy ($X(g) \longrightarrow X^+(g) + e^-$) of Period 3 elements in kilojoules per mole (kJ mol^{-1}).

In general, the first ionisation energy increases across Period 3 as the positive nuclear charge increases and electrons successively fill the third quantum shell. As electrons are in the same shell, the shielding effect is similar in atoms of each element. There are small 'dips' in the general trend across the period between Mg and Al, and between P and S. The same pattern appears in Period 2 for Be and B, and N and O. The explanation given on pages 41–2 also applies here in Period 3.

QUESTION

4 **a** What is the general trend in first ionisation energies across Period 3?

   b Explain why aluminium has a lower first ionisation energy than magnesium.

   c Explain why sulfur has a lower first ionisation energy than phosphorus.

   d Look at Period 4 in the Periodic Table (page 473). The first ionisation energies of the p-block elements are given in the table below.

      Predict the missing value for the first ionisation energy of selenium.

p-block element of Period 4	Atomic number	First ionisation energy / kJ mol^{-1}
gallium (Ga)	31	577
germanium (Ge)	32	762
arsenic (As)	33	966
selenium (Se)	34	
bromine (Br)	35	1140
krypton (Kr)	36	1350

153

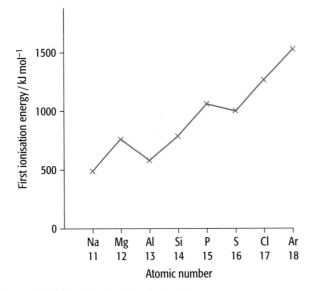

Figure 10.7 Plotting the first ionisation energy ($X(g) \longrightarrow X^+(g) + e^-$) against atomic number for the elements in Period 3.

REACTIONS OF PERIOD 3 ELEMENTS WITH OXYGEN

Sodium reacts vigorously when heated and placed in a gas jar of oxygen. The sodium burns with a bright yellow flame (Figure 10.8). The main product when sodium burns in a limited amount of oxygen is a white solid, sodium oxide:

$$4Na(s) + O_2(g) \longrightarrow 2Na_2O(s)$$

Figure 10.8 Sodium reacts vigorously with oxygen gas.

Magnesium also reacts vigorously when heated in oxygen, forming magnesium oxide. Aluminium metal is protected by a layer of aluminium oxide, but powdered aluminium does react well with oxygen. Both metals burn with bright white flames.

$$2Mg(s) + O_2(g) \longrightarrow 2MgO(s)$$
$$4Al(s) + 3O_2(g) \longrightarrow 2Al_2O_3(s)$$

Silicon reacts slowly with oxygen to form silicon(IV) oxide (silicon dioxide):

$$Si(s) + O_2(g) \longrightarrow SiO_2(s)$$

Phosphorus reacts vigorously with oxygen. A yellow or white flame is seen, and clouds of white phosphorus(V) oxide are produced:

$$4P(s) + 5O_2(g) \longrightarrow P_4O_{10}(s)$$

Sulfur powder, once ignited, burns gently with a blue flame in a gas jar of oxygen gas. Toxic fumes of sulfur dioxide gas are produced (Figure 10.9):

$$S(s) + O_2(g) \longrightarrow SO_2(g)$$

Figure 10.9 Sulfur burns gently in oxygen gas.

Further oxidation of sulfur dioxide gives sulfur trioxide. Their systematic names are sulfur(IV) oxide and sulfur(VI) oxide, respectively.

$$2SO_2(g) + O_2(g) \xrightleftharpoons{V_2O_5 \text{ catalyst}} 2SO_3(g)$$

Chlorine and argon do not react with oxygen.

Periodicity of chemical properties

We will now look at the chemistry of some of the elements of Period 3 and their compounds, focusing on the oxides and chlorides.

Reactions of Period 3 elements with chlorine

When sodium metal is heated then plunged into a gas jar of chlorine, there is a vigorous reaction, forming sodium chloride:

$$2Na(s) + Cl_2(g) \longrightarrow 2NaCl(s)$$

Magnesium and aluminium also react vigorously with chlorine gas:

$$Mg(s) + Cl_2(g) \longrightarrow MgCl_2(s)$$
$$2Al(s) + 3Cl_2(g) \longrightarrow Al_2Cl_6(s)$$

Silicon reacts slowly with chlorine, as it does with oxygen, giving silicon(IV) chloride:

$$Si(s) + 2Cl_2(g) \longrightarrow SiCl_4(l)$$

Phosphorus also reacts slowly with excess chlorine gas:

$$2P(s) + 5Cl_2(g) \longrightarrow 2PCl_5(l)$$

Sulfur does form chlorides, such as SCl_2 and S_2Cl_2, but you do not need to cover these for your examination.

Argon does not form a chloride.

REACTIONS OF SODIUM AND MAGNESIUM WITH WATER

Sodium reacts vigorously with cold water, melting into a ball of molten metal (Figure 10.10). It moves across the surface of the water, giving off hydrogen gas. It quickly gets smaller and smaller until it disappears, leaving a strongly alkaline solution (e.g. pH 14) of sodium hydroxide behind:

$$2Na(s) + 2H_2O(l) \longrightarrow 2NaOH(aq) + H_2(g)$$

Figure 10.10 Sodium reacts vigorously with water.

By contrast, magnesium reacts only very slowly with cold water, taking several days to produce a test tube of hydrogen gas. The solution formed is very weakly alkaline (e.g. pH 11), as any magnesium hydroxide formed is only slightly soluble. Therefore a lower concentration of $OH^-(aq)$ ions enter the solution compared with the result when sodium is added to water. This is because sodium hydroxide is much more soluble in water than magnesium hydroxide.

$$Mg(s) + 2H_2O(l) \xrightarrow{\text{slow reaction}} Mg(OH)_2(aq) + H_2(g)$$

When heated, magnesium does react vigorously with water in the form of steam to make magnesium oxide and hydrogen gas:

$$Mg(s) + H_2O(g) \longrightarrow MgO(s) + H_2(g)$$

155

QUESTION

5 a i The Group 1 metal lithium reacts in a similar way to sodium. It reacts with oxygen, producing lithium oxide. Write the balanced symbol equation, including state symbols, for this reaction.

ii Lithium also reacts with chlorine. Write the balanced symbol equation, including state symbols, for this reaction.

b i The Group 2 metal calcium reacts more vigorously with cold water than magnesium does, forming an alkaline solution. Write the balanced symbol equation, including state symbols, for this reaction.

ii The solution formed when 0.01 mol of calcium react completely with 1 dm³ of water is more alkaline than the solution formed when 0.01 mol of magnesium react completely with 1 dm³ of water. Explain why.

Oxides of Period 3 elements

Oxidation numbers of oxides

Table 10.7 shows the formulae of some of the common oxides of the Period 3 elements.

The maximum oxidation number of each element rises as we cross the period. This happens because the Period 3 element in each oxide can use all the electrons in its outermost shell in bonding to oxygen (ox. no. = −2). They all exist in positive oxidation states because oxygen has a higher electronegativity than any of the Period 3 elements. See page 60 for more about electronegativity.

Figure 10.11 The basic magnesium oxide or hydroxide reacts with acid in the stomach to form a salt plus water.

EFFECT OF WATER ON OXIDES AND HYDROXIDES OF PERIOD 3 ELEMENTS

The oxides of sodium and magnesium react with water to form hydroxides. The presence of excess aqueous hydroxide ions, $OH^-(aq)$, makes these solutions alkaline:

$$Na_2O(s) + H_2O(l) \longrightarrow 2NaOH(aq)$$
strongly alkaline
solution

$$MgO(s) + H_2O(l) \longrightarrow Mg(OH)_2(aq)$$
weakly alkaline
solution

Magnesium oxide and magnesium hydroxide are commonly used in indigestion remedies (Figure 10.11). These basic compounds neutralise excess acid in the stomach, relieving the pain:

$$MgO(s) + 2HCl(aq) \longrightarrow MgCl_2(aq) + H_2O(l)$$

$$Mg(OH)_2(s) + 2HCl(aq) \longrightarrow MgCl_2(aq) + 2H_2O(l)$$

Aluminium oxide does not react or dissolve in water, which is why an oxide layer can protect aluminium metal from corrosion. However, it does react and dissolve when added to acidic or alkaline solutions.

- With acid:

$$Al_2O_3(s) + 3H_2SO_4(aq) \longrightarrow Al_2(SO_4)_3(aq) + 3H_2O(l)$$

- With hot, concentrated alkali:

$$Al_2O_3(s) + 2NaOH(aq) + 3H_2O(l) \longrightarrow 2NaAl(OH)_4(aq)$$

When aluminium oxide reacts with an acid it behaves like a base – it forms a salt (aluminium sulfate in the example with dilute sulfuric acid above) plus water.

When it reacts with an alkali it behaves like an acid – reacting to form a salt (sodium tetrahydroxoaluminate in the example with sodium hydroxide above).

Compounds that can act as both acids and bases, such as aluminium oxide, are called **amphoteric**.

Silicon dioxide is also insoluble in water. Water cannot break down its giant molecular structure. However, it will react with and dissolve in hot, concentrated alkali:

$$SiO_2(s) + 2NaOH(aq) \longrightarrow Na_2SiO_3(aq) + H_2O(l)$$

Silicon dioxide acts as an acid when it reacts with sodium hydroxide, forming a salt (sodium silicate) plus water. It does not react with acids, so it is classed as an acidic oxide.

Period 3 element	sodium (Na)	magnesium (Mg)	aluminium (Al)	silicon (Si)	phosphorus (P)	sulfur (S)	chlorine (Cl)	argon (Ar)
Formula of oxide	Na_2O	MgO	Al_2O_3	SiO_2	P_4O_{10}	SO_2, SO_3	Cl_2O_7	–
Oxidation number of Period 3 element	+1	+2	+3	+4	+5	+4, +6	+7	–

Table 10.7 Oxidation numbers of the Period 3 elements in some common oxides. Chlorine has other oxides, such as Cl_2O, in which its oxidation number is +1, and Cl_2O_5, in which its oxidation number is +5.

Phosphorus(V) oxide reacts vigorously and dissolves in water to form an acidic solution of phosphoric(V) acid (pH 2):

$$P_4O_{10}(s) + 6H_2O(l) \longrightarrow 4H_3PO_4(aq)$$
$$\text{phosphoric(V) acid}$$

The oxides of sulfur, SO_2 and SO_3, both react and dissolve in water forming acidic solutions (pH 1):

$$SO_2(g) + H_2O(l) \longrightarrow H_2SO_3(aq)$$
$$\text{sulfurous acid (sulfuric(IV) acid)}$$

$$SO_3(g) + H_2O(l) \longrightarrow H_2SO_4(aq)$$
$$\text{sulfuric(VI) acid}$$

Summary of the acidic/basic nature of the Period 3 oxides

Table 10.8 shows a summary of the acidic/basic nature of the Period 3 oxides. You need to know this summary for your examination. We can explain the behaviour of the oxides by looking at their structure and bonding (Table 10.9 and Figure 10.12).

Going across a period the elements get more electronegative as electrons are more strongly attracted by the increasing positive nuclear charge (see page 60). The electronegativity values, which indicate the strength of

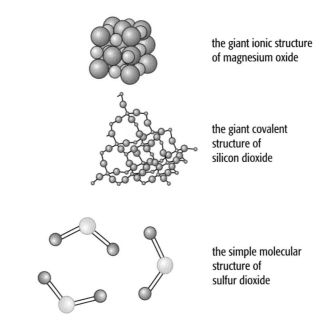

the giant ionic structure of magnesium oxide

the giant covalent structure of silicon dioxide

the simple molecular structure of sulfur dioxide

Figure 10.12 The structures of some Period 3 oxides.

the attraction of an atom for the electrons in a bond, are shown in Table 10.10.

The electronegativity of oxygen is 3.5. The greater the difference in electronegativity between the Period 3 element and oxygen, the more likely it is that the oxide will have ionic bonding. Electrons will be transferred

Period 3 oxide	Na_2O	MgO	Al_2O_3	SiO_2	P_4O_{10}	SO_2, SO_3
Acid/base nature	basic	basic	amphoteric	acidic	acidic	acidic

Table 10.8 The acid/base nature of the Period 3 oxides.

Period 3 oxide	Na_2O	MgO	Al_2O_3	SiO_2	P_4O_{10}	SO_2, SO_3
Relative melting point	high	high	very high	very high	low	low
Electrical conductivity when in liquid state	good	good	good	none	none	none
Chemical bonding	ionic	ionic	ionic (with a degree of covalent character)	covalent	covalent	covalent
Structure	giant ionic	giant ionic	giant ionic	giant covalent	simple molecular	simple molecular

Table 10.9 Some properties, chemical bonding and structure of some Period 3 oxides.

Period 3 element	sodium (Na)	magnesium (Mg)	aluminium (Al)	silicon (Si)	phosphorus (P)	sulfur (S)	chlorine (Cl)	argon (Ar)
Electronegativity	0.9	1.2	1.5	1.8	2.1	2.5	3.0	–

Table 10.10 Electronegativity values for Period 3 oxides (no data are available for argon).

157

from sodium, magnesium and aluminium atoms (forming positively charged ions) to oxygen atoms (forming O^{2-} ions) when their oxides are formed. The other Period 3 elements will form covalently bonded oxides in which bonding electrons are shared.

Notice the high melting points of the giant ionic and giant covalent structures, leading to the use of:

- magnesium oxide to line the inside of furnaces
- aluminium oxide and silicon dioxide to make ceramics, with giant covalent structures designed to withstand high temperatures and provide electrical insulation.

The oxides of the metals sodium and magnesium, with purely ionic bonding, produce alkaline solutions with water as their oxide ions, $O^{2-}(aq)$, become hydroxide ions, $OH^-(aq)$. The oxide ions behave as bases by accepting H^+ ions from water molecules:

$$O^{2-}(aq) + H_2O(l) \longrightarrow 2OH^-(aq)$$

By contrast, the covalently bonded non-metal oxides of phosphorus and sulfur dissolve and react in water to form acidic solutions. The acid molecules formed donate H^+ ions to water molecules, behaving as typical acids. For example, sulfuric(VI) acid:

$$H_2SO_4(aq) + H_2O(l) \longrightarrow H_3O^+(aq) + HSO_4^-(aq)$$

The insoluble oxides of aluminium and silicon show their acidic nature by reacting and dissolving in an alkaline solution, such as hot, concentrated sodium hydroxide solution, forming a soluble salt. This behaviour is typical of a covalently bonded oxide. However, aluminium oxide also reacts and dissolves in acidic solutions, forming a soluble salt – behaviour typical of a basic metal oxide with ionic bonding. This dual nature provides evidence that the chemical bonding in aluminium oxide is not purely ionic nor purely covalent, hence its amphoteric nature.

QUESTION

6 a The element germanium is in Group 14, in Period 4. It is classed as a semimetal or metalloid, as is silicon in Period 3.

   i Predict the chemical bonding and structure of the element germanium.

   ii Germanium(IV) oxide has properties similar to silicon dioxide. It is an acidic oxide. Write a balanced symbol equation, including state symbols, to show the reaction of germanium(IV) oxide with hot, concentrated sodium hydroxide solution.

   iii What would you expect to happen if germanium(IV) oxide was added to $2.0\,mol\,dm^{-3}$ hydrochloric acid?

 b Potassium oxide (K_2O) is a basic oxide. It reacts and dissolves in water, forming an alkaline solution.

   i Write a balanced symbol equation, including state symbols, to show the reaction of potassium oxide with water.

   ii Write a balanced symbol equation, including state symbols, to show the reaction of potassium oxide with dilute nitric acid.

   iii Predict the chemical bonding and structure of potassium oxide.

Chlorides of Period 3 elements

Oxidation numbers of the Period 3 elements in their chlorides

Table 10.11 shows the formulae of the common chlorides of the Period 3 elements.

The oxidation numbers rise as we cross Period 3, until we reach sulfur in Group 16. This happens because the Period 3 elements from sodium to phosphorus use all the electrons in their outermost shell, their valence electrons, in bonding to chlorine (ox. no. = −1). They all exist in positive oxidation states because chlorine has a higher electronegativity than any of the other Period 3 elements (see Table 10.11).

Period 3 element	sodium (Na)	magnesium (Mg)	aluminium (Al)	silicon (Si)	phosphorus (P)	sulfur (S)	chlorine (Cl)	argon (Ar)
Formula of chloride	NaCl	$MgCl_2$	Al_2Cl_6	$SiCl_4$	PCl_5	SCl_2	–	–
Oxidation number of Period 3 element	+1	+2	+3	+4	+5	+2	–	–

Table 10.11 Oxidation numbers of the Period 3 elements in their chlorides. Phosphorus also has a chloride with the formula PCl_3, in which its oxidation number is +3. Sulfur also has a chloride S_2Cl_2, in which its oxidation number is +1.

EFFECT OF WATER ON CHLORIDES OF PERIOD 3 ELEMENTS

As with the oxides of Period 3 elements, the chlorides also show characteristic behaviour when we add them to water. Once again, this is linked to their structure and bonding (Table 10.12).

At the start of Period 3, the ionic chlorides of sodium (NaCl) and magnesium ($MgCl_2$) do not react with water. The polar water molecules are attracted to the ions, dissolving the chlorides by breaking down the giant ionic structures. The solutions formed contain the positive metal ions and the negative chloride ions surrounded by water molecules. The metal ions and the chloride ions are called hydrated ions:

$$NaCl(s) \xrightarrow{\text{water}} Na^+(aq) + Cl^-(aq)$$

Aluminium chloride is sometimes represented as $AlCl_3$, which suggests that its chemical bonding is likely to be ionic – with Al^{3+} ions and Cl^- ions in a giant lattice. In solid hydrated aluminium chloride crystals, this is the case. However, without water it exists as Al_2Cl_6. This can be thought of as a dimer of $AlCl_3$ (two molecules joined together). This is a covalently bonded molecule (see Figure 10.13).

Once we add water, the dimers are broken down and aluminium ions and chloride ions enter the solution. Each relatively small and highly charged Al^{3+} ion is hydrated and causes a water molecule bonded to it to lose an H^+ ion, thus turning the solution acidic. We can show this in an equation as follows:

$$[Al(H_2O)_6]^{3+}(aq) \longrightarrow [Al(H_2O)_5OH]^{2+}(aq) + H^+(aq)$$

The non-metal chlorides, $SiCl_4$ and PCl_5, are hydrolysed in water, releasing white fumes of hydrogen chloride gas in a rapid reaction (Figure 10.14).

$$SiCl_4(l) + 2H_2O(l) \longrightarrow SiO_2O(s) + 4HCl(g)$$

The SiO_2 is seen as an off-white precipitate. Some of the hydrogen chloride gas produced dissolves in the water, leaving an acidic solution (hydrochloric acid).

Phosphorus(V) chloride also undergoes hydrolysis when added to water:

$$PCl_5(s) + 4H_2O(l) \longrightarrow H_3PO_4(aq) + 5HCl(g)$$

Both products are soluble in water and are highly acidic.

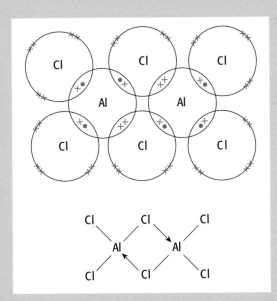

Figure 10.13 The chemical bonding in Al_2Cl_6.

Figure 10.14 Solid phosphorus(V) chloride is hydrolysed in water, releasing white fumes of hydrogen chloride gas.

Formula of chloride	NaCl	MgCl$_2$	Al$_2$Cl$_6$	SiCl$_4$	PCl$_5$	SCl$_2$
Chemical bonding	ionic	ionic	covalent	covalent	covalent	covalent
Structure	giant ionic	giant ionic	simple molecular	simple molecular	simple molecular	simple molecular
Observations when added to water	white solids dissolve to form colourless solutions		chlorides react with water, giving off white fumes of hydrogen chloride gas			
pH of solution formed with water	7	6.5	3	2	2	2

Table 10.12 The structure and bonding of the chlorides of Period 3 elements and the effect of water on these chlorides.

QUESTION

7 a The chloride of an unknown element, X, is a liquid at 20 °C. This chloride reacts with water, giving white fumes and leaving an acidic solution.

   i   Does element X belong to Group 1, Group 2 or Group 15 of the Periodic Table?

   ii What type of reaction takes place between X and water?

   iii Identify the white fumes given off when X reacts with water.

   b The chloride of an unknown element Y is a solid at 20 °C. This chloride does not react with water but dissolves to give a neutral solution. Does element Y belong to Group 1, Group 14 or Group 16 of the Periodic Table?

160

Summary

- Periods in the Periodic Table are rows of elements whose outermost electrons are in the same principal quantum shell.

- The atoms of neighbouring members differ by one proton and one electron (and usually by one or more neutrons).

- Periodic variations may be observed across periods in physical properties such as ionisation energies, atomic radii, ionic radii, melting points and electrical conductivities.

- The main influences on ionisation energies, atomic radii and ionic radii are:
   - the size of the positive nuclear charge
   - the distance of the outermost (valence) electrons from the nucleus
   - the shielding effect on outer electrons by electrons in filled inner shells.

- In general, ionisation energies tend to increase across a period.

- Atomic radii decrease across a period due to increasing nuclear charge.

- Positive ions are much smaller than their atoms. Negative ions are slightly larger than their atoms.

- Across a period, the structures of the elements change from giant metallic, through giant molecular to simple molecular. Group 18 elements consist of individual atoms.

- Across a period, the oxides of Period 3 elements change from basic compounds with ionic bonding through to giant molecular in the centre of the period (Group 14) with silicon, going on to acidic covalently bonded simple molecules of the non-metal oxides. Aluminium oxide (in Group 13) is amphoteric, exhibiting both basic and acidic behaviour.

- Across a period, the chlorides of Period 3 elements change from ionic compounds that dissolve in water to covalent compounds that are hydrolysed by water, releasing fumes of hydrogen chloride and leaving an acidic solution.

End-of-chapter questions

1 a Explain what is meant by the term 'periodic property'. [2]

b The graph shows how a periodic property varies when plotted against atomic number for Period 3 (sodium to argon).

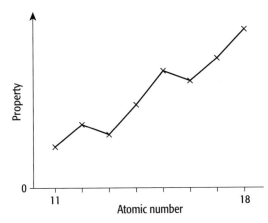

   i Identify the property. [1]

   ii Explain the overall trend across the period. [4]

Total = 7

2 The variation of melting point with atomic number for Periods 2 and 3 is shown in the graph below.

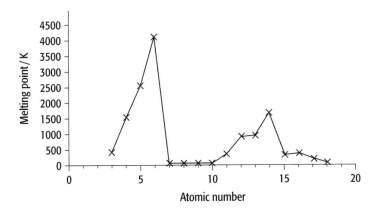

  a Explain what we mean when we say melting point is a periodic property. [1]

  b Explain the following.

    i The melting point of silicon is much greater than that of phosphorus. [4]

    ii The melting point of aluminium is greater than that of sodium. [5]

Total = 10

3 a i Describe how the atomic radius varies across Periods 2 and 3. [1]

    ii Explain this trend. [4]

  b i Describe how the atomic radius varies down each group of the Periodic Table. [1]

    ii Explain this trend. [1]

Total = 7

4 a Describe the acid–base nature of the solutions obtained when the following compounds are added to water. Use equations to illustrate your answers.

   i sodium chloride [2]

   ii sulfur trioxide [2]

   iii sodium oxide [2]

   iv phosphorus(V) chloride. [2]

  b i Write an equation for the reaction of magnesium with cold water. [1]

   ii Predict and explain the pH of the resulting solution. [2]

  c When magnesium is added to water, the reaction is very slow. In contrast, phosphorus(III) chloride (PCl_3) is a liquid that reacts vigorously with water. One of the products of this reaction is H_3PO_3, which forms in solution.

   i Write an equation, including state symbols, showing the reaction of phosphorus(III) chloride with water. [1]

   ii Predict the pH of the solution obtained. [1]

   iii State one observation a student watching the reaction would make. [1]

Total = 14

Chapter 11:
Group 2

Learning outcomes

You should be able to:

- describe the reactions of the Group 2 elements with oxygen, water and dilute acids

- describe the behaviour of the oxides, hydroxides and carbonates with water and with dilute acids

- describe the thermal decomposition of the nitrates and carbonates

- interpret, and make predictions from, the trends in properties of the elements and their compounds

- state the variation in the solubilities of the hydroxides and sulfates

- describe and explain the use of calcium hydroxide and calcium carbonate (powdered limestone) in agriculture

Introduction

Elements from Group 2 are used in a wide range of applications. For example, Group 2 metals produce coloured flames when heated, leading to their use in flares and fireworks. Magnesium is used in powdered form in flares. The large surface area in a fine powder increases the rate of reaction with oxygen. In military aircraft the heat given off from decoy magnesium flares confuses the infrared detection systems in missiles so enemy fire cannot focus in and target the aircraft.

Figure 11.1 A military plane releasing its decoy flares to protect it from missile attack.

Physical properties of Group 2 elements

The elements in Group 2 of the Periodic Table are sometimes referred to as the **alkaline earth metals**. As they are in Group 2, the elements have atoms whose electronic configurations end with two electrons in their outermost principal quantum shell. These two outer electrons occupy an s subshell. Here are the electronic configurations of the first five elements in Group 2:

Beryllium (Be)	$1s^2 2s^2$
Magnesium (Mg)	$1s^2 2s^2 2p^6 3s^2$
Calcium (Ca)	$1s^2 2s^2 2p^6 3s^2 3p^6 4s^2$
Strontium (Sr)	$1s^2 2s^2 2p^6 3s^2 3p^6 3d^{10} 4s^2 4p^6 5s^2$
Barium (Ba)	$1s^2 2s^2 2p^6 3s^2 3p^6 3d^{10} 4s^2 4p^6 4d^{10} 5s^2 5p^6 6s^2$

One way of describing the size of an atom is its metallic radius. The metallic radius is half the distance between the nuclei in a giant metallic lattice (Figure 11.2). See page 149 for other measures that describe the size of atoms.

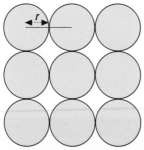

Figure 11.2 The metallic radius gives us a measure of the size of the atoms of metallic elements.

Look at the metallic radii of the Group 2 elements, shown in Table 11.1. The atoms of Group 2 elements get larger going down the group as the outer two electrons occupy a new principal quantum shell further from the nucleus.

Group 2 element	Metallic radius / nm
beryllium (Be)	0.122
magnesium (Mg)	0.160
calcium (Ca)	0.197
strontium (Sr)	0.215
barium (Ba)	0.217

Table 11.1 The metallic radii of the Group 2 elements.

There are also general trends in other physical properties, such as melting point and density, shown in Table 11.2 and Figures 11.3 and 11.4.

Group 2 element	Atomic number	Melting point / °C	Density / g cm⁻³
beryllium (Be)	4	1280	1.85
magnesium (Mg)	12	650	1.74
calcium (Ca)	20	838	1.55
strontium (Sr)	38	768	2.6
barium (Ba)	56	714	3.5

Table 11.2 The melting points and densities of the Group 2 elements.

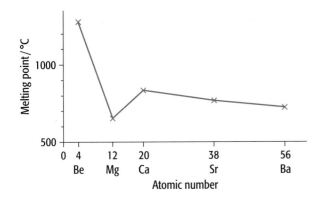

Figure 11.3 Melting points of the Group 2 elements.

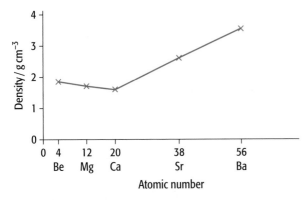

Figure 11.4 Densities of the Group 2 elements.

QUESTION

1 **a** Look at Figure 11.3.

    i What is the general trend in the melting points going down Group 2?

    ii Which element breaks the trend?

  b Explain why the atoms in Group 2, as in any other group, get larger with increasing atomic number.

  c Would you expect the 2+ ions of Group 2 elements to be larger or smaller than their atoms? Explain your answer.

  d Radium (Ra) is a radioactive element found below barium at the bottom of Group 2. Predict:

    i its melting point

    ii its density

    iii its metallic radius.

Reactions of Group 2 elements

The Group 2 metals form ionic compounds. When they react, their atoms lose the two electrons from their outermost s subshell and form an ion with the stable electronic configuration of a noble gas. This creates a 2+ ion. For example, in the ionisation of a magnesium atom to a magnesium ion:

$$Mg \longrightarrow Mg^{2+} + 2e^-$$

oxidation number   0   +2

The metals act as reducing agents. Their atoms give away electrons and so they are oxidised themselves as they react to form their 2+ ions. The ionisation energies shown in Table 11.3 show how easily the two outer electrons are removed from the Group 2 atoms.

Group 2 element	First ionisation energy / kJ mol^{-1}	Second ionisation energy / kJ mol^{-1}
beryllium (Be)	900	1760
magnesium (Mg)	736	1450
calcium (Ca)	590	1150
strontium (Sr)	548	1060
barium (Ba)	502	966

Table 11.3 The first and second ionisation energies of the Group 2 elements.

The metals in Group 2 get more reactive as we go down the group. As you can see from Table 11.3, it takes less energy (i.e. it gets easier) to remove the pair of outer electrons going down Group 2. So, although the positive charge on the nucleus increases down the group, the greater shielding effect provided by extra inner shells of electrons and the larger distance of the outermost electrons from the nucleus outweigh the attraction of the higher nuclear charge. This helps to explain the increase in reactivity going down the group, as it gets easier for the atoms to form their 2+ ions.

> The Group 2 metals get more reactive going down the group.

REACTION WITH OXYGEN

The Group 2 metals burn in air, and more rapidly in oxygen, forming white solid oxides. For example, magnesium ribbon burns with a bright white flame once ignited in a Bunsen flame (Figure 11.5):

$$2Mg(s) + O_2(g) \longrightarrow 2MgO(s)$$

Figure 11.5 Magnesium ribbon reacting with oxygen in the air.

The magnesium oxide formed is basic in character, as shown on page 156. Calcium oxide, CaO, reacts with water to form calcium hydroxide. If water is dripped onto the surface of a lump of calcium oxide it causes a vigorous reaction. It gives off so much heat that some of the water boils off as the solid lump appears to expand and cracks open:

$$CaO(s) + H_2O(l) \longrightarrow Ca(OH)_2(s)$$

In excess water, some of the slightly soluble calcium hydroxide dissolves to form a weakly alkaline solution. The excess aqueous hydroxide ions in the solution result in its pH of 11:

$$Ca(OH)_2(s) \xrightarrow{\text{water}} Ca^{2+}(aq) + 2OH^-(aq)$$

In general, the reaction and dissolving of the Group 2 metal oxides in water is described by the following ionic equation:

$$O^{2-}(s) + H_2O(l) \longrightarrow 2OH^-(aq)$$

The Group 2 metals get more reactive with oxygen going down the group. The larger atoms lose their outer two electrons more readily than the smaller atoms in the group. The reasons for this are given beneath Table 11.3.

The greater reactivity of barium metal is illustrated by the fact that it must be stored under oil to keep it out of contact with air.

Some of the Group 2 metals burn with characteristic flame colours. It is the 2+ ions formed in the reaction that cause the colours. We can test for calcium, strontium and barium in compounds using flame tests. A nichrome wire, cleaned with concentrated hydrochloric acid, is dipped into a sample of the salt to be tested and heated in a non-luminous Bunsen flame:

- calcium compounds give a brick-red colour
- strontium compounds give a scarlet/red colour
- barium compounds give an apple-green colour.

REACTION WITH WATER

We have seen on page 155 how magnesium reacts very slowly with cold water but will eventually form a weakly alkaline solution:

$$Mg(s) + 2H_2O(l) \longrightarrow Mg(OH)_2(aq) + H_2(g)$$

Hot magnesium does react vigorously with water in the form of steam to make magnesium oxide and hydrogen gas (Figure 11.6):

$$Mg(s) + H_2O(g) \longrightarrow MgO(s) + H_2(g)$$

REACTION WITH WATER (CONTINUED)

Figure 11.6 An experiment showing magnesium reacting with steam. The steam is given off from mineral wool soaked in water at the right-hand end of the test tube. The white magnesium oxide formed is visible inside the test tube and the hydrogen gas produced in the reaction has been ignited at the end of the straight tube.

Calcium reacts more readily than magnesium with water:

$$Ca(s) + 2H_2O(l) \longrightarrow Ca(OH)_2(aq) + H_2(g)$$

This reaction forms a cloudy white suspension of slightly soluble calcium hydroxide. The calcium hydroxide that does dissolve makes the solution weakly alkaline. The hydrogen gas is given off at a steady rate. Going down the group, hydrogen gas is released more and more rapidly by the reaction of the element with water (Figure 11.7).

Figure 11.7 Barium reacting vigorously with water.

The resulting solutions also get more alkaline going down the group. We can explain this by looking at the solubility of the hydroxides formed (see Table 11.4). Their **solubility increases** on going down Group 2. Therefore when adding and stirring magnesium hydroxide in water to make a saturated solution, then doing the same with barium hydroxide and water, there will be a higher concentration of hydroxide ions in the case of the saturated barium hydroxide solution. This results in a higher pH value for the barium hydroxide solution.

Not all Group 2 compounds get more soluble on descending the group. For example, their sulfates become **less** soluble – so barium sulfate is much less soluble than magnesium sulfate. (In fact the test for sulfate ions depends on the formation of a white precipitate of barium sulfate, produced when barium chloride solution is added to a solution of the compound being tested.)

You can read more about the reasons why the Group 2 sulfates get less soluble going down the group on page 267.

Group 2 element	Solubility of hydroxide at 298 K / mol / 100 g of water
magnesium hydroxide, $Mg(OH)_2$	2.0×10^{-5}
calcium hydroxide, $Ca(OH)_2$	1.5×10^{-3}
strontium hydroxide, $Sr(OH)_2$	3.4×10^{-3}
barium hydroxide, $Ba(OH)_2$	1.5×10^{-2}

Table 11.4 Solubility of the Group 2 hydroxides in water.

QUESTION

2 a Write a balanced chemical equation, including state symbols, for the reaction of:

  i strontium with oxygen

  ii strontium oxide with water.

 b i Write a balanced chemical equation, including state symbols, for the reaction of barium with water.

  ii Predict the pH of the solution formed in part **b i**.

 c Radium (Ra) is a radioactive element found below barium at the bottom of Group 2. Predict:

  i the formula of its ion

  ii the formula of its oxide and hydroxide

  iii its first ionisation energy

  iv its reactivity compared with barium

  v the relative pH of its saturated hydroxide solution compared with a saturated solution of calcium hydroxide

  vi the solubility of its sulfate compared with strontium sulfate.

 d Using Table 11.4 and the relative atomic mass data on page 473, calculate the mass of calcium hydroxide that will dissolve in 50 g of water at 298 K.

Reaction of Group 2 carbonates with water and with dilute acids

The carbonates of magnesium, calcium, strontium and barium are all **insoluble** in water. However, they all react in dilute acid, forming a salt and water and giving off carbon dioxide gas. For example, with dilute sulfuric acid:

$$MgCO_3(s) + H_2SO_4(aq) \longrightarrow MgSO_4(aq) + H_2O(l) + CO_2(g)$$

The magnesium sulfate salt formed in the reaction above is soluble in water so remains in aqueous solution, and no solid will remain in excess dilute sulfuric acid. However, the sulfates of the other Group 2 elements tend to form an insoluble sulfate layer on the carbonate, preventing further reaction after the initial effervescence of carbon dioxide gas is seen.

With dilute nitric acid, all the nitrate salts formed are soluble in water. For example:

$$CaCO_3(s) + 2HNO_3(aq)$$
$$\longrightarrow Ca(NO_3)_2(aq) + H_2O(l) + CO_2(g)$$

The reactions with dilute hydrochloric acid also form soluble salts, the chlorides. For example:

$$BaCO_3(s) + 2HCl(aq) \longrightarrow BaCl_2(aq) + H_2O(l) + CO_2(g)$$

Thermal decomposition of Group 2 carbonates and nitrates

The carbonates and nitrates of the Group 2 elements decompose when heated. The carbonates break down to form the metal oxide and give off carbon dioxide gas. For example:

$$MgCO_3(s) \xrightarrow{heat} MgO(s) + CO_2(g)$$

The temperature at which thermal decomposition takes place **increases** going down Group 2.

The Group 2 nitrates also undergo thermal decomposition. For example:

$$2Ca(NO_3)_2(s) \xrightarrow{heat} 2CaO(s) + 4NO_2(g) + O_2(g)$$

A brown gas is observed when a Group 2 nitrate is heated. This is toxic nitrogen dioxide, NO_2 (nitrogen(IV) oxide).

As with the carbonates, a higher temperature is needed to thermally decompose the nitrates as Group 2 is descended.

You can read an explanation of the trend in the thermal stability of the Group 2 carbonates and nitrates on page 264.

QUESTION

3 a Write a balanced symbol equation for the reaction of barium carbonate with dilute nitric acid.

 b Which one of the three compounds listed will decompose at the lowest temperature?

  i calcium carbonate, strontium carbonate, barium carbonate

  ii barium nitrate, calcium nitrate, magnesium nitrate

 c Write a balanced chemical equation, including state symbols, for the thermal decomposition of:

  i strontium carbonate

  ii barium nitrate.

Some uses of Group 2 compounds

We have just seen how the Group 2 carbonates decompose on heating. Limestone is made up mainly of calcium carbonate. There are many types of limestone, which provide useful rocks for building. They can be shaped into blocks that can be stuck to each other using mortar. Previously this mortar was made using lime and sand. Now it is more usual to use cement and sand, although the cement is made from lime – see below. Marble is another form of calcium carbonate used as a building material, for example to make expensive tiles.

However, most calcium carbonate is used to make cement. The first stage in the manufacture of cement is the roasting of limestone in a lime kiln (Figure 11.8). At the high temperatures in the kiln, calcium carbonate decomposes to form calcium oxide (also called lime or quicklime):

$$CaCO_3(s) \xrightarrow{\text{heat}} \underset{\text{lime}}{CaO(s)} + CO_2(g)$$

The calcium oxide made in the lime kiln goes on to be roasted with clay to make cement. Cement can be mixed with sand and small pieces of rock to make concrete, the most widely used building material in the world. Its tensile strength can be improved by letting the concrete set with iron rods running through it.

Slaked lime (calcium hydroxide, $Ca(OH)_2$) is also used by farmers to raise the pH of acidic soil. Calcium hydroxide is basic, so it will react with and neutralise acid, raising the pH of the soil.

Figure 11.8 In a rotating lime kiln, calcium carbonate undergoes thermal decomposition to form calcium oxide and carbon dioxide.

169

QUESTION

4 **a** How is limestone turned into lime in industry?

b Which major construction materials are made from cement?

c Both calcium carbonate and magnesium oxide have giant ionic structures. Why is magnesium oxide used to line furnaces but calcium carbonate is not?

d When lightning strikes during a thunderstorm, the rain that falls is a dilute solution of nitric acid (HNO_3). Use a balanced chemical equation, including state symbols, to show how slaked lime (calcium hydroxide) added to soil can neutralise nitric acid.

Summary

- The Group 2 elements magnesium to barium are typical metals with high melting points and they are good conductors of heat and electricity.

- Progressing down Group 2 from magnesium to barium, the atomic radius increases. This is due to the addition of an extra shell of electrons for each element as the group is descended.

- The Group 2 elements magnesium to barium react with water to produce hydrogen gas and the metal hydroxide, which may be only slightly soluble.

- The Group 2 elements magnesium to barium burn in air to form white solid oxides. These oxides form hydroxides with water. The hydroxides get more soluble in water going down the group so their solutions can become more alkaline.

- The sulfates of Group 2 elements get less soluble in water going down the group.

- Reactivity of the elements with oxygen or water increases down Group 2 as the first and second ionisation energies decrease.

- The Group 2 carbonates and nitrates get more resistant to thermal decomposition descending the group.

- Many of the compounds of Group 2 elements have important uses. Limestone, which contains mainly calcium carbonate, is used as a building material and is used to make cement, which is a component in the mixtures that make concrete and mortar. Slaked lime (calcium hydroxide) is used to neutralise acids in acidic soil.

End-of-chapter questions

You will need a copy of the Periodic Table (see page 473) to answer some of these questions.

1 Beryllium and radium are both in Group 2.
  a Write the electronic configuration of beryllium. [2]
  b Give the equations for the reactions of beryllium and radium with oxygen. [4]
  c Using dot-and-cross diagrams, and showing the outer electrons only, draw the electronic configurations of beryllium and oxygen before and after bonding. [5]
  d Draw a diagram to show the metallic bonding in both beryllium and radium. [3]
  e Using your diagram, explain why beryllium has a higher melting point than radium. [4]

  Total = 18

2 a Limewater is calcium hydroxide.
   i Give the formula of calcium hydroxide. [1]
   ii Explain why calcium hydroxide is used in agriculture. [2]
  b Exactly 0.1 moles of calcium hydroxide and barium hydroxide are added to separate beakers containing 100 cm^3 of water and stirred to form saturated solutions. Explain which solution has the higher pH value. [2]

  Total = 5

3 For the following reactions, state which element is oxidised and which one is reduced, and give the changes in oxidation number.
  a $Sr + Cl_2 \longrightarrow SrCl_2$ [3]
  b $Sr + 2H_2O \longrightarrow Sr(OH)_2 + H_2$ [3]
  c $2Mg + CO_2 \longrightarrow 2MgO + C$ [3]

  Total = 9

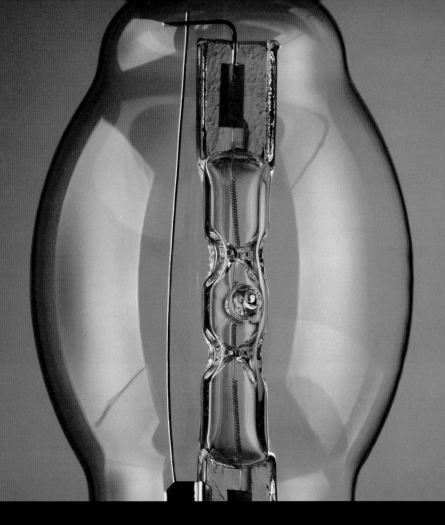

Chapter 12:
Group 17

Learning outcomes

You should be able to:

- describe the colours of, and explain the trend in volatility of, chlorine, bromine and iodine
- describe and explain
  - the relative reactivity of the elements as oxidising agents
  - the reactions of the elements with hydrogen
  - the relative thermal stabilities of the hydrides (in terms of bond energies)

- describe and explain the reactions of halide ions with
  - aqueous silver ions followed by aqueous ammonia
  - concentrated sulfuric acid
- describe and interpret the reaction of chlorine with cold, and with hot, aqueous sodium hydroxide
- explain the use of chlorine in water purification
- state the industrial importance and environmental significance of the halogens and their compounds

Introduction

Fluorine, found at the top of Group 17, is the most reactive of all the non-metallic elements and is a powerful oxidising agent. The next element in Group 17 is chlorine, also a toxic gas, but its compounds, such as trichlorophenol, are important disinfectants. Compounds of carbon, fluorine and chlorine are known as CFCs and have been responsible for most of the damage to the Earth's ozone layer. You can read more about uses of the halogens and their compounds on page 178.

Figure 12.1 Chlorine may be added to drinking water to kill harmful microorganisms.

Physical properties of Group 17 elements

In this chapter we will look at the elements in Group 17 of the Periodic Table, called the **halogens**. Their atoms all have seven electrons in the outer principal quantum shell. Here are the electronic configurations of the first four elements in Group 17:

Fluorine (F)	$1s^2 2s^2 2p^5$
Chlorine (Cl)	$1s^2 2s^2 2p^6 3s^2 3p^5$
Bromine (Br)	$1s^2 2s^2 2p^6 3s^2 3p^6 3d^{10} 4s^2 4p^5$
Iodine (I)	$1s^2 2s^2 2p^6 3s^2 3p^6 3d^{10} 4s^2 4p^6 4d^{10} 5s^2 5p^5$

The Group 17 elements are all non-metals. At room temperature, they exist as diatomic molecules, i.e. molecules made up of two atoms, F_2, Cl_2, Br_2 and I_2 (Figure 12.2). There is a single covalent bond between the two atoms in each molecule. Table 12.1 shows some of their physical properties.

Figure 12.2 Three of the Group 17 elements, known as the halogens.

Group 17 element	Atomic radius / nm	Melting point / °C	Boiling point / °C	Colour
fluorine (F_2)	0.072	−220	−188	pale yellow
chlorine (Cl_2)	0.099	−101	−35	green/yellow
bromine (Br_2)	0.114	−7	59	orange/brown
iodine (I_2)	0.133	114	184	grey/black solid, purple vapour

Table 12.1 Some physical properties of the Group 17 elements. The atomic radius value is taken from single covalent data (see page 51).

The melting points and boiling points of the halogens **increase** going down the group. The boiling point data gives us an idea of the volatility of the halogens, i.e. the ease with which they evaporate. All the values are relatively low because they have simple molecular structures. There are only weak van der Waals' forces between their diatomic molecules. These forces increase as the number of electrons in the molecules increases with increasing atomic number. The greater the number of electrons, the greater the opportunities for instantaneous dipoles arising within molecules, and for induced dipoles to be produced on neighbouring molecules. So the larger the molecules, the stronger the van der Waals' forces between molecules, making iodine the least volatile and fluorine the most volatile of the halogens we are considering.

The colours of the halogens get darker going down the group.

1
a What trend in volatility is seen going down Group 17?

b Using Table 12.1, what is the state of each halogen at 20 °C?

c What is the trend in the atomic radii of the halogens? Explain this trend.

d Astatine (At) lies below iodine at the bottom of Group 17. Predict its:

   i state at 20 °C

   ii colour

   iii atomic radius.

Reactions of Group 17 elements

The halogen atoms need to gain just one more electron to achieve the stable electronic configuration of the noble gas atoms to the right of them in the Periodic Table. Therefore they react with metallic elements, with each of their atoms gaining an electron from a metal atom to become ions with a 1– charge. For example:

$$Ca(s) + Cl_2(g) \longrightarrow Ca^{2+}Cl^-_2(s)$$

When a halogen reacts with a metal atom, the halogen atom gains one electron. Because of this, the halogens are oxidising agents (electron acceptors). In the process of oxidising another substance they themselves are reduced. Their oxidation number is reduced from 0 in the element usually to –1 in the compound formed.

$$Cl_2 \longrightarrow 2Cl^- + 2e^-$$

oxidation number $\quad$ 0 $\qquad$ –1

The halogens also react with many non-metals, each halogen atom sharing a pair of electrons with the other non-metal atom in a covalent bond, e.g. in hydrogen chloride, HCl.

$$H_2(g) + Cl_2(g) \longrightarrow 2HCl(g)$$

The reactions of chlorine with calcium and with hydrogen shown here can be repeated with the other halogens. In these experiments we find that the reactions of fluorine are more vigorous than those of chlorine. Bromine reacts less vigorously than chlorine, and iodine is less reactive than bromine.

The halogens get less reactive going down Group 17.

This pattern in reactivity corresponds to the trend in electronegativity going down the group, shown in Table 12.2.

Halogen	Electronegativity
fluorine (F)	4.0
chlorine (Cl)	3.0
bromine (Br)	2.8
iodine (I)	2.5

Table 12.2 Electronegativity values of the halogens.

A fluorine atom has the strongest pull on the pair of electrons in a covalent bond, while an iodine atom has the weakest attraction for electrons. We can explain this by looking at the atomic radii data in Table 12.1. The fluorine atom is the smallest in the group. Its outer shell is nearer to the attractive force of the nucleus and an electron entering its outer shell will also experience the least shielding from the attraction of the positive nuclear charge. These factors outweigh the fact that fluorine's nuclear charge is only 9+ compared with iodine's 53+. Therefore fluorine is a much stronger oxidising agent (acceptor of electrons) than iodine.

DISPLACEMENT REACTIONS

We can also judge the reactivity (or the oxidising power) of the halogens by looking at their displacement reactions with other halide ions in solution.

> A more reactive halogen can displace a less reactive halogen from a halide solution of the less reactive halogen.

Let's look at an example. When chlorine water, $Cl_2(aq)$, is added to a solution of sodium bromide, containing $Br^-(aq)$ ions, the solution changes to a yellowish brown colour. The colour is caused by the presence of dissolved bromine molecules, $Br_2(aq)$, as found in bromine water. The displacement reaction that takes place is:

$$Cl_2(aq) + 2NaBr(aq) \longrightarrow 2NaCl(aq) + Br_2(aq)$$

We say that chlorine has displaced bromine from solution.

This is summarised in the ionic equation for this displacement reaction:

$$Cl_2(aq) + 2Br^-(aq) \longrightarrow 2Cl^-(aq) + Br_2(aq)$$

The chlorine atoms are more electronegative than bromine atoms so have a stronger tendency to form negatively charged ions.

Likewise, bromine will displace iodine from an iodide solution:

$$Br_2(aq) + 2NaI(aq) \longrightarrow 2NaBr(aq) + I_2(aq)$$

or as an ionic equation:

$$Br_2(aq) + 2I^-(aq) \longrightarrow 2Br^-(aq) + I_2(aq)$$

The colours of the halogen molecules in solution are difficult to identify positively in these displacement reactions. However, the halogens dissolve well in cyclohexane (which is immiscible in water, forming two separate layers). The halogens dissolved in cyclohexane are distinctly different colours. Therefore adding some of this organic solvent after mixing the halogen/halide solutions, shaking the mixture and then allowing it to settle into layers shows clearly which halogen is present as its diatomic molecules (Figure 12.3).

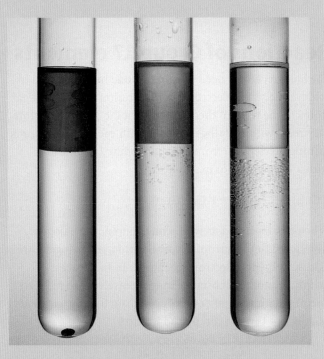

Figure 12.3 Cyclohexane forms a layer on top of water. Dissolved iodine is purple in this upper organic layer, bromine is orange and chlorine is very pale green.

Reactions with hydrogen

The halogens form hydrogen halides with hydrogen gas. One example of this is the reaction of hydrogen with chlorine to give hydrogen chloride (see page 173). The trend in reactivity is illustrated by their reactions (Table 12.3).

QUESTION

2 Chlorine water is mixed with a solution of potassium iodide in a test tube. $2\,cm^3$ of cyclohexane is added to the test tube, which is stoppered and shaken, then allowed to stand.

   a Write a balanced symbol equation, including state symbols, for the reaction that occurs.

   b Write an ionic equation for this reaction.

   c What colour is the cyclohexane layer at the end of the experiment?

174

Equation for reaction	Description of reaction
$H_2(g) + F_2(g) \longrightarrow 2HF(g)$	reacts explosively even in cool, dark conditions
$H_2(g) + Cl_2(g) \longrightarrow 2HCl(g)$	reacts explosively in sunlight
$H_2(g) + Br_2(g) \longrightarrow 2HBr(g)$	reacts slowly on heating
$H_2(g) + I_2(g) \rightleftharpoons 2HI(g)$	forms an equilibrium mixture on heating

Table 12.3 The reactions of hydrogen and the halogens, showing decreasing reactivity going down Group 17.

The hydrogen halides formed differ in their thermal stability. Hydrogen iodide can be decomposed by inserting a red-hot wire into a sample of hydrogen iodide gas. The purple fumes seen are iodine vapour:

$$2HI(g) \longrightarrow H_2(g) + I_2(g)$$

By contrast, hydrogen fluoride and hydrogen chloride are not decomposed in temperatures up to 1500 °C. Hydrogen bromide is not as stable as HF and HCl, but it is more resistant to decomposition than hydrogen iodide. At 430 °C in a closed container, 10% of a sample of HBr will decompose, whereas around 20% of HI decomposes at that temperature. We can explain this by looking at the bond energies of the hydrogen–halogen bonds (Table 12.4).

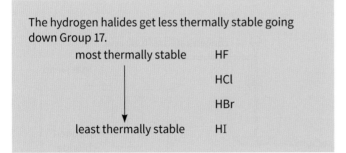

The hydrogen halides get less thermally stable going down Group 17.

most thermally stable   HF

HCl

HBr

least thermally stable   HI

Hydrogen–halogen bond	Bond energy / kJ mol^{-1}
H—F	562
H—Cl	431
H—Br	366
H—I	299

Table 12.4 Hydrogen–halogen bond energies.

As you can see in Table 12.4, the bond energies decrease going down Group 17, making it easier to break the hydrogen–halogen bond. This is because the iodine atom is the largest atom, so the overlap of its outer shell with a hydrogen atom gives a much longer bond length than with the other smaller halogen atoms. The longer the bond, the weaker it is, and the less energy required to break it. Hence HI is less thermally stable than HF.

QUESTION

3   a   Astatine (At) lies below iodine at the bottom of Group 17. Predict:
    i   the equation for its reaction with hydrogen
    ii   the vigour of its reaction with hydrogen
    iii   the thermal stability of its hydride.
  b   Explain why chlorine is a more powerful oxidising agent than bromine.

Reactions of the halide ions

In the following boxes, we consider the reactions of the ions formed by the halogens.

TESTING FOR HALIDE IONS

We can tell the halide ions, Cl$^-$(aq), Br$^-$(aq) and I$^-$(aq), apart by using simple chemical tests. If an unknown compound is dissolved in dilute nitric acid and silver nitrate solution is added, a precipitate will be formed if the unknown solution contains halide ions. The precipitate will be silver chloride (AgCl), silver bromide (AgBr) or silver iodide (AgI). Because these precipitates are similar in colour (see Figure 12.4), we can then add ammonia solution – dilute ammonia solution followed by concentrated ammonia solution – to verify the result. The results of the tests are shown in Table 12.5.

TESTING FOR HALIDE IONS (CONTINUED)

Figure 12.4 Colours of the silver halide precipitates: silver chloride (on the left), silver bromide and silver iodide (on the right).

The general equation for the precipitation reaction with silver nitrate solution is:

$$AgNO_3(aq) + X^-(aq) \longrightarrow AgX(s) + NO_3^-(aq)$$

where X^- represents the halide ion.

The aqueous nitrate ions can be left out to produce the ionic equation; they are spectator ions that do not get involved in the reaction:

$$Ag^+(aq) + X^-(aq) \longrightarrow AgX(s)$$

The added ammonia can form complex ions that are soluble:

- silver chloride forms complex ions with dilute ammonia
- silver bromide forms complex ions with concentrated ammonia.

Halide ion	Colour of silver halide precipitate on addition of silver nitrate solution	Effect on precipitate of adding dilute ammonia solution	Effect on precipitate of adding concentrated ammonia solution
chloride, Cl⁻(aq)	white	dissolves	dissolves
bromide, Br⁻(aq)	cream	remains insoluble	dissolves
iodide, I⁻(aq)	pale yellow	remains insoluble	remains insoluble

Table 12.5 The results of positive tests for halide ions.

Reactions of halide ions with concentrated sulfuric acid

Compounds that contain Cl^-, Br^- or I^- ions will react with concentrated sulfuric acid. All of these reactions produce one or more poisonous gases, so they must be performed with great care in a fume cupboard.

We can prepare hydrogen chloride gas by dropping concentrated sulfuric acid slowly onto crystals of sodium chloride (see the apparatus in Figure 12.5):

$$NaCl(s) + H_2SO_4(l) \longrightarrow NaHSO_4(s) + HCl(g)$$

The HCl produced is visible as white fumes.

However, we cannot use the same reaction to prepare samples of pure hydrogen bromide or hydrogen iodide. We saw on page 175 how it gets increasingly easy to decompose the hydrogen halides going down the group. When they decompose into their elements, the halide in HBr and HI is being oxidised. Concentrated sulfuric acid is a relatively strong oxidising agent. It is not strong enough to oxidise

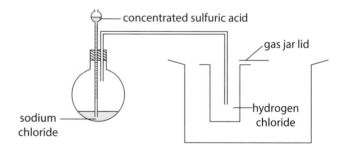

Figure 12.5 Preparing a sample of hydrogen chloride gas. The hydrogen chloride gas is denser than air so displaces the air from the gas jar as it collects.

HCl, but it will oxidise and decompose HBr and HI. So any HBr or HI formed in the reaction between sodium bromide, or sodium iodide, and concentrated sulfuric acid undergoes further reaction.

With sodium bromide, the sulfuric acid itself is reduced to sulfur dioxide gas as it oxidises the hydrogen bromide produced in the initial reaction:

$$NaBr(s) + H_2SO_4(l) \longrightarrow NaHSO_4(s) + HBr(g)$$

followed by oxidation of HBr(g):

$$2HBr(g) + H_2SO_4(l) \longrightarrow Br_2(g) + SO_2(g) + 2H_2O(l)$$

A reddish brown gas is seen; this is the element bromine.

With sodium iodide, the sulfuric acid is reduced to a variety of sulfur products as it oxidises the hydrogen iodide formed by different degrees. The products of the oxidation of HI are sulfur dioxide, sulfur and hydrogen sulfide, as shown in the reactions below:

$$NaI(s) + H_2SO_4(l) \longrightarrow NaHSO_4(s) + HI(g)$$

followed by oxidation of HI(g):

$$2HI(g) + H_2SO_4(l) \longrightarrow I_2(g) + SO_2(g) + 2H_2O(l)$$

and:

$$6HI(g) + H_2SO_4(l) \longrightarrow 3I_2(g) + S(s) + 4H_2O(l)$$

and:

$$8HI(g) + H_2SO_4(l) \longrightarrow 4I_2(g) + H_2S(g) + 4H_2O(l)$$

Several observations can be made here:

- sulfur is seen as a yellow solid
- hydrogen sulfide has a strong smell of bad eggs
- iodine is produced as a violet/purple vapour.

Therefore, a mixture of gases is produced when NaBr or NaI react with concentrated sulfuric acid, so this is not a good way to prepare a sample of the gases HBr or HI.

> It gets easier to oxidise the hydrogen halides going down Group 17.

QUESTION

4 a You suspect that a solid compound might be potassium bromide. Describe how you would test your idea and the positive results you would get if you were correct.

 b i What would you **see** in a test tube in which concentrated sulfuric acid is added dropwise to solid potassium iodide that you would **not** see if the acid was added to potassium chloride?

 ii Give equations to describe the reactions taking place in the test tube between concentrated sulfuric acid and potassium iodide.

Disproportionation

The element chlorine (Cl_2, oxidation number = 0) undergoes a type of redox reaction called **disproportionation** when it reacts with alkali. Disproportionation can be thought of as a 'self reduction/ oxidation' reaction. When chlorine reacts with dilute alkali some chlorine atoms are reduced and some are oxidised in the same reaction. The actual reaction that takes place depends on the temperature.

Chlorine in cold alkali (15 °C)

$$\underset{\text{sodium chlorate(I)}}{Cl_2(aq) + 2NaOH(aq) \longrightarrow NaCl(aq) + NaClO(aq) + H_2O(l)}$$

The ionic equation for the reaction is:

$$\underset{\substack{0 \\ \text{oxidation number of Cl}}}{Cl_2(aq)} + 2OH^-(aq) \longrightarrow \underset{-1}{Cl^-(aq)} + \underset{+1}{ClO^-(aq)} + H_2O(l)$$

The ionic equation for this redox reaction can be split into two half-equations, showing the reduction and oxidation.

- The **reduction** reaction (in which chlorine's oxidation number is reduced is):

$$\underset{\substack{\text{oxidation number of Cl} \quad 0}}{\tfrac{1}{2}Cl_2} + e^- \longrightarrow \underset{-1}{Cl^-}$$

- The **oxidation** reaction is:

$$\underset{\substack{\text{oxidation number of Cl} \quad 0}}{\tfrac{1}{2}Cl_2} + 2OH^- \longrightarrow \underset{+1}{ClO^-} + H_2O + e^-$$

Chlorine in hot alkali (70 °C)

When we add chlorine and hot concentrated aqueous sodium hydroxide a different disproportionation reaction takes place:

$$3Cl_2(aq) + 6NaOH(aq) \rightarrow 5NaCl(aq) + NaClO_3(aq) + 3H_2O(l)$$

177

178

QUESTION

5 a What type of reaction takes place between chlorine and hot aqueous sodium hydroxide?

b Write an ionic equation for the reaction of chlorine with hot aqueous sodium hydroxide.

c Write a half-equation to show the reduction reaction taking place in part **b**.

d Write a half-equation to show the oxidation reaction taking place in part **b**.

e Explain what happens in the reaction between chlorine and hot aqueous sodium hydroxide.

f Name the compound $NaClO_3$.

Uses of the halogens and their compounds

Chlorination of water

Adding a small amount of chlorine to a water supply will kill bacteria and make the water safer to drink. The chlorine undergoes disproportionation in water:

$$Cl_2(aq) + H_2O(l) \longrightarrow HCl(aq) + HClO(aq)$$

oxidation number of Cl: $0 \qquad -1 \qquad +1$

HClO is called chloric(I) acid. It decomposes slowly in solution. One theory suggests that it produces reactive oxygen atoms that can kill bacteria in water:

$$HClO \longrightarrow HCl + [O]$$

Bleach

Bleach is an equal mixture of sodium chloride (NaCl) and sodium chlorate(I) (NaClO), made from chlorine and cold alkali. It 'bleaches' colours and stains because oxygen atoms from the chlorate(I) ions oxidise dye and other coloured molecules. They also kill bacteria when toilets are cleaned with bleach (see Figure 12.6).

Figure 12.6 The reaction: $Cl_2(aq) + 2NaOH(aq)$ $\longrightarrow NaCl(aq) + NaClO(aq) + H_2O(l)$ is used in industry to produce bleach. The bleaching agent is the chlorate(I) ion.

Other uses

The halogens are found in many organic compounds such as the plastic PVC (poly(choroethene) or polyvinyl chloride) and halogenated hydrocarbons used as solvents, refrigerants and in aerosols. For more details see 'Uses of halogenoalkanes' on pages 222–3.

Summary

- The halogens chlorine, bromine and iodine exist as covalent diatomic molecules. They become increasingly less volatile and more deeply coloured on descending Group 17. The volatility decreases as van der Waals' forces between molecules increase.

- All the halogens are oxidising agents. Fluorine is the strongest oxidising agent and iodine is the weakest.

- The reactivity of the halogens decreases on descending the group.

- It gets easier to oxidise the hydrogen halides going down Group 17 as the strength of the hydrogen–halogen bond decreases.

- Chlorine reacts with cold hydroxide ions in a disproportionation ('self reduction-oxidation') reaction. This reaction produces commercial bleach.

- A different disproportionation reaction takes place between chlorine and hot alkali, producing NaCl(aq), $NaClO_3(aq)$ and water.

- The halogens all have important industrial uses, especially chlorine, which is used in the manufacture of many other useful products. Possibly the most important use of chlorine is in the prevention of disease by chlorination of water supplies.

End-of-chapter questions

You will need a copy of the Periodic Table (see page 473) to answer some of these questions.

1 a What is the molecular formula of bromine? [1]

  b Put the elements bromine, chlorine and iodine in order of boiling point, starting with the lowest. [2]

  c Explain the reasons for the trend described in part **b**. [2]

                                                  Total = 5

2 a Which of these mixtures will result in a chemical reaction?

    i bromine solution and sodium chloride solution [1]

    ii iodine solution and sodium bromide solution [1]

    iii chlorine solution and potassium bromide solution [1]

    iv bromine solution and sodium iodide solution [1]

  b Write a balanced chemical equation for each reaction that occurs in part **a**. [4]

  c What type of reaction occurs in part **a**? [1]

  d What trend do the reactions in part **a** show us? [1]

  e For one of the reactions that occurs in part **a**, identify the substance oxidised and the substance reduced. [2]

  f For one of the reactions that occurs in part **a**, rewrite the equation as an ionic equation. [1]

  g Chlorine is a stronger oxidising agent than bromine. Explain why. [2]

                                                  Total = 15

3 a Complete the equations below, including state symbols.

    i $AgNO_3(aq) + NaCl(aq) \longrightarrow \ldots$ [2]

    ii $AgNO_3(aq) + NaBr(aq) \longrightarrow \ldots$ [2]

    iii $AgNO_3(aq) + NaI(aq) \longrightarrow \ldots$ [2]

  b What would you observe in each reaction in part **a**? [4]

  c What would you observe in each case if dilute ammonia solution were subsequently added? [1]

  d What would you observe in each case if concentrated ammonia solution were subsequently added? [1]

                                                  Total = 12

4 a For the reaction of chlorine with water:

    i write a balanced chemical equation [2]

    ii give the oxidation numbers of chlorine before and after the reaction [3]

    iii give one use for the process. [1]

  b For the reaction of chlorine with cold dilute aqueous sodium hydroxide:

    i write a balanced chemical equation [2]

    ii give the oxidation numbers of chlorine before and after the reaction [3]

    iii give one use for the process. [1]

  c What name is given to the type of reaction in parts **a** and **b**? [1]

                                                  Total = 13

Chapter 13:
Nitrogen and sulfur

Learning outcomes

You should be able to:

- describe and explain:
  - the lack of reactivity of nitrogen gas
  - the basicity of ammonia (also see Chapter 8, page 130), and the formation and structure of the ammonium ion
  - the displacement of ammonia from its salts
- state the industrial importance of ammonia and nitrogen compounds derived from ammonia
- state and explain:
  - the environmental consequences of the uncontrolled use of nitrate fertilisers

- the natural and man-made occurrences of oxides of nitrogen and their catalytic removal from the exhaust gases of internal combustion engines
- why atmospheric oxides of nitrogen are pollutants, including their catalytic role in the oxidation of atmospheric sulfur dioxide (see also Chapter 9, page 144)
- describe the formation of sulfur dioxide gas from sulfur-contaminated fossil fuel, its role in the formation of acid rain and how acid rain affects the environment.

Introduction

The Group 15 element nitrogen makes up nearly four-fifths of the atmosphere on Earth. Nitrogen is a vital element in many of the processes of life, but as a pure gas it is unreactive. For this reason, nitrogen gas helps to prevent explosions when crude oil is pumped into or out of super-tankers, when the volatile fuel vapours can mix with oxygen from the air.

Sulfur is a Group 16 element that is mined for the production of sulfuric(VI) acid, one of the most important industrial chemicals, used in the manufacture of paints, dyes, plastics and fibres.

181

Figure 13.1 a Nitrogen gas is used in the hold of oil tankers above the crude oil as it is pumped ashore. This unreactive gas helps to prevent the chance of an explosive mixture of crude oil vapour and air forming inside the tanker. **b** Sulfur can be mined from underground deposits by pumping down super-heated water to melt the sulfur (it melts at about 115 °C). The molten sulfur is then forced to the surface under pressure and allowed to solidify back into a brittle, yellow solid. The 'crown-shaped' sulfur molecules, S_8, can pack together in regular patterns, forming crystals.

Nitrogen gas

Nitrogen is in Group 15 of the Periodic Table. It is a non-metallic element that makes up about 78% of the Earth's atmosphere. It exists as diatomic molecules, N_2. Nitrogen gas is the unreactive gas in air that dilutes the effects of the reactive gas, oxygen. To understand the lack of reactivity of nitrogen gas, we have to look at the bonding within its molecules.

The electronic configuration of a nitrogen atom is $1s^2 2s^2 2p^3$. Its atoms need to gain three electrons to achieve the noble gas configuration of neon. Nitrogen atoms do this by forming a triple covalent bond between two atoms (see Figure 13.2).

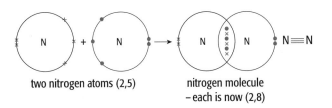

two nitrogen atoms (2,5)   nitrogen molecule – each is now (2,8)

Figure 13.2 The bonding in a nitrogen molecule, N_2.

The triple covalent bond is very strong; its bond energy is almost $1000\,kJ\,mol^{-1}$. It is difficult to break and so nitrogen gas will only react under extreme conditions. For example, the nitrogen and oxygen in the air react together during

Figure 13.3 Nitrogen oxides are formed when lightning strikes.

thunderstorms. Lightning provides the activation energy needed for this reaction to occur (Figure 13.3):

$$N_2(g) + O_2(g) \longrightarrow 2NO(g)$$
$$\text{nitrogen(II) oxide}$$

The nitrogen(II) oxide formed is further oxidised by oxygen in the air to give nitrogen(IV) oxide, NO_2.

$$2NO(g) + O_2(g) \longrightarrow 2NO_2(g)$$
$$\text{nitrogen(IV) oxide}$$

Nitrogen(IV) oxide dissolves in water droplets and forms nitric acid, which falls to earth in rain. This is a vital part of the natural nitrogen cycle:

$$2NO_2(g) + H_2O(l) + \tfrac{1}{2}O_2(g) \longrightarrow 2HNO_3(aq)$$
$$\text{nitric acid}$$

In this way, nitrogen gets into the soil in a soluble form that plants can absorb. They use the nitrate ions, NO_3^-, to make the proteins essential for growth.

Ammonia and ammonium compounds

Ammonia is a very important compound of nitrogen. It is an alkaline gas whose formula is NH_3. In industry it is made on a large scale in the Haber process (for details of the process see Chapter 8, page YY).

$$N_2(g) + 3H_2(g) \overset{Fe}{\rightleftharpoons} 2NH_3(g)$$
$$\text{nitrogen} \quad \text{hydrogen} \qquad \text{ammonia}$$

The bonding in ammonia is shown in Figure 13.4. You learned why the presence of a lone pair of electrons on

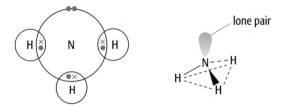

Figure 13.4 A dot-and-cross diagram showing the covalent bonding in an ammonia molecule and its pyramidal shape.

the nitrogen atom causes ammonia molecules to have a pyramidal shape on page 56.

You have also learnt that nitrogen's lone pair can be donated to an H^+ ion from an acid, forming a co-ordinate (or dative) covalent bond (see page 53). Ammonia is acting as a base in this reaction (because it is accepting an H^+ ion):

$$NH_3(aq) + H^+(aq) \longrightarrow NH_4^+(aq)$$
$$\text{ammonium ion}$$

Ammonium compounds are very important fertilisers. Nitrogen is removed from the soil as nitrates are absorbed through the roots when plants are growing. When crops are harvested by farmers the nitrogen is not replaced, as the plants do not die naturally and rot back into the soil. So farmers use ammonium compounds to replace this nitrogen in the soil. Common ammonium salts used in fertilisers include ammonium chloride, NH_4Cl, ammonium nitrate, NH_4NO_3, ammonium phosphate, $(NH_4)_3PO_4$, and ammonium sulfate, $(NH_4)_2SO_4$.

If we heat an ammonium salt with a base, the ammonium ion produces ammonia gas. We use this reaction to prepare ammonia gas in the laboratory. Ammonium chloride and calcium hydroxide, both in the solid state, are usually mixed then heated (see the apparatus in Figure 13.5).

$$2NH_4Cl(s) + Ca(OH)_2(s) \overset{heat}{\longrightarrow} CaCl_2(s) + 2H_2O(l) + 2NH_3(g)$$

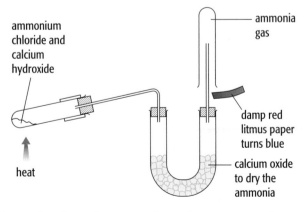

Figure 13.5 Preparing ammonia gas from an ammonium salt, NH_4Cl, and a base, $Ca(OH)_2$.

This reaction is used as the basis of the test for ammonium ions. If an unknown compound contains NH_4^+ ions it will give off ammonia when heated with a base. The ammonia given off is the only common alkaline gas. It turns red litmus blue.

Uses of ammonia and ammonium compounds

Farmers harvest crops to provide the world with food. Each year millions of tonnes of fertilisers are spread onto fields to replace the nitrogen and other plant nutrients lost from the soil. About 85% of the millions of tonnes of ammonia produced each year in the Haber process are used to make fertilisers. A relatively small amount of ammonia itself is used as fertiliser, mainly in the USA. This is injected into the soil. However, the vast majority of ammonia is reacted with acids to make solid ammonium salts.

The major nitrogen-based fertiliser is ammonium nitrate, NH_4NO_3. This is manufactured from ammonia and nitric acid:

$$NH_3(aq) + HNO_3(aq) \longrightarrow NH_4NO_3(aq)$$

The ammonium nitrate solution is heated to evaporate off the water and melt the solid. The molten solid is then sprayed into a tower with air blown into it. This solidifies the ammonium nitrate into pellets, which makes it convenient for farmers to spread from tractors (Figure 13.6). Ammonium sulfate, $(NH_4)_2SO_4$, and ammonium phosphate, $(NH_4)_3PO_4$, are other ammonium salts used in fertilisers.

The nitric acid used to make ammonium nitrate is itself made from ammonia in another chemical process. Fertiliser factories making ammonium nitrate often have three plants side by side, making:

- ammonia in the Haber process
- nitric acid from ammonia
- ammonium nitrate from nitric acid and ammonia.

Figure 13.6 Ammonium nitrate is spread as pellets onto the soil.

Concentrated nitric acid has other important uses. It is used to make many types of explosive, such as trinitrotoluene (TNT). About 10% of ammonium nitrate is used to make explosives. Nitric acid is also needed in the manufacture of detergents, paints, pigments, dyes and nylon.

Environmental problems caused by nitrogen compounds

Nitrate fertilisers

In order to work, nitrogen-based fertilisers, mainly ammonium nitrate and potassium nitrate (KNO_3), must be soluble in water. This has created an environmental problem. The nitrates can be washed, or leached, out of the soil by rain into groundwater. These can then find their way into rivers and lakes. Once in the rivers and lakes, the nitrates promote the growth of the water plants, which can 'strangle' a river. But the biggest problem is the growth of algae (a simple water plant) on the surface, causing **eutrophication** (Figure 13.7).

Figure 13.7 Fertilisers leached from farmland have caused eutrophication in this river.

- A bloom of algae can spread across the surface, blocking out the light for other plant life in the water.
- When the plants and algae die, bacteria in the water feed on them, decomposing the plant material.
- The bacteria multiply rapidly with so much food available, using up the dissolved oxygen in the water.
- Fish extract dissolved oxygen from water, taken in through their gills. Without this dissolved oxygen they die, affecting the whole ecosystem.

This isn't the only problem with fertilisers being leached from the soil. Nitrates have also been detected in our drinking water, especially in agricultural areas. People are worried that nitrates in drinking water cause 'blue baby' syndrome (when a newborn baby's blood is starved of oxygen), as well as stomach cancer. But others argue that links between nitrates and diseases have not been proven and that recommended nitrate levels are set unrealistically low.

Farmers can help limit the amount of nitrates in water courses by adding the most economical amounts of fertilisers at the right time of year. This will minimise the leaching of excess fertiliser from the soil and into our rivers and lakes.

Nitrogen oxides in the atmosphere

At the start of this chapter we saw how unreactive nitrogen gas is. However, in the extreme conditions in a thunderstorm, lightning can trigger the reaction between nitrogen and oxygen to form gaseous nitrogen oxides – nitrogen(II) oxide, NO and nitrogen(IV) oxide, NO_2. A similar oxidation of nitrogen takes place inside a car engine. In the engine's cylinders a mixture of air

(mainly nitrogen plus oxygen) and fuel is compressed and ignited by a spark. Under these conditions (high pressure and high temperature) nitrogen forms nitrogen oxides. These are released into the atmosphere in the car's exhaust fumes.

Nitrogen oxides are pollutants. They cause acid rain and photochemical smog. Nitrogen oxides also catalyse the oxidation of sulfur dioxide gas, SO_2, in the atmosphere during the formation of acid rain. The sulfur trioxide, SO_3, gas that is produced by this oxidation reacts with rainwater, forming sulfuric acid. The reactions below show the catalytic activity of the nitrogen oxides:

$$SO_2(g) + NO_2(g) \longrightarrow SO_3(g) + NO(g)$$

Then NO_2 is regenerated as NO reacts with oxygen in the air:

$$NO(g) + \tfrac{1}{2}O_2(g) \longrightarrow NO_2(g)$$

This NO_2 molecule can then go on to oxidise another sulfur dioxide molecule, at the same time producing an NO molecule to make another NO_2 molecule. This will oxidise another sulfur dioxide molecule, and so on. Therefore NO_2 catalyses the oxidation of SO_2.

Nowadays, car exhaust systems are fitted with catalytic converters to help reduce the pollutants from motor vehicles (see page 205). The reaction on the surface of the hot catalyst (e.g. platinum) reduces the nitrogen oxides to harmless nitrogen gas, which is released from the vehicle's exhaust pipe.

$$2CO(g) + 2NO(g) \longrightarrow 2CO_2(g) + N_2(g)$$

QUESTION

3   **a** Why is ammonia so important in providing enough food to feed the world?

  b Give one environmental problem and one possible health problem associated with nitrate fertilisers.

  c Explain how nitrogen oxides are involved in the formation of atmospheric sulfur trioxide (SO_3).

  d The following reaction takes place in a car's catalytic converter once it is warmed up:

$$2CO(g) + 2NO(g) \longrightarrow 2CO_2(g) + N_2(g)$$

  Use oxidation numbers to explain which species is reduced and which is oxidised in the reaction.

Sulfur and its oxides

We have just seen how sulfur dioxide in the atmosphere can be oxidised by nitrogen(IV) oxide to form sulfur(VI) oxide (also known as sulfur trioxide). This reacts with water to form sulfuric acid, which is the main cause of acid rain.

$$SO_3(g) + H_2O(l) \longrightarrow H_2SO_4(aq)$$

The sulfur dioxide is formed when we burn fossil fuels, especially coal. Crude oil, natural gas and coal have sulfur compounds present in them as impurities. When the fossil fuels (or fuels extracted from them, such as petrol or diesel) are burnt, the sulfur impurities get oxidised to sulfur dioxide. There are also large volumes of sulfur dioxide released naturally from volcanic activity.

Acid rain has harmful effects on:

- plants (especially trees)
- rivers, streams and lakes (and the fish and other animals in these habitats)
- buildings, statues (Figure 13.8) and metal structures.

Figure 13.8 This limestone carving has been chemically weathered by acid rain.

The acid rain leaches (washes out) nutrients from the soil, and so prevents the healthy growth of plants. Not only that, the acid rain can attack the waxy layer on leaves. This increases water loss and makes the plant more susceptible to disease and pests. Trees that grow at high altitudes are especially vulnerable, as they are often in contact with the tiny droplets of water (sulfuric acid solution) in clouds.

Acid rain falling into streams, rivers and lakes will lower the pH of the water. Many aquatic animals are very sensitive to changes in pH. Many insect larvae cannot survive even slight increases in acidity. Other animals higher up the food chain may be more resistant, but their numbers will decrease as their food source dies off.

In our cities, the acid rain attacks buildings and statues, especially those made from carbonate rock. The most common of these is limestone, containing calcium carbonate. The main metal used in construction, iron in the form of steel, is also corroded by acid rain.

Chemists have found ways to reduce sulfur dioxide emissions from fossil fuels. They now produce 'low-sulfur' versions of petrol and diesel. In power stations that burn fossil fuels, the sulfur is removed from the fuel before burning. Alternatively sulfur dioxide can be removed from the waste gases before they are released to the atmosphere through tall chimneys.

> **QUESTION**
>
> **4 a** Write a balanced equation, including state symbols, showing the formation of sulfuric acid from atmospheric sulfur trioxide, SO_3.
> **b** List three consequences of acid rain.

Sulfuric acid

Sulfuric(VI) acid, H_2SO_4, is one of the most important manufactured chemicals. It has been said that the amount of sulfuric acid used by a country is one of the best indicators of how well developed it is.

The chemical industry makes sulfuric acid in the Contact process (page 129). The raw materials needed are sulfur, air and water. Sulfur can be mined from underground (see Figure 13.1b at the start of this chapter). Poland and the USA export sulfur around the world. The sulfur extracted from the impurities in fossil fuels can also be used in the Contact process.

Like nitric acid, sulfuric acid is used to manufacture fertilisers, detergents, paints, pigments, dyes and synthetic fibres. It is also used to make various chemicals and plastics, as well as being used in car batteries, tanning leather and cleaning metal surfaces ('pickling').

Summary

■ Nitrogen, N_2, is a very unreactive gas because of the high bond energy of the $N\equiv N$ triple bond.

■ Ammonia, NH_3, is a common compound of nitrogen. An ammonia molecule can act as a base, accepting an H^+ ion to form an ammonium ion, NH_4^+.

■ Ammonia is manufactured in the Haber process (see page 129):

$$N_2(g) + 3H_2(g) \xrightarrow{\text{Fe}} 2NH_3(g)$$
$$\text{nitrogen} \quad \text{hydrogen} \qquad \text{ammonia}$$

■ Most ammonia is used to make ammonium salts in neutralisation reactions with different acids. The salts, such as ammonium nitrate, NH_4NO_3, are used as fertilisers,

■ Excess fertiliser can be leached out of soils into rivers and lakes, where it causes eutrophication, killing aquatic life.

■ Nitrogen oxides are formed naturally during lightning strikes, when nitrogen gas is oxidised. These gaseous oxides are also formed in internal combustion engines and become pollutants in the atmosphere, contributing to acid rain.

■ Sulfur can be mined as the element and is used as a raw material for manufacturing sulfuric acid in the Contact process (see page 129).

■ Sulfur dioxide is the main cause of acid rain. Its oxidation to sulfur trioxide is catalysed by oxides of nitrogen.

■ Acid rain causes the death of aquatic wildlife in rivers and lakes, kills trees and damages buildings and other structures.

End-of-chapter questions

1 Ammonia is made in the Haber process.

a What is the formula of ammonia? [1]

b Write a balanced equation for the formation of ammonia from nitrogen and hydrogen in the Haber process. [1]

c Give three uses of ammonia. [3]

d Give the formulae of the following ammonium salts:

   i ammonium chloride [1]

   ii ammonium nitrate [1]

   iii ammonium sulfate [1]

e Ammonium chloride reacts with calcium hydroxide when heated to produce ammonia gas.

   i Is this reaction carried out using solids or solutions? [1]

   ii Write the balanced equation for this reaction. [1]

Total = 10

2   The reaction

$$2SO_2(g) + O_2(g) \rightleftharpoons 2SO_3(g)$$

reaches dynamic equilibrium. The forward reaction is exothermic. The reaction is catalysed by vanadium(V) oxide, V_2O_5. You are given a vessel containing all three gases at equilibrium.

a   What will happen to the position of equilibrium if:

  i   you add more oxygen to the vessel?   [1]

  ii   you remove some sulfur trioxide from the vessel?   [1]

  iii the pressure in the vessel is lowered?   [1]

  iv   more V_2O_5 is added?   [1]

  v   the temperature in the vessel is increased?   [1]

b   i   Give three uses of sulfuric acid.   [3]

  ii   Why is it important that as little sulfur dioxide as possible is released into the atmosphere when sulfuric acid is manufactured?   [1]

  iii Explain, including a balanced equation, how sulfur dioxide enters the atmosphere from a coal-fired power station.   [3]

Total = 12

Chapter 14:
Introduction to organic chemistry

Learning outcomes

You should be able to:

- interpret, name and use the general, structural, displayed and skeletal formulae of the alkanes, alkenes, halogenoalkanes, alcohols (including primary, secondary and tertiary), aldehydes, ketones, carboxylic acids, esters, amines (primary only) and nitriles

- understand and use the following terminology associated with organic reactions:
    - functional group
    - homolytic and heterolytic fission
    - free radical, initiation, propagation, termination
    - nucleophile, electrophile
    - addition, substitution, elimination, hydrolysis, condensation
    - oxidation and reduction

- describe and explain the shape of, and bond angles in, the ethane and ethene molecules in terms of σ and π bonds and predict the shapes of, and bond angles in, other related molecules

- describe and explain the different types of structural isomerism and stereoisomerism.

Introduction

Living things are made of atoms covalently bonded to form molecules of organic compounds. All these molecules are based on carbon compounds. The complexity of life requires a great variety of different compounds. The great variety of organic compounds is possible because every carbon atom can bond with other carbon atoms to form chains and rings. These chains and rings are often found bonded to atoms of other elements, such as hydrogen, oxygen and nitrogen. This explains the millions of organic compounds that exist.

Note that not all carbon compounds are classified as organic compounds. The oxides of carbon and compounds containing carbonate and hydrogencarbonate ions are classed as inorganic compounds.

Figure 14.1 The substances that form the basis of all living things are organic compounds. Carbon atoms tend to form the 'backbone' of organic molecules – from the proteins in muscles and enzymes to the DNA (see above) that determines our characteristics.

Representing organic molecules

Figure 14.2 shows two types of three-dimensional (3D) diagram representing a selection of organic molecules. Chemists use various types of model for different purposes. The compounds shown are called **hydrocarbons**. Hydrocarbons are compounds of carbon and hydrogen only.

The colours used in the modelling of molecules are shown in Table 14.1.

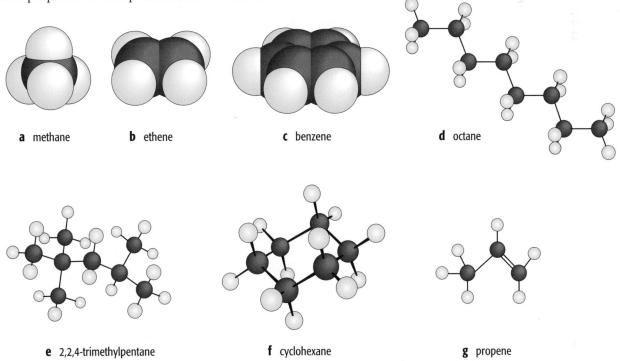

a methane **b** ethene **c** benzene **d** octane

e 2,2,4-trimethylpentane **f** cyclohexane **g** propene

Figure 14.2 Examples of the variety of hydrocarbons. **a–c** These hydrocarbons are shown as space-filling models. Such models show the region of space occupied by the atoms and the surrounding electrons. **d–g** These hydrocarbons are shown as ball-and-stick models, which enable bonds between atoms to be seen clearly.

Colour	Atom/electron cloud
white	hydrogen
dark grey	carbon
red	oxygen
blue	nitrogen
yellow-green	fluorine
green	chlorine
orange-brown	bromine
brown	phosphorus
violet	iodine
pale yellow	sulfur
yellow ochre	boron
pink	lone pair electron clouds
green	π-bond electron clouds

Table 14.1 Colours used in molecular modelling in this text.

We can represent organic molecules by a variety of different types of formula.

The **empirical formula** gives us the least detail. It tells us the simplest ratio of the different types of atoms present in the molecule. For example, an organic compound called propene has the empirical formula CH_2. This tells us that it has twice as many hydrogen atoms as carbon atoms in its molecules. We can calculate empirical formulae from experimental data on the mass of each element, and hence the number of moles of each element, in a sample of a compound.

The **molecular formula** shows us the actual numbers of each type of atom in a molecule. To find this we need to know the relative molecular mass of the compound. The relative molecular mass of propene is 42. We know that its empirical formula is CH_2; this CH_2 group of atoms has a relative mass of 14, as the relative atomic mass of C = 12 and H = 1. By dividing the relative molecular mass by the relative mass of the empirical formula (42/14 = 3), we see that there must be ($3 \times CH_2$) atoms in a propene molecule. So its molecular formula is C_3H_6.

Chemists can give more detail about a molecule by giving its **structural formula**. This tells us about the atoms bonded to each carbon atom in the molecule. The structural formula of propene is $CH_3HC{=}CH_2$ (also written as $CH_3CH{=}CH_2$ – but the central H atom does not form a double bond!). This tells us how many hydrogen atoms are bonded to each carbon atom, and that two of the carbon atoms in the molecule are joined by a double bond. Carbon–carbon double bonds are shown in a structural formula. However, **all the bonds** within a molecule are shown in its **displayed formula**. We can think of this

representation as a 2D, or flattened, version of the 'ball-and-stick' models shown in Figure 14.2. The displayed formula of propene is shown in Figure 14.3.

Figure 14.3 The displayed formula of propene, showing all the bonds in the molecule.

A simplified version of the displayed formula is called the **skeletal formula**. It has all the symbols for carbon and hydrogen atoms removed, as well as the carbon to hydrogen bonds. The carbon to carbon bonds are left in place. Figure 14.4 shows the skeletal formula of propene.

Figure 14.4 The skeletal formula of propene.

All other atoms that are not carbon or hydrogen, and their bonds, are included in the skeletal formula of an organic molecule. The displayed and skeletal formulae of an alcohol called butan-2-ol are shown in Figure 14.5. Notice that the H atom in an OH group is included in a skeletal formula.

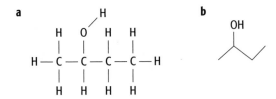

Figure 14.5 a The displayed formula of butan-2-ol; **b** the skeletal formula of butan-2-ol.

The 'zig-zag' in the carbon chain shown in a skeletal formula can be seen in the 3D representations of hydrocarbons in Figure 14.2. You will see more detailed 3D displayed formulae later in this chapter, when we look at optical isomers (see page 195). Figure 14.6 shows the 3D displayed formula of butan-2-ol.

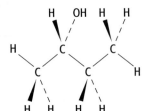

the 'wedge' bond is sticking out of the plane of the paper and the 'dashed-line' bond is sticking into the plane of the paper

Figure 14.6 The 3D displayed formula of butan-2-ol.

190

With complex molecules, chemists sometimes find it useful to combine structural and skeletal formulae when representing a molecule. The molecule of cholesterol shown in Figure 14.7 is one such example.

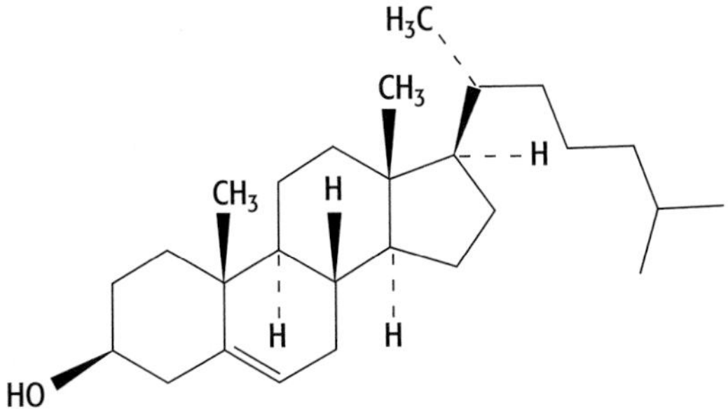

Figure 14.7 A useful way of combining structural and skeletal formulae.

1 a i On analysis a hydrocarbon was found to contain 0.72 g of carbon and 0.18 g of hydrogen. What is the empirical formula of the hydrocarbon?

   ii Further investigation showed that the relative molecular mass of the hydrocarbon was 30. What is its molecular formula?

 b A compound contains the elements carbon, hydrogen and oxygen. Its empirical formula is CH_2O and its relative molecular mass is 60. What is the molecular formula of the compound?

2 Draw the displayed formula of:

 a ethene (molecular formula C_2H_4)

 b propane (molecular formula C_3H_8).

3 a Draw the skeletal formula of pentane, a straight-chain hydrocarbon with a molecular formula of C_5H_{12}.

 b Draw the structural formulae of the molecules shown in Figure 14.2, parts **d**, **e** and **f**.

Structure of functional group	General formula	Name of an example	Structural formula of the example
alkenes, 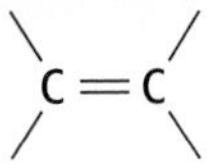 $\diagdown C=C \diagup$	C_nH_{2n}	ethene	$CH_2{=}CH_2$
arenes, 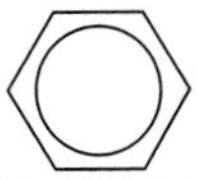 ⬡	$C_6H_5{-}$	benzene	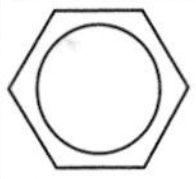 ⬡
halogenoalkanes, $-$X, where X = F, Cl, Br, I	$C_nH_{2n+1}X$	chloromethane	CH_3Cl
alcohols, $-$OH	$C_nH_{2n+1}OH$	methanol	CH_3OH
aldehydes, 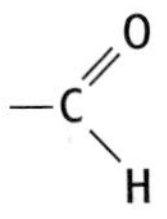 $-C\underset{H}{\overset{O}{\diagup}}$	$C_nH_{2n+1}CHO$	ethanal	CH_3CHO
ketones, 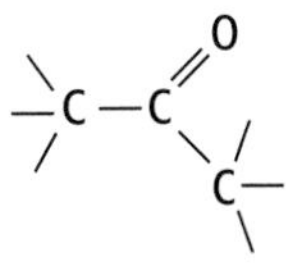 $\diagdown C-C\diagdown$	$C_nH_{2n+1}COC_mH_{2m+1}$	propanone	CH_3COCH_3
carboxylic acids, 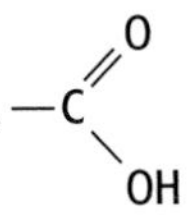 $-C\underset{OH}{\overset{O}{\diagup}}$	$C_nH_{2n+1}COOH$	ethanoic acid	CH_3COOH
esters, 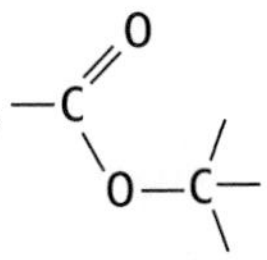 $-C\underset{O-C}{\overset{O}{\diagup}}$	$C_nH_{2n+1}COOC_mH_{2m+1}$	ethyl ethanoate	$CH_3COOC_2H_5$
amines, $-NH_2$	$C_nH_{2n+1}NH_2$	methylamine	CH_3NH_2
nitriles, $-C{\equiv}N$	$C_nH_{2n+1}CN$	ethanenitrile	CH_3CN

Table 14.2 Some common functional groups.

Functional groups

There are many classes of organic compound, some of which are shown in Table 14.2. Within a class of compounds all the compounds consist of molecules with a particular atom, or grouping of atoms, called a **functional group**. Different classes of compounds have different functional groups. The functional group determines the characteristic chemical properties of the compounds that contain that specific functional group. The functional group in an alkene is the C=C double bond. The functional group in a carboxylic acid is the —COOH group.

The **general formula** of the class of compounds is given in Table 14.2. By substituting a number for n in the general formula you get the molecular formula of a particular compound containing that functional group. Note that this formula assumes there is just one functional group present in the molecule.

Naming organic compounds

Chemists have a system of naming organic compounds that can be applied consistently. This means that they can communicate with each other clearly when referring to organic compounds.

The class of hydrocarbons called alkanes provide the basis of the naming system. The stem of each name indicates how many carbon atoms are in the longest chain in one molecule of the compound. Table 14.3 shows the names of the first ten alkanes and the stems used in naming other molecules.

Number of carbon atoms	Molecular formula of straight-chain alkane	Name of alkane	Stem used in naming
1	CH_4	methane	meth-
2	C_2H_6	ethane	eth-
3	C_3H_8	propane	prop-
4	C_4H_{10}	butane	but-
5	C_5H_{12}	pentane	pent-
6	C_6H_{14}	hexane	hex-
7	C_7H_{16}	heptane	hept-
8	C_8H_{18}	octane	oct-
9	C_9H_{20}	nonane	non-
10	$C_{10}H_{22}$	decane	dec-

Table 14.3 The stems used in naming simple organic compounds that contain a hydrocarbon chain.

The position of side-chains or functional groups is indicated by numbering the carbon atoms in the longest chain. The numbering starts at the end that produces the lowest possible numbers in the name (Figure 14.8).

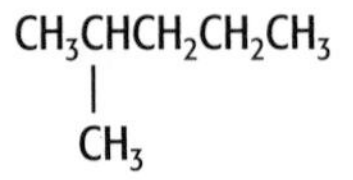

$$CH_3CHCH_2CH_2CH_3$$
$$|$$
$$CH_3$$

Figure 14.8 This is called 2-methylpentane, not 4-methylpentane.

Note that the hydrocarbon side-chain is named by adding –yl to the normal alkane stem, in this case a methyl group. This type of group is called an alkyl group. If there is more than one of the same alkyl side-chain or functional group we indicate how many by inserting di (for two), tri (for three) or tetra (for four) in front of its name. Figure 14.9 shows an example.

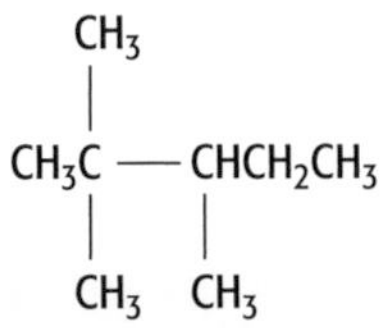

$$CH_3$$
$$|$$
$$CH_3C — CHCH_2CH_3$$
$$|\quad\quad|$$
$$CH_3\quad CH_3$$

Figure 14.9 This is 2,2,3-trimethylpentane.

Note that adjacent numbers in a name have a comma between them, whereas numbers and words are separated by hyphens.

If there is more than one type of alkyl side-chain, they are listed in the name in alphabetical order (Figure 14.10). The alkyl groups appear in its name in alphabetical order.

$$CH_2CH_3$$
$$|$$
$$CH_3CHCHCH_2CH_3$$
$$|$$
$$CH_3$$

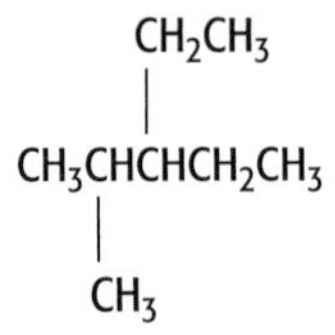

Figure 14.10 This is 3-ethyl-2-methylpentane.

QUESTION

4 **a** Draw the displayed formula of:

  i 2-methylbutane

  ii 3,5-diethylheptane

  iii 2,4,6-trimethyloctane.

  b What is the name of the following hydrocarbon?

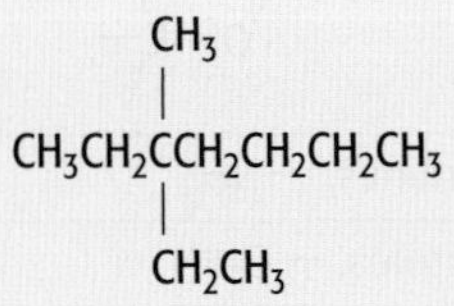

$$CH_3$$
$$|$$
$$CH_3CH_2CCH_2CH_2CH_2CH_3$$
$$|$$
$$CH_2CH_3$$

In Table 14.2 we saw the names of compounds with common functional groups. We also use the numbering system where necessary to indicate the position of the functional group in a molecule. For some functional groups no number is needed because the group can only be positioned at the end of a chain. Examples of this include carboxylic acids, such as butanoic acid, and aldehydes, such as pentanal.

As well as alkyl groups, you also have to recognise aryl groups. Aryl compounds contain at least one benzene ring. A benzene molecule has six carbon atoms arranged in a hexagon, with each carbon atom bonded to one hydrogen atom. Figure 14.11 shows the displayed and skeletal formulae of benzene.

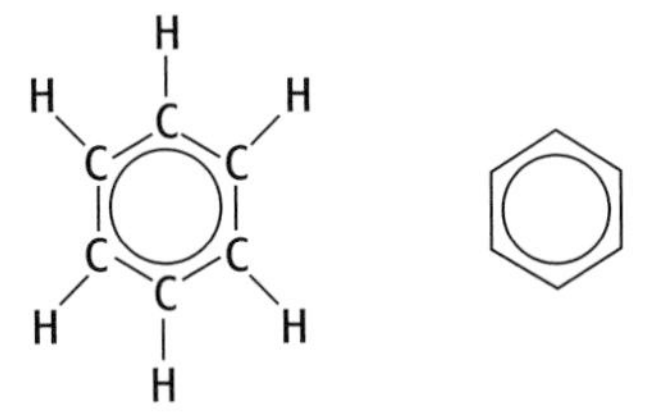

displayed formula   skeletal formula

Figure 14.11 Ways of representing benzene.

If only one alkyl group is bonded to a benzene ring, we do not have to include a number in the name as all six carbon atoms in the ring are equivalent. However, at A level, you will learn that with two or more alkyl groups we need to indicate their positions, as shown in Figure 14.12. (You do not need to recall this numbering for AS level.)

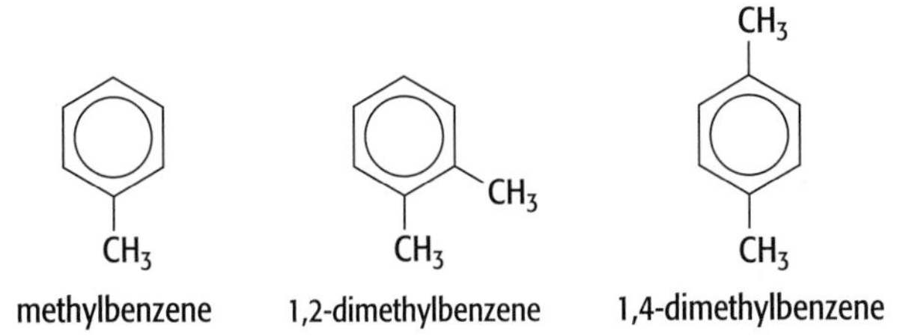

methylbenzene   1,2-dimethylbenzene   1,4-dimethylbenzene

Figure 14.12 Naming aryl compounds.

QUESTION

5   Draw the displayed formula of:

   a   propylbenzene

   b   1-ethyl-4-methylbenzene

   c   1,3,5-triethylbenzene,

       using the skeletal formula of benzene in the formulae as shown in Figure 14.11.

Bonding in organic molecules

The ability of a carbon atom to bond to other carbon atoms, and the shapes of the molecules formed, can be explained by looking closely at the bonding involved.

Sigma (σ) bonds

Each carbon atom has six electrons, with an electronic configuration of $1s^2 2s^2 2p^2$. This means that carbon has four electrons in its outermost shell. By forming **single covalent bonds** with four other atoms, a carbon atom can gain the electronic configuration of the noble gas neon (see page 49). These single covalent bonds are known as **sigma (σ) bonds**.

The pair of electrons in a σ bond is found in a region of space (described as a lobe) between the nuclei of the two atoms sharing the electrons. The electrostatic attraction between the negatively charged electrons and the two positively charged nuclei bonds the atoms to each other (see page 51).

In many organic compounds each carbon atom forms four σ bonds. The four bonding pairs of electrons around each carbon atom repel each other. They position themselves in a tetrahedral arrangement to get as far apart from each other as possible. The tetrahedral bond angle is 109.5° (see page 55). Figure 14.13 shows the shape of an ethane molecule.

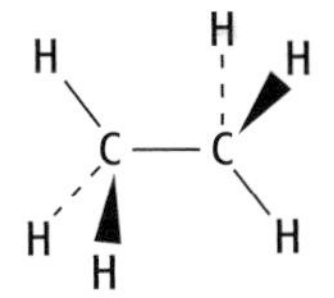

193

Figure 14.13 The bond angles are all close to 109.5° in an ethane molecule. The two carbon atoms, each forming four sigma bonds, are said to be sp³ hybridised (see page 57).

Pi (π) bonds

Carbon can also form double bonds between its atoms in organic molecules, as well as forming single bonds. A C=C double bond, as found in alkenes such as ethene, is made up of a σ bond and a **pi (π) bond**. The carbon atoms involved in the double bond will each form three σ bonds; an example of sp² hybridisation (see page 57). This leaves each carbon atom with one spare outer electron in a 2p orbital. When these two p orbitals overlap they form a π bond. Figure 14.14 shows how the π bond is formed in ethene.

The two lobes that make up the π bond lie above and below the plane of the atoms in an ethene molecule. This

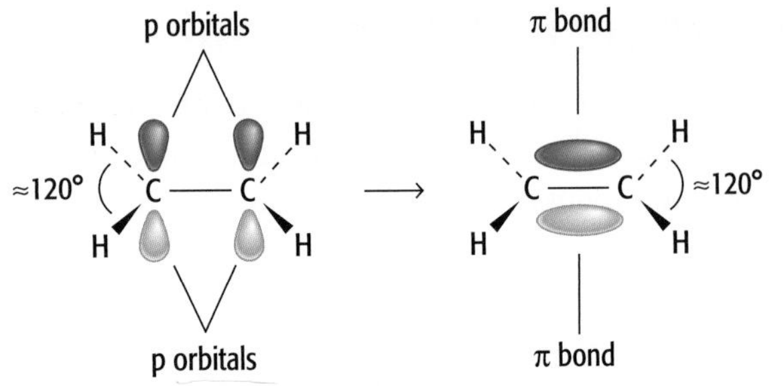

Figure 14.14 The overlap of p orbitals results in a π bond. Ethene is described as a **planar** molecule. The two carbon atoms are said to be sp² hybridised (see page 57). All the carbon and hydrogen atoms in the ethene molecule lie in the same plane.

maximises overlap of the p orbitals. The carbon atoms involved in the double bond are each surrounded by three pairs of electrons in the σ bonds. These are all in the plane of the molecule and repel each other to give bond angles of about 120°.

You can read about the special case of π bonding in a benzene molecule on page 382.

QUESTION

6 Draw a 3D formula for:

a propane

b propene.

Structural isomerism

We have seen how a compound's molecular formula tells us the number and type of each atom in one molecule of the compound. However, for a given molecular formula there may be different ways of arranging these atoms. This means different molecules can be formed, with different

Structural isomers have the same molecular formula but different structural formulae.

structures, resulting in different compounds. Such compounds with the same molecular formula but different structural formulae are called **structural isomers**. There are three types of structural isomerism:

1 position isomerism
2 functional group isomerism
3 chain isomerism.

1 Position isomerism

In position isomerism, it is the position of the functional group that varies in each isomer. An example is provided by the compound with the molecular formula $C_3H_6Br_2$. Its four possible isomers are shown in Figure 14.15.

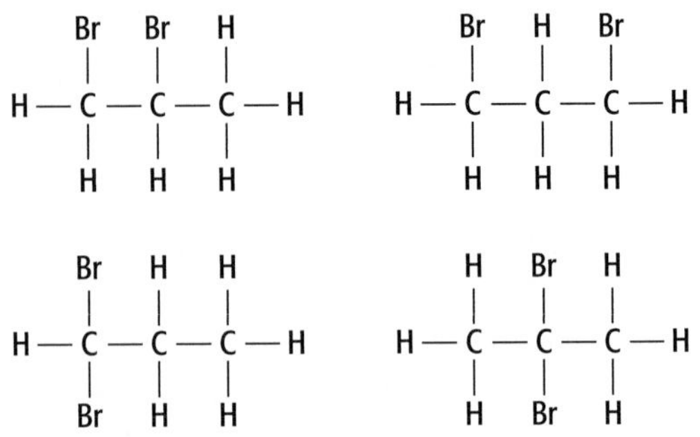

Figure 14.15 An example of position isomerism.

You need to take care when drawing the structural or displayed formula of different isomers not to repeat the same structure. Remember that there is free rotation about C—C single bonds. The three molecules shown in Figure 14.16 are all 1,2-dibromopropane; they are not three different isomers of $C_3H_6Br_2$.

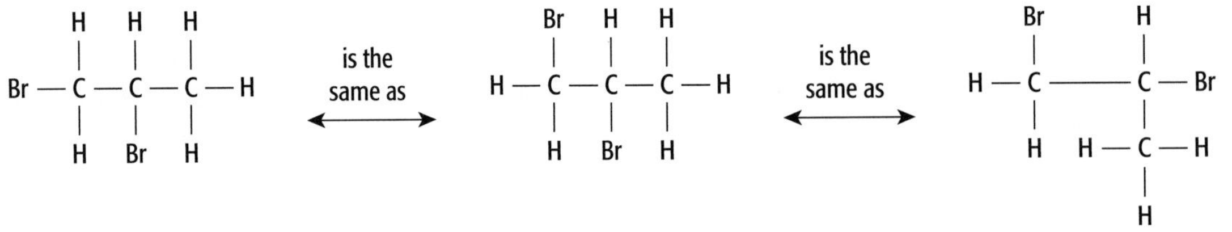

Figure 14.16 These are different ways of representing the **same molecule** because of free rotation about C—C single bonds.

2 Functional group isomerism

In functional group isomerism there are different functional groups present. For example, given the molecular formula C_3H_8O we can draw both an alcohol and an ether (Figure 14.17).

These two isomers have different functional groups and so have very different chemical properties.

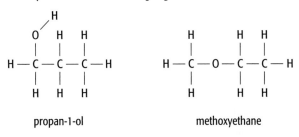

Figure 14.17 An example of functional group isomerism.

3 Chain isomerism

Chain isomers differ in the structure of their carbon 'skeleton'. For example, butane and methylpropane are chain isomers, both with the molecular formula of C_4H_{10} (Figure 14.18).

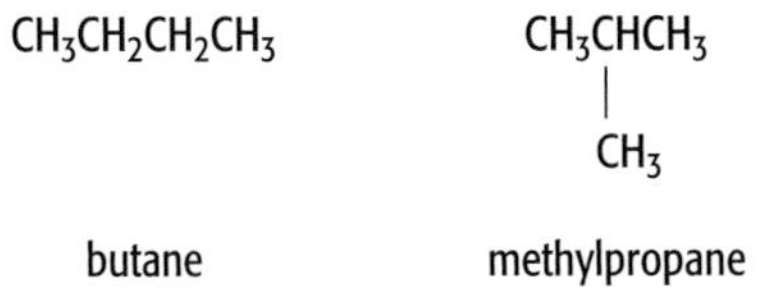

$$CH_3CH_2CH_2CH_3 \qquad CH_3CHCH_3$$
$$\qquad\qquad\qquad\qquad | $$
$$\qquad\qquad\qquad\qquad CH_3$$

butane   methylpropane

Figure 14.18 An example of chain isomerism.

QUESTIONS

7 a Name the four isomers in Figure 14.15.

  b Draw the displayed formulae and name the structural isomers of C_3H_7Cl.

8 a Draw the displayed formulae and name the functional group isomers of C_3H_6O that are:

    i an aldehyde

    ii a ketone.

  b Draw the displayed formula and name an isomer of C_3H_8O that could be used as an example of positional isomerism of one of the isomers in Figure 14.17.

9 Draw the displayed formulae and give the names of the isomers of C_5H_{12}.

Stereoisomerism

In **stereoisomerism** we have compounds whose molecules have the same atoms bonded to each other but with different arrangements of the atoms in space.

There are two types of stereoisomerism:

1   *cis–trans* isomerism

2   optical isomerism.

1 *Cis-trans* isomerism

Unlike a C—C single bond, there is **no free rotation** about a C=C double bond. This results in the possibility of a different type of isomerism in unsaturated organic compounds. Figure 14.19 gives an example.

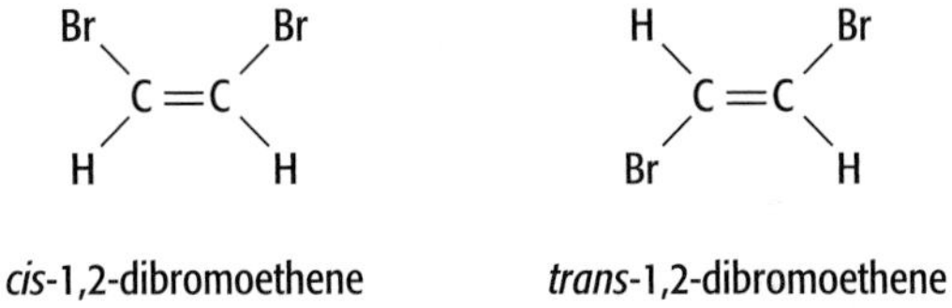

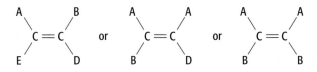

cis-1,2-dibromoethene   trans-1,2-dibromoethene

Figure 14.19 An example of *cis–trans* isomerism.

In *cis*-1,2-dibromoethene both the Br atoms remain fixed on the same side of the C=C double bond. On the other hand, in *trans*-1,2-dibromoethene, the Br atoms are positioned across the C=C double bond. (Remember that the prefix 'trans-' means across.) These two stereoisomers have different arrangements of the atoms in space so they are different compounds with different physical properties and some different chemical properties, e.g. differing rates for the same reaction. Whenever we have unsaturated compounds with the structures shown in Figure 14.20, we can have this *cis–trans* type of isomerism.

Figure 14.20 These three arrangements can result in *cis–trans* isomerism because there is restricted rotation about the C=C double bond.

2 Optical isomerism

If a molecule contains a carbon atom that is bonded to four different atoms or groups of atoms, it can form two optical isomers. The two different molecules are mirror images of each other and cannot be superimposed (Figure 14.21). The carbon atom with the four different groups attached is called the **chiral centre** of the molecule.

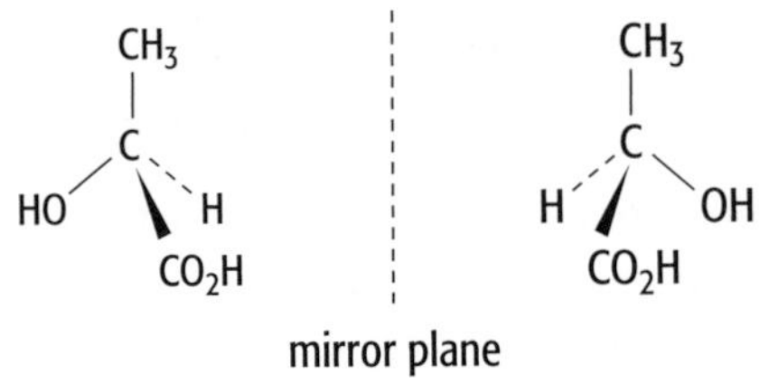

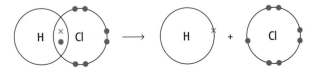

Figure 14.21 These two molecules are optical isomers, sometimes referred to as enantiomers. Trying to superimpose the two isomers is like trying to superimpose your left hand on top of your right hand – it can't be done.

Optical isomers differ in their effect on polarised light. Normal light is unpolarised. It can be thought of as fluctuating electric and magnetic fields, vibrating at right angles to each other in every possible direction. Passing this unpolarised light through a polariser results in polarised light, which vibrates in only one plane. A pair of optical isomers will rotate the plane of polarised light by equal amounts but in opposite directions. One will rotate polarised light clockwise and the other anticlockwise.

QUESTION

10 a Draw the displayed formulae and name the *cis– trans* isomers of but-2-ene.

b The molecule CHBrClF exhibits optical isomerism. Draw the 3D displayed formulae of both optical isomers.

Organic reactions – mechanisms

Chemists find it useful to explain organic reactions by summarising the overall reaction in a series of steps called a reaction mechanism. Like all chemical reactions, organic reactions involve the breaking and making of chemical bonds. There are two ways in which covalent bonds can break:

- homolytic fission
- heterolytic fission.

Homolytic fission

In this type of bond breaking, both the atoms at each end of the bond leave with one electron from the pair that formed the covalent bond. This is shown in Figure 14.22, using the simple example of a hydrogen chloride molecule.

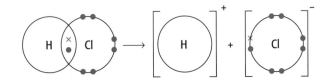

Figure 14.22 Homolytic fission of a covalent bond.

The species produced when a bond breaks homolytically are called **free radicals**. We can show the formation of free radicals by using an equation:

$$HCl \longrightarrow H\bullet + Cl\bullet$$

H• and Cl• are free radicals. All free radicals have an unpaired electron (represented by the dot) and are very reactive.

You can read more about a free-radical reaction on page 207.

- This type of reaction involves the formation of the free radicals in an **initiation step**. This requires an input of energy to break a covalent bond, resulting in two free radicals.
- The radicals formed can then attack reactant molecules, generating more free radicals. These reactions are called **propagation steps**. They can be thought of as a chain reaction, which only stops when free radicals react with each other.
- Two free radicals reacting together will form a molecule, with no free radicals generated. Therefore this is called a **termination step**.

Heterolytic fission

The second type of bond breaking involves the 'uneven' breaking of a covalent bond. In heterolytic fission the more electronegative atom takes both the electrons in the covalent bond. Again we can use hydrogen chloride to illustrate this (Figure 14.23).

Figure 14.23 Heterolytic fission of a covalent bond.

We can show this type of bond breaking in an equation. A small curly arrow shows the movement of a pair of electrons:

$$H - Cl \longrightarrow H^+ + Cl^-$$

The heterolytic fission of a bond can involve a C—X bond, where X is an atom more electronegative than carbon. For example:

$$H_3C - Br \longrightarrow CH_3^+ + Br^-$$

In this case, as the bond breaks, the Br atom takes both the shared electrons, forming a bromide anion (a negatively charged ion). This leaves the methyl group one electron short, resulting in the formation of a positively charged ion. This type of alkyl ion is called a **carbocation**. These positively charged carbocations often appear in reaction mechanisms (see page 221). There are three types of carbocations that you need to consider: primary, secondary and tertiary carbocations (Figure 14.24).

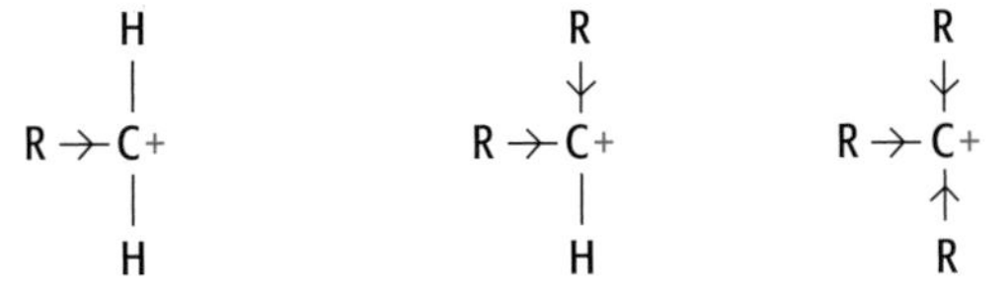

primary carbocation   secondary   tertiary carbocation
(least stable)   carbocation   (most stable)

Key: where R = an alkyl group

Figure 14.24 Note that the carbon atom with the positive charge only has three covalent bonds, not the usual four, making it electron deficient. Alkyl groups have the effect of spreading out the charge on the carbocation. The more alkyl groups adjacent to the positively charged carbon atom, the more stable the carbocation.

The type of carbocation formed in a reaction mechanism can affect the products formed in some organic reactions, such as addition reactions to alkenes (see page 208). Alkyl groups (e.g. $-CH_3$, $-C_2H_5$, $-C_3H_7$, etc.) tend to 'push' the electrons away from themselves. We say that the electron-donating nature of alkyl groups has a **positive inductive effect** on adjacent groups. Therefore, in carbocations the more alkyl groups attached to the positively charged carbon, the less the charge density is on the carbon atom with the three covalent bonds. Organic intermediates formed in the course of a reaction are energetically more stable when any charge on a species is not concentrated in one place but is spread over several atoms. So when carbocations are formed as intermediates in reactions, the tertiary carbocation is most likely to form as its positive charge is, in effect, 'smeared' over the C^+ atom and the three carbon atoms it is bonded to.

Carbocations are an example of a species called an **electrophile**.

An electrophile is an acceptor of a pair of electrons.

When an electrophile accepts a pair of electrons this results in the formation of a new covalent bond (see page 209).

You will also meet **nucleophiles** when studying organic reactions. These are electron-rich species, i.e. they carry a negative, or partial negative, charge.

A nucleophile is a donator of a pair of electrons.

When a nucleophile donates a pair of electrons, this leads to the formation of a new covalent bond with the electron-deficient atom under attack (see page 237).

QUESTION

11 a Write an equation to show the homolytic fission of the Cl—Cl bond in a chlorine molecule, Cl_2.

b Write an equation to show the heterolytic fission of the C—Cl bond in chloromethane. Include a curly arrow in your answer.

c Which one of the following species is likely to act as a nucleophile: H_2, H^+, OH^-?

d Explain your answer to part **c**.

e Which one of the following species is likely to act as an electrophile: H_2, H^+, OH^-?

f Explain your answer to part **e**.

g Which of these carbocations is most likely to form as an intermediate in an organic reaction? Explain your answer.

197

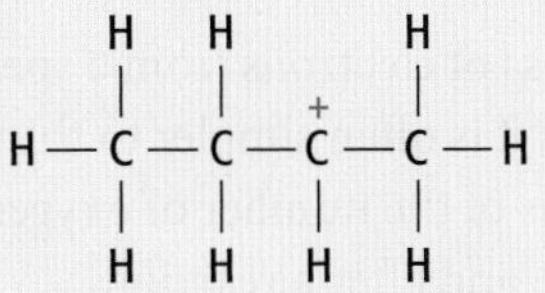

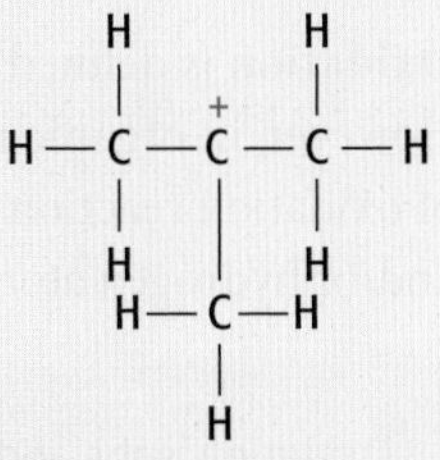

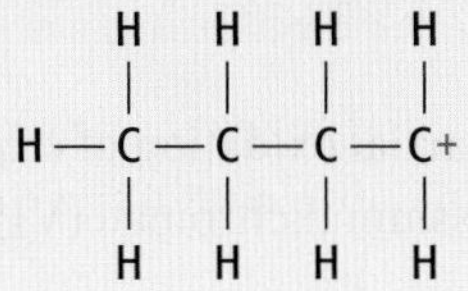

Types of organic reaction

Addition reactions involve the formation of a single product from two reactant molecules. An example is the addition reaction between an alkene and bromine (see page 209):

$$C_2H_4 + Br_2 \longrightarrow C_2H_4Br_2$$

Elimination reactions result in the removal of a small molecule from a larger one. An example is the dehydration of an alcohol by concentrated sulfuric acid (see page 230):

$$C_2H_5OH \xrightarrow{\text{conc. } H_2SO_4} C_2H_4 + H_2O$$

Substitution reactions involve the replacement of one atom, or a group of atoms, by another. For example, the free-radical substitution of alkanes by chlorine in sunlight (see page 207):

$$CH_4 + Cl_2 \xrightarrow{\text{UV light}} CH_3Cl + HCl$$

Here an H atom in CH_4 has been replaced by a Cl atom.

Hydrolysis is the breakdown of a molecule by water. This type of reaction is often speeded up by acid or alkali. For example, the hydrolysis of a halogenoalkane by water to give an alcohol (see page 219):

$$C_2H_5Br + H_2O \longrightarrow C_2H_5OH + HBr$$

Hydrolysis with alkali is faster, and gives slightly different products:

$$C_2H_5Br + NaOH \longrightarrow C_2H_5OH + NaBr$$

Oxidation is defined as the loss of electrons from a species. However, in organic reactions it is often simpler to think of oxidation reactions in terms of the number of oxygen and/or hydrogen atoms before and after a reaction.

> Oxidation is the addition of oxygen atoms to a molecule and/or the removal of hydrogen atoms from a molecule.

An example is the partial oxidation of ethanol to ethanal using acidified potassium dichromate(VI) solution (see page 231):

$$C_2H_5OH + [O] \longrightarrow CH_3CHO + H_2O$$

- before the reaction ethanol contains one O atom and six H atoms
- after the reaction ethanal contains one O atom and four H atoms.

In effect, the ethanol loses two H atoms, so we can say it has been oxidised.

Notice the use of [O] to simplify the chemical equation used to describe oxidation reactions. This is commonly used, but the equation must still be balanced – just like a normal equation. For example, in the complete oxidation of ethanol to ethanoic acid, using the reagents above but under harsher conditions (see page 231):

$$C_2H_5OH + 2[O] \longrightarrow CH_3COOH + H_2O$$

[O] represents an oxygen atom from the oxidising agent. The 2 in front of the [O] is needed to balance the equation for oxygen atoms.

Reduction is the chemical opposite of oxidation.

For example, in the reduction of a ketone, using sodium tetrahydridoborate, $NaBH_4$ (see page 237):

$$CH_3COCH_3 + 2[H] \longrightarrow CH_3CHOHCH_3$$

Notice the use of [H] to simplify the chemical equation used to describe reduction reactions. [H] represents a hydrogen atom from the reducing agent. The 2 in front of the [H] is necessary to balance the equation for hydrogen atoms.

> **QUESTION**
>
> 12 Classify these reactions, choosing from the types of reaction described above:
>
> a $C_3H_7I + H_2O \longrightarrow C_3H_7OH + HI$
>
> b $CH_3CHO + 2[H] \longrightarrow CH_3CH_2OH$
>
> c $C_2H_5Br \longrightarrow C_2H_4 + HBr$
>
> d $C_2H_4 + H_2O \longrightarrow C_2H_5OH$
>
> e $C_2H_6 + Cl_2 \longrightarrow C_2H_5Cl + HCl$

Summary

- We can represent an organic molecule, with increasing detail, by using its:
  - empirical formula
  - molecular formula
  - structural formula
  - displayed formula
  - 3D displayed formula.
- The presence of functional groups give organic compounds their characteristic reactions.
- Important functional groups include alcohols, halogenoalkanes, aldehydes, ketones, carboxylic acids, amines and nitriles.
- The shapes of organic molecules can be explained by the σ and π bonds between carbon atoms.

- There are two types of isomer – structural isomers and stereoisomers.
- Structural isomers have the same molecular formula but different structural formulae. We can group these into position, functional group or chain isomers.
- Stereoisomers have the same molecular formula but different arrangement of their atoms in space.
  - *Cis–trans* isomers arise because of the restricted rotation around a C=C double bond.
  - Optical isomers contain a chiral centre (a carbon atom bonded to four different atoms or groups of atoms), resulting in mirror images of the molecule that cannot be superimposed.

End-of-chapter questions

1 A carbon compound **P** has the percentage composition 85.7% carbon and 14.3% hydrogen. Its relative molecular mass was found to be 56.

   a   **i**   Calculate its empirical formula.   [4]

        ii   Calculate its molecular formula.   [1]

   b   Write down the **names** and **displayed formulae** of all the non-cyclic isomers of compound **P** which have the following characteristics:

        i   straight chain   [6]

        ii   branched chain.   [2]

                                          Total = 13

2 A chemist was investigating the best way to produce 1,2-dichloroethane. He devised two methods, **I** and **II**, of doing this.

   I   He reacted ethane with chlorine in the presence of UV light by the following reaction:

      $C_2H_6(g) + 2Cl_2(g) \longrightarrow C_2H_4Cl_2(l) + 2HCl(g)$

      After doing this he found that 600 g of ethane gave 148.5 g of $C_2H_4Cl_2$.

   a   **i**   How many moles of ethane are there in 600 g?   [1]

        ii   How many moles of 1,2-dichloroethane would have been formed if the yield had been 100%?   [1]

        iii   How many moles of 1,2-dichloroethane are there in 148.5 g?   [1]

        iv   Calculate the percentage yield of 1,2-dichloroethane.   [1]

II He reacted ethene with chlorine in the dark by the following reaction:

$$C_2H_4(g) + Cl_2(g) \longrightarrow C_2H_4Cl_2(l)$$

In this reaction 140 g of ethene gave 396 g of $C_2H_4Cl_2$.

b Calculate the percentage yield for this reaction. Show your working. [3]

c There are isomers of the compound $C_2H_4Cl_2$. Draw the displayed formulae of the isomers and name them. [4]

d Choose from redox, substitution, elimination, addition and hydrolysis to give the type of reaction for:

   i reaction I [1]

   ii reaction II. [1]

Total = 13

Chapter 15:
Hydrocarbons

Learning outcomes

You should be able to:

- understand the general unreactivity of alkanes, and describe the combustion of ethane and the free-radical substitution of methyl groups (as well as the mechanism) by chlorine and by bromine
- suggest how cracking can be used to obtain more useful alkanes and alkenes of lower M_r from larger hydrocarbon molecules separated from crude oil
- describe the chemistry of alkenes as shown by their addition, oxidation and polymerisation, identifying monomers and repeat units in polymers (see also Chapter 28, page 412)

- describe the mechanism of electrophilic addition in alkenes and explain the inductive effects of alkyl groups on the stability of cations formed
- describe the difficulty of the disposal of polyalkenes
- describe the environmental consequences of burning hydrocarbon fuels in vehicles and the removal of pollutants in catalytic converters
- outline the use of infrared spectroscopy in monitoring air pollution (see also Chapter 18, page 241).

Introduction

Crude oil is our main source of hydrocarbons. Hydrocarbons are compounds containing carbon and hydrogen only. They provide us with fuels such as petrol, diesel and kerosene. Hydrocarbons are also the starting compounds we use to make many new compounds, such as most of the plastics we meet in everyday life.

Figure 15.1 Crude oil is extracted from porous seams of rock found beneath an impervious layer of rock within the Earth's crust.

The homologous group of alkanes

The majority of compounds found in the mixture of hydrocarbons we call crude oil are **alkanes**. We have met the first ten members of this homologous series in Table 14.3 (page 192). The general formula for the alkanes is C_nH_{2n+2}. For example, the molecular formula of pentane, in which $n = 5$, is C_5H_{12}. Figure 15.2 shows some different ways of representing pentane molecules.

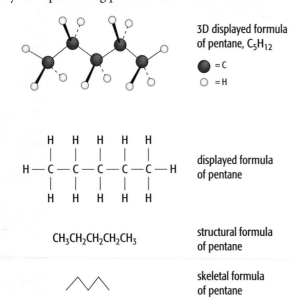

3D displayed formula of pentane, C_5H_{12}

● = C
○ = H

displayed formula of pentane

$CH_3CH_2CH_2CH_2CH_3$ — structural formula of pentane

skeletal formula of pentane

Figure 15.2 The 3D displayed formula shows the tetrahedral arrangement of atoms around each carbon atom (approximate bond angles of 109.5°).

Note that all the carbon–carbon bonds are single covalent bonds. The carbon atoms all display sp^3 hybridisation (see page 193). This means that alkanes have the maximum number of hydrogen atoms in their molecules and are known as **saturated hydrocarbons**.

QUESTION

1 Eicosane is a straight-chain alkane whose molecules contain 20 carbon atoms.

    a What is the molecular formula of eicosane?

    b Draw the skeletal formula of eicosane.

Sources of the alkanes

Crude oil is found trapped in layers of rock beneath the surface of the Earth. The actual composition of crude oil varies in different oilfields around the world.

- Crude oil is a complex mixture of hydrocarbons – alkanes, cycloalkanes and aromatic compounds.
- Cycloalkanes are saturated hydrocarbons in which there is a 'ring' consisting of three or more carbon atoms. Imagine the two carbon atoms at each end of a straight-chain alkane bonding to each other. These two carbon atoms could then only bond to two hydrogen atoms each, not three as in the straight-chain alkane. Cyclohexane, C_6H_{12}, is an example (Figure 15.3).

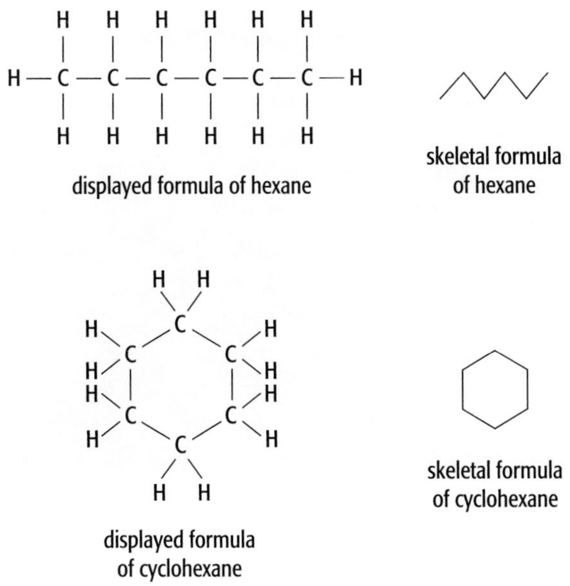

Figure 15.3 Hexane, C_6H_{14}, and cyclohexane, C_6H_{12}.

Note that a cycloalkane does not follow the general alkane formula, C_nH_{2n+2}. This is because the two end carbon atoms in an alkane chain bond to each other, forming a closed ring. Therefore there are two fewer hydrogen atoms in a cycloalkane compared with its equivalent straight-chain alkane.

Another class of hydrocarbons called aromatic hydrocarbons, which are also known as arenes, are based on hexagonal benzene rings (see Chapter 25).

The crude oil is brought to the surface at oil wells and transported to an oil refinery. At the refinery the crude oil is processed into useful fuels. The first step is fractional distillation of the oil. This separates the wide range of different hydrocarbons into fractions. The hydrocarbons in each fraction will have similar boiling points. This is carried out in tall fractionating columns (Figure 15.4).

The lower the relative molecular mass of the hydrocarbons, the more volatile they are. They have lower boiling points and are collected nearer the top of the fractionating columns. These compounds are in high demand – especially the gasoline fraction (providing petrol) and the naphtha fraction (providing the starting compounds for making many other chemicals in industry).

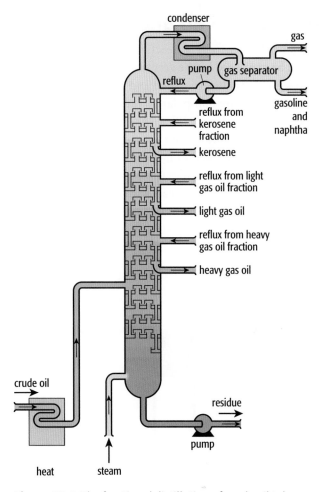

Figure 15.4 The fractional distillation of crude oil takes place in a fractionating column. The top of the column is at a lower temperature than the bottom of the column. The crude oil enters as vapour and liquid. The liquids are drawn off at the bottom of the column while more volatile hydrocarbons rise up the column. They condense at different levels as the temperature gradually falls and are collected as liquids. The most volatile hydrocarbons, which are short-chain alkanes (methane to butane), leave the top of the column as gases.

203

QUESTION

2 a Draw the displayed formula and the skeletal formula of cyclopentane.

  b What is the general formula of cycloalkanes?

  c Give two differences between a molecule of cyclopentane and a molecule of pentane.

  d Which alkane would be collected at a higher temperature from a fractionating column in an oil refinery: ethane or decane?

Reactions of alkanes

The alkanes are generally unreactive compounds. This can be explained by the very small difference in electronegativity between carbon and hydrogen. The alkane molecules are non-polar, so they are not attacked by nucleophiles or electrophiles. They have no partial positive charges on any of their carbon atoms to attract nucleophiles, neither do they have areas of high electron density to attract electrophiles (see page 197).

However, the alkanes do react with oxygen in combustion reactions and also undergo substitution by halogens in sunlight. These reactions are covered in the next sections.

Figure 15.5 Non-polar alkanes do not react with polar compounds such as water. The hexane (which is dyed with iodine to make it more clearly visible) and water shown here are immiscible – they do not mix and they do not react with each other.

Combustion of alkanes

Alkanes are often used as fuels (Figure 15.6). We burn them for many reasons:

- to generate electricity in power stations
- to heat our homes and cook our food
- to provide energy needed in industrial processes
- to provide power for ships, aeroplanes, trains, lorries, buses, cars and motorbikes.

If an alkane is burnt in plenty of oxygen, it will undergo complete combustion. The carbon will be oxidised fully to form carbon dioxide and the hydrogen will be oxidised to form water:

$$\text{alkane} + \text{oxygen} \xrightarrow[\text{combustion}]{\text{complete}} \text{carbon dioxide} + \text{water}$$

Figure 15.6 Alkanes are useful fuels.

For example, octane can be found in petrol. Some of it will undergo complete combustion in a car engine:

$$\text{octane} + \text{oxygen} \longrightarrow \text{carbon dioxide} + \text{water}$$
$$2C_8H_{18} + 25O_2 \longrightarrow 16CO_2 + 18H_2O$$

The equation can also be written as:

$$C_8H_{18} + 12\tfrac{1}{2}O_2 \longrightarrow 8CO_2 + 9H_2O$$

Pollution from burning hydrocarbon fuels

When the petrol or diesel is mixed with air inside a car engine, there is a limited supply of oxygen. Under these conditions, not all the carbon in the hydrocarbon fuel is fully oxidised to carbon dioxide. Some of the carbon is only partially oxidised to form carbon monoxide gas. This is called incomplete combustion. For example:

$$\text{octane} + \text{oxygen} \xrightarrow[\text{combustion}]{\text{incomplete}} \text{carbon monoxide} + \text{water}$$
$$2C_8H_{18} + 17O_2 \longrightarrow 16CO + 18H_2O$$

or

$$C_8H_{18} + 8\tfrac{1}{2}O_2 \longrightarrow 8CO + 9H_2O$$

Carbon monoxide is a toxic gas that bonds with the haemoglobin in your blood. The haemoglobin molecules can then no longer bond to oxygen and so cannot transport oxygen around your body. Victims of carbon monoxide poisoning will feel dizzy, then lose consciousness. If not removed from the toxic gas, the victim will die. Carbon monoxide is odourless, so this adds to the danger. This is why faulty gas heaters in which incomplete combustion occurs can kill unsuspecting people in rooms with poor ventilation.

As well as carbon monoxide, road traffic also releases acidic nitrogen oxides. These contribute to the problem of acid rain. Acid rain can kill trees and aquatic animals in lakes (Figure 15.7). Acid raid also corrodes metals, such as iron.

Figure 15.7 These trees have been badly damaged by acid rain.

In normal combustion, nitrogen gas in the air does not get oxidised. However, in the very high temperatures in car engines oxidation of nitrogen does take place. A variety of nitrogen oxides can be formed and released in the car's exhaust fumes (Figure 15.8). For example:

$$N_2(g) + O_2(g) \rightleftharpoons 2NO(g)$$

Figure 15.8 The vast numbers of cars on the roads pollute our atmosphere.

As well as toxic carbon monoxide and acidic nitrogen oxides, cars also release unburnt hydrocarbons, often referred to as volatile organic compounds (VOCs) into the air. Some of these are carcinogens (they cause cancers).

Cars can now be fitted with a catalytic converter in their exhaust system (Figure 15.9). Once warmed up, a catalytic converter can cause the following reactions to take place:

- the oxidation of carbon monoxide to form carbon dioxide
- the reduction of nitrogen oxides to form harmless nitrogen gas
- the oxidation of unburnt hydrocarbons to form carbon dioxide and water.

Unfortunately, catalytic converters can do nothing to reduce the amount of carbon dioxide (a greenhouse gas) given off in the exhaust gases of cars.

Figure 15.9 Catalytic converters reduce the pollutants from car exhausts. Precious metals, such as platinum, are coated on a honeycomb structure to provide a large surface area on which the reactions can occur.

The following equation describes the reaction between carbon monoxide and nitrogen monoxide. It takes place on the surface of the precious metal catalyst in a catalytic converter:

$$2CO + 2NO \longrightarrow 2CO_2 + N_2$$

Note that more carbon dioxide is released in place of carbon monoxide. Carbon dioxide is not a toxic gas, but it is still considered a pollutant because of its contribution to enhanced global warming.

Carbon dioxide occurs naturally in the air. The gas absorbs infrared radiation given off by the Earth as it cools down at night. This helps to keep the Earth at the right temperature to support life. Without it all the water on our planet would be constantly frozen. The problem of **enhanced global warming** has arisen because of the huge increase in the amount of CO_2 produced by human activity in the last 200 years. This extra CO_2 traps more heat, and most scientists accept that this is causing the average temperature of the Earth to rise. This increase in temperature could cause rising sea levels, resulting in the flooding of low-lying areas of land. The climate will also change around the world, with more extreme weather predicted.

Environmental scientists can monitor the pollutant gases in the air using an instrumental technique called infrared spectroscopy (see Chapter 18, page 241). It works quickly and accurately to monitor pollutants, including nitrogen dioxide, sulfur dioxide, carbon monoxide and carbon dioxide, as well as more than a hundred VOCs and low-level ozone. The scientists can use the characteristic wavelengths of infrared radiation absorbed by the molecules of the pollutants to identify them. They can also analyse the intensity of the absorptions to find the concentration of each pollutant present in a sample. Monitored over a period of time, the scientists provide useful information on the effectiveness of pollution control measures introduced locally and on a global level.

Substitution reactions of alkanes

QUESTIONS

3 **a** What would happen if octane was added to a solution of sodium hydroxide?

   b Explain your answer to part **a**.

4 Give the balanced symbol equations for:

   a the complete combustion of heptane, C_7H_{16}, giving carbon dioxide and water

   b the incomplete combustion of methane, CH_4, giving carbon monoxide and water

   c the incomplete combustion of nonane, C_9H_{20}.

5 **a** Name two pollutants from a car engine that are oxidised in a catalytic converter.

   b Name a pollutant that is reduced in a catalytic converter.

   c Which pollutant from a car engine is not diminished by the use of a catalytic converter? What environmental problem does this pollutant contribute to?

   d What information about air pollution can the technique of infrared spectroscopy reveal to an environmental scientist?

The alkanes will undergo substitution reactions with halogens in sunlight. For example:

$$CH_4 + Cl_2 \xrightarrow{\text{sunlight}} CH_3Cl + HCl$$

methane   chloromethane

In this reaction a hydrogen atom in the methane molecule gets replaced by a chlorine atom. However, the reaction does not take place in darkness (Figure 15.10). So what role does the sunlight play in the mechanism of the substitution reaction?

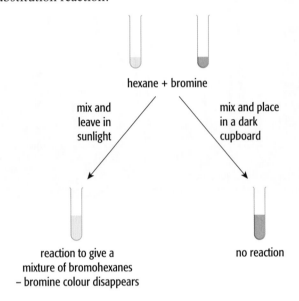

Figure 15.10 A substitution reaction takes place between alkanes and bromine in sunlight, but there is no reaction in darkness.

Initiation step

The first step in the mechanism is the breaking of the Cl—Cl bond by ultraviolet light from the Sun. This is an example of homolytic fission of a covalent bond (see page 196). This is called the initiation step in the mechanism:

$$Cl_2 \xrightarrow{\text{UV light}} 2Cl\bullet$$

As the Cl—Cl bond breaks, each chlorine atom takes one electron from the pair of electrons in the Cl—Cl bond. Two Cl• atoms are formed. These Cl• atoms, each with an unpaired electron, are called free radicals.

Propagation steps

Free radicals are very reactive. They will attack the normally unreactive alkanes. A chlorine free radical will attack the methane molecule:

$$CH_4 + Cl\bullet \longrightarrow \bullet CH_3 + HCl$$

In this propagation step, a C—H bond in CH_4 breaks

homolytically. A methyl free radical, $\cdot CH_3$, is produced. This can then attack a chlorine molecule, forming chloromethane and regenerating a chlorine free radical:

$$\cdot CH_3 + Cl_2 \longrightarrow CH_3Cl + Cl\cdot$$

Then the first propagation step can be repeated as the chlorine free radical can attack another methane molecule. This forms the methyl free radical, which regenerates another chlorine free radical, and so on …

The word 'propagation' usually refers to growing new plants. In this mechanism the substitution reaction progresses (grows) in a kind of chain reaction.

This reaction is not really suitable for preparing specific halogenoalkanes, because we get a mixture of substitution products. In the reaction between methane and chlorine, the products can include dichloromethane, trichloromethane and tetrachloromethane as well as chloromethane. These other products result from propagation steps in which a chlorine free radical attacks a halogenoalkane already formed. For example:

$$CH_3Cl + Cl\cdot \longrightarrow \cdot CH_2Cl + HCl$$

This can then be followed by:

$$\cdot CH_2Cl + Cl_2 \longrightarrow CH_2Cl_2 + Cl\cdot$$
$$\text{dichloromethane}$$

The more chlorine gas in the reaction mixture to start with, the greater the proportions of CH_2Cl_2, $CHCl_3$ and CCl_4 formed as products.

Termination steps

Whenever two free radicals meet they will react with each other. A single molecule is the only product. As no free radicals are made that can carry on the reaction sequence, the chain reaction stops. Examples of termination steps include:

$$\cdot CH_3 + Cl\cdot \longrightarrow CH_3Cl$$
$$\cdot CH_3 + \cdot CH_3 \longrightarrow C_2H_6$$

- In the initiation step we start with a molecule and get two free radicals formed.
- In the propagation steps we start with a molecule plus a free radical and get a different molecule and a different free radical formed.
- In the termination steps we start with two free radicals and end up with a molecule and no free radicals.

Overall, the reaction between alkanes and halogens, involving initiation, propagation and termination steps, is called **free-radical substitution**.

QUESTION

6 Bromine can react with ethane to form bromoethane.
   a What conditions are needed for the reaction between ethane and bromine to take place?
   b What do we call this type of reaction?
   c Write an equation to show the reaction of ethane and bromine to form bromoethane.
   d Why is this reaction not a good way to prepare a pure sample of bromoethane?
   e i   Name the three steps in the mechanism of this reaction.
      ii Write an equation to show the first step in the mechanism.
      iii What type of bond breaking does this first step involve?

The alkenes

We have looked at the nature of the double bond found in the hydrocarbons called **alkenes** on pages 193–4. Alkenes with one double bond per molecule have the general formula C_nH_{2n}. One example is ethene, C_2H_4. Alkanes are described as saturated hydrocarbons; however, alkenes are described as **unsaturated hydrocarbons**.

Oil refineries provide useful alkenes for the chemical industry. On page 203 we saw how crude oil is separated into fractions at a refinery. Oil companies find that the demand for the each fraction differs. The lighter fractions, such as the gasoline fraction, are in high demand. So, some of the excess heavier fractions are converted to lighter hydrocarbons. The large, less useful hydrocarbon molecules are broken down into smaller, more useful molecules. The process is called **cracking**.

The larger hydrocarbon molecules are fed into a steel chamber that contains no oxygen, so combustion does not take place. The larger hydrocarbon molecules are heated to a high temperature and are passed over a catalyst (Figure 15.11).

When large alkane molecules are cracked they form smaller alkane molecules and alkene molecules. One possible example of a cracking reaction is:

$$CH_3(CH_2)_8CH_3 \longrightarrow CH_3(CH_2)_4CH_3 + CH_2{=}CHCH_2CH_3$$
$$C_{10}H_{22} \longrightarrow C_6H_{14} + C_4H_8$$

207

a

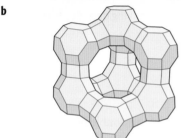

b

Figure 15.11 a A catalytic cracker occupies the bulk of the central part of this view of an oil refinery. **b** A computer graphic showing a zeolite catalyst used to crack hydrocarbons.

The low-molecular mass alkanes formed (C_6H_{14} in this example) make very useful fuels and are in high demand. However, the alkenes produced (C_4H_8 in this example) are also very useful. They are more reactive than the alkanes because of their double bonds. This makes them useful for the chemical industry as the starting compounds (feedstock) for making many new products. These include most plastics (see page YYY).

QUESTION

7 a Name the first member of the homologous series of alkenes.

  b What is the molecular formula of the alkene containing 18 carbon atoms and one C=C bond?

  c Look at the equation for cracking given in the text. Write a word equation for this reaction.

  d Write a balanced equation to show the cracking of nonane into heptane and ethene.

Addition reactions of the alkenes

Most reactions of the alkenes are examples of **addition** reactions. In these reactions one of the two bonds in the carbon–carbon double bond is broken and a new single bond is formed from each of the two carbon atoms. The general addition reactions are shown in Figure 15.12.

Figure 15.12 General equations for addition reactions of the alkenes: **a** with a hydrogen halide such as hydrogen bromide, and **b** with a halogen such as chlorine. In an addition reaction a single product is always formed.

Addition of hydrogen, $H_2(g)$

When hydrogen and an alkene are passed over a finely divided nickel catalyst at 140 °C, the addition reaction produces an alkane:

$$CH_2{=}CH_2 + H_2 \xrightarrow{\text{Ni catalyst}} CH_3CH_3$$

ethene → ethane

The addition reaction with hydrogen is used in the manufacture of margarine (Figure 15.13).

Figure 15.13 Unsaturated oils, such as sunflower oil, contain hydrocarbon chains with several C=C double bonds. These become partially saturated by reacting them with hydrogen. This raises the melting points of the oils, changing them from liquids to soft solids that can be spread easily.

Addition of steam, H₂O(g)

The addition of steam to alkenes is used in industry to make alcohols. Steam and the gaseous alkene, in the presence of concentrated phosphoric acid as the catalyst, are reacted at a temperature of 330 °C and a pressure of 6 MPa. When the alkene is ethene, the product is ethanol (Figure 15.14). However, the ethanol found in alcoholic drinks is always produced by the fermentation of glucose.

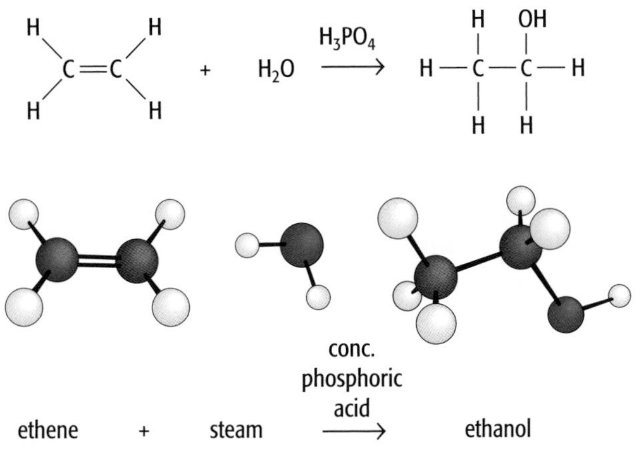

Figure 15.14 The reaction between ethene and steam.

Addition of hydrogen halides, HX(aq)

When an alkene is bubbled through a concentrated solution of a hydrogen halide (HF, HCl, HBr, HI) at room temperature, the product is a halogenoalkane. For example:

$$CH_2{=}CH_2 + HBr \longrightarrow CH_3CH_2Br$$
ethene   bromoethane

With longer, asymmetric alkenes there are always two possible products that could be formed. For example, with propene:

$$CH_3CH{=}CH_2 + HBr \longrightarrow CH_3CH_2CH_2Br$$
propene   1-bromopropane

and

$$CH_3CH{=}CH_2 + HBr \longrightarrow CH_3CHBrCH_3$$
propene   2-bromopropane

Where two products are formed, the major product is the one that has the halogen atom bonded to the carbon with the least number of hydrogen atoms (in this case $CH_3CHBrCH_3$). This is because the $CH_3CHBrCH_3$ is formed from a secondary carbocation intermediate. On page 197 we saw that this ion is more stable than the primary carbocation so is more readily formed in the course of a reaction. The mechanism that follows shows how a carbocation forms and is then attacked by a negative ion to give the product of the addition reaction.

Addition of halogens, X₂(aq)

If we bubble an alkene through a solution of chlorine or bromine at room temperature, we again get an addition reaction. The colour of the halogen molecules in solution, which is pale green for chlorine water and orange/yellow for bromine water, is removed. In fact, bromine water is used to test for the presence of the C=C bond in compounds. The compound to be tested is shaken with bromine water. If it is unsaturated, the bromine water will be decolorised (Figure 15.15).

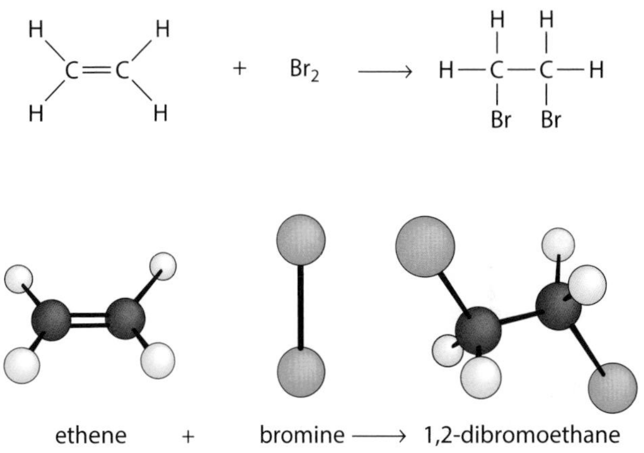

Figure 15.15 The reaction between ethene and bromine.

The mechanism of electrophilic addition to alkenes

On pages 193–4 we saw how the double bond in ethene is formed from a σ bond and a π bond. There are four electrons in total in these two bonds. So although ethene is a non-polar molecule, there is an area of high electron density around the C=C bond. This makes the alkenes open to attack by electrophiles (see page 197).

Remember that an electrophile is an acceptor of a pair of electrons. HBr is a polar molecule because of the difference in electronegativity between the H atom and the Br atom. In a molecule of HBr, the H atom carries a partial positive charge and the Br atom carries a partial negative charge. In the mechanism of addition, the H atom acts as the electrophile, accepting a pair of electrons from the C=C bond in the alkene.

But how can a non-polar molecule such as Br₂ act as an electrophile? As the bromine molecule and ethene molecules approach each other, the area of high electron density around the C=C bond repels the pair of electrons in the Br—Br bond away from the nearer Br atom. This makes the nearer Br atom slightly positive and the further Br atom slightly negative. Figure 15.16 shows the mechanism of electrophilic addition.

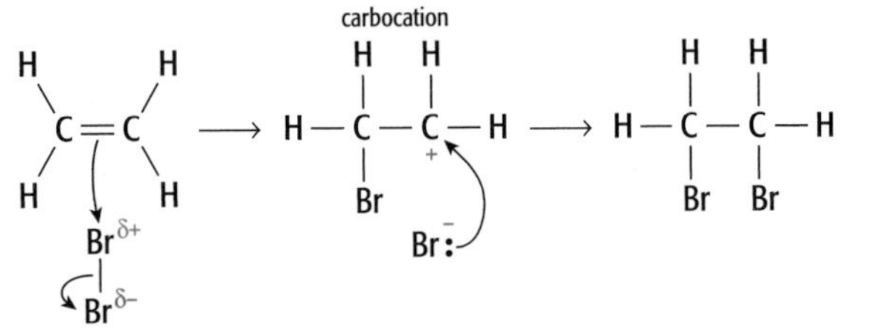

Figure 15.16 The mechanism of electrophilic addition of bromine to ethene.

As the new bond between the C and Br atom forms, the Br—Br bond breaks heterolytically (see page 196). The Br⁻ ion formed then attacks the highly reactive carbocation intermediate. So one bromine atom bonds to each carbon atom, producing 1,2-dibromoethane.

QUESTIONS

8 a State the conditions used in the reaction between an alkene and hydrogen.

   b Name the product formed when propene reacts with chlorine.

   c Ethanol can be used as a solvent. How is this ethanol made in industry?

   d What will be formed when ethene gas is bubbled through a concentrated solution of hydrochloric acid?

9 a Define the term **electrophile**.

   b Explain how a chlorine molecule can act as an electrophile in its reaction with an alkene.

   c Draw the mechanism for the reaction between ethene and chlorine.

Oxidation of the alkenes

Alkenes can be oxidised by acidified potassium manganate(VII) solution, which is a powerful oxidising agent. The products formed will depend on the conditions chosen for the reaction. In Figure 15.17, the R, R¹ and R² are alkyl groups.

COLD DILUTE ACIDIFIED MANGANATE(VII) SOLUTION

If an alkene is shaken with a dilute solution of acidified potassium manganate(VII) at room temperature, the pale purple solution turns colourless. The alkene is converted into a diol, i.e. a compound with two alcohol (—OH) groups:

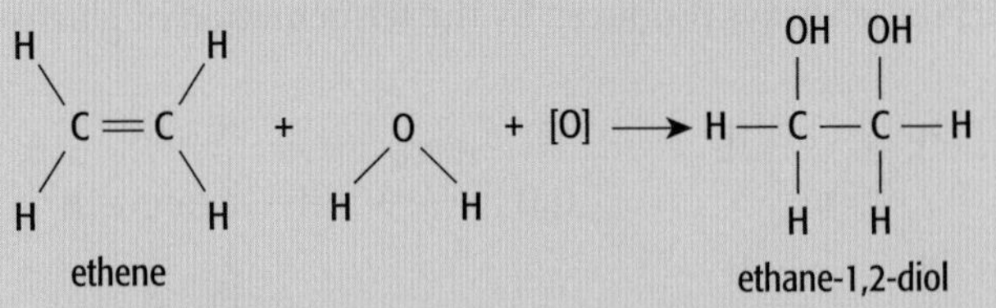

This reaction can be used as a test to find out whether a compound is unsaturated. However, the decolorisation of bromine water is a more commonly used test (see page 209).

Hot, concentrated manganate(VII) solution

Under these harsher conditions, the C=C bond in the alkene is broken completely. The O—H groups in the diol formed initially are further oxidised to ketones, aldehydes, carboxylic acids or carbon dioxide gas. The actual products depend on what is bonded to the carbon atoms involved in the C=C bond. Figure 15.17 shows the oxidation products from each type of group bonded to a carbon atom in the C=C bond.

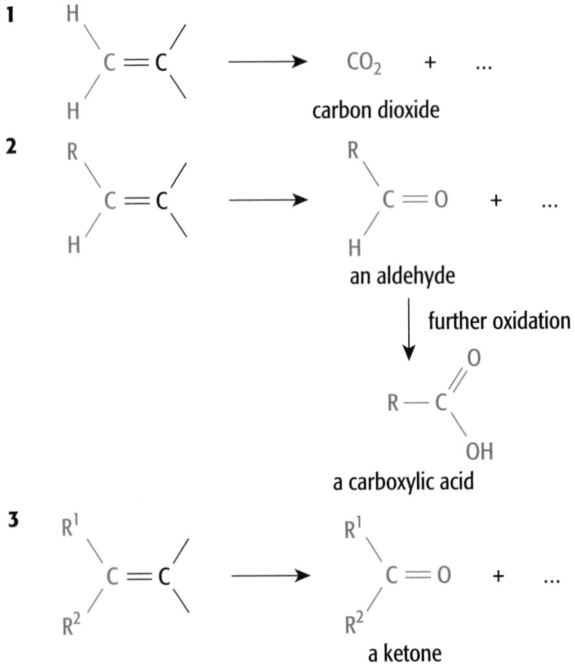

Figure 15.17 Oxidation with hot, concentrated manganate(VII) solution.

To see what is formed when 2-methylprop-1-ene is heated with hot, concentrated potassium manganate(VII), look at equations 1 and 3 in Figure 15.17. The actual oxidation can be represented as:

$$(CH_3)_2C{=}CH_2 + 4[O] \longrightarrow (CH_3)_2C{=}O + CO_2 + H_2O$$
2-methylprop-1-ene $\qquad\qquad$ propanone, a ketone

We can use this reaction to determine the position of the double bond in larger alkenes. To do this we would need to identify the products of the oxidation reaction and work backwards to deduce the original alkene. If, for example, carbon dioxide is given off in the oxidation, this tells us that the double bond was between the end two carbon atoms in the alkene.

We can summarise the oxidations under harsh conditions (using a hot, concentrated solution of potassium managanate(VII)) in three reactions.

1 $H_2C{=}CH_2 \longrightarrow CO_2 + CO_2$

If a carbon atom is bonded to two hydrogen atoms we get oxidation to a CO_2 molecule.

2 $RHC{=}CHR \longrightarrow RCHO + RCHO$
$\qquad\qquad\qquad\longrightarrow RCOOH + RCOOH$

If a carbon atom is bonded to one hydrogen atom and one alkyl group we get oxidation to a $-COOH$ (carboxylic acid) group.

3 $R^1R^2C{=}CR^3R^4 \longrightarrow R^1R^2C{=}O + R^3R^4C{=}O$

If a carbon atom is bonded to two alkyl groups we get oxidation to a C=O (ketone) group.

Addition polymerisation

Probably the most important addition reaction of the alkenes forms the basis of much of the plastics industry. Molecules of ethene, as well as other unsaturated compounds, can react with each other under the right conditions to form **polymer** molecules. A polymer is a long-chain molecule made up of many repeating units. The small, reactive molecules that react together to make the polymer are called **monomers**. Up to 10 000 ethene monomers can bond together to form the polymer chains of poly(ethene). Poly(ethene) is commonly used to make carrier bags. Other alkenes also polymerise to make polymers with different properties. Examples of other poly(alkenes) include poly(propene) and poly(phenylethene).

We can show the polymerisation reaction of ethene as:

$$nC_2H_4 \longrightarrow {\left[C_2H_4 \right]}_n$$
ethene $\qquad$ poly(ethene)

or by using the displayed formulae:

n is very large, e.g. up to 10 000

The section of the polymer shown in the brackets is the repeat unit of the polymer.

The reaction is called **addition polymerisation**. As in other addition reactions, it involves the breaking of the π bond in each C=C bond, then the monomers link together.

211

We can also use substituted alkenes, such as chloroethene, as monomers:

$$n\text{H}_2\text{C}=\text{CHCl} \longrightarrow \text{+H}_2\text{C}-\text{CHCl+}_n$$

chloroethene   poly(chloroethene)

The $\text{+H}_2\text{C}-\text{CHCl+}$ section of the polymer chain is the repeat unit of poly(chloroethene) (Figure 15.18). In poly(alkenes) made of one type of monomer, the repeat unit is the same as the monomer except that the C=C double bond is changed to a C—C single bond. Notice that, as in any other addition reaction of the alkenes, addition polymerisation yields only one product.

Figure 15.18 A 3D displayed formula of a small section of the poly(chloroethene) molecule. Its common name is PVC, as the old name for chloroethene was vinyl chloride.

Remember that:

- the section of the polymer chain shown inside the brackets in its structural or displayed formula is called its repeat unit
- addition polymerisation is characterised by:
  - monomers which are unsaturated, e.g. contain a C=C double bond
  - the polymer being the only product of the reaction.

Disposal of poly(alkene) plastics

Plastics are widely used in many aspects of everyday life. However, the large-scale use of poly(alkene)s has created a problem when we come to dispose of them. During their useful life, one of the poly(alkene)s' useful properties is their lack of reactivity. As they are effectively huge alkane molecules, they are resistant to chemical attack. So they can take hundreds of years to decompose when dumped in landfill sites, taking up valuable space. They are non-biodegradable. Therefore throwing away poly(alkenes) creates rubbish that will pollute the environment for centuries (Figure 15.19).

Burning plastic waste

One way to solve this problem would be to burn the poly(alkene)s and use the energy released to generate electricity. As we have seen on page 204, if hydrocarbons burn in excess oxygen the products are carbon dioxide

Figure 15.19 A beach littered with poly(alkene) plastic waste.

and water. So this solution would not help combat global warming, but would help to conserve our supplies of fossil fuels that currently generate most of our electricity. However, we have also seen that toxic carbon monoxide is produced from incomplete combustion of hydrocarbons.

Another problem is the difficulty recycling plants have in separating other plastic waste from the poly(alkene)s when objects have just been thrown away without being sorted according to their recycling code. Then if poly(chloroethene) is burnt, acidic hydrogen chloride gas will be given off, as well as toxic compounds called dioxins. Acidic gases would have to be neutralised before releasing the waste gas into the atmosphere and very high temperatures used in incinerators to break down any toxins.

QUESTIONS

12 Tetrafluoroethene, C_2F_4, is the monomer for the polymer PTFE, which is used in the non-stick coating on pans.

   a What does PTFE stand for?

   b What do we call the type of reaction used to form PTFE?

   c Write a chemical equation to show the formation of PTFE from C_2F_4.

   d Draw the structure of the repeat unit in PTFE.

13 a How could poly(alkene) waste be used to conserve fossil fuels?

   b Why would your answer to part **a** add to the problem of enhanced global warming?

   c A waste batch of poly(ethene) pellets was burnt in an inefficient industrial incinerator. Name a toxic gas that would be released.

Tackling questions on addition polymers

In your exam, you might be asked to:

1 deduce the repeat unit of a polymer obtained from a given unsaturated monomer

2 identify the monomer(s) present in a given section of a polymer molecule.

1 Deducing the repeat unit of an addition polymer for given monomer(s)

Given a monomer with a C=C bond, simply turn the double bond into a C—C single bond and show the bonds either side of the two C atoms that would continue the chain:

monomer   repeat unit

2 Identifying the monomer(s) present in a given section of an addition polymer molecule

First of all you should split the polymer chain into its repeat units.

With an addition polymer, you then need to put the

C=C double bond back into the monomer:

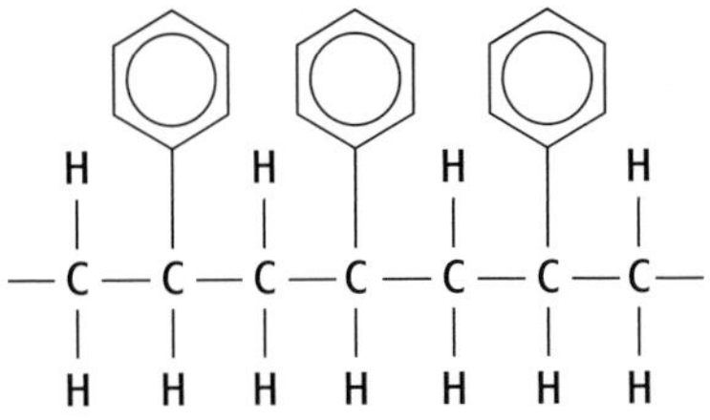

part of addition polymer

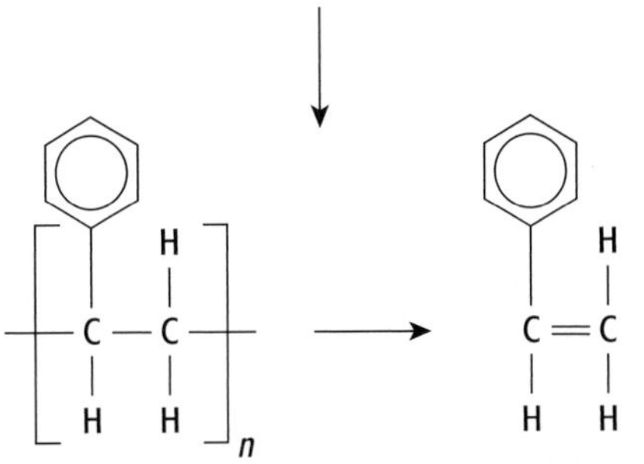

repeat unit   monomer

QUESTION

14 Name the monomer used to make this polymer:

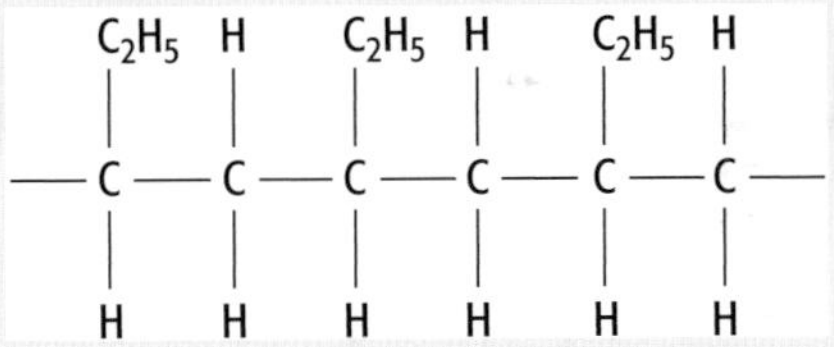

Summary

- Alkanes are saturated hydrocarbons with the general formula C_nH_{2n+2}.

- Alkanes are relatively unreactive as they are non-polar. Most reagents are polar and do not usually react with non-polar molecules.

- Alkanes are widely used as fuels. When they burn completely they produce carbon dioxide and water. However, they produce toxic carbon monoxide gas when they burn in a limited supply of oxygen, e.g. in a car engine. This gas, and other pollutants in the air, can be monitored using infra-red spectroscopy (see page 241 for more details of this instrumental technique).

- Cracking of the less useful fractions from the fractional distillation of crude oil produces a range of more useful alkanes with lower molecular masses, as well as alkenes.

- Chlorine atoms or bromine atoms can substitute for hydrogen atoms in alkanes in the presence of ultraviolet light, producing halogenoalkanes. This is called a free radical substitution reaction. The Cl—Cl or Br—Br bond undergoes homolytic fission in ultraviolet light, producing reactive Cl• or Br• free radicals. This initiation step of free-radical substitution is followed by propagation steps involving a chain reaction which regenerates the halogen free radicals. Termination steps occur, when two free radicals combine.

- Alkenes are unsaturated hydrocarbons with one carbon–carbon double bond consisting of a σ bond and a π bond. Their general formula is C_nH_{2n}.

- Alkenes are more reactive than alkanes because they contain a π bond. The characteristic reaction of the alkenes is addition, which occurs across the π bond:
  - ethene produces ethane when reacted with hydrogen over a nickel catalyst
  - ethene produces 1,2-dibromoethane when reacted with bromine at room temperature
  - ethene produces chloroethane when reacted with hydrogen chloride at room temperature
  - ethene produces ethanol when reacted with steam in the presence of concentrated H_3PO_4 catalyst.

- The mechanism of the reaction of bromine with ethene is electrophilic addition. Electrophiles accept a pair of electrons from an electron-rich atom or centre, in this case the π bond. A carbocation intermediate is formed after the addition of the first bromine atom. This rapidly reacts with a bromide ion to form 1,2-dibromoethane.

- Mild oxidation of alkenes by cold, dilute acidified manganate(VII) solution gives a diol. However, a hot, concentrated acidified manganate(VII) solution will break the C=C bond and give two oxidation products. Identifying the two products formed will indicate the position of the C=C bond in the original alkene.

- Alkenes produce many useful polymers by addition polymerisation. For example, poly(ethene) is made from $CH_2=CH_2$ and poly(chloroethene) is made from $CH_2=CHCl$.

- The disposal of poly(alkene) plastic waste is difficult, as much of it is chemically inert and non-biodegradable. When burnt, waste plastics may produce toxic products, such as hydrogen chloride from PVC (poly(chloroethene)).

End-of-chapter questions

1   2-Methylpentane, 3-ethylpentane and 2,3-dimethylbutane are alkanes.

   a   For each one give:

      i   its molecular formula [3]

      ii   its structural formula [3]

      iii   its displayed formula [3]

      iv   its skeletal formula. [3]

   b   Give the general formula that is used to represent alkanes. [1]

   c   Two of the alkanes in this question are isomers of each other. Identify which two and identify the type of isomerism they show. [2]

   d   Using terms from part **a** of this question, define **isomers**. [2]

   e   Name the alkane whose structural formula is $CH_3CH(CH_3)CH_2CH(CH_3)_2$ [1]

                                                  Total = 18

2   **a**   Alkanes are saturated hydrocarbons. Explain the words **saturated** and **hydrocarbons**. [2]

   b   Alkanes are generally unreactive. Explain why this is so. [2]

   c   Write balanced symbol equations for the complete combustion of:

      i   methane [2]

      ii   ethane. [2]

                                                  Total = 8

3 Use the passage below and your own knowledge to answer the questions that follow.

Methane reacts with bromine to give bromomethane and hydrogen bromide. The mechanism for the reaction is called free-radical substitution and involves homolytic fission of chemical bonds. The reaction proceeds via initiation, propagation and termination steps.

    a By what mechanism does bromine react with methane? [1]

    b Write a balanced symbol equation for this reaction. [2]

    c Bonds break in this reaction. What type of bond breaking is involved? [1]

    d What essential conditions are required for this reaction? Why? [2]

    e For this reaction, write down an equation for:

        i an initiation step [2]

        ii a propagation step [2]

        iii a termination step. [2]

Total = 12

4 In a similar reaction to the one in question **3**, 1.50 g of ethane reacts with chlorine. 1.29 g of chloroethane is formed.

(A_r values: H = 1.0, C = 12.0, Cl = 35.5)

Calculate:

    a the number of moles of ethane that were used [2]

    b the number of moles of chloroethane that were formed [2]

    c the percentage yield [2]

    d the number of grams of chloroethane that would have formed if the percentage yield had been 60.0%. [2]

Total = 8

5 Propene, *cis*-pent-2-ene and *trans*-pent-2-ene are alkenes.

    a For each one give:

        i its molecular formula [3]

        ii its structural formula [3]

        iii its displayed formula [3]

        iv its skeletal formula. [3]

    b Give the general formula that is used to represent alkenes. [1]

    c Two of these alkenes are isomers of each other. Identify which two. [1]

    d Why is it not possible to change one of these two isomers into the other at room temperature? [2]

    e Give displayed formulae and the names of the four alkenes with molecular formula C_4H_8. [8]

    f 3-Methylpent-2-ene has two *cis–trans* isomers. Draw and name the **two** isomers. [3]

Total = 27

6 Using structural formulae throughout, give balanced symbol equations for the following reactions.

    a Propene with bromine. [1]

    b Propene with hydrogen. Name the catalyst used. Which industrial process uses a similar reaction? [3]

    c Propene with hydrogen bromide. Give structural formulae for both possible products. [2]

    d Propene with steam. Give structural formulae for both possible products. Give the formula of the catalyst used. [3]

Total = 9

7 a Alkenes are unsaturated hydrocarbons. Explain the word **unsaturated**. [1]

    b Describe the bonding between the two carbon atoms in ethene. [2]

    c Describe and draw the shape of an ethene molecule, labelling all bond angles. [2]

    d Explain the meaning of the term **functional group**. Which functional group is present in all alkenes? [2]

    e Describe a simple chemical test to determine whether an unknown hydrocarbon is unsaturated. Describe the result if the test is positive. [2]

Total = 9

8 Use the passage below and your own knowledge to answer the questions that follow.
Ethene reacts with bromine to give 1,2-dibromoethane as the only product. The mechanism for the reaction is electrophilic addition and involves heterolytic fission of chemical bonds.
The bromine molecules behave as electrophiles in this reaction.
   a   By what mechanism does bromine react with ethene?   [1]
   b   Write a balanced symbol equation for this reaction.   [2]
   c   Bonds break in this reaction. What type of bond breaking is involved?   [1]
   d   Show the mechanism of the reaction as fully as you can, using curly arrows.   [5]
   e   Which substance behaves here as an electrophile? Explain what is meant by the term **electrophile**. [2]

Total = 11

9 In a similar reaction to the reaction described in question **8**, 2.80 g of ethene react with chlorine. 8.91 g of dichloroethane are formed.
(A_r values: H = 1.0, C = 12.0, Cl = 35.5)
Calculate:
   a   the number of moles of ethene that were used   [2]
   b   the number of moles of dichloroethane that were formed   [2]
   c   the percentage yield   [2]
   d   the number of grams of dichloroethane that would have formed if the percentage yield had been 80.0%. [2]

Total = 8

10 Alkenes are important industrial chemicals, particularly as raw materials for the manufacture of polymers. Ethene can be used to make poly(ethene). Ethene is used to make chloroethene, which is then used to make poly(chloroethene), and ethene is also used to make tetrafluoroethene, which is used to make poly(tetrafluoroethene).
   a   Use displayed formulae to write an equation for the formation of poly(chloroethene) from chloroethene. [3]
   b   Why do waste (used) poly(alkene)s cause problems in a landfill site?   [2]
   c   Burning halogenated polymers such as PVC can release toxic waste products, such as HCl, into the environment. Explain how this can be minimised.   [2]

Total = 7

Chapter 16:
Halogenoalkanes

Learning outcomes

You should be able to:

- write equations for the reactions of halogenoalkanes when they undergo:
  - nucleophilic substitution, such as hydrolysis, formation of nitriles, formation of primary amines by reaction with ammonia
  - elimination of hydrogen bromide (for example, from 2-bromopropane)
- describe and explain the S_N1 and S_N2 mechanisms of nucleophilic substitution in halogenoalkanes

- interpret the different reactivities of halogenoalkanes
- explain the uses of fluoroalkanes and fluorohalogenoalkanes in terms of their relative lack of reactivity
- explain the concern about the effect of chlorofluoroalkanes on the ozone layer.

Introduction

Halogenoalkanes are used in many industrial chemical processes. Unlike some of the elements from which they are formed, such as fluorine and chlorine, many halogenoalkanes are relatively unreactive under normal conditions. This leads to their use as flame retardants and anaesthetics.

If you have ever had an operation, you may have a halogenoalkane to thank for putting you to sleep. You might have heard of an early anaesthetic called chloroform. Its systematic name is trichloromethane. Nowadays you may receive a gas known as 'halothane':

$$
\begin{array}{ccc}
 & F & Cl \\
 & | & | \\
F - & C - C & - Br \\
 & | & | \\
 & F & H
\end{array}
$$

However, under other conditions, such as high in the Earth's stratosphere, some halogenoalkanes react in completely different ways.

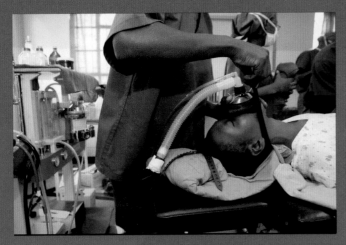

Figure 16.1 An anaesthetist putting a patient to sleep before an operation.

Nucleophilic substitution reactions

We can think of the halogenoalkanes as alkanes that have one or more hydrogen atoms replaced by halogen atoms.

> Remember that the halogens are the elements in Group 17 of the Periodic Table, namely fluorine (F), chlorine (Cl), bromine (Br) and iodine (I).

The simplest halogenoalkanes, whose molecules contain just one halogen atom, will have the general formula $C_nH_{2n+1}X$, where X is F, Cl, Br or I. The presence of the halogen atom has a huge effect on the reactivity of the halogenoalkanes compared with that of the alkanes.

1 Substitution reactions with aqueous alkali, OH⁻(aq)

When an aqueous solution of sodium hydroxide is added to a halogenoalkane, a nucleophilic substitution reaction takes place. The halogen atom in the halogenoalkane is replaced by an —OH, hydroxyl group, so the organic product formed is an alcohol:

$$CH_3CH_2Br + NaOH \longrightarrow CH_3CH_2OH + NaBr$$
bromoethane \qquad\qquad\qquad ethanol

We can also show this equation as:

$$CH_3CH_2Br + OH^- \longrightarrow CH_3CH_2OH + Br^-$$

The aqueous hydroxide ion behaves as a nucleophile here, because it is donating a pair of electrons to the carbon atom bonded to the halogen in the halogenoalkane. This is why the reaction is called a **nucleophilic** substitution.

HYDROLYSIS OF A HALOGENOALKANE

The reaction is carried out under reflux in the laboratory. This enables us to heat the reaction mixture without evaporating off the volatile organic compounds in the reaction flask. The apparatus is shown in Figure 16.2.

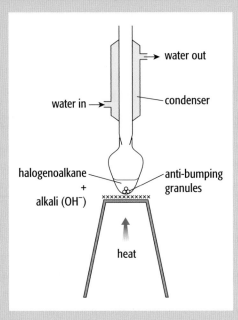

Figure 16.2 Reflux apparatus for hydrolysis of a halogenoalkane.

Similar reactions occur with other halogenoalkanes, but the reaction rates differ. We can investigate the rate of hydrolysis using aqueous silver nitrate solution. The water in the silver nitrate solution acts as the nucleophile, and again an alcohol is formed. The reaction is called hydrolysis (meaning 'breakdown by water'):

$$CH_3CH_2Br + H_2O \longrightarrow CH_3CH_2OH + H^+ + Br^-$$

It is a very similar reaction to the reaction that takes place with aqueous alkali.

However, the hydrolysis with water occurs more slowly than with OH⁻(aq). This is because the negatively charged hydroxide ion is a more effective nucleophile than a neutral water molecule.

From the equation above, you can see that a halide ion, in this case Br⁻, is produced in the reaction.

On page 175 we used silver nitrate solution to test for halide ions. Remember that aqueous chlorides give a white precipitate (silver chloride), bromides give a cream precipitate (silver bromide) and iodides produce a pale yellow precipitate (silver iodide). The water in the silver nitrate solution will hydrolyse a halogenoalkane.

Observing this reaction, we can time how long it takes for test tubes containing the halogenoalkanes and aqueous silver nitrate solution to become opaque.

We find that:

■ the fastest nucleophilic substitution reactions take place with the iodoalkanes
■ the slowest nucleophilic substitution reactions take place with the fluoroalkanes.

The substitution reaction involves the breaking of the carbon—halogen bond. Looking at the bond energies

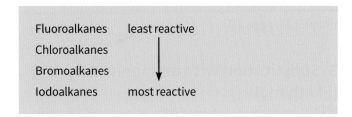

(Table 16.1) helps us to explain the rates of reaction. Notice that the C–I bond is the weakest, so it is broken most easily. It forms an I⁻ ion during the substitution reaction. This is shown clearly in an ionic equation:

$$\underset{\text{iodooethane}}{CH_3CH_2I} + OH^- \longrightarrow \underset{\text{ethanol}}{CH_3CH_2OH} + I^-$$

There is more about the mechanism of nucleophilic substitution on pages 220–1.

Bond	Bond energy / kJ mol⁻¹
C—F	467 (strongest bond)
C—Cl	346
C—Br	290
C—I	228 (weakest bond)

Table 16.1 Bond energy values of the carbon–halogen bonds.

2 Substitution with cyanide ions, CN⁻ (in ethanol)

In this reaction the nucleophile is the cyanide, CN⁻, ion. To carry out the reaction, a solution of potassium cyanide, KCN, in ethanol (known as an ethanolic or alcoholic

219

solution of potassium cyanide) is made up. This is then heated under reflux with the halogenoalkane. An ionic equation for this reaction is:

$$CH_3CH_2Br + CN^- \longrightarrow CH_3CH_2CN + Br^-$$
bromoethane   propanenitrile

Note that in the reaction with the cyanide ion, an extra carbon atom is added to the original halogenoalkane chain. In this case, bromoethane is converted to propanenitrile.

Sometimes in industry chemists need to make a new compound with one more carbon atom than the best available organic raw material (the starting compound). Therefore, if we can convert the starting compound to a halogenoalkane, we can then reflux with ethanolic KCN to make a nitrile. We now have an intermediate nitrile with the correct number of carbon atoms.

We will consider nitriles and their subsequent conversion to carboxylic acids and amines again in Chapter 18, page 231.

3 Substitution with ammonia, NH$_3$ (in ethanol)

If a halogenoalkane is heated with an excess of ammonia dissolved in ethanol under pressure, an amine is formed.

$$CH_3CH_2Br + NH_3 \longrightarrow CH_3CH_2NH_2 + HBr$$
bromoethane   ethylamine

Here the nucleophile is the ammonia molecule. Ethylamine is a primary amine, as the nitrogen atom is attached to only one alkyl group. If the ammonia is not in excess, we get a mixture of amine products. This is because the primary amine product will act as a nucleophile itself and will attack halogenoalkane molecules, forming secondary amines, and so on. The secondary amine formed above would be $(CH_3CH_2)_2NH$, called diethylamine. You can read more about amines in Chapter 27, page 401.

QUESTIONS

1   a   Why does the hydrolysis of a halogenoalkane happen more quickly with OH$^-$(aq) ions than with water molecules?

     b   Explain why silver nitrate solution can be used to investigate the rate of hydrolysis of the halogenoalkanes. Include ionic equations for the formation of the precipitates.

QUESTIONS (CONTINUED)

2   a   Why can ammonia and amine molecules act as nucleophiles?

     b   When ammonia is reacted with an excess of a halogenoalkane, a mixture of amines can be formed. If we start with an excess of 1-bromopropane, give the structural formula and name of the **tertiary** amine formed.

Mechanism of nucleophilic substitution in halogenoalkanes

Many of the reactions of halogenoalkanes are nucleophilic substitutions. In these reactions, the nucleophile attacks the carbon atom bonded to the halogen. Remember from Chapter 14 that nucleophiles are donors of an electron pair and are attracted to electron-deficient atoms.

The carbon–halogen bond is polarised because the halogen is more electronegative than carbon. Therefore the carbon atom carries a partial positive charge as the electron pair in the carbon–halogen bond is drawn nearer to the halogen atom (shown in Figure 16.3). The halogen atom is replaced by the nucleophile in the substitution reaction.

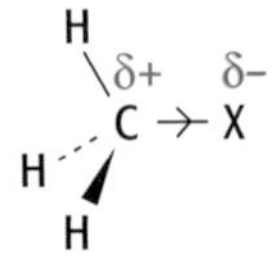

Figure 16.3   The carbon–halogen bond is polarised.

There are two possible mechanisms that can operate in the nucleophilic substitution reactions of halogenoalkanes. The mechanism is determined by the structure of the halogenoalkane involved in the reaction.

Mechanism for primary halogenoalkanes (S$_N$2)

In primary halogenoalkanes containing one halogen atom, the halogen atom is bonded to a carbon atom, which is itself bonded to one other carbon atom and two hydrogen atoms. This means that the carbon atom bonded to the halogen is attached to one alkyl group. For example, 1-chloropropane, $CH_3CH_2CH_2Cl$, is a primary halogenoalkane. On page 220 we looked at the hydrolysis of bromoethane, another primary halogenoalkane. Figure 16.4 shows the mechanism for that reaction.

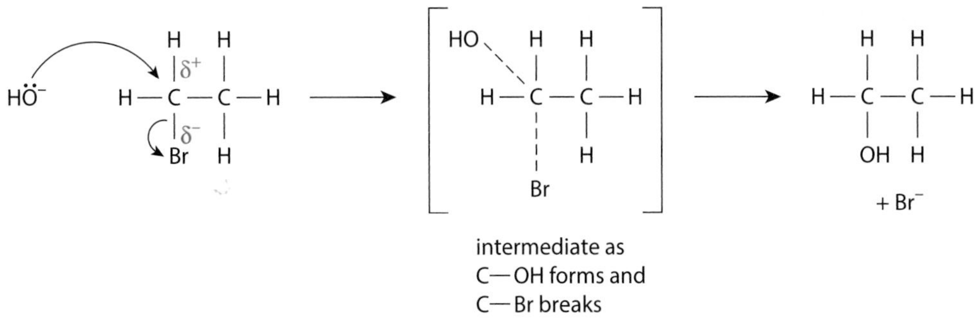

intermediate as
C—OH forms and
C—Br breaks

Figure 16.4 The mechanism of nucleophilic substitution in a primary halogenoalkane.

The OH$^-$ ion donates a pair of electrons to the δ+ carbon atom, forming a new covalent bond. At the same time, the C—Br bond is breaking. The Br atom takes both the electrons in the bond (an example of heterolytic fission of a covalent bond, see page 196) and leaves as a Br$^-$ ion.

This mechanism is called an **S$_N$2 mechanism**. The 'S' stands for substitution and the 'N' stands for nucleophilic. The '2' tells us that the rate of the reaction, which is determined by the slow step in the mechanism (see page 141), involves two reacting species. Experiments show us that the rate depends on both the concentration of the halogenoalkane and the concentration of the hydroxide ions present.

Mechanism for tertiary halogenoalkanes (S$_N$1)

In a tertiary halogenoalkane, the carbon atom bonded to the halogen atom is also bonded to three other carbon atoms (alkyl groups). For example, 2-bromo-2-methylpropane is a tertiary halogenoalkane. Its structure is shown in Figure 16.5.

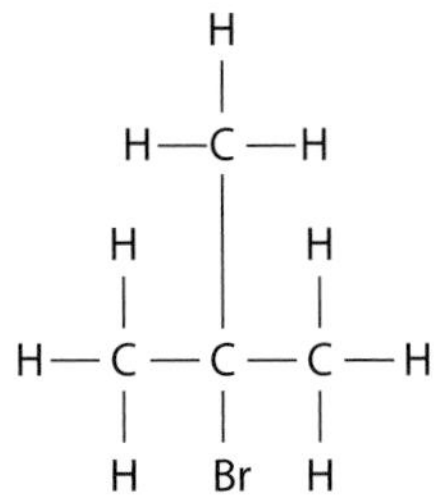

Figure 16.5 A tertiary halogenoalkane, 2-bromo-2-methylpropane.

A tertiary halogenoalkane reacts with a hydroxide ion by a two-step mechanism. The first step in the mechanism

is the breaking of the carbon–halogen bond. This forms a tertiary carbocation, which is attacked immediately by the hydroxide ion (Figure 16.6).

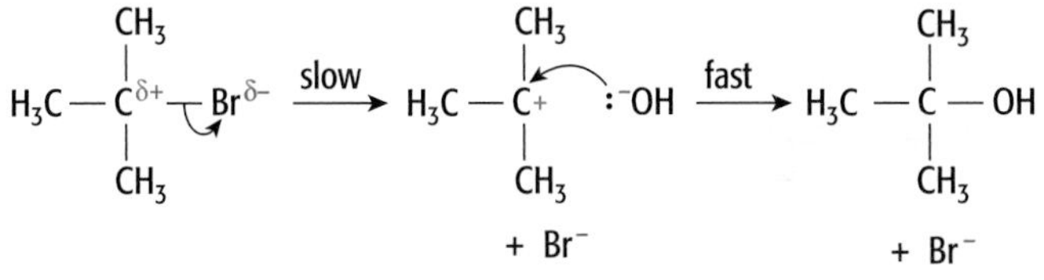

Figure 16.6 The mechanism of nucleophilic substitution in a tertiary halogenoalkane.

This mechanism is known as an **S$_N$1 mechanism**. The '1' tells us that the rate of the reaction only depends on one reagent, in this case the concentration of the halogenoalkane, as shown in the first (slow) step of the mechanism.

Once again, this breaking of the C—Br bond is an example of heterolytic fission.

The Br$^-$ ion forms again, as in the S$_N$2 mechanism, but in this mechanism a carbocation ion forms. This does not happen with primary halogenoalkanes. This is because tertiary carbocations are more stable than primary carbocations due to the inductive effect of the alkyl groups attached to the carbon atom bonded to the halogen. Alkyl groups tend to release electrons to atoms attached to them. So a tertiary carbocation has three alkyl groups donating electrons towards the positively charged carbon atom, reducing its charge density. This makes it more stable than a primary carbocation, which just has one alkyl group releasing electrons (Figure 16.7).

The S$_N$1 mechanism and the S$_N$2 mechanism are both likely to play a part in the nucleophilic substitution of **secondary** halogenoalkanes.

221

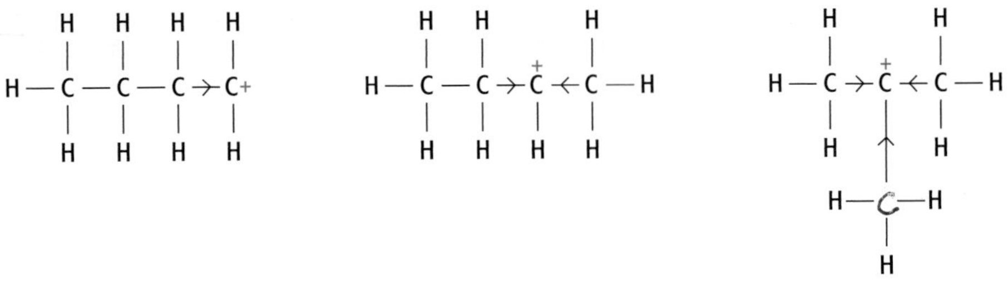

primary carbocation
(least stable)

secondary carbocation

tertiary carbocation
(most stable)

Figure 16.7 The trend in the stability of primary, secondary and tertiary carbocations.

QUESTIONS

3   Show the mechanism, including appropriate curly arrows, for the hydrolysis of 1-chloropropane, $CH_3CH_2CH_2Cl$, by alkali.

4   **a**   Draw the structure (displayed formula) of 2-chloro-2-methylbutane.

    b   Show the mechanism for the hydrolysis of 2-chloro-2-methylbutane by alkali.

Elimination reactions

Halogenoalkanes also undergo elimination reactions. An elimination reaction involves the loss of a small molecule from the original organic molecule. In the case of halogenoalkanes, this small molecule is a hydrogen halide, such as HCl or HBr.

The reagent used in these elimination reactions is ethanolic sodium hydroxide:

$$CH_3CHBrCH_3 + NaOH(ethanol)$$
2-bromopropane

$$\longrightarrow CH_2{=}CHCH_3 + H_2O + NaBr$$
propene

The original 2-bromopropane molecule has lost an H atom and a Br atom. We can think of it as HBr being eliminated from the halogenoalkane. The ethanolic OH^- ion acts as a base, accepting an H^+ from the halogenoalkane to form water. The C—Br bond breaks heterolytically, forming a Br^- ion and leaving an alkene as the organic product.

Notice the importance of the conditions used in organic reactions. If we use NaOH(aq), a nucleophilic substitution reaction occurs and an alcohol is produced. If we use NaOH(ethanol), an elimination reaction occurs and an alkene is produced.

QUESTION

5   Write a balanced equation for the reaction of bromoethane with ethanolic sodium hydroxide.

Uses of halogenoalkanes

Halogenoalkanes are rarely found naturally but they are important in the chemical industry. They are frequently made as intermediates for making other useful substances but have also found some uses themselves. We have already seen at the start of this chapter how some halogenoalkanes are important anaesthetics, for example 2-bromo-2-chloro-1,1,1-trifluoroethane (halothane). One of the essential properties of an anaesthetic is chemical inertness, and each halothane molecule contains three very strong C—F bonds that are difficult to break, making halothane inert and safe to use in the aqueous environment inside the body.

The non-stick lining of pans is a 'fluoropolymer'. Its name is poly(tetrafluoroethene) – often referred to by its trade name Teflon®. The strength of the C—F bond means that it can be used at high temperatures during cooking without breaking down. The polymer is now finding uses in ice-skating blades because of its durability and its 'low-friction' properties.

CFC substitutes containing fluorine

CFCs are chlorofluorocarbons. Chemists refer to them as chlorofluoroalkanes. These organic compounds are all chemically inert (very unreactive). They are not flammable and are not toxic. These properties made volatile CFCs useful as aerosol propellants, solvents and as the refrigerants inside fridges. They were also used as blowing agents for polymers such as expanded polystyrene.

Dichlorodifluoromethane is an example of a CFC used for these purposes.

When the compounds were discovered in the 1930s, people could see no drawbacks to using the new 'wonder compounds'. However, CFCs have caused a serious environmental issue – the depletion of the ozone layer in the upper atmosphere. The ozone layer protects the Earth by absorbing harmful UV radiation arriving from the Sun.

It turns out that CFCs are unreactive in normal conditions, but high up in the atmosphere they become totally different. The CFCs can persist in the atmosphere for about a hundred years. They diffuse up to the stratosphere – and that's where the problem starts. The UV light from the Sun breaks the C—Cl bonds in the CFC molecules. This releases highly reactive chlorine atoms, called chlorine free radicals. These chlorine free radicals react with ozone molecules. In a sequence of chain reactions, it has been estimated that each chlorine free radical can destroy a million ozone molecules (Figure 16.8).

Governments have tackled the problem, and most industrialised countries have now banned the use of CFCs. Chemists developed new compounds for fridges and aerosols, such as hydrofluorocarbons (HFCs): for example, CH_2FCF_3. These non-chlorinated compounds break down more quickly once released into the air because of the presence of hydrogen in their molecules, so they never rise in the atmosphere as far as the ozone layer. There are now signs that the ozone layer is recovering from the effects of CFCs. The hole in the ozone layer is very slowly closing up.

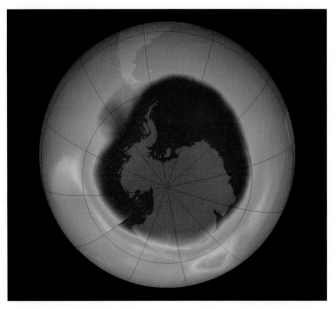

Figure 16.8 Banning the use of CFCs has meant that the hole in the ozone layer over Antarctica is now getting smaller.

HFEs are hydrofluoroethers, which are solvents marketed as 'low global warming' and are used in industry for cleaning and drying. When fluorine replaces chlorine in a solvent the new compound is more stable, again due to C—F being stronger than C—Cl.

223

QUESTION

6 How can such unreactive compounds as CFCs cause so much damage to the ozone layer?

Summary

- If one or more of the hydrogen atoms in an alkane molecule are replaced by halogen atoms, the compound is called a halogenoalkane.

- Iodoalkanes are the most reactive halogenoalkanes, whereas fluoroalkanes are the least reactive. This is explained by the trend in the bond strength of the carbon–halogen bonds. The C—F bond is the strongest bond, and the C—I bond is the weakest bond. So the C—I bond is most easily broken during its reactions.

- Halogenoalkanes are attacked by nucleophiles. This happens because the carbon bonded to the halogen carries a partial positive charge due to the higher electronegativity of the halogen. Halogenoalkanes undergo nucleophilic substitution.

- Suitable nucleophiles include aqueous alkali, OH^- (aq), cyanide, CN^-, and ammonia, NH_3.

- The reaction with OH^- ions (or with water) is known as hydrolysis, and an alcohol is formed.

- Halogenoalkanes will also undergo elimination reactions when heated with ethanolic sodium hydroxide, forming alkenes.

- The fluoroalkanes and fluorohalogenoalkanes have many uses, including anaesthetics, solvents, refrigerants and aerosol propellants.

- Chlorofluoroalkanes have been responsible for damaging the Earth's ozone layer, but alternative inert compounds, such as fluoroalkanes, are now replacing the use of CFCs.

End-of-chapter questions

1 1-bromobutane will undergo reactions when heated, as shown by reactions A and B.

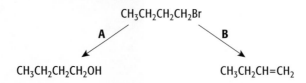

a   For reactions A and B give the reagents used in each case.   [2]

b   Reaction A was repeated using 1-iodobutane instead of 1-bromobutane. Explain any difference in the
    rate of reaction observed.   [2]

c   What type of organic reaction is A?   [1]

d   Show the mechanism for reaction A.   [3]

e   Reaction A was repeated with 2-bromo-2-methylpropane instead of 1-bromobutane.

   i   Name the organic compound formed.   [1]

   ii The mechanism of the reaction with 2-bromo-2-methylpropane differs from the mechanism of
       reaction A. Describe how the mechanisms differ.   [2]

f   What type of reaction is B?   [1]

g   If reaction B was repeated with 2-bromobutane, name the other organic products that can form as
    well as the product shown above.   [2]

Total = 14

2 Bromochlorodifluoromethane has been used in fire extinguishers. However, its breakdown products
  were found to be toxic.

a   Draw the displayed formula of bromochlorodifluoromethane.   [1]

b CF_3CH_2F is being introduced as a replacement for various CFCs in refrigerants and aerosols.
    Name this compound.   [1]

c   What is the main environmental problem caused by the use of CFCs?   [1]

Total = 3

Chapter 17:
Alcohols, esters and carboxylic acids

Learning outcomes

You should be able to:

- recall the chemistry of alcohols, such as ethanol, in combustion, substitution to give halogenoalkanes, reaction with sodium, oxidation to carbonyl compounds and carboxylic acids, and dehydration to alkenes
- classify hydroxy compounds into primary, secondary and tertiary alcohols
- suggest characteristic distinguishing reactions, e.g. mild oxidation
- describe the acid and base hydrolysis of esters

- state the major commercial uses of esters, e.g. solvents, perfumes, flavourings
- describe the formation of carboxylic acids from alcohols, aldehydes and nitriles
- describe the reactions of carboxylic acids in the formation of:
  - salts, by the use of reactive metals, alkalis or carbonates
  - alkyl esters, by reaction with alcohols
  - alcohols, by use of LiAlH$_4$.

Introduction

Ethanol, C_2H_5OH, is the most widely used of the homologous series of alcohols. The sugar extracted from crops such as sugar cane and sugar beet can be fermented with yeast to make ethanol. Ethanol is a 'biofuel' and burns with a clean flame. This process is becoming increasingly important as our supplies of crude oil diminish and cleaner, easier to produce biofuels are needed to take the place of petrol and diesel.

Figure 17.1 The sugar extracted from sugar cane can be fermented with yeast to make ethanol.

The homologous series of alcohols

Alcohols are organic molecules containing the hydroxyl group, —OH. With one hydroxyl group substituted into an alkane molecule, the general formula is $C_nH_{2n+1}OH$. The alcohols are named by adding '-anol' to the alkane stem. For example, CH_3OH is called methanol. For alcohol molecules with three or more carbon atoms, the position of the hydroxyl group is shown by inserting a number to indicate which carbon atom is bonded to the OH group. Figure 17.2 gives some examples.

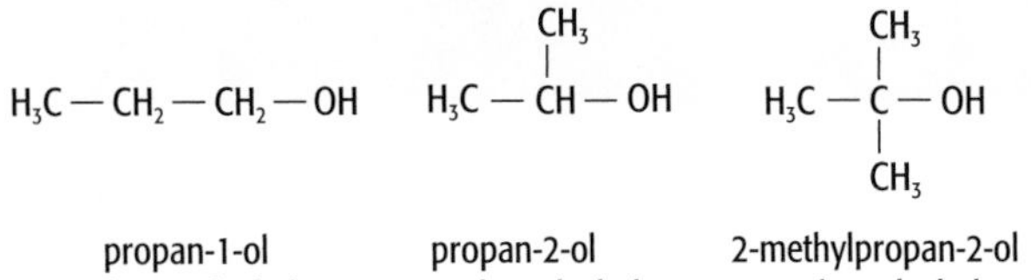

Figure 17.2 Note that the numbering to show the position of the OH group in an alcohol starts from the end of the molecule that gives the smaller number.

Propan-1-ol is classified as a **primary alcohol**. The carbon atom bonded to the —OH group is attached to one other carbon atom (alkyl group). Propan-2-ol is a **secondary alcohol** as the carbon atom bonded to the —OH group is attached to two other carbon atoms (alkyl groups). With three alkyl groups attached, 2-methylpropan-2-ol is an example of a **tertiary alcohol**.

The alcohols have higher boiling points than expected when compared with other organic molecules with similar relative molecular masses. Even methanol, the alcohol with the lowest molar mass, is a liquid at room temperature. This occurs because of hydrogen bonding between alcohol molecules (see page 64). Hydrogen bonding also explains why the smaller alcohol molecules mix and dissolve so well in water.

QUESTION

1 **a** Explain how hydrogen bonds arise:
   i between ethanol molecules
   ii between ethanol and water molecules.
b Ethanol mixes with water in all proportions but hexan-1-ol is less miscible with water. Why is this?

Reactions of the alcohols

1 Combustion

When ignited, the alcohols react with oxygen in the air. The products of complete combustion are carbon dioxide and water. For example, ethanol burns with a clean blue flame in a good supply of air:

alcohol + oxygen ⟶ carbon dioxide + water

$$\underset{\text{ethanol}}{C_2H_5OH} + 3O_2 \longrightarrow 2CO_2 + 3H_2O$$

Ethanol is sometimes used in Brazil as a car fuel. This reduces the use of petrol.

A country like Brazil has few oil reserves but can grow plenty of sugar cane, which can be fermented to make ethanol, which is used as a fuel either in pure form or in mixtures with other fuels (Figure 17.3). As well as conserving the world's diminishing supplies of crude oil, sugar cane has the advantage of absorbing CO_2 as it grows. Although the CO_2 is effectively returned to the atmosphere during fermentation and when the ethanol burns, **biofuels** such as ethanol are said to be 'carbon neutral'. Overall, they do not increase the greenhouse gases in the air (in theory). Even if we take into account the CO_2 produced in growing, harvesting, transporting and processing the sugar cane, it is still much better for the environment to use 'bio-ethanol' as a fuel than petrol or diesel from crude oil.

Figure 17.3 The fuel called 'gasohol' is a mixture of ethanol and petrol.

Ethanol is used as a solvent as well as a fuel. We often use it as 'methylated spirits', which contains about 90% ethanol.

QUESTION

2 a Write a balanced equation for the complete combustion of:

   i propan-1-ol

   ii butan-1-ol.

 b Glucose can be fermented with yeast in anaerobic conditions. Name the products of the reaction.

2 Substitution to form a halogenoalkane

In this substitution reaction with a hydrogen halide, such as hydrogen chloride, the —OH group in the alcohol is replaced by a halogen atom to produce a halogenoalkane. The carbon atom bonded to the hydroxyl group in the alcohol will carry a partial positive charge (as oxygen is more electronegative than carbon). This makes the carbon atom open to nucleophilic attack. The initial attack on the alcohol is by the partially negative halogen atom in the hydrogen halide:

$$\overset{\delta+}{H} \rightarrow \overset{\delta-}{X} \quad \text{where X = halogen atom}$$

alcohol + hydrogen halide $\longrightarrow$ halogenoalkane + water

For example:

$$CH_3CH_2OH + HCl \longrightarrow CH_3CH_2Cl + 3H_2O$$

ethanol   chloroethane

The dry hydrogen chloride gas for this reaction can be made *in situ* (in the reaction vessel). Sodium chloride and concentrated sulfuric acid are used for this:

$$NaCl + H_2SO_4 \longrightarrow NaHSO_4 + HCl$$

HALOGENATION OF AN ALCOHOL

The alcohol is heated under reflux (see apparatus on page 219) with the reactants to make the halogenoalkane. The halogenoalkane made can then be distilled off from the reaction mixture and collected as oily droplets under water (Figure 17.4).

Figure 17.4 Bromoethane being distilled off following the reaction between ethanol and hydrogen bromide. The white solid visible in the pear-shaped flask is sodium bromide (as crystals). The sodium bromide reacts with concentrated sulfuric acid to make the hydrogen bromide needed for the reaction.

227

Sulfur dichloride oxide, $SOCl_2$, can also be used to substitute a chlorine atom into an alcohol molecule, as shown below:

$$C_2H_5OH + SOCl_2 \longrightarrow C_2H_5Cl + HCl + SO_2$$

Note that in this reaction the two byproducts of the reaction (HCl and SO_2) are both gases. These escape from the reaction mixture, leaving the halogenoalkane, without the need to distil it off as in the hydrogen halide reaction.

We can also use phosphorus halides to provide the halogen atoms for this substitution reaction.

For chloroalkanes we can use solid phosphorus(V) chloride, PCl_5:

$$C_2H_5OH + PCl_5 \xrightarrow{\text{room temperature}} C_2H_5Cl + HCl + POCl_3$$

The release of acidic hydrogen chloride gas from this reaction can be used as a test for the hydroxyl group. The HCl gas causes acidic 'steamy fumes' to be observed.

Phosphorus(III) chloride can also be used to halogenate an alcohol, but this reaction does require heating.

For bromoalkanes and iodoalkanes we can make the phosphorus(III) halide, PBr_3 or PI_3, *in situ* using red phosphorus and bromine or iodine. These are warmed with the alcohol. For example:

$$3C_2H_5OH + PI_3 \longrightarrow \underset{\text{iodoethane}}{3C_2H_5I} + H_3PO_3$$

QUESTION

3 a Write a balanced equation to show the reaction between ethanol and hydrogen bromide.

   b What are the reagents and conditions used for this reaction?

   c What do we call this type of reaction?

---

3 Reaction with sodium metal

In the reaction with hydrogen halides, the C—O bond in the alcohol breaks. However, in some other reactions the O—H bond in the alcohol breaks. The reaction with sodium metal is an example:

$$\underset{\text{ethanol}}{C_2H_5OH} + \underset{\text{sodium}}{Na} \longrightarrow \underset{\text{sodium ethoxide}}{C_2H_5O^-Na^+} + \underset{\text{hydrogen}}{H_2}$$

The reaction is similar to sodium's reaction with water, but less vigorous. In both cases hydrogen gas is given off and

a basic ionic compound is formed. With ethanol, if the excess ethanol is evaporated off after the reaction, a white crystalline solid is left. This is the sodium ethoxide.

Other alcohols react in a similar way with sodium. For example, propan-1-ol would produce sodium propoxide plus hydrogen gas.

In general:

$$\text{alcohol} + \text{sodium} \longrightarrow \text{sodium alkoxide} + \text{hydrogen}$$

We find that the longer the hydrocarbon chain, the less vigorous the reaction.

Figure 17.5 Sodium reacting with ethanol. The pink colour is from a colourless phenolphthalein indicator that has been added to the ethanol, showing the basic nature of the sodium ethoxide formed.

QUESTION

4 Lithium reacts with alcohols in a similar way to sodium. A small piece of lithium metal is dropped onto a watch-glass containing propan-1-ol.

   a What would you observe?

   b Name the products of the reaction.

   c What difference would you expect to see if you used sodium instead of lithium in this reaction?

4 Esterification

ALCOHOL PLUS CARBOXYLIC ACID

Another reaction that involves the breaking of the O—H bond in alcohols is **esterification**, i.e. the making of esters. An esterification reaction is usually between an alcohol and a carboxylic acid. The general equation is:

$$\text{carboxylic acid} + \text{alcohol} \underset{}{\overset{\text{acid catalyst}}{\rightleftharpoons}} \text{ester} + \text{water}$$

For this reaction to take place, the carboxylic acid and alcohol are heated under reflux with a **strong** acid catalyst (usually concentrated sulfuric acid). The reaction is reversible, so an equilibrium can be established with all the reactants and products shown in the general equation present.

The esters formed usually have sweet, fruity smells. They are present naturally in fruits, and we use them in artificial flavourings and perfumes (Figure 17.6). They are also used as solvents, e.g. in nail varnish remover.

Here is an example of an esterification reaction:

$$C_2H_5OH + CH_3C\overset{O}{\underset{OH}{\diagdown}} \overset{H_2SO_4}{\rightleftharpoons} CH_3C\overset{O}{\underset{OC_2H_5}{\diagdown}} + H_2O$$

ethanol   ethanoic acid   ethyl ethanoate   water

The ester formed is called ethyl ethanoate.

What would be the name of the ester formed if ethanol was reacted with propanoic acid? Would it be propyl ethanoate or ethyl propanoate? The answer

Figure 17.6 Esters contribute to the complex mixture of substances blended in a perfume.

is ethyl propanoate. That's because the first part of an ester's name comes from the alcohol: in this case ethanol, giving 'ethyl …'. The second part comes from the carboxylic acid, in this case propanoic acid, giving '… propanoate', thus making the name of the ester formed 'ethyl propanoate':

$$\underset{\text{propanoic acid}}{CH_3CH_2COOH} + \underset{\text{ethanol}}{C_2H_5OH}$$

$$\overset{H_2SO_4}{\rightleftharpoons} \underset{\text{ethyl propanoate}}{CH_3CH_2COOC_2H_5} + \underset{\text{water}}{H_2O}$$

Hydrolysis of esters

Esters can be hydrolysed by heating under reflux with either an acid or a base.

Refluxing with an acid simply reverses the preparation of the ester from an alcohol and a carboxylic acid. The acid catalyses the reaction. The reaction is reversible and an equilibrium mixture is established. In acid hydrolysis, there are always both reactants (ester + water) and products (carboxylic acid + alcohol) present after the reaction. The equation for the acid hydrolysis of the ester ethyl ethanoate is:

$$H_3C-C\overset{O}{\underset{O-CH_2CH_3}{\diagdown}} + H_2O \overset{H^+(aq)}{\rightleftharpoons} H_3C-C\overset{O}{\underset{O-H}{\diagdown}} + CH_3CH_2OH$$

However, when an ester is refluxed with an alkali (a soluble base), such as aqueous sodium hydroxide, it is fully hydrolysed. Unlike acid hydrolysis, this is not a reversible reaction, so all the ester present can be broken down by excess alkali. An alcohol and the sodium salt of the carboxylic acid are formed. The equation for the base hydrolysis of ethyl ethanoate is:

$$H_3C - C\overset{\displaystyle O}{\underset{\displaystyle O-CH_2CH_3}{\big\langle}} + NaOH \longrightarrow H_3C-C\overset{\displaystyle O}{\underset{\displaystyle O^-Na^+}{\big\langle}} + CH_3CH_2OH$$

sodium ethanoate

QUESTION

5 **a** Name the ester formed in each of the following reactions:
   i butan-1-ol + ethanoic acid
   ii ethanol + hexanoic acid
   iii pentan-1-ol and methanoic acid.

b Write the structural formula of each ester formed in part **a**.

5 Dehydration

Alcohols can also undergo elimination reactions in which water is lost and alkenes are formed. As the small molecule removed from the alcohol molecule is H_2O, this reaction is also known as **dehydration**.

$$\text{alcohol} \xrightarrow{\text{catalyst}} \text{alkene} + \text{water}$$

The reaction takes place when alcohol vapour is passed over a hot catalyst of aluminium oxide powder. Pieces of porous pot or pumice also catalyse the reaction. For example:

$$\underset{\text{ethanol}}{C_2H_5OH} \xrightarrow{Al_2O_3 \text{ catalyst}} \underset{\text{ethene}}{CH_2{=}CH_2} + \underset{\text{water}}{H_2O}$$

Figure 17.7 shows how the ethene gas formed can be collected.

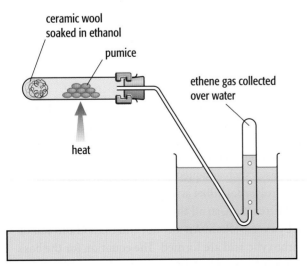

Figure 17.7 The dehydration of ethanol to give ethene.

QUESTION

6 Concentrated sulfuric acid or phosphoric acid can also be used to catalyse the dehydration of an alcohol. The alcohol and concentrated acid are heated to about 170 °C. The concentrated acid does not change chemically during the reaction.

a Write an equation showing the dehydration of ethanol using concentrated sulfuric acid.

b If propan-1-ol was used instead of ethanol, name the organic product formed.

6 Oxidation

On page 226 we saw how alcohols can be classified as primary, secondary or tertiary. For many of their reactions, the class of alcohol makes no difference to the type of products formed. In organic chemistry, we can usually generalise for the whole homologous series. However, when alcohols are oxidised, different products are obtained from primary, secondary and tertiary alcohols.

Alcohols can be oxidised by potassium dichromate(VI) solution, $K_2Cr_2O_7$, acidified with dilute sulfuric acid. The solution's orange colour is caused by the dichromate(VI) ions, $Cr_2O_7{}^{2-}(aq)$. When the dichromate(VI) ions react as an oxidising agent, they themselves are reduced and turn into chromium(III) ions, $Cr^{3+}(aq)$, which form a green solution. The reaction mixture needs to be warmed before the oxidation takes place.

The product formed when an alcohol is oxidised can be used to distinguish between primary, secondary and tertiary alcohols. You can learn about the chemical tests for the products on pages 238–9.

■ With tertiary alcohols, a mixture of the tertiary alcohol, dilute sulfuric acid and potassium dichromate(VI) solution remains orange when warmed. No reaction takes place under these relatively mild conditions.

■ A secondary alcohol, such as propan-2-ol, will be oxidised to form a ketone. In this case propanone is formed and the reaction mixture turns green:

$$H_3C-\overset{\displaystyle OH}{\underset{\displaystyle H}{\overset{\displaystyle |}{\underset{\displaystyle |}{C}}}}-CH_3 + [O] \longrightarrow H_3C-\overset{\displaystyle O}{\overset{\displaystyle \|}{C}}-CH_3 + H_2O$$

propanone

These oxidation equations use [O] to show the oxygen added from the oxidising agent. You have met this type of simplified equation for oxidation reactions before on page 198.

■ With a primary alcohol, such as ethanol, the alcohol is oxidised to an aldehyde. Ethanol is oxidised to ethanal:

$$CH_3CH_2OH + [O] \longrightarrow H_3C - \overset{\overset{\displaystyle O}{\|}}{C} - H + H_2O$$
ethanal

The ethanal formed can be further oxidised to form ethanoic acid, a carboxylic acid. This is achieved by refluxing with excess acidified potassium dichromate(VI):

$$H_3C - \overset{\overset{\displaystyle O}{\|}}{C} - H + [O] \longrightarrow H_3C - \overset{\overset{\displaystyle O}{\|}}{C} - OH$$
ethanoic acid

DISTINGUISHING TERTIARY ALCOHOLS

Given three unknown alcohols, one primary, one secondary and one tertiary, it would be easy to distinguish the tertiary alcohol. Figure 17.8 shows the results of warming each class of alcohol with a solution of acidified potassium dichromate(VI). More details of these reactions are given on page 236.

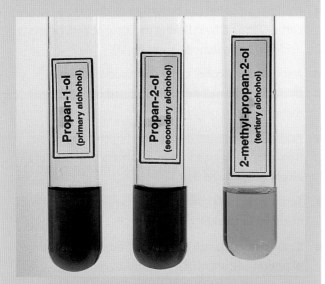

Figure 17.8 Before warming with the labelled alcohol, each of these tubes contained orange acidified potassium dichromate(VI) solution. After warming, the orange dichromate(VI) ions have been reduced to green chromium(III) ions by the primary and secondary alcohols. This shows that both the primary and secondary alcohols have been oxidised but the tertiary alcohol, 2-methylpropan-2-ol, has not.

QUESTION

7 Propan-1-ol can be oxidised to propanal, CH_3CH_2CHO, and then to propanoic acid, CH_3CH_2COOH.
   a What reagents and conditions should be used to oxidise propan-1-ol to propanal?
   b Write a balanced chemical equation for this oxidation. Oxygen from the oxidising agent should be shown as [O].
   c What reagents and conditions should be used to oxidise propan-1-ol to propanoic acid?
   d Write a balanced chemical equation for this oxidation. Again, show oxygen from the oxidising agent as [O].

Carboxylic acids

Reactions that form carboxylic acids

We have already seen how primary alcohols can be oxidised to aldehydes and then further oxidation of the aldehyde formed yields the carboxylic acid.

Carboxylic acids are also made from nitriles, $R - C \equiv N$. When a nitrile is refluxed with dilute hydrochloric acid hydrolysis occurs, and the $-C \equiv N$ group at the end of the hydrocarbon chain is converted to the $-COOH$ group, forming a carboxylic acid (see page 237). For example:

$$CH_3CH_2CN + HCl + 2H_2O \longrightarrow CH_3CH_2COOH + NH_4Cl$$
propanenitrile   propanoic acid

Reacting as acids

Carboxylic acids are described as weak acids because their molecules do not dissociate (ionise) completely when added to water. However a small proportion of the molecules do dissociate, releasing the $H^+(aq)$ ions that characterise all acidic solutions with a pH value less than 7. For example, ethanoic acid forms aqueous hydrogen ions and ethanoate ions in water:

$$CH_3COOH(aq) \rightleftharpoons CH_3COO^-(aq) + H^+(aq)$$
ethanoic acid   ethanoate ion

You can learn more about the dissociation of carboxylic acids in Chapter 26 (pages 394–5).

The presence of $H^+(aq)$ ions in solutions of carboxylic acids means that they undergo all the usual reactions of acids. They react with

■ alkalis to form a salt and water:
$$CH_3COOH + NaOH \longrightarrow CH_3COONa + H_2O$$

■ reactive metals to form a salt and hydrogen gas:
$$2CH_3COOH + Mg \longrightarrow (CH_3COO)_2Mg + H_2$$

■ carbonates to form a salt, water and carbon dioxide gas:
$$2CH_3COOH + K_2CO_3 \longrightarrow 2CH_3COOK + H_2O + CO_2$$

The salts formed in the three reactions above are called sodium ethanoate, magnesium ethanoate and potassium ethanoate, respectively.

Reduction of carboxylic acids

Carboxylic acids can be reduced to their corresponding primary alcohol by using the reducing agent lithium tetrahydridoaluminate, $LiAlH_4$, in dry ether at room temperature. Dry ether is used because $LiAlH_4$ reacts violently with water.

In the simplified reduction equation, the symbol [H] can be used to represent the hydrogen atoms from the reducing agent (remember that in organic chemistry, reduction can be thought of as the addition of hydrogen atoms). So for ethanoic acid being reduced to ethanol, we can show the reaction as:

$$CH_3COOH + 4[H] \longrightarrow CH_3CH_2OH + H_2O$$

QUESTION

8 a How would you make ethanoic acid from ethanenitrile?

 b Write a balanced equation, using structural formulae for the organic compounds, to show the formation of:

 i sodium methanoate, using sodium hydroxide as one of the reactants

 ii potassium ethanoate, using potassium metal as one of the reactants

 iii lithium propanoate, using lithium carbonate as one of the reactants.

 c Name and give the formula of the reducing agent used to convert carboxylic acids to primary alcohols, stating the conditions for the reaction.

Summary

- The complete combustion of alcohols forms carbon dioxide and water.

- A nucleophilic substitution reaction takes place between alcohols and hydrogen halides to form halogenoalkanes.

- Alcohols react with sodium metal to give sodium alkoxides and hydrogen gas.

- An alcohol will react with a carboxylic acid, in the presence of a strong acid catalyst, to form an ester and water. Esters are used as solvents, perfumes and flavourings.

- Esters can be hydrolysed by an acid or by a base. Acid hydrolysis is a reversible reaction but base hydrolysis is not reversible.

- Elimination of water from an alcohol produces an alkene; the reaction is a dehydration. Dehydration may be carried out by passing alcohol vapour over heated pumice, porous pot or aluminium oxide catalysts.

- A primary alcohol can be oxidised to an aldehyde by heating the alcohol gently with acidified potassium dichromate(VI) (and distilling out the aldehyde as it forms – see page 236).

- A primary alcohol can be further oxidised to a carboxylic acid by refluxing the alcohol with excess acidified potassium dichromate(VI).

- A secondary alcohol can be oxidised to a ketone by heating the alcohol with acidified potassium dichromate(VI).

- Acidified potassium dichromate(VI) changes colour from orange to green when a primary or secondary alcohol is oxidised by it.

- Tertiary alcohols cannot be oxidised by refluxing with acidified potassium dichromate(VI).

- Carboxylic acids can be formed from the oxidation of primary alcohols or aldehydes by refluxing with excess potassium dichromate(VI) and dilute sulfuric(VI) acid. They can also be made by refluxing nitriles with dilute hydrochloric acid.

- Carboxylic acids are weak acids that react with reactive metals, alkalis or carbonates to form carboxylate salts.

- The carboxylic acids can be reduced by $LiAlH_4$ in dry ether to form primary alcohols.

End-of-chapter questions

1 Pentan-2-ol, butan-1-ol and 2-methylpropan-2-ol are alcohols.

    a For each one:

        i give its molecular formula [3]

        ii give its structural formula [3]

        iii give its displayed formula [3]

        iv give its skeletal formula [3]

        v state whether it is a primary, secondary or tertiary alcohol. [3]

    b Give the general formula that is used to represent alcohols. [1]

    c Two of the alcohols in this question are isomers of each other. Identify which two and identify the type of isomerism they show. [2]

    d Name the alcohol whose structural formula is $CH_3CH_2COH(CH_3)_2$. [1]

                                                        Total = 19

2 Write a balanced chemical equation for each of the following processes. Structural or displayed formulae should be used for all organic substances.

    a Making ethanol using ethene as feedstock. Include the formula of the catalyst used. [2]

    b The complete combustion of ethanol in oxygen. [2]

    c The dehydration of butan-2-ol when passed over hot Al_2O_3. Give three equations, one for each of the three possible products. [3]

    d The reaction of ethanoic acid with ethanol. Name the catalyst used, the type of reaction and the products. [4]

                                                        Total = 11

3 Primary and secondary alcohols can be oxidised by heating with a mixture of potassium dichromate(VI) and dilute sulfuric(VI) acid.

    ■ A primary alcohol can be oxidised to two different products, depending on the conditions used.

    ■ A secondary alcohol forms one product when oxidised.

    ■ Tertiary alcohols cannot be oxidised.

    a What is the formula of potassium dichromate(VI)? [1]

    b Using a primary alcohol of your choice as an example:

        i give the displayed formulae of the two products it could be oxidised to [2]

        ii state the conditions needed to give each product [2]

        iii state which homologous series each product belongs to [2]

        iv write a balanced chemical equation for each reaction (the convention [O] may be used for the oxidising agent). [2]

    c Using a secondary alcohol of your choice as an example:

        i give the displayed formula of the product it could be oxidised to [2]

        ii state which homologous series the product belongs to [1]

        iii write a balanced chemical equation for the reaction (the convention [O] may be used for the oxidising agent). [1]

    d Why are tertiary alcohols resistant to oxidation? [1]

                                                        Total = 14

Chapter 18:
Carbonyl compounds

Learning outcomes

You should be able to:

- describe:
  - the formation of aldehydes and ketones from oxidation of primary and secondary alcohols
  - the reduction of aldehydes and ketones, e.g. using $NaBH_4$ or $LiAlH_4$
  - the reaction of aldehydes and ketones with HCN and NaCN
- describe the mechanism of the nucleophilic addition reactions of hydrogen cyanide
- describe the detection of carbonyl compounds by the use of 2,4-dinitrophenylhydrazine (2,4-DNPH) reagent

- distinguish between aldehydes and ketones by testing with Fehling's and Tollens' reagents
- describe the reaction of CH_3CO- compounds with alkaline aqueous iodine to give tri-iodomethane
- deduce the presence of a $CH_3CH(OH)-$ group in an alcohol from its reaction with alkaline aqueous iodine to form tri-iodomethane
- analyse an infra-red spectrum of a simple molecule to identify functional groups.

Introduction

Aromatic carbonyl compounds have very distinctive, almond-like odours. Benzaldehyde is used to make almond essence, the flavouring used in some cakes and puddings. Benzaldehyde is also a component of the mixtures that make up the smells and flavours of many fruits such as mangoes, cherries, apricots, plums and peaches. The structures of heptan-2-one and benzaldehyde are shown on the right:

heptan–2–one   benzaldehyde

Figure 18.1 a Heptan-2-one, a ketone, is responsible for the smell of blue cheese. **b** Benzaldehyde, an aldehyde, contributes to the flavours of many fruits and nuts. The structures of heptan-2-one and benzaldehyde are shown above by their displayed formulae.

The homologous series of aldehydes and ketones

You have met aldehydes and ketones, the main classes of carbonyl compounds, in Chapter 17. Remember:

- aldehydes can be formed from the oxidation of primary alcohols
- ketones can be formed from the oxidation of secondary alcohols (see page 236).

In aldehydes the carbon atom in the carbonyl group, $C=O$, is bonded to a carbon atom and a hydrogen atom. In other words, the carbonyl group is positioned at the end of a carbon chain.

In ketones the carbonyl group is attached to two other carbon atoms. Tables 18.1 and 18.2 give examples from the start of these homologous series.

Name	Structural formula
methanal	HCHO
ethanal	CH_3CHO
propanal	CH_3CH_2CHO
butanal	$CH_3CH_2CH_2CHO$
pentanal	$CH_3CH_2CH_2CH_2CHO$

Table 18.1 The names of aldehydes are derived from the name of the equivalent alkane, with the '-e' at the end of the name replaced by '-al'. Note that numbers are not needed when naming aldehydes, as the carbonyl group is always at the end of the carbon chain.

Name	Structural formula
propanone	CH_3COCH_3
butanone	$CH_3COCH_2CH_3$
pentan-2-one pentan-3-one	$CH_3COCH_2CH_2CH_3$ $CH_3CH_2COCH_2CH_3$

Table 18.2 Ketones are named by replacing the '-e' with '-one'. However, in ketone molecules larger than butanone we need to indicate the position of the carbonyl group.

QUESTION

1 **a** Name the following compounds:

   i $CH_3CH_2CH_2CH_2CH_2CHO$

   ii $CH_3CH_2CH_2CH_2CH_2CH_2COCH_3$

  b Draw the displayed formula of:

   i methanal

   ii propanal

   iii pentan-3-one.

  c Draw the skeletal formula of the compounds listed in part **a**.

Preparation of aldehydes and ketones

1 OXIDATION OF A PRIMARY ALCOHOL

The general equation for the reaction in which an aldehyde is made from a primary alcohol is:

primary alcohol + oxygen atom from oxidising agent
$\longrightarrow$ aldehyde + water

For example:

$$CH_3CH_2CH_2OH + [O] \longrightarrow CH_3CH_2CHO + H_2O$$
propan-1-ol   propanal

The oxidising agent used is a solution of potassium dichromate(VI), which is orange, acidified with dilute sulfuric acid. To make the aldehyde, the primary alcohol is heated gently with acidified dichromate solution. The reaction mixture turns green as the orange dichromate ions, $Cr_2O_7{}^{2-}$(aq), are reduced to green Cr^{3+}(aq) ions.

The oxidising agent is added one drop at a time to the warm alcohol. The aldehyde made needs to be distilled off as it forms in the reaction vessel. This can be done because the aldehyde product will always have a lower boiling point than its corresponding alcohol. If the aldehyde is not distilled off as soon as it is formed, further heating

1 OXIDATION OF A PRIMARY ALCOHOL (CONTINUED)

with acidified dichromate solution will oxidise the aldehyde produced to a carboxylic acid. The apparatus used to prepare a sample of ethanal is shown in Figure 18.2.

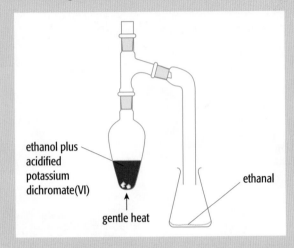

ethanol plus acidified potassium dichromate(VI)

ethanal

gentle heat

Figure 18.2 Distilling off and collecting the aldehyde, ethanal, formed in the mild oxidation of a primary alcohol, ethanol. The aqueous ethanal formed smells like rotting apples.

2 OXIDATION OF A SECONDARY ALCOHOL

The general equation for making a ketone is:

secondary alcohol + oxygen atom from oxidising agent
$\longrightarrow$ ketone + water

For example:

$$CH_3CH(OH)CH_3 + [O] \longrightarrow CH_3COCH_3 + H_2O$$
propan-2-ol   propanone

Once again, the oxidising agent used is a solution of potassium dichromate(VI), acidified with dilute sulfuric acid. To produce a ketone, this oxidising agent must be heated with a secondary alcohol. The ketone formed cannot be further oxidised, even if we reflux the reaction mixture and add excess oxidising agent. Therefore we do not need to distil out the ketone product immediately.

2 a i Write a balanced equation for the oxidation of ethanol to ethanal, using [O] to represent an oxygen atom from the oxidising agent.

ii Give practical details to explain how you would use the reaction described in part **a i** to prepare and collect a sample of ethanal.

b i Write a balanced equation for the oxidation of butan-2-ol to butanone, using [O] to represent an oxygen atom from the oxidising agent.

ii What do you observe in the reaction vessel if the oxidising agent used in part **b i** is potassium dichromate(VI) solution, acidified with dilute sulfuric acid, and the reaction mixture is heated?

3 a Write a balanced equation for the reaction that takes place when propanal is warmed with an aqueous alkaline solution of sodium tetrahydridoborate, using the symbol [H] to represent a hydrogen atom from the reducing agent.

b Name the product formed in the reduction reaction if pentan-3-one is added to lithium tetrahydridoaluminate in dry ether.

Reduction of aldehydes and ketones

Chemical reduction of an aldehyde or ketone produces an alcohol.

aldehyde + reducing agent $\longrightarrow$ primary alcohol
ketone + reducing agent $\longrightarrow$ secondary alcohol

The reducing agent used is usually an aqueous alkaline solution of sodium tetrahydridoborate, $NaBH_4$, or lithium tetrahydridoaluminate, $LiAlH_4$, in dry ether.

The reduction reaction is carried out by either:

- warming the aldehyde or ketone with an aqueous alkaline solution of sodium tetrahydridoborate
- adding lithium tetrahydridoaluminate dissolved in a dry ether, such as diethyl ether, at room temperature. The organic solvent has to be dry because lithium tetrahydridoaluminate is a more powerful reducing agent than sodium tetrahydridoborate and reacts vigorously in water.

In the same way that we have used the symbol [O] in organic oxidation equations, we use the symbol [H] in reduction equations. [H] represents a hydrogen atom from the reducing agent. Look at the equations below used to summarise these reduction reactions:

$$CH_3CHO + 2[H] \longrightarrow CH_3CH_2OH$$
ethanal   ethanol

$$CH_3COCH_3 + 2[H] \longrightarrow CH_3CH(OH)CH_3$$
propanone   propan-2-ol

Nucleophilic addition with HCN

The addition reactions we have met so far have involved electrophilic addition across the $C=C$ bond in alkene molecules (see page 209). Aldehydes and ketones both undergo addition reactions with hydrogen cyanide, HCN. In this case, addition of HCN takes place across the $C=O$ bond. However, the attack is by a nucleophile, not an electrophile. We can show this using the **nucleophilic addition** reaction of propanal with HCN. The HCN is generated *in situ* (in the reaction vessel) by the reaction of sodium cyanide, NaCN, and dilute sulfuric acid.

propanal   2-hydroxybutanenitrile

Note that a carbon atom has been added to the propanal molecule by the addition of the nitrile group ($-C\equiv N$). This is a useful reaction in synthetic chemistry, as it increases the length of the hydrocarbon chain in the original aldehyde molecule by one carbon atom.

The nitrile group ($-C\equiv N$) can then be easily:

- hydrolysed to a carboxylic acid
- reduced to an amine.

The hydrolysis can be carried out by refluxing with dilute hydrochloric acid:

$$-CN + H^+ + H_2O \longrightarrow -COOH + NH_4^+$$

The reduction of the nitrile group to an amine can be carried out using sodium and ethanol:

$$-CN + 4[H] \longrightarrow -CH_2NH_2$$

237

Mechanism of nucleophilic addition

The carbonyl group, C=O, in aldehydes and ketones is polarised due to the high electronegativity of the oxygen atom. The electrons in the C=O bond are drawn nearer to the O atom, giving it a partial negative charge and leaving the C atom with a partial positive charge. This makes the C atom open to attack by a nucleophile, such as the cyanide ion, CN^-.

First step

The negatively charged intermediate formed in the first step in the mechanism is highly reactive and quickly reacts with an H^+ ion (from HCN, from dilute acid or from water present in the reaction mixture). This forms the **2-hydroxynitrile** product.

Second step

All aldehydes and ketones form '2-hydroxynitriles' when they undergo nucleophilic addition as the —OH (hydroxyl) group will always be on the adjacent carbon atom to the nitrile group.

However, starting with the aldehyde methanal, HCHO, the hydroxynitrile formed in its nucleophilic addition with HCN would be called hydroxyethanenitrile. In this case there is no need to insert the '2' at the start of its name as the —OH group could only possibly bond to the carbon atom that is next to the nitrile group.

QUESTION

4 a Name the organic product that would be formed in the nucleophilic addition of HCN to:

   i   ethanal

   ii propanone.

 b Use diagrams and curly arrows to describe the mechanism of the reaction in part **a i**.

Testing for aldehydes and ketones

Testing for the carbonyl group

TESTING WITH 2,4-DNPH

The presence of a carbonyl group in an aldehyde or ketone can be easily tested for by adding a solution of 2,4-dinitrophenylhydrazine (often abbreviated to 2,4-DNPH). If an aldehyde or ketone is present, a deep-orange precipitate is formed (Figure 18.3).

Figure 18.3 The orange precipitate formed from 2,4-DNPH in a test with propanone, a ketone.

The structure of 2,4-dinitrophenylhydrazine is:

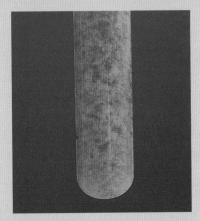

The precipitate formed can be purified by recrystallisation and its melting point can be measured experimentally. The identity of the compound that precipitated out can then be found by referring to melting point data. From this, the specific aldehyde or ketone used in the test can be identified.

The reaction of an aldehyde or ketone with 2,4-dinitrophenylhydrazine is an example of a **condensation reaction**. In a condensation reaction, two molecules join together and in the process eliminate a small molecule, in this case water. The equation for the reaction of ethanal with 2,4-DNPH is:

2,4-dinitrophenylhydrazine

atoms lost in condensation reaction to form water

a 2,4-dinitrophenylhydrazone

Other classes of organic compound that also contain the carbonyl group (such as carboxylic acids and esters) do not form precipitates.

Distinguishing between aldehydes and ketones

As we saw on page 236, aldehydes can be further oxidised to form carboxylic acids, but ketones cannot be oxidised easily. We can use this difference to distinguish between an aldehyde and a ketone in simple chemical tests. The two tests most commonly used involve Tollens' reagent and Fehling's solution.

TESTING WITH TOLLENS' REAGENT

Tollens' reagent is an aqueous solution of silver nitrate in excess ammonia solution, sometimes called ammoniacal silver nitrate solution. The silver ions, Ag^+, in the solution act as a mild oxidising agent. When warmed, the Ag^+ ions will oxidise an aldehyde to form a carboxylate ion.

Under alkaline conditions any carboxylic acid formed is immediately neutralised to the carboxylate ion, $-COO^-$, as H^+ is removed from $-COOH$ and a salt is formed.

In the redox reaction with an aldehyde, the Ag^+ ions themselves are reduced to silver atoms. The silver atoms form a 'mirror' on the inside of the tube, giving a positive test for an aldehyde (Figure 18.4).

There will be no change observed when a ketone is warmed with Tollens' reagent as no redox reaction takes place. It remains a colourless mixture in the test tube.

Figure 18.4 The 'before' and 'after' observations when Tollens' reagent is warmed with an aldehyde, such as ethanal.

TESTING WITH FEHLING'S SOLUTION

Fehling's solution is an alkaline solution containing copper(II) ions. When warmed with an aldehyde, the Cu^{2+} ions act as an oxidising agent. The aldehyde is oxidised to a carboxylate ion while the Cu^{2+} ions are reduced to Cu^+ ions. The clear blue Fehling's solution turns an opaque red/orange colour as a precipitate of copper(I) oxide forms throughout the solution (Figure 18.5).

Once again, ketones are not oxidised, so the Fehling's solution remains blue when warmed.

Figure 18.5 The 'before' and 'after' observations when Fehling's solution is warmed with an aldehyde, such as ethanal.

5 The melting points of the derivatives of the reaction between 2,4-DNPH and various aldehydes and ketones are shown in the table.

Product of reaction between 2,4-DNPH and ...	Melting point / °C
ethanal	168
propanal	155
butanal	126
propanone	126
butanone	116

a What would be observed when each of the carbonyl compounds in the table is mixed with 2,4-DNPH?

b A derivative was formed between 2,4-DNPH and an unknown carbonyl compound.

  i The melting point of the derivative was 126 °C. What does this result tell you?

  ii The unknown carbonyl compound formed an orange precipitate when warmed with Fehling's solution. Name the unknown compound.

  iii Describe and explain the different results obtained when the compound named in part b ii is warmed with Tollens' reagent in a test tube and then the same test is performed on butanone.

c Write a half-equation to show silver ions acting as an oxidising agent in a positive test for an aldehyde.

d Write a half-equation to show copper(II) ions acting as an oxidising agent in a positive test for an aldehyde.

Figure 18.6 The yellow precipitate of tri-iodomethane forming.

The reaction involves two steps:

1 the carbonyl compound is halogenated – the three hydrogen atoms in the CH_3 group are replaced by iodine atoms

2 the intermediate is hydrolysed to form the yellow precipitate of tri-iodomethane, CHI_3 (Figure 18.6).

When separated from the reaction mixture, the yellow crystals of tri-iodomethane can be positively identified by their melting point of 119 °C.

Here R is an alkyl group in a methyl ketone:

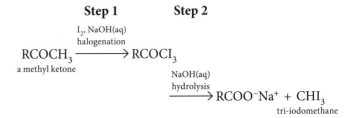

Reactions to form tri-iodomethane

Tri-iodomethane (iodoform) forms as a yellow precipitate with methyl ketones, i.e. compounds containing the CH_3CO— group (Figure 18.6). Note that ethanal, CH_3CHO, an aldehyde, also contains the CH_3CO— group. Chemists use the appearance of the yellow precipitate as evidence of the CH_3CO— group in an unknown compound.

The reagent used is an alkaline solution of iodine, which is warmed together with the substance being tested.

Testing for the $CH_3CH(OH)$— group

The tri-iodomethane test can also be used to identify the presence of a secondary alcohol group on the carbon atom adjacent to a methyl group. This $CH_3CH(OH)$— group is firstly oxidised by the alkaline iodine solution. This oxidation forms a methyl ketone, $RCOCH_3$, which then reacts via the two steps shown above to give the yellow tri-iodomethane precipitate, CHI_3.

You should note that there are two organic products formed in this reaction: one is tri-iodomethane and the other is the sodium salt of a carboxylic acid.

QUESTION

6 a i When propanone is warmed with alkaline iodine solution, a yellow precipitate is formed. Name and draw the displayed formula of the yellow precipitate.

ii Give the structural formulae of the organic products formed in both steps of the reaction in part **i**.

b Explain, naming any organic products formed, why ethanol gives a positive test when warmed with alkaline iodine solution.

c Which of these compounds will give a yellow precipitate when treated with alkaline aqueous iodine?

i	butanone	**iv**	pentan-2-one
ii	butanal	**v**	ethanal
iii	pentan-3-one	**vi**	methanal

Infra-red spectroscopy

In **infra-red spectroscopy** a sample being analysed is irradiated with electromagnetic waves in the infra-red region of the electromagnetic spectrum. The machine used is called a spectrophotometer, and it detects the intensity of the wavelengths of infra-red radiation that passes through the sample.

This analytical technique is particularly useful for organic chemists because all organic molecules absorb radiation in the infra-red range of wavelengths. The energy absorbed corresponds to changes in the vibration of the bonds between atoms. The bonds can vibrate by stretching, bending and twisting. They have a natural frequency at which they vibrate. If we irradiate the molecules with energy that corresponds to this frequency, it stimulates larger vibrations and energy is absorbed. This is called the **resonance frequency** of that vibration.

Each type of vibration will absorb characteristic wavelengths of infra-red radiation. These are often expressed as the reciprocal of the wavelength in a unit called wavenumbers (measured in cm^{-1}). We cannot be too specific when quoting the characteristic absorption frequency of a bond – the nature of the rest of the molecule shifts the energy absorbed in each particular molecule. However, we can say, for example, that the amine group (—NH$_2$) absorbs in the range 3300 to 3500 cm^{-1}.

Therefore we can identify the presence (or absence) of different functional groups from the absorbance pattern on an infra-red spectrum. Look at the infra-red spectrum of ethylamine in Figure 18.7:

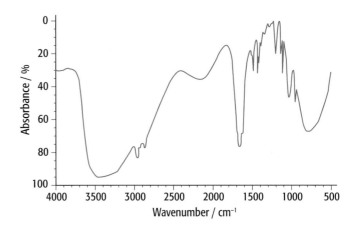

Figure 18.7 The infra-red spectrum of ethylamine, $CH_3CH_2NH_2$. Note that the percentage absorbance and the wavenumbers on the axes both get smaller in magnitude along each axis.

We can use the characteristic infra-red spectrum of an unknown compound to identify it by 'fingerprinting' from a database of known spectra. Some characteristic absorption ranges and appearances of the peaks are shown in Table 18.3.

Bond	Functional groups containing the bond	Absorption range (in wavenumbers) / cm^{-1}	Appearance of peak (s = strong, w = weak)
C—O	alcohols, ethers, esters	1040–1300	s
C=C	aromatic compounds, alkenes	1500–1680	w unless conjugated
C=O	amides ketones and aldehydes esters	1640–1690 1670–1740 1715–1750	s s s
C≡C	alkynes	2150–2250	w unless conjugated
C≡N	nitriles	2200–2250	w
C—H	alkanes, CH$_2$—H alkenes/arenes, =C—H	2850–2950 3000–3100	s w
N—H	amines, amides	3300–3500	w
O—H	carboxylic acids, RCO$_2$—H H-bonded alcohol, RO—H free alcohol, RO—H	2500–3000 3200–3600 3580–3650	s and very broad s s and sharp

Table 18.3 Some characteristic infra-red absorbance bands and their intensities.

These values will usually be given to you. You can see that absorption bands overlap considerably. That is why we **need to use a variety of techniques**, such as NMR, infrared spectroscopy and mass spectrometry, to work out the structure of a new organic compound (see Chapter 29).

As well as their wavenumber bands, particular absorbances have characteristic widths (broad or sharp peaks) and intensities (strong or weak) on the infra-red spectrum. For example, the presence of hydrogen bonding makes the absorbance of the O—H bonds in alcohols and carboxylic acids broad. By contrast, the C=O bond in carbonyl groups has a strong, sharp absorbance peak. Look at the infra-red spectra of ethanol, ethanoic acid and ethyl ethanoate shown in Figures 18.8–18.10.

Using the data in Table 18.3, note the broad bands in Figures 18.8 and 18.9 arising from the O—H groups involved in hydrogen bonding in the alcohol and in the

carboxylic acid. Contrast the width of these peaks with the sharp peak of the carbonyl group in the ester, ethyl ethanoate in Figure 18.10.

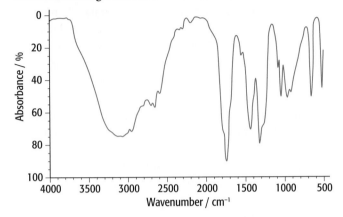

Figure 18.9 The infra-red spectrum of ethanoic acid, CH_3COOH.

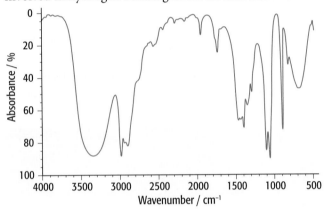

Figure 18.8 The infra-red spectrum of ethanol, CH_3CH_2OH.

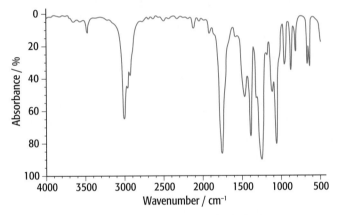

Figure 18.10 The infra-red spectrum of ethyl ethanoate, $CH_3COOCH_2CH_3$.

QUESTION

7 Look at the two infra-red spectra below:

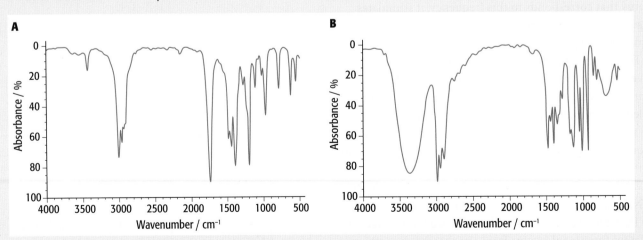

a Which one of the infra-red spectra is that of butanone and which one is of butan-2-ol?

b Explain your reasoning in part **a**.

Summary

- Aldehydes and ketones contain the carbonyl group, $C=O$:
  - in aldehydes, the carbonyl group is joined to just one other carbon atom
  - in ketones, the carbonyl group is joined to two other carbon atoms.

- The names of aldehydes are derived from the name of the alkane with the '-e' at the end replaced by '-al'.

- Similarly, ketones are named with the '-e' replaced by '-one'.

- Carbonyl compounds are readily reduced by aqueous $NaBH_4$ or $LiAlH_4$ dissolved in dry ether:
  - reduction of an aldehyde forms a primary alcohol
  - reduction of a ketone produces a secondary alcohol.

- Aldehydes are readily oxidised under mild conditions to carboxylic acids. Ketones are not oxidised under mild conditions.

- The polar nature of the carbonyl group in aldehydes and ketones enables them to undergo nucleophilic addition by reacting with the cyanide ions (CN^-) from HCN. The product is a 2-hydroxynitrile.

- The reagent 2,4-dinitrophenylhydrazine (2,4-DNPH) can be used to identify the presence of a carbonyl group in an aldehyde or ketone. It produces an orange precipitate. The melting point of the product is used to identify particular aldehydes and ketones.

- As aldehydes are readily oxidised, they may be distinguished from ketones on warming with suitable oxidising reagents:
  - with aldehydes, Tollens' reagent produces a silver mirror inside a warmed test tube and Fehling's solution turns from a blue solution to a red/orange precipitate when warmed
  - with ketones, there is no oxidation reaction, so no changes are observed when ketones are warmed with Tollens' reagent or Fehling's solution.

- Chemists can use alkaline iodine solution to test for:
  - methyl ketones
  - ethanol or secondary alcohols with an adjacent methyl group.

  A yellow precipitate of tri-iodomethane is formed in a positive test.

- Infra-red spectroscopy helps to identify organic compounds by their absorption of energy in the infra-red range of wavelengths, matching their spectrum to a database of known infra-red spectra.

243

End-of-chapter questions

1 a Name the following compounds:

    i CH_3COCH_3 [1]

    ii $CH_3CH_2CH_2OH$ [1]

    iii CH_3CHO [1]

    iv $CH_3CH(OH)CH_3$ [1]

    v $CH_3COCH_2CH_3$ [1]

    vi CH_3CH_2CHO [1]

  b Which of the compounds in part **a** are alcohols and which are carbonyl compounds?   [1]

  c Which of the carbonyl compounds in part **a** are aldehydes and which are ketones?   [1]

  d Two of the compounds in part **a** could be made by oxidising two of the others.

     i Identify these four compounds, stating which could be made from which. [4]

     ii State the reagents and conditions you would use to carry out each oxidation and write a balanced chemical equation for each oxidation. [O] can be used in oxidation equations. [4]

  e Ethanol could be made by the reduction of one of the compounds in part **a**.

     i Identify which compound this is. [1]

     ii State the reagent you would use to carry out the reduction. [1]

     iii Write a balanced chemical equation for the reduction. [H] can be used in reduction equations. [1]

Total = 19

2 **a** What reagent would you add to an unknown compound to see if it contains a carbonyl group? [1]

    b What result would you get if the unknown compound did contain a carbonyl group? [1]

    c Why would it be useful to find the melting point of the product of this test? [1]

Total = 3

3 **a** Draw the skeletal formulae of:

     i pentan-2-one [1]

     ii pentan-3-one [1]

     iii pentanal. [1]

    b Describe the results you would expect to see if pentan-3-one and pentanal were separately treated with Tollens' reagent. Where a reaction takes place, name the organic product and name the type of reaction that takes place. [4]

Total = 7

4 Ethanol can be made from ethanal using sodium tetrahydridoborate(III) as a reducing agent.

    a Give the formula of sodium tetrahydridoborate(III). [1]

    b What other reagent is necessary for the reaction to take place? [1]

    c The reaction mechanism proceeds in a similar way to the steps in the reaction of ethanal with HCN, but the initial attack is by the H^- ion instead of the CN^- ion. The intermediate then gains an H^+ ion from a water molecule to form the product, ethanol. Name the mechanism and describe it as fully as you can, using curly arrows to show the movement of electron pairs. [7]

Total = 9

5 A compound, X, has the following percentage composition: 66.7% carbon, 11.1% hydrogen and 22.2% oxygen.

    a Calculate the empirical formula of X. [3]

    b The relative molecular mass of X is 72. Calculate the molecular formula. [1]

    c Give the structural formulae and names of the three isomers of X that are carbonyl compounds. [3]

    d Explain how you could identify X using chemical means. [5]

Total = 12

6   An alcohol has the molecular formula C_3H_8O. When warmed with an alkaline solution of iodine it forms a yellow precipitate.

   a   Name the yellow precipitate. [1]

   b   Draw the displayed formula of the alcohol. [1]

   c   The first stage in the reaction of the alcohol with alkaline iodine solution is an oxidation reaction. Name the organic product of this first stage. [1]

   d   There are four isomeric alcohols with the formula C_4H_9OH.

      i   Name the four isomeric alcohols. [1]

      ii Classify each one as a primary, secondary or tertiary alcohol. [1]

      iii Which of the four isomeric alcohols will give a yellow precipitate when warmed with an alkaline solution of iodine? [1]

Total = 6

7   Use data from the table below of characteristic infra-red absorptions in organic molecules to answer the following question.

Bond	Location	Wavenumber / cm^{-1}
C—O	alcohols, esters	1000–1300
C=O	aldehydes, ketones, carboxylic acids, esters	1680–1750
O—H	hydrogen bonded in carboxylic acids	2500–3300 (broad)
N—H	primary amines	3100–3500
O—H	hydrogen bonded in alcohols, phenols	3230–3550
O—H	free	3580–3670

One of the three spectra labelled **A** to **C** below is produced when ethanal is analysed in an infra-red spectrophotometer:

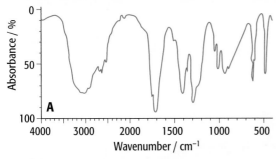

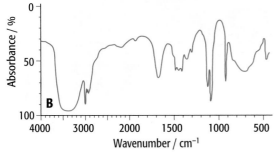

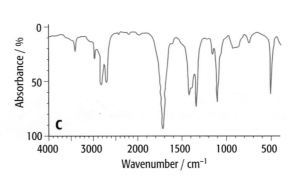

Which infra-red spectrum is most likely to be produced by ethanal? Give three reasons for your choice. [3]

Total = 3

Chapter P1:
Practical skills 1

Introduction

The analytical skills of chemists are still important despite the development of new increasingly rapid and sensitive instrumental techniques (see Chapter 29). Your practical skills make an important contribution to the grade you achieve in your chemistry qualification.

Figure P1.1 Chemist performing a titration.

Review of practical knowledge and understanding

In scientific investigations we are often interested in finding out how one variable affects another. For example, we might want to investigate a precipitation reaction to find out how the concentration of a reactant affects the rate at which the precipitate forms. You might have seen the reaction between sodium thiosulfate and dilute hydrochloric acid, which is a commonly investigated precipitation reaction. Sulfur is the precipitate formed:

$$Na_2S_2O_3(aq) + 2HCl(aq)$$
$$\longrightarrow 2NaCl(aq) + S(s) + H_2O(l) + SO_2(g)$$

This type of investigation involves changing only the variable under investigation (in this case the concentration of a reactant) and keeping all other relevant variables constant. We can judge the effect of changing the concentration by devising a way to measure how quickly the precipitate forms, such as timing how long it takes for the solution to become opaque.

We now have the question we are investigating and the structure of the investigation in terms of its key variables:

In a precipitation reaction, how does the concentration of a reactant affect the rate of precipitation (as measured by the time it takes for the solution to become opaque)?

- The **independent variable** is the one under investigation, which is changed systematically and for which we can choose different values (in this case, the concentration of reactant).
- The **dependent variable** is the one we measure to judge the effect of changing the independent variable (in this case, the time it takes for the solution to become opaque).
- The **control variables** are those that we must keep constant to ensure a fair test is carried out (in this case, we should control the temperature and total volume of reactants used).

Note that we can express the question in this type of investigation generally as:

How does the independent variable affect the dependent variable?

When asked to plan and/or carry out an investigation, it is important that you state the question under investigation clearly and list the independent, dependent and control variables before you start writing down your proposed method or planning how to record and present your results.

The type of variable under investigation will determine whether you display the data collected in a table as a line graph or as a bar chart. To decide which type of graph to draw, you need to know the difference between continuous variables – which are measured so can have any numerical value within the range of results – and categoric variables – which are described by words. We can assume that the dependent variable is continuous, as it measures the effect of varying the independent variable. Then if the independent variable is continuous, we draw a line graph. If the independent variable is categoric, we draw a bar chart. So if you investigate the effect of temperature on rate of reaction, the data can be presented as a line graph, whereas if you investigate the rate of different metals reacting with dilute acid, the data can be presented as a bar chart (as there are no values between those chosen for the independent variable). See the graphs in Figure P1.2.

In the Cambridge International AS and A Level Advanced Practical Skills examination (Paper 3), you will need to follow instructions to carry out an investigation into an unknown substance or mixture of substances. Always read through all of the instructions before carrying out the tests. Testing for unknown substances will require you to describe your observations in detail. You will be able to refer to tables of tests for cations, anions and gases in the Qualitative Analysis Notes in your examination paper (see Appendix 3, page 475) to draw your conclusions.

You will also carry out a quantitative task (based on measurements) rather than a qualitative task (based on observations). Examples of problems that need you to collect quantitative data could be a titration (a volumetric analysis) or an enthalpy change experiment. This type of task will require you to read scales on measuring instruments such as burettes, measuring cylinders, gas syringes and balances. For instruments with an analogue scale, such as a burette, you should be able to read measurements to within half the value of the fine line divisions on the scale. So a burette with fine line divisions every $0.10\,cm^3$ should be read to the nearest $0.05\,cm^3$. A

thermometer with fine line divisions every $1\,°C$ should be read to the nearest $0.5\,°C$ (see Figure P1.3).

However, if a measuring instrument has very fine calibration (tightly grouped marks), it should be read to the nearest calibrated mark.

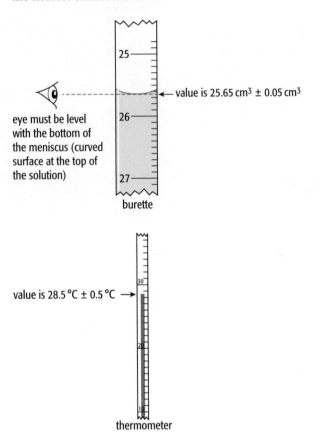

Figure P1.3 Taking readings from a magnified burette scale and a thermometer with an analogue scale.

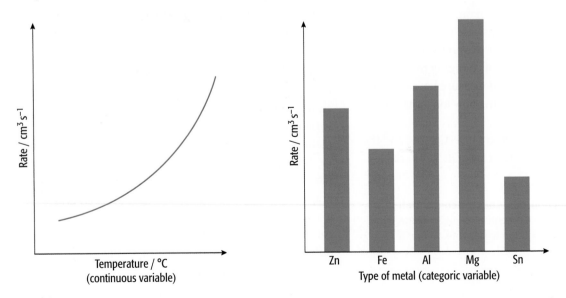

Figure P1.2 A continuous independent variable ⟶ a line graph; a categoric independent variable ⟶ a bar chart.

Useful definitions to know, because you may need to decide upon or recognise these in a task, are:

- **Range:** The minimum and maximum values for the independent or the dependent variable. For example, in the rate of precipitation investigation, the range of the independent variable (the concentration) might be $0.2\,mol\,dm^{-3}$ to $1.0\,mol\,dm^{-3}$.
- **Interval:** The difference chosen between consecutive values of the independent variable. For example, in the rate of precipitation investigation you might choose to test concentrations of 0.2, 0.4, 0.6, 0.8 and $1.0\,mol\,dm^{-3}$, giving an interval of $0.2\,mol\,dm^{-3}$.
- **Anomalous result:** A result that does not follow an established pattern.
- **Precise results:** Results in which each set of repeat readings are grouped closely together.
- **Accurate results:** Results that reflect the true value of a quantity.

QUESTION

1 A student was investigating how temperature affects the rate of a reaction between magnesium and dilute hydrochloric acid. The student decided to measure the volume of gas given off in 30 seconds for different concentrations of acid. She decided to use temperatures of 10, 20, 30, 40 and 50 °C.

  a Name the independent variable.

  b Name the dependent variable.

  c List two control variables.

  d Give the range of the independent variable.

  e What is the value of the interval chosen for the independent variable?

  f Which type of graph would you use to display the results of an investigation to find out how different transition metal oxides affect the rate of reaction?

In order to address the Cambridge International AS and A Level Advanced Practical Skills examination (Paper 3), you will need to master the expectations set out throughout this chapter.

Manipulation, measurement and observation

Expectations

You should be able to:

Successful collection of data and observations

- set up apparatus correctly
- follow instructions given in the form of written instructions or diagrams

- use the apparatus to collect an appropriate quantity of data or observations, including subtle differences in colour, solubility or quantity of materials
- make measurements using pipettes, burettes, measuring cylinders, thermometers and other common laboratory apparatus.

Quality of measurements or observations

- make accurate and consistent measurements and observations.

Decisions relating to measurements or observations

- decide how many tests or observations to perform
- make measurements that span a range and have a distribution appropriate to the experiment
- decide how long to leave experiments running before making readings
- identify where repeated readings or observations are appropriate
- replicate readings or observations as necessary
- identify where confirmatory tests are appropriate and the nature of such tests
- choose reagents to distinguish between given ions.

Points to remember

- When describing a liquid or solution that is not coloured and is transparent, always use the word 'colourless'. Some people make the mistake of just writing 'clear' – but a solution of copper(II) sulfate is clear (i.e. transparent) but blue in colour.
- A solution that appears white and opaque in a chemical test probably contains a fine suspension of a white precipitate, for example when testing for carbon dioxide gas.
- When carrying out a titration, you should repeat the test until you have two titres that are within $0.1\,cm^3$ of each other. Ideally you should be aiming for two concordant titres with the same values – but judging the end-point can be tricky. That is why we carry out repeat sets of each test in many investigations – to make our results more accurate by reducing experimental error. You can read more about sources of error on page 251.
- The first titre measured is always a rough value to establish approximately where the actual end-point lies. When obtaining subsequent values, you should be able to add the solution from the burette one drop at a time near the end-point.
- Sometimes a result is clearly incorrect. For example, it might be very different from the others in a repeat set of readings or does not follow a well-established pattern in a series of tests. If you have time, try it again. If not, discard it – do not include it in your calculation of the mean or ignore the point when drawing a line of best fit on a graph.

■ When plotting a line graph of the data collected, a minimum of five values of the independent variable (which is plotted along the horizontal axis) must be recorded to be confident of any pattern observed.

■ Note that it is possible to have precise results that are not particularly accurate. For example, if you measure the mass of a product formed three times and the results are all the same, they are precise. However, if the balance was not set to zero for any of the measurements, the mass will **not** be accurate.

QUESTION

2 a A student carried out a titration four times and got results for the titre of 13.25, 12.95, 12.65 and then 12.65 cm^3. What is the most accurate value of the titre to use in any calculations?

b What do we call a mixture of water and fine particles of a insoluble solid dispersed throughout the liquid?

c Describe any similarities and differences you observe when looking at a test tube of dilute sulfuric acid and a test tube of 0.05 mol dm^{-3} copper(II) sulfate solution.

d Name the white precipitate formed in the test for carbon dioxide gas.

e In **Question 1** on page 249, what piece of apparatus could the student use to measure:

   i the independent variable

   ii the dependent variable.

Presentation of data and observations

Expectations

You should be able to:

Recording data or observations

■ present numerical data, values or observations in a single table of results

■ draw up the table in advance of taking readings/making observations so that you do not have to copy up your results

■ include in the table of results, if necessary, columns for raw data, for calculated values and for analyses or conclusions

■ use column headings that include both the quantity and the unit and that conform to accepted scientific conventions

■ record raw readings of a quantity to the same degree of precision and observations to the same level of detail.

Display of calculation and reasoning

■ show your working in calculations, and the key steps in your reasoning

■ use the correct number of significant figures for calculated quantities.

Data layout

■ choose a suitable and clear method of presenting the data, e.g. tabulations, graphs or a mixture of presentation methods

■ select which variables to plot against which and decide whether a graph should be drawn as a straight line or a curve

■ plot appropriate variables on clearly labelled x- and y-axes

■ choose suitable scales for graph axes

■ plot all points or bars to an appropriate accuracy

■ follow the Association for Science Education (ASE) recommendations for putting lines on graphs (see the 'Points to remember' referring to graphs, below).

Points to remember

■ There are certain conventions to observe when designing and drawing a table to use to record your experimental data. Generally, the independent variable goes in the first column and the dependent variable goes in the second column. Sometimes, if space on the page is an issue, a table can be organised horizontally. In this case, the independent variable again goes first but at the start of the first row in the table, with the dependent variable beneath it, not next to it as in a conventional table.

■ When recording quantitative data you will often need columns for repeat results and calculations of the mean. This is achieved by subdividing the column for the dependent variable into the required number of columns. For example, in the rate of precipitation investigation described at the beginning of this chapter, the table to record three repeat readings and their means would be organised as:

Concentration / mol dm^{-3}	Time for reaction mixture to turn opaque / s			
	1st test	2nd test	3rd test	Mean

■ Note that the headings in the table have their units included – therefore you do not need to record the units for each entry you make in the table.

■ On graphs, always plot the independent variable along the horizontal (x) axis and the dependent variable up the vertical (y) axis.

- Draw the lines in tables and graphs in pencil, labelling the axes as in the corresponding table headings with their units.
- In the table above, there could be an extra column on the right-hand side for values of the reciprocal of the mean time taken for the reaction mixture to become opaque (headed '1 / time'). This could be plotted on a graph of 1/time against concentration to see how the rate of reaction varies with temperature (as rate is proportional to 1/time, so the greater the time, the slower the rate). See the graphs in Figure P1.4.
- The labelled axes must be longer than half the size of the graph grid in both directions, selecting a sensible scale (e.g. 1, 2 or 5 units per 20 mm square on the grid – **not** 3 units).
- The points should be plotted as small, neat x's with a sharp pencil. The line drawn through the points should not be 'dot-to-dot' but should be a line of best fit – either drawn with a ruler for a straight line or a smooth free-hand line for a curve. Think of the best-fit line as the 'average' line though the points.
- Always show your working out in calculations.
- Only give answers produced by calculation to correspond to the number of significant figures of the least accurate experimental data used. So if calculating a concentration using titre volumes such as 15.35 cm^3, then the value of the concentration of the unknown solution can be given to 4 significant figures (e.g. 1.244 or 0.9887 mol dm^{-3}). However, if the known concentration of one of the reactants is given to three significant figures (e.g. 0.0250 mol dm^{-3} or 0.200 mol dm^{-3}), then the calculated concentration could be given to three or four significant figures.
- When recording qualitative descriptions in a table, if there is 'no change visible', write that and do not just put in a dash.

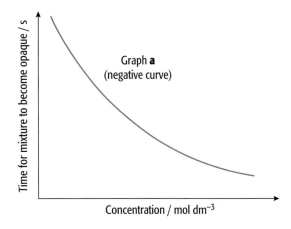

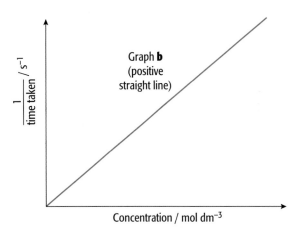

Figure P1.4 Graphs that could be drawn from the data in a table using concentrations and mean times.

Analysis, conclusions and evaluation

Expectations

You should be able to:

Interpretation of data or observations and identifying sources of error

- describe the patterns and trends shown by tables and graphs
- describe and summarise the key points of a set of observations
- find an unknown value by using co-ordinates or intercepts on a graph
- calculate other quantities from data, or calculate the mean from replicate values, or make other appropriate calculations
- determine the gradient of a straight-line graph
- evaluate the effectiveness of control variables

251

QUESTION

3   In an experiment to find the enthalpy change of a reaction between two solutions, the mass of solutions mixed together was 50.0 g and the temperature increased by 7.5 °C. The following equation is used:

energy transferred = mass × specific heat capacity × change in temperature

where the specific heat capacity of the solutions was taken as 4.18 J g^{-1} °C^{-1}.

   a   Calculate the energy transferred in joules (J) to an appropriate number of significant figures.

   b   Explain the number of significant figures chosen in part **a**.

- identify the most significant sources of error in an experiment
- estimate, quantitatively, the uncertainty in quantitative measurements
- express such uncertainty in a measurement as an actual or percentage error
- show an understanding of the distinction between systematic errors and random errors.

Drawing conclusions

- draw conclusions from an experiment, giving an outline description of the main features of the data, considering whether experimental data support a given hypothesis, and making further predictions
- draw conclusions from interpretations of observations, data and calculated values
- make scientific explanations of the data, observations and conclusions that have been described.

Suggesting improvements

- suggest modifications to an experimental arrangement that will improve the accuracy of the experiment or the accuracy of the observations that can be made
- suggest ways in which to extend the investigation to answer a new question
- describe such modifications clearly in words or diagrams.

Points to remember

To measure the gradient (slope) of a straight line on a graph, choose two points on the line at least half as far apart as its total length. Then construct a right-angled triangle, as shown in Figure P1.5. The gradient tells us the rate of change of y (the dependent variable) per unit change of x (the independent variable):

$$\text{gradient} = \frac{\text{change in } y}{\text{change in } x}$$

When evaluating the quality of the data collected, there are two types of error to consider: **random errors** and **systematic errors**. Whenever we carry out an experiment there are always errors involved. They might be due to the experimenter not reading the scale on a measuring instrument correctly or choosing a measuring instrument with an inappropriate scale. These examples of human error could equally make the values of data too high or too low, so they are called random errors. Repeating tests and taking the mean value helps to reduce the effect of random errors.

However, other errors can result in consistently high or low values being recorded. These are called systematic errors. Examples would be reading the volume of liquid

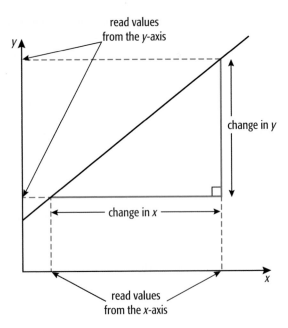

Figure P1.5 Finding the gradient of a straight-line graph. Choosing to construct a large triangle reduces the percentage error in the values read from the axes, which are then used to calculate the gradient.

in a burette to the upper level of the liquid instead of to the bottom of the meniscus. It should noted though that these consistently high measurements of volume would not result in an incorrect value for the titre, because the final volume is subtracted from the initial volume. Not ensuring the measuring instrument is correctly set on zero is another example of a systematic error, which if not corrected during an investigation can result in consistently high or low masses being measured on balances.

Other systematic errors can be caused by errors when planning an investigation. This might result in data being collected that does not really answer the question under investigation. For example, a control variable might not be kept constant or taken into account, or the dependent variable chosen might not be a true measure of the effect of varying the independent variable. Such error will make the data collected invalid.

You will have to estimate the error inherent in reading scales, as described at the beginning of this chapter, and the evaluation is the place to discuss the effect these measurement errors might have on the validity of the data and conclusions you can draw from them. In the example of a thermometer with 1 °C calibration marks, you can quote values to the nearest 0.5 °C. The actual effect of this margin of error on confidence levels will depend on the magnitude of the temperature being measured. When reading a low temperature of, say, 5.0 °C, plus or minus

0.5 °C will have a bigger effect than when reading a higher temperature, such as 92.5 °C. For this reason it is best to quote percentage errors, worked out using the equation:

$$\text{percentage error} = \frac{\text{margin of error}}{\text{actual or mean measurement}} \times 100\%$$

WORKED EXAMPLE

In the case of the two temperatures 5 °C and 92.5 °C, for 5 °C the percentage error will be:

$$\frac{0.5 \times 100}{5} = 10\%$$

whereas for 92.5 °C the percentage error is:

$$\frac{0.5 \times 100}{92.5} = 0.54\%$$

So there is a significant error in reading 5 °C compared with reading 92.5 °C.

In enthalpy change investigations you often have to measure temperature differences, subtracting the final temperature from the initial temperature. In this case, using the thermometer just described, the error would be plus or minus 1 °C, as the two 0.5 °C margins of error should be added together. In this case you should suggest increasing the temperature change. For example, when evaluating enthalpies of combustion of alcohols by heating water in a copper calorimeter, you could use a smaller volume of water to heat. However, this change would have to be balanced against the increase in percentage error in measuring the smaller volume of water, to see which gives the least percentage error overall.

You might need to suggest how to make your data more accurate. For example, in the rate of precipitation investigation you could improve the accuracy of judging the time when the reaction reaches a certain point in each test carried out. Whereas judging the moment when a pencil mark can no longer be seen through the reaction mixture is subjective, you could use a light source and lightmeter to make more objective judgements. You could stop the timer when the level of light passing through the reaction mixture drops to the same level as measured by the lightmeter in each test. This will make your repeat (or replicate) data more precise and improve the accuracy of your results.

Your evaluation might lead beyond suggestions to change the method to ideas to investigate new questions. For example, evaluating the rate of precipitation, you will have tried to control the temperature – probably by ensuring both solutions started mixing at the same temperature. However, if the reaction is exothermic, this might cause the temperature to change between the different concentrations investigated. This could lead to a new investigation to compare the energy transferred in a precipitation reaction at different concentrations. The question could be phrased as 'How does the concentration of a reactant solution affect the energy transferred in the reaction?'.

When drawing conclusions from investigations involving the manipulation of variables, you should refer to your graph when commenting on the relationship between the independent and dependent variables, explaining your findings using the data and your scientific knowledge and understanding. When drawing conclusions from qualitative tests to identify an unknown substance, where possible try to carry out or suggest a further confirmatory test for the same substance from the table provided in Paper 3.

Any hypotheses you were testing can only be refuted (disproved) by a practical investigation you carry out; they cannot be proved because of the limitations of your investigation. So hypotheses can only be 'supported' by the data collected. If your hypothesis predicts that the rate of reaction increases with increasing concentration, with a justification using collision theory, and data from your investigation supports this, you cannot say whether this relationship is true beyond the range of concentrations tested. There might be a point at higher concentrations where increasing the concentration of one reactant will start to have less, or even no, effect because there is such excess that the rate of collisions with the other reactant particles is not affected by further increases of concentration – so this would give you another idea to test!

QUESTION

4 **a** A student measured the average rate of a reaction by timing how long it took to collect $20 \, \text{cm}^3$ of the gas liberated in the reaction. What calculation would the student do to work out the average rate in $\text{cm}^3 \, \text{s}^{-1}$?

   b The student finds that the rate of a reaction is directly proportional to the concentration of a reactant, X.

   i Sketch a graph to show this relationship.

   ii Explain how to work out the gradient of the line on the graph.

   iii If the student changed the concentration of X from $0.50 \, \text{mol dm}^{-3}$ to $0.25 \, \text{mol dm}^{-3}$, what would happen to the rate of reaction?

   c Explain the quantitative relationship that the student found in this investigation using your scientific knowledge and understanding.

Summary

■ The following table summarises the breakdown of skills and the marks allocated to each skill area each skill area as it is assessed in the Cambridge International AS and A Level Advanced Practical Skills examination (Paper 3).

Skill	Minimum mark allocation*	Breakdown of skills	Minimum mark allocation*
Manipulation, measurement and observation	12 marks	Successful collection of data and observations	8 marks
		Quality of measurements or observations	2 marks
		Decisions relating to measurements or observations	2 marks
Presentation of data and observations	6 marks	Recording data or observations	2 marks
		Display of calculation and reasoning	2 marks
		Data layout	2 marks
Analysis, conclusions and evaluation	10 marks	Interpretation of data or observations and identifying sources of error	4 marks
		Drawing conclusions	5 marks
		Suggesting improvements	1 mark

* The remaining 12 marks will be allocated across the skills in this grid and their allocation may vary from paper to paper.

End-of-chapter questions

1 A student investigated the ease with which various metal carbonates decompose on heating. She decide to heat equal masses of each carbonate and time how long it took for the carbon dioxide given off to turn limewater in a test tube cloudy.

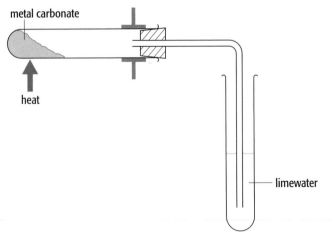

a i Name the independent variable in the investigation. [1]

ii Name the dependent variable. [1]

iii Name the control variable described at the start of this question. [1]

b The student decided to repeat the test on each of five metal carbonates provided three times.

    i Why is it a good idea to collect replicate data in investigations? [1]

    ii Draw a table that the student could fill in as the investigation was carried out. [3]

c **i** The test tube contained $10\,cm^3$ of limewater. The student measured this volume in a $10\,cm^3$ measuring cylinder with calibration marks every $0.1\,cm^3$. What is the margin of error when reading this scale and what is the percentage error in measuring the volume of limewater for this investigation? [2]

    ii Explain what is likely to be the greatest source of error in this investigation. [2]

d What type of graph should the student use to display the data from the investigation? [1]

Total = 12

2 The rate of the following reaction between hydrogen peroxide (H_2O_2) and iodide ions can be monitored using sodium thiosulfate and starch indicator:

$$2H^+(aq) + H_2O_2(aq) + 2I^-(aq) \longrightarrow 2H_2O(l) + I_2(aq)$$

A mixture of starch solution, potassium iodide solution, sulfuric acid and sodium thiosulfate is made. This mixture can then be reacted with varying concentrations of 10-volume hydrogen peroxide, made by making measured volumes of the peroxide solution up to $25\,cm^3$ with distilled water. When the hydrogen peroxide solution is added to the original mixture containing starch in a flask, the time for the contents of the flask to turn a blue/black colour can be measured.

This procedure, using a range of volumes of hydrogen peroxide, can determine how the concentration of hydrogen peroxide affects the rate of the reaction shown above. Here is a set of results obtained from one such investigation.

Volume of hydrogen peroxide used / cm^3	Time, t, for blue/black colour to appear / s	
1	300	
2	200	
4	90	
6	60	
8	44	
10	37	
12	28	

a A student wants to use these results to draw a graph that will show how the concentration of hydrogen peroxide affects the rate of reaction. Record the heading and values that the student could use to complete the third column of the table (to 2 significant figures). [3]

b What piece of measuring equipment would be used to make up the volumes of hydrogen peroxide solution to $25\,cm^3$? [1]

c The student was provided with a stopclock measuring to the nearest second to measure the time taken for the solution to turn blue/black but asked for a stopwatch measuring to one-hundredth of a second. The teacher said that would not be necessary. Explain the teacher's response. [2]

d The original mixture was made up using a solution of $40\,cm^3$ of $0.10\,mol\,dm^{-3}$ potassium iodide. How many moles of iodide ions are in the reaction mixture? [2]

e What role does the sodium thiosulfate play in this investigation? [3]

Total = 11

3   You have to identify an unknown compound, X.

Test	Observations made
To a small spatula measure of sodium carbonate in a test tube, add enough distilled water to make a solution. Add 1 cm depth of **X** solution.	White ppt
To a small spatula measure of sodium sulfate in a test tube, add enough distilled water to make a solution. Add 1 cm depth of **X** solution.	White ppt
To 1 cm depth of **X** solution in a test tube, add aqueous sodium hydroxide.	White ppt that is soluble in excess sodium hydroxide
Carefully heat the solid **X** in the test tube provided. Note: two gases are released.	Brown gas is given off (nitrogen dioxide is a brown gas). The gas re-lights a glowing splint (showing oxygen is present). The solid turns yellow and crackles as it is heated.

a   From the results of the tests above, and the Tables of Qualitative Analysis notes on page 475, identify the cation present in **X**.   [1]

b   Suggest another reagent to confirm the cation present in **X** giving the predicted observation.   [2]

c   Suggest the identity of **X**.   [1]

Total = 4

Chapter 19:
Lattice energy

Learning outcomes

You should be able to:

- explain and use the term **lattice energy**
- explain and use the terms **ionisation energy**, **enthalpy change of atomisation** and **electron affinity**
- construct Born–Haber cycles
- use Born–Haber cycles to calculate lattice energies
- explain, in qualitative terms, the effect of ionic charge and ionic radius on the numerical magnitude of a lattice energy

- interpret and explain qualitatively the trend in the thermal stability of the nitrates and carbonates of Group 2 elements in terms of the charge density of the cation and the polarisability of the large anion
- apply Hess's law to construct energy cycles to determine enthalpy changes of solution and enthalpy changes of hydration
- interpret and explain qualitatively the variation in solubility of Group 2 sulfates in terms of the relative values of the enthalpy change of hydration and the corresponding lattice energy.

Introduction

In Chapters 4 and 5 we introduced the idea of ionic bonding as the electrostatic force of attraction between positive and negative ions in the crystal lattice. In this chapter we show how we can use enthalpy changes to calculate the strength of ionic bonding, and explain differences in solubility and ease of thermal decomposition of ionic compounds.

Figure 19.1 A model of the sodium chloride lattice. The energy released when gaseous ions combine to form a lattice is called the lattice energy.

Defining lattice energy

When ions combine to form an ionic solid there is a huge release of energy. The reaction is highly exothermic. The energy given out when ions of opposite charges come together to form a crystalline lattice is called the lattice energy, $\Delta H^{\ominus}_{latt}$.

Equations describing the lattice energy of sodium chloride and magnesium chloride are shown here.

> Lattice energy is the enthalpy change when 1 mole of an ionic compound is formed from its gaseous ions under standard conditions.

$$Na^+(g) + Cl^-(g) \longrightarrow NaCl(s) \qquad \Delta H^{\ominus}_{latt} = -787\,kJ\,mol^{-1}$$

$$Mg^{2+}(g) + 2Cl^-(g) \longrightarrow MgCl_2(s) \quad \Delta H^{\ominus}_{latt} = -2526\,kJ\,mol^{-1}$$

Note that:

- it is the **gaseous** ions that combine to form the ionic solid
- the lattice energy is always exothermic: the value of $\Delta H^{\ominus}_{latt}$ is always negative, because the definition specifies the bonding together of ions, not the separation of ions.

The large exothermic value of the lattice energy shows that the ionic lattice is very stable with respect to its gaseous ions. The more exothermic the lattice energy, the stronger the ionic bonding in the lattice.

It is impossible to determine the lattice energy of a compound by a single direct experiment. We can, however, calculate a value for $\Delta H^{\ominus}_{latt}$ using several experimental values and an energy cycle called a Born–Haber cycle. In order to do this, we first need to introduce two more types of enthalpy change.

Note that the quantity we have defined as lattice energy is more accurately called the lattice enthalpy. However, the term **lattice energy** is commonly applied to lattice enthalpy as well. Lattice energy is the internal energy change when 1 mole of an ionic compound is formed from its gaseous ions at 0 K. Lattice enthalpy values are very close to the corresponding lattice energy values.

> QUESTION
>
> 1 a Give values for the standard conditions of temperature and pressure.
>
> b Write equations describing the lattice energy of:
>
>   i magnesium oxide
>
>   ii potassium bromide
>
>   iii sodium sulfide.

Enthalpy change of atomisation and electron affinity

Enthalpy change of atomisation

> The standard enthalpy change of atomisation, $\Delta H^{\ominus}_{at}$, is the enthalpy change when 1 mole of gaseous atoms is formed from its element under standard conditions.

The standard enthalpy change of atomisation of lithium relates to the equation:

$$Li(s) \longrightarrow Li(g) \qquad \Delta H^{\ominus}_{at} = +161\,kJ\,mol^{-1}$$

The standard enthalpy change of atomisation of chlorine relates to the equation:

$$\tfrac{1}{2}Cl_2(g) \longrightarrow Cl(g) \qquad\qquad \Delta H^{\ominus}_{at} = +122\,kJ\,mol^{-1}$$

Values of $\Delta H^{\ominus}_{at}$ are always positive (endothermic) because energy must be supplied to break the bonds holding the atoms in the element together.

QUESTION

2 a The bond energy of the chlorine molecule is +244 kJ mol^{-1}. Why is the standard enthalpy change of atomisation half this value?

b Write equations, including state symbols, that represent the enthalpy change of atomisation of:

  i oxygen

  ii barium

  iii bromine.

c What is the numerical value of the enthalpy change of atomisation of helium? Explain your answer.

Electron affinity

The energy change occurring when a gaseous non-metal atom accepts one electron is called the **electron affinity**. The symbol for electron affinity is $\Delta H^{\ominus}_{ea}$.

The first electron affinity, $\Delta H^{\ominus}_{ea1}$, is the enthalpy change when 1 mole of electrons is added to 1 mole of gaseous atoms to form 1 mole of gaseous 1– ions under standard conditions.

Equations representing the first electron affinity of chlorine and sulfur are:

$$Cl(g) + e^- \longrightarrow Cl^-(g) \qquad \Delta H^{\ominus}_{ea1} = -348\,kJ\,mol^{-1}$$

$$S(g) + e^- \longrightarrow S^-(g) \qquad \Delta H^{\ominus}_{ea1} = -200\,kJ\,mol^{-1}$$

Note that:

- the change is from gaseous atoms to gaseous 1– ions
- the enthalpy change for the first electron affinity, $\Delta H^{\ominus}_{ea1}$ is generally exothermic: $\Delta H^{\ominus}_{ea}$ is negative.

When an element forms an ion with more than one negative charge, we must use successive electron affinities (this is rather like the successive ionisation energies we used on page 34). The 1st, 2nd and 3rd electron affinities have symbols $\Delta H^{\ominus}_{ea1}$, $\Delta H^{\ominus}_{ea2}$ and $\Delta H^{\ominus}_{ea3}$.

The **second electron affinity**, $\Delta H^{\ominus}_{ea2}$, is the enthalpy change when 1 mole of electrons is added to 1 mole of gaseous 1– ions to form 1 mole of gaseous 2– ions under standard conditions.

The equations representing the 1st and 2nd electron affinities of oxygen are:

1st electron affinity:
$$O(g) + e^- \longrightarrow O^-(g) \quad \Delta H^{\ominus}_{ea1} = -141\,kJ\,mol^{-1}$$

2nd electron affinity:
$$O^-(g) + e^- \longrightarrow O^{2-}(g) \quad \Delta H^{\ominus}_{ea2} = +798\,kJ\,mol^{-1}$$

Note that 2nd electron affinities are always endothermic ($\Delta H^{\ominus}_{ea2}$ is positive), and so are 3rd electron affinities.

The overall enthalpy change in forming an oxide ion, O^{2-}, from an oxygen atom is found by adding together the 1st and 2nd electron affinities:

$$O(g) + 2e^- \longrightarrow O^{2-}(g)$$

$$\Delta H^{\ominus}_{ea1} + \Delta H^{\ominus}_{ea2} = (-141) + (+798) = +657\,kJ\,mol^{-1}$$

259

QUESTION

3 a Suggest why the 2nd and 3rd electron affinities are always endothermic.

b The 1st electron affinity of sulfur is –200 kJ mol^{-1}. The second electron affinity of sulfur is +640 kJ mol^{-1}. Calculate a value for the enthalpy change S(g) + 2e$^-$ $\longrightarrow$ S^{2-}(g)

c Write equations representing:

  i the 1st electron affinity of iodine

  ii the 2nd electron affinity of sulfur.

Born–Haber cycles

Components of the Born–Haber cycle

We have seen how we can apply Hess's law in energy cycles to work out enthalpy changes (page 97). A **Born–Haber cycle** is a particular type of enthalpy cycle used to calculate lattice energy. In simple terms it can be represented by Figure 19.2.

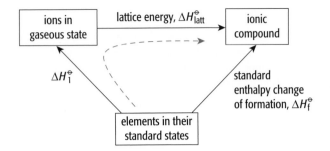

Figure 19.2 A simple enthalpy cycle that can be used to calculate lattice energy. The dashed line shows the two-step route: using Hess's law, $\Delta H_1^\ominus + \Delta H_{latt}^\ominus = \Delta H_f^\ominus$.

We can determine the lattice energy of a compound if we know:

- its enthalpy change of formation, $\Delta H_f^\ominus$
- the enthalpy changes involved in changing the elements from their standard states to their gaseous ions, $\Delta H_1^\ominus$.

According to Hess's law, Figure 19.2 shows that:

$$\Delta H_1^\ominus + \Delta H_{latt}^\ominus = \Delta H_f^\ominus$$

Rearranging this equation we get:

$$\Delta H_{latt}^\ominus = \Delta H_f^\ominus - \Delta H_1^\ominus$$

The enthalpy change $\Delta H_1^\ominus$ involves several steps.

Taking lithium fluoride as an example, the relevant enthalpy cycle can be written to show these steps (Figure 19.3).

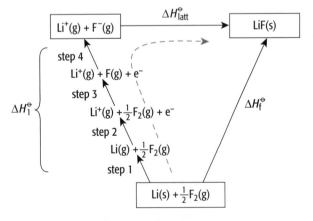

Figure 19.3 An enthalpy cycle that can be used to calculate the lattice energy of lithium fluoride. The dashed line shows the two-step route.

The enthalpy changes needed to calculate $\Delta H_1^\ominus$ are as follows.

Step 1 Convert solid lithium to gaseous lithium atoms: the enthalpy change required is the enthalpy change of atomisation of lithium, $\Delta H_{at}^\ominus$.

$$Li(s) \longrightarrow Li(g) \qquad \Delta H_{at}^\ominus = +161 \text{ kJ mol}^{-1}$$

Step 2 Convert gaseous lithium atoms to gaseous lithium ions: the enthalpy change required is the 1st ionisation energy of lithium, $\Delta H_{i1}^\ominus$ (see page 34).

$$Li(g) \longrightarrow Li+(g) + e^- \qquad \Delta H_{i1}^\ominus = +520 \text{ kJ mol}^{-1}$$

Step 3 Convert fluorine molecules to fluorine atoms: the enthalpy change required is the enthalpy change of atomisation of fluorine, $\Delta H_{at}^\ominus$.

$$\tfrac{1}{2}F_2(g) \longrightarrow F(g) \qquad \Delta H_{at}^\ominus = +79 \text{ kJ mol}^{-1}$$

Step 4 Convert gaseous fluorine atoms to gaseous fluoride ions: the enthalpy change required is the 1st electron affinity of fluorine, $\Delta H_{ea1}^\ominus$.

$$F(g) + e^- \longrightarrow F^-(g) \qquad \Delta H_{ea1}^\ominus = -328 \text{ kJ mol}^{-1}$$

Step 5 By adding all these values together, we get a value for $\Delta H_1^\ominus$.

The enthalpy change of formation of lithium fluoride is -617 kJ mol^{-1}. We now have all the information we need to calculate the lattice energy.

Calculating lattice energies

Applying Hess's law to find the lattice energy of lithium fluoride:

$$\Delta H_{latt}^\ominus = \Delta H_f^\ominus - \Delta H_1^\ominus$$

We know that:

$$\Delta H_1^\ominus = \Delta H_{at}^\ominus [Li] + \Delta H_{i1}^\ominus [Li] + \Delta H_{at}^\ominus [F] + \Delta H_{ea1}^\ominus [F]$$

So

$$\Delta H_{latt}^\ominus = \Delta H_f^\ominus - \{\Delta H_{at}^\ominus [Li] + \Delta H_{i1}^\ominus [Li] + \Delta H_{at}^\ominus [F] + \Delta H_{ea1}^\ominus [F]\}$$

Putting in the figures:

$$\Delta H_{latt}^\ominus = (-617) - \underbrace{\{(+161) + (+520) + (+79) + (-328)\}}_{= +432}$$

$$\Delta H_{latt}^\ominus = (-617) - (+432) = -1049 \text{ kJ mol}^{-1}$$

Note: take care to account for the signs of the enthalpy changes. The values of the enthalpy changes of formation and the electron affinity may be negative or positive.

4 a Write equations to represent:

    i the 1st ionisation energy of caesium

    ii the 3rd ionisation energy of aluminium

    iii the enthalpy change of formation of calcium oxide

    iv the enthalpy change of formation of iron(III) chloride.

b Calculate the lattice energy for sodium chloride, given that:

$$\Delta H_f^\ominus [NaCl] = -411 \, kJ \, mol^{-1}$$

$$\Delta H_{at}^\ominus [Na] = +107 \, kJ \, mol^{-1}$$

$$\Delta H_{at}^\ominus [Cl] = +122 \, kJ \, mol^{-1}$$

$$\Delta H_{i1}^\ominus [Na] = +496 \, kJ \, mol^{-1}$$

$$\Delta H_{ea1}^\ominus [Cl] = -348 \, kJ \, mol^{-1}$$

The Born–Haber cycle as an energy level diagram

We can show the Born–Haber cycle as an energy level diagram (Figure 19.4). This is the best, and clearest, type of diagram for a Born–Haber cycle. You should therefore choose to draw this type of diagram to show a Born–Haber cycle.

To draw the cycle you:

- start by putting down the elements in their standard state on the left-hand side
- add the other enthalpy changes in the order of steps 1 to 4 shown in Figure 19.4
- complete the cycle by adding the enthalpy change of formation and lattice energy.

Note that the arrows going upwards represent an increase in energy ($\Delta H^\ominus$ is positive) and the arrows going downwards represent a decrease in energy ($\Delta H^\ominus$ is negative).

5 a Draw a fully labelled Born–Haber cycle for potassium bromide, naming each step.

b State the name of the enthalpy changes represented by the following equations:

    i $I_2(s) \longrightarrow I(g)$

    ii $N(g) + e^- \longrightarrow N^-(g)$

    iii $Sr(s) + Cl_2(g) \longrightarrow SrCl_2(s)$

    iv $Cd^{2+}(g) + 2Cl^-(g) \longrightarrow CdCl_2(s)$

261

The Born–Haber cycle for magnesium chloride

The Born–Haber cycle for magnesium chloride is shown in Figure 19.5.

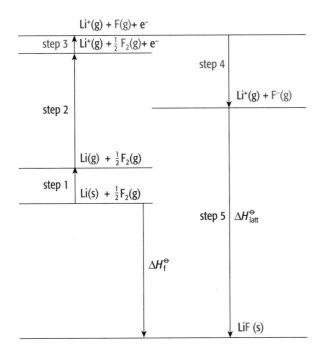

Figure 19.4 Born–Haber cycle for lithium fluoride.

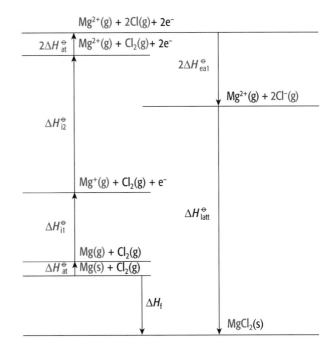

Figure 19.5 Born–Haber cycle for magnesium chloride.

There are a few minor differences between this cycle and the one for lithium fluoride.

1 The magnesium ion is Mg^{2+}, so the 1st and the 2nd ionisation energies need to be taken into account:

$$Mg(g) \longrightarrow Mg^+(g) + e^- \qquad \Delta H^{\ominus}_{i1} = +736\,kJ\,mol^{-1}$$

$$Mg^+(g) \longrightarrow Mg^{2+}(g) + e^- \qquad \Delta H^{\ominus}_{i2} = +1450\,kJ\,mol^{-1}$$

2 There are two chloride ions in $MgCl_2$, so the values of the enthalpy change of atomisation and the first electron affinity of chlorine must be multiplied by 2.

$$Cl_2(g) \longrightarrow 2Cl(g) \quad 2\Delta H^{\ominus}_{at} = 2 \times (+122) = +244\,kJ\,mol^{-1}$$

$$2Cl(g) + 2e^- \longrightarrow 2Cl^-(g)$$
$$2\Delta H^{\ominus}_{ea1} = 2 \times (-348) = -696\,kJ\,mol^{-1}$$

In order to calculate the lattice energy we need some additional information:

$$\Delta H^{\ominus}_f\,[MgCl_2] = -641\,kJ\,mol^{-1}$$

$$\Delta H^{\ominus}_{at}\,[Mg] = +148\,kJ\,mol^{-1}$$

According to Hess's law:

$$\Delta H^{\ominus}_{latt} = \Delta H^{\ominus}_f - \{\Delta H^{\ominus}_{at}\,[Mg] + \Delta H^{\ominus}_{i1}\,[Mg] + \Delta H^{\ominus}_{i2}\,[Mg] + 2\Delta H^{\ominus}_{at}\,[Cl] + 2\Delta H^{\ominus}_{ea1}\,[Cl]\}$$

$$\Delta H^{\ominus}_{latt} = (-641) - \{(+148) + (+736) + (+1450) + 2 \times (+122) + 2 \times (-348)\}$$
$$= +1882$$

$$\Delta H^{\ominus}_{latt} = (-641) - (+1882) = -2523\,kJ\,mol^{-1}$$

QUESTION

6 Draw fully labelled Born–Haber cycles for:

a MgO

b Na_2O.

Constructing a Born–Haber cycle for aluminium oxide

Aluminium oxide, Al_2O_3, contains two aluminium ions (Al^{3+}) and three oxide ions (O^{2-}).

■ In order to form 1 mole of gaseous Al^{3+} ions from 1 mole of Al(s), we apply the following sequence of enthalpy changes:

$$Al(s) \xrightarrow{\Delta H^{\ominus}_{at}} Al(g) \xrightarrow{\Delta H^{\ominus}_{i1}} Al^+(g) \xrightarrow{\Delta H^{\ominus}_{i2}} Al^{2+}(g) \xrightarrow{\Delta H^{\ominus}_{i3}} Al^{3+}(g)$$
$$+326\,kJ\,mol^{-1} \quad +577\,kJ\,mol^{-1} \quad +1820\,kJ\,mol^{-1} \quad +2470\,kJ\,mol^{-1}$$

■ In order to form 1 mole of gaseous O^{2-} ions from oxygen molecules, we apply the following sequence of enthalpy changes:

$$O_2(g) \xrightarrow{\Delta H^{\ominus}_{at}} O(g) \xrightarrow{\Delta H^{\ominus}_{ea1}} O^-(g) \xrightarrow{\Delta H^{\ominus}_{ea2}} O^{2-}(g)$$
$$+249\,kJ\,mol^{-1} \quad -141\,kJ\,mol^{-1} \quad +798\,kJ\,mol^{-1}$$

QUESTION

7 a Draw a Born–Haber cycle for aluminium oxide.

b Calculate a value for the lattice energy of aluminium oxide using the data under the arrows in the sequences above and given that $\Delta H^{\ominus}_f\,[Al_2O_3] = -1676\,kJ\,mol^{-1}$. Remember that there are 2 moles of Al^{3+} ions and 3 moles of O^{2-} ions in 1 mole of Al_2O_3.

Factors affecting the value of lattice energy

Lattice energy arises from the electrostatic force of attraction of oppositely charged ions when the crystalline lattice is formed. The size and charge of these ions can affect the value of the lattice energy.

Lattice energy and ion size

As the size of the ion increases, the lattice energy becomes less exothermic. This applies to both anions and cations. Figure 19.6 shows that:

■ for any given anion, e.g. F^-, the lattice energy gets less exothermic as the size of the cation increases from Li^+ to Cs^+

■ for any given cation, e.g. Li^+, the lattice energy gets less exothermic as the size of the anion increases from F^- to I^-.

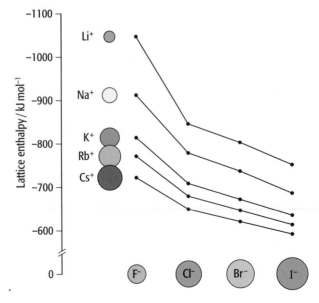

Figure 19.6 Lattice enthalpies of the Group 1 halides.

Ions with the same ionic charge have a lower charge density if their radius is larger. This is because the same charge is spread out over a larger volume. A lower charge density results in weaker electrostatic forces of attraction in the ionic lattice. Sodium fluoride has a less exothermic lattice energy than lithium fluoride. This reflects the lower charge density on sodium ions compared with lithium ions.

Lattice energy and charge on the ions

The lattice energy becomes more exothermic as the ionic charge increases.

We can see this by comparing lithium fluoride, LiF, with magnesium oxide, MgO. These compounds have the same arrangement of ions in their lattice structure. The cations Li^+ and Mg^{2+} have similar sizes. The anions F^- and O^{2-} are fairly similar in size (although they are much larger than the cations). The major physical difference between LiF and MgO is the ionic charge. This affects the lattice energy:

$$\Delta H^{\ominus}_{latt}[LiF] = -1049\,kJ\,mol^{-1}$$

$$\Delta H^{\ominus}_{latt}[MgO] = -3923\,kJ\,mol^{-1}$$

Magnesium oxide has a greater lattice energy than lithium fluoride. The doubly charged Mg^{2+} and O^{2-} ions in magnesium oxide attract each other more strongly than the singly charged ions of the same size in LiF. For ions of similar size, the greater the ionic charge, the higher the charge density. This results in stronger ionic bonds being formed.

QUESTIONS

8 a For each pair of compounds, suggest which will have the most exothermic lattice energy.

   i   KCl and BaO (ionic radii are similar)

   ii MgI_2 and SrI_2

   iii CaO and NaCl (ionic radii are similar).

  b Place the following compounds in order of increasingly exothermic lattice energy. Explain your answer.

     LiF   MgO   RbCl

9 Students taking physics A level learn that the electrostatic force between two charged particles is proportional to

   $$\frac{Q_1 \times Q_2}{r^2}$$ where Q_1 and Q_2 are the charges on the particles

QUESTIONS (CONTINUED)

and r is the distance between the centres of the particles. Use this relationship to explain why:

a magnesium oxide has a greater lattice energy than lithium fluoride

b lithium fluoride has a greater lattice energy than potassium bromide.

Ion polarisation

In our model of an ionic lattice, we have thought of the ions as being spherical in shape. This is not always the case. In some cases, the positive charge on the cation in an ionic lattice may attract the electrons in the anion towards it. This results in a distortion of the electron cloud of the anion and the anion is no longer spherical (Figure 19.7). We call this distortion **ion polarisation**. The ability of a cation to attract electrons and distort an anion is called the **polarising power** of the cation.

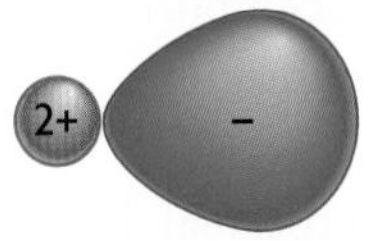

Figure 19.7 Ion polarisation. A small highly charged cation can distort the shape of the anion.

Factors affecting ion polarisation

The degree of polarisation of an anion depends on:

- the charge density of the cation
- the ease with which the anion can be polarised
  – its polarisability.

An anion is more likely to be polarised if:

- the cation is small
- the cation has a charge of 2+ or 3+
- the anion is large
- the anion has a charge of 2– or 3–.

A small highly charged cation such as Fe^{3+} can attract electrons and distort a larger anion to such an extent that the bond formed has a considerable amount of covalent character. Pure ionic bonding and pure covalent bonding are extremes. Many ionic compounds have some covalent character due to ion polarisation. Many covalent compounds have some degree of charge separation, i.e. they are polar, due to bond polarisation (see Chapter 4, pages 60–61).

263

QUESTION

10 a Explain why a cation with a smaller ionic radius has a higher charge density.

   b Which one of the following ions will be the best polariser of the large nitrate ion? Explain your answer.

   Cs⁺   Li⁺   Na⁺   K⁺

   c Which one of these ions will be most polarised by a Mg²⁺ ion? Explain your answer.

   Br⁻   Cl⁻   F⁻   I⁻

The thermal stability of Group 2 carbonates and nitrates

The Group 2 carbonates decompose to their oxides and carbon dioxide on heating. For example:

$$CaCO_3(s) \xrightarrow{\text{heat}} CaO(s) + CO_2(g)$$

Table 19.1 shows the decomposition temperature and enthalpy change of reaction, $\Delta H^{\ominus}_r$, for some Group 2 carbonates.

   The relative ease of thermal decomposition is shown by the values of the enthalpy changes of reaction. The more positive the enthalpy change, the more stable the carbonate relative to its oxide and carbon dioxide. This is also reflected by the decomposition temperatures: the further down the group, the higher the temperature required to decompose the carbonate (see page 168).

Group 2 carbonate	Decomposition temperature / °C	Enthalpy change of reaction / kJ mol⁻¹
magnesium carbonate	540	+117
calcium carbonate	900	+176
strontium carbonate	1280	+238
barium carbonate	1360	+268

Table 19.1 Enthalpy change of reaction values for the decomposition of some Group 2 carbonates.

So the relative stabilities of these carbonates increases down the group in the order:

$$BaCO_3 > SrCO_3 > CaCO_3 > MgCO_3.$$

We can explain this trend using ideas about ion polarisation:

- the carbonate ion has a relatively large ionic radius so it is easily polarised by a small highly charged cation
- the Group 2 cations increase in ionic radius down the group:

  $Mg^{2+} < Ca^{2+} < Sr^{2+} < Ba^{2+}$

- the smaller the ionic radius of the cation, the better it is at polarising the carbonate ion (Figure 19.8)
- so the degree of polarisation of the carbonate ion by the Group 2 cation follows the order

  $Mg^{2+} > Ca^{2+} > Sr^{2+} > Ba^{2+}$

- the greater the polarisation of the carbonate ion, the easier it is to weaken a carbon–oxygen bond in the carbonate and form carbon dioxide and the oxide on heating.

A similar pattern is observed with the thermal decomposition of Group 2 nitrates: these decompose to form the oxide, nitrogen dioxide and oxygen. For example:

$$2Mg(NO_3)_2(s) \longrightarrow 2MgO(s) + 4NO_2(g) + O_2(g)$$

The order of stability with respect to the products is in the order:

$$Ba(NO_3)_2 > Sr(NO_3)_2 > Ca(NO_3)_2 > Mg(NO_3)_2.$$

Figure 19.8 Magnesium ions are better polarisers of carbonate ions than calcium ions.

The difference in thermal stability of Group 2 carbonates can be analysed by comparing Born–Haber cycles involving the lattice energies of calcium carbonate and calcium oxide. The unequal changes in the lattice energies of calcium carbonate and calcium oxide as the cation size increases can be related to the increasing thermal stability down the group.

QUESTION

11 Use ideas about ion polarisation to explain why magnesium nitrate undergoes thermal decomposition at a much lower temperature than barium nitrate.

Enthalpy changes in solution

When an ionic solid dissolves in water, the crystal lattice breaks up and the ions separate. It requires a large amount of energy to overcome the attractive forces between the ions. How does this happen, even when the water is not heated? We will answer this question in this section.

Enthalpy change of solution

> The enthalpy change of solution, $\Delta H^{\ominus}_{sol}$, is the energy absorbed or released when 1 mole of an ionic solid dissolves in sufficient water to form a very dilute solution.

The enthalpy changes of solution for magnesium chloride and sodium chloride are described by the equations below:

$$MgCl_2(s) + aq \longrightarrow MgCl_2(aq) \qquad \Delta H^{\ominus}_{sol} = -55\,kJ\,mol^{-1}$$

or

$$MgCl_2(s) + aq \longrightarrow Mg^{2+}(aq) + 2Cl^-(aq)$$
$$\Delta H^{\ominus}_{sol} = -55\,kJ\,mol^{-1}$$

$$NaCl(s) + aq \longrightarrow NaCl(aq) \qquad \Delta H^{\ominus}_{sol} = +3.9\,kJ\,mol^{-1}$$

or

$$NaCl(s) + aq \longrightarrow Na^+(aq) + Cl^-(aq) \quad \Delta H^{\ominus}_{sol} = +3.9\,kJ\,mol^{-1}$$

Note that:

- the symbol for enthalpy change of solution is $\Delta H^{\ominus}_{sol}$
- the symbol 'aq' represents the very large amount of water used
- enthalpy changes of solution can be positive (endothermic) or negative (exothermic)
- a compound is likely to be soluble in water only if $\Delta H^{\ominus}_{sol}$ is negative or has a small positive value; substances with large positive values of $\Delta H^{\ominus}_{sol}$ are relatively insoluble.

QUESTION

12 a Write equations to represent the enthalpy change of solution of:

   i potassium sulfate

   ii zinc chloride.

  b The enthalpies of solution of some metal halides are given below. What do these values tell you about the relative solubilities of these four compounds?

   sodium chloride, $\Delta H^{\ominus}_{sol} = +3.9\,kJ\,mol^{-1}$

   silver chloride, $\Delta H^{\ominus}_{sol} = +65.7\,kJ\,mol^{-1}$

   sodium bromide, $\Delta H^{\ominus}_{sol} = -0.6\,kJ\,mol^{-1}$

   silver bromide, $\Delta H^{\ominus}_{sol} = +84.5\,kJ\,mol^{-1}$

'Soluble' and 'insoluble' are only relative terms. Magnesium carbonate is regarded as being insoluble because only 0.6 g of the salt dissolves in every dm^3 of water. No metallic salts are absolutely insoluble in water. Even lead carbonate, which is regarded as insoluble, dissolves to a very small extent: 0.000 17 g dissolves in every dm^3 of water. If salts were completely insoluble they could not have a value for $\Delta H^{\ominus}_{sol}$.

Enthalpy change of hydration

The lattice energy for sodium chloride is $-788\,kJ\,mol^{-1}$. This means that we need to supply (at least) $+788\,kJ\,mol^{-1}$ to overcome the forces of attraction between the ions. But $\Delta H^{\ominus}_{sol}$ [NaCl] is only $+3.9\,kJ\,mol^{-1}$. Where does the energy needed to separate the ions come from? The answer is that it comes from the strong attraction between the ions and the water molecules.

When an ionic solid dissolves in water, bonds are formed between water molecules and the ions. These bonds are called ion–dipole bonds. Water is a polar molecule. The δ– oxygen atoms in water molecules are attracted to the positive ions in the ionic compound. The δ+ hydrogen atoms in water molecules are attracted to the negative ions in the ionic compound (Figure 19.9).

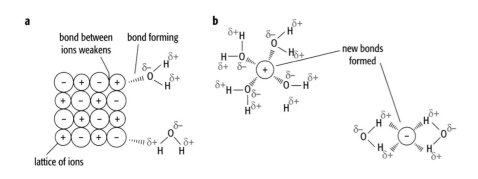

Figure 19.9 a Water molecules forming ion–dipole bonds with an ionic compound. **b** Hydrated ions in solution.

The energy released in forming ion–dipole bonds is sufficient to compensate for the energy that must be put in to separate the anions and cations that are bonded together in the crystal lattice.

The energy released when gaseous ions dissolve in water is called the **enthalpy change of hydration**.

> The enthalpy change of hydration, $\Delta H^{\ominus}_{hyd}$, is the enthalpy change when 1 mole of a specified gaseous ion dissolves in sufficient water to form a very dilute solution.

The enthalpy changes of hydration for calcium ions and chloride ions are described by the equations below:

$$Ca^{2+}(g) + aq \longrightarrow Ca^{2+}(aq) \qquad \Delta H^{\ominus}_{hyd} = -1650\,kJ\,mol^{-1}$$

$$Cl^{-}(g) + aq \longrightarrow Cl^{-}(aq) \qquad \Delta H^{\ominus}_{hyd} = -364\,kJ\,mol^{-1}$$

Note that:

- the symbol for enthalpy change of hydration is $\Delta H^{\ominus}_{hyd}$
- the enthalpy change of hydration is always exothermic
- the value of $\Delta H^{\ominus}_{hyd}$ is more exothermic for ions with the same charge but smaller ionic radii, e.g. $\Delta H^{\ominus}_{hyd}$ is more exothermic for Li^+ than for Na^+
- the value of $\Delta H^{\ominus}_{hyd}$ is more exothermic for ions with the same radii but a larger charge, e.g. $\Delta H^{\ominus}_{hyd}$ is more exothermic for Mg^{2+} than for Li^+.

QUESTIONS

13 a Why is the enthalpy change of hydration always exothermic?

b Write equations to represent:

i the hydration of a sodium ion

ii the hydration of a chloride ion.

c Draw diagrams to show:

i 4 water molecules hydrating a magnesium ion

ii 2 water molecules hydrating a bromide ion.

Show the dipole on each water molecule.

d Explain why the value of $\Delta H^{\ominus}_{hyd}$ for magnesium ions is much more exothermic than $\Delta H^{\ominus}_{hyd}$ for potassium ions.

14 Name the changes associated with the equations below:

a $KBr(s) + aq \longrightarrow KBr(aq)$ (for 1 mole of KBr)

b $K^+(g) + aq \longrightarrow K^+(aq)$ (for 1 mole of K^+ ions)

c $K^+(g) + Br^-(g) \longrightarrow KBr(s)$ (for 1 mole of KBr)

d $Br^-(g) + aq \longrightarrow Br^-(aq)$ (for 1 mole of Br^- ions)

Calculating enthalpy changes in solution

We can calculate the enthalpy change of solution or the enthalpy change of hydration by constructing an enthalpy cycle and using Hess's law (Figure 19.10).

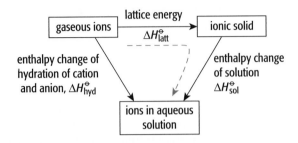

Figure 19.10 An enthalpy cycle involving lattice energy, enthalpy change of hydration and enthalpy change of solution.

We can see from this enthalpy cycle that:

$$\Delta H^{\ominus}_{latt} + \Delta H^{\ominus}_{sol} = \Delta H^{\ominus}_{hyd}$$

Note that the $\Delta H^{\ominus}_{hyd}$ values for both anions and cations are added together to get the total value of $\Delta H^{\ominus}_{hyd}$.

We can use this energy cycle to calculate:

- the value of $\Delta H^{\ominus}_{sol}$
- the value of $\Delta H^{\ominus}_{hyd}$.

WORKED EXAMPLES

1 Determine the enthalpy change of solution of sodium fluoride using the following data:

- lattice energy $= -902\,kJ\,mol^{-1}$
- enthalpy change of hydration of sodium ions $= -406\,kJ\,mol^{-1}$
- enthalpy change of hydration of fluoride ions $= -506\,kJ\,mol^{-1}$

Step 1: draw the enthalpy cycle (Figure 19.11)

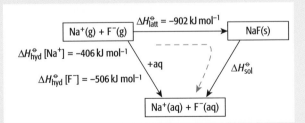

Figure 19.11 An enthalpy cycle to determine $\Delta H^{\ominus}_{sol}$ of NaF.

Step 2: rearrange the equation and substitute the figures to find $\Delta H^{\ominus}_{sol}$

$$\Delta H^{\ominus}_{latt} + \Delta H^{\ominus}_{sol} = \Delta H^{\ominus}_{hyd}$$

WORKED EXAMPLES (CONTINUED)

so

$$\Delta H^{\ominus}_{sol} = \Delta H^{\ominus}_{hyd} - \Delta H^{\ominus}_{latt}$$

$$\Delta H^{\ominus}_{sol} = (-406) + (-506) - (-902)$$

$$= -912 + 902$$

$$\Delta H^{\ominus}_{sol} [NaF] = -10\,kJ\,mol^{-1}$$

An energy level diagram for this enthalpy cycle is shown in Figure 19.12.

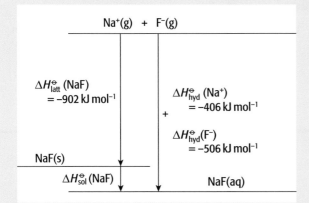

Figure 19.12 An energy level diagram to determine $\Delta H^{\ominus}_{sol}$ of NaF.

2 Determine the enthalpy change of hydration of the chloride ion using the following data.

- lattice energy of lithium chloride = $-846\,kJ\,mol^{-1}$
- enthalpy change of solution of lithium chloride = $-37\,kJ\,mol^{-1}$
- enthalpy change of hydration of lithium ion = $-519\,kJ\,mol^{-1}$

Step 1: draw the enthalpy cycle (Figure 19.13).

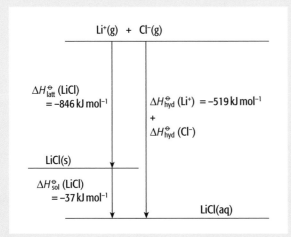

Figure 19.13 An enthalpy cycle to determine $\Delta H^{\ominus}_{hyd} [Cl^-]$.

WORKED EXAMPLES (CONTINUED)

Step 2: rearrange the equation and substitute the figures to find $\Delta H^{\ominus}_{hyd} [Cl^-]$.

$$\Delta H^{\ominus}_{latt} + \Delta H^{\ominus}_{sol} = \Delta H^{\ominus}_{hyd} [Li^+] + \Delta H^{\ominus}_{hyd} [Cl^-]$$

so

$$\Delta H^{\ominus}_{hyd} [Cl^-] = \Delta H^{\ominus}_{latt} + \Delta H^{\ominus}_{sol} - \Delta H^{\ominus}_{hyd} [Li^+]$$

$$\Delta H^{\ominus}_{hyd} [Cl^-] = (-846) + (-37) - (-519)$$

$$= -883 + 519$$

$$\Delta H^{\ominus}_{hyd} [Cl^-] = -364\,kJ\,mol^{-1}$$

QUESTION

15 a Draw an enthalpy cycle to calculate the enthalpy of hydration of magnesium ions when magnesium chloride dissolves in water.

 b Calculate the enthalpy of hydration of magnesium ions given that:

$$\Delta H^{\ominus}_{latt} [MgCl_2] = -2592\,kJ\,mol^{-1}$$

$$\Delta H^{\ominus}_{sol} [MgCl_2] = -55\,kJ\,mol^{-1}$$

$$\Delta H^{\ominus}_{hyd} [Cl^-] = -364\,kJ\,mol^{-1}$$

The solubility of Group 2 sulfates

Table 19.2 shows the solubility in water of some Group 2 sulfates. The solubility decreases as the radius of the metal ion increases. We can explain this variation in solubility in terms of the relative values of enthalpy change of hydration and the corresponding lattice energy.

Compound	Solubility / mol dm^{-3}
magnesium sulfate	1.83
calcium sulfate	4.66×10^{-2}
strontium sulfate	7.11×10^{-4}
barium sulfate	9.43×10^{-6}

Table 19.2 Solubilities in water of some Group 2 sulfates.

267

Change in hydration enthalpy down the group

- Smaller ions (with the same charge) have greater enthalpy changes of hydration
- so the enthalpy change of hydration decreases (gets less exothermic) in the order $Mg^{2+} > Ca^{2+} > Sr^{2+} > Ba^{2+}$
- this decrease is relatively large down the group and it depends entirely on the increase in the size of the cation, as the anion is unchanged (it is the sulfate ion in every case).

Change in lattice energy down the group

- Lattice energy is greater if the ions (with the same charge) forming the lattice are small
- so the lattice energy decreases in the order $Mg^{2+} > Ca^{2+} > Sr^{2+} > Ba^{2+}$
- the lattice energy is also inversely proportional to the sum of the radii of the anion and cation
- the sulfate ion is much larger than the group 2 cations
- so the sulfate ion contributes a relatively greater part to the change in the lattice energy down the group
- so the decrease in lattice energy is relatively smaller down the group and it is determined more by the size of the large sulfate ion than the size of the cations.

Difference in enthalpy change of solution of Group 2 sulfates

On page 265 we saw that substances that have a very low solubility in water are likely to have $\Delta H^{\ominus}_{sol}$ with a high positive (endothermic) value. As a rough guide, the higher the positive value of $\Delta H^{\ominus}_{sol}$ the less soluble the salt.

We have seen that:

- the lattice energy of the sulfates decreases (gets less exothermic) by relatively smaller values down the group
- the enthalpy change of hydration decreases (gets less exothermic) by relatively larger values down the group
- so applying Hess's law, the value of $\Delta H^{\ominus}_{sol}$ gets more endothermic down the group (Figure 19.14)
- so the solubility of the Group 2 sulfates decreases down the group.

QUESTION

16 a Draw an enthalpy cycle as an energy level diagram showing the relationship between lattice energy, enthalpy change of solution and enthalpy change of hydration for barium sulfate.

$\Delta H^{\ominus}_{sol}$ [BaSO$_4$] is very endothermic.

b Explain why magnesium sulfate is more soluble than barium sulfate by referring to the relative values of the lattice energies and enthalpy changes of hydration.

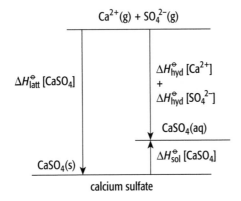

calcium sulfate

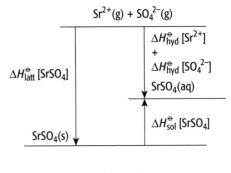

strontium sulfate

Figure 19.14 Enthalpy cycles comparing the enthalpy change of solution of calcium sulfate and strontium sulfate.

Summary

- The lattice energy ($\Delta H^{\ominus}_{latt}$) is the energy change when gaseous ions come together to form 1 mole of a solid lattice (under standard conditions).

- The standard enthalpy change of atomisation ($\Delta H^{\ominus}_{at}$) is the enthalpy change when 1 mole of gaseous atoms is formed from the element in its standard state under standard conditions.

- The 1st ionisation energy of an element ($\Delta H^{\ominus}_{i1}$) is the energy needed to remove one electron from each atom in 1 mole of atoms of the element in the gaseous state to form gaseous 1+ ions.

- The 1st electron affinity ($\Delta H^{\ominus}_{ea1}$) is the enthalpy change when 1 mole of electrons is added to 1 mole of gaseous atoms to form 1 mole of gaseous 1– ions under standard conditions.

- A Born–Haber cycle is a type of enthalpy cycle (Hess cycle) that includes lattice energy, enthalpy change of formation and relevant electron affinities, enthalpy changes of atomisation and enthalpy changes of ionisation.

- Lattice energies can be calculated from a Born–Haber cycle.

- Lattice energies are exothermic. The greater the value of the lattice energy, the stronger the ionic bonding holding the lattice together.

- The value of the lattice energy depends on:
  - the size of the ions (the smaller the ion, the more exothermic the lattice energy)
  - the charge on the ions (the greater the charge on the ions, the more exothermic the lattice energy).

- The thermal stability of the carbonates and nitrates of Group 2 elements depends on the degree to which the Group 2 cation is able to polarise the larger anion:
  - smaller cations have a higher charge density and are better polarisers of a given anion
  - larger anions are more polarised by a given cation.

- The standard enthalpy change of solution ($\Delta H^{\ominus}_{sol}$) is the enthalpy change when 1 mole of an ionic solid dissolves in sufficient water to form a very dilute solution. $\Delta H^{\ominus}_{sol}$ may be exothermic or endothermic.

- The enthalpy change of hydration ($\Delta H^{\ominus}_{hyd}$) is the enthalpy change when 1 mole of gaseous ions dissolves in sufficient water to form a very dilute solution. $\Delta H^{\ominus}_{hyd}$ is always exothermic.

- The value of $\Delta H^{\ominus}_{hyd}$ depends on:
  - the size of the ion ($\Delta H^{\ominus}_{hyd}$ is more exothermic the smaller the ion)
  - the charge on the ion ($\Delta H^{\ominus}_{hyd}$ is more exothermic the greater the charge).

- Hess's law can be applied to construct energy cycles to determine enthalpy changes of solution and enthalpy changes of hydration.

- The decrease in solubility of Group 2 sulfates down the group can be explained in terms of the relative values of the enthalpy change of hydration and the corresponding lattice energy.

End-of-chapter questions

Learn a mental check list to help you construct Born–Haber cycles:

- have I included the enthalpy of formation?
- have I included both enthalpies of atomisation?
- have I converted all atoms into ions of the **correct charge**?
- have I considered **how many moles of each ion** are in 1 mole of the compound?

The last two points get forgotten most often, especially the final one – which is important in question **1**, parts **a** and **b**, question **3**, part **b ii**, and question **4**, part **c**.

1 The table shows the enthalpy changes needed to calculate the lattice energy of potassium oxide, K_2O.

Type of enthalpy change	Value of enthalpy change / kJ mol^{-1}
1st ionisation energy of potassium	+418
1st electron affinity of oxygen	−141
2nd electron affinity of oxygen	+798
enthalpy change of formation of K_2O	−361
enthalpy change of atomisation of potassium	+89
enthalpy change of atomisation of oxygen	+249

a Copy the incomplete Born–Haber cycle shown below. On the lines **A** to **E** of your copy of the Born–Haber cycle, write the correct symbols relating to potassium and oxygen. [5]

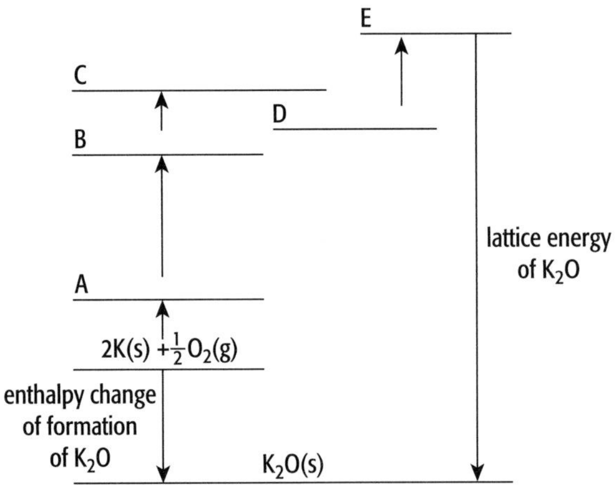

b Use the data in the table above to calculate the lattice energy of potassium oxide. [2]

c Describe how, and explain why, the lattice energy of sodium oxide differs from that of potassium sulfide, K_2S. [4]

d Explain why the 2nd electron affinity of oxygen has a positive value. [1]

Total = 12

2   The lattice energy of sodium chloride can be calculated using the following enthalpy changes:
- enthalpy change of formation of sodium chloride
- enthalpy changes of atomisation of sodium and chlorine
- 1st ionisation energy of sodium
- 1st electron affinity of chlorine.

  a State the meaning of the terms:
     i   first ionisation energy [3]
     ii enthalpy change of atomisation. [2]
  b Draw and label a Born–Haber cycle to calculate the lattice energy of sodium chloride. [4]
  c Explain why the lattice energy of sodium chloride has a value that is lower than the lattice energy of lithium chloride. [2]

                                                   Total = 11

3   a   Draw an enthalpy (Hess's law) cycle to show the dissolving of magnesium iodide in water. [5]
  b The table shows the values for all but one of the enthalpy changes relevant to this cycle.

Enthalpy change	Value / kJ mol^{-1}
lattice energy	−2327
enthalpy change of hydration of Mg^{2+} ion	−1920
enthalpy change of hydration of I^- ion	−314

     i   Define **enthalpy change of hydration**. [2]
     ii Use the values in the table to calculate the value for the enthalpy change of solution of magnesium iodide. [3]
  c Draw a diagram to show how water molecules are arranged around a magnesium ion. [2]
  d Explain why the enthalpy change of hydration of a magnesium ion is more exothermic than the enthalpy change of hydration of a sodium ion. [3]

                                                   Total = 15

4   The lattice energy of magnesium bromide, $MgBr_2$, can be calculated using the enthalpy changes shown in the table.

Type of enthalpy change	Value of enthalpy change / kJ mol^{-1}
1st ionisation energy of magnesium	+736
2nd ionisation energy of magnesium	+1450
1st electron affinity of bromine	−325
enthalpy change of formation of $MgBr_2$	−524
enthalpy change of atomisation of magnesium	+150
enthalpy change of atomisation of bromine	+112

  a State the meaning of the terms:
     i   **lattice energy** [2]
     ii **2nd ionisation energy**. [3]
  b Draw and label a Born–Haber cycle to calculate the lattice energy of magnesium bromide. [4]
  c Calculate the lattice energy of magnesium bromide. [2]

                                                   Total = 11

5   a   For each of the following pairs of compounds, state with reasons which one you would expect to have the higher lattice energy.

   i   NaCl and KBr   [2]

   ii KCl and SrS.   [2]

   b   In some crystal lattices, some of the ions are polarised.

   i   State the meaning of the term **ion polarisation**.   [2]

   ii Explain why a magnesium ion is better than a sodium ion at polarising an iodide ion.   [2]

   iii Use ideas about ion polarisation to explain why barium carbonate is more stable to thermal decomposition than magnesium carbonate.   [3]

                                                                                          Total = 11

6   The diagram shows the enthalpy changes when sodium chloride is dissolved in water.

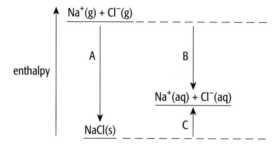

   a   Define the following terms:

   i   **enthalpy change of solution**   [2]

   ii **enthalpy change of hydration**.   [2]

   b   Write symbol equations that describe the following:

   i   enthalpy change of solution of sodium chloride   [2]

   ii enthalpy change of hydration of the chloride ion.   [2]

   c   Name the enthalpy changes labelled **A**, **B** and **C**.   [3]

   d   Draw the water molecules around magnesium ions and sulfate ions in a solution of magnesium sulfate.   [3]

   e   Explain, in terms of differences of lattice energies and enthalpy changes of hydration, why magnesium sulfate is more soluble in water than calcium sulfate.   [5]

                                                                                          Total = 19

Chapter 20:
Electrochemistry

Learning outcomes

You should be able to:

- describe electrolytic cells and the redox reactions occurring at the anode and cathode during electrolysis
- state the relationship, $F = Le$, between the Faraday constant, the Avogadro constant and the charge on the electron
- predict the identity of the substance liberated during electrolysis from:
  - the state of electrolyte (molten or aqueous)
  - the position of the ions (in the electrolyte) in the redox series (electrode potential)
  - the concentration of the ions in the electrolyte
- calculate:
  - the quantity of charge passed during electrolysis
  - the mass and/or volume of substance liberated during electrolysis, including those in the electrolysis of $H_2SO_4(aq)$ and $Na_2SO_4(aq)$
- describe the determination of a value of the Avogadro constant by an electrolytic method
- define the terms:
  - **standard electrode (redox) potential**
  - **standard cell potential**
- describe the standard hydrogen electrode

- describe methods used to measure the standard electrode potentials of:
  - metals or non-metals in contact with their ions in aqueous solution
  - ions of the same element in different oxidation states
- calculate a standard cell potential by combining two standard electrode potentials
- use standard cell potential to:
  - deduce and explain the direction of electron flow in a simple cell
  - predict the feasibility of a reaction
- construct redox equations using the relevant half-equations
- describe and deduce from electrode potential values the relative reactivity of the Group 17 elements as oxidising agents
- predict qualitatively how the value of an electrode potential varies with the concentration of the aqueous ion
- use the Nernst equation to predict quantitatively how the value of an electrode potential varies with the concentration of the aqueous ion
- state the possible advantages of developing other types of cell, e.g. the H_2/O_2 fuel cell, and improved batteries (as in electric vehicles) in terms of smaller size, lower mass and higher voltage.

Introduction

The element manganese is used to form many alloys, for example adding hardness to steel. Manganese(IV) oxide is used to decolourise glass and to depolarise dry electrochemical cells. Manganese(II) oxide is a powerful oxidising agent. One of the most useful aspects of manganese is that it can exist in a number of oxidation states (Figure 20.1).

Figure 20.1 a manganese(0), the metal; **b** manganese(II) as $Mn^{2+}(aq)$ ions; **c** manganese(III) as $Mn^{3+}(aq)$ ions; **d** manganese(IV) as MnO_2; **e** Mn(VI) as MnO_4^{2-} as with parts **b** and **c** ions; **f** Mn(VII) as MnO_4^- as with parts **b** and **c** ions. Manganese metal is a good reductant, whereas $MnO_4^-(aq)$ in acidic solution is a good oxidant.

Redox reactions revisited

In Chapter 7 (page 108) you learnt to construct equations for redox reactions from relevant half-equations. You also used the concept of oxidation numbers to show whether a particular reactant has been oxidised or reduced during a chemical reaction.

Electrons may be gained or lost in redox reactions.

- The species (atom, ion or molecule) losing electrons is being oxidised. It acts a reducing agent.
- The species gaining electrons is being reduced. It acts an oxidising agent.

Make sure that you can do questions **1** and **2** before continuing with this chapter. Refer back to Chapter 7 (page 107) if you need some help.

QUESTIONS

1   In each of the chemical reactions **a** to **c**:

    i   Which species gains electrons?

    ii   Which species loses electrons?

    iii   Which species is the oxidising agent?

    iv   Which species is the reducing agent?

  a $CuCl_2 + Fe \longrightarrow FeCl_2 + Cu$

  b $Cu + Br_2 \longrightarrow Cu^{2+} + 2Br^-$

  c $PbO_2 + SO_2 \longrightarrow PbSO_4$

2   Construct full redox equations from the following pairs of half-equations.

  a   The reaction of iodide ions with hydrogen peroxide:

$$I^- \longrightarrow \tfrac{1}{2}I_2 + e^-$$
$$H_2O_2 + 2H^+ + 2e^- \longrightarrow 2H_2O$$

  b   The reaction of chloride ions with acidified manganese(IV) oxide:

$$Cl^- \longrightarrow \tfrac{1}{2}Cl_2 + e^-$$
$$MnO_2 + 4H^+ + 2e^- \longrightarrow Mn^{2+} + 2H_2O$$

  c   The reaction of acidified MnO_4^- ions with Fe^{2+} ions:

$$Fe^{2+} \longrightarrow Fe^{3+} + e^-$$
$$MnO_4^- + 8H^+ + 5e^- \longrightarrow Mn^{2+} + 4H_2O$$

Electrolysis

Electrolytic cells

Electrolysis is the decomposition of a compound into its elements by an electric current. It is often used to extract metals that are high in the reactivity series. These metals cannot be extracted by heating their ores with carbon. Electrolysis is also used to produce non-metals such as chlorine and to purify some metals. Electrolysis is generally carried out in an electrolysis cell (Figure 20.2).

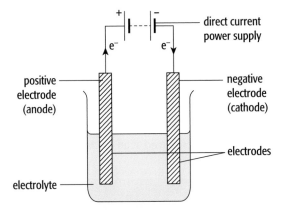

Figure 20.2 The main parts of an electrolysis cell. The actual structure of the cell will vary according to the element extracted. The e^- shows the direction of travel of the electrons around the external circuit.

In the electrolysis cell:

- the **electrolyte** is the compound that is decomposed; it is either a molten ionic compound or a concentrated aqueous solution of ions
- the **electrodes** are rods, made from either carbon (graphite) or metal, which conduct electricity to and from the electrolyte
  - the **anode** is the positive electrode
  - the **cathode** is the negative electrode
- the power supply must be direct current.

QUESTION

3 a Why does an ionic compound have to be molten to undergo electrolysis?

b Give two properties of graphite that make it a suitable material for use as an electrode. Explain your answers.

Redox reactions in electrolysis

During electrolysis, the positive ions (**cations**) move to the cathode. When they reach the cathode they gain electrons from the cathode. For example:

$$Cu^{2+} + 2e^- \longrightarrow Cu$$

$$2H^+ + 2e^- \longrightarrow H_2$$

Gain of electrons is reduction. Reduction always occurs at the cathode. If metal atoms are formed, they may be deposited as a layer of metal on the cathode. Alternatively they may form a molten layer in the cell. If hydrogen gas is formed, it bubbles off.

The negative ions (**anions**) move to the anode. When they reach the anode they lose electrons to the anode. For example:

$$2Cl^- \longrightarrow Cl_2 + 2e^-$$

$$4OH^- \longrightarrow O_2 + 2H_2O + 4e^-$$

Loss of electrons is oxidation. Oxidation always occurs at the anode.

Electrolysis is a redox reaction. For example, when molten zinc chloride is electrolysed the electrode reactions are:

cathode: $Zn^{2+} + 2e^- \longrightarrow Zn$ (reduction)

anode: $2Cl^- \longrightarrow Cl_2 + 2e^-$ (oxidation)

The electron loss at the anode balances the electron gain at the cathode. Overall, the reaction is:

$$ZnCl_2 \longrightarrow Zn + Cl_2$$

QUESTION

4 a Explain why cations move towards the cathode during electrolysis.

b When lead iodide, PbI_2, is electrolysed the following reactions occur:

$Pb^{2+} + 2e^- \longrightarrow Pb$ and $2I^- \longrightarrow I_2 + 2e^-$

i Which of these equations describes the reaction at the cathode? Explain your answer.

ii What is the ox. no. change of each iodide ion in the reaction

$2I^- \longrightarrow I_2 + 2e^-$?

275

Quantitative electrolysis

The mass of substance deposited during electrolysis

The mass of a substance produced at an electrode during electrolysis is proportional to:

- the time over which a constant electric current passes
- the strength of the electric current.

Combining current and time, we get the relationship:

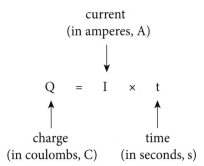

$$Q = I \times t$$

The mass of a substance produced at (or removed from) an electrode during electrolysis is proportional to the quantity of electricity (in coulombs) which passes through the electrolyte.

The quantity of electricity is often expressed in terms of a unit called the Faraday (symbol F). 1 Faraday is the quantity of electric charge carried by 1 mole of electrons or 1 mole of singly charged ions. Its value is $96\,500\,C\,mol^{-1}$ (to 3 significant figures).

During the electrolysis of silver nitrate solution, silver is deposited at the cathode:

$$\underset{\text{1 mol}}{Ag^+} + \underset{\text{1 mol}}{e^-} \longrightarrow \underset{\text{1 mol}}{Ag}$$

1 Faraday of electricity ($96\,500\,C$) is required to deposit 1 mole of silver.

During the electrolysis of copper(II) sulfate solution, copper is deposited at the cathode:

$$\underset{\text{1 mol}}{Cu^{2+}} + \underset{\text{2 mol}}{2e^-} \longrightarrow \underset{\text{1 mol}}{Cu}$$

The equation shows that 2 moles of electrons are needed to produce 1 mole of copper from Cu^{2+} ions. So it requires 2 Faradays of electricity ($2 \times 96\,500\,C$) to deposit 1 mole of copper.

During the electrolysis of molten sodium chloride, chlorine is produced at the anode:

$$\underset{\text{2 mol}}{2Cl^-} \longrightarrow \underset{\text{1 mol}}{Cl_2} + \underset{\text{2 mol}}{2e^-}$$

The equation shows that 2 moles of electrons are released when 1 mole of chlorine gas is formed from 2 moles of Cl^- ions. So it requires 2 Faradays of electricity ($2 \times 96\,500\,C$) to produce 1 mole of Cl_2.

During the electrolysis of an aqueous solution of sulfuric acid or aqueous sodium sulfate, oxygen is produced at the anode:

$$4OH^-(aq) \longrightarrow O_2(g) + 2H_2O(l) + 4e^-$$

The equation shows that 4 moles of electrons are released when 1 mole of oxygen gas is formed from 4 moles of OH^- ions. So it requires 4 Faradays of electricity ($4 \times 96\,500\,C$) to produce 1 mole of O_2.

Calculating amount of substance produced during electrolysis

We can use the value of F to calculate:

- the mass of substance deposited at an electrode
- the volume of gas produced at an electrode.

WORKED EXAMPLES

1   Calculate the mass of lead deposited at the cathode during electrolysis when a current of 1.50 A flows through molten lead(II) bromide for 20.0 min. (A_r value: [Pb] = 207; $F = 96\,500\,C\,mol^{-1}$)

Step 1 Write the half-equation for the reaction.

$$Pb^{2+} + 2e^- \longrightarrow Pb$$

Step 2 Find the number of coulombs required to deposit 1 mole of product at the electrode.

2 moles of electrons are required per mole of Pb formed

$$= 2F$$
$$= 2 \times 96\,500$$
$$= 193\,000\,C\,mol^{-1}$$

Step 3 Calculate the charge transferred during the electrolysis.

$$Q = I \times t$$
$$= 1.50 \times 20 \times 60$$
$$= 1800\,C$$

Step 4 Calculate the mass by simple proportion using the relative atomic mass.

$193\,000\,C$ deposits 1 mole Pb, which is 207 g Pb

so $1800\,C$ deposits $\dfrac{1800}{193\,000} \times 207 = 1.93\,g\,Pb$

WORKED EXAMPLES (CONTINUED)

2   Calculate the volume of oxygen produced at r.t.p. when a concentrated aqueous solution of sulfuric acid, H_2SO_4, is electrolysed for 30.0 min using a current of 0.50 A.

($F = 96500\,C\,mol^{-1}$; 1 mole of gas occupies $24.0\,dm^3$ at r.t.p.)

Step 1 Write the half-equation for the reaction.

$$4OH^-(aq) \longrightarrow O_2(g) + 2H_2O(l) + 4e^-$$

Step 2 Find the number of coulombs required to produce 1 mole of gas.

4 moles of electrons are released

per mole of O_2 formed

$= 4F$

$= 4 \times 96500$

$= 386000\,C\,mol^{-1}$

Step 3 Calculate the charge transferred during the electrolysis.

$Q = I \times t$

$\quad = 0.50 \times 30 \times 60$

$\quad = 900\,C$

Step 4 Calculate the volume by simple proportion using the relationship 1 mole of gas occupies $24.0\,dm^3$ at r.t.p.

386000 C produces 1 mole O_2, which is $24\,dm^3\,O_2$

so 900 C produces $\dfrac{900}{386000} \times 24.0$

$\qquad\qquad\qquad = 0.0560\,dm^3\,O_2$ at r.t.p.

QUESTIONS

5   Calculate the mass of silver deposited at the cathode during electrolysis when a current of 1.80 A flows through an aqueous solution of silver nitrate for 45.0 min.

(A_r value: [Ag] = 108; $F = 96500\,C\,mol^{-1}$)

6   Calculate the volume of hydrogen produced at r.t.p. when a concentrated aqueous solution of sulfuric acid is electrolysed for 15.0 min using a current of 1.40 A.

($F = 96500\,C\,mol^{-1}$; 1 mole of gas occupies $24.0\,dm^3$ at r.t.p.)

7   Calculate the volume of oxygen produced at r.t.p. when a concentrated aqueous solution of sodium sulfate is electrolysed for 55.0 min using a current of 0.70 A.

($F = 96500\,C\,mol^{-1}$; 1 mole of gas occupies $24.0\,dm^3$ at r.t.p.)

Calculating the Avogadro constant by an electrolytic method

The Avogadro constant, L, is the number of specified particles in 1 mole (see page 5).

We can use an electrolytic method to find a value for the Avogadro constant by calculating the charge associated with 1 mole of electrons.

$$L = \frac{\text{charge on 1 mole of electrons}}{\text{charge on 1 electron}}$$

We can calculate the charge on the electron by experiment. The results show us that the charge on the electron is approximately $1.60 \times 10^{-19}\,C$.

FINDING THE CHARGE ON 1 MOLE OF ELECTRONS

The charge on 1 mole of electrons can be found from a simple electrolytic experiment. The apparatus for this is shown in Figure 20.3.

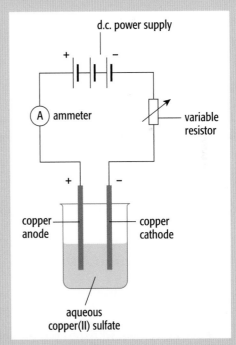

Figure 20.3 Apparatus for calculating the mass of copper deposited during the electrolysis of aqueous copper(II) sulfate.

The procedure is:

- weigh the pure copper anode and pure copper cathode separately
- arrange the apparatus as shown in Figure 20.3; the variable resistor is used to keep the current constant
- pass a constant electric current for a measured time interval

277

FINDING THE CHARGE ON 1 MOLE OF ELECTRONS (CONTINUED)

- remove the cathode and anode and wash and dry them with distilled water and then with propanone
- reweigh the cathode and anode.

The cathode increases in mass because copper is deposited. The anode decreases in mass because the copper goes into solution as copper ions. The decrease in mass of the anode is measured. This is preferred because the copper does not always 'stick' to the cathode very well.

A sample calculation is shown below, using a current of 0.20 A for 34 min.

- mass of anode at start of the experiment = 56.53 g
- mass of anode at end of experiment = 56.40 g
- mass of copper removed from anode = 0.13 g
- quantity of charge passed $Q = I \times t$
$$= 0.20 \times 34 \times 60$$
$$= 408\,C$$

To deposit 0.13 g of copper requires 408 C, so to deposit 1 mole of copper (63.5 g) requires $\frac{63.5}{0.13} \times 408\,C$

But the equation for the electrolysis shows that 2 moles of electrons are needed to produce 1 mole of copper:

$$Cu^{2+} + 2e^- \longrightarrow Cu$$

The charge on 1 mole of electrons $= \frac{63.5}{0.13} \times 408 \times \frac{1}{2}$
$$= 99\,600\,C$$

If the charge on one electron is $1.60 \times 10^{-19}\,C$,

$$L = \frac{99\,600}{1.60 \times 10^{-19}} = 6.2 \times 10^{23}\,mol^{-1}$$

(to 2 significant figures)

This is in good agreement with the accurate value of $6.02 \times 10^{23}\,mol^{-1}$.

QUESTIONS

8 A student passed a constant electric current of 0.15 A through a solution of silver nitrate, using pure silver electrodes, for 45 min exactly. The mass of the anode decreased by 0.45 g. Use this data to calculate the charge on a mole of electrons.

(A_r value: [Ag] = 108)

9 An accurate value of the Faraday constant is $96485\,C\,mol^{-1}$. An accurate value for the charge on one electron is $1.6022 \times 10^{-19}\,C$. Use these values to calculate a value of the Avogadro constant to 5 significant figures.

Electrode potentials

Introducing electrode potentials

A redox equilibrium exists between two chemically related species that are in different oxidation states. For example, when a copper rod is placed in contact with an aqueous solution of its ions the following equilibrium exists:

$$Cu^{2+}(aq) + 2e^- \rightleftharpoons Cu(s)$$

There are two opposing reactions in this equilibrium.

- Metal atoms from the rod entering the solution as metal ions. This leaves electrons behind on the surface of the rod. For example:

$$Cu(s) \longrightarrow Cu^{2+}(aq) + 2e^-$$

- Ions in solution accepting electrons from the metal rod and being deposited as metal atoms on the surface of the rod. For example:

$$Cu^{2+}(aq) + 2e^- \longrightarrow Cu(s)$$

The redox equilibrium is established when the rate of electron gain equals the rate of electron loss.

For unreactive metals such as copper, if this equilibrium is compared with the equilibrium set up by other metals, the equilibrium set up by copper lies further over to the right.

$$Cu^{2+}(aq) + 2e^- \rightleftharpoons Cu(s)$$

$Cu^{2+}(aq)$ ions are therefore relatively easy to reduce. They gain electrons readily to form copper metal.

For reactive metals such as vanadium, the equilibrium lies further over to the left.

$$V^{2+}(aq) + 2e^- \rightleftharpoons V(s)$$

$V^{2+}(aq)$ ions are therefore relatively difficult to reduce. They gain electrons much less readily by comparison.

The position of equilibrium differs for different combinations of metals placed in solutions of their ions.

When a metal is put into a solution of its ions an electric potential (voltage) is established between the metal and the metal ions in solution. We cannot measure this potential directly. But we can measure the difference in potential between the metal/metal ion system and another system. We call this value the electrode potential, E. Electrode potential is measured in volts. The system we use for comparison is the standard hydrogen electrode.

It is thought that the absolute electrical potentials that we cannot measure are caused by the formation of an electrical double layer when an element is placed in a solution of its ions. For example, when zinc is placed in a solution containing zinc ions, a tiny number of zinc atoms on the surface of the metal are converted to zinc ions, which go into solution. This leaves an excess of electrons on the surface of the zinc. The solution around the metal now has excess Zn^{2+} ions. Some of these cations near the surface of the zinc are attracted to its surface. So an electrical double layer is formed. This build up of charge causes an electric potential (voltage) between the metal and the metal ions in solution (Figure 20.4).

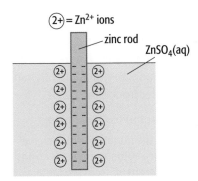

Figure 20.4 The separation of charge when a zinc rod is placed in a solution of Zn^{2+} ions results in an electrical double layer.

THE STANDARD HYDROGEN ELECTRODE

The standard hydrogen electrode is one of several types of half-cell that can be used as reference electrodes. Figure 20.5 shows a standard hydrogen electrode.

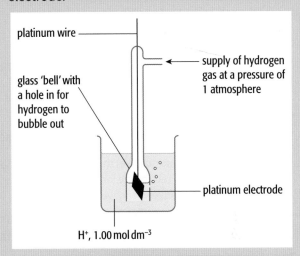

Figure 20.5 The standard hydrogen electrode.

This electrode consists of:

- hydrogen gas at 101 kPa pressure, in equilibrium with
- H^+ ions of concentration $1.00\,mol\,dm^{-3}$
- a platinum electrode covered with platinum black in contact with the hydrogen gas and the H^+ ions.

The platinum black is finely divided platinum, which allows close contact of hydrogen gas and H^+ ions in solution so that equilibrium between H_2 gas and H^+ ions is established quickly. The platinum electrode is inert so it does not take part in the reaction.

Standard electrode potential $E^{\ominus}$ values for all half-cells are measured relative to this electrode. When connected to another half-cell, the value read on the voltmeter gives the standard electrode potential for that half-cell.

The half-equation for the hydrogen electrode can be written:

$$2H^+(aq) + 2e^- \rightleftharpoons H_2(g)$$

or

$$H^+(aq) + e^- \rightleftharpoons \tfrac{1}{2}H_2(g)$$

The way that the half-equation is balanced makes no difference to the value of $E^{\ominus}$. The equation does not affect the tendency for the element to gain electrons.

279

Electrode potential and redox reactions

Electrode potential values give us an indication of how easy it is to reduce a substance.

Note that:

- By convention, the electrode potential refers to the reduction reaction. So the electrons appear on the left-hand side of the half-equation. For example:

$$Al^{3+}(aq) + 3e^- \rightleftharpoons Al(s)$$

- The more positive (or less negative) the electrode potential, the easier it is to reduce the ions on the left. So the metal on the right is relatively unreactive and is a relatively poor reducing agent. For example:

$$Ag^+(aq) + e^- \rightleftharpoons Ag(s) \qquad \text{voltage} = +0.80\,V$$

- The more negative (or less positive) the electrode potential, the more difficult it is to reduce the ions on the left. So the metal on the right is relatively reactive and is a relatively good reducing agent. For example:

$$Zn^{2+}(aq) + 2e^- \rightleftharpoons Zn(s) \qquad \text{voltage} = -0.76\,V$$

QUESTION

10 Refer to the list of electrode potentials below to answer parts **a** to **d**.

$Ag^+(aq) + e^- \rightleftharpoons Ag(s)$	voltage = +0.80 V
$Co^{2+}(aq) + 2e^- \rightleftharpoons Co(s)$	voltage = −0.28 V
$Cu^{2+}(aq) + 2e^- \rightleftharpoons Cu(s)$	voltage = +0.34 V
$Pb^{2+}(aq) + 2e^- \rightleftharpoons Pb(s)$	voltage = −0.13 V
$Zn^{2+}(aq) + 2e^- \rightleftharpoons Zn(s)$	voltage = −0.76 V

  a Which metal in the list is the best reducing agent?

  b Which metal ion in the list is most difficult to reduce?

  c Which metal in the list is most reactive?

  d Which metal ion in the list is the easiest to reduce?

COMBINING HALF-CELLS

In order to measure the electrode potential relating to the half-equation

$$Cu^{2+}(aq) + 2e^- \longrightarrow Cu(s)$$

we place a pure copper rod in a solution of $Cu^{2+}(aq)$ ions (for example copper(II) sulfate solution). This Cu^{2+}/Cu system is called a half-cell (Figure 20.6).

We use the following standard conditions to make the half-cell:

- the $Cu^{2+}(aq)$ ions have a concentration of $1.00\,mol\,dm^{-3}$
- the temperature is 25 °C (298 K)
- the copper rod must be pure.

If we connect two half-cells together we have made an electrochemical cell. We can measure the voltage between these two half-cells. Figure 20.7 shows a Cu^{2+}/Cu half-cell connected to a Zn^{2+}/Zn half-cell to make a complete electrochemical cell.

Half-cells are connected together using:

- wires connecting the metal rods in each half-cell to a high-resistance voltmeter; the electrons flow round this external circuit from the metal with the more negative (or less positive) electrode potential to the metal with the less negative (or more positive) electrode potential
- a salt bridge to complete the electrical circuit allowing the movement of ions between the two half-cells so that ionic balance is maintained; a salt bridge does not allow the movement of electrons.

A salt bridge can be made from a strip of filter paper (or other inert porous material) soaked in a saturated solution of potassium nitrate.

Figure 20.6 The Cu^{2+}/Cu half-cell.

COMBINING HALF-CELLS (CONTINUED)

The voltages for the half-cells in Figure 20.7 can be represented by the following half-equations:

$$Cu^{2+}(aq) + 2e^- \rightleftharpoons Cu(s) \qquad \text{voltage} = +0.34\,V$$

$$Zn^{2+}(aq) + 2e^- \rightleftharpoons Zn(s) \qquad \text{voltage} = -0.76\,V$$

The relative values of these voltages tell us that Zn^{2+} ions are more difficult to reduce than Cu^{2+} ions. So Cu^{2+} ions will accept electrons from the Zn^{2+}/Zn half-cell and zinc will lose electrons to the Cu^{2+}/Cu half-cell.

Half-equations can be used to show us the contents of half-cells. A half-cell does not have to be a metal/metal ion system. We can construct half-cells for any half-equation written. For example:

$$Fe^{3+}(aq) + e^- \rightleftharpoons Fe^{2+}(aq)$$

$$Cl_2(g) + 2e^- \rightleftharpoons 2Cl^-(aq)$$

$$MnO_4^-(aq) + 8H^+(aq) + 5e^- \rightleftharpoons Mn^{2+}(aq) + 4H_2O(l)$$

Note that the oxidised species (having the higher oxidation number) is always written on the left-hand side and the reduced form on the right-hand side.

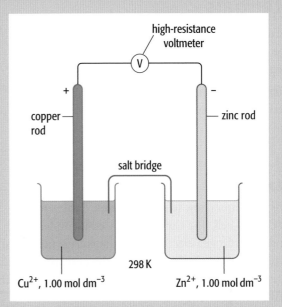

Figure 20.7 One type of electrochemical cell is made by connecting a Cu^{2+}/Cu half-cell to a Zn^{2+}/Zn half-cell. The voltage generated by this cell is +1.10 V.

281

11 a Suggest why aqueous silver nitrate is not used in a salt bridge when connecting a half-cell containing Zn and $1.00\,mol\,dm^{-3}$ $ZnCl_2(aq)$ to another half-cell.

b Write half-equations for the reactions taking place in the half-cells below. Write each equation as a reduction (electrons on the left-hand side of the equation).

   i Cr^{2+}/Cr^{3+}

   ii $Br_2/2Br^-$

   iii $O_2 + H_2O/OH^-$ (make sure that you balance the equation)

   iv $VO^{2+} + H_2O/VO_2^+ + H^+$ (make sure that you balance the equation)

Standard electrode potential

The position of equilibrium of a reaction may be affected by changes in the concentration of reagents, temperature and pressure of gases. The voltage of an electrochemical cell will also depend on these factors, so we should use standard conditions when comparing electrode potentials. These are:

- concentration of ions at $1.00\,mol\,dm^{-3}$
- a temperature of 25 °C (298 K)
- any gases should be at a pressure of 1 atmosphere (101 kPa)
- the value of the electrode potential of the half-cell is measured relative to the standard hydrogen electrode.

Under these conditions, the electrode potential we measure is called the **standard electrode potential**. This has the symbol, $E^{\ominus}$. It is spoken of as 'E standard'.

> The standard electrode potential for a half-cell is the voltage measured under standard conditions with a standard hydrogen electrode as the other half-cell.

Measuring standard electrode potentials

There are three main types of half-cell whose $E^{\ominus}$ value can be obtained when connected to a standard hydrogen electrode:

- metal/metal ion half-cell
- non-metal/non-metal ion half-cell
- ion/ion half-cell.

Half-cells containing metals and metal ions

Figure 20.8 shows how to measure the $E^{\ominus}$ value for a Cu^{2+}/Cu half-cell. The Cu^{2+}/Cu half-cell is connected to a standard hydrogen electrode and the voltage measured. The voltage is +0.34 V. The copper is the positive terminal (positive pole) of the cell and the hydrogen electrode is the negative terminal. The two half-equations are:

$$Cu^{2+}(aq) + 2e^- \rightleftharpoons Cu(s) \qquad E^{\ominus} = +0.34\,V$$

$$H^+(aq) + e^- \rightleftharpoons \tfrac{1}{2}H_2(g) \qquad E^{\ominus} = 0.00\,V$$

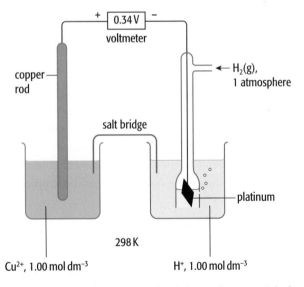

Figure 20.8 Measuring the standard electrode potential of a Cu^{2+}/Cu half-cell.

- The $E^{\ominus}$ values show us that Cu^{2+} ions are easier to reduce than H^+ ions (they have a more positive $E^{\ominus}$ value).
- Cu^{2+} ions are more likely to gain electrons than H^+ ions.
- So Cu^{2+} ions will accept electrons from the H^+/H_2 half-cell and H_2 will lose electrons to the Cu^{2+}/Cu half-cell.

Figure 20.9 shows how to measure the $E^{\ominus}$ value for a Zn^{2+}/Zn half-cell. The voltage of the Zn^{2+}/Zn half-cell is −0.76 V. The zinc is the negative terminal (negative pole) of the cell and the hydrogen electrode is the positive terminal. The two half-equations are:

$$H^+(aq) + e^- \rightleftharpoons \tfrac{1}{2}H_2(g) \qquad E^{\ominus} = 0.00\,V$$

$$Zn^{2+}(aq) + 2e^- \rightleftharpoons Zn(s) \qquad E^{\ominus} = -0.76\,V$$

- The $E^{\ominus}$ values show us that Zn^{2+} ions are more difficult to reduce than H^+ ions (they have a more negative $E^{\ominus}$ value).
- Zn^{2+} ions are less likely to gain electrons than H^+ ions.
- So Zn will lose electrons to the H^+/H_2 half-cell and H^+ ions will gain electrons from the Zn^{2+}/Zn half-cell.

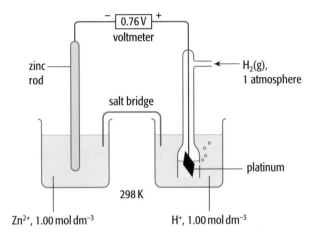

Figure 20.9 Measuring the standard electrode potential of a Zn^{2+}/Zn half-cell.

From these two examples, we can see that:

- Reduction takes place at the positive terminal of the cell. For example, in the Zn^{2+}/Zn; H^+/H_2 cell:

$$H^+(aq) + e^- \rightleftharpoons \tfrac{1}{2}H_2(g)$$

- Oxidation takes place at the negative terminal of the cell. For example, in the Zn^{2+}/Zn: H^+/H_2 cell:

$$Zn(s) \longrightarrow Zn^{2+}(aq) + 2e^-$$

12 a Write half-equations for the three reactions taking place in the half-cells shown on the left in Figure 20.10.

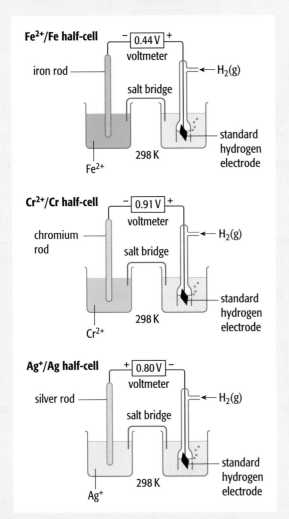

Figure 20.10 Measuring standard electrode potentials.

b What are the standard electrode potentials for these half-cell reactions?

c List all the necessary conditions in each cell.

Half-cells containing non-metals and non-metal ions

In half-cells that do not contain a metal, electrical contact with the solution is made by using platinum wire or platinum foil as an electrode. The redox equilibrium is established at the surface of the platinum. The platinum electrode is inert so plays no part in the reaction.

The platinum must be in contact with both the element and the aqueous solution of its ions.

Figure 20.11 shows a Cl_2/Cl^- half-cell connected to a standard hydrogen electrode. The voltage of the Cl_2/Cl^- half-cell is +1.36 V. So the Cl_2/Cl^- half-cell forms the positive terminal of the cell and the hydrogen electrode is the negative terminal. The two half-equations are:

$$\tfrac{1}{2}Cl_2(g) + e^- \rightleftharpoons Cl^-(aq) \qquad\qquad E^\ominus = +1.36\ \text{V}$$

$$H^+(aq) + e^- \rightleftharpoons \tfrac{1}{2}H_2(g) \qquad\qquad E^\ominus = 0.00\ \text{V}$$

- The $E^\ominus$ values show us that Cl_2 molecules are easier to reduce than H^+ ions (they have a more positive $E^\ominus$ value).
- Cl_2 molecules are more likely to gain electrons than H^+ ions.
- So Cl_2 molecules will gain electrons from the $H^+/\tfrac{1}{2}H_2$ half-cell and H_2 molecules will lose electrons to the $\tfrac{1}{2}Cl_2/Cl^-$ half-cell.

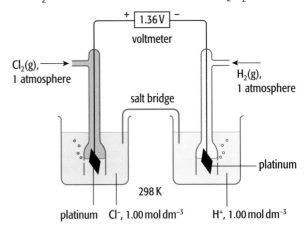

Figure 20.11 Measuring the standard electrode potential of a Cl_2/Cl^- half-cell.

13 a Look at Figure 20.12. Write a half-equation for the half-cell on the left-hand side.

b What is the $E^\ominus$ value for this half-cell?

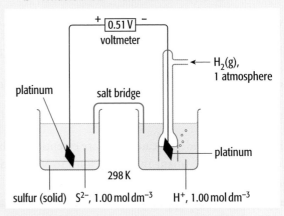

Figure 20.12 Measuring the standard electrode potential of an S/S^{2-} half-cell.

283

Half-cells containing ions of the same element in different oxidation states

Half-cells can contain two ions of different oxidation states derived from the same element. For example a mixture of Fe^{3+} and Fe^{2+} ions can form a half-cell using a platinum electrode. In this type of half-cell, the concentration of each ion present is $1.00 \, mol \, dm^{-3}$. Figure 20.13 shows the set-up for a cell used to measure the standard electrode potential of the Fe^{3+}/Fe^{2+} half-cell.

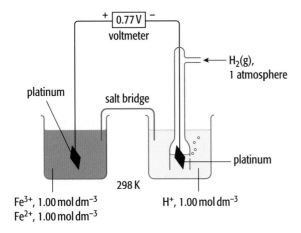

Figure 20.13 Measuring the standard electrode potential of the Fe^{3+}/Fe^{2+} half-cell.

The voltage of this half-cell is +0.77 V.

$$Fe^{3+}(aq) + e^- \rightleftharpoons Fe^{2+}(aq) \qquad E^\ominus = +0.77 \, V$$

Some reactions involve several ionic species. For example:

$$MnO_4^-(aq) + 8H^+(aq) + 5e^- \rightleftharpoons Mn^{2+}(aq) + 4H_2O(l)$$

The H^+ ions are included because they are essential for the conversion of MnO_4^- (manganate(VII) ions) to Mn^{2+} ions. So the half-cell contains:

- $1.00 \, mol \, dm^{-3} \, MnO_4^-(aq)$ ions
- $1.00 \, mol \, dm^{-3} \, Mn^{2+}(aq)$ ions
- $1.00 \, mol \, dm^{-3} \, H^+(aq)$ ions.

Figure 20.14 shows the set-up of a cell used to measure the standard electrode potential of the MnO_4^-/Mn^{2+} half-cell.

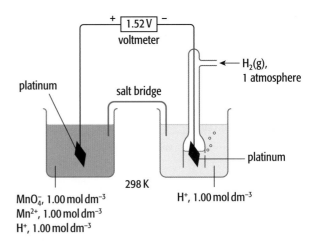

Figure 20.14 Measuring the standard electrode potential of the MnO_4^-/Mn^{2+} half-cell.

Using $E^\ominus$ values

Using $E^\ominus$ values to predict cell voltages

We can use $E^\ominus$ values to calculate the voltage of an electrochemical cell made up of two half-cells, even when neither of them is a standard hydrogen electrode. The voltage measured is the difference between the $E^\ominus$ values of the two half-cells. We call this value the **standard cell potential**.

For the electrochemical cell shown in Figure 20.15, the two relevant half-equations are:

$$Ag^+(aq) + e^- \rightleftharpoons Ag(s) \qquad E^\ominus = +0.80 \, V$$

$$Zn^{2+}(aq) + 2e^- \rightleftharpoons Zn(s) \qquad E^\ominus = -0.76 \, V$$

The voltage of this cell is +0.80 − (−0.76) = +1.56 V (Figure 20.16).

Note that in order to calculate the cell voltage, we always subtract the less positive $E^\ominus$ value from the more positive $E^\ominus$ value.

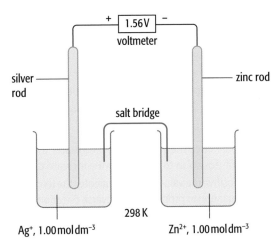

Figure 20.15 An Ag^+/Ag, Zn^{2+}/Zn electrochemical cell.

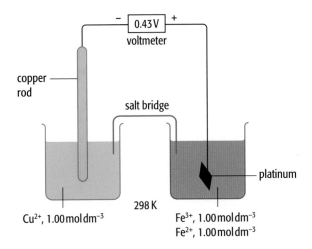

Figure 20.17 An Cu^+/Cu, Fe^{3+}/Fe^{2+} electrochemical cell.

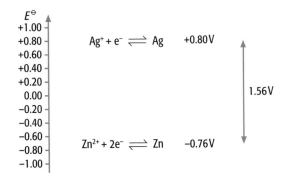

Figure 20.16 The difference between +0.80 V and −0.76 V is +1.56 V.

The $E^{\ominus}$ value for the Ag^+/Ag half-cell is more positive than for the Zn^{2+}/Zn half-cell. So the Ag^+/Ag half-cell is the positive pole and the Zn^{2+}/Zn half-cell is the negative pole of the cell.

For the electrochemical cell shown in Figure 20.17, the relevant half-equations are:

$$Fe^{3+}(aq) + e^- \rightleftharpoons Fe^{2+}(aq) \qquad E^{\ominus} = +0.77 \text{ V}$$

$$Cu^{2+}(aq) + 2e^- \rightleftharpoons Cu(s) \qquad E^{\ominus} = +0.34 \text{ V}$$

The voltage of this cell is +0.77 − (+0.34) = +0.43 V.

The $E^{\ominus}$ value for the Fe^{3+}/Fe^{2+} half-cell is more positive than for the Cu^{2+}/Cu half-cell. So the Fe^{3+}/Fe^{2+} half-cell is the positive pole and the Cu^{2+}/Cu half-cell is the negative pole of the cell.

18 a Draw a diagram of an electrochemical cell consisting of a Cr^{3+}/Cr half-cell and a Cl_2/Cl^- half-cell.

b Use the data in Appendix 2 (page 474) to calculate the cell voltage.

c Which half-cell is the positive pole?

19 a Draw a diagram of an electrochemical cell consisting of a Mn^{2+}/Mn half-cell and a Pb^{2+}/Pb half-cell.

b Use the data in Appendix 2 (page 474) to calculate the cell voltage.

c Which half-cell is the positive pole?

$E^{\ominus}$ values and the direction of electron flow

We can deduce the direction of electron flow in the wires in the external circuit by comparing the $E^{\ominus}$ values for the two half-cells which make up the electrochemical cell. For example in Figure 20.15 these voltages are:

$$Ag^+(aq) + e^- \rightleftharpoons Ag(s) \qquad E^{\ominus} = +0.80 \text{ V}$$

$$Zn^{2+}(aq) + 2e^- \rightleftharpoons Zn(s) \qquad E^{\ominus} = -0.76 \text{ V}$$

The relative values of these voltages tell us that Zn^{2+} ions are more difficult to reduce than Ag^+ ions. So:

■ Zn metal will lose electrons to the Ag^+/Ag half-cell
■ Ag^+ ions will accept electrons from the Zn^{2+}/Zn half-cell.

The electrons move through the wires in the external circuit. They do not travel through the electrolyte solution.

So the electron flow is from the Zn^{2+}/Zn half-cell to the Ag^+/Ag half-cell. In other words, the flow is from the negative pole to the positive pole. It may help you to remember that the more **positive** pole attracts the **negative** electrons.

In the electrochemical cell in Figure 20.17, the electrons move in the external circuit from the Cu^{2+}/Cu half-cell to the Fe^{3+}/Fe^{2+} half-cell.

$$Fe^{3+}(aq) + e^- \rightleftharpoons Fe^{2+}(aq) \qquad E^\ominus = +0.77\,V$$

$$Cu^{2+}(aq) + 2e^- \rightleftharpoons Cu(s) \qquad E^\ominus = +0.34\,V$$

The negative pole of this cell is provided by the Cu^{2+}/Cu half-cell. This because the Cu^{2+}/Cu half-cell is better at losing electrons than the Fe^{3+}/Fe^{2+} half-cell.

QUESTION

20 State the direction of the electron flow in the electrochemical cells represented by the following pairs of half-equations. Use the data in Appendix 2 (page 474) to help you.

a $F_2 + 2e^- \rightleftharpoons 2F^-$ and $Mn^{2+} + 2e^- \rightleftharpoons Mn$

b $Sn^{4+} + 2e^- \rightleftharpoons Sn^{2+}$ and $I_2 + 2e^- \rightleftharpoons 2I^-$

c $Cr_2O_7{}^{2-} + 14H^+ + 6e^- \rightleftharpoons 2Cr^{3+} + 7H_2O$ and $Cu^{2+} + 2e^- \rightleftharpoons Cu$

d $Ni^{2+} + 2e^- \rightleftharpoons Ni$ and $Fe^{3+} + 3e^- \rightleftharpoons Fe$

Using $E^\ominus$ values to predict if a reaction will occur

Standard electrode potential values, $E^\ominus$, give us a measure of how easy or difficult it is to oxidise or reduce a species. We can compare the oxidising and reducing powers of

elements and ions by comparing the $E^\ominus$ values for their half reactions.

Figure 20.18 compares the oxidising and reducing powers of selected elements and ions. The $E^\ominus$ values are listed in order of increasingly negative values. For each half-equation, the more oxidised form is on the left and the more reduced form is on the right.

■ The more positive the value of $E^\ominus$, the greater the tendency for the half-equation to proceed in the forward direction.
■ The less positive the value of $E^\ominus$, the greater the tendency for the half-equation to proceed in the reverse direction.
■ The more positive the value of $E^\ominus$, the easier it is to reduce the species on the left of the half-equation.
■ The less positive the value of $E^\ominus$, the easier it is to oxidise the species on the right of the half-equation.

We can make an electrochemical cell from the two half-cells:

$$Cu^{2+}(aq) + 2e^- \rightleftharpoons Cu(s) \qquad E^\ominus = +0.34\,V$$

$$Zn^{2+}(aq) + 2e^- \rightleftharpoons Zn(s) \qquad E^\ominus = -0.76\,V$$

When these two half-cells are connected together, a reaction takes place in each of the half-cells. The $E^\ominus$ values can be used to predict whether the reaction happening in each half-cell is a reduction (i.e. forward direction) reaction, or an oxidation (i.e. backwards direction) reaction. If the reactions happening in each half-cell are combined, we can produce an ionic equation for the reaction that takes place in the electrochemical cell as a whole.

Cu^{2+} has a greater tendency to gain electrons than Zn^{2+}, so the chemical reaction that proceeds in this half-cell is in the forward direction:

$$Cu^{2+}(aq) + 2e^- \longrightarrow Cu(s)$$

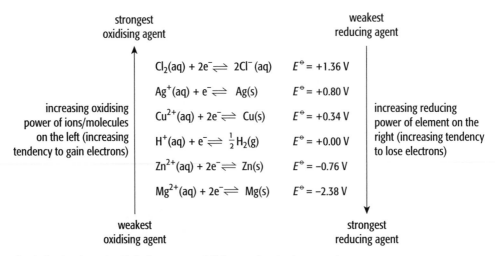

Figure 20.18 Standard electrode potentials for some oxidising and reducing agents.

Zn has a greater tendency to lose electrons than Cu, so the chemical reaction that proceeds in this half-cell is in the reverse direction:

$$Zn(s) \longrightarrow Zn^{2+}(aq) + 2e^-$$

We can combine these two half-equations to show the direction of the reaction in the electrochemical cell as a whole.

$$Zn(s) + Cu^{2+}(aq) \longrightarrow Zn^{2+}(aq) + Cu(s)$$

This is the reaction taking place in the electrochemical cell. But it is also the reaction that takes place if a piece of zinc metal is placed directly into a $1.00\,mol\,dm^{-3}$ solution of Cu^{2+} ions. A reaction is said to be **feasible** if it is likely to occur. The reaction between zinc metal and copper ions is feasible.

If the forward reaction is feasible, the reverse reaction (between Cu metal and zinc ions) is not feasible. If a piece of copper metal is placed directly into a $1.00\,mol\,dm^{-3}$ solution of Zn^{2+} ions no reaction takes place.

Figure 20.19 As predicted by the $E^\ominus$ values, zinc reacts with Cu^{2+} ions but copper does not react with Zn^{2+} ions.

We can predict whether a reaction is likely to occur by referring to a list of half-reactions with their $E^\ominus$ values listed in descending order from most positive to most negative (see Figure 20.18). When we select two

half-equations, the direction of the reaction is given by a clockwise pattern (reactant, product, reactant, product) starting from the top left as shown in Figure 20.20 for the cell made from the two half-cells Cu^{2+}/Cu and Zn^{2+}/Zn.

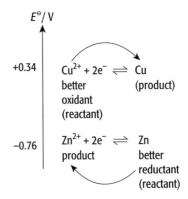

Figure 20.20 A reaction occurs in a direction so that the stronger oxidising agent reacts with the stronger reducing agent.

Here are some examples of using $E^\ominus$ values to predict whether a reaction occurs or not.

WORKED EXAMPLES

3 Will chlorine oxidise Fe^{2+} ions to Fe^{3+} ions?

■ Write down the two half-equations with the more positive $E^\ominus$ value first.

$$\tfrac{1}{2}Cl_2(g) + e^- \rightleftharpoons Cl^-(aq) \qquad\qquad E^\ominus = +1.36\,V$$

$$Fe^{3+}(aq) + e^- \longrightarrow Fe^{2+}(aq) \qquad\qquad E^\ominus = +0.77\,V$$

■ Identify the stronger oxidising agent and the stronger reducing agent.

Cl_2 is the better oxidising agent. This is because the more positive value of $E^\ominus$ indicates that Cl_2 molecules are more likely to accept electrons than are Fe^{3+} ions.

Fe^{2+} is the better reducing agent. This is because the more negative value of $E^\ominus$ indicates that Fe^{2+} ions are more likely to release electrons than are Cl^- ions.

■ The stronger oxidising agent reacts with the stronger reducing agent, meaning that the reaction is feasible.

■ The top reaction goes in the forward direction and the bottom reaction goes in the reverse direction:

$$\tfrac{1}{2}Cl_2(g) + e^- \rightleftharpoons Cl^-(aq)$$

$$Fe^{2+}(aq) \rightleftharpoons Fe^{3+}(aq) + e^-$$

■ Combine the two half-equations:

$$\tfrac{1}{2}Cl_2(g) + Fe^{2+}(aq) \longrightarrow Cl^-(aq) + Fe^{3+}(aq)$$

287

This reaction is feasible. The prediction made using $E^{\ominus}$ values is correct, this reaction takes place in a suitable electrochemical cell, or when Cl_2 gas is bubbled into a $1.00\,mol\,dm^{-3}$ solution of Fe^{2+} ions.

This means that this reaction

$$Cl^-(aq) + Fe^{3+}(aq) \longrightarrow \tfrac{1}{2}Cl_2(g) + Fe^{2+}(aq)$$

is not feasible. If a $1.00\,mol\,dm^{-3}$ solution of Fe^{3+} ions is added to a $1.00\,mol\,dm^{-3}$ solution of Cl^- ions, no reaction takes place. This prediction has been made using $E^{\ominus}$ values, and it is correct.
$E^{\ominus}$ values are a very powerful tool for predicting which redox reactions are feasible, and which ones are not feasible.

4   Will iodine, I_2, oxidise Fe^{2+} ions to Fe^{3+} ions?

▪ Give the two half-equations, with most positive $E^{\ominus}$ value first.

$$Fe^{3+}(aq) + e^- \rightleftharpoons Fe^{2+}(aq) \qquad E^{\ominus} = +0.77\,V$$

$$\tfrac{1}{2}I_2(aq) + e^- \rightleftharpoons I^-(aq) \qquad E^{\ominus} = +0.54\,V$$

▪ Identify the stronger oxidising agent and the stronger reducing agent.

Fe^{3+} is the better oxidising agent. It is more likely to accept electrons than I_2 molecules.

I^- is the better reducing agent. It is more likely to release electrons than Fe^{2+} ions.

▪ I_2 is a relatively weaker oxidising agent and Fe^{2+} is a relatively weaker reducing agent. So the reaction is NOT feasible. (The reaction that is feasible is the reaction between Fe^{3+} ions and I^- ions.)

5   Will hydrogen peroxide, H_2O_2, reduce acidified manganate(VII) ions, MnO_4^-, to Mn^{2+} ions?

▪ Write down the two half-equations with the more positive $E^{\ominus}$ value first.

$$MnO_4^-(aq) + 8H^+(aq) + 5e^- \rightleftharpoons Mn^{2+}(aq) + 4H_2O(l)$$
$$E^{\ominus} = +1.52\,V$$

$$O_2(g) + 2H^+(aq) + 2e^- \rightleftharpoons H_2O_2(aq) \quad E^{\ominus} = +0.68\,V$$

▪ Identify the stronger oxidising agent and the stronger reducing agent.

The system $MnO_4^- + H^+$ is the better oxidising agent. It is more likely to accept electrons than the system $O_2 + 2H^+$.

H_2O_2 is the better reducing agent. It is more likely to release electrons than Mn^{2+} ions.

▪ The stronger oxidising agent reacts with the stronger reducing agent, so the reaction is feasible.

▪ The top reaction goes in the forward direction and the bottom reaction goes in the reverse direction:

$$MnO_4^-(aq) + 8H^+(aq) + 5e^- \rightleftharpoons Mn^{2+}(aq) + 4H_2O(l)$$

$$H_2O_2(aq) \rightleftharpoons O_2(g) + 2H^+(aq) + 2e^-$$

▪ Balance the electrons, so that ten electrons are involved in each half-equation:

$$2MnO_4^-(aq) + 16H^+(aq) + 10e^-$$
$$\rightleftharpoons 2Mn^{2+}(aq) + 8H_2O(l)$$

$$5H_2O_2(aq) \rightleftharpoons 5O_2(g) + 10H^+(aq) + 10e^-$$

▪ Combine the two half-equations:

$$2MnO_4^-(aq) + 6H^+(aq) + 5H_2O_2(aq)$$
$$\rightleftharpoons 2Mn^{2+}(aq) + 8H_2O(l) + 5O_2(g)$$

Note that 10 H^+ ions have been cancelled from each side.

Figure 20.21 If the $KMnO_4(aq)$ is acidified, would it be safe to do this in an open lab or would chlorine gas be produced? You will answer this question in question **21**, part **a**.

We can use the relative voltage of the half-cells to predict whether a reaction takes place without considering which species is the best oxidant or reductant. The procedure is given in the examples below.

WORKED EXAMPLES

6 Will bromine oxidise silver to silver ions?

Step 1 Write the equation for the suggested reaction.

$$\tfrac{1}{2}Br_2 + Ag \longrightarrow Br^- + Ag^+$$

Step 2 Write the two half-equations:

$$\tfrac{1}{2}Br_2 + e^- \rightleftharpoons Br^-$$

$$Ag \rightleftharpoons Ag^+ + e^-$$

Step 3 Include the value of $E^{\ominus}$ for each half-reaction but reverse the sign of the half-equation showing oxidation (loss of electrons). This is because the data book values are always for the reduction reaction.

$$\tfrac{1}{2}Br_2 + e^- \rightleftharpoons Br^- \qquad E^{\ominus} = +1.07\,V$$

$$Ag \rightleftharpoons Ag^+ + e^- \qquad E^{\ominus} = -0.80\,V$$

Step 4 Add the two voltages. This is because we are combining the two half-equations.

$$= +1.07 + (-0.80) = +0.27\,V$$

Step 5 If the value of the sum of the two voltages is positive the reaction will occur as written. If the value of the sum of the two voltages is negative the reaction will not occur.

In this case the sum of the two voltages is positive so bromine will oxidise silver to silver ions.

7 Will iodine oxidise silver to silver ions?

Step 1 Write the equation for the suggested reaction.

$$\tfrac{1}{2}I_2 + Ag \longrightarrow I^- + Ag^+$$

Step 2 The two half-equations are:

$$\tfrac{1}{2}I_2 + e^- \rightleftharpoons I^-$$

$$Ag \rightleftharpoons Ag^+ + e^-$$

Step 3 Write the $E^{\ominus}$ values, with the sign reversed for the oxidation reaction.

$$\tfrac{1}{2}I_2 + e^- \rightleftharpoons I^- \qquad E^{\ominus} = +0.54\,V$$

$$Ag \rightleftharpoons Ag^+ + e^- \qquad E^{\ominus} = -0.80\,V$$

Step 4 Add the two voltages.

$$= +0.54 + (-0.80) = -0.26\,V$$

Step 5 The sum of the two voltages is negative, so iodine will not oxidise silver to silver ions.

QUESTIONS

21 Use the data in Appendix 2 (page 474) to predict whether or not the following reactions are feasible. If a reaction does occur, write a balanced equation for it.

  a Can MnO_4^- ions oxidise Cl^- ions to Cl_2 in acidic conditions?

  b Can MnO_4^- ions oxidise F^- ions to F_2 in acidic conditions?

  c Can H^+ ions oxidise V^{2+} ions to V^{3+} ions?

  d Can H^+ ions oxidise Fe^{2+} ions to Fe^{3+} ions?

22 Suggest a suitable reagent that can carry out each of the following oxidations or reductions. Use the data in Appendix 2 (page 474) to help you.

  a The reduction of Zn^{2+} ions to Zn.

  b The oxidation of Br^- ions to Br_2.

  c The reduction of acidified SO_4^{2-} ions to SO_2.

  d The oxidation of Cl^- ions to Cl_2.

23 Use the cell voltage method described in Worked examples **6** and **7** above to answer question **21**, parts **a** to **d**.

$E^{\ominus}$ values and oxidising and reducing agents

Look back at Figure 20.18 (page 286). Note the following as the values of $E^{\ominus}$ for each of these reduction reactions gets more negative.

- The species on the left of the equation become weaker oxidising agents. They accept electrons less readily.
- The species on the right of the equation become stronger reducing agents. They release electrons more readily.

Cu will not reduce Zn^{2+} ions to Zn. So how can we reduce Zn^{2+} ions? The answer is to react the Zn^{2+} ions with a stronger reducing agent, which should have an $E^{\ominus}$ value more negative than the $E^{\ominus}$ value for Zn^{2+}/Zn. In Figure 20.18 we see that the half-equation Mg^{2+}/Mg has a more negative $E^{\ominus}$ value. So Mg is a suitable reducing agent.

$$Zn^{2+}(aq) + e^- \rightleftharpoons Zn(s) \qquad E^{\ominus} = -0.76\,V$$

$$Mg^{2+}(aq) + 2e^- \rightleftharpoons Mg(s) \qquad E^{\ominus} = -2.38\,V$$

Zn^{2+} is the better oxidising agent. It is more likely to accept electrons than Mg^{2+} ions. Mg is the better reducing agent. It is more likely to release electrons than Zn.

Nitric acid is a good oxidising agent, but it will not oxidise chloride ions to chlorine. So how can we oxidise Cl^- ions? The answer is to react the Cl^- ions with a stronger oxidising agent, which should have an $E^\ominus$ value more positive than the $E^\ominus$ value for Cl_2/Cl^-. The half-equation

$$MnO_4^-(aq) + 8H^+(aq) + 5e^- \rightleftharpoons Mn^{2+}(aq) + 4H_2O(l)$$

provides a suitable oxidising agent.

This half-equation has a more positive $E^\ominus$ value than that for the Cl_2/Cl^- half-equation. So acidified MnO_4^- ions are a suitable oxidising agent to oxidise chloride ions to chlorine (see Figure 20.21).

$$MnO_4^-(aq) + 8H^+(aq) + 5e^- \rightleftharpoons Mn^{2+}(aq) + 4H_2O(l)$$
$$E^\ominus = +1.52\,V$$

$$\tfrac{1}{2}Cl_2(g) + e^- \rightleftharpoons Cl^-(aq) \qquad E^\ominus = +1.36\,V$$

Acidified MnO_4^- is the better oxidising agent. It is more likely to accept electrons than Cl_2 molecules. Cl^- is the better reducing agent. It is more likely to release electrons than Mn^{2+}.

We can explain the relative oxidising abilities of the halogens in a similar way. The standard electrode potentials for the halogens are:

$$\tfrac{1}{2}F_2 + e^- \rightleftharpoons F^- \qquad E^\ominus = +2.87\,V$$

$$\tfrac{1}{2}Cl_2 + e^- \rightleftharpoons Cl^- \qquad E^\ominus = +1.36\,V$$

$$\tfrac{1}{2}Br_2 + e^- \rightleftharpoons Br^- \qquad E^\ominus = +1.07\,V$$

$$\tfrac{1}{2}I_2 + e^- \rightleftharpoons I^- \qquad E^\ominus = +0.54\,V$$

Based on these $E^\ominus$ values, as we go down Group 17 from F_2 to I_2, the oxidising ability of the halogen decreases and the ability of halide ions to act as reducing agents increases.

Figure 20.22 Aqueous chlorine displaces bromine from a solution of potassium bromide. We can use $E^\ominus$ values to explain why a halogen higher in Group 17 displaces a halogen lower in the group from a solution of its halide ions.

290

24 Use the $E^\ominus$ values for the halogens (see page 474) to explain the following:

   a Why bromine can oxidise an aqueous solution of iodide ions.

   b Why bromine does not react with chloride ions.

25 Use the data in Appendix 2 (page 474) to answer these questions.

   a Of the ions Ag^+, Cr^{2+} and Fe^{2+}, which one needs the strongest reducing agent to reduce it to metal atoms?

   b Of the atoms Ag, Cr and Fe, which one needs the strongest oxidising agent to oxidise it to an ion?

How does the value of $E^\ominus$ vary with ion concentration?

In Chapter 8 (pages 119–123) we saw that the position of an equilibrium reaction is affected by changes in concentration, temperature and pressure. Redox equilibria are no different. When we compare the voltage of a standard half-cell, X, with a standard hydrogen electrode, we are measuring $E^\ominus$ for the half-cell X. If we change the concentration or temperature of half-cell X, the electrode potential also changes. Under these non-standard conditions we use the symbol E for the electrode potential.

What happens to the electrode potential when we change the concentration of ions in a half-cell? Let us take an example of a metal/metal ion equilibrium:

$$Zn^{2+}(aq) + e^- \rightleftharpoons Zn(s) \qquad E^\ominus = -0.76\,V$$

- If $[Zn^{2+}]$ is greater than $1.00\,mol\,dm^{-3}$, the value of E becomes less negative / more positive (for example $-0.61\,V$).

- If $[Zn^{2+}]$ is less than $1.00\,mol\,dm^{-3}$, the value of E becomes more negative / less positive (for example $-0.80\,V$).

We can apply Le Chatelier's principle to redox equilibria. If we increase the concentration of the species on the left of the equation, the position of equilibrium will shift to the right. So the value of E becomes more positive / less negative.

If two different ions are present in the half-cell, we have to consider both ions.

Let us take the equilibrium between Fe^{3+} ions and Fe^{2+} ions as an example.

$$\underset{1.00\,mol\,dm^{-3}}{Fe^{3+}} + e^- \rightleftharpoons \underset{1.00\,mol\,dm^{-3}}{Fe^{2+}} \qquad E^\ominus = +0.77\,V$$

- If $[Fe^{3+}]$ is greater than $1.00\,mol\,dm^{-3}$
  (keeping $[Fe^{2+}] = 1.00\,mol\,dm^{-3}$) the value of E becomes
  more positive (for example $+0.85\,V$).

- If $[Fe^{3+}]$ is less than $1.00\,mol\,dm^{-3}$
  (keeping $[Fe^{2+}] = 1.00\,mol\,dm^{-3}$) the value of E becomes less
  positive (for example $+0.70\,V$).

- If $[Fe^{2+}]$ is greater than $1.00\,mol\,dm^{-3}$
  (keeping $[Fe^{3+}] = 1.00\,mol\,dm^{-3}$) the value of E becomes less
  positive (for example $+0.70\,V$).

- If $[Fe^{2+}]$ is less than $1.00\,mol\,dm^{-3}$
  (keeping $[Fe^{3+}] = 1.00\,mol\,dm^{-3}$) the value of E becomes
  more positive (for example $+0.85\,V$).

You can see from the above that if we increase the concentration of both the Fe^{3+} and Fe^{2+} ions, these effects may cancel each other out.

How can we predict whether or not a given reaction will occur under non-standard conditions? The answer is that if the $E^{\ominus}$ values of the two half-reactions involved differ by more than $0.30\,V$, then the reaction predicted by the $E^{\ominus}$ values is highly likely to occur. So chlorine is likely to oxidise Fe^{2+} ions even if the conditions are not standard. This is because the difference in their $E^{\ominus}$ values is $0.59\,V$, which is considerably greater than $0.30\,V$.

$$\tfrac{1}{2}Cl_2(g) + e^- \rightleftharpoons Cl^-\,(aq) \qquad E^{\ominus} = +1.36\,V$$

$$Fe^{3+}(aq) + e^- \rightleftharpoons Fe^{2+}(aq) \qquad E^{\ominus} = +0.77\,V$$

We cannot, however, predict with confidence whether the reaction between MnO_4^- ions and Cl_2 will take place if the conditions are too far from standard.

$$MnO_4^-(aq) + 8H^+(aq) + 5e^- \rightleftharpoons Mn^{2+}(aq) + 4H_2O(l)$$
$$E^{\ominus} = +1.52\,V$$

$$\tfrac{1}{2}Cl_2(g) + e^- \rightleftharpoons Cl^-(aq) \qquad E^{\ominus} = +1.36\,V$$

This is because the difference in $E^{\ominus}$ values is $0.16\,V$, which is considerably smaller than $0.30\,V$.

The figure $0.30\,V$ given here to enable us to tell if a reaction will still occur under non-standard conditions is a rough guide only. If $E^{\ominus}$ values differ by less than $0.30\,V$, non-standard conditions may result in an unexpected outcome.

QUESTION

26 The half-cell

$$Cr_2O_7^{2-} + 14H^+ + 6e^- \rightleftharpoons 2Cr^{3+} + 7H_2O$$

has an $E^{\ominus}$ value of $+1.33\,V$.

a Suggest how the value of $E^{\ominus}$ changes if the other species are kept at $1.00\,mol\,dm^{-3}$ but:

  i $[Cr_2O_7^{2-}]$ is increased

  ii $[H^+]$ is decreased

  iii $[Cr^{3+}]$ is increased.

b What effect would each of these concentration changes have on the strength of the acidified $Cr_2O_7^{2-}$ solution as an oxidising agent?

c What conditions would you use to make a solution of $Cr_2O_7^{2-}$ as strong an oxidising agent as possible?

d Use Le Chatelier's principle to explain your answer to part c.

The Nernst equation

If we consider a cell made up from a silver/silver ion electrode and a copper/copper(II) ion electrode, the reaction taking place is:

$$Cu(s) + 2Ag^+(aq) \rightleftharpoons Cu^{2+}(aq) + 2Ag(s) \qquad E^{\ominus} = +0.46\,V$$

standard conditions and change the concentration of the silver ions, we obtain the graph shown in Figure 20.23. Note that we have plotted the value of E_{cell} (non-standard conditions for the cell as a whole) against the logarithm of the silver ion concentration.

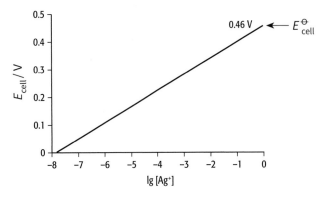

Figure 20.23 Increasing the concentration of silver ions in the cell reaction $Cu(s) + 2Ag^+(aq) \rightleftharpoons Cu^{2+}(aq) + 2Ag(s)$ makes the value of E_{cell} more positive.

The effect of concentration and temperature on the value of E_{cell} can be deduced using the Nernst equation. For a given electrode, e.g. a $Cu(s)/Cu^{2+}(aq)$ electrode, the relationship is:

$$E = E^{\ominus} + \frac{RT}{zF} \ln \frac{[\text{oxidised form}]}{[\text{reduced form}]}$$

where

E is the electrode potential under non-standard conditions

$E^{\ominus}$ is the standard electrode potential

R is the gas constant, 8.314, in $J\,K^{-1}\,mol^{-1}$

T is the kelvin temperature

z is the number of electrons transferred in the reaction

F is the value of the Faraday constant in $C\,mol^{-1}$

ln is the natural logarithm

[oxidised] refers to the concentration of the oxidised form in the half-equation.

Fortunately for us, for a metal/metal ion electrode, we can simplify this equation in three ways:

- The natural logarithm, ln, is related to log to the base 10 by the relationship
  $\ln x = 2.303 \log_{10} x$
- At standard temperature the values of R, T and F are constant
- For a metal/metal ion electrode, e.g.
  $Cu^{2+}(aq) + 2e^{-} \rightleftharpoons Cu(s)$ the reduced form is the metal. The concentration of the metal does not change. So the ratio [oxidised form]/[reduced form] can be written [oxidised form], e.g. $[Cu^{2+}(aq)]$

So the relationship becomes:

$$E = E^{\ominus} + \frac{0.059}{z} \log_{10} [\text{oxidised form}]$$

Note that if the temperature is not 25 °C the full form of the Nernst equation must be used.

QUESTION

27 a Calculate the value of the electrode potential at 298 K of a $Ni(s)/Ni^{2+}(aq)$ electrode that has a concentration of $Ni^{2+}(aq)$ ions of $1.5\,mol\,dm^{-3}$. $E^{\ominus} = -0.25\,V$.

b Calculate the electrode potential of a silver/silver ion electrode, $Ag(s)/Ag^{+}(aq)$, at 0 °C when the concentration of $Ag^{+}(aq)$ ions is $0.0002\,mol\,dm^{-3}$. $E^{\ominus} = +0.80\,V$.

WORKED EXAMPLE

8 Calculate the value of the electrode potential at 298 K of a $Cu(s)/Cu^{2+}(aq)$ electrode that has a concentration of $Cu^{2+}(aq)$ ions of $0.001\,mol\,dm^{-3}$. $E^{\ominus} = +0.34\,V$

Substituting the values in the relationship:

$$E = E^{\ominus} + \frac{0.059}{z} \log_{10} [Cu^{2+}(aq)]$$

$$E = +0.34 + \frac{0.059}{2} \log_{10} (0.001)$$

$$E = +0.34 - 0.089 = +0.25\,V$$

Note how $\log_{10}$ [oxidised form] changes the sign of the second term in the equation:

- If the concentration is $1\,mol\,dm^{-3}$, $\log_{10}$ [oxidised form] is 0 and $E = E^{\ominus}$.
- If the concentration is less than $1\,mol\,dm^{-3}$, $\log_{10}$ [oxidised form] is negative and E is less positive than $E^{\ominus}$.
- If the concentration is greater than $1\,mol\,dm^{-3}$, $\log_{10}$ [oxidised form] is positive and E is more positive than $E^{\ominus}$.

Feasibility predictions based on $E^{\ominus}$ don't always work!

The feasibility of a reaction based on $E^{\ominus}$ values is no guarantee that a reaction will proceed quickly. It only tells us that a reaction is possible, and that the reverse reaction does not occur. Some reactions are feasible, but they proceed so slowly that they do not **seem** to be taking place. Take, for example, the lack of reactivity of zinc with cold water. Remember that water contains H^{+} ions. The relevant half-equations are:

$$H^{+} + e^{-} \rightleftharpoons \tfrac{1}{2}H_2(g) \qquad\qquad E^{\ominus} = 0.00\,V$$

$$Zn^{2+}(aq) + 2e^{-} \rightleftharpoons Zn(s) \qquad\qquad E^{\ominus} = -0.76\,V$$

Even when the low concentration of H^{+} ions is taken into account, $E^{\ominus}$ values predict that a reaction should occur. The rate of reaction between zinc and water, however, is extremely slow. It is the rate of reaction rather than the value of $E^{\ominus}$ which is determining the lack of reactivity.

QUESTIONS

28 An industrial process relies on a reaction that is impractically slow under normal conditions. How might you try to solve this problem? Use your knowledge of reaction rates to suggest several different approaches.

29 Describe two limitations to using $E^{\ominus}$ values to predict the feasibility of a reaction.

Cells and batteries

The variety of cells

The ordinary dry cells used in torches, toys and radios have voltages ranging from 1.5 V to 2.0 V. Several of these cells are often needed to produce enough power and the voltage of these 'batteries' drops gradually during their lifetime.

A wide variety of electrochemical cells have been developed for specific functions in recent years. Many cells are small but they do not necessarily produce a high voltage for a long time. Batteries of several cells joined together give a higher voltage but take up more space. When selecting a cell for a particular job we need to consider:

- whether or not the cell can be recharged
- the size and mass of the cell
- the voltage of the cell
- the nature of the electrolyte
- how long the cell can deliver its maximum voltage
- the cost of the cell.

Rechargeable cells

The electrochemical cells that you have studied so far are called primary cells. In these cells the redox reactions continue until the reactants reach a low concentration and the voltage of the cell declines. The cell is then no longer of any use. Some electrochemical cells can be recharged by passing an electric current through them. The products are then changed back to reactants so the cell can function again. These cells are called secondary cells or storage cells.

A car battery is a secondary cell that consists of plates of lead and lead(IV) oxide immersed in sulfuric acid (Figure 20.24). The voltage of each cell is 2 V. In order to operate the car's starter motor, a higher voltage is

required. So a car battery consists of six of these cells in series to provide 12 V. The battery is recharged by the car's alternator while the car engine is running. Lead–acid batteries are very heavy but are cheap to manufacture.

Improved batteries for electric vehicles have been developed.

- Nickel–cadmium cells are smaller and have a lower mass than lead–acid cells but they give a lower voltage. They do not 'run down' as quickly.
- Aluminium–air batteries are lightweight and produce a higher voltage than a lead–acid battery. They are expensive and are not true secondary cells because the aluminium anode has to be replaced from time to time.

Solid state cells

In recent years, primary cells have been developed with improved voltage and reduced size. Cells the size of a large button are used in heart pacemakers, hearing aids and other medical uses as well as in watches and calculators. They have several advantages:

- they are lightweight and small
- they give a high voltage, for example 3.0 V
- they give a constant voltage over time
- they do not contain liquids or paste, so they do not leak.

Commonly used 'button' cells use lithium or zinc as the negative pole and iodine, manganese(IV) oxide or silver oxide as the positive pole.

Figure 20.25 Button cells like these are used to power watches and hearing aids.

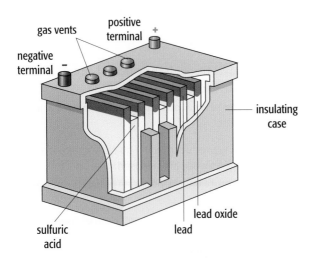

Figure 20.24 The storage cell used in a car.

293

Figure 20.26 Fuel cells may eventually replace petrol and diesel engines in cars.

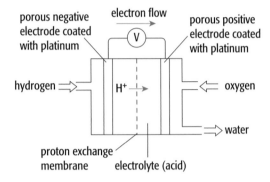

Figure 20.27 A hydrogen–oxygen fuel cell.

30 The nickel–cadmium cell is rechargeable. The half-equations for the electrode reactions are:

$$Cd(OH)_2 + 2e^- \longrightarrow Cd + 2OH^- \qquad E^{\ominus} = -0.81\,V$$

$$NiO_2 + 2H_2O + 2e^- \longrightarrow Ni(OH)_2 + 2OH^- \quad E^{\ominus} = +0.49\,V$$

a Which of these reactions proceeds in a forward direction when electrical energy is being taken from the cell?

b Predict the cell voltage, assuming that all conditions are standard.

c Write an equation for the cell reaction that occurs when electrical energy is being taken from the cell.

d Write an equation for the cell reaction that occurs when the cell is being recharged.

31 Lithium is often used as the negative pole in 'button' cells used to power watches.

a Explain why lithium is often used to make electrochemical cells.

b The half-equations for a lithium/iodine button cell are:

$$Li^+ + e^- \rightleftharpoons Li \qquad\qquad E^{\ominus} = -3.04\,V$$

$$\tfrac{1}{2}I_2(s) + e^- \rightleftharpoons I^-(aq) \qquad E^{\ominus} = +0.54\,V$$

  i Predict the cell voltage of this cell using the $E^{\ominus}$ values for the two half-equations above.

  ii The actual voltage of a lithium/iodine button cell is 2.8 V. Suggest why this is different from the value you calculated in part **i**.

c Give **two** advantages of a lithium/iodine cell compared with an ordinary dry cell.

Hydrogen–oxygen fuel cells

A **fuel cell** is an electrochemical cell in which a fuel gives up electrons at one electrode and oxygen gains electrons at the other electrode. Fuel cells are increasingly used instead of petrol to power buses and cars. The fuel is stored in tanks in the vehicle and oxygen comes from the air. The energy released in a fuel cell produces a voltage which can be used to power the electric motor of the vehicle.

One type of fuel cell is the hydrogen–oxygen fuel cell. Hydrogen gas and oxygen gas are bubbled through two porous platinum-coated electrodes where the half-reactions take place. Electrons flow through the external circuit from the negative to the positive pole. As they do

so, their energy is used to drive an electric motor or other device. The overall reaction is:

$$2H_2 + O_2 \longrightarrow 2H_2O$$

A hydrogen–oxygen fuel cell with an acidic electrolyte is shown in Figure 20.27.

At the negative electrode, hydrogen gas loses electrons:

$$H_2(g) \longrightarrow 2H^+(aq) + 2e^-$$

The electrons move round the external circuit where they can do a useful job of work, e.g. drive an electric motor. The H^+ ions diffuse through the membrane to the positive electrode. The reaction at the positive electrode is:

$$4H^+(aq) + O_2(g) + 4e^- \longrightarrow 2H_2O$$

The electrons travel through the external circuit from the negative electrode to the positive electrode.

Fuel cells have several advantages over petrol and diesel engines.

- Water is the only product made – no carbon dioxide or harmful nitrogen oxides are released.
- They produce more energy per gram of fuel burnt than petrol engines do.
- They are very efficient – the transmission of energy from the fuel cell to the motor is direct. There are no moving parts in which energy is wasted as heat.

There are several limitations to hydrogen–oxygen fuel cells.

- High cost: the materials used to make the electrodes and membrane are expensive.
- Manufacturing of fuel cells involves the production of toxic by-products.
- Storage of hydrogen: high-pressure tanks are needed in order to store a sufficient amount of fuel. At present refuelling has to be done more often compared with a petrol engine.
- Manufacturing hydrogen: the hydrogen needed for fuel cells can only be produced cheaply by using fossil fuels.
- Fuel cells do not work well at low temperatures: if the temperature falls much below 0 °C, the fuel cell 'freezes'.

QUESTIONS

32 A car's fuel tank holds 40 kg of petrol.
- 1 kg of petrol releases 5×10^7 J of energy when it burns.
- Only 40% of the energy released when the petrol burns is converted into useful work.
- 1×10^6 J of work is needed to drive the car 1 km.
- **a** How many joules of energy are released when 40 kg of petrol burns?
- **b** How many of these joules of energy are available to move the car forward?
- **c** How far can the car travel on 40 kg of petrol?

33 A fuel cell vehicle with a similar volume fuel tank can store 400 g of hydrogen at high pressure.
- 2 g of hydrogen release 286 000 J of energy when used in the vehicle's fuel cells.
- 60% of the energy released from the fuel cell is converted into useful work.
- 1×10^6 J of work is needed to drive the car 1 km.
- **a** How many joules of energy are released when 400 g of hydrogen is used in the vehicle's fuel cells?
- **b** How many of these joules of energy are available to move the car forward?
- **c** How far can the car travel on 400 g of hydrogen?

34 Compare and comment on your answers to questions 32 and 33.

More about electrolysis

On page 276 we studied the electrolysis of molten sodium chloride. During electrolysis:

- cations (positive ions) move towards the cathode where they gain electrons; gain of electrons is reduction
- anions (negative ions) move towards the anode where they lose electrons; loss of electrons is oxidation.

In this section we shall find out how the nature of the electrolyte and the concentration of aqueous electrolytes affects the products of electrolysis.

Electrolysis of molten electrolytes

When pure molten ionic compounds containing two simple ions are electrolysed, a metal is formed at the cathode and a non-metal at the anode. Some examples are shown in Table 20.1.

Let us take the electrolysis of molten zinc chloride as an example.

Compound electrolysed	Cathode product	Anode product
aluminium oxide	aluminium	oxygen
magnesium bromide	magnesium	bromine
sodium chloride	sodium	chlorine
zinc iodide	zinc	iodine

Table 20.1 The products formed at the cathode and anode when some molten salts are electrolysed.

At the cathode, the metal ions gain electrons and are reduced to the metal.

$$Zn^{2+} + 2e^- \longrightarrow Zn$$

At the anode, the non-metal ions lose electrons and are oxidised to a non-metal.

$$2Cl^- \longrightarrow Cl_2 + 2e^-$$

Electrolysis of aqueous solutions

Aqueous solutions of electrolytes contain more than one cation and more than one anion. For example, an aqueous solution of sodium chloride contains Na^+, Cl^-, H^+ and OH^- ions. The H^+ and OH^- ions arise from the ionisation of water:

$$H_2O \rightleftharpoons H^+ + OH^-$$

So – we have to ask, which ions are discharged (changed into atoms or molecules) during the electrolysis of aqueous solutions?

Among other things this depends on:

- the relative electrode potential of the ions
- the concentration of the ions.

295

Electrolysis products and electrode potentials

When an aqueous ionic solution is electrolysed using inert electrodes, there is usually only one product obtained at each electrode. The ease of discharge of cations at the cathode is related to their electrode potentials. Figure 20.28 shows some half-reactions and their electrode potentials.

$E^\ominus$ / V

+0.80	$Ag^+(aq) + e^- \rightleftharpoons Ag(s)$
+0.34	$Cu^{2+}(aq) + 2e^- \rightleftharpoons Cu(s)$
0.00	$H^+(aq) + e^- \rightleftharpoons \frac{1}{2}H_2(g)$
−0.13	$Pb^{2+}(aq) + 2e^- \rightleftharpoons Pb(s)$
−0.76	$Zn^{2+}(aq) + 2e^- \rightleftharpoons Zn(s)$
−2.38	$Mg^{2+}(aq) + 2e^- \rightleftharpoons Mg(s)$
−2.71	$Na^+(aq) + e^- \rightleftharpoons Na(s)$

increasing ease of discharge of cation at cathode

Figure 20.28 The ease of discharge of ions at a cathode in electrolysis is related to the electrode potential of the ions.

The cation that is most easily reduced is discharged at the cathode. So the cation in the half-equation with the most positive $E^\ominus$ value will be discharged.

When a concentrated aqueous solution of sodium chloride ($1.00\,mol\,dm^{-3}$) is electrolysed, H^+ ions and Na^+ ions are present in the solution. Hydrogen rather than sodium is formed at the cathode because H^+ ions are more easily reduced than Na^+ ions.

$$H^+ + e^- \rightleftharpoons \frac{1}{2}H_2 \qquad E^\ominus = 0.00\,V$$

$$Na^+(aq) + e^- \rightleftharpoons Na(s) \qquad E^\ominus = -2.71\,V$$

When a concentrated aqueous solution of copper(II) sulfate ($1.00\,mol\,dm^{-3}$) is electrolysed, H^+ ions and Cu^{2+} ions are present in the solution. Copper rather than hydrogen is formed at the cathode because Cu^{2+} ions are more easily reduced than H^+ ions.

$$Cu^{2+}(aq) + 2e^- \rightleftharpoons Cu(s) \qquad E^\ominus = +0.34\,V$$

$$H^+ + e^- \rightleftharpoons \frac{1}{2}H_2 \qquad E^\ominus = 0.00\,V$$

At the anode, using graphite electrodes, the ease of discharge of anions follows the order:

$$SO_4^{2-}(aq), NO_3^-(aq), Cl^-(aq), OH^-(aq), Br^-(aq), I^-(aq)$$

increasing ease of discharge
increasing ease of oxidation

When a concentrated aqueous solution of sodium sulfate ($1.00\,mol\,dm^{-3}\,Na_2SO_4$) is electrolysed, OH^- ions and

SO_4^{2-} ions are present in the solution. Hydroxide ions are discharged at the anode because OH^- ions are more easily oxidised than SO_4^{2-} ions. The OH^- ions are oxidised to oxygen, which bubbles off at the anode.

$$4OH^-(aq) \longrightarrow O_2(g) + 2H_2O(l) + 4e^-$$

When a concentrated aqueous solution of sodium iodide ($1.00\,mol\,dm^{-3}$) is electrolysed, I^- ions and OH^- ions are present in the solution. Iodide ions are discharged at the anode because I^- ions are more easily oxidised than OH^- ions.

$$I^-(aq) \longrightarrow \frac{1}{2}I_2(aq) + e^-$$

Note that in the discussion above, we have used standard electrode potentials. If conditions are standard, the concentration of the aqueous solution is $1.00\,mol\,dm^{-3}$ with respect to the ionic compound dissolved in water. But the concentration of hydrogen and hydroxide ions in solution is very low. We saw on page 286 that we can use electrode potential values to predict whether or not a reaction will occur under non-standard conditions. As long as the difference in electrode potentials is greater than 0.30 V, we can be fairly sure that the predictions will be correct.

QUESTIONS

35 An aqueous solution of sodium sulfate, Na_2SO_4, is electrolysed using carbon electrodes.

   a Explain why hydrogen is formed at the cathode and not sodium.

   b Write a half-equation for the reaction occurring at the anode.

36 Predict the electrolysis products at the anode and cathode when the following are electrolysed:

   a molten aluminium iodide

   b a concentrated aqueous solution of magnesium chloride

   c a concentrated aqueous solution of sodium bromide

   d molten zinc oxide.

Electrolysis products and solution concentration

When aqueous solutions are electrolysed, the ions are rarely present at concentrations of $1.00\,mol\,dm^{-3}$. On page 290 we saw that the value of E changes with the concentration of the ion. An ion, Z, higher in the discharge series may be discharged in preference to one below it if Z is present at a relatively higher concentration than normal. For this to be possible, the E values of the competing ions are usually less than 0.30 V different from each other.

When a concentrated solution of sodium chloride is electrolysed, chloride ions are discharged at the anode in preference to hydroxide ions. This is because chloride ions are present in a much higher concentration than hydroxide ions. The chloride ions fall below the hydroxide ions in the discharge series.

But what happens when we electrolyse an extremely dilute solution of sodium chloride?

We find that oxygen, rather than chlorine, is formed at the anode. This is because the relatively lower concentration of Cl^- ions allows OH^- ions to fall below

Cl^- ions in the discharge series. In reality, the electrolysis of a dilute aqueous solution of sodium chloride gives a mixture of chlorine and oxygen at the anode. The proportion of oxygen increases the more dilute the solution.

QUESTION

37 A concentrated aqueous solution of hydrochloric acid is electrolysed.

    a Write half-equations to show the reactions at:
        i the cathode
        ii the anode.

    b A very dilute solution of hydrochloric acid is electrolysed. What substance or substances are formed at the anode? Explain your answer.

Summary

- An electrolytic cell consists of a direct current power supply connected to two electrodes which dip into an electrolyte.

- An electrolyte is a compound that is decomposed during electrolysis.

- During electrolysis reduction occurs at the cathode (negative electrode) because ions gain electrons from the cathode.

- During electrolysis oxidation occurs at the anode (positive electrode) because ions lose electrons to the anode.

- The Faraday constant (F) is the electric charge, in coulombs, on 1 mole of electrons.

- The relationship between the Faraday constant, the Avogadro constant (L) and the charge on an electron (e) is given by $F = Le$.

- A value for the Avogadro constant can be determined by an electrolytic method using the relationship $F = Le$.

- The nature of the substances liberated during electrolysis depends on:
  - the state of the electrolyte (molten or aqueous); a metal is formed at the cathode when molten metal salts are electrolysed; hydrogen may be formed at the cathode when dilute aqueous solutions of metal salts are electrolysed
  - the position of the ions (in the electrolyte) in the redox series; ions lower in the redox series are

more likely to be discharged than those higher in the series
  - the concentration of the ions in the electrolyte; when different ions are not very far apart in the redox series, the ion present in greater concentration is more likely to be discharged.

- The quantity of charge, in coulombs, passed during electrolysis is found by multiplying the current, in amps, by time, in seconds, $Q = It$.

- The mass and/or volume of substance liberated during electrolysis can be calculated from the quantity of charge and the number of Faradays required to discharge 1 mole of ions.

- A half-cell can consist of an element in contact with its aqueous ions or two different aqueous ions of the same element in different oxidation states in contact with a platinum electrode.

- Two half-cells joined together form an electrochemical cell.

- A standard hydrogen electrode is a half-cell in which hydrogen gas at a pressure of 101 kPa bubbles through a solution of $1.00 \, mol \, dm^{-3}$ $H^+(aq)$ ions.

- The standard electrode potential of a half-cell ($E^{\ominus}$) is the voltage of the half-cell under standard conditions compared with a standard hydrogen electrode.

- The standard cell potential ($E^{\ominus}_{cell}$) is the voltage developed under standard conditions when two half-cells are joined.

- The standard cell potential is calculated from the difference between the standard electrode potentials of two half-cells.

- The direction of electron flow in a simple cell is from the half-cell that has the more negative (or less positive) electrode potential to the half-cell that has the less negative (or more positive) electrode potential.

- The value of E_{cell} can be used to predict whether a reaction is likely to take place (whether the reaction is feasible).

- A particular redox reaction will occur if the $E^\ominus$ of the half-equation involving the species being reduced is more positive than the $E^\ominus$ of the half-equation of the species being oxidised.

- The ability of the halogens to act as oxidising agents depends on the $E^\ominus$ of the half-equation involving $X_2 + 2e^- \rightleftharpoons 2X^-$ (where X is a halogen atom). The more positive the value of $E^\ominus$ for this half-reaction, the better the halogen is as an oxidising agent.

- Redox equations can be constructed by combining the relevant half-equations.

- The value of the $E^\ominus$ of a half-cell containing a metal in contact with its aqueous ions becomes more negative as the concentration of the aqueous ion decreases.

- The Nernst equation shows the relationship between the concentration of aqueous ions in each half-cell and the electrode potential.

- A fuel cell uses the energy from reaction of a fuel (such as hydrogen) with oxygen to generate a voltage.

- Improved batteries (as in electric vehicles) have advantages in terms of smaller size, lower mass and higher voltage.

End-of-chapter questions

1 The diagram shows an electrochemical cell designed to find the standard electrode potential for zinc.

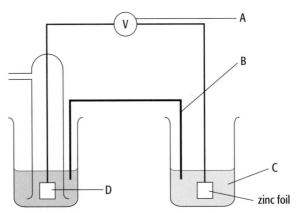

a	Name the apparatus labelled **A** and give a characteristic it should have.	[2]
b	**i** Name part **B** and give its two functions.	[3]
	ii Describe how part **B** can be prepared.	[2]
c	What is **C**?	[2]
d	Name part **D** and give its two functions.	[3]
e	Give the three standard conditions for the measurement of a standard electrode potential.	[3]

Total = 15

Question **2**, part **c**, involves three questions in which you have two choices of answer. To be sure of getting your answers the right way round, apply the rules carefully. To start with, the half-cell with the more positive $E^\ominus$ value will attract and accept electrons, so reduction takes place here. Remember OIL RIG – Oxidation Is Loss, Reduction Is Gain (of electrons).

2   The diagram shows an electrochemical cell involving two metal/metal-ion systems.

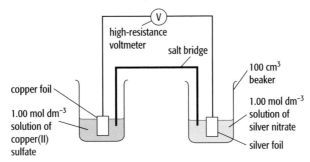

The standard electrode potentials for the half-cells are:

$Ag^+ + e^- \rightleftharpoons Ag$ $E^\ominus = +0.80\,V$

$Cu^{2+} + 2e^- \rightleftharpoons Cu$ $E^\ominus = +0.34\,V$

a   Calculate a value for the cell voltage. Show your working.   [2]
b   Write the balanced ionic equation for the overall cell reaction.   [2]
c   In this reaction:
   i   Which substance is oxidised? Explain your answer.   [1]
   ii Which substance is reduced? Explain your answer.   [1]
   iii In which direction do the electrons flow? Explain your answer.   [2]
d   The contents of the Cu^{2+}/Cu half-cell are diluted with water. The contents of the Ag^+/Ag half-cell are kept the same. Suggest what effect this will have on the value of the cell voltage, E. Explain your answer.   [3]

Total = 11

Question **3**, part **a**, is another definition! Make sure you learn these. Question **3**, part **b**, includes the word 'standard', so don't forget standard conditions when you are labelling. This is also relevant for several of the other questions that follow.

3   a   Define the term **standard electrode potential**.   [3]
    b   Draw a labelled diagram to show how the standard electrode potential of a half-cell containing chlorine gas and chloride ions can be measured.   [5]
    c   Write a half-equation for this half-cell.   [1]
    d   The standard electrode potential of a Cl_2/Cl^- half-cell is +1.36 V. This Cl_2/Cl^- half-cell was connected to a standard half-cell containing solid iodine in equilibrium with iodide ions. The standard electrode potential of an I_2/I^- half-cell is +0.54 V.
       i   Calculate the standard cell voltage for this cell.   [1]
       ii Write the balanced ionic equation for the overall cell reaction.   [2]

Total = 12

4 a In the presence of acid, the manganate(VII) ion is a powerful oxidising agent. The half-equation for its reduction in acid solution is:

$$MnO_4^-(aq) + 8H^+(aq) + 5e^- \rightleftharpoons Mn^{2+}(aq) + 4H_2O(l) \qquad E^\ominus = +1.51\,V$$

    i Explain why the presence of an acid is necessary for the $Mn_4^-(aq)$ to function as an oxidising agent. [1]

    ii Give two reasons for the $MnO_4^-(aq)$ acting as an oxidising agent in acidic solution. [2]

b Iodide ions are oxidised to iodine according to the half-cell equation:

$$\tfrac{1}{2}I_2(aq) + e^- \rightleftharpoons I^-(aq) \qquad E^\ominus = +0.54\,V$$

    i Explain why an acidified solution of manganate(VII) ions can be used to oxidise iodide ions to iodine. [5]

    ii Write the balanced equation for this reaction. [2]

Total = 10

5 Liquid bromine is added to an aqueous solution of potassium iodide. The following reaction takes place.

$$Br_2(l) + 2I^-(aq) \longrightarrow 2Br^-(aq) + I_2(aq) \qquad E^\ominus_{cell} = +0.53\,V$$

a Write two half-equations for this reaction. [2]

b Draw a labelled diagram to show two linked half-cells that could be used to measure the standard cell potential for this reaction. [7]

c The standard cell potential for this reaction is +0.53 V. Does the position of equilibrium favour the reactants or the products? Explain your answer. [4]

d The standard electrode potentials for a number of half-equations are shown below:

$$Fe^{3+}(aq) + e^- \longrightarrow Fe^{2+}(aq) \qquad E^\ominus = +0.77\,V$$

$$I_2(aq) + 2e^- \longrightarrow 2I^-(aq) \qquad E^\ominus = +0.54\,V$$

$$Ni^{2+}(aq) + 2e^- \longrightarrow Ni(s) \qquad E^\ominus = -0.25\,V$$

$$Pb^{4+}(aq) + 2e^- \longrightarrow Pb^{2+}(aq) \qquad E^\ominus = +1.69\,V$$

    Which atom or ion in this list will reduce iodine to iodide ions? Explain your answer. [4]

Total = 17

6 The list below gives the standard electrode potentials for five half-reactions.

$$Cu^{2+}(aq) + e^- \longrightarrow Cu(s) \qquad E^\ominus = +0.34\,V$$

$$Fe^{2+}(aq) + 2e^- \longrightarrow Fe(s) \qquad E^\ominus = -0.44\,V$$

$$Fe^{3+}(aq) + e^- \longrightarrow Fe^{2+}(aq) \qquad E^\ominus = +0.77\,V$$

$$I_2(aq) + 2e^- \longrightarrow 2I^-(aq) \qquad E^\ominus = +0.54\,V$$

$$Zn^{2+}(aq) + 2e^- \longrightarrow Zn(s) \qquad E^\ominus = -0.76\,V$$

a What is the meaning of **standard electrode potential**? [3]

b Which species in the list is:

    i the strongest oxidising agent? [1]

    ii the strongest reducing agent? [1]

c A cell was set up as shown below.

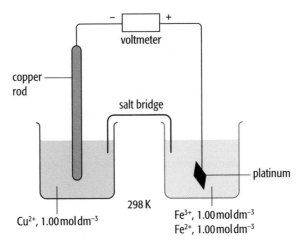

i   Calculate the standard cell potential of this cell. [1]

ii In which direction do the electrons flow in the external circuit? Explain your answer. [2]

iii Write an equation for the complete cell reaction. [2]

d The concentration of copper(II) ions in the left-hand electrode was increased from $1.00\,mol\,dm^{-3}$ to $1.30\,mol\,dm^{-3}$. The concentration of ions in the right-hand cell was not changed.

i   What effect does this change have on the E value of the Cu^{2+}/Cu half-cell? [1]

ii What effect does this change have on the E value for the complete electrochemical cell? [1]

iii Why is the direction of the cell reaction unlikely to be altered by this change in concentration? [1]

e Lithium–iodine button cells are often used to power watches. Suggest two reasons, other than size, why button cells are used to power watches rather than ordinary 'dry cells'. [2]

Total = 15

7 An electric current of $1.04\,A$ was passed through a solution of dilute sulfuric acid for $6.00\,min$. The volume of hydrogen produced at r.t.p. was $43.5\,cm^3$.

a How many coulombs of charge were passed during the experiment? [1]

b How many coulombs of charge are required to liberate 1 mole of hydrogen gas? ($F = 96\,500\,C\,mol^{-1}$) [2]

c In another experiment, copper(II) sulfate was electrolysed using copper electrodes. Copper was deposited at the cathode.

i   Write a half-equation for this reaction. [1]

ii A student conducted an experiment to calculate a value for the Faraday constant, F. An electric current of $0.300\,A$ was passed through the solution of copper(II) sulfate for exactly $40\,min$. $0.240\,g$ of copper was deposited at the cathode. Use this information to calculate a value for F. Express your answer to 3 significant figures. (A_r value: [Cu] = 63.5) [3]

iii The charge on one electron is approximately $1.60 \times 10^{-19}\,C$. Use this information and your answer to part **ii** to calculate a value for the Avogadro constant. [2]

Total = 9

301

8   An aqueous solution of silver nitrate is electrolysed.
 a **i** Explain why silver rather than hydrogen is produced at the cathode. [2]
  ii Write an equation for the reaction occurring at the cathode. [1]
 b **i** Write an equation for the reaction occurring at the anode. [1]
  ii Is the anode reaction an oxidation or reduction reaction? Explain your answer. [1]
 c Explain why the silver nitrate solution becomes acidic during this electrolysis. [3]
 d Calculate the mass of silver deposited at the cathode when the electrolysis is carried out for exactly 35 min using a current of 0.18 A. (A_r[Ag] = 108; F = 96 500 C mol^{-1}) [3]

                          Total = 11

9   The reaction taking place in an electrochemical cell under standard conditions is

$$Fe^{2+}(aq) + Ag^+(aq) \longrightarrow Fe^{3+}(aq) + Ag(s)$$

 a Write two half-equations for this reaction. For each, state whether oxidation or reduction is occurring. [2]
 b The standard electrode potential for the half-cell containing $Fe^{2+}(aq)$ and $Fe^{3+}(aq)$ is +0.77 V.

  i Use the relationship $E = E^{\ominus} + \dfrac{0.059}{z} \log_{10} \dfrac{[\text{oxidised form}]}{[\text{reduced form}]}$

   to calculate the electrode potential at 298 K if the concentration of $Fe^{2+}(aq)$ is 0.02 mol dm^{-3} and the concentration of $Fe^{3+}(aq)$ is 0.1 mol dm^{-3}. [3]

  ii Use the relationship above to explain why the standard electrode potential for the half-cell containing $Fe^{2+}(aq)$ and $Fe^{3+}(aq)$ is always +0.77 V if there are equimolar concentrations of $Fe^{2+}(aq)$ and $Fe^{3+}(aq)$. [2]
 c The standard electrode potential for the half-cell containing $Ag^+(aq)$ and $Ag(s)$ is +0.80 V. Calculate the electrode potential at 298 K if the concentration of $Ag^+(aq)$ is 0.05 mol dm^{-3}. [2]
 d Use your results to parts **b i** and **c** to predict whether the reaction $Fe^{2+}(aq) + Ag^+(aq) \longrightarrow Fe^{3+}(aq) + Ag(s)$ is likely to occur at the concentrations $Fe^{2+}(aq)$ 0.05 mol dm^{-3}, $Fe^{3+}(aq)$ 0.1 mol dm^{-3} and $Ag^+(aq)$ 0.05 mol dm^{-3}. Explain your answer. [4]

                          Total = 13

10 Concentrated aqueous sodium chloride can be electrolysed in the laboratory using graphite electrodes.
 a Write the formulae for all the ions present in an aqueous solution of sodium chloride. [2]
 b Write half-equations to show the reactions at:
  i the anode (positive electrode) [1]
  ii the cathode (negative electrode). [1]
 c Explain why the reaction at the anode is classed as oxidation. [1]
 d After a while, the solution near the cathode becomes very alkaline. Explain why. [3]
 e The chlorine produced at the anode can react with warm concentrated sodium hydroxide:

  $$Cl_2 + 6NaOH \longrightarrow 5NaCl + NaClO_3 + 3H_2O$$

  What are the oxidation number changes per atom of chlorine when
  i Cl_2 is converted to NaCl? [1]
  ii Cl_2 is converted to $NaClO_3$? [1]
 f Give the systematic name for the compound $NaClO_3$. [1]

                          Total = 11

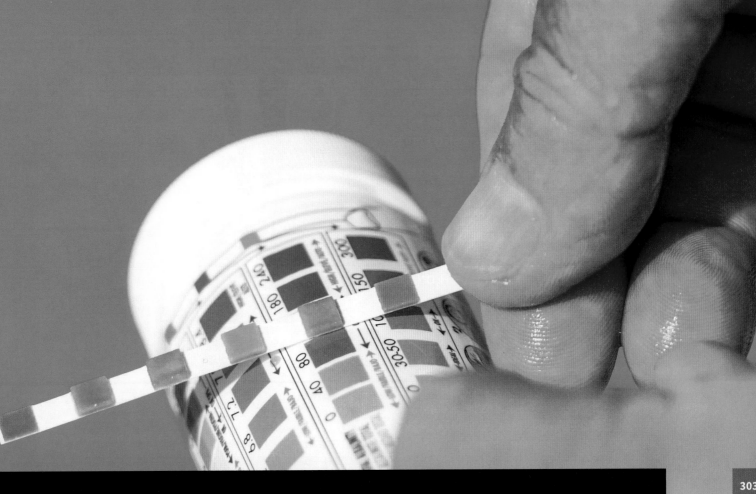

Chapter 21:
Further aspects of equilibria

Learning outcomes

You should be able to:

- explain the terms **pH**, **pK_a** and K_w and use them in calculations
- calculate [H$^+$(aq)] and pH values for strong and weak acids and strong bases
- explain the choice of suitable indicators for acid–base titrations, given appropriate data
- describe the changes in pH during acid–base titrations and explain these changes in terms of the strengths of the acids and bases
- explain how buffer solutions control pH
- describe and explain the uses of buffer solutions, including the role of HCO$_3^-$ in controlling pH in the blood

- calculate the pH of buffer solutions, given appropriate data
- show understanding of and use the concept of solubility product, K_{sp}
- calculate K_{sp} from concentrations and vice versa
- show understanding of the common ion effect
- state what is meant by the term **partition coefficient**
- calculate and use a partition coefficient for a system in which the solute is in the same molecular state in the two solvents.

Introduction

In Chapter 8 (pages 133–4) we learnt that acids and bases can be classed as strong or weak.

- Strong acids ionise completely in water. For example, aqueous hydrochloric acid consists entirely of $H_3O^+(aq)$ and $Cl^-(aq)$:

$$HCl(g) + H_2O(l) \longrightarrow H_3O^+(aq) + Cl^-(aq)$$

- Weak acids only ionise to a small extent in water.

For example, aqueous ethanoic acid consists mostly of un-ionised $CH_3COOH(aq)$:

$$CH_3COOH(aq) + H_2O(l) \rightleftharpoons CH_3COO^-(aq) + H_3O^+(aq)$$

The pH of the resulting solutions can be related to the concentration of H_3O^+ ions formed.

In this chapter:

- we shall use hydrogen ion concentrations to calculate pH values for solutions of strong acids
- we shall use equilibrium expressions to calculate hydrogen ion concentrations for solutions of weak acids, in order to calculate their pH values
- we shall also learn about ionic equilibria related to the solubility of salts.

Figure 21.1 Compost in a compost bin. The pH of compost changes as the plant material is broken down by bacterial action. The chemical reactions in compost involve weak acids and weak bases.

The ionic product of water, K_w

Water is able to act as either an acid (by donating protons, H^+) or a base (by accepting protons). In pure water, the following equilibrium exists.

H+ donated

$$H_2O(l) + H_2O(l) \rightleftharpoons \underset{\text{acid}}{H_3O^+(aq)} + \underset{\text{base}}{OH^-(aq)}$$

We can simplify this equation by writing hydroxonium ions, H_3O^+, as simple hydrogen ions, H^+:

$$H_2O(l) \rightleftharpoons H^+(aq) + OH^-(aq)$$

The equilibrium expression for this reaction is:

$$K_c = \frac{[H^+(aq)]\,[OH^-(aq)]}{[H_2O(l)]}$$

The extent of ionisation of water is very low. The concentration of hydrogen ions and hydroxide ions in pure water (and hence the value of K_c) is extremely small. Because of this, we can regard the concentration of water as being constant.

We can therefore incorporate this into the value of K_c. The equilibrium expression then becomes:

$$K_w = [H^+]\,[OH^-]$$

K_w is called the **ionic product of water**. Its value at 298 K is $1.00 \times 10^{-14}\,mol^2\,dm^{-6}$.

We can use this equation to find the hydrogen ion concentration in pure water; for simplicity we will now omit the state symbol (aq). For each molecule of water that ionises, one H^+ ion and one OH^- ion are produced.

$$[H^+] = [OH^-]$$

We can rewrite the equilibrium expression

$$K_w = [H^+]\,[OH^-]$$

as:

$$K_w = [H^+]^2$$

Rearranging this equation to find the hydrogen ion concentration $[H^+]$ in pure water:

$$[H^+] = \sqrt{K_w} = \sqrt{1.00 \times 10^{-14}} = 1.00 \times 10^{-7}\,mol\,dm^{-3}$$

pH calculations

We know that the lower the hydrogen ion concentration, the higher the pH. The pH values of some familiar aqueous solutions are shown in Table 21.1.

The range of possible hydrogen ion concentrations in different solutions is very large. It can range from $10^{-15}\,mol\,dm^{-3}$ to $10\,mol\,dm^{-3}$. In order to overcome the problem of dealing with a wide range of numbers, the Danish chemist Søren Sørensen introduced the **pH** scale.

Solution	pH
hydrochloric acid ($1.00\,mol\,dm^{-3}$)	0.0
stomach 'juices' (contains HCl(aq))	1.0–2.0
lemon juice	2.3
vinegar	3
coffee	around 5
rainwater (normal)	5.7
saliva	6.3–6.8
fresh milk	around 6.5
pure water	7.0
sea water	around 8.5
milk of magnesia	10
soapy water (cheap soap!)	11
bench sodium hydroxide ($1.00\,mol\,dm^{-3}$)	14

Table 21.1 pH values of some familiar aqueous solutions.

> pH is defined as the negative logarithm to the base 10 of the hydrogen ion concentration. In symbols this is written:
>
> $$pH = -\log_{10}[H^+]$$

Note that:

- the negative sign is introduced to make the pH values positive in most cases
- the logarithms used are to the base 10 (not to the base e), so make sure that when doing calculations you press the log or lg button on your calculator (not the ln button)
- we can use this equation to convert $[H^+]$ to pH or pH to $[H^+]$.

Calculating pH values from [H⁺]

Here is an example of the use of logarithms to calculate pH from hydrogen ion concentrations.

> **WORKED EXAMPLE**
>
> 1 Calculate the pH of a solution whose H^+ ion concentration is $5.32 \times 10^{-4}\,mol\,dm^{-3}$.
>
> $$\begin{aligned} pH &= -\log_{10}[H^+] \\ &= -\log_{10}(5.32 \times 10^{-4}) \\ &= 3.27 \end{aligned}$$
>
> Use your own calculator to check that you can get the correct answer. Try it several times. If you cannot get this answer (3.27) check with your calculator's instruction booklet, or find your teacher or a member of your teaching group to work with to solve this problem.

> **QUESTION**
>
> 1 Calculate the pH of the following solutions:
>
> a $[H^+] = 3.00 \times 10^{-4}\,mol\,dm^{-3}$
>
> b $[H^+] = 1.00 \times 10^{-2}\,mol\,dm^{-3}$
>
> c $[H^+] = 4.00 \times 10^{-8}\,mol\,dm^{-3}$
>
> d $[H^+] = 5.40 \times 10^{-12}\,mol\,dm^{-3}$
>
> e $[H^+] = 7.80 \times 10^{-10}\,mol\,dm^{-3}$

You should notice that the solutions in question **1**, parts **c**, **d** and **e**, are alkalis; they all have pH values greater than 7. Even though they are alkalis they each still have a small concentration of H^+ ions, and this concentration is used to calculate the pH. They each have a small concentration of H^+ ions because $H_2O \rightleftharpoons H^+ + OH^-$ is an equilibrium. Even when there is an excess of OH^- ions there is still a small concentration of H^+ ions. In the same way, the solutions in question **1**, parts **a** and **b**, have a small concentration of OH^- ions, even though the solutions are acids.

Calculating [H⁺] from pH

Here is an example of the use of logarithms to calculate hydrogen ion concentration from pH. Use your own calculator to check that you get the correct answer.

WORKED EXAMPLE

2 Calculate the hydrogen ion concentration of a solution whose pH is 10.5.

$$pH = -\log_{10}[H^+]$$
$$[H^+] = 10^{-pH}$$
$$= 10^{-10.5}$$
$$= 3.16 \times 10^{-11}\,mol\,dm^{-3}$$

Use your own calculator to check that you can get the correct answer. Try it several times. If you cannot get this answer (3.16×10^{-11}) check with your calculator's instruction booklet, or find your teacher or a member of your teaching group to work with to solve this problem.

QUESTION

2 Calculate the concentration of hydrogen ions in solutions having the following pH values:

a pH 2.90   b pH 3.70   c pH 11.2

d pH 5.40   e pH 12.9

The pH of strong acids

Monobasic acids contain only one replaceable hydrogen atom per molecule. Strong monobasic acids such as hydrochloric acid are completely ionised in solution. It follows from this that the concentration of hydrogen ions in solution is approximately the same as the concentration of the acid. (We are making the assumption that the concentration of H^+ ions arising from the ionisation of water molecules is very small compared with those arising from the acid.)

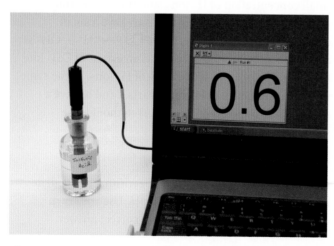

Figure 21.2 A pH electrode allows us to determine pH accurately.

■ pH of $0.1\,mol\,dm^{-3}$ HCl is $-\log(1 \times 10^{-1}\,mol\,dm^{-3}) = pH\,1$
■ pH of $0.01\,mol\,dm^{-3}$ HCl is $-\log(1 \times 10^{-2}\,mol\,dm^{-3}) = pH\,2$
■ pH of $0.001\,mol\,dm^{-3}$ HCl is $-\log(1 \times 10^{-3}\,mol\,dm^{-3}) = pH\,3$

Diluting the acid 10 times reduces the value of the H^+ ion concentration by one-tenth and increases the pH by a value of one.

Calculating the pH of strong bases

Strong bases, such as sodium hydroxide, ionise completely in solution. The concentration of hydroxide ions in a solution of sodium hydroxide is therefore approximately the same as the concentration of the sodium hydroxide.

To calculate the pH of a solution of strong base we need to know:

■ the concentration of OH^- ions in solution
■ the equilibrium expression for the ionisation of water:
  $$K_w = [H^+][OH^-]$$
■ the value of K_w for water.

As $K_w = [H^+][OH^-]$

$$[H^+] = \frac{K_w}{[OH^-]}$$

We can calculate the $[H^+]$ and then calculate the pH.

WORKED EXAMPLE

3 Calculate the pH of a solution of sodium hydroxide of concentration $0.0500\,mol\,dm^{-3}$.

$K_w = 1.00 \times 10^{-14}\,mol^2\,dm^{-6}$ (at 298 K).

Step 1 Write the expression relating $[H^+]$ to K_w and $[OH^-]$

$$[H^+] = \frac{K_w}{[OH^-]}$$

Step 2 Substitute the values into the expression to calculate $[H^+]$.

$$[H^+] = \frac{1.00 \times 10^{-14}}{0.0500} = 2.00 \times 10^{-13}\,mol\,dm^{-3}$$

Step 3 Calculate the pH.

$$pH = -\log_{10}[H^+]$$
$$= -\log_{10}(2.00 \times 10^{-13})$$
$$= 12.7$$

A quick way to get the same answer is to:

■ find $-\log_{10}[OH^-]$ (here $-\log_{10}[OH^-] = -\log_{10}(0.0500) = 1.3$).

■ subtract this value from 14 (in this example $14 - 1.3 = 12.7$).

This works because $-\log_{10}[H^+] - \log_{10}[OH^-] = 14$.

3 Find the pH of the following strong acids and strong bases:

a 1.00 mol dm^{-3} HNO$_3$

b 0.500 mol dm^{-3} HNO$_3$

c an aqueous solution containing 3.00 g HCl per dm^3

d 0.001 00 mol dm^{-3} KOH
($K_w = 1.00 \times 10^{-14}$ mol^2 dm^{-6})

e an aqueous solution containing 0.200 g of NaOH per dm^3
($K_w = 1.00 \times 10^{-14}$ mol^2 dm^{-6})

Weak acids – using the acid dissociation constant, K_a

K_a and pK_a

The equilibrium law (see page 123) can be applied to aqueous solutions of weak acids and weak bases. For example, when ethanoic acid dissolves in water the following equilibrium results:

$$CH_3COOH(aq) + H_2O(l) \rightleftharpoons H_3O^+(aq) + CH_3COO^-(aq)$$

We can simplify this equation to:

$$\underset{\text{ethanoic acid}}{CH_3COOH(aq)} \rightleftharpoons H^+(aq) + \underset{\text{ethanoate ion}}{CH_3COO^-(aq)}$$

The equilibrium expression for this reaction is:

$$K_a = \frac{[H^+][CH_3COO^-]}{[CH_3COOH]}$$

K_a is called the **acid dissociation constant**. At 298 K the value of K_a for the dissociation of ethanoic acid is 1.74×10^{-5} mol dm^{-3}.

The units of K_a are determined in the same way as for K_c (see page 123). For the dissociation of a monobasic acid the units are mol dm^{-3}.

We can write the general formula for a monobasic acid as HA. The balanced equation for the partial ionisation of this weak acid is:

$$HA(aq) \rightleftharpoons H^+(aq) + A^-(aq)$$

The general equilibrium expression applying to a monobasic acid then becomes:

$$K_a = \frac{[H^+][A^-]}{[HA]}$$

Figure 21.3 Friedrich Ostwald (1853–1932) was a German chemist who developed the idea of 'degree of dissociation' of weak acids and bases. He was one of the most famous physical chemists of his day. But strangely enough, he didn't accept the atomic theory until 1906.

The value of K_a indicates the extent of dissociation of the acid.

- A high value for K_a (for example, 40 mol dm^{-3}) indicates that the position of equilibrium lies to the right. The acid is almost completely ionised.

- A low value for K_a (for example, 1.0×10^{-4} mol dm^{-3}) indicates that the position of equilibrium lies to the left. The acid is only slightly ionised and exists mainly as HA molecules and comparatively few H$^+$ and A$^-$ ions.

As K_a values for many acids are very low, we can use pK_a values to compare their strengths.

$$pK_a = -\log_{10} K_a$$

Table 21.2 shows the range of values of K_a and pK_a for various acids. Note that the less positive the value of pK_a, the more acidic is the acid.

4 a Write equilibrium expressions for the following reactions:

i $C_6H_5COOH(aq) \rightleftharpoons H^+(aq) + C_6H_5COO^-(aq)$

ii $HCO_3^-(aq) \rightleftharpoons H^+(aq) + CO_3^{2-}(aq)$

iii $NH_4^+(aq) \rightleftharpoons H^+(aq) + NH_3(aq)$

b Look at Table 21.2. For the following acids or ions (shown in the left-hand column) work out which species in the equilibrium are Brønsted–Lowry acids and which are their conjugate bases:

i hydrated Fe^{3+} ion

ii nitric(III) (acid)

iii carbonic (acid)

iv hydrogensilicate ion.

307

Acid or ion	Equilibrium in aqueous solution	K_a / mol dm^{-3}	pK_a
nitric	$HNO_3 \rightleftharpoons H^+ + NO_3^-$	about 40	−1.4
sulfuric(IV)	$H_2SO_3 \rightleftharpoons H^+ + HSO_3^-$	1.5×10^{-2}	1.82
hydrated Fe^{3+} ion	$[Fe(H_2O)_6]^{3+} \rightleftharpoons H^+ + [Fe(H_2O)_5(OH)]^{2+}$	6.0×10^{-3}	2.22
hydrofluoric	$HF \rightleftharpoons H^+ + F^-$	5.6×10^{-4}	3.25
nitric(III)	$HNO_2 \rightleftharpoons H^+ + NO_2^-$	4.7×10^{-4}	3.33
methanoic	$HCOOH \rightleftharpoons H^+ + HCOO^-$	1.6×10^{-4}	3.80
benzoic	$C_6H_5COOH \rightleftharpoons H^+ + C_6H_5COO^-$	6.3×10^{-5}	4.20
ethanoic	$CH_3COOH \rightleftharpoons H^+ + CH_3COO^-$	1.7×10^{-5}	4.77
propanoic	$CH_3CH_2COOH \rightleftharpoons H^+ + CH_3CH_2COO^-$	1.3×10^{-5}	4.89
hydrated Al^{3+} ion	$[Al(H_2O)_6]^{3+} \rightleftharpoons H^+ + [Al(H_2O)_5(OH)]^{2+}$	1.0×10^{-5}	5.00
carbonic	$CO_2 + H_2O \rightleftharpoons H^+ + HCO_3^-$	4.5×10^{-7}	6.35
silicic	$SiO_2 + H_2O \rightleftharpoons H^+ + HSiO_3^-$	1.3×10^{-10}	9.89
hydrogencarbonate ion	$HCO_3^- \rightleftharpoons H^+ + CO_3^{2-}$	4.8×10^{-11}	10.3
hydrogensilicate ion	$HSiO_3^- \rightleftharpoons H^+ + SiO_3^{2-}$	1.3×10^{-12}	11.9
water	$H_2O \rightleftharpoons H^+ + OH^-$	1.0×10^{-14}	14.0

Table 21.2 Acid dissociation constants, K_a, for a range of acids, for aqueous solutions in the region of 0.0–0.01 mol dm^{-3}.

Calculating K_a for a weak acid

We can calculate the value of K_a for a weak acid if we know:

- the concentration of the acid
- the pH of the solution.

From the general equation:

$$HA(aq) \rightleftharpoons H^+ + A^-$$

we can see that for each molecule of HA that ionises, one H$^+$ ion and one A$^-$ ion are produced. (This assumes that we ignore the H$^+$ ions arising from the ionisation of water.)

$$[H^+] = [A^-]$$

We can rewrite the equilibrium expression

$$K_a = \frac{[H^+][A^-]}{[HA]}$$

as

$$K_a = \frac{[H^+]^2}{[HA]}$$

In order to calculate the value of K_a we make two assumptions.

- We ignore the concentration of hydrogen ions produced by the ionisation of the water molecules present in the solution. This is reasonable because the ionic product of

water (1.00×10^{-14} mol^2 dm^{-6}) is negligible compared with the values for most weak acids (see Table 21.2).

- We assume that the ionisation of the weak acid is so small that the concentration of undissociated HA molecules present at equilibrium is approximately the same as that of the original acid.

Worked example 4 shows how to calculate the value of K_a using the pH and the concentration of the weak acid.

WORKED EXAMPLE

4   Calculate the value of K_a for methanoic acid. A solution of 0.010 mol dm^{-3} methanoic acid, HCOOH, has a pH of 2.90.

Step 1   Convert pH to [H$^+$].
$$[H^+] = 10^{-2.90}$$
$$= 1.26 \times 10^{-3} \text{ mol dm}^{-3}$$

Step 2   Write the equilibrium expression.
$$K_a = \frac{[H^+]^2}{[HA]} \quad \text{or} \quad K_a = \frac{[H^+]^2}{[HCOOH]}$$

Step 3   Enter the values into the expression and calculate the answer.
$$K_a = \frac{(1.26 \times 10^{-3})^2}{(0.010)}$$
$$= 1.59 \times 10^{-4} \text{ mol dm}^{-3}$$

5 a Calculate the value of K_a for the following acids:

   i $0.0200 \, mol \, dm^{-3}$ 2-aminobenzoic acid, which has a pH of 4.30

   ii $0.0500 \, mol \, dm^{-3}$ propanoic acid, which has a pH of 3.10

   iii $0.100 \, mol \, dm^{-3}$ 2-nitrophenol, which has a pH of 4.10

   b Calculate pK_a values for each of the acids in part **a**.

Calculating the pH of a weak acid

We can calculate the pH value (or $[H^+]$) of a weak acid if we know:

- the concentration of the acid
- the value of K_a for the acid.

Again, we make the same assumptions about the concentration of hydrogen ions produced by the ionisation of water and the equilibrium concentration of the weak acid. The value of the pH calculated will not be significantly affected by these factors unless we require great accuracy (for example calculating pH to the 3rd decimal place).

Worked example 5 shows how to calculate pH from the value of K_a and concentration of the weak acid.

WORKED EXAMPLE

5 Calculate the pH of $0.100 \, mol \, dm^{-3}$ ethanoic acid, CH_3COOH.

   ($K_a = 1.74 \times 10^{-5} \, mol \, dm^{-3}$)

   Step 1 Write the equilibrium expression for the reaction.

   $$CH_3COOH(aq) \rightleftharpoons H^+(aq) + CH_3COO^-(aq)$$

   $$K_a = \frac{[H^+]^2}{[HA]} \quad \text{or} \quad K_a = \frac{[H^+]^2}{[CH_3COOH]}$$

   Step 2 Enter the values into the expression.

   $$1.74 \times 10^{-5} = \frac{[H^+]^2}{(0.100)}$$

   Step 3 Rearrange the equation.

   $$[H^+]^2 = 1.74 \times 10^{-5} \times 0.100 = 1.74 \times 10^{-6}$$

   Step 4 Take the square root.

   $$[H^+] = \sqrt{1.74 \times 10^{-6}} = 1.32 \times 10^{-3} \, mol \, dm^{-3}$$

   Step 5 Calculate pH.

   $$pH = -\log_{10}[H^+]$$
   $$= -\log_{10}(1.32 \times 10^{-3})$$
   $$= 2.88 \text{ (to 3 significant figures)}$$

6 Use the data from Table 21.2 to work out the pH values of the following solutions:

   a $0.0200 \, mol \, dm^{-3}$ aqueous benzoic acid

   b $0.0100 \, mol \, dm^{-3}$ hydrated aluminium ions

   c $0.100 \, mol \, dm^{-3}$ aqueous methanoic acid.

Indicators and acid–base titrations

In Chapter 1 (page 15) we learnt that indicators are used to detect the end-point in acid–alkali titrations. You may also have used indicators such as litmus to test whether a substance is acidic or alkaline. In this section we shall look more closely at how specific indicators are used in titrations involving strong and weak acids and bases.

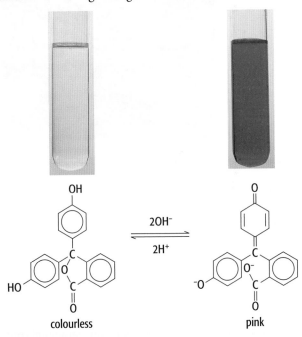

colourless   pink

Figure 21.4 The colour change in phenolphthalein is due to small differences in the structure of its molecule when hydrogen ions or hydroxide ions are added.

Introducing indicators

An **acid–base indicator** is a dye or mixture of dyes that changes colour over a specific pH range. In simple terms, many indicators can be considered as weak acids in which the acid (HIn) and its conjugate base (In^-) have different colours.

$$HIn \rightleftharpoons H^+ + In^-$$

un-ionised indicator colour A   conjugate base colour B

309

- Adding an acid to this indicator solution shifts the position of equilibrium to the left. There are now more molecules of colour A.
- Adding an alkali shifts the position of equilibrium to the right. There are now more ions of colour B.
- The colour of the indicator depends on the relative concentrations of HIn and In⁻. The colour of the indicator during a titration depends on the concentration of H^+ ions present.

Indicators usually change colour over a pH range of between 1 and 2 pH units. In the middle of the range there is a recognisable end-point where the indicator has a colour in between the two extremes of colour. For example, bromothymol blue is yellow in acidic solution and blue in alkaline solution. The colour change takes place between pH 6.0 and pH 7.6. The end-point, which is a greyish-green colour, occurs when the pH is 7.0.

The pH at which indicators begin to change colour varies considerably. Table 21.3 shows the colours, ranges and end-points of some indicators.

Figure 21.5 The red petals of pelargonium (geranium) contain the dye pelargonidin. Hydrogen ions or hydroxide ions can make small changes in its molecular structure to produce different colours.

Name of dye	Colour at lower pH	pH range	End-point	Colour at higher pH
methyl violet	yellow	0.0–1.6	0.8	blue
methyl yellow	red	2.9–4.0	3.5	yellow
methyl orange	red	3.2–4.4	3.7	yellow
bromophenol blue	yellow	2.8–4.6	4.0	blue
bromocresol green	yellow	3.8–5.4	4.7	blue
methyl red	red	4.2–6.3	5.1	yellow
bromothymol blue	yellow	6.0–7.6	7.0	blue
phenolphthalein	colourless	8.2–10.0	9.3	pink/violet
alizarin yellow	yellow	10.1–13.0	12.5	orange/red

Table 21.3 Some of the chemical indicators used to monitor pH, with their pH ranges of use and pH of end-point.

In Chapter 1 (page 15) we described the titration procedure for determining the amount of acid required to neutralise an alkali. Figure 21.6 shows the apparatus used to follow the changes in pH when a base is titrated with an acid.

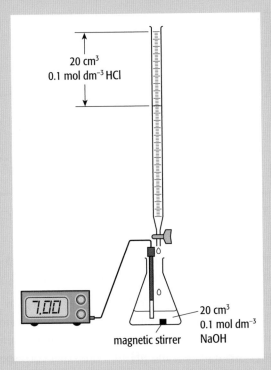

Figure 21.6 Measuring the pH change during the titration of sodium hydroxide with hydrochloric acid.

The procedure is:
- set up the apparatus with the pH electrode connected to the computer via a data logger
- switch on the magnetic stirrer
- deliver the acid at a constant slow rate from the burette into the alkali in the flask
- stop when the pH has reached a nearly constant low value.

The pH of the reaction mixture can also be monitored manually. You record the pH after fixed volumes of acid have been added to the flask.

The graphs recorded on the computer or drawn by hand show how pH varies with the volume of acid added. The shapes of these graphs are characteristic and depend on whether the acid and base used in the titration are strong or weak.

Strong acids with strong bases

Figure 21.7 shows how the pH changes when $0.100 \, mol \, dm^{-3}$ sodium hydroxide (a strong base) is titrated with $0.100 \, mol \, dm^{-3}$ hydrochloric acid (a strong acid) in the presence of bromothymol blue indicator.

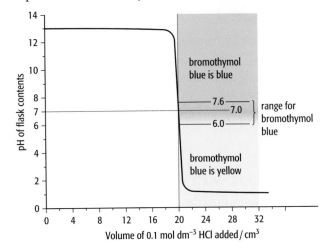

Figure 21.7 A strong acid–strong base titration with bromothymol blue as indicator.

These results show:
- a sharp fall in the graph line between pH 10.5 and pH 3.5; in this region tiny additions of H^+ ions result in a rapid change in pH
- a midpoint of the steep slope at pH 7
- the midpoint of the sharp fall corresponds to the point at which the H^+ ions in the acid have exactly reacted with the OH^- ions in the alkali; this is the end-point of the titration
- that bromothymol blue indicator changed from blue to yellow over the range 7.6 to 6.0 where the slope is steepest.

Because there is a sharp change in pH over the region pH 3.5 to 10.5 we can use other indicators that change colour within this region. For example, phenolphthalein changes colour in the pH range 8.2 to 10.0 (Figure 21.8).

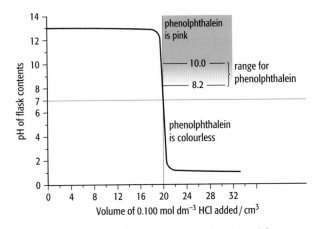

Figure 21.8 A strong acid–strong base titration with phenolphthalein as indicator.

311

Because the sharp pH change occurs over such a wide pH range, there are many indicators that can be used to determine the end-point of the reaction of a strong acid with a strong base.

> **QUESTION**
>
> **7** Use Table 21.3 to identify:
>
> **a** those indicators which could be used for a strong acid–strong base titration like the one in Figure 21.8.
>
> **b** those indicators that could not be used.

Strong acids with weak bases

Figure 21.9 shows how the pH changes when $0.100 \, mol \, dm^{-3}$ aqueous ammonia (a weak base) is titrated with $0.100 \, mol \, dm^{-3}$ nitric acid (a strong acid).

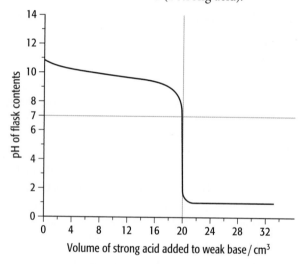

Figure 21.9 A typical strong acid–weak base titration.

These results show:

- a sharp fall in the graph line between pH 7.5 and pH 3.5
- that the midpoint of the steep slope is at about pH 5.

Because there is a sharp change in pH over the region 3.5 to 7.5 we can use methyl red as an indicator for this titration. This is because methyl red changes colour between pH 4.2 and pH 6.3, values that correspond with the region of sharpest pH change. Phenolphthalein would not be a suitable indicator to use because it only changes colour in alkaline regions (pH 8.2–10) that do not correspond to the sharp pH change. The phenolphthalein would change colour only gradually as more and more acid is added, instead of changing suddenly on the addition of a single drop at the end-point.

Weak acids with strong bases

Figure 21.10 shows how the pH changes when $0.100 \, mol \, dm^{-3}$ aqueous sodium hydroxide (a strong base) is titrated with $0.100 \, mol \, dm^{-3}$ benzoic acid (a weak acid).

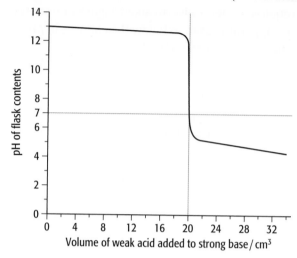

Figure 21.10 A typical weak acid–strong base titration.

These results show:

- a sharp fall in the graph line between pH 11 and pH 7.5
- that the midpoint of the steep slope is at about pH 9.

Because there is a sharp change in pH over the region pH 7.5 to 11 we can use phenolphthalein as an indicator for this titration. This is because phenolphthalein changes colour between pH 8.2 and pH 10, values that correspond with the region of sharpest pH change. Methyl orange would not be a suitable indicator to use because it only changes colour in acidic regions that do not correspond to the sharp pH change.

Weak acids with weak bases

Figure 21.11 shows how the pH changes when $0.100 \, mol \, dm^{-3}$ aqueous ammonia (a weak base) is titrated with $0.100 \, mol \, dm^{-3}$ aqueous benzoic acid (a weak acid).

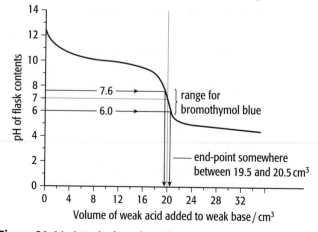

Figure 21.11 A typical weak acid–weak base titration.

These results show that there is no sharp fall in the graph line. No acid–base indicator is suitable to determine the end-point of this reaction. In the example shown bromothymol blue:

- starts changing colour when 19.50 cm^3 of acid have been added
- finishes changing colour when 20.50 cm^3 of acid have been added.

Such a gradual colour change on addition of acid is not acceptable when accuracy of reading the end-point to the nearest 0.05 cm^3 is required.

Buffer solutions

What is a buffer solution?

A **buffer solution** is a solution in which the pH does not change significantly when small amounts of acids or alkalis are added. A buffer solution is used to keep pH (almost) constant.

One type of buffer solution is a mixture of a weak acid and one of its salts. An example is an aqueous mixture of ethanoic acid and sodium ethanoate. Mixtures of ethanoic acid and sodium ethanoate in different proportions act as buffers between pH values of 4 and 7. We can understand how a buffer solution works by referring to the equilibria involved.

Ethanoic acid is a weak acid. So it stays mostly in the un-ionised form (CH_3COOH) and only gives rise to a low concentration of ethanoate ions in solution:

$$CH_3COOH(aq) \rightleftharpoons H^+(aq) + CH_3COO^-(aq)$$
ethanoic acid   ethanoate ion

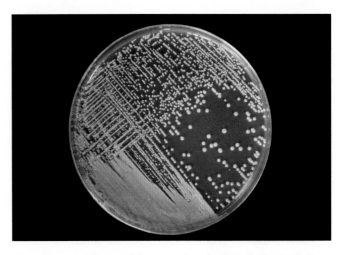

Figure 21.12 The pH of this agar plate for growing bacteria is kept constant by using a buffer solution. The buffer solution is incorporated in the agar jelly used to make the plate.

Sodium ethanoate is fully ionised in aqueous solution:

$$CH_3COONa(s) + aq \longrightarrow Na^+(aq) + CH_3COO^-(aq)$$
sodium ethanoate   ethanoate ion

The buffer solution contains relatively high concentrations of both CH_3COOH and CH_3COO^-. We say that there are reserve supplies of the acid (CH_3COOH) and its conjugate base (CH_3COO^-). The pH of a buffer solution depends on the ratio of the concentration of the acid and the concentration of its conjugate base. If this does not change very much, the pH changes very little.

In the buffer solution ethanoic acid molecules are in equilibrium with hydrogen ions and ethanoate ions:

$$CH_3COOH(aq) \rightleftharpoons H^+(aq) + CH_3COO^-(aq)$$
relatively high   relatively high
concentration   concentration
of ethanoic acid   of ethanoate ions

We can use this equation to explain how buffer solutions work.

An increase in hydrogen ion concentration would greatly lower the pH of water, but when H^+ ions are added to the buffer solution:

- addition of H^+ ions shifts the position of equilibrium to the left because H^+ ions combine with CH_3COO^- ions to form more CH_3COOH until equilibrium is re-established
- the large reserve supply of CH_3COO^- ensures that the concentration of CH_3COO^- ions in solution does not change significantly
- the large reserve supply of CH_3COOH ensures that the concentration of CH_3COOH molecules in solution does not change significantly
- so the pH does not change significantly.

313

An increase in hydroxide ion concentration would greatly increase the pH of water, but when OH$^-$ ions are added to the buffer solution:

- the added OH$^-$ ions combine with H$^+$ ions to form water
- this reduces the H$^+$ ion concentration
- the position of equilibrium shifts to the right
- so CH$_3$COOH molecules ionise to form more H$^+$ and CH$_3$COO$^-$ ions until equilibrium is re-established
- the large reserve supply of CH$_3$COOH ensures that the concentration of CH$_3$COOH molecules in solution does not change significantly
- the large reserve supply of CH$_3$COO$^-$ ensures that the concentration of CH$_3$COO$^-$ ions in solution does not change significantly
- so the pH does not change significantly.

In unpolluted regions of the Earth, rainwater has a pH of 5.7. This is because carbon dioxide dissolves in the rainwater to form a dilute solution of the weak acid carbonic acid, H$_2$CO$_3$. This acid and its conjugate base, HCO$_3^-$, act as a buffer solution. It minimises changes in pH if very small amounts of acid or alkali are added to the rainwater. But in regions where there is pollution caused by the emission of acidic oxides of nitrogen and sulfur, the pH of the rainwater falls to around 4. The rainwater can no longer act as a buffer because the concentrations of the H$_2$CO$_3$ and HCO$_3^-$ are not high enough to cope with the large amounts of acidic pollution involved.

No buffer solution can cope with the excessive addition of acids or alkalis. If very large amounts of acid or alkali are added, the pH will change significantly.

Buffer solutions that resist changes in pH in alkaline regions are usually a mixture of a weak base and its conjugate acid. An example is a mixture of aqueous ammonia with ammonium chloride.

Aqueous ammonia is a weak base, so there is only a low concentration of ammonium ions in ammonia solution:

$$NH_3(aq) + H_2O(l) \rightleftharpoons NH_4^+(aq) + OH^-(aq)$$

Ammonium chloride is fully ionised in aqueous solution. This supplies the reserve supplies of the conjugate acid, NH$_4^+$.

$$NH_4Cl(aq) \longrightarrow NH_4^+(aq) + Cl^-(aq)$$

QUESTION

9   A mixture of 0.500 mol dm^{-3} aqueous ammonia and 0.500 mol dm^{-3} ammonium chloride acts as a buffer solution.

   a   Explain how this buffer solution minimises changes in pH on addition of

   i   dilute hydrochloric acid

   ii   dilute sodium hydroxide.

   b   Explain why dilute aqueous ammonia alone will not act as a buffer solution.

Calculating the pH of a buffer solution

We can calculate the pH of a buffer solution if we know:

- the K_a of the weak acid
- the equilibrium concentration of the weak acid and its conjugate base (salt).

To do the calculation we use the equilibrium expression for the particular reaction.

WORKED EXAMPLE

6   Calculate the pH of a buffer solution containing 0.600 mol dm^{-3} propanoic acid and 0.800 mol dm^{-3} sodium propanoate.
   (K_a propanoic acid = 1.35×10^{-5} mol dm^{-3})

   Step 1   Write the equilibrium expression.

   $$K_a = \frac{[H^+][C_2H_5COO^-]}{[C_2H_5COOH]}$$

   Step 2   Rearrange the equilibrium expression to make [H$^+$] the subject.

   $$[H^+] = \frac{K_a \times [C_2H_5COOH]}{[C_2H_5COO^-]}$$

   Note that in this expression, the ratio determining [H$^+$], and hence pH, is the ratio of the concentration of the acid to the salt (conjugate base).

   Step 3   Substitute the data given.

   $$[H^+] = 1.35 \times 10^{-5} \times \frac{(0.600)}{0.800}$$

   $$= 1.01 \times 10^{-5} \text{ mol dm}^{-3}$$

   Step 4   Calculate the pH.

   $$pH = -\log_{10}[H^+]$$

   $$= -\log_{10}(1.01 \times 10^{-5})$$

   $$= -(-4.99)$$

   $$= 4.99$$

We can make the numbers easier to deal with in calculations involving buffer solutions by using logarithms throughout. So instead of using the expression:

$$[H^+] = K_a \times \frac{[acid]}{[salt]}$$

we can use the expression:

$$pH = pK_a + \log_{10}\left(\frac{[salt]}{[acid]}\right)$$

QUESTION

10 a Calculate the pH of the following buffer solutions:

    i $0.0500\,\text{mol}\,\text{dm}^{-3}$ methanoic acid and $0.100\,\text{mol}\,\text{dm}^{-3}$ sodium methanoate.

         (K_a of methanoic acid = $1.60 \times 10^{-4}\,\text{mol}\,\text{dm}^{-3}$)

    ii $0.0100\,\text{mol}\,\text{dm}^{-3}$ benzoic acid and $0.0400\,\text{mol}\,\text{dm}^{-3}$ sodium benzoate.

         (K_a of benzoic acid = $6.3 \times 10^{-5}\,\text{mol}\,\text{dm}^{-3}$)

b How many moles of sodium ethanoate must be added to $1.00\,\text{dm}^3$ of $0.100\,\text{mol}\,\text{dm}^{-3}$ ethanoic acid to produce a buffer solution of pH 4.90?

     (K_a of ethanoic acid = $1.74 \times 10^{-5}\,\text{mol}\,\text{dm}^{-3}$)

     Hint: first find the hydrogen ion concentration, then rearrange the equilibrium expression to make [(sodium) ethanoate] the subject of the expression.

Uses of buffer solutions

Buffer solutions play an important part in many industrial processes, including electroplating, the manufacture of dyes and in the treatment of leather. They are also used to make sure that pH meters record the correct pH.

Many animals depend on buffers to keep a constant pH in various parts of their bodies. In humans, the pH of the blood is kept between 7.35 and 7.45 by a number of different buffers in the blood:

- hydrogencarbonate ions, HCO_3^-
- haemoglobin and plasma proteins
- dihydrogenphosphate ($H_2PO_4^-$) and hydrogenphosphate (HPO_4^{2-}) ions.

The cells in our body produce carbon dioxide as a product of aerobic respiration (the oxidation of glucose to provide energy). Carbon dioxide combines with water in the blood to form a solution containing hydrogen ions.

$$CO_2(aq) + H_2O(aq) \rightleftharpoons H^+(aq) + HCO_3^-(aq)$$

$$\text{hydrogencarbonate ion}$$

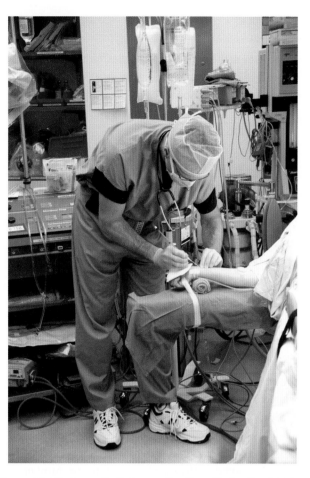

Figure 21.13 Anaesthetists monitor the pH of patients' blood.

This reaction is catalysed by the enzyme carbonic anhydrase. When the blood passes through the small blood vessels around our lungs hydrogencarbonate ions are rapidly converted to carbon dioxide and water. The carbon dioxide escapes into the lungs.

The production of H^+ ions, if left unchecked, would lower the pH of the blood and cause 'acidosis'. This may disrupt some body functions and eventually lead to coma. The equilibrium between carbon dioxide and hydrogencarbonate is the most important buffering system in the blood.

If the H^+ ion concentration increases:

- the position of this equilibrium shifts to the left
- H^+ ions combine with HCO_3^- ions to form carbon dioxide and water until equilibrium is restored
- this reduces the concentration of hydrogen ions in the blood and helps keep the pH constant.

If the H^+ ion concentration decreases:

- the position of this equilibrium shifts to the right
- some carbon dioxide and water combine to form H^+ and HCO_3^- ions until equilibrium is restored
- this increases the concentration of hydrogen ions in the blood and helps keep the pH constant.

QUESTION

11 a One of the buffers in blood plasma is a mixture of dihydrogenphosphate ions ($H_2PO_4^-$) and hydrogenphosphate (HPO_4^{2-}) ions.

    i Identify the conjugate acid and base in this buffer.

    ii Write a balanced equation for the equilibrium between these two ions.

b Some proteins in the blood can act as buffers. The equation below shows a simplified equilibrium equation for this reaction. (Pr = protein)

$$HPr \rightleftharpoons H^+ + Pr^-$$

Explain how this system can act as a buffer to prevent the blood getting too acidic.

Equilibrium and solubility

In Chapter 4 (page 66) we learnt that most ionic compounds dissolve in water and in Chapter 19 (page 265) we related solubility to enthalpy change of solution. Some ionic compounds, however, are insoluble or only slightly soluble in water. But even 'insoluble' ionic compounds may dissolve to a very small extent in water. Solubility is generally quoted as the number of grams or number of moles of compound needed to saturate 100 g or 1 kg of water at a given temperature. We say that a solution is saturated when no more solute dissolves in it.

- Sodium chloride is regarded as a soluble salt: a saturated solution contains 36 g per 100 g of water.
- Lead(II) chloride is regarded as an insoluble salt: a saturated solution contains 0.99 g per 100 g of water.

Solubility product

An equilibrium is established when an undissolved ionic compound is in contact with a saturated solution of its ions. The ions move from the solid to the saturated solution at the same rate as they move from the solution to the solid (Figure 21.14).

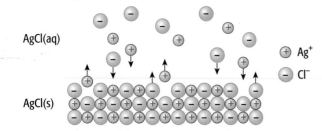

AgCl(aq)

AgCl(s)

⊕ Ag^+
⊖ Cl^-

Figure 21.14 An equilibrium is established between solid silver chloride and its saturated solution. The water molecules are not shown.

When solid silver chloride dissolves it is in contact with saturated silver chloride solution and the following equilibrium is set up:

$$AgCl(s) \rightleftharpoons Ag^+(aq) + Cl^-(aq)$$

The equilibrium expression relating to this equation is:

$$K_c = \frac{[Ag^+(aq)][Cl^-(aq)]}{[AgCl(s)]}$$

For any solid, the concentration of the solid phase remains constant and can be combined with the value of K_c.

So we can write this equilibrium expression as:

$$K_{sp} = [Ag^+(aq)][Cl^-(aq)]$$

K_{sp} is called the **solubility product**. Values are quoted at 298 K.

Solubility product is the product of the concentrations of each ion in a saturated solution of a sparingly soluble salt at 298 K, raised to the power of their relative concentrations.

$$K_{sp} = [C^{y+}(aq)]^a[A^{x-}(aq)]^b$$

where a is the number of C^{y+} cations in one formula unit of the compound and b is the number of A^{x-} anions in one formula unit of the compound

So for Fe_2S_3 (which contains Fe^{3+} ions and S^{2-} ions) the equilibrium is:

$$Fe_2S_3(s) \rightleftharpoons 2Fe^{3+}(aq) + 3S^{2-}(aq)$$

and the equilibrium expression is:

$$K_{sp} = [Fe^{3+}(aq)]^2[S^{2-}(aq)]^3$$

The idea of solubility product only applies to ionic compounds that are only slightly soluble.

The units of solubility product depend on the number of each type of ion present in solution. You can work the units out in the same way as for general equilibrium expressions (see page 123), but you don't have to do any cancelling. For example, for the expression:

$$
\begin{aligned}
K_{sp} &= [Mg^{2+}(aq)] \times [OH^-(aq)]^2 \\
&= mol\,dm^{-3} \times (mol\,dm^{-3})^2 \\
&= mol^3\,dm^{-9}
\end{aligned}
$$

The idea of solubility product is only useful for sparingly soluble salts. The smaller the value of K_{sp} the lower is the solubility of the salt. Some values of K_{sp} are given in Table 21.4.

Compound	$K_{sp}/(\text{mol dm}^{-3})^{x+y}$
AgCl	1.8×10^{-10}
Al(OH)$_3$	1.0×10^{-32}
BaCO$_3$	5.5×10^{-10}
BaSO$_4$	1.0×10^{-10}
CaCO$_3$	5.0×10^{-9}
CoS	2.0×10^{-26}
CuS	6.3×10^{-36}
Fe(OH)$_2$	7.9×10^{-16}
Fe$_2$S$_3$	1.0×10^{-88}
HgI$_2$	2.5×10^{-26}
Mn(OH)$_2$	1.0×10^{-11}
PbCl$_2$	1.6×10^{-5}
Sb$_2$S$_3$	1.7×10^{-93}
SnCO$_3$	1.0×10^{-9}
Zn(OH)$_2$	2.0×10^{-17}
ZnS	1.6×10^{-23}

Table 21.4 Some values of solubility product at 298 K.

QUESTION

12 a Write equilibrium expressions for the solubility products of the following:
  i Fe(OH)$_2$
  ii Fe$_2$S$_3$
  iii Al(OH)$_3$
 b State the units of solubility product for each of the compounds in part **a**.

Solubility product calculations

You may be asked to calculate the solubility product of a compound from its solubility, or you may be asked to calculate the solubility of a compound from its solubility product. An example of each of these types of calculation is shown next.

WORKED EXAMPLES

7 Calculating solubility product from solubility.

A saturated solution of magnesium fluoride, MgF$_2$, has a solubility of 1.22×10^{-3} mol dm^{-3}. Calculate the solubility product of magnesium fluoride.

Step 1 Write down the equilibrium equation.

$MgF_2(s) \rightleftharpoons Mg^{2+}(aq) + 2F^-(aq)$

Step 2 Calculate the concentration of each ion in solution.

When 1.22×10^{-3} mol dissolves to form 1 dm^3 of solution the concentration of each ion is:
$[Mg^{2+}] = 1.22 \times 10^{-3}$ mol dm^{-3}
$[F^-] = 2 \times 1.22 \times 10^{-3}$ mol dm$^{-3} = 2.44 \times 10^{-3}$ mol dm^{-3}

(The concentration of F$^-$ is $2 \times 1.22 \times 10^{-3}$ mol dm^{-3} because each formula unit contains $2 \times$ F$^-$ ions.)

Step 3 Write down the equilibrium expression.
$K_{sp} = [Mg^{2+}][F^-]^2$

Step 4 Substitute the values.
$K_{sp} = (1.22 \times 10^{-3}) \times (2.44 \times 10^{-3})^2$
$= 7.26 \times 10^{-9}$

Step 5 Add the correct units.
$(\text{mol dm}^{-3}) \times (\text{mol dm}^{-3})^2 = \text{mol}^3 \text{dm}^{-9}$
Answer $= 7.26 \times 10^{-9}$ mol^3 dm^{-9}

8 Calculating solubility from solubility product
Calculate the solubility of copper(II) sulfide in mol dm^{-3}.
(K_{sp} for CuS $= 6.3 \times 10^{-36}$ mol^2 dm^{-6})

Step 1 Write down the equilibrium equation.
$CuS(s) \rightleftharpoons Cu^{2+}(aq) + S^{2-}(aq)$

Step 2 Write the equilibrium expression in terms of one ion only.
From the equilibrium equation $[Cu^{2+}] = [S^{2-}]$
So $K_{sp} = [Cu^{2+}][S^{2-}]$ becomes $K_{sp} = [Cu^{2+}]^2$

Step 3 Substitute the value of K_{sp}.
$(6.3 \times 10^{-36}) = [Cu^{2+}]^2$

Step 4 Calculate the concentration.
In this case we take the square root of K_{sp}.
$[Cu^{2+}] = \sqrt{K_{sp}}$
$[Cu^{2+}] = \sqrt{6.3 \times 10^{-36}} = 2.5 \times 10^{-18}$ mol dm^{-3}

QUESTION

13 a Calculate the solubility product of the following solutions:

  i a saturated aqueous solution of cadmium sulfide, CdS (solubility = 1.46×10^{-11} mol dm^{-3})

  ii a saturated aqueous solution of calcium fluoride, CaF$_2$, containing 0.0168 g dm^{-3} CaF$_2$

b Calculate the solubility in mol dm^{-3} of zinc sulfide, ZnS.
(K_{sp} = 1.6×10^{-23} mol^2 dm^{-6})

c Calculate the solubility of silver carbonate, Ag$_2$CO$_3$.
(K_{sp} = 6.3×10^{-12} mol^3 dm^{-9})

Hint: you have to divide by 4 then take the cube root – can you see why? You should have a cube root button on your calculator ($\sqrt[3]{\ }$).

Predicting precipitation

The solubility product can be used to predict whether precipitation will occur when two solutions are mixed. For example: will we get a precipitate when we mix a solution of barium chloride, BaCl$_2$, with a very dilute solution of sodium carbonate?

Both barium chloride and sodium carbonate are soluble salts, but barium carbonate is relatively insoluble. We must consider the equilibrium for the insoluble salt dissolving in water:

$$BaCO_3(s) \rightleftharpoons Ba^{2+}(aq) + CO_3^{2-}(aq)$$

The solubility product is given by:

$$K_{sp} = [Ba^{2+}][CO_3^{2-}] = 5.5 \times 10^{-10} \text{ mol}^2 \text{ dm}^{-6}$$

If $[Ba^{2+}][CO_3^{2-}]$ is greater than 5.5×10^{-10} mol^2 dm^{-6} a precipitate will form.

If $[Ba^{2+}][CO_3^{2-}]$ is less than 5.5×10^{-10} mol^2 dm^{-6} no precipitate will form.

WORKED EXAMPLE

9 Will a precipitate form if we mix equal volumes of solutions of 1.00×10^{-4} mol dm^{-3} Na$_2$CO$_3$ and 5.00×10^{-5} mol dm^{-3} BaCl$_2$?

  ◻ $[Ba^{2+}] = 2.50 \times 10^{-5}$ mol dm^{-3}

  ◻ $[CO_3^{2-}] = 5.00 \times 10^{-5}$ mol dm^{-3}

$[Ba^{2+}][CO_3^{2-}] = (2.50 \times 10^{-5}) \times (5.00 \times 10^{-5})$
$= 1.25 \times 10^{-9}$ mol^2 dm^{-6}

This value is greater than the solubility product, so a precipitate of barium carbonate forms.

Figure 21.15 The shell of this nautilus is composed mainly of calcium carbonate. The nautilus adjusts conditions so shell material is formed when the concentration of calcium ions and carbonate ions in seawater are high enough to precipitate calcium carbonate.

The common ion effect

The **common ion effect** is the reduction in the solubility of a dissolved salt achieved by adding a solution of a compound which has an ion in common with the dissolved salt. This often results in precipitation.

An example of the common ion effect can be seen when we add a solution of sodium chloride to a saturated solution of silver chloride and silver chloride precipitates. Why is this?

In a saturated solution of silver chloride in water, we have the following equilibrium:

$$AgCl(s) \rightleftharpoons Ag^+(aq) + Cl^-(aq)$$

We now add a solution of sodium chloride:

- the chloride ion is common to both sodium chloride and silver chloride
- the added chloride ions shift the position of equilibrium to the left
- silver chloride is precipitated.

The addition of the common ion, Cl$^-$, has reduced the solubility of the silver chloride because its solubility product has been exceeded. When $[Ag^+][Cl^-]$ is greater than the K_{sp} for silver chloride a precipitate will form.

The solubility of an ionic compound in aqueous solution containing a common ion is less than its solubility in water.

For example, the solubility of barium sulfate, $BaSO_4$, in water is $1.0 \times 10^{-5}\,mol\,dm^{-3}$ and the solubility of barium sulfate in $0.100\,mol\,dm^{-3}$ sulfuric acid, H_2SO_4, is only $1.0 \times 10^{-9}\,mol\,dm^{-3}$.

We can explain the lower solubility in sulfuric acid by referring to the solubility product of barium sulfate:

$$K_{sp} = [Ba^{2+}][SO_4{}^{2-}] = 1.0 \times 10^{-10}\,mol^2\,dm^{-6}$$

If we ignore the very small amount of $SO_4{}^{2-}(aq)$ from the barium sulfate then $[SO_4{}^{2-}]$ is $0.1\,mol\,dm^{-3}$ (from the sulfuric acid). This gives:

$$1.0 \times 10^{-10} = [Ba^{2+}] \times [0.1]$$

$$[Ba^{2+}] = 1.0 \times 10^{-9}\,mol\,dm^{-3}$$

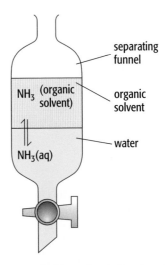

Figure 21.16 Ammonia (the solute) dissolves in both solvents, water and the organic solvent. A state of dynamic equilibrium is established.

ammonia molecules are moving from the aqueous layer to the organic layer at the same rate as they are moving from the organic layer to the aqueous layer:

$$NH_3(aq) \rightleftharpoons NH_3(\text{organic solvent})$$

We can calculate a value for the equilibrium constant (see page 123). We call this the **partition coefficient** (K_{pc}). The partition coefficient is the equilibrium constant that relates the concentration of a solute partitioned between two immiscible solvents at a particular temperature.

319

> ### QUESTION
>
> **14 a** Thallium(I) chloride is a salt that is sparingly soluble in water. When hydrochloric acid is added to a saturated solution of thallium(I) chloride, a precipitate is formed. Explain why a precipitate is formed.
>
> **b** Calcium sulfate is a sparingly soluble salt that can be made by mixing solutions containing calcium and sulfate ions. A $0.001\,00\,mol\,dm^{-3}$ solution of aqueous calcium chloride, $CaCl_2$, is mixed with an equal volume of $0.001\,00\,mol\,dm^{-3}$ solution of aqueous sodium sulfate, Na_2SO_4.
>
>   **i** Calculate the concentration of calcium and sulfate ions when equal volumes of these solutions of calcium chloride and sodium sulfate are mixed.
>
>   **ii** Will a precipitate of calcium sulfate form? (K_{sp} of calcium sulfate = $2.0 \times 10^{-5}\,mol^2\,dm^{-6}$)

Partition coefficients

The principle of partition of a **solute** between two solvents helps us to understand more fully how the components in a mixture are separated in chromatography (see page 434). Let us consider ammonia dissolved in two immiscible solvents, i.e. solvents that do not dissolve in each other and so form two separate layers (Figure 21.16).

A separating funnel is shaken with the organic solvent and an aqueous solution of ammonia. The ammonia is soluble in both solvents so when the mixture is left to settle, a dynamic equilibrium is established. At this point,

> ### WORKED EXAMPLE
>
> **10** $100\,cm^3$ of a $0.100\,mol\,dm^{-3}$ solution of ammonia in water at $20\,°C$ was shaken with $50\,cm^3$ of an organic solvent and left in a separating funnel for equilibrium to be established.
>
> A $20.0\,cm^3$ portion of the aqueous layer was run off and titrated against $0.200\,mol\,dm^{-3}$ dilute hydrochloric acid. The end-point was found to be $9.40\,cm^3$ of acid.
>
> What is the partition coefficient of ammonia between these two solvents at $20\,°C$?
>
> The alkaline ammonia solution is neutralised by dilute hydrochloric acid:
>
> $$NH_3(aq) + HCl(aq) \longrightarrow NH_4Cl(aq)$$
>
> 1 mole of ammonia reacts with 1 mole of the acid.
>
> In the titration we used:
>
> $$\frac{9.40}{1000} \times 0.200\,\text{moles of HCl}$$
>
> $$= 1.88 \times 10^{-3}\,\text{moles}$$

WORKED EXAMPLE (CONTINUED)

This reacts with ammonia in the ratio 1:1 so there must be 1.88×10^{-3} moles of NH_3 in the $20.0\,cm^3$ portion titrated.

Therefore in the $100\,cm^3$ aqueous layer there are

$1.88 \times 10^{-3} \times \dfrac{100}{20.0}\,mol$

$= 9.40 \times 10^{-3}\,mol$

The number of moles of ammonia in the organic layer must be equal to the initial number of moles of ammonia minus the amount left in the aqueous layer at equilibrium

initial number of moles of ammonia

$= 0.100 \times \dfrac{100}{1000}$

$= 0.0100\,mol$

final number of moles of ammonia in organic layer

$= 0.0100 - 9.40 \times 10^{-3}\,mol$

$= 6.00 \times 10^{-4}\,mol$

Now we need to change the numbers of moles of ammonia in each layer into concentrations (i.e. the number of moles in $1000\,cm^3$ or $1\,dm^3$) to substitute into the equilibrium expression for the partition coefficient, K_{pc}.

The concentration of ammonia in $100\,cm^3$ of the aqueous layer

$= 9.40 \times 10^{-3} \times \dfrac{1000}{100}$

$= 0.094\,mol\,dm^{-3}$

The concentration of ammonia in $50\,cm^3$ of the organic solvent

$= 6.00 \times 10^{-4} \times \dfrac{1000}{50}$

$= 0.012\,mol\,dm^{-3}$

The expression for the partition coefficient, K_{pc} is:

$K_{pc} = \dfrac{[NH_3(\text{organic solvent})]}{[NH_3(aq)]} = \dfrac{0.012}{0.094}$

$= 0.128\,(\text{no units})$

This value is less than 1, which shows us that ammonia is more soluble in water than in the organic solvent.

In general for a solute X partitioned between two solvents A and B, the equilibrium expression is given by

$K_{pc} = \dfrac{[X(\text{solvent A})]}{[X(\text{solvent B})]}$

In paper chromatography the different partition coefficients of the components in a mixture correspond to their relative solubilities in the two solvents. In the worked example above the relative solubility of ammonia in water is greater than in the organic solvent. In paper chromatography the mobile phase is the solvent chosen. The other solvent is the water trapped in the paper's structure, which is the stationary phase. Figure 21.17 shows solute molecules partitioned between the mobile phase and a stationary liquid phase on a solid support.

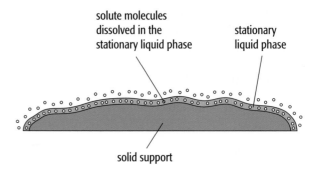

Figure 21.17 Partition chromatography. The mobile phase moves over the stationary liquid phase, carrying solute particles with it. The filter paper is the solid support in paper chromatography.

The solutes in the mixture being separated are partitioned to different extents between the solvents in the mobile and stationary phases. The greater the relative solubility in the mobile phase, the faster the rate of movement as the mobile phase passes over the stationary phase.

QUESTION

15 A solution of butanedioic acid (BDA) in ether contains $0.034\,mol$ of BDA in $20\,cm^3$ of ether. This solution is shaken with $50\,cm^3$ of water. The mass of BDA extracted into the water layer after shaking was $0.032\,mol$.

   a Calculate the concentration of BDA in the water layer after shaking.

   b Calculate the concentration of BDA in the ether layer after shaking.

   c Determine the value of the partition coefficient, K_{pc}.

Summary

- pH is a measure of the hydrogen ion concentration: $pH = -\log_{10}[H^+(aq)]$.

- K_a is the dissociation constant for an acid. It is the equilibrium constant for the dissociation of a weak acid, HA(aq):

$$A \rightleftharpoons H^+(aq) + A^-(aq)$$

- Acid strengths can be compared using pK_a values: $pK_a = -\log_{10}K_a$.

- A lower value of pK_a means greater acid strength.

- K_w is the ionic product for water:

$$K_w = [H^+(aq)][OH^-aq] = 1.00 \times 10^{-14}\,mol^2\,dm^{-6}$$
$$pK_w = -\log_{10}K_w$$

- For weak acids hydrogen ion concentration (and therefore pH) can be calculated from the equilibrium concentrations in the equilibrium expression:

$$K_a = \frac{[H^+(aq)][A^-aq]}{[HA(aq)]}$$

when the value of K_a is known.

- The pH value of a strong base can be calculated by using the expression $K_w = [H^+(aq)][OH^-aq]$.

- pH titration curves enable end-points for acid–base titrations to be found.

- The exact shape of a pH titration curve depends on the strengths of the acid and base used.

- pH titration curves can be used to suggest appropriate indicators for particular acid–base titrations.

- A buffer solution minimises pH changes on addition of a small amount of acid or base.

- A buffer solution is a mixture of a weak acid and its conjugate base.

- Buffer solutions control pH by maintaining a fairly constant ratio of weak acid and its conjugate base.

- The pH of a buffer solution can be calculated by using the equilibrium concentrations of the weak acid and its conjugate base and the K_a value of the weak acid.

- Buffer solutions have many uses. In our bodies, the HCO_3^- ion acts as a buffer, which prevents the blood from becoming too acidic.

- The solubility product, K_{sp}, is the equilibrium expression showing the equilibrium concentrations of the ions in a saturated solution of a sparingly soluble salt taking into account the relative number of each ion present.

- The addition of a common ion to a saturated solution of a sparingly soluble salt (e.g. adding a concentrated solution of (sodium) chloride to a saturated solution of silver chloride) causes precipitation of the sparingly soluble salt.

- The partition coefficient, K_{pc}, is the equilibrium constant which relates the concentration of a solute partitioned between two immiscible solvents at a particular temperature.

- The partition coefficient of a solute X between two solvents A and B is described by the equilibrium expression:

$$K_{pc} = \frac{[X(solvent\ A)]}{[X(solvent\ B)]}$$

End-of-chapter questions

You have to know how to calculate the pH of four different types of solution:
- ☐ a strong acid   ☐ a weak acid   ☐ a strong base   ☐ a buffer.

Each of these requires a different approach. Practise them until you always choose the correct method for each one.

1 a Write general expressions for the terms:

  i pH [1]

  ii K_w [1]

  iii K_a [1]

  b What is the pH of $0.00400\,mol\,dm^{-3}$ HCl(aq)? Show your working. [2]

  c What is the pH of $0.00400\,mol\,dm^{-3}$ butanoic acid(aq)? ($K_a = 1.51 \times 10^{-5}\,mol\,dm^{-3}$) [3]

  d $0.25\,mol$ of sodium hydroxide is dissolved in $2.00\,dm^3$ of water. Calculate the concentration and pH of the sodium hydroxide solution. ($K_w = 1.00 \times 10^{-14}\,mol^2\,dm^{-6}$) [3]

  Total = 11

2 a Sketch the graph of pH that would be obtained when $10.0\,cm^3$ of $0.200\,mol\,dm^{-3}$ HCl is titrated against $0.200\,mol\,dm^{-3}$ aqueous ammonia. [3]

  b Explain why methyl orange is a suitable indicator for this titration but phenolphthalein is not. [2]

  c Sketch the graph that would be obtained if $25.0\,cm^3$ of $0.200\,mol\,dm^{-3}$ sodium hydroxide is titrated against $0.100\,mol\,dm^{-3}$ ethanoic acid solution. [3]

  d Explain why phenolphthalein is a suitable indicator for this titration but methyl orange is not. [2]

  e Bromocresol green and bromothymol blue are indicators. Their pK_a values are: bromocresol green = 4.7 and bromothymol blue = 7.0. Would either of these indicators be suitable for the titration in part **a** or the titration in part **c**? Explain your answer. [4]

  Total = 14

3 a What is the pH of a solution containing $0.100\,mol\,dm^{-3}$ ethanoic acid and $0.100\,mol\,dm^{-3}$ sodium ethanoate? (K_a of $CH_3COOH = 1.74 \times 10^{-5}\,mol\,dm^{-3}$) [3]

  b How many moles of sodium ethanoate must be added to $2.00\,dm^3$ of $0.0100\,mol\,dm^{-3}$ ethanoic acid to produce a buffer solution of pH 5.40? [5]

  c Explain why the pH of a solution containing $0.100\,mol\,dm^{-3}$ ethanoic acid and $0.100\,mol\,dm^{-3}$ sodium ethanoate does not change significantly when a small amount of hydrochloric acid is added. [3]

  Total = 11

4 Copper(I) bromide, CuBr, is a sparingly soluble salt. ($K_{sp} = 3.2 \times 10^{-8}\,mol^2\,dm^{-6}$)

  a What do you understand by the terms:

  i **solubility product** [2]

  ii **common ion effect** [2]

  b Calculate the solubility of CuBr in:

  i pure water [2]

  ii an aqueous solution of $0.0100\,mol\,dm^{-3}$ sodium bromide. [1]

  iii Explain the difference in your answers to part **b, ii** and **iii**. [2]

  Total = 9

5 A buffer solution consists of 6.00 g of ethanoic acid (CH_3COOH) and 12.3 g of sodium ethanoate (CH_3COONa) in 200 cm³ of aqueous solution.
(A_r values: H = 1.0, C = 12.0, O = 16.0, Na = 23.0; K_a for $CH_3COOH = 1.74 \times 10^{-5}$ mol dm⁻³)

  a What is the concentration of ethanoic acid in the buffer? [2]

  b What is the concentration of sodium ethanoate in the buffer? [2]

  c Calculate the pH of the buffer solution. [2]

  d Using this solution as an example, explain why the pH of a buffer solution changes very little when small amounts of hydrogen ions or hydroxide ions are added to it. [3]

  e Explain how the carbon dioxide/hydrogencarbonate buffer helps control blood pH. [3]

                                                               Total = 12

6 A saturated solution of copper(I) sulfide, Cu_2S, contains 1.91×10^{-12} g of Cu_2S dissolved in 1 dm³ of water.
(A_r values: Cu = 63.5, S = 32.1)

  a Write an equilibrium expression for the solubility product of copper(I) sulfide. [1]

  b Calculate the value of the solubility product of copper(I) sulfide, stating the units. [5]

  c Copper(II) chromate has a solubility of 1.9×10^{-3} mol dm⁻³ in water. Copper(II) sulfate has a solubility of 1.4×10^{-1} mol dm⁻³ in water. What will you observe when 10 cm³ of an aqueous solution of 0.0100 mol dm⁻³ copper(II) sulfate is added to an equal volume of a saturated solution of copper(II) chromate. Explain your answer. [3]

                                                               Total = 9

7 **a** What is the pH of 0.25 mol dm⁻³ HCl(aq)? [1]

  b What is the pH of 0.0500 mol dm⁻³ sodium hydroxide? ($K_w = 1.00 \times 10^{-14}$ mol² dm⁻⁶) [2]

  c The graph shows how the pH changes when 0.100 mol dm⁻³ ethanoic acid is titrated with 0.100 mol dm⁻³ sodium hydroxide.

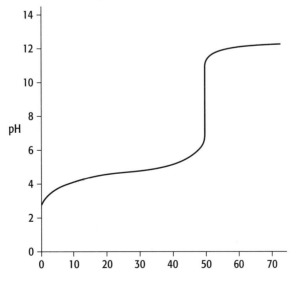

    i Explain why methyl orange (pK_a = 3.7) is not a suitable indicator to use for this titration. [1]

    ii Would phenolphthalein be a suitable indicator to use for this titration? Explain your answer. [1]

  d Propanoic acid is a weak acid. A 0.0500 mol dm⁻³ solution of propanoic acid has a pH of 3.1. Calculate the value of K_a for propanoic acid. Show all your working. [4]

                                                               Total = 9

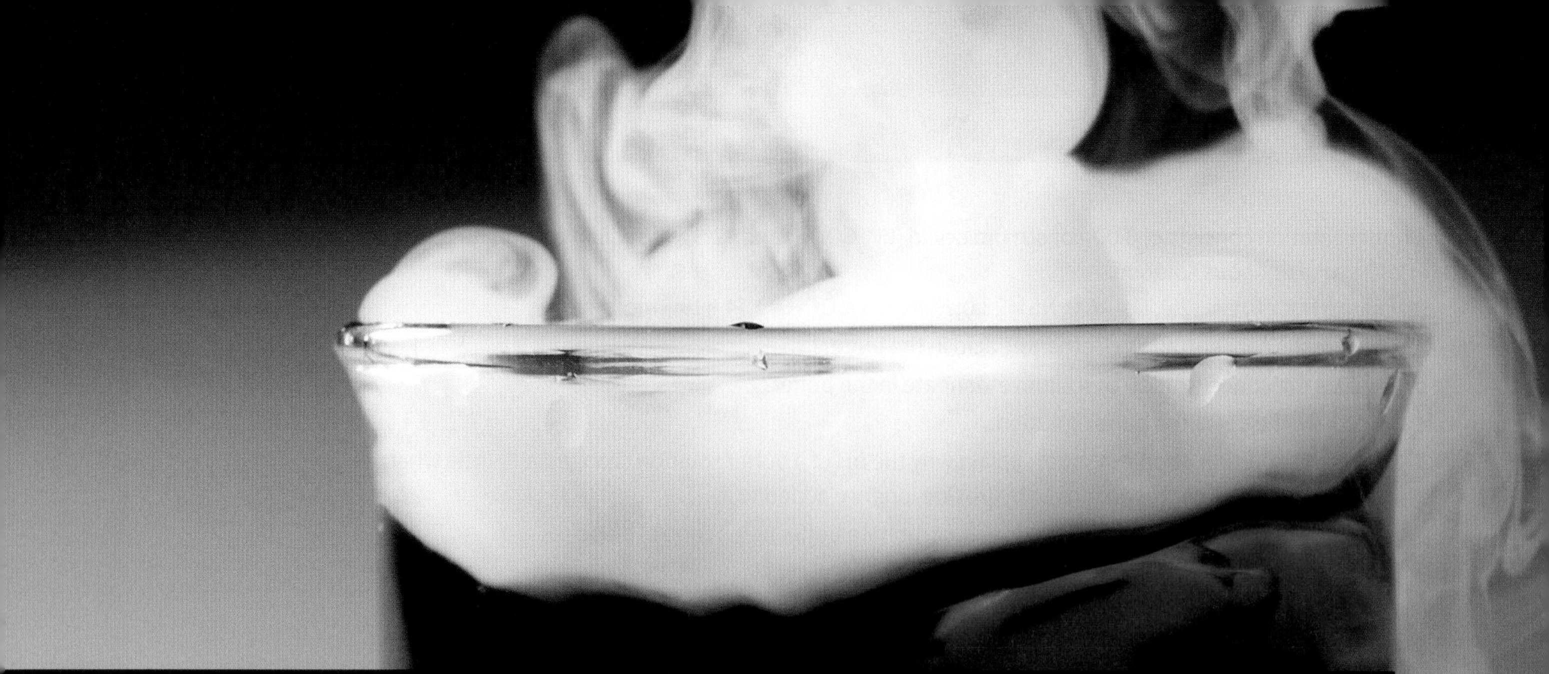

Chapter 22:
Reaction kinetics

Learning outcomes

You should be able to:

- explain and use the terms:
  - **rate equation**
  - **order of reaction**
  - **rate constant**
  - **half-life of a reaction**
  - **rate-determining step**
- construct and use rate equations of the form rate = $k[A]^m[B]^n$ (limited to simple cases of single-step reactions and of multi-step processes with a rate-determining step for which m and n are 0, 1 or 2) including:
  - deducing the order of a reaction by the initial rates method
  - justifying, for zero- and first-order reactions, the order of reaction from concentration–time graphs
  - verifying that a suggested reaction mechanism is consistent with the observed kinetics
  - predicting the order that would result from a given reaction mechanism (and vice versa)
  - calculating an initial rate using concentration data (not including integrated forms of the rate equation)

- show understanding that the half-life of a first-order reaction is independent of concentration
- use the half-life of a first-order reaction in calculations
- calculate a rate constant using the initial rates or half-life method
- for a multi-step reaction:
  - suggest a reaction mechanism that is consistent with the rate equation and the equation for the overall reaction
  - predict the order that would result from a given reaction mechanism (and vice versa)
- devise a suitable experimental technique for studying the rate of a reaction, from given information
- outline the different modes of action of homogeneous and heterogeneous catalysts, including:
  - the Haber process
  - the catalytic removal of oxides of nitrogen in the exhaust gases from car engines
  - the catalytic role of atmospheric oxides of nitrogen in the oxidation of atmospheric sulfur dioxide
  - the catalytic role of Fe^{3+} in the $I^-/S_2O_3^{2-}$ reaction.

Introduction

The Northern Lights (*aurora borealis*) are the result of many complex reactions taking place in the upper atmosphere. A knowledge of reaction rates is needed to understand the natural reactions involved and how these might be disturbed by artificial emissions.

Figure 22.1 Northern Lights over the Arctic Circle.

Factors affecting reaction rate

In Chapter 9 you learnt why reaction rate is increased when:

- the concentrations of the reactants are increased
- the temperature is increased
- a catalyst is added to the reaction mixture.

In this chapter you will review the definition of the rate of reaction, and find out about:

- quantitative aspects of reaction rates
- how the data gathered from experiments on rates of reaction can be used to confirm possible reaction mechanisms
- more about how catalysts speed up reaction rates.

Rate of reaction

Defining rate of reaction

We calculate rate of reaction by measuring a decrease in concentration of a particular reactant or an increase in concentration of a particular product over a period of time.

$$\text{rate of reaction} = \frac{\text{change in concentration}}{\text{time taken for this change}}$$

Units of concentration are usually expressed in $mol\,dm^{-3}$, units of time are usually expressed in seconds, so the units of rate of reaction are normally $mol\,dm^{-3}\,s^{-1}$. For very slow reactions, you may see the units of rates expressed as $mol\,dm^{-3}\,min^{-1}$ or $mol\,dm^{-3}\,h^{-1}$.

QUESTION

1 Convert the following rates into the units of $mol\,dm^{-3}\,s^{-1}$:

   a 0.254 g of I_2 consumed in 1.00 h in a reaction mixture of volume 1 dm^3

     ($A_r[I] = 127$)

   b 0.0440 g ethyl ethanoate formed in 1.00 min from a reaction mixture of volume 400 cm^3.

     ($M_r\,[CH_3COOC_2H_5] = 88.0$)

METHODS FOR FOLLOWING THE COURSE OF A REACTION

In order to find out how the rate of reaction changes with time we need to select a suitable method to follow the progress of a reaction. This method will measure either the rate of disappearance of a reactant, or the rate of appearance of a product. There are two main types of method: sampling and continuous.

METHODS FOR FOLLOWING THE COURSE OF A REACTION (CONTINUED)

1 Sampling

This method involves taking small samples of the reaction mixture at various times and then carrying out a chemical analysis on each sample. An example is the alkaline hydrolysis of bromobutane:

$$C_4H_9Br + OH^- \longrightarrow C_4H_9OH + Br^-$$

Samples are removed at various times and 'quenched' to stop or slow down the reaction, e.g. by cooling the sample in ice. The hydroxide ion concentration can be found by titration with a standard solution of a strong acid.

2 Continuous

In this method a physical property of the reaction mixture is monitored over a period of time. Some examples are using colorimetry, a conductivity meter or measuring changes in gas volume or gas pressure.

Colorimetry can be used to monitor the change in colour of a particular reactant. For example, this method can be used to follow the reaction of iodine with propanone:

$$CH_3COCH_3 + I_2 \longrightarrow CH_3COCH_2I + HI$$

As the reaction proceeds, the colour of the iodine fades.

Changes in electrical conductivity of the solution can be measured. For example, this method can be used to follow the reaction:

$$(CH_3)_3CBr + H_2O \longrightarrow (CH_3)_3COH + H^+ + Br^-$$

As the reaction proceeds, the electrical conductivity of the solution increases because ions are being formed in the reaction. This method can sometimes be used even if there are ions on both sides of the equation. This is due to the fact that ions vary in their conductivities. For example the small H^+ and OH^- ions have very high conductivities but Br^- ions have a low conductivity.

Changes in gas volume or gas pressure can be measured. For example, this method can be used to follow the reaction of benzenediazonium chloride, $C_6H_5N{\equiv}N^+Cl^-$, with water.

$$C_6H_5N{\equiv}N^+Cl^-(aq) + H_2O(l)$$
$$\longrightarrow C_6H_5OH(aq) + N_2(g) + HCl(aq)$$

Figure 22.2 A colorimeter can be used to monitor the progress of a reaction. It measures the transmission of light through a 'cell' containing the reaction mixture. The less concentrated the colour of the reaction mixture, the more light is transmitted through the 'cell'.

The reaction can be monitored by measuring the change in volume of gas released with time. You may have used this method to follow the rate of the reaction between calcium carbonate and hydrochloric acid. If you did, you will have measured the change in volume of carbon dioxide gas released with time.

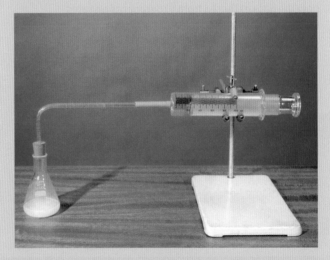

Figure 22.3 Rate of reaction can be followed by measuring the change in volume of a gas given off in a reaction. In this experiment CO_2 is being given off when $CaCO_3$ reacts with HCl.

METHODS FOR FOLLOWING THE COURSE OF A REACTION (CONTINUED)

The progress of some reactions can be followed by measuring small changes in the volume of the reaction mixture. For example, during the hydration of methylpropene, the volume decreases.

$$(CH_3)_2C{=}CH_2 + H_2O \xrightarrow{\text{H}^+} (CH_3)_3COH$$

An instrument called a dilatometer (Figure 22.4) is used to measure the small changes in volume. The temperature has to be controlled to an accuracy of ±0.001 °C. Can you think why?

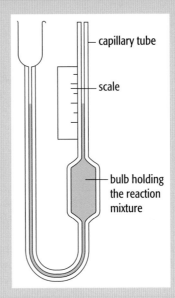

Figure 22.4 A dilatometer.

QUESTION

2 **a** Suggest a suitable method for following the progress of each of these reactions:

  i $H_2O_2(aq) + 2I^-(aq) + 2H^+(aq)$
  $$\longrightarrow 2H_2O(l) + I_2(aq)$$

  ii $HCOOCH_3(aq) + H_2O(l)$
  $$\longrightarrow HCOOH(aq) + CH_3OH(aq)$$

  iii $2H_2O_2(aq) \longrightarrow 2H_2O(l) + O_2(g)$

  iv $BrO_3^-(aq) + 5Br^-(aq) + 6H^+(aq)$
  $$\longrightarrow 3Br_2(aq) + 3H_2O(l)$$

 b Why is it essential that the temperature is kept constant when measuring the progress of a reaction?

Calculating rate of reaction graphically

Rate of reaction usually changes as the reaction proceeds. This is because the concentration of reactants is decreasing. Taking the isomerisation of cyclopropane to propene as an example:

$$\underset{\text{cyclopropane}}{\overset{H_2C}{\underset{H_2C}{\diagdown}}{\diagup}CH_2(g)} \longrightarrow \underset{\text{propene}}{CH_3CH{=}CH_2(g)}$$

The progress of this reaction can be followed by measuring the decrease in concentration of cyclopropane or increase

in concentration of propene. Table 22.1 shows these changes at 500 °C. The measurements were all made at the same temperature because reaction rate is affected markedly by temperature.

Time / min	[cyclopropane] / mol dm^{-3}	[propene] / mol dm^{-3}
0	1.50	0.00
5	1.23	0.27
10	1.00	0.50
15	0.82	0.68
20	0.67	0.83
25	0.55	0.95
30	0.45	1.05
35	0.37	1.13
40	0.33	1.17

Table 22.1 Concentrations of reactant (cyclopropane) and product (propene) at 5-minute intervals (temperature = 500 °C (773 K)).

Note that we put square brackets, [ ], around the cyclopropane and propene to indicate concentration; [propene] means 'concentration of propene'.

  Figure 22.5 shows how the concentration of propene changes with time.

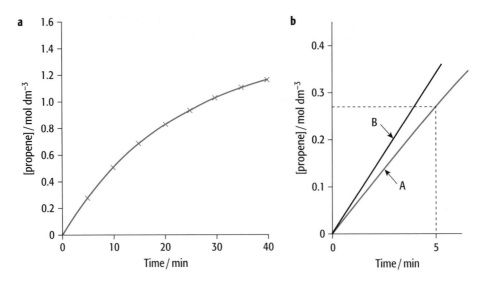

Figure 22.5 How the concentration of propene changes with time in the reaction cyclopropane $\longrightarrow$ propene: **a** the whole curve; **b** the first part of the curve magnified. Line A shows the average rate over the first 5 minutes. Line B shows the actual initial rate found by drawing a tangent at the start of the curve.

We can see from Figure 22.5b that the concentration of propene increases from 0.00 to 0.27 mol dm^{-3} in the first 5 minutes. In Chapter 6 (page 91) we used the symbol Δ (Greek capital 'delta') to represent a change in a particular quantity. So we can write:

$$\text{rate of reaction} = \frac{\Delta[\text{propene}]}{\Delta \text{ time}} = \frac{0.27}{5}$$

$$= 0.054 \text{ mol dm}^{-3} \text{min}^{-1}$$

This gives the average rate of reaction over the first 5 minutes. You will notice, however, that the graph is a curve which becomes shallower with time. So the rate decreases with time. By measuring the change in concentration over shorter and shorter time intervals we get an increasingly accurate value of the reaction rate. If we make the time interval over which we measure the reaction almost zero, we obtain a reaction rate at a particular instant. We do this by drawing tangents at particular points on the curve. Line B in Figure 22.5b shows a tangent drawn at the start of the curve. This gives a much more accurate value of the initial rate of reaction.

Figure 22.6 shows how to draw a tangent and calculate the rate at a particular point on a curve. In this case, we are using a graph of concentration of cyclopropane against time.

The procedure is:

■ Select a point on the graph corresponding to a particular time (10 minutes in this example).

■ Draw a straight line at this point so that it just touches the line. The two angles between the straight line and the curve should look very similar.

■ Extend the tangent to meet the axes of the graph.

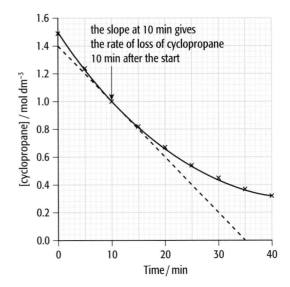

Figure 22.6 The rate of decrease of cyclopropane concentration over times as the reaction proceeds. The rate of reaction at a given time can be found by drawing a tangent and measuring the gradient.

■ Calculate the slope (gradient) of the tangent. This is a measure of the rate of reaction. In this example the slope is:

$$\text{slope} = \frac{0.00 - 1.40}{35 \times 60} = -6.67 \times 10^{-4} \text{ mol dm}^{-3} \text{s}^{-1}$$

Note:

■ we convert the minutes to seconds by multiplying by 60

■ the sign of the slope is negative because the reactant concentration is decreasing

■ the value of -6.67×10^{-4} mol dm^{-3} s^{-1} refers to the rate of change of cyclopropane concentration

■ this is the rate of reaction when the cyclopropane concentration is 1.00 mol dm^{-3}.

Changes in rate as the reaction proceeds

As time passes, the concentration of cyclopropane falls. We can find the rate at different concentrations of cyclopropane by drawing tangents at several points on the graph. Figure 22.7 shows how this is done for cyclopropane concentrations of $1.50\,mol\,dm^{-3}$ (the initial rate), $1.00\,mol\,dm^{-3}$ and $0.05\,mol\,dm^{-3}$. The data is summarised in Table 22.2.

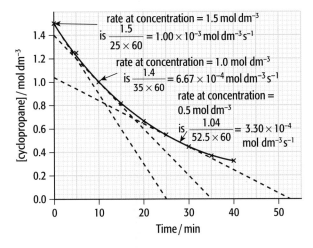

Figure 22.7 Calculation of the rate of decrease of cyclopropane concentration, made at regular intervals.

[cyclopropane] / mol dm^{-3}	Rate / mol dm^{-3} s^{-1}	$\dfrac{\text{Rate}}{\text{[cyclopropane]}}$ /s^{-1}
1.50	1.00×10^{-3}	6.67×10^{-4}
1.00	6.67×10^{-4}	6.67×10^{-4}
0.50	3.30×10^{-4}	6.60×10^{-4}

Table 22.2 Rates of decrease for cyclopropane at different concentrations, calculated from Figure 22.7.

A graph of rate of reaction against concentration of cyclopropane (Figure 22.8) shows us that the rate is directly proportional to the concentration of cyclopropane. So, if the concentration of cyclopropane is doubled the rate of reaction is doubled, and if the concentration of cyclopropane falls by one-third, the rate of reaction falls by one-third.

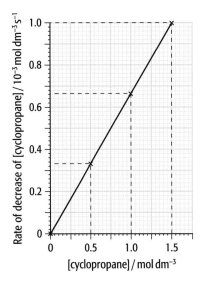

Figure 22.8 The rate of decrease of cyclopropane. Note how the gradient (rate/concentration) is constant.

MONITORING VERY FAST REACTIONS

The complete course of some very fast reactions can be monitored using stopped-flow spectrophotometry. In this technique, very small volumes of reactants are driven at high speed into a mixing chamber. From here they go to an observation cell, where the progress of the reaction is monitored (usually by measuring the transmission of ultraviolet radiation through the sample). A graph of rate of reaction against time can be generated automatically.

QUESTION

3 a i Plot the data in Table 22.1 for increase in propene concentration with time.

  ii Calculate the rate after 10 minutes (when the propene concentration is $0.50\,mol\,dm^{-3}$) by drawing a tangent.

 b Use the same method to calculate the rate of reaction at propene concentrations of $0.00\,mol\,dm^{-3}$, $0.30\,mol\,dm^{-3}$ and $0.90\,mol\,dm^{-3}$.

 c i Calculate the concentration of cyclopropane when the concentration of propene is 0.00, 0.30, 0.50 and $0.90\,mol\,dm^{-3}$.

  ii Plot a graph of rate of reaction against [cyclopropane]. Note that the graph is for cyclopropane concentration NOT [propene] as it is the concentration of the reactant that is affecting the rate not the product.

329

Rate equations

The rate constant and rate equations

The third column in Table 22.2 shows that the rate of the reaction is proportional to cyclopropane concentration (within the limits of experimental error). We can express this mathematically as:

$$\text{rate of reaction} = k \times [\text{cyclopropane}]$$

The proportionality constant, k, is called the rate constant.

The overall expression (rate of reaction = $k \times$ [cyclopropane]) is the rate equation for this particular reaction. Rate equations are generally written without the $\times$ sign. For example:

$$\text{rate} = k[\text{cyclopropane}]$$

Rate equations can only be determined from experimental data. They cannot be found from the stoichiometric equation.

Some experimentally determined rate equations are shown in Table 22.3.

You can see from equation 1 that the rate of reaction is proportional to the concentration of both H_2 and I_2; however, in equation 2, CO and O_2 do not appear in the rate equation, even though they are present in the stoichiometric equation. Similarly in reactions 3 and 4 there is no relationship between the rate equation and the stoichiometry of the chemical equation.

Stoichiometric equation	Rate equation
1 $H_2(g) + I_2(g) \longrightarrow 2HI(g)$	rate = $k[H_2][I_2]$
2 $NO(g) + CO(g) + O_2(g)$ $\longrightarrow NO_2(g) + CO_2(g)$	rate = $k[NO]^2$
3 $2H_2(g) + 2NO(g)$ $\longrightarrow 2H_2O(g) + N_2(g)$	rate = $k[H_2][NO]^2$
4 $BrO_3^-(aq) + 5Br^-(aq) + H^+(aq)$ $\longrightarrow 3Br_2(aq) + 3H_2O(l)$	rate = $k[BrO_3^-][Br^-][H^+]^2$

Table 22.3 Rate equations for some reactions.

In order to find the rate equation we have to conduct a series of experiments. Using reaction 3 as an example:

- first find how the concentration of $H_2(g)$ affects the rate by varying the concentration of $H_2(g)$, while keeping the concentration of NO(g) constant
- the results show that the rate is proportional to the concentration of hydrogen (rate = $k_1[H_2]$)

- then find how the concentration of NO(g) affects the rate by varying the concentration of NO(g) while keeping the concentration of $H_2(g)$ constant
- the results show that the rate is proportional to the square of the concentration of NO (rate = $k_2[NO]^2$).

Combining the two rate equations we get the overall rate equation: rate = $k[H_2][NO]^2$.

The rate equations for some reactions may include compounds that are not present in the chemical equation.

QUESTION

4 Write rate equations for each of the following reactions:

a cyclopropane $\longrightarrow$ propene

where rate is proportional to the concentration of cyclopropane

b $2HI(g) \longrightarrow H_2(g) + I_2(g)$

where rate is proportional to the square of the hydrogen iodide concentration

c $C_{12}H_{22}O_{11}(g) + H_2O(l) \xrightarrow{H+} 2C_6H_{12}O_6(aq)$

where rate is proportional to the concentration of $C_{12}H_{22}O_{11}$ and to the concentration of H^+ ions

d $2HgCl_2(aq) + K_2C_2O_4(aq)$ $\longrightarrow Hg_2Cl_2(s) + 2KCl(aq) + 2CO_2(g)$

where rate is proportional to the concentration of $HgCl_2$ and to the square of the concentration of $K_2C_2O_4$

e $CH_3COCH_3 + I_2 \xrightarrow{H+} CH_3COCH_2I + HI$

where rate is proportional to the concentration of CH_3COCH_3 and to the concentration of H^+ ions, but the concentration of I_2 has no effect on the rate.

Order of reaction

The order of a reaction shows how the concentration of a reagent affects the rate of reaction.

The order of reaction with respect to a particular reactant is the power to which the concentration of that reactant is raised in the rate equation.

For example, for a rate equation involving only one particular reactant, the order is the power of the concentration shown in the rate equation. For equation **2** in Table 22.3, the rate equation is rate = $k[NO]^2$ and so the order is 2 with respect to [NO].

When you are writing about order of reaction, you must distinguish carefully between the order with respect to a particular reactant and the overall order of reaction. Taking equation **3** in Table 22.3 as an example:

rate = $k[H_2][NO]^2$

We say that this reaction is:

- first-order with respect to H_2
  (as rate is proportional to $[H_2]^1$)
- second-order with respect to NO
  (as rate is proportional to $[NO]^2$)
- third-order overall (as the sum of the powers is $1 + 2 = 3$).

In general terms, for a reaction $A + B \longrightarrow$ products, the rate equation can be written in the form:

rate of reaction = $k[A]^m[B]^n$

In this equation:

- [A] and [B] are the concentrations of the reactants
- m and n are the orders of the reaction
- the values of m and n can be 0, 1, 2, 3 or rarely higher
- when the value of m or n is 0 we can ignore the concentration term because any number to the power of zero = 1.

Orders of reaction are not always whole numbers. A few reactions have fractional orders. For example, the reaction:

$$CH_3CHO(g) \longrightarrow CH_4(g) + CO(g)$$

has an overall order of 1.5. The rate equation for this reaction is:

rate = $k[CH_3CHO]^{1.5}$

Many reactions involving free radicals have fractional orders of reaction.

QUESTION

5   For each of the reactions **a** to **e** in question 4, state:
   i   the order of reaction with respect to each reactant
   ii the overall order of reaction.

Units of k

The units of k vary according to the form of the rate equation.

WORKED EXAMPLES

1   From equation 1 in Table 22.3.

Step 1 Write the rate equation

rate = $k[H_2][I_2]$

Step 2 Rearrange the equation in terms of k.

$k = \dfrac{\text{rate}}{[H_2][I_2]}$

Step 3 Substitute the units.

$k = \dfrac{mol\,dm^{-3}\,s^{-1}}{(mol\,dm^{-3}) \times (mol\,dm^{-3})}$

Step 4 Cancel mol dm^{-3}.

$k = \dfrac{\cancel{mol\,dm^{-3}}\,s^{-1}}{(\cancel{mol\,dm^{-3}}) \times (mol\,dm^{-3})}$

Step 5 Units of k.

units of $k = s^{-1}\,mol^{-1}\,dm^3 = dm^3\,mol^{-1}\,s^{-1}$

- when writing the units on one line, the indices on the bottom change sign
- we usually put the unit with the positive index first
- don't forget the s^{-1} arising from the units of rate.

2   From equation 3 in Table 22.3.

Step 1 Write the rate equation.

rate = $k[H_2][NO]^2$

Step 2 Rearrange the equation in terms of k.

$k = \dfrac{\text{rate}}{[H_2][NO]^2}$

Step 3 Substitute the units.

$k = \dfrac{mol\,dm^{-3}\,s^{-1}}{(mol\,dm^{-3}) \times (mol\,dm^{-3})^2}$

Step 4 Cancel mol dm^{-3}.

$k = \dfrac{\cancel{mol\,dm^{-3}}\,s^{-1}}{(\cancel{mol\,dm^{-3}}) \times (mol\,dm^{-3})^2}$

Step 5 Units of k.

units of $k = s^{-1}\,mol^{-2}\,dm^6 = dm^6\,mol^{-2}\,s^{-1}$

6 State the units of k corresponding to each of the following rate equations:

a   rate = $k[NO]^2$

b   rate = $k[NH_3]^0$

c   rate = $k[BrO_3^-][Br^-][H^+]^2$

d   rate = $k[cyclopropane]$

Which order of reaction?

We can identify the order of a reaction in three ways:

- plot a graph of reaction rate against concentration of reactant
- plot a graph of concentration of reactant against time
- deduce successive half-lives from graphs of concentration against time.

Graphs of reaction rate against concentration

A graph of reaction rate against concentration tells us whether a reaction is zero, first, second or third order with respect to a particular reagent (or overall). It is very rare to obtain an order with respect to a particular reagent higher than second order. Figure 22.9 shows the shapes of the graphs expected for different orders of reaction.

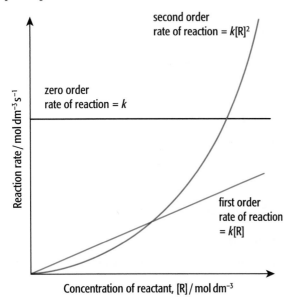

Figure 22.9 Zero-, first- and second-order reactions: how changes in the concentration of a reactant affect the reaction rate.

We shall now look at some examples of zero-, first- and second-order reactions.

Zero-order

$$2NH_3(g) \xrightarrow{\text{hot tungsten}} N_2(g) + 3H_2(g)$$

The rate equation derived from experiments is:

rate = $k[NH_3]^0$

The plot of reaction rate against concentration is a horizontal straight line (see Figure 22.9). The reaction rate does not change with concentration. For a zero-order reaction, k is numerically equal to the reaction rate:

rate = k

This is because any number to the power of zero = 1.

First-order

$$2N_2O(g) \xrightarrow{\text{gold}} 2N_2(g) + O_2(g)$$

The rate equation derived from experiments is:

rate = $k[N_2O]^1$

This is usually written as:

rate = $k[N_2O]$

The plot of reaction rate against concentration is an inclined straight line going through the origin (see Figure 22.9). The rate is directly proportional to the concentration of N_2O. So doubling the concentration of N_2O doubles the rate of reaction.

Second-order

$$NO_2(g) + CO(g) \longrightarrow NO(g) + CO_2(g)$$

The rate equation derived from experiments is:

rate = $k[NO_2]^2$

The plot of reaction rate against concentration is an upwardly curved line (see Figure 22.9).

In this case, reaction rate is directly proportional to the square of the concentration of $NO_2(g)$. When the concentration of $NO_2(g)$ doubles, the rate of reaction increases four-fold. If we consider the second-order rate equation as written above, we can see that this is true by comparing the rates at two different concentrations, $1\,mol\,dm^{-3}$ and $2\,mol\,dm^{-3}$.

rate at $1\,mol\,dm^{-3}$ = $k(1)^2 = 1k$

rate at $2\,mol\,dm^{-3}$ = $k(2)^2 = 4k$

7 Draw sketch graphs of reaction rate against concentration of the reactant in bold for each of the following reactions:

a **NO**(g) + CO(g) + O_2(g) $\longrightarrow$ NO_2(g) + CO_2(g)

for which the rate equation is:

rate = $k[NO]^2$

b **2HI**(g) $\overset{gold}{\longrightarrow}$ H_2(g) + I_2(g)

for which the rate equation is:

rate = k

Note: the catalyst influences the order here – the order is not the same as for the uncatalysed reaction.

c **$(CH_3)_3CCl$** + OH^- $\longrightarrow$ $(CH_3)_3COH$ + Cl^-

for which the rate equation is:

$k[(CH_3)_3CCl]$

Graphs of concentration of reactant against time

Figure 22.10 shows how we can distinguish between zero-, first- and second-order reactions by plotting a graph of concentration against time.

For a zero-order reaction, the graph is a descending straight line. The rate of reaction is the slope (gradient) of the graph. The reaction proceeds at the same rate whatever the concentration of the reactant.

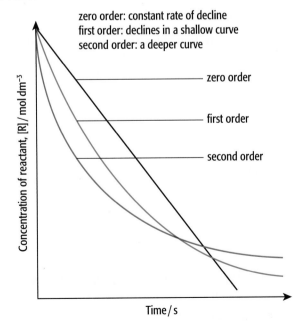

zero order: constant rate of decline
first order: declines in a shallow curve
second order: a deeper curve

Figure 22.10 Zero-, first- and second-order reactions: how changes in the concentration of a reactant affect the time taken for a reaction to proceed.

For first- and second-order reactions, the graph is a curve. The curve for the second-order reaction is much deeper than for a first-order reaction. It also appears to have a relatively longer 'tail' as it levels off. We can also distinguish between these two curves by determining successive half-lives of the reaction.

8 For each of the reactions **a** to **c** in question **7**, draw a sketch graph to show how the concentration of the bold reactant changes with time.

Half-life and reaction rates

Half-life, $t_{\frac{1}{2}}$, is the time taken for the concentration of a reactant to fall to half of its original value.

Figure 22.11 shows how half-life is measured for the cyclopropane to propene reaction that we studied earlier. Three successive half-lives are shown. Table 22.4 shows the values of the successive half-lives obtained from Figure 22.11.

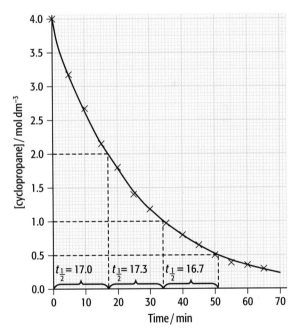

Figure 22.11 Measurement of half-life for cyclopropane isomerisation.

Δ[cyclopropane] / mol dm⁻³	Half-life / min
4.00 to 2.00	17.0
2.00 to 1.00	34.3 – 17.0 = 17.3
1.00 to 0.50	51.0 – 34.3 = 16.7

Table 22.4 A constant half-life indicates a first-order reaction.

333

You can see that the successive half-lives have values that are fairly close to each other (17.0, 17.3, 16.7). The mean half-life is 17.0 minutes for this reaction. We can tell that this reaction is first order because the successive half-lives are more or less constant. In a first-order reaction like this the half-life is independent of the original concentration of reactant. This means that whatever the starting concentration of cyclopropane, the half-life will always be 17 minutes.

We can distinguish zero-, first- and second-order reactions from their successive half-lives (Figure 22.12).

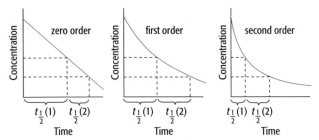

Figure 22.12 The half-life of zero-, first- and second-order reactions can be determined from graphs of concentration against time.

- A zero-order reaction has successive half-lives which decrease with time.
- A first-order reaction has a half-life which is constant.
- Second-order reactions have successive half-lives which increase with time. (This also applies to reactions with a higher order for a particular reagent but we will not be discussing these.)

QUESTION

9 Benzenediazonium chloride, $C_6H_5N_2Cl$, decomposes at room temperature:

$$C_6H_5N_2Cl(aq) + H_2O(l) \longrightarrow C_6H_5OH(aq) + N_2(g) + HCl(aq)$$

a Describe how this reaction can be monitored.

b Using the data in the table, plot a graph of concentration of $C_6H_5N_2Cl$ against time.

Time / s	$[C_6H_5N_2Cl]$ / 10^{-4} mol dm^{-3}
0	5.8
200	4.4
400	3.2
600	2.5
800	1.7
1000	1.2
1200	0.8
1400	0.5
1600	0.3

c From your graph, find the value of two successive half-lives.

d Use the values of these half-lives to deduce the order of the reaction.

Calculations involving the rate constant, k

Calculating k from initial concentrations and initial rate

In the presence of hydrogen ions, hydrogen peroxide, H_2O_2, reacts with iodide ions to form water and iodine:

$$H_2O_2(aq) + 2I^-(aq) + 2H^+(aq) \longrightarrow 2H_2O(l) + I_2(aq)$$

The rate equation for this reaction is:

$$\text{rate of reaction} = k[H_2O_2][I^-]$$

The progress of the reaction can be followed by measuring the initial rate of formation of iodine. Table 22.5 shows the rates of reaction obtained using various initial concentrations of each reactant.

The procedure for calculating k is shown below, using the data for experiment 1.

Step 1 Write out the rate equation.

$$\text{rate of reaction} = k[H_2O_2][I^-]$$

Step 2 Rearrange the equation in terms of k

$$k = \frac{\text{rate}}{[H_2O_2][I^-]}$$

Step 3 Substitute the values

$$k = \frac{3.50 \times 10^{-6}}{(0.0200) \times (0.0100)}$$

$$k = 1.75 \times 10^{-2}\,\text{dm}^3\,\text{mol}^{-1}\,\text{s}^{-1}$$

Note: the concentration of hydrogen ions is ignored because $[H^+]$ does not appear in the rate equation. The reaction is zero order with respect to $[H^+]$.

Calculating k from half-life

For a first-order reaction, half-life is related to the rate constant by the expression:

$$t_{\frac{1}{2}} = \frac{0.693}{k}, \text{ where } t_{\frac{1}{2}} \text{ is the half-life, measured in s}$$

We can rewrite this in the form:

$$k = \frac{0.693}{t_{\frac{1}{2}}}$$

So, for the first-order reaction cyclopropane to propene, for which the half-life is 17.0 min, we:

- convert minutes to seconds
- then substitute the half-life into the expression:

$$k = \frac{0.693}{t_{\frac{1}{2}}} = \frac{0.693}{17.0 \times 60} = 6.79 \times 10^{-4}\,\text{dm}^3\,\text{mol}^{-1}\,\text{s}^{-1}$$

Experiment	$[H_2O_2]$ / mol dm^{-3}	$[I^-]$ / mol dm^{-3}	$[H^+]$ / mol dm^{-3}	Initial rate of reaction / mol dm^{-3} s^{-1}
1	0.0200	0.0100	0.0100	3.50×10^{-6}
2	0.0300	0.0100	0.0100	5.30×10^{-6}
3	0.0050	0.0200	0.0200	1.75×10^{-6}

Table 22.5 Rates of reaction obtained using different initial concentrations of H_2O_2, I^- ions and H^+ ions.

This value is very close to the ones quoted in Table 22.2. Rate constants for zero- and second-order reactions can also be calculated from half-lives but the calculations are more complex.

We can also use the expression $k = \dfrac{0.693}{t_{\frac{1}{2}}}$ to calculate the half-life of a first-order reaction if we know the rate constant.

QUESTION

10 a Use the data from experiments **2** and **3** in Table 22.5 to calculate the rate constant for the following reaction.

$H_2O_2(aq) + 2I^-(aq) + 2H^+(aq) \longrightarrow 2H_2O(l) + I_2(aq)$

The rate equation for this reaction is:

rate of reaction = $k[H_2O_2][I^-]$

b Use the formula $t_{\frac{1}{2}} = \dfrac{0.693}{k}$ to calculate a value for the rate constant of a reaction which is first order and has a half-life of 480 s.

c A first-order reaction has a rate constant of 9.63×10^{-5} s^{-1}. Calculate a value for the half-life of this reaction.

Deducing order of reaction from raw data

We can use any of the methods mentioned on page 330 to determine the order of a reaction. In this section we shall look in detail at some more complex examples.

Using data from the course of a reaction

In this method we carry out one or more experiments with known initial concentrations of reactants and follow the course of the reaction until it is complete (or nearly complete).

The steps in analysing the data are as follows.

Step 1 Plot a graph to show how the concentration of a particular reactant (or product) changes with time.

Step 2 Take tangents at various points along the curve which correspond to particular concentrations of the reactant.

Step 3 Calculate the slope (gradient) at each concentration selected. The rate of reaction is calculated from the slope of the graph.

Step 4 Plot a graph of rate of reaction against concentration.

WORKED EXAMPLE

3 Methanol reacts with hydrochloric acid at 25 °C. The products are chloromethane and water.

$CH_3OH(aq) + HCl(aq) \longrightarrow CH_3Cl(g) + H_2O(l)$

Equimolar amounts of methanol and hydrochloric acid are mixed at 25 °C. The progress of the reaction is followed by
- taking a small sample of the reaction mixture from time to time, then
- titrating each sample with a standard solution of sodium hydroxide.

The data obtained are shown in Table 22.6

Time / min	$[HCl]$ / mol dm^{-3}	$[CH_3OH]$ / mol dm^{-3}
0	1.84	1.84
200	1.45	1.45
400	1.22	1.22
600	1.04	1.04
800	0.91	0.91
1000	0.81	0.81
1200	0.72	0.72
1400	0.66	0.66
1600	0.60	0.60
1800	0.56	0.56
2000	0.54	0.54

Table 22.6 Data for the reaction between methanol and hydrochloric acid.

335

WORKED EXAMPLE (CONTINUED)

Step 1 Draw a graph of concentration (of hydrochloric acid) against time (Figure 22.13).

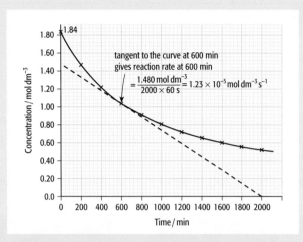

Figure 22.13 The concentration of hydrochloric acid and methanol fall at the same rate as time passes.

Step 2 Draw tangents to the curve at various places corresponding to a range of concentrations. In Figure 22.13 the tangent drawn corresponds to $[HCl] = 1.04\,mol\,dm^{-3}$.

Step 3 For each tangent drawn, calculate the gradient and then the rate of reaction. In Figure 22.13, the rate corresponding to $[HCl] = 1.04\,mol\,dm^{-3}$ is

$$\frac{1.480}{2000 \times 60} = 1.23 \times 10^{-5}\,mol\,dm^{-3}\,s^{-1}$$

(multiply by 60 to convert minutes to seconds)

Table 22.7 shows the rates corresponding to five different concentrations of hydrochloric acid.

Time / min	Concentration / mol dm^{-3}	Rate from graph / mol dm^{-3} min^{-1}	Rate from graph / mol dm^{-3} s^{-1}
0	1.84	2.30×10^{-3}	3.83×10^{-5}
200	1.45	1.46×10^{-3}	2.43×10^{-5}
400	1.22	1.05×10^{-3}	1.75×10^{-5}
600	1.04	0.74×10^{-3}	1.23×10^{-5}
800	0.91	0.54×10^{-3}	0.90×10^{-5}

Table 22.7 Values calculated for the reaction between methanol and hydrochloric acid.

Step 4 Plot a graph of rate of reaction against concentration.

Figure 22.14 shows a plot of rate against the concentration of [HCl] or [CH$_3$OH]. We have included

WORKED EXAMPLE (CONTINUED)

the [CH$_3$OH] because if you look at the data in Table 22.6, you will see that the concentration of CH$_3$OH is decreasing at the same rate as the decrease in concentration of HCl.

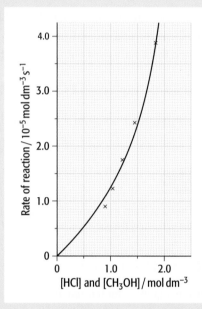

Figure 22.14 A graph showing how concentration changes of hydrochloric acid or methanol affect rate of reaction. The curve shows that the reaction is likely to be second order.

Figure 22.14 shows an upward curve. This indicates that the reaction is second order. But second order with respect to what? As the concentrations of both HCl and CH$_3$OH are decreasing at the same rate, either of these may be second order. The possibilities are:

- rate = $k[CH_3OH][HCl]$
- rate = $k[CH_3OH]^2$
- rate = $k[HCl]^2$

Further experiments would have to be carried out to confirm one or other of these possibilities. The only thing we can be sure of is that the reaction is second order overall.

QUESTION

11 Suggest how the experiment for the reaction between methanol and hydrochloric acid might be re-designed to obtain evidence for the effect of changing the HCl concentration whilst controlling the CH$_3$OH concentration.

Using initial rates

The initial rates method is often used when the rate of reaction is slow.

- Carry out several experiments with different known initial concentrations of each reactant.
- Measure the initial rates of reaction by either:
  - taking the tangent of the curve at the start of each experiment or
  - measuring the concentration of a reactant or product soon after the experiment has started.
- For each reactant, plot a graph of initial rate against concentration of that particular reactant.

WORKED EXAMPLE

4 Nitrogen(V) oxide, N_2O_5, decomposes to nitrogen(IV) oxide and oxygen.

$$2N_2O_5(g) \longrightarrow 4NO_2(g) + O_2(g)$$

Table 22.8 shows how the initial rate of reaction varies with the initial concentration of N_2O_5.

Initial concentration, $[N_2O_5]$ / mol dm^{-3}	Initial rate / 10^{-5} mol dm^{-3} s^{-1}
3.00	3.15
1.50	1.55
0.75	0.80

Table 22.8 Data for the decomposition of nitrogen(V) oxide.

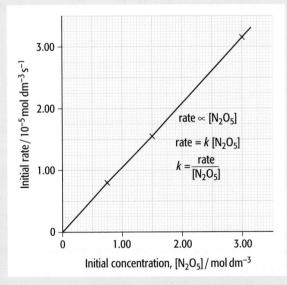

Figure 22.15 The initial rate of decomposition of nitrogen(V) oxide is directly proportional to the initial concentration.

WORKED EXAMPLE (CONTINUED)

A graph of the data (Figure 22.15) shows that the initial rate of reaction is directly proportional to the initial concentration of N_2O_5.

rate of reaction $\propto [N_2O_5]$

$\quad\quad = k[N_2O_5]$

QUESTION

12 a State the order of reaction for the decomposition of nitrogen(V) oxide.

b Use the data for 3.00 mol dm^{-3} N_2O_5 in Table 22.8 to calculate a value for the rate constant for this decomposition.

WORKED EXAMPLE

5 The equation below describes the reaction of propanone with iodine. Hydrogen ions catalyse this reaction.

$$CH_3COCH_3 + I_2 \xrightarrow{H^+} CH_3COCH_2I + HI$$

The progress of the reaction can be followed by using a colorimeter. The brown colour of the iodine fades as the reaction proceeds. The experimental results are shown in Table 22.9.

Experi-ment	[HCl] / mol dm^{-3}	[propanone] / 10^{-3} mol dm^{-3}	[iodine] / 10^{-3} mol dm^{-3}	Initial rate / 10^{-6} mol dm^{-3} s^{-1}
1	1.25	0.50	1.25	10.9
2	0.625	0.50	1.25	5.4
3	1.25	0.25	1.25	5.1
4	1.25	0.50	0.625	10.7

Table 22.9 Experimental results for the reaction of propanone with iodine at varying aqueous concentrations.

Note that:

- the data is from real experiments, so experimental errors have to be taken into account
- the hydrogen ions have been provided by the hydrochloric acid.

In this method we see how changing the concentration of each reactant in turn affects the rate of reaction. In order to make a fair comparison, we must make sure that the concentrations of the other reactants are kept constant.

WORKED EXAMPLE (CONTINUED)

Compare experiments 1 and 2 (propanone and iodine concentrations are constant):

- doubling the concentration of H⁺ ions from 0.625 to 1.25 mol dm⁻³ doubles the rate of reaction
- the reaction is first order with respect to H⁺ ions.

Compare experiments 1 and 3 (hydrochloric acid and iodine concentrations are constant):

- doubling the concentration of propanone from 0.25×10^{-3} to 0.50×10^{-3} mol dm⁻³ doubles the rate of reaction
- the reaction is first order with respect to propanone.

Compare experiments 1 and 4 (hydrochloric acid and propanone concentrations are constant):

- doubling the concentration of iodine from 0.625×10^{-3} to 1.25×10^{-3} mol dm⁻³ has no effect on the rate of reaction
- the reaction is zero order with respect to iodine.

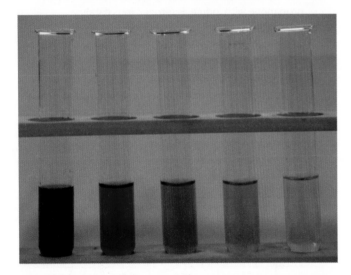

Figure 22.16 The rate of reaction between propanone and iodine can be followed by the loss of colour of the reaction mixture as the reaction proceeds.

QUESTION

13 a Write the rate equation for the acid-catalysed reaction of iodine with propanone.

b Use your rate equation and the information in Table 22.9 (experiment **1**) to calculate a value for the rate constant for this reaction.

Kinetics and reaction mechanisms

The rate-determining step

In Worked example 5 you saw that for the reaction:

$$CH_3COCH_3 + I_2 \xrightarrow{H^+} CH_3COCH_2I + HI$$

the iodine did not appear in the rate equation but the H⁺ ions did.

- A reactant that appears in the chemical equation may have no affect on reaction rate.
- A substance that is not a reactant in the chemical equation can affect reaction rate.

In organic chemistry, you have met the idea that reactions occur in a number of steps. We call this the reaction mechanism. These steps do not take place at the same rate. The overall rate of reaction depends on the slowest step. We call this the rate-determining step. If the concentration of a reactant appears in the rate equation, then that reactant (or substances that react together to form it) appears in the rate-determining step. If a substance does not appear in the overall rate equation it does not take part in the rate-determining step. So, for the reaction between propanone and iodine, H⁺ ions are involved in the rate-determining step but iodine is not.

Verifying possible reaction mechanisms

We can use kinetic data to confirm proposed reaction mechanisms. It is important to realise that the mechanism is not deduced from the kinetic data. The kinetic data simply show us that a proposed reaction mechanism is possible.

Various mechanisms have been proposed for the reaction

$$CH_3COCH_3 + I_2 \xrightarrow{H^+} CH_3COCH_2I + HI$$

Figure 22.17 shows one proposed mechanism.

The rate equation for this reaction is

$$\text{rate} = k[CH_3COCH_3][H^+]$$

We could not have deduced this reaction mechanism from the rate equation. But the mechanism is consistent with the rate equation.

The slow step (the rate-determining step) does not involve either propanone or hydrogen ions directly. However, the intermediate with the formula

$$CH_3 - \overset{\overset{\displaystyle +OH}{\|}}{C} - CH_3$$

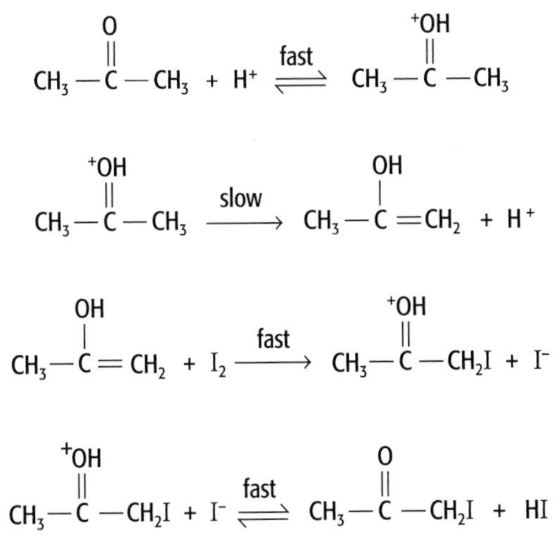

$$CH_3-\overset{\overset{\displaystyle O}{\|}}{C}-CH_3 + H^+ \xrightleftharpoons{\text{fast}} CH_3-\overset{\overset{\displaystyle ^+OH}{\|}}{C}-CH_3$$

$$CH_3-\overset{\overset{\displaystyle ^+OH}{\|}}{C}-CH_3 \xrightarrow{\text{slow}} CH_3-\overset{\overset{\displaystyle OH}{|}}{C}=CH_2 + H^+$$

$$CH_3-\overset{\overset{\displaystyle OH}{|}}{C}=CH_2 + I_2 \xrightarrow{\text{fast}} CH_3-\overset{\overset{\displaystyle ^+OH}{\|}}{C}-CH_2I + I^-$$

$$CH_3-\overset{\overset{\displaystyle ^+OH}{\|}}{C}-CH_2I + I^- \xrightleftharpoons{\text{fast}} CH_3-\overset{\overset{\displaystyle O}{\|}}{C}-CH_2I + HI$$

Figure 22.17 Propanone molecules rapidly accept hydrogen ions to form an intermediate that slowly forms propen-2-ol. This reacts rapidly with iodine to give the products.

is derived from substances that react together to form it (propanone and hydrogen ions). So both $[CH_3COCH_3]$ and $[H^+]$ appear in the rate equation.

The reaction between iodine and the intermediate

$CH_3C(OH){=}CH_2$ is fast and iodine molecules are not involved in the mechanism until after the rate-determining step. So the rate of reaction does not depend on the concentration of iodine.

On page 337 we saw that the rate equation for the reaction

$$2N_2O_5(g) \longrightarrow 4NO_2(g) + O_2$$

is rate $= k[N_2O_5]$. Figure 22.18 shows a suggested mechanism for this reaction. The rate equation suggests that a single N_2O_5 molecule is involved in the rate-determining step. This fits in with the proposed mechanism that suggests that the decomposition of N_2O_5 to form NO_2 and NO_3 is the slow step. The steps that follow the slow step are relatively fast and so have no effect on reaction rate.

If there is only a single species (atom, ion or molecule) in the rate-determining step we call the reaction unimolecular. If two species (which can be the same or different) are involved in the rate-determining step, we say that the reaction is bimolecular. Mechanisms that involve a trimolecular step are rare. This is because it is unlikely that three species will collide at the same time.

339

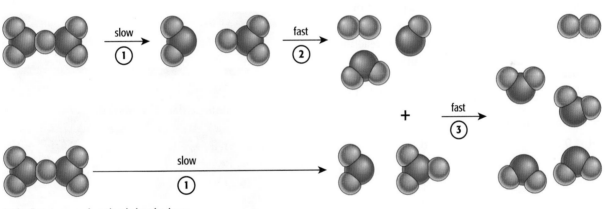

in the first step – each molecule breaks down, they don't collide in pairs

Reaction steps:
(1) $N_2O_5 \xrightarrow{\text{slow}} NO_2 + NO_3$
(2) $NO_2 + NO_3 \xrightarrow{\text{fast}} NO + NO_2 + O_2$
(3) $NO + NO_3 \xrightarrow{\text{fast}} 2NO_2$

(note that two molecules of N_2O_5 need to have reacted for subsequent steps to be completed)

Figure 22.18 The rate equation tells us that the decomposition of individual molecules of nitrogen(V) oxide is the rate-determining step. The subsequent reactions are very much faster by comparison, and do not influence the overall rate. Try to match the reaction steps with the illustrations to get a picture of what is happening.

QUESTION

14 An acidified solution of hydrogen peroxide reacts with iodide ions.

$$H_2O_2(aq) + 2H^+(aq) + 2I^-(aq) \longrightarrow 2H_2O(l) + I_2(aq)$$

The rate equation for this reaction is

rate = $[H_2O_2][I^-]$

The mechanism below has been proposed for this reaction.

$$H_2O_2 + I^- \xrightarrow{\text{slow}} H_2O + IO^-$$

$$H^+ + IO^- \xrightarrow{\text{fast}} HIO$$

$$HIO + H^+ + I^- \xrightarrow{\text{fast}} I_2 + H_2O$$

Explain why this mechanism is consistent with the rate equation.

Predicting the order of a reaction from reaction mechanisms

We can predict the order of reaction from a given reaction mechanism if we know the intermediates present in the rate-determining step (or substances that react together to form the intermediate). Take, for example, the reaction of propanone with bromine in alkaline solution.

$$CH_3COCH_3 + Br_2 + OH^- \longrightarrow CH_3COCH_2Br + H_2O + Br^-$$

The reaction mechanism is shown in Figure 22.19.

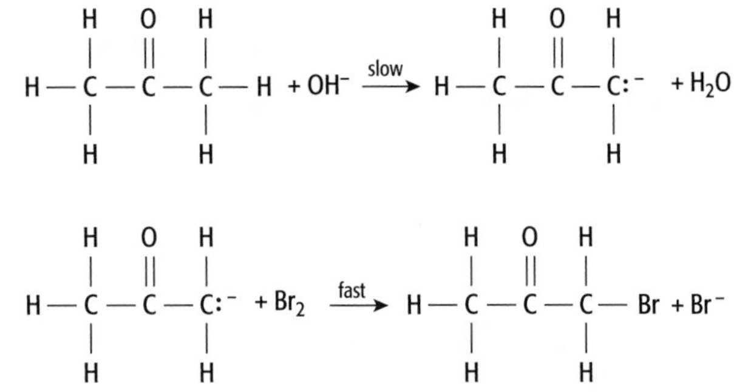

Figure 22.19 The reaction mechanism for the bromination of propanone in alkaline conditions.

The rate-determining step in this reaction is the slow step. The slow step involves one molecule of propanone and one hydroxide ion, so only these two species appear in the rate equation. The reaction is second order overall, first order with respect to propanone and first order with respect to hydroxide ions.

rate = $k[CH_3COCH_3][OH^-]$

Bromine does not appear in the rate equation, as it takes part in a fast step after the rate-determining step.

Catalysis

In Chapter 9 (page 144) you saw that catalysts increase the rate of a chemical reaction. They do this by providing an alternative pathway for the reaction with lower activation energy. We can divide catalysts into two main classes.

- **Homogeneous catalysis** occurs when the catalyst is in the same phase as the reaction mixture. For example: hydrogen ions catalyse the hydrolysis of esters.

$$CH_3COOC_2H_5(aq) + H_2O(l) \underset{}{\overset{H^+(aq)}{\rightleftharpoons}} CH_3COOH(aq) + C_2H_5OH(aq)$$

In this reaction the reactants, products and catalyst are all in the aqueous phase.

- **Heterogeneous catalysis** occurs when the catalyst is in a different phase to the reaction mixture. For example, the decomposition of aqueous hydrogen peroxide catalysed by manganese(IV) oxide.

$$2H_2O_2(aq) \xrightarrow{MnO_2(s)} 2H_2O(l) + O_2(g)$$

The manganese(IV) oxide is in the solid phase, whereas the hydrogen peroxide is in aqueous solution.

Figure 22.20 Addition polymers are produced using metallocene catalysts such as $[(C_5H_5)_2 ZrCH_3]^+$. The strength and puncture resistance of this polymer film is being shown with a ball-point pen.

Homogeneous catalysis

Homogeneous catalysis often involves changes in oxidation number of the ions involved in catalysis. For example, small amounts of iodide ions catalyse the decomposition of hydrogen peroxide. In the catalysed reaction, iodide ions, I^-, are first oxidised to iodate(I) ions, IO^-. The IO^- ions then react with further molecules of hydrogen peroxide and are reduced back to iodide ions.

$$H_2O_2(aq) + I^-(aq) \longrightarrow H_2O(l) + IO^-(aq)$$

$$H_2O_2(aq) + IO^-(aq) \longrightarrow H_2O(l) + I^-(aq) + O_2(g)$$

The overall equation is:

$$2H_2O_2(aq) \xrightarrow{\;I^-\;} 2H_2O(l) + O_2(g)$$

Ions of transition elements are often good catalysts because of their ability to change oxidation number.

Examples of homogeneous catalysis

The iodine–peroxodisulfate reaction

Peroxodisulfate (persulfate) ions, $S_2O_8^{2-}$, oxidise iodide ions to iodine. This reaction is very slow.

$$S_2O_8^{2-}(aq) + 2I^-(aq) \longrightarrow 2SO_4^{2-}(aq) + I_2(aq)$$

The peroxodisulfate and iodide ions both have a negative charge. In order to collide and react, these ions need considerable energy to overcome the repulsive forces when like charges approach each other.

$Fe^{3+}(aq)$ ions catalyse this reaction. The catalysis involves two redox reactions.

- Reaction 1: reduction of Fe^{3+} ions to Fe^{2+} ions by I^- ions:

$$2Fe^{3+}(aq) + 2I^-(aq) \longrightarrow 2Fe^{2+}(aq) + I_2(aq)$$

- Reaction 2: oxidation of Fe^{2+} ions back to Fe^{3+} by $S_2O_8^{2-}$ ions:

$$2Fe^{2+}(aq) + S_2O_8^{2-}(aq) \longrightarrow 2Fe^{3+}(aq) + 2SO_4^{2-}(aq)$$

In both reactions 1 and 2, positively charged iron ions react with negatively charged ions. As ions with unlike charges are attracted to each other, these reactions are more likely to occur than direct reaction between $S_2O_8^{2-}$ and I^- ions.

You should notice that it doesn't matter what the order is of the two reactions. The oxidation of Fe^{2+} ions to Fe^{3+} by $S_2O_8^{2-}$ ions could happen first:

$$2Fe^{2+}(aq) + S_2O_8^{2-}(aq) \longrightarrow 2Fe^{3+}(aq) + 2SO_4^{2-}(aq)$$

followed by

$$2Fe^{3+}(aq) + 2I^-(aq) \longrightarrow 2Fe^{2+}(aq) + I_2(aq)$$

This reaction is catalysed by $Fe^{3+}(aq)$ and it is also catalysed by $Fe^{2+}(aq)$.

Figure 22.21 shows an energy level profile for the catalysed and the uncatalysed reactions. Note that the catalysed reaction has two energy 'humps' because it is a two-stage reaction.

In order for this catalysis to work, the standard electrode potentials for the reactions involving the catalyst must lie between the electrode potentials involving the two reactants (Figure 22.22). The use of electrode potentials in this way only predicts that the catalysis is possible. It does not give any information about the rate of reaction.

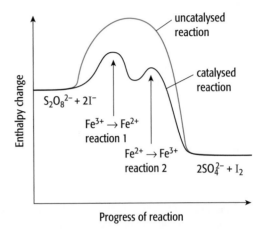

Figure 22.21 Energy level profiles for the catalysed and uncatalysed reactions of peroxodisulfate ions with iodide ions.

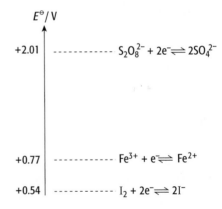

Figure 22.22 The electrode potential diagram for the catalysis of the reaction $S_2O_8^{2-} + 2I^- \longrightarrow 2SO_4^{2-} + I_2$.

Oxides of nitrogen and acid rain

Sulfur dioxide is produced when fossil fuels containing sulfur are burnt. When sulfur dioxide escapes into the atmosphere it contributes to acid rain. One of the steps in the formation of acid rain is the oxidation of sulfur dioxide to sulfur trioxide.

$$SO_2(g) + \tfrac{1}{2}O_2(g) \longrightarrow SO_3(g)$$

This oxidation is catalysed by a wide variety of mechanisms. Nitrogen(IV) oxide present in the atmosphere from a variety of sources (see page 184) can

341

catalyse the oxidation of sulfur dioxide. The nitrogen(IV) oxide is reformed by reaction with atmospheric oxygen.

$$SO_2(g) + NO_2(g) \longrightarrow SO_3(g) + NO(g)$$

$$NO + \tfrac{1}{2}O_2 \longrightarrow NO_2(g)$$

15 a State which pairs of substances **i** to **iv** below might catalyse the reaction:

$$S_2O_8^{2-}(aq) + 2I^-(aq) \longrightarrow 2SO_4^{2-}(aq) + I_2(aq)$$

Explain your answer.

i	$Ni^{2+}(aq) / Ni(s)$	$E^\ominus = -0.25\,V$
ii	$Mn^{3+}(aq) / Mn^{2+}(aq)$	$E^\ominus = +1.49\,V$
iii	$Ce^{4+}(aq) / Ce^{3+}(aq)$	$E^\ominus = +1.70\,V$
iv	$Cu^{2+}(aq) / Cu^+(aq)$	$E^\ominus = +0.15\,V$

b Describe in terms of oxidation number change, which species are being oxidised and which are being reduced in these equations:

i $SO_2(g) + NO_2(g) \longrightarrow SO_3(g) + NO(g)$

ii $NO + \tfrac{1}{2}O_2 \longrightarrow NO_2(g)$

Heterogeneous catalysis

Heterogeneous catalysis often involves gaseous molecules reacting at the surface of a solid catalyst. The mechanism of this catalysis can be explained using the theory of **adsorption**. Chemical adsorption (also called chemisorption) occurs when molecules become bonded to atoms on the surface of a solid. Transition elements such as nickel are particularly good at chemisorbing hydrogen gas. Figure 22.23 shows the process of adsorption of hydrogen onto a nickel surface.

You must be careful to distinguish between the words adsorb and absorb. **Adsorb** means to bond to the surface of a substance. **Absorb** means to move right into the substance – rather like a sponge absorbs water.

The stages in adsorption of hydrogen onto nickel are:

- hydrogen gas diffuses to the surface of the nickel
- the hydrogen is physically adsorbed onto the surface – weak van der Waals' forces link the hydrogen molecules to the nickel
- the hydrogen becomes chemically adsorbed onto the surface – this causes stronger bonds to form between the hydrogen and the nickel
- this causes weakening of the hydrogen–hydrogen covalent bond.

Examples of heterogeneous catalysis

Iron in the Haber process

Particular conditions of temperature and pressure are required to form ammonia from nitrogen and hydrogen (see page 182). The reaction is catalysed by iron. The catalyst works by allowing hydrogen and nitrogen molecules to come close together on the surface of the iron. They are then more likely to react. Figure 22.24 shows the five steps in this heterogeneous catalysis.

1 Diffusion: nitrogen gas and hydrogen gas diffuse to the surface of the iron.

2 Adsorption: the reactant molecules are chemically adsorbed onto the surface of the iron. The bonds formed between the reactant molecules and the iron are:

- strong enough to weaken the covalent bonds within the nitrogen and hydrogen molecules so the atoms can react with each other
- weak enough to break and allow the products to leave the surface.

3 Reaction: the adsorbed nitrogen and hydrogen atoms react on the surface of the iron to form ammonia.

4 Desorption: the bonds between the ammonia and the surface of the iron weaken and are eventually broken.

5 Diffusion: ammonia diffuses away from the surface of the iron.

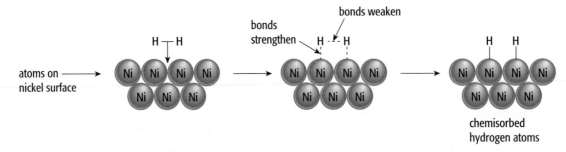

Figure 22.23 The adsorption of hydrogen onto a nickel surface.

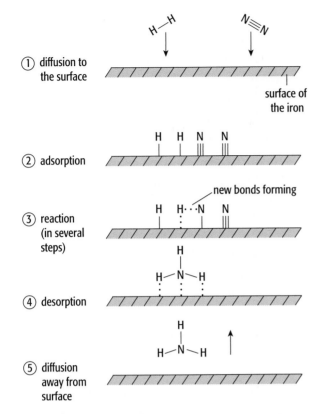

Figure 22.24 A possible mechanism for catalysis in the Haber process.

① diffusion to the surface

surface of the iron

② adsorption

new bonds forming

③ reaction (in several steps)

④ desorption

⑤ diffusion away from surface

Transition elements in catalytic converters

In Chapter 15 (page 205) you learnt how catalytic converters convert harmful nitrogen oxides and carbon monoxide present in the exhaust gases from car engines to harmless gases. The 'honeycomb' structure inside the catalytic converter contains small beads coated with platinum, palladium or rhodium. These act as heterogeneous catalysts. Possible steps in the catalytic process include:

■ adsorption of nitrogen oxides and carbon monoxide onto the catalyst surface

■ weakening of the covalent bonds within the nitrogen oxides and carbon monoxide

■ formation of new bonds between

   – adjacent nitrogen atoms (to form nitrogen molecules)

   – carbon monoxide and oxygen atoms to form carbon dioxide

■ desorption of nitrogen molecules and carbon dioxide molecules from the surface of the catalyst.

> **QUESTION**
>
> **16 a** Describe in general terms what is meant by **desorption**.
>
> **b** Nickel acts as a catalyst for the hydrogenation of alkenes. For example:
>
> $$CH_2{=}CH_2 + H_2 \xrightarrow{\text{Ni}} CH_3{-}CH_3$$
>
> Suggest how nickel catalyses this reaction by referring to the processes of adsorption, reaction on the metal surface and desorption.
>
> **c** In catalytic converters, rhodium catalyses the reduction of nitrogen(II) oxide, NO, to nitrogen. Draw diagrams to suggest:
>
> **i** how NO is adsorbed onto the surface of the rhodium metal
>
> **ii** how nitrogen is formed.

343

Summary

■ Rate of reaction is a measure of the rate at which reactants are used up or the rate at which products are formed. The units of rate are $mol\,dm^{-3}\,s^{-1}$.

■ Rate of reaction is related to concentrations of reactants by a rate equation, which can only be determined by experiment.

■ The general form of the rate equation is:

rate = $k[A]^m[B]^n$, where:

   – k is the rate constant

   – [A] and [B] are the concentrations of those reactants that affect the rate of reaction

   – m is the order of the reaction with respect to A and n is the order of reaction with respect to B.

■ The overall order of reaction is the sum of the orders in the rate equation. For the previous example:

overall order is $m + n$

■ The order of reaction for a given reactant can be determined experimentally by either:

   – measuring the initial rate of reaction using different concentrations of a given reactant while keeping the concentrations of all other reactants fixed, or

   – determining the change in concentration of a specific reactant as the experiment proceeds, the rate being calculated from tangents taken at several points on the graph.

- The order of reaction can be determined from graphs of reaction rate against concentration.

- The half-life of a reaction is the time taken for the concentration of a reactant to halve.

- In a first-order reaction the half-life is independent of the concentration(s) of the reactant(s).

- The half-life of a first-order reaction may be used in calculations to find the first-order rate constant using the relationship

$$t_{\frac{1}{2}} = \frac{0.693}{k}$$

- The rate-determining step is the slowest step in a reaction mechanism. The rate-determining step determines the overall rate of reaction.

- The order of reaction with respect to a particular reactant shows how many molecules of that reactant are involved in the rate-determining step of a reaction.

- The rate equation provides evidence to support the suggestion of a reaction mechanism.

- The order of a reaction can be predicted from a given reaction mechanism knowing the rate-limiting step.

- Homogeneous catalysis occurs when a catalyst and the reactants are in the same phase.

- The mechanism of homogeneous catalysis usually involves redox reactions.

- Examples of homogeneous catalysis include:
  - the catalytic role of atmospheric oxides of nitrogen in the atmospheric oxidation of sulfur dioxide
  - Fe^{2+} or Fe^{3+} ions catalysing the reaction between iodide ions and peroxodisulfate ions.

- Heterogeneous catalysis occurs when a catalyst is in a different phase from the reactants.

- The mechanism of heterogeneous catalysis involves the processes of adsorption, reaction and desorption.

- Examples of heterogeneous catalysis include:
  - the use of iron in the Haber process
  - the catalytic removal of oxides of nitrogen in the exhaust gases from car engines.

End-of-chapter questions

Questions **1a**, **4b** and **6a** all require you to plot a graph. Make sure that you do the following:

- the axes (e.g. 0–120 minutes and 0–0.080 mol dm^{-3}) take up more than half of the graph paper you use
- label the axes sensibly so that plotting is easy; for example, if on your time axis, two large squares = 30 minutes, it is much easier to make plotting mistakes
- plot points precisely with a sharp pencil
- draw a smooth curve through the points, with care.

These skills are all essential and should be practised every time you plot a graph.

1 The rate of reaction between butanone and iodine is studied. In this experiment, iodine is in excess. The concentration of butanone is measured at various time intervals. The results are shown in the table below.

Time / min	0	10	20	30	40	50	60	80	100	120
[butanone] / mol dm^{-3}	0.080	0.055	0.035	0.024	0.015	0.010	0.007	0.003	0.001	0.001

a   Plot these data on a suitable graph.   [3]

b   Show from your graph that these data are consistent with the reaction being first order with respect to butanone.   [2]

c   Find the gradient of your graph when the butanone concentration is:

■ $0.070 \, \text{mol dm}^{-3}$

■ $0.040 \, \text{mol dm}^{-3}$

■ $0.010 \, \text{mol dm}^{-3}$ [2]

d   Use your answers to part **c** to plot a suitable graph to show rate of reaction (on the vertical axis) against concentration (on the horizontal axis).   [3]

e   Explain how the graph you plotted in part **d** is consistent with the reaction being first order with respect to butanone.   [2]

Total = 12

2   The reaction

$$A + B + C \longrightarrow ABC$$

is zero order with respect to one reactant, first order with respect to another reactant and second order with respect to another reactant.

a **i** Explain what is meant by the term **order of reaction** with respect to a given reactant.   [2]

    ii Use the data in the table below to deduce the order with respect to each of the reactants, **A**, **B** and **C**.

Experiment	$[A] / \text{mol dm}^{-3}$	$[B] / \text{mol dm}^{-3}$	$[C] / \text{mol dm}^{-3}$	Rate $/ \text{mol dm}^{-3} \, \text{s}^{-1}$
1	0.100	1.00	1.00	0.00783
2	0.200	1.00	1.00	0.00802
3	0.300	1.00	1.00	0.00796
4	1.00	0.100	1.00	0.00008
5	1.00	0.200	1.00	0.00031
6	1.00	0.300	1.00	0.00073
7	1.00	1.00	0.100	0.00078
8	1.00	1.00	0.200	0.00158
9	1.00	1.00	0.300	0.00236

[9]

b **i** Write the rate equation for this reaction.   [1]

    ii State the overall order of the reaction.   [1]

    iii Calculate the value of the rate constant using experiment **6**. Include the units in your answer.   [3]

c   Suggest a possible mechanism consistent with the rate equation you have proposed and the chemical equation

$$A + B + C \longrightarrow ABC$$

[3]

Total = 19

345

3 The rate equation for the reaction between iodine and propanone is:

rate = $k[CH_3COCH_3][H^+][I_2]^0$

a State the order of reaction with respect to iodine. [1]

b State the overall order of reaction. [1]

c i What is meant by the term **half-life**? [1]

 ii In an experiment a large excess of iodine is reacted with a small concentration of propanone in the presence of $H^+(aq)$. The concentration of propanone is measured at regular time intervals. What happens to the value of the half-life of the propanone concentration as the concentration of propanone decreases? [1]

d Copy the sketch graph. Plot additional points at 10-second intervals up to 50 s. Join all the points with a smooth curve. [4]

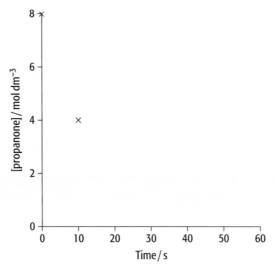

e Explain the term **rate-determining step**. [2]

f Suggest a possible mechanism for the rate-determining step for the reaction between iodine and propanone. [3]

Total = 13

4 The decomposition of hydrogen peroxide, H_2O_2, to oxygen and water is catalysed by manganese(IV) oxide.

a Define the term **catalyst**. [2]

b The results for the decomposition of a sample of hydrogen peroxide are shown in the table.

Time / min	0	1	2	3	4	5	6	7	8
$[H_2O_2]$ / mol dm^{-3}	1.60	1.04	0.61	0.40	0.25	0.16	0.10	0.06	0.04

 i Draw a graph of concentration of hydrogen peroxide (vertical axis) against time (horizontal axis). Draw a curve of best fit. [3]

 ii Use your graph to determine the half-life of the reaction. Show your working. [2]

 iii Use your graph to find the rate of reaction after 2 min. [4]

c i Give the rate equation for the reaction. Explain your answer. [3]

 ii Use your answer to part **b, iii**, to calculate the value of the rate constant, k, and give the units. [3]

 iii Using your rate equation, find the rate of reaction when $[H_2O_2] = 2$ mol dm^{-3}. [2]

Total = 19

5 Peroxodisulfate ions, $S_2O_8^{2-}$, react with iodide ions in aqueous solution to form iodine and sulfate ions.

$S_2O_8^{2-}(aq) + 2I^-(aq) \longrightarrow 2SO_4^{2-}(aq) + I_2(aq)$ **equation 1**

The initial rates of reaction are compared by timing how long it takes to produce a particular amount of iodine using four different initial concentrations of $S_2O_8^{2-}$. The results are shown in the table.

$[S_2O_8^{2-}]/mol\,dm^{-3}$	Initial rate of reaction$/s^{-1}$
0.0200	4.16×10^{-3}
0.0150	3.12×10^{-3}
0.0120	2.50×10^{-3}
0.0080	1.70×10^{-3}

a Plot a suitable graph to calculate rate of reaction.   [3]

b Deduce the order of reaction with respect to peroxodisulfate ions. Explain your answer.   [2]

c The reaction is first order with respect to iodide ions. Use this information and your answer to part **b** to write the overall rate equation for the reaction.   [1]

d The reaction between peroxodisulfate ions and iodide ions is slow. The reaction can be speeded up by adding a few drops of Fe^{3+} (aq) ions. The following reactions then take place:

$2I^-(aq) + 2Fe^{3+}(aq) \longrightarrow I_2(aq) + 2Fe^{2+}(aq)$ **equation 2**

$2Fe^{2+}(aq) + S_2O_8^{2-}(aq) \longrightarrow 2Fe^{3+}(aq) + 2SO_4^{2-}(aq)$ **equation 3**

  i What type of catalysis is occurring here? Explain your answer.   [2]

  ii By referring to equations **1**, **2** and **3** above, suggest why Fe^{3+}(aq) ions catalyse the reaction between peroxodisulfate ions and iodide ions.   [4]

Total = 12

6 The rate of reaction between butanone and iodine is studied. In this experiment, butanone is in excess. The concentration of iodine is measured every 10 minutes for 1 hour. The results are shown in the table.

Time / min	0	10	20	30	40	50	60
$[I_2]/mol\,dm^{-3}$	0.060	0.051	0.041	0.032	0.022	0.012	0.003

a Plot these data on a suitable graph.   [3]

b Show from the graph that these data are consistent with the reaction being zero order with respect to iodine.   [1]

c The balanced chemical equation for the reaction is

$CH_3CH_2COCH_3 + I_2 \longrightarrow CH_3CH_2COCH_2I + HI$

Could this reaction occur in a single step? Explain your answer.   [2]

d The rate equation for the reaction is

$rate = k[CH_3CH_2COCH_3]$

Explain the different meanings of the balanced chemical equation and the rate equation.   [4]

Total = 10

7 Nitrogen oxides can be removed from the exhaust gases of a car engine by using a catalytic converter. Many catalytic converters contain metals such as platinum and rhodium. These act as heterogeneous catalysts.

   a **i** What is meant by the term **heterogeneous catalysis**? [2]

       ii Explain in general terms how heterogeneous catalysts work. [4]

   b Nitrogen(IV) oxide and carbon monoxide from car exhausts can react in a catalytic converter.

$$NO_2(g) + CO(g) \longrightarrow NO(g) + CO_2(g)$$

The rate equation for this reaction is

$$\text{rate} = k[NO_2]^2$$

Suggest a two-step reaction mechanism for this reaction that is consistent with this rate equation. [2]

   c Nitrogen(IV) oxide is formed when nitrogen(II) oxide reacts with oxygen.

$$2NO(g) + O_2(g) \longrightarrow 2NO_2(g)$$

The table shows the data obtained from a series of experiments to investigate the kinetics of this reaction.

Experiment	$[NO]$ / mol dm^{-3}	$[O_2]$ / mol dm^{-3}	Initial rate / mol dm^{-3} s^{-1}
1	0.00100	0.00300	21.3
2	0.00100	0.00400	28.4
3	0.00300	0.00400	256

     i Deduce the order of reaction with respect to each reactant. In each case, show your reasoning. [4]

     ii Deduce the rate equation for this reaction. [1]

     iii State the units of the rate constant, k, for this reaction. [1]

Total = 14

8 Bromate(V) ions react with bromide ions in acidic solution to form bromine.

$$BrO_3^-(aq) + 5Br^-(aq) + 6H^+(aq) \longrightarrow 3Br_2(aq) + 3H_2O(l)$$

   a Suggest two methods of following the progress of this reaction. For each method explain your answer. [4]

   b The initial rates of reaction were compared using the initial concentrations of reactants shown in the table.

Experiment	$[BrO_3^-]$ / mol dm^{-3}	$[Br^-]$ / mol dm^{-3}	$[H^+]$ / mol dm^{-3}	Relative rate of formation of bromine
1	0.040	0.20	0.24	1
2	0.040	0.20	0.48	4
3	0.080	0.20	0.48	8
4	0.040	0.10	0.48	2

     i Deduce the order of reaction with respect to each reactant. In each case, show your reasoning. [6]

     ii Deduce the rate equation for this reaction. [1]

     iii State the units of the rate constant, k, for this reaction. [1]

Total = 12

Chapter 23:
Entropy and Gibbs free energy

Learning outcomes

You should be able to:

- explain that **entropy**, ΔS, is the measure of the disorder of a system and that a system becomes energetically more stable when it becomes more disordered

- explain the difference in magnitude of entropy:
  - for a change in state
  - for a change in temperature
  - for a reaction in which there is a change in the number of gaseous molecules

- predict whether the entropy change for a given process is positive or negative

- calculate the entropy change for a reaction, $\Delta S^{\ominus}$, given the standard entropies of the reactants and products

- define **standard Gibbs free energy change of reaction** by means of the equation

  $$\Delta G^{\ominus} = \Delta H^{\ominus} - T\Delta S^{\ominus}$$

- state whether a reaction or process will be spontaneous by using the sign $\Delta G^{\ominus}$

- predict the effect of temperature change on the spontaneity of a reaction given standard enthalpy and entropy changes.

Introduction

About 150 years ago, many scientists thought that all chemical reactions gave off heat to the surroundings. They thought that all chemical reactions were exothermic. We now know this not true. Many chemical reactions and processes are endothermic. Enthalpy changes alone cannot help us predict whether or not a reaction will occur. If we want to predict this, we need to consider the entropy change of the reaction.

The term entropy was first given by German physicist Rudolf Clausius in 1865. From experimental results, he suggested a relationship between entropy change (ΔS), the energy transferred reversibly from the surroundings (q) and the temperature (T):

$$\Delta S = \frac{q}{T}$$

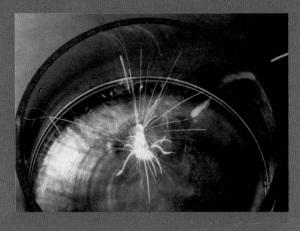

Figure 23.1 Potassium reacts spontaneously with water.

Introducing entropy

Entropy is a measure of the dispersal of energy at a specific temperature. Entropy can also be thought of as a measure of the randomness or disorder of a system. The higher the randomness or disorder, the greater the entropy of the system. A **system** is the part under investigation. In chemistry this is the chemical reaction itself, i.e. reactants being converted to products. The system of magnesium reacting with sulfuric acid in a test tube to form magnesium sulfate and hydrogen releases energy to the surroundings. The surroundings include:

- the solvent (in this case water)
- the air around the test tube
- the test tube itself
- anything dipping into the test tube (e.g. a thermometer).

Changes that tend to continue to happen naturally are called **spontaneous changes**. Once started, a spontaneous change will carry on. When a light is applied, methane gas reacts with oxygen in a spontaneous reaction to form carbon dioxide and water. The reaction is spontaneous because the methane continues to burn in the oxygen until either the methane or oxygen is completely used up. For a reaction to be spontaneous, it does not need to happen rapidly. Many spontaneous reactions are slow or need an input of energy to start them.

Entropy can also be thought of as a dispersal of energy, either from the system to the surroundings or from the surroundings to the system. The system becomes energetically more stable when it becomes more disordered.

Chance and spontaneous change

Diffusion

If you spill a few drops of perfume in a closed room with no air draughts, the smell spreads gradually throughout the room. The molecules in the perfume vapour, which are responsible for the smell, move randomly in straight lines until they collide with air molecules, other perfume molecules or with the walls of the room. After collision, the perfume molecules change direction. This process of random movement and random collisions of molecules is called diffusion. The reason molecules in a vapour diffuse is because of the laws of chance and probability.

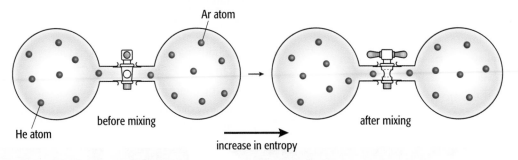

Figure 23.2 The spontaneous mixing of helium atoms (●) with argon atoms (●).

We can make a model to show how, during a spontaneous process, the entropy of the system increases. Figure 23.2 shows a system of two flasks connected by a stopcock. One flask contains helium and the other contains argon. These gases do not react.

When the stopcock is opened, the gas atoms move spontaneously by diffusion. After mixing, the gases are mixed up and there is more disorder than before mixing. The entropy has increased.

Diffusion and number of ways

We can show that the molecules in a vapour diffuse by chance by thinking about the probability of finding them at one place at any one time. Consider the simplified model shown below.

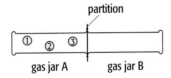

The three molecules in gas jar A cannot move into gas jar B.

In this model we assume that:

■ there are only a few molecules in gas jar A
■ there are no other particles present
■ the molecules move randomly and change directions when they collide.

After we remove the partition, the molecules can move randomly not only within gas jar A but also into gas jar B. There are three molecules and two places in which they can be (gas jar A and gas jar B). The number of ways of arranging the molecules after removing the partition is shown in Figure 23.3.

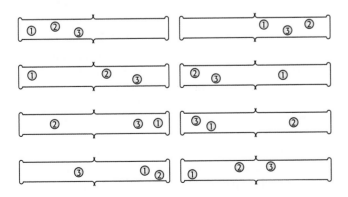

Figure 23.3 The eight possible arrangements of molecules after removing the partition between the gas jars.

There are eight different ways of arranging the three molecules between two gas jars. We can express this as:

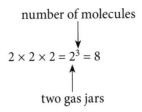

$$2 \times 2 \times 2 = 2^3 = 8$$

Each of these ways is equally likely (probable). So the chance that all the molecules will stay in gas jar A is 1 in 8. Similarly, the chance that all three molecules will move over to gas jar B is 1 in 8. The molecules diffuse because there are more ways of them being spread out than remaining in the same place.

If we started with five molecules in gas jar A, the number of ways of arranging the molecules is $2^5 = 32$ different ways. If we scaled this up to the numbers of gas molecules that we might find in a container in the laboratory, the number of ways of arranging the molecules is extremely large; for example, for a million molecules between two gas jars it would be $2^{1\,000\,000}$, a number that is too large for your calculator to deal with. So diffusion happens because there is an overwhelming likelihood of it taking place as a result of the large number of ways of arranging the molecules. The idea of the 'number of ways' of arranging either molecules or the energy within molecules dictates whether the changes that take place are the ones that are most likely to happen. This applies to chemical reactions as well as to physical processes such as diffusion.

351

QUESTION

1 a For this question refer back to Figure 23.3. If there are four molecules in the gas jar on the left, how many ways of arranging the molecules are there when the partition is removed?

b What is the probability of finding all four molecules in the right-hand gas jar?

c Which of the following changes are likely to be spontaneous?

i sugar dissolving in water

ii the smell from an open bottle of aqueous ammonia diffusing throughout a room

iii water turning to ice at 10 °C

iv ethanol vaporising at 20 °C

v water mixing completely with cooking oil

vi limestone (calcium carbonate) decomposing at room temperature

Comparing entropy values

To make any comparison of entropy values fair, we must use standard conditions. These standard conditions are the same as those used for ΔH:

- a pressure of 10^5 Pa
- a temperature of 298 K (25 °C)
- each substance involved in the reaction is in its normal physical state (solid, liquid or gas) at 10^5 Pa and 298 K.

Under these conditions and for a mole of substance, the unit of standard molar entropy, $S^{\ominus}$, is $J\,K^{-1}\,mol^{-1}$. Standard molar entropy is the entropy of one mole of substance in its standard state. The symbol $^{\ominus}$ indicates that the entropy is at standard conditions.

Table 23.1 shows some values for some standard molar entropies.

Substance	$S^{\ominus}/$ $J\,K^{-1}\,mol^{-1}$	Substance	$S^{\ominus}/$ $J\,K^{-1}\,mol^{-1}$
diamond (s)	2.4	methanol (l)	239.7
graphite (s)	5.7	water (l)	69.9
calcium (s)	41.4	carbon monoxide (g)	197.6
lead (s)	64.8	hydrogen (g)	130.6
calcium oxide (s)	39.7	helium (g)	126.0
calcium carbonate (s)	92.9	ammonia (g)	192.3
mercury (l)	76.0	oxygen (g)	205.0
bromine (l)	151.6	carbon dioxide (g)	213.6

Table 23.1 Standard molar entropy values of some solids, liquids and gases. The states are shown as state symbols after each substance.

The values of all standard molar entropies are positive. Remember that elements have positive standard molar entropy values. Do not get this muddled with the case of enthalpies, where the elements in their standard states have entropy values of zero. The entropy values are compared to a theoretically perfect crystal. The Third Law of Thermodynamics states that 'All perfect crystals have the same entropy at a temperature of absolute zero'. The nearest we can get to this is a perfect diamond weighing 12 g cooled to as low a temperature as possible.

From the values in the table and other data we can make some generalisations:

- Gases generally have much higher entropy values than liquids, and liquids have higher entropy values than solids. There are exceptions to this. For example, calcium

Figure 23.4 A diamond has a very low entropy value because it is a solid element with atoms regularly arranged. Bromine has a high entropy value because it tends to spread out.

carbonate (solid) has a higher entropy value than mercury (liquid).

- Simpler substances with fewer atoms have lower entropy values than more complex substances with a greater number of atoms. For example, for calcium oxide, CaO, $S^{\ominus} = 39.7\,J\,K^{-1}\,mol^{-1}$ but for calcium carbonate, $CaCO_3$, $S^{\ominus} = 92.9\,J\,K^{-1}\,mol^{-1}$. Carbon monoxide, CO, has a lower entropy value than carbon dioxide, CO_2.
- For similar types of substances, harder substances have a lower entropy value. For example, diamond has a lower entropy value than graphite and calcium has a lower entropy value than lead.
- For a given substance the entropy increases as a solid melts and then changes to a vapour (see Figure 23.5). For example, the molar entropy of ice just below its melting point is $48.0\,J\,K^{-1}\,mol^{-1}$; the molar entropy for water is $69.9\,J\,K^{-1}\,mol^{-1}$, but just above its boiling point, the value increases to $188.7\,J\,K^{-1}\,mol^{-1}$. There is a gradual increase in entropy as the temperature of a substance is increased. Increasing the temperature of a solid makes the molecules, atoms or ions vibrate more. Increasing the temperature of a liquid or gas increases the entropy because it increases the disorder of the particles. When a substance melts or vaporises, there is a large increase in entropy because there is a very large increase in the disorder of the particles.

When a solid changes to a liquid:

- the regularly arranged lattice of particles close together in the solid changes to
- an irregular arrangement of particles, which are close together but rotate and slide over each other in the liquid.

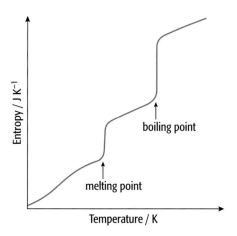

Figure 23.5 The change in entropy as a substance melts and then boils.

When a liquid changes to a vapour:

- the irregular arrangement of particles in the liquid which are close together and rotating changes to
- an irregular arrangement of particles, which are free to move around rapidly because they are far apart from each other.

QUESTION

2 Explain the difference in the entropy of each of the following pairs of substances in terms of their state and structure.

a $Br_2(l)$ $S^\ominus = 151.6 \, J \, K^{-1} \, mol^{-1}$
and $I_2(s)$ $S^\ominus = 116.8 \, J \, K^{-1} \, mol^{-1}$

b $H_2(g)$ $S^\ominus = 130.6 \, J \, K^{-1} \, mol^{-1}$
and $CH_4(g)$ $S^\ominus = 186.2 \, J \, K^{-1} \, mol^{-1}$

c $Hg(l)$ $S^\ominus = 76.00 \, J \, K^{-1} \, mol^{-1}$
and $Na(s)$ $S^\ominus = 51.20 \, J \, K^{-1} \, mol^{-1}$

d $SO_2(g)$ $S^\ominus = 248.1 \, J \, K^{-1} \, mol^{-1}$
and $SO_3(l)$ $S^\ominus = 95.60 \, J \, K^{-1} \, mol^{-1}$

Entropy changes in reactions

In a chemical reaction, if we compare the entropies of the reactants and products, we can try to explain the magnitude of the entropy change and whether or not it increases or decreases. We will assume that gases have high entropy and solids have low entropy. If there is a change in the number of gaseous molecules in a reaction, there is likely to be a significant entropy change. This is because high values of entropy are associated with gases. The more gas molecules, there are, the greater is the number of ways of arranging them and the higher the entropy. For example in the reaction:

$$CaCO_3(s) \longrightarrow CaO(s) + CO_2(g)$$

there is an increase in entropy of the system because the a gas is being produced (high entropy) but the reactant, calcium carbonate, is a solid (low entropy).

In the reaction

$$2N_2O_5(g) \longrightarrow 4NO_2(g) + O_2(g)$$

we should expect an increase of entropy of the system because there are a greater number of moles of gas molecules in the products (5 molecules) than in the reactants (2 molecules). In addition, there are two different product molecules but only one type of reactant molecule. This also contributes to a greater disorder in the products compared with the reactants. The system becomes energetically more stable when it becomes more disordered.

In the reaction

$$N_2(g) + 3H_2(g) \longrightarrow 2NH_3(g)$$

we should expect a decrease in the entropy of the system because there is a reduction in the number of gas molecules as the reaction proceeds. So the entropy change of the system is negative. The reactants, hydrogen and nitrogen, are more stable than the product, ammonia.

QUESTION

3 For each of the following reactions, suggest whether the entropy of the reactants or the products will be greater or whether it is difficult to decide. Explain your answers.

a $NH_3(g) + HCl(g) \longrightarrow NH_4Cl(s)$

b $S(l) + O_2(g) \longrightarrow SO_2(g)$

c $2Mg(s) + CO_2(g) \longrightarrow 2MgO(s) + C(s)$

d $2Li(s) + Cl_2(g) \longrightarrow 2LiCl(s)$

e $H_2O(g) + C(s) \longrightarrow H_2(g) + CO(g)$

f $2HI(g) \rightleftharpoons H_2(g) + I_2(g)$

g $2K(s) + 2H_2O(l) \longrightarrow 2KOH(aq) + H_2(g)$

h $MgCO_3(s) \longrightarrow MgO(s) + CO_2(g)$

353

Calculating entropy changes

Entropy changes in exothermic and endothermic reactions

Energy can be transferred from the system to the surroundings (exothermic change) or from the surroundings to the system (endothermic change). The surroundings are so large that when energy exchange takes place there is such a small change in temperature or pressure that we can ignore these.

- For an exothermic reaction, the energy released to the surroundings increases the number of ways of arranging the energy. This is because the energy goes into rotation and translation (movement from place to place) of molecules in the surroundings. So there is likely to be an increase in entropy and an increased probability of the chemical change occurring spontaneously.
- For an endothermic reaction, the energy absorbed from the surroundings decreases the number of ways of arranging the energy. So there is likely to be a decrease in entropy and a decreased probability of the chemical change occurring spontaneously.

Total entropy change

We can use entropy values to predict whether a chemical reaction will occur spontaneously or not. When a chemical reaction takes place there is a change in entropy because the reactants and products have different entropy values. The symbol for standard entropy change is $\Delta S^{\ominus}$. The total entropy change involves both the system and the surroundings. For the system (reactants and products) we write the entropy change as $\Delta S^{\ominus}_{system}$.

For the surroundings we write the entropy change as $\Delta S^{\ominus}_{surroundings}$.

The total entropy change is given by:

$$\Delta S^{\ominus}_{total} = \Delta S^{\ominus}_{system} + \Delta S^{\ominus}_{surroundings}$$

If the total entropy change increases, the entropy change is positive, e.g. $\Delta S^{\ominus}_{total}$ is $+40\,J\,K^{-1}\,mol^{-1}$. The reaction will then occur spontaneously. We say that the reaction is feasible.

If the total entropy change decreases, the entropy change is negative, e.g. $\Delta S^{\ominus}_{total}$ is $-40\,J\,K^{-1}\,mol^{-1}$. The reaction is then not likely to occur.

Calculating the entropy change of the system

In order to calculate the entropy change of the system we use the relationship:

$$\Delta S^{\ominus}_{system} = S^{\ominus}_{products} - S^{\ominus}_{reactants}$$

Note that:

1 We need to take account of the stoichiometry of the equation (as we did in calculations involving $\Delta H^{\ominus}$).

2 When looking up entropy values in tables of data, we need to choose the data for the correct state, solid, liquid or gas.

WORKED EXAMPLES

1 Calculate the entropy change of the system for the reaction:

$$2Ca(s) + O_2(g) \longrightarrow 2CaO(s)$$

The standard entropy values are:

$S^{\ominus}[Ca(s)] = 41.40\,J\,K^{-1}\,mol^{-1}$

$S^{\ominus}[O_2(g)] = 205.0\,J\,K^{-1}\,mol^{-1}$

$S^{\ominus}[CaO(s)] = 39.70\,J\,K^{-1}\,mol^{-1}$

$\Delta S^{\ominus}_{system} = S^{\ominus}_{products} - S^{\ominus}_{reactants}$

$= 2 \times S^{\ominus}[CaO(s)] - \{2 \times S^{\ominus}[Ca(s)] + S^{\ominus}[O_2(g)]\}$

$= 2 \times 39.70 - \{(2 \times 41.40) + 205.0\}$

$= 79.40 - 287.8$

$\Delta S^{\ominus}_{system} = -208.4\,J\,K^{-1}\,mol^{-1}$

The negative value for the entropy change shows that the entropy of the system has decreased. We know, however, that calcium reacts spontaneously with oxygen. So the entropy of the surroundings must also play a part because the total entropy change must be positive for the reaction to be feasible.

2 Calculate the entropy change of the system for the reaction:

$$CH_4(g) + 2O_2(g) \longrightarrow CO_2(g) + 2H_2O(g)$$

The standard entropy values are:

$S^{\ominus}[CH_4(g)] = 186.2\,J\,K^{-1}\,mol^{-1}$

$S^{\ominus}[O_2(g)] = 205.0\,J\,K^{-1}\,mol^{-1}$

$S^{\ominus}[CO_2(g)] = 213.6\,J\,K^{-1}\,mol^{-1}$

$S^{\ominus}[H_2O(g)] = 188.7\,J\,K^{-1}\,mol^{-1}$

$\Delta S^{\ominus}_{system} = S^{\ominus}_{products} - S^{\ominus}_{reactants}$

$= \{S^{\ominus}[CO_2(g)] + 2 \times S^{\ominus}[H_2O(g)]\}$
$\qquad\qquad - \{S^{\ominus}[CH_4(g)] + 2 \times S^{\ominus}[O_2(g)]\}$

$= \{213.6 + (2 \times 188.7)\} - \{186.2 + (2 \times 205.0)\}$

$= 591.0 - 596.2$

$\Delta S^{\ominus}_{system} = -5.2\,J\,K^{-1}\,mol^{-1}$

The negative value for the entropy change shows that the entropy of the system has decreased slightly. We know, however, that methane burns in oxygen once it is ignited. So the entropy of the surroundings must also play a part in the overall entropy change.

QUESTION

4 Calculate the standard entropy change of the system in each of the following reactions using the standard molar entropy values given here.

(Values for $S^{\ominus}$ in $J K^{-1} mol^{-1}$: $Cl_2(g) = 165.0$, $Fe(s) = 27.30$, $Fe_2O_3(s) = 87.40$, $H_2(g) = 130.6$, $H_2O(l) = 69.90$, $H_2O_2(l) = 109.6$, $Mg(s) = 32.70$, $MgO(s) = 26.90$, $Na(s) = 51.20$, $NaCl(s) = 72.10$, $NH_4NO_3(s) = 151.1$, $N_2O(g) = 219.7$, $O_2(g) = 205.0$)

a $2H_2O_2(l) \longrightarrow 2H_2O(l) + O_2(g)$

b $NH_4NO_3(s) \longrightarrow N_2O(g) + 2H_2O(g)$

c $2Mg(s) + O_2(g) \longrightarrow 2MgO(s)$

d $2Na(s) + Cl_2(g) \longrightarrow 2NaCl(s)$

e $3Mg(s) + Fe_2O_3(s) \longrightarrow 3MgO(s) + 2Fe(s)$

Calculating the entropy change of the surroundings

Many chemical reactions are accompanied by large enthalpy changes. These enthalpy changes change the number of ways of arranging the energy in the surroundings. So, in many chemical reactions the value of the entropy changes in the surroundings cannot be ignored.

The entropy change of the surroundings is calculated using the relationship:

$$\Delta S^{\ominus}_{surroundings} = \frac{-\Delta H^{\ominus}_{reaction}}{T}$$

where

- $\Delta H^{\ominus}_{reaction}$ is the standard enthalpy change of the reaction
- T is the temperature in kelvin. At standard temperature, this value is 298 K.

Note:

1 When performing calculations to find $\Delta S^{\ominus}_{surroundings}$ the value of $\Delta H^{\ominus}_{reaction}$ in $kJ mol^{-1}$ should be multiplied by 1000. This is because entropy changes are measured in units of joules per kelvin per mole.

2 The negative sign in front of $\Delta H^{\ominus}_{reaction}$ is part of the equation and not the sign of the enthalpy change. If the enthalpy change is negative, the whole $-\Delta H^{\ominus}/T$ term becomes positive.

WORKED EXAMPLES

3 Calculate the entropy change of the surroundings for the reaction:

$2Ca(s) + O_2(g) \longrightarrow 2CaO(s)$
$$\Delta H^{\ominus}_{reaction} = -1270.2 \, kJ \, mol^{-1}$$

Step 1 Convert the enthalpy change into $J mol^{-1}$ by multiplying by 1000.

$-1270.2 \times 1000 = -1\,270\,200 \, J \, mol^{-1}$

Step 2 Apply the relationship

$$\Delta S^{\ominus}_{surroundings} = \frac{-\Delta H^{\ominus}_{reaction}}{T}$$

$$= \frac{-(-1\,270\,200)}{298}$$

$$= +4262.4 \, J \, K^{-1} \, mol^{-1}$$

4 Calculate the entropy change of the surroundings for the reaction:

$CH_4(g) + 2O_2(g) \longrightarrow CO_2(g) + 2H_2O(g)$
$$\Delta H^{\ominus}_{reaction} = -890.3 \, kJ \, mol^{-1}$$

Step 1 Convert the enthalpy change into $J mol^{-1}$ by multiplying by 1000.

$-890.3 \times 1000 = -890\,300 \, J \, mol^{-1}$

Step 2 Apply the relationship

$$\Delta S^{\ominus}_{surroundings} = \frac{-\Delta H^{\ominus}_{reaction}}{T}$$

$$= \frac{-(-890\,300)}{298}$$

$$= +2987.6 \, J \, K^{-1} \, mol^{-1}$$

QUESTION

5 Calculate the entropy change of the surroundings in each of the following reactions. Assume that the value of ΔH does not change with temperature.

a $C(s) + O_2(g) \longrightarrow CO_2(g)$ $\quad \Delta H^{\ominus}_{reaction} = -393.5 \, kJ \, mol^{-1}$

carried out at 0 °C

b $2C(s) + N_2(g) \longrightarrow C_2N_2(g)$ $\quad \Delta H^{\ominus}_{reaction} = +307.9 \, kJ \, mol^{-1}$

carried out at 300 °C

c $H_2(g) + F_2(g) \longrightarrow 2HF(g)$ $\Delta H^{\ominus}_{\text{reaction}}$
    $= -271.1\,\text{kJ}\,\text{mol}^{-1}$

carried out at standard temperature

d $Si(s) + 2H_2(g) \longrightarrow SiH_4(g)$ $\Delta H^{\ominus}_{\text{reaction}}$
    $= +34.30\,\text{kJ}\,\text{mol}^{-1}$

carried out at $-3\,°C$

Calculating total entropy change

The total entropy change is given by:

$$\Delta S^{\ominus}_{\text{total}} = \Delta S^{\ominus}_{\text{system}} + \Delta S^{\ominus}_{\text{surroundings}}$$

We can also write this as:

$$\Delta S^{\ominus}_{\text{total}} = \Delta S^{\ominus}_{\text{system}} - \Delta H^{\ominus}_{\text{reaction}}/T$$

The total entropy change for the examples given above for the reaction of calcium with oxygen and the combustion of methane are calculated by simply adding the entropy change of the system to the entropy change of the surroundings.

WORKED EXAMPLES

5 Calculate the total entropy change for the reaction:

$$2Ca(s) + O_2(g) \longrightarrow 2CaO(s)$$

$\Delta S^{\ominus}_{\text{system}}$ $= -208.4\,\text{J}\,\text{K}^{-1}\,\text{mol}^{-1}$

$\Delta S^{\ominus}_{\text{surroundings}} = +4262.4\,\text{J}\,\text{K}^{-1}\,\text{mol}^{-1}$

So:

$\Delta S^{\ominus}_{\text{total}} = \Delta S^{\ominus}_{\text{system}} + \Delta S^{\ominus}_{\text{surroundings}}$

$= -208.4 + 4262.4$

$\Delta S^{\ominus}_{\text{total}} = +4054.0\,\text{J}\,\text{K}^{-1}\,\text{mol}^{-1}$

6 Calculate the total entropy change for the reaction:

$$CH_4(g) + 2O_2(g) \longrightarrow CO_2(g) + 2H_2O(g)$$

$\Delta S^{\ominus}_{\text{system}}$ $= -5.2\,\text{J}\,\text{K}^{-1}\,\text{mol}^{-1}$

$\Delta S^{\ominus}_{\text{surroundings}} = +2987.6\,\text{J}\,\text{K}^{-1}\,\text{mol}^{-1}$

So:

$\Delta S^{\ominus}_{\text{total}} = \Delta S^{\ominus}_{\text{system}} + \Delta S^{\ominus}_{\text{surroundings}}$

$= -5.2 + 2987.6$

$\Delta S^{\ominus}_{\text{total}} = +2982.4\,\text{J}\,\text{K}^{-1}\,\text{mol}^{-1}$

You can see that in both of these worked examples, the large positive entropy change of the surroundings has more than compensated for the negative entropy change of the system. The total entropy change is positive and the reactions are feasible.

6 Calculate the total standard entropy change in each of the following reactions using the standard molar entropy values given here.

(Values for $S^{\ominus}$ in $\text{J}\,\text{K}^{-1}\,\text{mol}^{-1}$: C(graphite) = 5.700, $C_2N_2(g)$ = 242.1, $C_3H_8(g)$ = 269.9, $CO_2(g)$ = 213.6, $H_2(g)$ = 130.6, $H_2O(l)$ = 69.90, $H_2S(g)$ = 205.7, $N_2(g)$ = 191.6, $O_2(g)$ = 205.0, P(s) = 41.10, $P_4O_{10}(s)$ = 228.9, S(s) = 31.80)

a $S(s) + H_2(g) \longrightarrow H_2S(g)$
    $\Delta H^{\ominus}_{\text{reaction}} = -20.6\,\text{kJ}\,\text{mol}^{-1}$

b $2C(graphite) + N_2(g) \longrightarrow C_2N_2(g)$
    $\Delta H^{\ominus}_{\text{reaction}} = +307.9\,\text{kJ}\,\text{mol}^{-1}$

c $4P(s) + 5O_2(g) \longrightarrow P_4O_{10}(s)$
    $\Delta H^{\ominus}_{\text{reaction}} = -2984.0\,\text{kJ}\,\text{mol}^{-1}$

d $C_3H_8(g) + 5O_2(g) \longrightarrow 3CO_2(g) + 4H_2O(l)$
    $\Delta H^{\ominus}_{\text{reaction}} = -2219.2\,\text{kJ}\,\text{mol}^{-1}$

Entropy in equilibrium reactions

In equilibrium reactions both products and reactants are present. How can the total entropy change be positive in both directions? There is an additional increase in disorder and hence an increase in entropy associated with this mixing. Figure 23.6 shows how the increase in entropy changes as a reaction progresses, starting either from pure reactants or pure products to reach equilibrium.

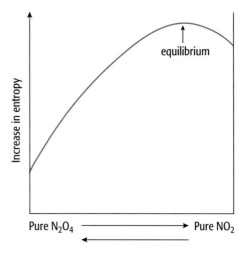

Figure 23.6 The total entropy change, $\Delta S^{\ominus}_{\text{total}}$, when N_2O_4 is converted to an equilibrium mixture of NO_2 and N_2O_4 and NO_2 is converted to the same equilibrium mixture.

As mixing proceeds, the rate of increasing disorder decreases as more and more NO_2 molecules are formed from N_2O_4. At some stage in the reaction, the rate of the forward reaction equals the rate of the backward reaction. Equilibrium has been reached. The same argument applies to the reverse reaction. At the position of equilibrium the total entropy change of the forward reaction equals the total entropy change of the backward reaction, and under standard conditions the overall entropy change is zero.

Entropy and temperature

We have seen that the entropy change of the surroundings is given by

$$\Delta S^{\ominus}_{surroundings} = \frac{-\Delta H^{\ominus}_{reaction}}{T}$$

If we carry out reactions at temperatures above standard temperature, an increase in temperature makes the entropy change of the surroundings less negative or more positive. If we carry out reactions at temperatures below standard temperature, a decrease in temperature makes the entropy change of the surroundings more negative or less positive. In both these cases we make the assumption that $\Delta H^{\ominus}_{reaction}$ does not change significantly with temperature. In reality $\Delta H^{\ominus}_{reaction}$ does change slightly with temperature, but we can often disregard this change.

We can see how increasing the temperature affects the ability of zinc carbonate to undergo thermal decomposition by comparing the entropy changes at 298 K and 550 K. However, we have to take into account both the surroundings and the system. We assume that neither the standard molar entropies nor the enthalpy change of formation change with temperature.

$$ZnCO_3(s) \longrightarrow ZnO(s) + CO_2(g)$$
$$\Delta H^{\ominus}_{reaction} = +72.3\,kJ\,mol^{-1}$$

For this reaction $S^{\ominus}_{system} = +174.8\,J\,K^{-1}\,mol^{-1}$ (the same for both temperatures).

Reaction at 298 K

$$\Delta S^{\ominus}_{surroundings} = \frac{-72\,300}{298}$$

$$= -242.6\,J\,K^{-1}\,mol^{-1}$$

$$\Delta S^{\ominus}_{total} = +174.8 - 242.6\,J\,K^{-1}\,mol^{-1}$$

$$\Delta S^{\ominus}_{total} = -67.8\,J\,K^{-1}\,mol^{-1}$$

Reaction at 550 K

$$\Delta S^{\ominus}_{surroundings} = \frac{-72\,300}{550}$$

$$= -131.5\,J\,K^{-1}\,mol^{-1}$$

$$\Delta S^{\ominus}_{total} = +174.8 - 131.5\,J\,K^{-1}\,mol^{-1}$$

$$\Delta S^{\ominus}_{total} = +43.3\,J\,K^{-1}\,mol^{-1}$$

You can see that at 298 K the total entropy change is negative, so the reaction does not occur at this temperature. At 550 K the total entropy change is positive, so the reaction is spontaneous at this temperature.

- When the total entropy change in a reaction shows a large increase, e.g. $+200\,J\,K^{-1}\,mol^{-1}$, the reaction can be regarded as going to completion. It is definitely spontaneous.
- When the total entropy change shows a large decrease, e.g. $-600\,J\,K^{-1}\,mol^{-1}$, we can deduce that there is very little likelihood of a reaction occurring.

QUESTION

7 The decomposition of calcium carbonate, $CaCO_3(s) \longrightarrow CaO(s) + CO_2(g)$, does not take place at room temperature.

a Explain in terms of entropy changes why heating the calcium carbonate to a high temperature increases the likelihood of this reaction taking place.

b In a closed system at high temperature, the reactants and products are in equilibrium.

$$CaCO_3(s) \rightleftharpoons CaO(s) + CO_2(g)$$

i Explain the meaning of the term **closed system.**

ii Explain in terms of entropy changes what happens when the pressure on this system is increased.

iii What is the value of the standard total entropy change at equilibrium?

357

Entropy, enthalpy changes and free energy

For an exothermic reaction such as:

$$CH_4(g) + 2O_2(g) \longrightarrow CO_2(g) + 2H_2O(g)$$
$$\Delta H^{\ominus}_{reaction} = -890.3\,kJ\,mol^{-1}$$

the entropy change of the system is negative. But the large negative value of the enthalpy change more than compensates for the negative entropy change of the system because it causes the term $-\Delta H^{\ominus}_{reaction}/T$ to have a high positive value. So the total entropy change is positive and the reaction, once started, is spontaneous. In highly exothermic reactions, where the value of $\Delta H^{\ominus}_{\text{reaction}}$ is large and negative, the enthalpy change is the driving force of the reaction.

In endothermic reactions, the entropy term tends to be more important. The term $-\Delta H^{\ominus}_{\text{reaction}}/T$ has a negative value. If the value of $\Delta S^{\ominus}_{\text{system}}$ and $\Delta S^{\ominus}_{\text{surroundings}}$ are both negative, then the reaction will not be spontaneous. However, if the value of $\Delta S^{\ominus}_{\text{system}}$ is positive and large enough, it can compensate for the negative value of the $\Delta S^{\ominus}_{\text{surroundings}}$ so that $\Delta S^{\ominus}_{\text{total}}$ becomes positive. The reaction is spontaneous.

Chemists are usually interested in the system of reactants and products rather than having to consider the energy changes with the surroundings. Fortunately for us, there is a way in which we can take account of both system and surroundings in a more straightforward way. This involves a quantity called Gibbs free energy or, more simply, free energy. It can also be called Gibbs energy or Gibbs function, G.

Figure 23.7 Gibbs free energy is named after American scientist Josiah Willard Gibbs, who applied the concept of entropy and 'applied energy' changes to chemical reactions and physical processes.

Gibbs free energy

What is Gibbs free energy?

In determining whether a chemical reaction is likely to be spontaneous we use the quantity Gibbs free energy change, ΔG. The Gibbs free energy change is given by the relationship:

$$\Delta G = -T\Delta S_{\text{total}}$$

We can also write the expression without having to consider the entropy changes of the surroundings:

$$\Delta G = \Delta H_{\text{reaction}} - T\Delta S_{\text{system}}$$

Where T is the temperature in kelvin.

Gibbs free energy is a useful concept because it includes both enthalpy change and entropy change.

To make any comparison of Gibbs free energy values fair, we must use standard conditions. These standard conditions are the same as those used for ΔH and ΔS:

- pressure of 10^5 Pa
- temperature of 298 K (25 °C)
- each substance involved in the reaction is in its normal physical state (solid, liquid or gas) at 10^5 Pa and 298 K.

The **standard molar Gibbs free energy of formation** is the free energy change that accompanies the formation of one mole of a compound from its elements in their standard state.

The symbol for standard molar Gibbs free energy of formation is $\Delta G^{\ominus}_{\text{f}}$. The units are kJ mol^{-1}.

For example:

$$\text{Mg(s)} + \tfrac{1}{2}\text{O}_2\text{(g)} \longrightarrow \text{MgO(s)} \qquad \Delta G^{\ominus}_{\text{f}} = -569.4 \text{ kJ mol}^{-1}$$

Derivation

Gibbs free energy can easily be derived from the equation relating total entropy to the entropy changes of system and surroundings.

As:

$$\Delta S^{\ominus}_{\text{total}} = \Delta S^{\ominus}_{\text{system}} - \frac{\Delta H^{\ominus}}{T}$$

Multiplying by $-T$: $-T\Delta S^{\ominus}_{\text{total}} = -T\Delta S^{\ominus}_{\text{system}} + \Delta H^{\ominus}$

The term $-T\Delta S^{\ominus}_{\text{system}} + \Delta H^{\ominus}$ is equivalent to the Gibbs free energy change of the reaction system $\Delta G^{\ominus}$.

So $-T\Delta S^{\ominus}_{\text{total}} = \Delta G^{\ominus}$ and so $\Delta G^{\ominus} = \Delta H^{\ominus} - T\Delta S^{\ominus}_{\text{system}}$.

Gibbs free energy and spontaneous reactions

For a reaction to be spontaneous, $\Delta S^{\ominus}_{\text{total}}$ must be positive. The value of T is always positive on the absolute (kelvin) temperature scale. So applying these signs to the relationship $\Delta G^{\ominus} = -T\Delta S^{\ominus}_{\text{total}}$, the value of ΔG must be negative for a reaction to be spontaneous. So, when a spontaneous reaction occurs at constant temperature and pressure, the Gibbs free energy decreases. If the value of ΔG is positive, the reaction is not spontaneous.

Applying the equation
$\Delta G^{\ominus} = \Delta H^{\ominus} - T\Delta S^{\ominus}_{system}$

We can calculate the Gibbs free energy change for a reaction if we know:

- the entropy change of the system in $J\,K^{-1}\,mol^{-1}$
- the enthalpy change of the system in $J\,mol^{-1}$; we have to multiply the value of the enthalpy change by 1000 because the entropy change is in joules per kelvin per mol
- the temperature; under standard conditions, this is 298 K.

WORKED EXAMPLE

7 Calculate the Gibbs free energy change for the decomposition of zinc carbonate at 298 K.

$ZnCO_3(s) \longrightarrow ZnO(s) + CO_2(g)$ $\Delta H^{\ominus}_r = +71.0\,kJ\,mol^{-1}$

(Values for $S^{\ominus}$ in $J\,K^{-1}\,mol^{-1}$: $CO_2(g) = +213.6$, $ZnCO_3(s) = +82.4$, $ZnO(s) = +43.6$)

Step 1 Convert the value of $\Delta H^{\ominus}_r$ to $J\,mol^{-1}$:

$+71.0 \times 1000 = 71\,000\,J\,mol^{-1}$

Step 2 Calculate $\Delta S^{\ominus}_{system}$:

$\Delta S^{\ominus}_{system} = S^{\ominus}_{products} - S^{\ominus}_{reactants}$

$= S^{\ominus}[ZnO(s)] + S^{\ominus}[CO_2(g)] - S^{\ominus}[ZnCO_3(s)]$

$= 43.6 + 213.6 - 82.4$

$\Delta S^{\ominus}_{system} = +174.8\,J\,K^{-1}\,mol^{-1}$

Step 3 Calculate $\Delta G^{\ominus}$:

$\Delta G^{\ominus} = \Delta H^{\ominus}_{reaction} - T\Delta S^{\ominus}_{system}$

$= 71\,000 - 298 \times (+174.8)$

$\Delta G^{\ominus} = +18\,909.6\,J\,mol^{-1}$

$= +18.9\,kJ\,mol^{-1}$ (to 3 significant figures)

As the value of $\Delta G^{\ominus}$ is positive, the reaction is not spontaneous at 298 K.

QUESTION

8 Calculate the standard Gibbs free energy of reaction in each of the following using the standard molar entropy values given. Express your answers to 3 significant figures in $kJ\,mol^{-1}$, and in each case state whether the reaction is spontaneous or not under standard conditions.

(Values for $S^{\ominus}$ in $J\,K^{-1}\,mol^{-1}$: $Ag_2CO_3(s) = 167.4$, $Ag_2O(s) = 121.3$, $CH_4(g) = 186.2$, $Cl_2(g) = 165$, $CO_2(g) = 213.6$, $H_2(g) = 130.6$, $HCl(g) = 186.8$, $H_2O(l) = 69.9$, $Mg(s) = 37.2$, $MgCl_2(s) = 89.6$, $Na(s) = 51.2$, $Na_2O_2(s) = 95.0$, $O_2(g) = 205.0$)

QUESTION (CONTINUED)

a $H_2(g) + Cl_2(g) \longrightarrow 2HCl(g)$

$\Delta H^{\ominus}_r = -184.6\,kJ\,mol^{-1}$

b $CH_4(g) + 2O_2(g) \longrightarrow CO_2(g) + 2H_2O(l)$

$\Delta H^{\ominus}_r = -890.3\,kJ\,mol^{-1}$

c $2Na(s) + O_2(g) \longrightarrow Na_2O_2(s)$

$\Delta H^{\ominus}_r = -510.9\,kJ\,mol^{-1}$

d $Mg(s) + Cl_2(g) \longrightarrow MgCl_2(s)$

$\Delta H^{\ominus}_r = -641.3\,kJ\,mol^{-1}$

e $Ag_2CO_3(s) \longrightarrow Ag_2O(s) + CO_2(g)$

$\Delta H^{\ominus}_r = +167.5\,kJ\,mol^{-1}$

Temperature change and reaction spontaneity

For a reaction to be spontaneous, ΔG must be negative. The temperature can influence the spontaneity of a reaction. We can deduce this by considering the Gibbs free energy as a combination of two terms in the relationship

$$\Delta G = \underbrace{\Delta H_{reaction}}_{\text{first term}} - \underbrace{T\Delta S_{system}}_{\text{second term}}$$

Assuming that the value of $\Delta H_{reaction}$ does not change much with temperature, we can see that the value of $T\Delta S_{system}$ may influence the value of ΔG.

- For an exothermic reaction, the first term ($\Delta H_{reaction}$) has a negative value.

  - If the value of ΔS_{system} is positive, the second term ($-T\Delta S_{system}$) is negative and the reaction will be spontaneous because both $\Delta H_{reaction}$ and $-T\Delta S_{system}$ are negative. So ΔG is negative.

  - If the value of ΔS_{system} is negative, the second term is positive. The reaction is likely to be spontaneous if the temperature is low because $\Delta H_{reaction}$ is more likely to have a greater negative value than the positive value of the second term. So ΔG is negative. If the temperature is very high, the second term may be positive enough to overcome the negative value of $\Delta H_{reaction}$ and make ΔG positive. So the reaction is less likely to be spontaneous at a higher temperature. This mirrors what we know about the effect of temperature on equilibrium: for an exothermic reaction, a higher temperature shifts the position of equilibrium in favour of the reactants.

359

■ For an endothermic reaction, the first term ($\Delta H_{reaction}$) has a positive value.

  – If the value of ΔS_{system} is negative, the second term is positive. The reaction will not occur because both terms are positive, making the value of ΔG positive.

  – If the value of ΔS_{system} is positive, the second term is negative. The reaction is unlikely to be spontaneous if the temperature is low because $\Delta H_{reaction}$ is more likely to have a greater positive value than the negative value of the second term. So ΔG is positive. If the temperature is very high, the second term may be negative enough to overcome the positive value of $\Delta H_{reaction}$ and make ΔG negative. So the reaction is more likely to be spontaneous at a higher temperature. This mirrors what we know about the effect of temperature on equilibrium: for an endothermic reaction, a higher temperature shifts the position of equilibrium in favour of the products.

We can see the effect of temperature on the spontaneity of the reaction if we rework Worked Example 7 at a temperature of 1200 K.

WORKED EXAMPLE

8 Calculate the Gibbs free energy change for the decomposition of zinc carbonate at 1200 K.

$$ZnCO_3(s) \longrightarrow ZnO(s) + CO_2(g) \quad \Delta H^{\ominus}_r = +71.0\,kJ\,mol^{-1}$$

(Values for $S^{\ominus}$ in $J\,K^{-1}\,mol^{-1}$: $CO_2(g) = +213.6$, $ZnCO_3(s) = +82.4$, $ZnO(s) = +43.6$)

$\Delta H^{\ominus}_r = +71.0\,kJ\,mol^{-1}$ $\Delta S^{\ominus}_{system} = +174.8\,J\,K^{-1}\,mol^{-1}$

$\Delta G^{\ominus} = \Delta H^{\ominus}_{reaction} - T\Delta S^{\ominus}_{system}$

$\quad\quad = 71\,000 - 1200 \times (+174.8)$

$\quad\quad = 71\,000 - 209\,760$

$\Delta G^{\ominus} = -139\,kJ\,mol^{-1}$

As the value of $\Delta G^{\ominus}$ is negative, the reaction is spontaneous at 1200 K.

Comparing Gibbs free energy values

Table 23.2 shows some values for some standard molar Gibbs free energy changes of formation.

You learnt in Chapter 6 (page 92) that the standard enthalpy change of an element is zero. Similarly, the standard Gibbs free energy change of formation of an element is zero. Many compounds in the solid state have high negative values of Gibbs free energy change of formation. Many gases and liquids have standard Gibbs free energy change values that are negative but many others, such as ethene, have positive values. The standard Gibbs free energy change of formation also depends on the state. For example, $\Delta G^{\ominus}_f$ [$H_2O(l)$] is $-237.2\,kJ\,mol^{-1}$ but $\Delta G^{\ominus}_f$ [$H_2O(g)$] is $-228.6\,kJ\,mol^{-1}$.

Gibbs free energy calculations

Gibbs free energy change of reaction

The **standard Gibbs free energy change of reaction** is the Gibbs free energy change when the amounts of the reactants shown in the stoichiometric equation react under standard conditions to give products. The reactants and products must be in their standard states.

The method of calculating Gibbs free energy change of reaction uses an energy cycle similar to the enthalpy cycles you used to calculate the enthalpy change of reaction in Chapter 6 (see Figure 23.8).

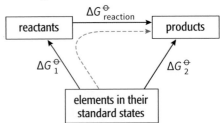

Figure 23.8 A free energy cycle for calculating the standard Gibbs free energy of reaction. The dashed line shows the indirect (two-step) route.

Substance	$\Delta G^{\ominus}_f$ / kJ mol^{-1}	Substance	$\Delta G^{\ominus}_f$ / kJ mol^{-1}
carbon (s)	0	water (l)	−237.2
calcium (s)	0	methanol (l)	−166.4
bromine (l)	0	chlorobenzene (l)	+93.6
helium (g)	0	water (g)	−228.6
calcium oxide (s)	−604.0	ethane (g)	+68.2
calcium carbonate (s)	−1128.8	ammonia (g)	−16.5
magnesium oxide (s)	−569.4	magnesium ion, Mg^{2+} (aq)	−454.8
zinc sulfide (s)	−201.3	carbonate ion, CO_3^{2-} (aq)	−527.9

Table 23.2 Standard molar Gibbs free energy changes of some solids, liquids, gases and aqueous ions. The states are shown as state symbols after each substance.

Using the same ideas as in Hess's law, we see that:

$$\Delta G_2^\ominus = \Delta G_1^\ominus + \Delta G_{reaction}^\ominus$$

So:

$$\Delta G_{reaction}^\ominus = \Delta G_2^\ominus - \Delta G_1^\ominus$$

Another way of writing this is:

$$\Delta G_{reaction}^\ominus = \Delta G_{products}^\ominus - \Delta G_{reactants}^\ominus$$

To calculate the Gibbs free energy change of reaction from an energy cycle like this, we use the following procedure:

- write the balanced equation at the top
- draw the cycle with the elements at the bottom
- draw in all arrows making sure that they go in the correct directions
- calculate $\Delta G_{reaction}^\ominus = \Delta G_2^\ominus - \Delta G_1^\ominus$ taking into account the number of moles of reactants and products.

WORKED EXAMPLES

9 Draw a Gibbs free energy cycle to calculate the standard Gibbs free energy change of decomposition of sodium hydrogencarbonate.

$$2NaHCO_3(s) \longrightarrow Na_2CO_3(s) + CO_2(g) + H_2O(l)$$

The relevant Gibbs free energy values are:

$\Delta G_f^\ominus[NaHCO_3(s)] = -851.0\,kJ\,mol^{-1}$

$\Delta G_f^\ominus[Na_2CO_3(s)] = -1044.5\,kJ\,mol^{-1}$

$\Delta G_f^\ominus[CO_2(g)] = -394.4\,kJ\,mol^{-1}$

$\Delta G_f^\ominus[H_2O(l)] = -237.2\,kJ\,mol^{-1}$

The Gibbs free energy cycle is shown in Figure 23.9.

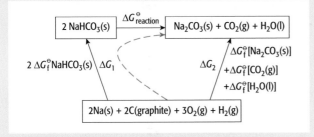

Figure 23.9 The free energy cycle for the decomposition of sodium hydrogencarbonate. The dashed line shows the two-step route.

WORKED EXAMPLES (CONTINUED)

$\Delta G_{reaction}^\ominus = \Delta G_2^\ominus - \Delta G_1^\ominus$

$\Delta G_{reaction}^\ominus = \Delta G_f^\ominus[Na_2CO_3(s)] + \Delta G_f^\ominus[CO_2(g)]$
$\qquad\qquad + \Delta G_f^\ominus[H_2O(l)] - 2 \times \Delta G_f^\ominus[NaHCO_3(s)]$

$\qquad = (-1044.5) + (-394.4) + (-237.2) - \{2 \times (-851.0)\}$

$\qquad = -1676.1 - (-1702)$

$\qquad = +25.9\,kJ$

The value of $\Delta G_{reaction}^\ominus$ is positive. So under standard conditions, the reaction is not spontaneous. However, $\Delta G_{reaction}^\ominus$ does vary with temperature. At a higher temperature the reaction is spontaneous.

10 Calculate the standard Gibbs free energy change of the reaction between hydrogen and oxygen.

$$2H_2(g) + O_2(g) \longrightarrow 2H_2O(l)$$

(The relevant Gibbs free energy value is:
$\Delta G_f^\ominus[H_2O(l)] = -237.2\,kJ\,mol^{-1}$)

Note that the values of $\Delta G_f^\ominus$ for both hydrogen and oxygen are zero, as they are elements in their standard states.

$\Delta G_{reaction}^\ominus = \Delta G_{products}^\ominus - \Delta G_{reactants}^\ominus$

$\Delta G_{reaction}^\ominus$
$\qquad = 2 \times \Delta G_f^\ominus[H_2O(l)] - \{2 \times \Delta G_f^\ominus[H_2(g)] + \Delta G_f^\ominus[O_2(g)]\}$

$\qquad = 2 \times (-273.2) - 0 + 0$

$\Delta G_{reaction}^\ominus = -546.4\,kJ$

The value of $\Delta G_{reaction}^\ominus$ is negative. So under standard conditions, the reaction is spontaneous.

Gibbs free energy and work

Gibbs free energy change can be thought of as part of the enthalpy change that is needed to do work. If we rearrange the equation $\Delta G = \Delta H - T\Delta S$ as $\Delta H = \Delta G + T\Delta S$, we can regard the $+T\Delta S$ part as being the energy unavailable to do work because it is involved with the disorder of the system. The ΔG part is free energy that is available to do work, e.g. driving the charge in electrochemical cells.

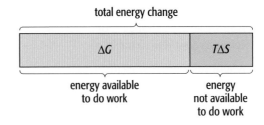

Figure 23.10 The enthalpy change of a reaction at constant temperature can be split into two parts.

361

Gibbs free energy change and direction of chemical change

Gibbs free energy of formation is a measure of the stability of a compound. The more negative the value of $\Delta G_f^\ominus$, the greater the stability of the compound. It is unlikely to decompose. If $\Delta G_f^\ominus$ is positive, the compound is likely to be unstable with respect to its elements. For example:

$$\tfrac{1}{2}H_2(g) + \tfrac{1}{2}I_2(s) \longrightarrow HI(g) \quad \Delta G_f^\ominus[HI(g)] = +1.7\,kJ\,mol^{-1}$$

The Gibbs free energy change of reaction is also a measure of the feasibility of a reaction. Reactions with negative values of $\Delta G_{reaction}^\ominus$ are likely to be feasible (spontaneous), whereas those with positive values are less likely to be spontaneous.

- When a system is in chemical equilibrium and the amounts of products and reactants balance, the value of $\Delta G_{reaction}^\ominus$ is zero ($\Delta G_{reaction}^\ominus = 0$).
- The products predominate if the value of $\Delta G_{reaction}^\ominus$ has a fairly low negative value, e.g. $-10\,kJ\,mol^{-1}$.
- The reactants predominate if the value of $\Delta G_{reaction}^\ominus$ has a slightly positive value, e.g. $+10\,kJ\,mol^{-1}$.
- The reaction can be regarded as complete if the value of $\Delta G_{reaction}^\ominus$ is high and negative, e.g. $-60\,kJ\,mol^{-1}$.

- The reaction can be regarded as not being feasible (spontaneous) at all if the value of $\Delta G_{reaction}^\ominus$ is high and positive, e.g. $+60\,kJ\,mol^{-1}$.

QUESTION

9   Calculate the standard Gibbs free energy change of reaction in each of the following using the standard molar values for Gibbs free energy change given here. In each case, comment on whether the reaction is spontaneous or not, under standard conditions.

(Values for $G^\ominus$ in $kJ\,mol^{-1}$: $C_3H_8(g) = -23.4$, $CO_2(g) = -394.4$, $Fe_2O_3(s) = -742.2$, $H_2O(l) = -273.2$, $H_2O_2(l) = -120.4$, $MgO(s) = -569.4$, $NaCl(s) = -384.2$, $NH_4NO_3(s) = -184.0$, $N_2O(g) = +104.2$)

a $2H_2O_2(l) \longrightarrow 2H_2O(l) + O_2(g)$

b $NH_4NO_3(s) \longrightarrow N_2O(g) + 2H_2O(g)$

c $2Mg(s) + O_2(g) \longrightarrow 2MgO(s)$

d $C_3H_8(g) + 5O_2(g) \longrightarrow 3CO_2(g) + 4H_2O(l)$

e $3Mg(s) + Fe_2O_3(s) \longrightarrow 3MgO(s) + 2Fe(s)$

Summary

- **Entropy** (S) is related to the degree of randomness or disorder in a system. The greater the disorder, the greater the entropy.

- **Standard molar entropy** ($S^\ominus$) is the entropy when the substance is in its normal state at 298 K and $10^5\,Pa$.

- In a chemical reaction, the **system** is the chemical reactants and products themselves and the **surroundings** is everything not involved in the system, e.g. the air around the reaction vessel.

- A system becomes energetically more stable when it becomes more disordered

- A **spontaneous change** is one that, once started, tends to continue to happen.

- A **spontaneous** change involves an increase in total entropy (ΔS is **positive**). If a reaction is not spontaneous, there is a decrease in entropy (ΔS is **negative**).

- The entropy increases as a substance changes state from solid to liquid to gas.

- Solids generally have smaller entropies than liquids, and liquids have smaller entropies than gases.

- A knowledge of the structures and states of the reactants and products helps us to make generalisations about whether the entropy of the reactants or products is greater.

- The total entropy change in a reaction is given by $\Delta S_{total} = \Delta S_{system} + \Delta S_{surroundings}$

- The entropy change in the system is given by $\Delta S_{system} = \Delta S_{products} - \Delta S_{reactants}$

- The entropy change in the surroundings is given by $\Delta S_{surroundings} = -\Delta H_{reaction}/T$, where T is the temperature in kelvin.

- An increase in temperature makes the entropy change of the surroundings less negative.

- **Standard Gibbs free energy of formation** is the Gibbs free energy change when 1 mole of a compound is formed from its elements in their normal states under standard conditions.

■ **Standard Gibbs free energy of reaction** is the Gibbs free energy change when the amounts of reactants shown in the stoichiometric equation react under standard conditions to form the products.

■ Gibbs free energy is related to the enthalpy change of reaction and entropy change of the system by the relationship $\Delta G^{\ominus} = \Delta H^{\ominus}_{\text{reaction}} - T\Delta S^{\ominus}_{\text{system}}$

■ The Gibbs free energy change of a reaction can be calculated from Gibbs free energy changes of formation using the relationship is related to

the enthalpy change of reaction and entropy change of the system by the relationship
$\Delta G^{\ominus}_{\text{reaction}} = \Delta G^{\ominus}_{\text{products}} - \Delta G^{\ominus}_{\text{reactants}}$

■ The Gibbs free energy change of formation of an element is zero.

■ **Spontaneous** (**feasible**) chemical changes involve a decrease in Gibbs free energy (ΔG is **negative**).

■ Chemical reactions tend not to be spontaneous if there is an increase in Gibbs free energy (ΔG is **positive**).

End-of-chapter questions

1 Graphite and diamond are both forms of carbon. Their standard molar entropies are:

$\Delta S^{\ominus}_{\text{graphite}} = 5.70 \, \text{J K}^{-1} \text{mol}^{-1}$, $\Delta S^{\ominus}_{\text{diamond}} = 2.40 \, \text{J K}^{-1} \text{mol}^{-1}$

   a i Suggest why the standard molar entropy of graphite is greater than that of diamond.   [2]

      ii Calculate the entropy change of the process $C_{\text{graphite}} \longrightarrow C_{\text{diamond}}$ at 298 K   [1]

      iii Explain why you would be unlikely to make diamonds from graphite at atmospheric temperature and pressure.   [1]

   b The standard molar enthalpy change for $C_{\text{graphite}} \longrightarrow C_{\text{diamond}}$ is +2.00 kJ mol^{-1}.

      i Calculate the total entropy change for this reaction at 25.0 °C.   [4]

      ii Explain why you would be unlikely to make diamonds from graphite at atmospheric temperature and pressure.   [1]

   c Graphite reacts with oxygen to form carbon dioxide. Would you expect the entropy of the products to be greater or less than the entropy of the reactants? Explain your answer.   [1]

                                    Total = 10

2 3268 kJ are required to change 1 mole of ethanol into its gaseous atoms.

$C_2H_5OH(g) \longrightarrow 2C(g) + 6H(g) + O(g)$

   a Calculate the entropy change of the surroundings during this process when it is carried out at 150 °C.   [3]

   b Explain why the total entropy change of this reaction is likely to be negative.   [2]

   c When ethanol undergoes combustion, carbon dioxide and water are formed.

      $C_2H_5OH(l) + 3O_2(g) \longrightarrow 2CO_2(g) + 3H_2O(l)$ $\Delta H^{\ominus}_{\text{reaction}} = -1367 \, \text{kJ mol}^{-1}$

      Calculate the total standard entropy change for this reaction.

      (Values for $S^{\ominus}$ in J K^{-1} mol^{-1}: $C_2H_5OH(l)$ = 160.7, CO_2 = 213.6, $H_2O(l)$ = 69.90, $O_2(g)$ = 205.0)   [6]

                                    Total = 11

3 At 10 °C ice changes to water.

$$H_2O(s) \longrightarrow H_2O(l) \qquad \Delta H^{\ominus} = +6.01 \, kJ \, mol^{-1}$$

   a Explain why the entropy change of the system is positive. [2]

   b The entropy change for the system is $+22.0 \, J \, K^{-1} \, mol^{-1}$. Calculate the total entropy change at 10.0 °C. [4]

   c Explain why the process shown in the equation does not occur at −10.0 °C. [2]

   d At 273 K ice and water are in equilibrium.

$$H_2O(s) \rightleftharpoons H_2O(l) \qquad \Delta H^{\ominus} = +6.01 \, kJ \, mol^{-1}$$

     i Calculate the entropy change of the surroundings for this process. [2]

     ii What main assumption did you make when doing this calculation? [1]

     iii Use your answer to part **d i** to deduce the value of ΔS_{system} at 278 K. Explain your answer fully. [3]

   e At −10.0 °C, the value of ΔS_{system} is $-22.0 \, J \, K^{-1} \, mol^{-1}$ and the value of $\Delta S_{surroundings}$ is $+22.9 \, J \, K^{-1} \, mol^{-1}$. Calculate the total entropy change in the process. Include the correct sign. [2]

Total = 16

4 Barium carbonate decomposes when heated.

$$BaCO_3(s) \longrightarrow BaO(s) + CO_2(g)$$

   a Use your knowledge of Hess cycles from Chapter 6 to calculate the enthalpy change of this reaction. Express your answer to three significant figures.

$$\Delta H^{\ominus}_f \, [BaCO_3(s)] = -1216.0 \, kJ \, mol^{-1}$$
$$\Delta H^{\ominus}_f \, [BaO(s)] \quad = -553.5 \, kJ \, mol^{-1}$$
$$\Delta H^{\ominus}_f \, [CO_2(g)] \quad = -393.5 \, kJ \, mol^{-1} \qquad [2]$$

   b Use your answer to part **a** and the data below to calculate ΔS_{total} for this reaction under standard conditions. Express your answer to three significant figures.

$$\Delta S^{\ominus} \, [BaCO_3(s)] = +112.1 \, J \, K^{-1} \, mol^{-1}$$
$$\Delta S^{\ominus} \, [BaO(s)] \quad = +70.40 \, J \, K^{-1} \, mol^{-1}$$
$$\Delta S^{\ominus} \, [CO_2(g)] \quad = +213.6 \, J \, K^{-1} \, mol^{-1} \qquad [5]$$

   c Is this reaction spontaneous (feasible) at 298 K? Explain your answer. [1]

   d **i** Calculate the temperature at which this reaction has a total entropy value of zero. [4]

     ii What main assumption did you make in your calculation in part **d i**? [1]

Total = 13

5 **a** For each of the following changes state whether the entropy of the system decreases or increases. In each case, explain your answer in terms of the order or disorder of the particles

     i $NaCl(s) + aq \longrightarrow Na^+(aq) + Cl^-(aq)$ [5]

     ii $H_2O(g) \longrightarrow H_2O(l)$ [3]

   b The table shows the formula, state and standard molar entropies of the first six straight-chain alkanes.

Alkane	$CH_4(g)$	$C_2H_6(g)$	$C_3H_8(g)$	$C_4H_{10}(g)$	$C_5H_{12}(l)$
$\Delta S^{\ominus} \, / \, J \, K^{-1} \, mol^{-1}$	186.2	229.5	269.9	310.1	261.2

     i Describe and explain the trend in the standard molar entropies of these alkanes. [4]

     ii Estimate the value of the standard molar entropy of the straight-chain alkane with the formula C_6H_{14}. [1]

Total = 13

6 a i Define **standard free energy change of formation**. [2]

 ii Write a balanced equation to represent the standard free energy change of formation of ethane. Include state symbols in your answer. [2]

 b The standard free energy change of formation of ethane is $-32.9 \, kJ \, mol^{-1}$. The standard entropy change of the system for this reaction is $-173.7 \, J \, K^{-1} \, mol^{-1}$.

 i State the relationship between standard free energy change of formation, standard entropy change of the system and the enthalpy change. [1]

 ii Explain why the reaction can be regarded as spontaneous, even though the value of the standard entropy change of the system is negative. [3]

 c Ethane undergoes combustion to form carbon dioxide and water.

$$C_2H_6(g) + 3\tfrac{1}{2}O_2(g) \longrightarrow 2CO_2(g) + 3H_2O(l)$$

 Calculate the free energy change of combustion for this reaction.

 (Values for $\Delta G_f^{\ominus}$ in $kJ \, mol^{-1}$: $C_2H_6(g) = -32.9$, $CO_2(g) = -394.4$, $H_2O(l) = -237.2$) [3]

 Total = 11

7 Calcium carbonate decomposes when heated to form calcium oxide and carbon dioxide.

$$CaCO_3(s) \longrightarrow CaO(s) + CO_2(g)$$

 a Calculate the entropy change of the system for this reaction.

 (Values for $S^{\ominus}$ in $J \, K^{-1} \, mol^{-1}$: $CaCO_3(s) = +92.9$, $CaO(s) = +39.7$, $CO_2(g) = +213.6$) [2]

 b Calculate the enthalpy change for this reaction.

 (Values for $\Delta H_f^{\ominus}$ in $kJ^{-1} \, mol^{-1}$: $CaCO_3(s) = -1206.9$, $CaO(s) = -635.1$, $CO_2(g) = -393.5$) [2]

 c Use your answers to parts **a** and **b** to calculate the Gibbs free energy change of this reaction at 298 K by a method that does not include calculating the entropy change of the surroundings. [5]

 d Explain why the reaction is not spontaneous at 298 K even though the entropy change of the system has a positive value. [3]

 Total = 12

8 Water is formed when hydrogen burns in oxygen.

$$2H_2(g) + O_2(g) \longrightarrow 2H_2O(l) \qquad \Delta H_r^{\ominus} = -561.6 \, kJ^{-1} \, mol^{-1}$$

 a Calculate the entropy change of the system for this reaction.

 (Values for $S^{\ominus}$ in $J \, K^{-1} \, mol^{-1}$: $H_2(g) = +130.6$, $O_2(g) = +205.0$, $H_2O(g) = +69.9$) [3]

 b Use your answer to part **a** and the information at the start of the question to calculate a value for the Gibbs free energy change of this reaction. [5]

 c Is the reaction spontaneous at room temperature? Explain your answer. [1]

 d Use your answer to part **b** to suggest a value for the standard Gibbs free energy of formation of $H_2O(l)$. Explain your answer. [2]

 Total = 11

Chapter 24:
Transition elements

Learning outcomes

You should be able to:

- explain what is meant by a **transition element**, in terms of d-block elements forming one or more stable ions with incomplete d orbitals

- state the electronic configuration of a first-row transition element and of its ions

- contrast, qualitatively, the melting point, density, atomic radius, ionic radius, first ionisation energy and conductivity of the transition elements with those of calcium as a typical s-block element

- describe the tendency of transition elements to have variable oxidation states

- predict from a given electronic configuration, the likely oxidation states of a transition element

- describe and explain the use of Fe^{3+}/Fe^{2+}, MnO_4^-/Mn^{2+} and $Cr_2O_7^{2-}/Cr^{3+}$ as examples of redox systems (see also Chapter 19)

- predict, using $E^\ominus$ values, the likelihood of redox reactions

- define the term ligand as a species that contains a lone pair of electrons that forms a dative covalent bond to a central metal atom/ion including monodentate, bidentate and polydentate ligands

- describe and explain the reactions of transition elements with ligands to form complexes, including the complexes of copper(II) and cobalt(II) ions with water and ammonia molecules and hydroxide and chloride ions

- describe the types of stereoisomerism (*cis-trans* and optical isomerism) shown by complexes, including those associated with bidentate ligands

- describe the use of *cis*-platin as an anticancer drug

- explain qualitatively that ligand exchange may occur, including the complexes of copper(II) ions with water, hydroxide and ammonia

- describe and explain ligand exchanges in terms of competing equilibria

- describe the term **stability constant**, K_{stab}, of a complex ion as the equilibrium constant for the formation of the complex ion in a solvent from its constituent ions or molecules

- deduce expressions for the stability constant in ligand substitution

- explain ligand exchange in terms of stability constants and understand that a large value of K_{stab} is due to the formation of a stable complex ion.

- sketch the general shape of a d orbital

- describe the splitting of degenerate d orbitals into two energy levels in octahedral complexes using the complexes of copper(II) ions with water and ammonia as examples

- explain the origin of colour in transition element complexes resulting from the absorption of light energy as an electron moves between two non-degenerate d orbitals

- describe, in qualitative terms, the effects of different ligands on the absorption of light, and hence colour, using the complexes of copper(II) ions with water, hydroxide and ammonia as examples.

Introduction

Many transition elements and their compounds are used in construction and engineering. Iron and copper have been used for many centuries (Figure 24.1). In more recent times, we have discovered how to extract and use other, rarer transition elements. For example, titanium is used in jet turbines because it can withstand high temperatures and is very strong.

Figure 24.1 The transition elements iron and copper are very important in the construction industry.

What is a transition element?

The transition elements are found in the d block of the Periodic Table, between Groups 2 and 13. However, not all d-block elements are classified as transition elements.

> A transition element is a d-block element that forms one or more stable ions with an incomplete d subshell.

We do not define Sc and Zn as transition elements.

- Scandium forms only one ion (Sc^{3+}) and this has no electrons in its 3d subshell – the electronic configuration of Sc^{3+} is (Ar) $3d^0 4s^0$.
- Zinc forms only one ion (Zn^{2+}) and this has a complete 3d subshell – the electronic configuration of Zn^{2+} is (Ar) $3d^{10} 4s^0$.

In this chapter we will be looking at the transition elements in the first row of the d block. These are the metals titanium (Ti) through to copper (Cu), according to the definition above.

Electronic configurations

Atoms

Table 24.1 shows the electronic configurations of the atoms in the first row of the transition elements.

In atoms of the transition elements, the 4s subshell is normally filled and the rest of the electrons occupy orbitals in the 3d subshell. However, chromium and copper atoms are the exceptions. Chromium atoms have just one electron in the 4s subshell. The remaining five electrons are arranged in the 3d subshell so that each orbital is occupied by one electron. Copper atoms also have just one electron in the 4s subshell. The remaining ten electrons are arranged in the 3d subshell so that each orbital is filled by two electrons.

Element	Electronic configuration
titanium (Ti)	$1s^2 2s^2 2p^6 3s^2 3p^6 3d^2 4s^2$
vanadium (V)	$1s^2 2s^2 2p^6 3s^2 3p^6 3d^3 4s^2$
chromium (Cr)	$1s^2 2s^2 2p^6 3s^2 3p^6 3d^5 4s^1$
manganese (Mn)	$1s^2 2s^2 2p^6 3s^2 3p^6 3d^5 4s^2$
iron (Fe)	$1s^2 2s^2 2p^6 3s^2 3p^6 3d^6 4s^2$
cobalt (Co)	$1s^2 2s^2 2p^6 3s^2 3p^6 3d^7 4s^2$
nickel (Ni)	$1s^2 2s^2 2p^6 3s^2 3p^6 3d^8 4s^2$
copper (Cu)	$1s^2 2s^2 2p^6 3s^2 3p^6 3d^{10} 4s^1$

Table 24.1 Electronic configurations of the first row of transition elements.

367

Ions

The transition elements are all metals. In common with all metals, their atoms tend to lose electrons so they form positively charged ions. However, each transition metal can form more than one ion. For example, the common ions of copper are Cu^+ and Cu^{2+}. We say that the transition metals have **variable oxidation states**. The resulting ions are often different colours (Figure 24.2).

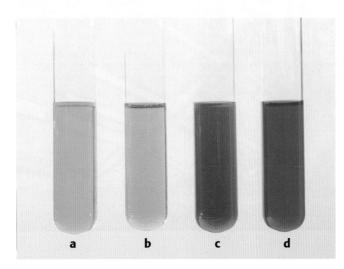

Figure 24.2 Vanadium and its oxidation states: **a** a solution containing VO_2^+ ions; **b** a solution containing VO^{2+} ions; **c** a solution containing V^{3+} ions; **d** a solution containing V^{2+} ions.

Table 24.2 shows the most common oxidation states of the first row of the transition elements.

Element	Most common oxidation states
titanium (Ti)	+3, +4
vanadium (V)	+2, +3, +4, +5
chromium (Cr)	+3, +6
manganese (Mn)	+2, +4, +6, +7
iron (Fe)	+2, +3
cobalt (Co)	+2, +3
nickel (Ni)	+2
copper (Cu)	+1, +2

Table 24.2 Common oxidation states of the transition elements.

The existence of variable oxidation states means that the names of compounds containing transition elements must have their oxidation number included, e.g. manganese(IV) oxide, cobalt(II) chloride.

When transition elements form ions, their atoms lose electrons from the 4s subshell first, followed by 3d electrons.

Notice the partially filled d subshells (see definition of transition element on the previous page) in the following examples of ions:

$$V \text{ atom} = 1s^2\,2s^2\,2p^6\,3s^2\,3p^6\,3d^3\,4s^2$$
$$\longrightarrow V^{3+} \text{ ion} = 1s^2\,2s^2\,2p^6\,3s^2\,3p^6\,3d^2\,4s^0$$

$$Fe \text{ atom} = 1s^2\,2s^2\,2p^6\,3s^2\,3p^6\,3d^6\,4s^2$$
$$\longrightarrow Fe^{3+} \text{ ion} = 1s^2\,2s^2\,2p^6\,3s^2\,3p^6\,3d^5\,4s^0$$

$$Cu \text{ atom} = 1s^2\,2s^2\,2p^6\,3s^2\,3p^6\,3d^{10}\,4s^1$$
$$\longrightarrow Cu^{2+} \text{ ion} = 1s^2\,2s^2\,2p^6\,3s^2\,3p^6\,3d^9\,4s^0$$

The most common oxidation state is +2, usually formed when the two 4s electrons are lost from the atoms. The maximum oxidation number of the transition elements at the start of the row involves all the 4s and 3d electrons in the atoms. For example, vanadium's maximum oxidation state is +5, involving its two 4s electrons and its three 3d electrons. At the end of the row, from iron onwards, the +2 oxidation state dominates as 3d electrons become increasingly harder to remove as the nuclear charge increases across the period.

QUESTION

1 **a** State the electronic configurations of the following atoms or ions:

    i Ti   **iv** Fe^{3+}

    ii Cr   **v** Ni^{2+}

    iii Co   **vi** Cu^+

b Explain why scandium (which forms only one ion, Sc^{3+}) and zinc (which forms only one ion, Zn^{2+}) are not called transition elements.

c Why is the maximum oxidation state of manganese +7?

d Look back at the different oxidation states of vanadium shown in Figure 24.2. State the oxidation state of the vanadium in each photo **a**–**d**.

e Zirconium (Zr) is in the second row of transition elements beneath titanium in the Periodic Table. Its electronic configuration is $[Kr]4d^2\,5s^2$, where [Kr] represents the electronic configuration of krypton, the noble gas with atomic number 36.

    i Predict the maximum stable oxidation state of zirconium and explain your answer.

    ii Give the formula of the oxide of zirconium, assuming zirconium exhibits the oxidation state given in **e**, part **i**.

The higher oxidation states of the transition elements are found in complex ions or in compounds formed with oxygen or fluorine. Common examples are the chromate(VI) ion, CrO_4^{2-}, and the manganate(VII) ion, MnO_4^-.

Physical properties of the transition elements

The transition elements commonly have physical properties that are typical of most metals:

- they have high melting points
- they have high densities
- they are hard and rigid, and so are useful as construction materials
- they are good conductors of electricity and heat.

The first ionisation energy, the atomic radius and the ionic radius of transition elements do not vary much as we go across the first row. The data are given in Table 24.3.

Element	1st ionisation energy / kJ mol^{-1}	Atomic radius / nm	Ionic radius / nm
titanium (Ti)	661	0.132	Ti^{2+} 0.090
vanadium (V)	648	0.122	V^{3+} 0.074 or V^{2+} 0.090
chromium (Cr)	653	0.117	Cr^{3+} 0.069 or Cr^{2+} 0.085
manganese (Mn)	716	0.117	Mn^{2+} 0.080
iron (Fe)	762	0.116	Fe^{2+} 0.076
cobalt (Co)	757	0.116	Co^{2+} 0.078
nickel (Ni)	736	0.115	Ni^{2+} 0.078
copper (Cu)	745	0.117	Cu^{2+} 0.069

Table 24.3 There are comparatively small variations in 1st ionisation energy, atomic radius and ionic radius of the first-row transition elements.

From previous work looking at periodic properties in Chapter 10, we would expect the 1st ionisation energy, atomic radius and ionic radius of positively charged ions to vary across a period. In general, the 1st ionisation energy would increase as the increasing nuclear charge has a tighter hold on electrons filling the same main energy level or shell, and the shielding effect stays roughly the same. For similar reasons the atomic radius and ionic radius of a positively charged ion would be expected to decrease

across a period. However, the transition elements show only a very small variation.

Comparing the transition elements with an s-block element

The s-block metal that lies immediately before the first row of d-block elements in the Periodic Table is calcium (Ca), in Group 2. When we compare the properties of calcium with the first row of transition elements we find some differences despite the fact that they are all metals. You need to know the following comparisons:

- the melting point of calcium (839 °C) is **lower** than that of a transition element (e.g. titanium at 1660 °C)
- the density of calcium (1.55 g cm^{-3}) is **lower** than that of a transition element (e.g. nickel at 8.90 g cm^{-3})
- the atomic radius of calcium (0.197 nm) is **larger** than that of a transition element (e.g. iron at 0.116 nm)
- the ionic radius of the calcium ion, Ca^{2+}, (0.099 nm) is **larger** than that of a transition element (e.g. Mn^{2+} at 0.080 nm)
- the first ionisation energy of calcium (590 kJ mol^{-1}) is **lower** than that of a transition element (e.g. chromium at 653 kJ mol^{-1} or cobalt at 757 kJ mol^{-1})
- the electrical conductivity of calcium is **higher** than that of a transition element (with the exception of copper).

369

QUESTION

2 a Explain why the 1st ionisation energy of calcium is lower than that of cobalt.

b Explain why the density of calcium is lower than the density of nickel.

Redox reactions

We have seen how the transition elements can exist in various oxidation states. When a compound of a transition element is treated with a suitable reagent, the oxidation state of the transition element can change. Whenever a reaction involves reactants changing their oxidation states the reaction is a redox reaction, involving the transfer of electrons. Remember that a species is reduced when its oxidation state is reduced (gets lower in value). Its oxidation state is lowered when it gains electrons, and, as well as being reduced, it is acting as an oxidising agent. For example, in the half-equation:

$$Fe^{3+}(aq) + e^- \longrightarrow Fe^{2+}(aq)$$
pale yellow → pale green

Fe^{3+} has been reduced to Fe^{2+} by gaining one electron. In the equation as shown Fe^{3+} is acting as an oxidising agent. For this reaction to happen another half-equation is needed in which the reactant loses one or more electrons, i.e. acts as a reducing agent. In Chapter 20 (page 286) we saw how we can use standard electrode potential values, $E^{\ominus}$, to predict whether or not such reactions should take place.

Another half-equation we could consider would be:

$$MnO_4^-(aq) + 8H^+(aq) + 5e^- \longrightarrow Mn^{2+}(aq) + 4H_2O(l)$$
<small>purple</small> <small>pale pink</small>

Both half-equations are written below as they appear in tables of data showing standard electrode potentials:

$$Fe^{3+}(aq) + e^- \longrightarrow Fe^{2+}(aq) \qquad E^{\ominus} = +0.77\,V$$

$$MnO_4^-(aq) + 8H^+(aq) + 5e^- \longrightarrow Mn^{2+}(aq) + 4H_2O(l)$$
$$E^{\ominus} = +1.52\,V$$

Can Fe^{3+} ions oxidise Mn^{2+} to MnO_4^- ions, or can MnO_4^- ions in acid solution oxidise Fe^{2+} ions to Fe^{3+} ions?

The magnitude of the positive values provides a measure of the tendency of the half-equations to proceed to the right-hand side. The values show us that $MnO_4^-(aq)$ is more likely to accept electrons and proceed in the forward direction, changing to $Mn^{2+}(aq)$, than $Fe^{3+}(aq)$ is to accept electrons and change to $Fe^{2+}(aq)$. $MnO_4^-(aq)$ is a more powerful oxidising agent than $Fe^{3+}(aq)$. Therefore $MnO_4^-(aq)$ ions are capable of oxidising $Fe^{2+}(aq)$ ions to form $Fe^{3+}(aq)$, and the top half-equation proceeds in the reverse direction.

We can now combine the two half-cells to get the overall reaction. Note that the sign of the Fe(III)/Fe(II) half-cell has changed by reversing its direction. The Fe^{2+}/Fe^{3+} equation also has to be multiplied by 5 so that the electrons on either side of the equation cancel out (this does not affect the value of $E^{\ominus}$).

$$5Fe^{2+}(aq) \longrightarrow 5Fe^{3+}(aq) + 5e^- \qquad E^{\ominus} = -0.77\,V$$

$$MnO_4^-(aq) + 8H^+(aq) + 5e^- \longrightarrow Mn^{2+}(aq) + 4H_2O(l)$$
$$E^{\ominus} = +1.52\,V$$

$$MnO_4^-(aq) + 5Fe^{2+}(aq) + 8H^+(aq) \longrightarrow$$
$$Mn^{2+}(aq) + 5Fe^{3+}(aq) + 4H_2O(l)$$
$$E^{\ominus} = +0.75\,V$$

The relatively large positive value of $E^{\ominus}$ (+0.75 V) tells us that the reaction is likely to proceed in the forward direction as written. In fact we use this reaction to calculate the amount of iron (Fe^{2+} ions) in a sample, such as an iron tablet, by carrying out a titration.

- A known volume (e.g. 25 cm³) of an unknown concentration of $Fe^{2+}(aq)$ is placed in a conical flask.
- A solution of a known concentration of potassium manganate(VII) is put in a burette.
- The potassium manganate(VII) solution is titrated against the solution containing $Fe^{2+}(aq)$ in the conical flask.
- The purple colour of the manganate(VII) ions is removed in the reaction with $Fe^{2+}(aq)$. The end-point is reached when the $Fe^{2+}(aq)$ ions have all reacted and the first permanent purple colour appears in the conical flask.

Figure 24.3 Manganate(VII) ions can be used to determine the percentage of Fe^{2+} in an iron tablet.

You can achieve a more accurate result for the mass of Fe^{2+} in a solution by using dichromate(VI) ions, $Cr_2O_7^{2-}(aq)$, to oxidise it in a titration. This is because compounds such as potassium dichromate(VI) can be prepared to a higher degree of purity than potassium manganate(VII). In a titration with $Fe^{2+}(aq)$ and dichromate(VI) we need an indicator of the end-point that will be oxidised as soon as the $Fe^{2+}(aq)$ has all reacted.

The half-equation and value for $E^{\ominus}$ for the use of dichromate as an oxidising agent is:

$$Cr_2O_7^{2-}(aq) + 14H^+(aq) + 6e^- \longrightarrow 2Cr^{3+}(aq) + 7H_2O(l)$$
$$E^{\ominus} = +1.33\,V$$

WORKED EXAMPLE

1 0.420 g of iron ore were dissolved in acid, so that all of the iron present in the original ore was then present as Fe^{2+}(aq). The solution obtained was titrated against $0.0400\,mol\,dm^{-3}$ $KMnO_4$(aq). The titre was $23.50\,cm^3$.

a Calculate the number of moles of MnO_4^- in the titre.

Use the equation:

$n = V \times c$

where n = number of moles, V = volume of solution in dm^3 and c = concentration

$n = \dfrac{23.50}{1000} \times 0.0400 = 0.000\,940\,mol$

b Calculate the number of moles of Fe^{2+} in the solution.

The equation for the reaction in the titration is:

$5Fe^{2+} + MnO_4^- + 8H^+ \longrightarrow 5Fe^{3+} + Mn^{2+} + 4H_2O(l)$

number of moles of $Fe^{2+} = 5\,0 \times 0.000\,940$

$= 0.004\,70\,mol$

c Calculate the mass of iron in the solution (A_r of iron is 55.8).

moles of Fe = moles of Fe^{2+} = $0.004\,70\,mol$

mass of Fe = $n \times A_r$

$= 0.004\,70 \times 55.8$

$= 0.262\,g$

d Calculate the percentage mass of iron in the 0.420 g of iron ore.

percentage mass of iron = $\dfrac{0.262}{0.420} \times 100\%$

$= 62.4\%$

QUESTIONS

3 a Write two half-equations for the reactions that take place when Fe^{2+}(aq) is oxidised by dichromate(VI) ions.

b Combine the two half-equations and write the equation for the oxidation of Fe^{2+}(aq) by dichromate(VI) ions.

c Work out the $E^{\ominus}$ value of the cell made when the two half-cells in part a are connected and the reaction in part b takes place. Explain what this value predicts about the likelihood of Fe^{2+}(aq) being oxidised by dichromate(VI) ions.

d How many moles of Fe^{2+}(aq) can 1 mole of dichromate(VI) oxidise?

e In a titration, $25.0\,cm^3$ of an solution containing Fe^{2+}(aq) ions was completely oxidised by $15.30\,cm^3$ of $0.00100\,mol\,dm^{-3}$ potassium dichromate(VI) solution.

i How many moles of potassium dichromate(VI) are there in $15.30\,cm^3$ of $0.00\,100\,mol\,dm^{-3}$ solution?

ii How many moles of Fe^{2+} were present in the $25.0\,cm^3$ of solution?

iii What was the concentration of the Fe^{2+}(aq) in the flask at the start of the titration?

371

Ligands and complex formation

In the previous section on redox reactions we have learnt about the oxidation of Fe^{2+}(aq) ions. When these ions are in solution the Fe^{2+} ion is surrounded by six water molecules. Each water molecule bonds to the central Fe^{2+} ion by forming a dative (co-ordinate) bond from the oxygen atom into vacant orbitals on the Fe^{2+} ion (Figure 24.4). The water molecules are called ligands and the resulting ion is called a complex ion. Its formula is written as $[Fe(H_2O)_6]^{2+}$. The shape of a complex with six ligands is octahedral.

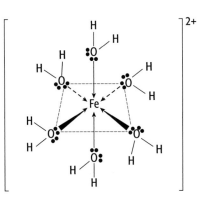

Figure 24.4 $[Fe(H_2O)_6]^{2+}$; the complex ion formed between an Fe^{2+} ion and six water molecules. It is called a hexaaquairon(II) ion.

Figure 24.5 shows the shape of complexes with four ligands.

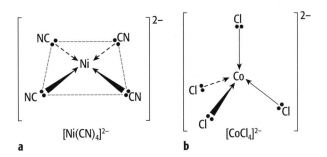

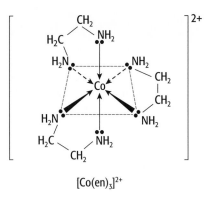

$[Co(en)_3]^{2+}$

Figure 24.5 The complex ion formed between a transition metal ion and a larger ligand can only fit four ligands around the central ion. These are arranged in either a square planar shape (as in **a** $[Ni(CN)_4]^{2-}$) or a tetrahedral shape (as in **b** $[CoCl_4]^{2-}$).

Figure 24.6 $[Co(en)_3]^{2+}$ is an example of a complex ion containing the bidentate ligand $NH_2CH_2CH_2NH_2$ (abbreviated to 'en').

All ligands can donate an electron pair to a central transition metal ion. The **co-ordination number** of a complex is the number of co-ordinate (dative) bonds to the central metal ion. Some ligands can form two co-ordinate bonds from each ion or molecule to the transition metal ion. These are called **bidentate** ligands, as shown in Figure 24.6. Most ligands, such as water and ammonia, form just one co-ordinate bond and are called **monodentate** ligands.

A few transition metal ions, e.g. copper(I), silver(I), gold(I), form linear complexes with ligands. The co-ordination number in these complexes is 2 (Figure 24.7). Table 24.4 shows some common ligands.

Note in Table 24.4 that the charge on a complex is simply the sum of the charges on the central metal ion and on each ligand in the complex. Some complexes will carry no charge, e.g. $Cu(OH)_2(H_2O)_4$.

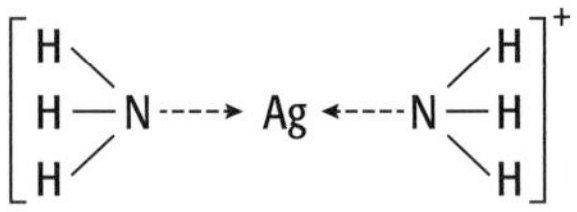

Figure 24.7 The diamminesilver(I) cation has a linear structure.

Name of ligand	Formula	Example of complex	Co-ordination number	Shape of complex
water	H_2O	$[Fe(H_2O)_6]^{2+}$	6	octahedral (see Figure 24.4)
ammonia	NH_3	$[Co(NH_3)_6]^{3+}$	6	octahedral
chloride ion	Cl^-	$[CuCl_4]^{2-}$	4	tetrahedral (see Figure 24.5b)
cyanide ion	CN^-	$[Ni(CN)_4]^{2-}$	4	square planar (see Figure 24.5a)
hydroxide ion	OH^-	$[Cr(OH)_6]^{3-}$	6	octahedral
thiocyanate ion	SCN^-	$[FeSCN]^{2+}$ or $[Fe(SCN)(H_2O)_5]^{2+}$	6	octahedral
ethanedioate ion (abbreviated as 'ox' in the formulae of complexes)	$^-OOC-COO^-$	$[Mn(ox)_3]^{3-}$	6	octahedral
1,2-diaminoethane (abbreviated as 'en' in the formulae of complexes)	$NH_2CH_2CH_2NH_2$	$[Co(en)_3]^{3+}$	6	octahedral (see Figure 24.6)

Table 24.4 Some common ligands and their complexes.

372

373

QUESTION

4 a What is the oxidation number of the transition metal in each of the following complexes?

   i $[Co(NH_3)_6]^{3+}$

   ii $[Ni(CN)_4]^{2-}$

   iii $[Cr(OH)_6]^{3-}$

   iv $[Co(en)_3]^{3+}$

   v $Cu(OH)_2(H_2O)_4$

b EDTA^{4-} ions can act as ligands. A single EDTA^{4-} ion can form six co-ordinate bonds to a central transition metal ion to form an octahedral complex. It is called a hexadentate ligand. Give the formula of such a complex formed between Ni^{2+} and EDTA^{4-}.

c Which ligands in Table 24.4 are bidentate?

Stereoisomerism in transition metal complexes

In Chapter 14 (pages 195–6) we learnt about two types of stereoisomerism: geometric isomerism and optical isomerism. The presence of a double bond in 1,2-dibromoethane means that two geometrical isomers (*cis-trans* isomers) are possible. Geometric isomerism is also possible in transition metal complexes, where no double bond exists. In this case, the term **geometric isomerism** refers to complexes with the same molecular formula but different geometrical arrangements of their atoms. Examples are *cis-* and *trans*-platin (Figure 24.8). In *cis*-platin, the chlorine atoms are next to each other in the square complex but in *trans*-platin, they are opposite. The properties of these geometrical isomers are slightly different.

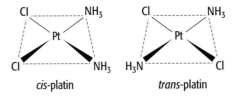

Figure 24.8 The geometrical isomers, *cis*-platin and *trans*-platin.

Cis-platin has been used as an anti-cancer drug. It acts by binding to sections of the DNA in cancer cells, preventing cell division.

Stereoisomerism is commonly shown by octahedral (six co-ordinate) complexes associated with bidentate ligands. An example is the complex containing nickel as the transition metal and 1,2-diaminoethane $(NH_2CH_2CH_2NH_2)$ as the bidentate ligand (Figure 24.9). The two isomers are stereoisomers because the two different molecules are mirror images of each other and cannot be superimposed.

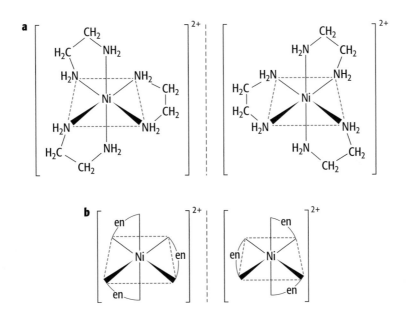

Figure 24.9 The two non-superimposable optical isomers of Ni(NH$_2$CH$_2$CH$_2$NH$_2$)$_3$$^{2+}$: **a** the full structure; **b** a simplified structure with 'en' representing a molecule of 1,2-diaminoethane.

5 a Cobalt forms a complex with the simplified structure:

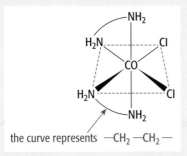

the curve represents —CH$_2$—CH$_2$—

  i Give the co-ordination number in this complex.

  ii Draw the stereoisomer of this complex.

  iii Explain why this is a stereoisomer.

b Draw the two geometrical isomers of Ni(CN)$_2$(Cl)$_2$$^{2-}$. Label the *cis*-isomer and the *trans*-isomer.

Substitution of ligands

The ligands in a complex can be exchanged, wholly or partially, for other ligands. This is a type of substitution reaction. It happens if the new complex formed is more stable than the original complex. The complexes of copper(II) ions can be used to show ligand substitution reactions.

Whenever we write Cu^{2+}(aq) we are really referring to the complex ion [Cu(H$_2$O)$_6$]$^{2+}$. This ion gives a solution of copper sulfate its blue colour. On adding sodium hydroxide solution, we see a light blue precipitate forming.

Two water ligands are replaced by two hydroxide ligands in the reaction:

$$[Cu(H_2O)_6]^{2+}(aq) + 2OH^-(aq)$$
blue solution

$$\longrightarrow Cu(OH)_2(H_2O)_4(s) + 2H_2O(l)$$
pale blue precipitate

If you now add concentrated ammonia solution, the pale blue precipitate dissolves and we get a deep blue solution:

$$Cu(OH)_2(H_2O)_4(s) + 4NH_3(aq)$$
$$\longrightarrow [Cu(H_2O)_2(NH_3)_4]^{2+}(aq) + 2H_2O(l) + 2OH^-(aq)$$
deep blue solution

The first reaction can also be achieved by adding concentrated ammonia solution to copper sulfate solution drop by drop or by adding a dilute solution of ammonia. The pale blue precipitate formed will then dissolve and form the deep blue solution when excess ammonia is added. The structure of [Cu(H$_2$O)$_2$(NH$_3$)$_4$]$^{2+}$(aq) is shown in Figure 24.10.

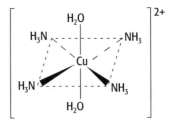

Figure 24.10 The structure of [Cu(H$_2$O)$_2$(NH$_3$)$_4$]$^{2+}$(aq).

Water ligands in [Cu(H$_2$O)$_6$]$^{2+}$ can also be exchanged for chloride ligands if we add concentrated hydrochloric acid drop by drop. A yellow solution forms, containing the complex ion [CuCl$_4$]$^{2-}$ (Figure 24.11):

[CuCl$_4$]$^{2-}$
this yellow complex forms on adding concentrated HCl

[Cu(H$_2$O)$_6$]$^{2+}$
the well-known blue Cu^{2+} complex with water

[Cu(H$_2$O)$_2$(NH$_3$)$_4$]$^{2+}$
this dark blue complex forms on adding concentrated NH$_3$

Figure 24.11 The equations for the changes are:

[Cu(H$_2$O)$_6$]$^{2+}$ + 4Cl$^-$ $\rightleftharpoons$ [CuCl$_4$]$^{2-}$ + 6H$_2$O and [Cu(H$_2$O)$_6$]$^{2+}$ + 4NH$_3$ $\rightleftharpoons$ [Cu(H$_2$O)$_2$(NH$_3$)$_4$]$^{2+}$ + 4H$_2$O.

$[Cu(H_2O)_6]^{2+}(aq) + 4Cl^-(aq)$
blue solution
$$\longrightarrow [CuCl_4]^{2-}(aq) + 6H_2O(l)$$
yellow solution

Aqueous cobalt(II) compounds also form complex ions. Whenever we write $Co^{2+}(aq)$, we are referring to the complex ion $[Co(H_2O)_6]^{2+}$. This ion gives an aqueous solution of cobalt(II) sulfate its pink colour. On adding sodium hydroxide solution, we see a blue precipitate of cobalt(II) hydroxide forming, which turns red when warmed if the alkali is in excess. Water ligands in $[Co(H_2O)_6]^{2+}$ can also be exchanged for ammonia ligands if we add concentrated aqueous ammonia drop by drop.

$[Co(H_2O)_6]^{2+}(aq) + 6NH_3(aq)$
$$\longrightarrow [Co(NH_3)_6]^{2+}(aq) + 6H_2O(l)$$

The addition of concentrated hydrochloric acid drop by drop to an aqueous solution of cobalt(II) ions results in the formation of a blue solution containing the tetrahedral complex $[CoCl_4]^{2-}(aq)$.

$[Co(H_2O)_6]^{2+}(aq) + 4Cl^-(aq)$
$$\longrightarrow [CoCl_4]^{2-}(aq) + 6H_2O(l)$$

Aqueous cobalt(II) ions usually form tetrahedral complexes with monodentate anionic ligands such as Cl^-, SCN^- and OH^-.

QUESTION

6 a Blue cobalt chloride paper gets its blue colour from $[CoCl_4]^{2-}$ ions. What is the oxidation number of the cobalt in this complex ion?

b Blue cobalt chloride paper is used to test for water. If water is present the paper turns pink as a complex forms between the cobalt ion and six water ligands (Figure 24.12). Write an equation to show the ligand substitution reaction that takes place in a positive test for water.

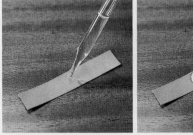

Figure 24.12 A positive test for the presence of water using anhydrous cobalt chloride paper.

Stability constants

Aqueous solutions of transition element ions are hydrated. They are complex ions with water as a ligand. Different ligands form complexes with different stabilities. For example when we add concentrated aqueous ammonia to an aqueous solution of copper(II) sulfate, the ammonia ligands displace water ligands in a stepwise process.

$[Cu(H_2O)_6]^{2+}(aq) + NH_3(aq)$
$$\rightleftharpoons [Cu(NH_3)(H_2O)_5]^{2+}(aq) + H_2O(l)$$

$[Cu(NH_3)(H_2O)_5]^{2+}(aq) + NH_3(aq)$
$$\rightleftharpoons [Cu(NH_3)_2(H_2O)_4]^{2+}(aq) + H_2O(l)$$

As we increase the concentration of ammonia, this process continues until four of the water molecules are replaced by ammonia to form a deep blue solution. The overall process is:

$[Cu(H_2O)_6]^{2+} + 4NH_3(aq)$
$$\rightleftharpoons [Cu(NH_3)_4(H_2O)_2]^{2+}(aq) + 4H_2O(l)$$

We can think of this exchange of ligands in terms of competing equilibria of the forward and backward reactions. The position of equilibrium lies in the direction of the more stable complex. In this case, the complex with ammonia as a ligand is more stable than the complex with just water as a ligand. If we dilute the complex with water, the position of equilibrium shifts to the left and a complex with more water molecules as ligands is formed.

The stability of the complex is expressed in terms of the equilibrium constants for ligand displacement. This is called the **stability constant**. Usually an overall stability constant, K_{stab}, is given rather than the stepwise constants. The stability constant is the equilibrium constant for the formation of the complex ion in a solvent from its constituent ions or molecules. The method for writing equilibrium expressions for stability constants is similar to the one we used for writing K_c (see page 304). So for the equilibrium

$[Cu(H_2O)_6]^{2+} + 4Cl^-(aq) \rightleftharpoons [CuCl_4]^{2-}(aq) + 6H_2O(l)$

the expression is:

$$K_{stab} = \frac{[[CuCl_4]^{2-}(aq)]}{[[Cu(H_2O)_6]^{2+}][Cl^-(aq)]^4}$$

Note:

- water does not appear in the equilibrium expression because it is in such a large excess that its concentration is regarded as being constant

375

- the units for the stability constant are worked out in the same way as for the units of K_c (see page 124). For example, in the above case:

$$K_{stab} = \frac{[[CuCl_4]^{2-}(aq)]}{[[Cu(H_2O)_6]^{2+}][Cl^-(aq)]^4} \frac{(mol\,dm^{-3})}{(mol\,dm^{-3}) \times (mol\,dm^{-3})^4}$$

$$= dm^{12}\,mol^{-4}$$

Stability constants are often given on a $\log_{10}$ scale. When expressed on a $\log_{10}$ scale, they have no units. Stability constants can be used to compare the stability of any two ligands. The values quoted usually give the stability of the complex relative to the aqueous ion where the ligand is water. The higher the value of the stability constant, the more stable the complex. Table 24.5 gives some values of stability constants for various copper(II) complexes relative to their aqueous ions.

Ligand	$\log_{10} K_{stab}$
chloride, Cl^-	5.6
ammonia, NH_3	13.1
2-hydroxybenzoate	16.9
1,2-dihydroxybenzene	25.0

Table 24.5 The stability constants of some complexes of copper.

From the table you can see that, in general, complexes with bidentate ions (2-hydroxybenzoate and 1,2-dihydroxybenzene) have higher stability constants than those with monodentate ligands. We can use the values of the stability constants to predict the effect of adding different ligands to complex ions. For example, the addition of excess ammonia to the complex $[CuCl_4]^{2-}(aq)$ should result in the formation of a dark blue solution of the ammonia complex because the stability constant of the ammonia complex is higher than that of the chloride complex. The position of equilibrium is shifted to the right in the direction of the more stable complex. Addition of excess 1,2-dihydroxybenzene to the dark blue ammonia complex results in the formation of a green complex with 1,2-dihydroxybenzene. This is because the stability constant with the 1,2-dihydroxybenzene is higher than that for ammonia:

QUESTION

7 a Write expressions for the stability constants for the following reactions:

   i $[PtCl_4]^{2-}(aq) + 2NH_3(aq)$

$$\rightleftharpoons PtCl_2(NH_3)_2(aq) + 2Cl^-(aq)$$

   ii $[Cr(H_2O)_6]^{3+}(aq) + 2Cl^-(aq)$

$$\rightleftharpoons [Cr(H_2O)_4Cl_2]^+(aq) + 2H_2O(l)$$

   iii $[Ni(H_2O)_6]^{2+}(aq) + 4NH_3(aq)$

$$\rightleftharpoons [Ni(NH_3)_4(H_2O)_2]^{2+}(aq) + 4H_2O(l)$$

b An iron(III) ion, Fe^{3+}, in aqueous solution has six water molecules bonded to it as ligands.

   i Draw the structure of this ion.

   ii When thiocyanate ions, SCN^-, are added to an aqueous solution of iron(III) ions, the solution turns red and one water molecule is replaced by a thiocyanate ion. Use the concept of stability constants to explain why the reaction occurs.

   iii Deduce the formula of the ion forming the red solution.

   iv The stability constant for aqueous Fe^{3+} ions with SCN^- as a ligand is $891\,dm^3\,mol^{-1}$. The stability constant for aqueous Fe^{3+} ions with fluoride ions, F^-, as a ligand is $2 \times 10^5\,dm^3\,mol^{-1}$. A solution containing fluoride ions is added to the red solution. Would you expect to observe any changes? Explain your answer.

The colour of complexes

You cannot fail to notice the striking colours of complexes containing transition metal ions. But how do these colours arise? White light is made up of all the colours of the visible spectrum. When a solution containing a transition metal ion in a complex appears coloured, part of the visible spectrum is absorbed by the solution. However, that still doesn't explain why part of the spectrum is absorbed by transition metal ions. To answer this question we must look in more detail at the d orbitals in the ions.

The five d orbitals in an isolated transition metal atom or ion are described as **degenerate**, meaning they are all at the same energy level (Figure 24.13).

In the presence of ligands a transition metal ion is not isolated. The co-ordinate bonding from the ligands causes the five d orbitals in the transition metal ion to split into two sets of **non-degenerate** orbitals at slightly different energy levels (Figure 24.14). In a complex with six

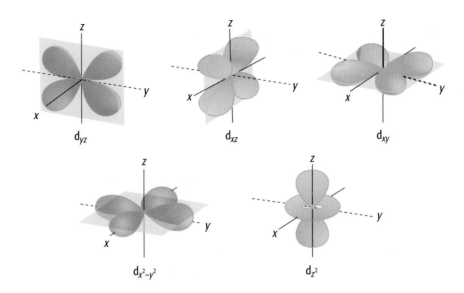

Figure 24.13 The degenerate d orbitals in a transition metal atom.

ligands, the ligands are arranged in an octahedral shape around the central metal ion. The lone pairs donated by the ligands into the transition metal ion repel electrons in the two $d_{x^2-y^2}$ and d_{z^2} orbitals shown in Figure 24.13 more than those in the other three d orbitals. This is because these d orbitals line up with the co-ordinate bonds in the complex's octahedral shape and so they are closer to the bonding electrons in the octahedral arrangement, increasing repulsion between electrons. Therefore the orbitals are split, with these two d orbitals at a slightly higher energy level than the d_{yz}, d_{xz} and d_{xy} orbitals (Figure 24.14).

A Cu^{2+} ion has an electronic configuration of [Ar] $3d^9$. Figure 24.14 shows how the nine d electrons are distributed between the non-degenerate orbitals formed

in a complex with ligands. The difference in the energy between the non-degenerate d orbitals is labelled ΔE. ΔE is part of the visible spectrum of light. So, when light shines on the solution containing the $Cu(H_2O)_6^{2+}$ complex, an electron absorbs this amount of energy. It uses this energy to jump into the higher of the two non-degenerate energy levels. In copper complexes, the rest of the visible spectrum that passes through the solution makes it appear blue in colour.

The exact energy difference (ΔE) between the non-degenerate d orbitals in a transition metal ion is affected by many factors. One of these factors is the identity of the ligands that surround the transition metal ion. As you have seen, a solution containing $Cu(H_2O)_6^{2+}$ is a light blue, whereas a solution containing $Cu(NH_3)_2(H_2O)_2^{2+}$ is a very

377

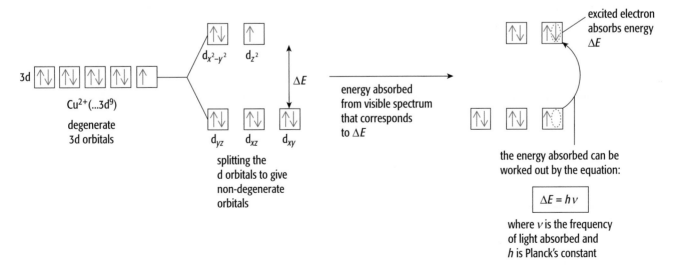

Figure 24.14 The splitting of the 3d orbitals in a $Cu(H_2O)_6^{2+}$ complex ion.

deep shade of blue. The colour change arises because the presence of the ammonia ligands causes the d orbitals to split by a different amount of energy. This means that the size of ΔE changes and this results in a slightly different amount of energy being absorbed by electrons jumping up to the higher orbitals. Therefore a different colour is absorbed from visible light, so a different colour is seen.

QUESTIONS

8 **a** What do we mean by **degenerate atomic orbitals**?

   b Explain why an octahedral complex of a transition element is coloured.

   c Draw the non-degenerate 3d orbitals in a Ni^{2+} ion on a diagram similar to Figure 24.14. The electrons should be shown in the configuration that gives the lowest possible energy.

9 **a** A solution of Sc^{3+} ions is colourless. Suggest a reason for this.

   b A solution of Zn^{2+} ions is colourless. Suggest a reason for this.

Summary

- Each of the transition elements forms at least one ion with a partially filled d orbital. They are metals with similar physical and chemical properties.

- When a transition element is oxidised, it loses electrons from the 4s subshell first and then the 3d subshell to form a positively charged ion.

- Transition elements can exist in several oxidation states.

- Many reactions involving transition elements are redox reactions. Some redox reactions are used in titrations to determine concentrations.

- A ligand is a molecule or ion with one or more lone pairs of electrons available to donate to a transition metal ion.

- Transition elements form complexes by combining with ligands. Ligands bond to transition metal ions by one or more co-ordinate bonds.

- Ligands can be exchanged for other ligands in a complex. This can result in a change of colour.

- Some transition element complexes exist as geometrical (*cis-trans*) isomers, e.g. *cis-* and *trans-*platin; others, especially those associated with bidentate ligands with co-ordination number 6, may exist as optical isomers.

- *cis*-platin can be used as an anti-cancer drug by binding to DNA in cancer cells and preventing cell division.

- Ligand exchange can be described in terms of competing equilibria.

- The stability constant, K_{stab}, of a complex ion is the equilibrium constant for the formation of the complex ion in a solvent from its constituent ions or molecules.

- The higher the value of the stability constant, the more stable is the complex ion formed.

- Transition metal compounds are often coloured because of d orbital splitting, caused by ligands. Different ligands will split the d orbitals by different amounts, resulting in differently coloured complexes.

End-of-chapter questions

1 Define the following terms:

   a transition element [1]

   b ligand [1]

   c complex ion. [2]

                     Total = 4

2 Use subshell notation ($1s^2 2s^2 2p^6$, etc.) to give the electronic configurations of the following:

   a an Fe atom [1]

   b a Co^{2+} ion [1]

   c a Ti^{3+} ion. [1]

                     Total = 3

3 a Give the formulae of two iron compounds in which iron has different oxidation states. Give the oxidation states of the iron in each compound. [4]

   b Explain why complexes of iron compounds are coloured. [3]

                     Total = 7

4 Write balanced ionic equations and describe the observations for the reactions that occur when:

   a sodium hydroxide solution is added to a solution containing $[Cu(H_2O)_6]^{2+}(aq)$ [2]

   b excess concentrated ammonia solution is added to a solution containing $[Cu(H_2O)_6]^{2+}(aq)$. [3]

                     Total = 5

5 The half-cell reactions given below are relevant to the questions that follow.

$$Cl_2 + 2e^- \longrightarrow 2Cl^- \qquad E^\ominus = +1.36\,V$$

$$Fe^{3+} + e^- \longrightarrow Fe^{2+} \qquad E^\ominus = +0.77\,V$$

$$MnO_4^- + 8H^+ + 5e^- \longrightarrow Mn^{2+} + 4H_2O \qquad E^\ominus = +1.51\,V$$

$$SO_4^{2-} + 4H^+ + 2e^- \longrightarrow SO_2 + 2H_2O \qquad E^\ominus = +0.17\,V$$

In order to standardise a solution of $KMnO_4$, a student weighed out 5.56 g of $FeSO_4.7H_2O$, dissolved it in sulfuric acid and then made it up to a total volume of 250 cm^3 with distilled water. She then took 25.0 cm^3 portions of this solution, and added 10 cm^3 of 2.00 mol dm^{-3} sulfuric acid to each. She then titrated these solutions against the potassium manganate(VII) solution. The average titre was 21.2 cm^3.

   a Using the electrode potentials, explain why she used sulfuric acid and not hydrochloric acid in her titrations. [4]

   b What was the concentration of the iron(II) sulfate solution? [3]

   c **i** Write the full ionic equation for the reaction between the manganate(VII) solution and the iron(II) sulfate. [2]

       ii How does the student know that she has reached the end-point for the reaction? [1]

   d What is the concentration of the manganate(VII) solution? [2]

   e If the student passed sulfur dioxide gas through 25.0 cm^3 of the manganate(VII) solution, what volume of gas would be required to completely decolorise the manganate(VII)? (1 mol of gas occupies 24.0 dm^3 at room temperature and pressure) [5]

                     Total = 17

6 Copper forms complexes with chloride ions and with ammonia.

$\log_{10} K_{stab}$ for aqueous Cu^{2+} ions with Cl^- as a ligand is 2.80.

$\log_{10} K_{stab}$ for aqueous Cu^{2+} ions with NH_3 as a ligand is 4.25.

a A few drops of hydrochloric acid are added to blue aqueous copper(II) sulfate.

   i Copy and complete the equation for this reaction.

   $[Cu(H_2O)_6]^{2+}(aq) +$ _____ $\rightleftharpoons [CuCl_4]^{2-} (aq) +$ _____
   light blue   yellow-green   [2]

   ii Describe and explain what happens when excess water is then added to the reaction mixture in part i. [3]

   iii Explain what happens in terms of ligand exchange, when concentrated aqueous ammonia is added to the reaction mixture from part ii. [2]

b Aqueous copper ions form a complex with 1,2-diaminoethane, $NH_2CH_2CH_2NH_2$. They also form a complex with 1,3-diaminopropane $NH_2CH_2CH_2CH_2NH_2$.

   $\log_{10} K_{stab}$ for aqueous Cu^{2+} ions with 1,2-diaminoethane as a ligand is 20.3

   $\log_{10} K_{stab}$ for aqueous Cu^{2+} ions with 1,3-diaminopropane as a ligand is 17.7

   i What type of ligands are 1,2-diaminoethane and 1,3-diaminopropane? Explain your answer. [2]

   ii Which one of these ligands forms a more stable complex? Explain your answer. [1]

   iii 1,2-diaminoethane can be abbreviated as 'en'.

   A complex of nickel ions, Ni^{2+}, with 1,2-diaminoethane is octahedral in shape with a co-ordination number of 6. Draw the structures of the two stereoisomers of this complex. [4]

   Total = 14

Chapter 25:
Benzene and its compounds

Learning outcomes

You should be able to:

- interpret, name and use the general, structural, displayed and skeletal formulae of benzene and simple aryl compounds

- describe and explain the shape of, and bond angles in, benzene molecules in terms of σ and π bonds

- describe the reactions of arenes, such as benzene and methylbenzene, in:
  - substitution reactions with chlorine and with bromine
  - nitration
  - Friedel–Crafts alkylation and acylation
  - complete oxidation of the side-chain to give a benzoic acid

  - hydrogenation of the benzene ring to form a cyclohexane ring

- describe the mechanism of electrophilic substitution in arenes and the effect of the delocalisation of electrons in such reactions

- interpret the difference in reactivity between benzene and chlorobenzene

- predict whether halogenation will occur in the side-chain or in the benzene ring in arenes depending on reaction conditions

- apply knowledge relating to position of substitution in the electrophilic substitution of arenes (see Table 25.4).

Introduction

In the English language, 'aromatic' means 'having an agreeable, sweet or spicy odour'. In chemistry, the word 'aromatic' was once used to describe chemical compounds containing a particular structure of six carbon atoms arranged in a ring – the benzene ring. These compounds are now called aryl compounds. However, many chemicals with structures containing one or more benzene rings do have strong odours.

Figure 25.1 This is a vanilla orchid. Its seed pods contain a substance called vanillin. Its molecules are based on a benzene ring – as represented by the hexagon with a circle inside in the structure shown below. Vanillin is used to flavour foods such as ice cream and chocolate. Its structure is:

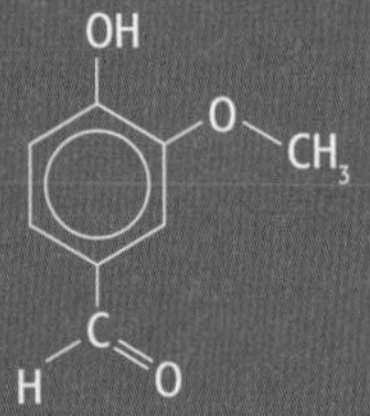

The benzene ring

The 'benzene ring' is a particularly important functional group found in many organic compounds. A benzene ring is a hexagon made of six carbon atoms bonded together in a particular way. Benzene rings are found in many compounds that are commercially important – for example as medicines, dyes and plastics.

Organic hydrocarbons containing one or more benzene rings are called **arenes**. In general, compounds of benzene are known as **aryl compounds** or aromatic compounds; an example is chlorobenzene, which is one of the halogenoarenes.

The simplest arene is benzene itself. Its formula is C_6H_6. The early organic chemists struggled to work out its structure. However, around 1865 Friedrich August Kekulé seemed to have solved the problem. He proposed a hexagonal ring of carbon atoms, each bonded to one hydrogen atom. In Kekulé's structure the hexagonal ring contained three double C=C bonds (Figure 25.2).

This is reflected in benzene's name, which has the same ending as the alkenes.

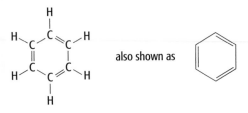

also shown as

Figure 25.2 Kekulé's structure of benzene.

As analytical techniques were developed, however, chemists found out that the benzene molecule was a planar, perfectly symmetrical molecule. Kekulé's structure would suggest three shorter double C=C bonds and three longer single C—C bonds in the ring. This would produce a distorted hexagonal shape, not the perfect hexagonal arrangement of carbon atoms in benzene's actual molecules. Figure 25.3 shows how we represent benzene's skeletal formula.

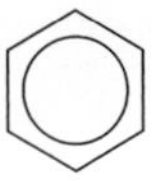

Figure 25.3 The skeletal formula of benzene. It can also be used in displayed formulae of aryl compounds, as on the previous page showing the structure of vanillin.

We can now measure actual bond lengths. This was impossible in the 19th century when Kekulé worked. Table 25.1 shows that the bond length of the carbon–carbon bonds in benzene lie between the values for C—C single bonds and C=C double bonds.

Bond	Bond length / nm
C—C	0.154
C=C	0.134
carbon to carbon bond in benzene	0.139

Table 25.1 Comparing bond lengths.

The chemistry of benzene also suggests that the Kekulé structure is incorrect. If there were three C=C bonds in benzene it would undergo addition reactions like the alkenes (see page 209). However, this is not the case. For example, ethene will decolorise bromine water on mixing, but benzene needs much harsher conditions.

The actual structure of benzene can be explained by considering the bonding in the molecule. Each carbon atom in the hexagonal ring is sp^2 hybridised (see page 57), sharing:

■ one pair of electrons with one of its neighbouring carbon atoms
■ one pair of electrons with its other neighbouring carbon atom
■ one pair of electrons with a hydrogen atom.

These are σ (sigma) bonds; covalent bonds with the pair of electrons found mainly between the nuclei of the atoms bonded to each other. Each carbon atom forms three σ bonds. That leaves one electron spare on each of the six carbon atoms. Each carbon atom contributes this one electron to a π (pi) bond (see page 57). However, the π bonds formed are not localised between pairs of carbon atoms as in an alkene C=C bond (see page 193). Instead, the π bonds in benzene spread over all six carbon atoms in the hexagonal ring. The six electrons in the π bonds are said to be **delocalised**.

The π bonding in benzene is formed by the overlap of carbon p atomic orbitals, one from each of the six carbon atoms. To achieve maximum overlap, the benzene molecule must be planar. The lobes of the p orbitals overlap to form a ring of delocalised electrons above and below the plane of the carbon atoms in the benzene molecule. This is shown in Figure 25.4.

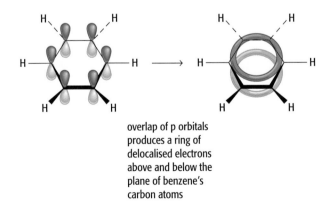

overlap of p orbitals produces a ring of delocalised electrons above and below the plane of benzene's carbon atoms

Figure 25.4 The π bonding in benzene. The three bond angles around each of the sp^2 hybridised carbon atoms are 120°.

Naming aryl compounds

You saw how to name aryl compounds with alkyl side-chains on page 193. Some aryl compounds have functional groups that are substituted directly into the benzene ring in place of a hydrogen atom. You need to know the names of the compounds in Table 25.2.

Skeletal formula of aryl compound	Name
Cl	chlorobenzene
NO_2	nitrobenzene
OH	phenol
OH, Br, Br, Br	2,4,6-tribromophenol: note the numbering of the carbon atoms in the benzene ring to describe the position of each substituted group (see page 193)
NH_2	phenylamine

Table 25.2 The names of some aryl compounds. The phenyl group can be written as C_6H_5; e.g. the structural formula of phenylamine is $C_6H_5NH_2$.

383

QUESTIONS

1   **a** How many electrons are involved in the π bonding system in a benzene molecule?

    b From which type of atomic orbital do the electrons in part **a** come from?

    c What do we mean by the term 'delocalised electrons' in benzene?

    d What is the difference between the π bonding in benzene and the π bonding in hex-3-ene?

2   **a** Draw the displayed or skeletal formula of:

    i   1,3,5-tribromobenzene

    ii 1,3-dichloro-5-nitrobenzene.

    b Name the molecules below:

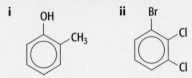

Reactions of arenes

Most reactions of benzene maintain the highly stable delocalised ring of π bonding electrons intact. This occurs by substituting an atom, or group of atoms, for one or more hydrogen atoms attached to the benzene ring. The initial attack is usually by an electrophile, which is attracted to the high electron density around the benzene ring.

Electrophilic substitution with chlorine or bromine

Benzene will react with bromine in the presence of an anhydrous iron(III) bromide catalyst. The catalyst can be made in the reaction vessel by adding iron filings to the benzene and bromine. The substitution reaction is:

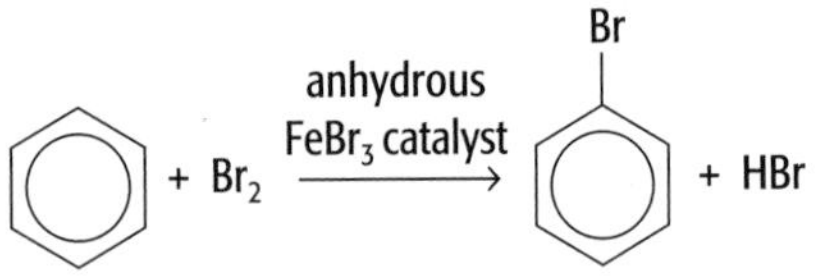

At first sight the electrophile that starts the attack on benzene is not obvious. The electrophile is created when an iron(III) bromide molecule polarises a bromine molecule. The Br_2 molecule forms a dative (co-ordinate) bond with iron(III) bromide by donating a lone pair of electrons from one bromine atom into an empty 3d orbital in the iron. This draws electrons from the other bromine atom in the Br_2 molecule making it partially positive, creating the electrophile.

We can think of the electrophile as a Br^+ cation:

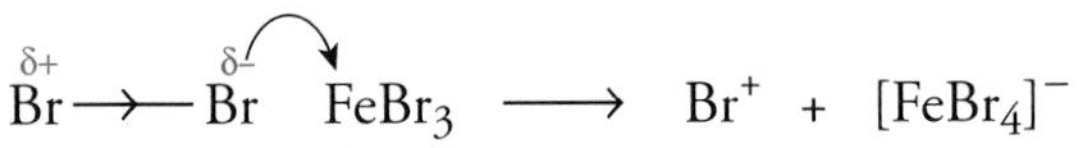

$$\overset{\delta+}{Br} \longrightarrow \overset{\delta-}{Br} \quad FeBr_3 \longrightarrow Br^+ + [FeBr_4]^-$$

The Br^+ cation and the 'electron-rich' benzene ring are attracted to each other, as the mechanism below shows. Remember that the curly arrows show the movement of a pair of electrons.

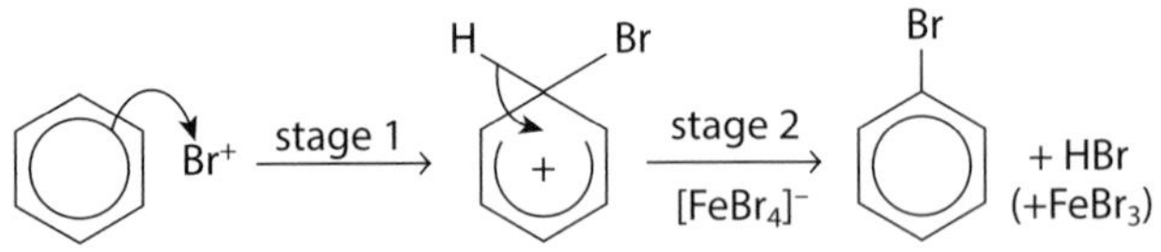

A similar reaction happens when chlorine gas is bubbled through benzene at room temperature in the presence of a catalyst such as iron(III) chloride or aluminium chloride. The products of this electrophilic substitution are chlorobenzene and hydrogen chloride. The catalysts in these reactions, i.e. $FeBr_3$, $AlCl_3$ and $FeCl_3$, are known as 'halogen carriers'.

When we halogenate methylbenzene or other alkylarenes, the halogen atom substitutes into the benzene ring at positions 2 or 4. These positions are 'activated' by any electron-donating groups bonded directly to the benzene ring (see Table 25.4 on page 390). Other examples of benzene compounds that are activated in these positions are phenol and phenylamine. So when we react methylbenzene with chlorine gas, using an anhydrous aluminium chloride catalyst, two products can be made:

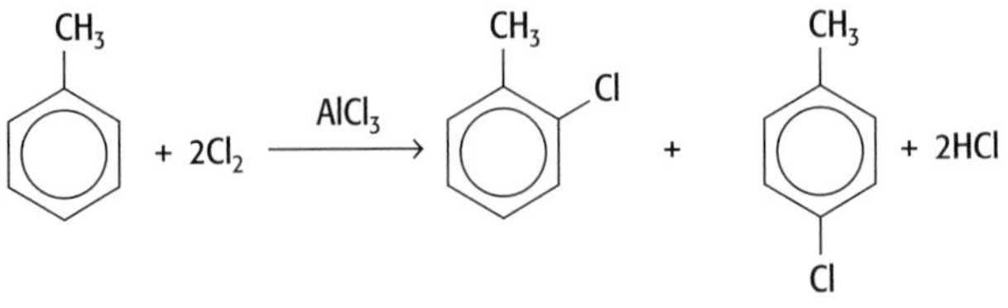

2-chloromethyl-
benzene

4-chloromethyl-
benzene

If excess chlorine gas is bubbled through, we can form 1-methyl-2,4-dichlorobenzene, 1-methyl-2,6-dichlorobenzene and 1-methyl-2,4,6-trichlorobenzene. (Remember that the 2 and 6 positions in substituted arenes are equivalent.)

The carbon–halogen bond in halogenoarenes is stronger than the equivalent bond in a halogenoalkane because one of the lone pairs on the halogen atom overlaps slightly with the π bonding system in the benzene ring. This gives the carbon–halogen bond a partial double bond character.

Notice that the methyl side-chain is not affected under the conditions used in the reaction above. However, we learnt on page 206 that chlorine will react with alkanes in the presence of ultraviolet (UV) light or strong sunlight. This is a free radical substitution reaction. So if the chlorine gas is passed into boiling methylbenzene, in the presence of UV light, the following reaction takes place:

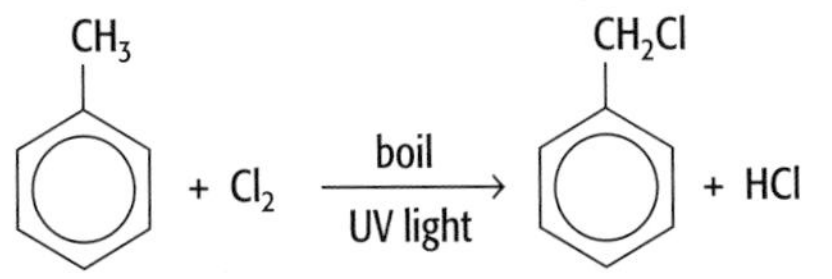

chloromethyl-
benzene

Note that there is no substitution into the benzene ring under these conditions. In excess chlorine, eventually all three of the hydrogen atoms on the methyl side-chain will be replaced by chlorine atoms.

QUESTION

3   a   Write the equation for the reaction of chlorine with benzene in the presence of an iron(III) chloride catalyst.

    b   What do we call this type of mechanism for the reaction in part **a**?

    c   Draw the mechanism of the reaction in part **a**, with Cl$^+$ as the attacking species and using curly arrows to show the movement of electron pairs.

    d   Draw the displayed formula of the 'tri-substituted' halogenoarene produced if methylbenzene is added to excess bromine at room temperature in the presence of iron(III) bromide.

    e   How would the reaction in part **d** differ if the methylbenzene and bromine were boiled in the presence of UV light?

    f   Name the mechanism of the reaction in part **e**.

Nitration of benzene

The nitration of benzene is another example of an electrophilic substitution. Nitration refers to the introduction of the NO_2 group into a molecule. In this reaction the electrophile is the NO_2^+ ion, known as the nitronium ion (or nitryl cation). This is made from a mixture of concentrated nitric acid and concentrated sulfuric acid:

$$HNO_3 + 2H_2SO_4 \longrightarrow NO_2^+ + 2HSO_4^- + H_3O^+$$

This 'nitrating mixture' is refluxed with benzene at about 55 °C to make nitrobenzene:

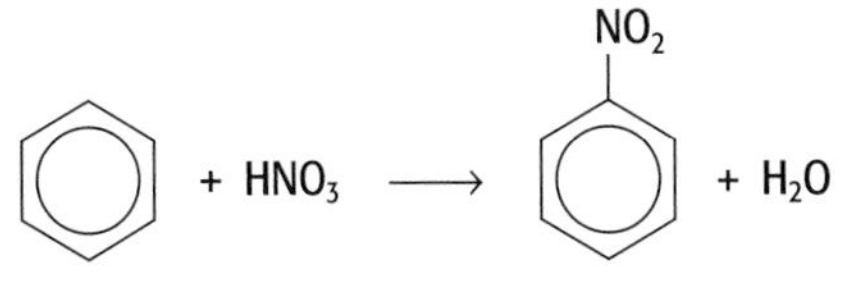

The mechanism of the electrophilic substitution is:

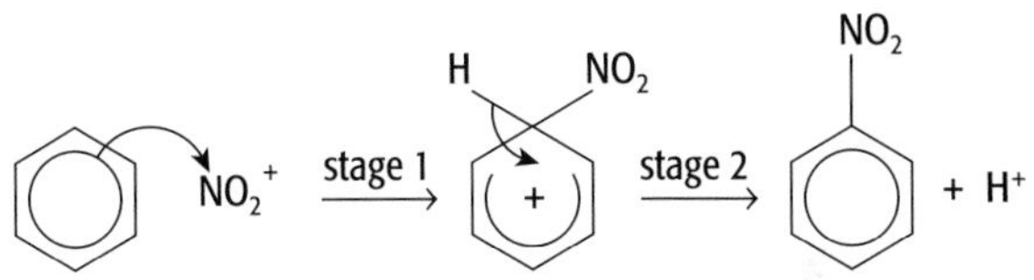

In stage 1 in the mechanism, the electrophile, NO_2^+, is attracted to the high electron density of the π bonding system in benzene. A pair of electrons from the benzene ring is donated to the nitrogen atom in NO_2^+, and forms a new covalent bond. At this point, benzene's delocalised ring of electrons is disrupted. There are now four π bonding electrons and a positive charge spread over five carbon atoms.

However, the full delocalised ring is restored in stage 2 when the C—H bond breaks heterolytically. Both electrons in the C—H covalent bond go into nitrobenzene's π bonding system, and hydrogen leaves as an H$^+$ ion. There are now six electrons spread over the six carbon atoms, so the chemical stability of the benzene ring is retained in this substitution reaction.

Further nitration of the nitrobenzene produces 1,3-dinitrobenzene and 1,3,5-trinitrobenzene. Unlike the electron-donating methyl group in methylbenzene (which activates the 2 and 4 positions in the benzene ring), the NO_2 group is electron-withdrawing. This type of group (which includes COOH) deactivates the 2 and 4 positions in the benzene ring. Therefore, when there is a nitro group bonded to the benzene ring, further substitution takes place at the 3 and 5 positions (see Table 25.4, page 390).

QUESTION

4 a Copy and complete the two equations below, which can be used to show the nitration of methylbenzene:

i $C_6H_5CH_3 + NO_2^+ \longrightarrow$ ______ + ______

ii $C_6H_5CH_3 + HNO_3 \xrightarrow{H_2SO_4}$ ______ + ______

iii Name the possible mono-substituted products in parts **i** and **ii**.

iv 1-methyl-2,4-dinitrobenzene and 1-methyl-2,4,6-trinitrobenzene are formed on further nitration of methylbenzene. Draw the displayed formula of each compound.

b Benzene also undergoes electrophilic substitution when refluxed with fuming sulfuric acid for several hours. This is called sulfonation. The electrophile is the SO_3 molecule and the product formed is benzenesulfonic acid, $C_6H_5SO_3H$.

i Which atom in the SO_3 molecule accepts an electron pair in the mechanism of sulfonation?

ii Write an equation in the style of part **a i** for the sulfonation of benzene to form benzenesulfonic acid.

Alkylation (or acylation) of benzene (Friedel–Crafts reaction)

Friedel–Crafts reactions, named after the chemists who first discovered them, are a third example of **electrophilic substitution** into the benzene ring.

Sometimes chemists need to change the structure of an arene in order to make a new product. Examples include the manufacture of detergents or the reactants needed to make plastics, such as poly(phenylethene) – commonly known as polystyrene. They can use a Friedel–Crafts reaction to substitute a hydrogen in the benzene ring for an alkyl group, such as a methyl ($—CH_3$) or an ethyl ($—C_2H_5$) group:

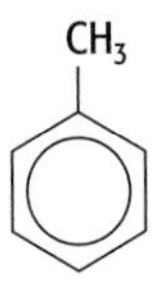

methylbenzene

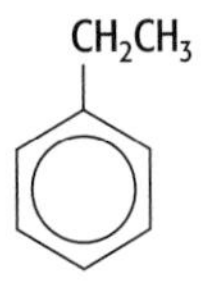

ethylbenzene

The same type of reaction can also be used to introduce an acyl group into a benzene ring. An acyl group contains an alkyl group and a carbonyl (C=O) group:

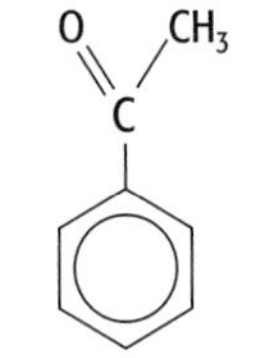

phenylethanone

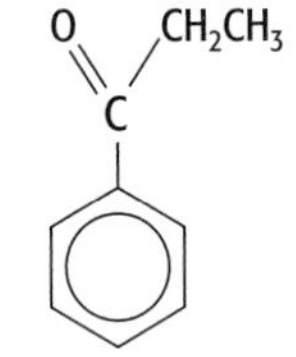

phenylpropanone

Friedel–Crafts reactions result in **the introduction of a side-chain** into a benzene ring.

They are also called alkylation or acylation reactions.

For example:

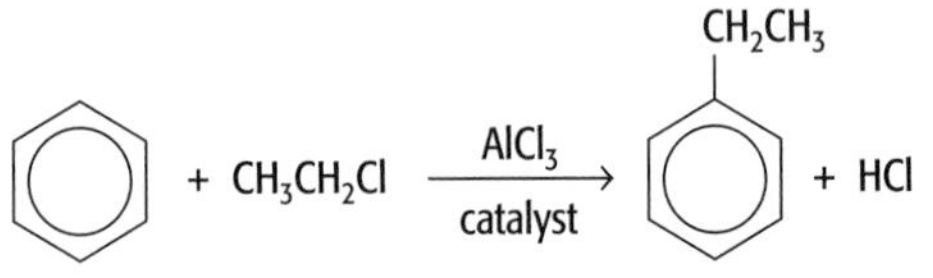

ethylbenzene

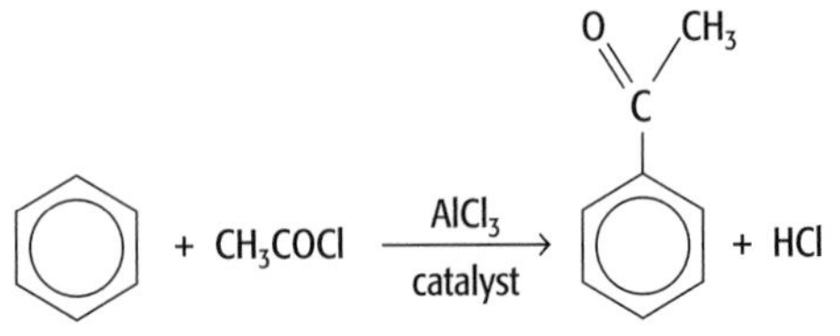

phenylethanone

The reactions involve attack on the benzene ring by an **electrophile** carrying a positive charge on a carbon atom, i.e. a carbocation.

The electrophile is often formed by adding an aluminium chloride catalyst to a halogenoalkane. This creates the carbocation electrophile:

1st step

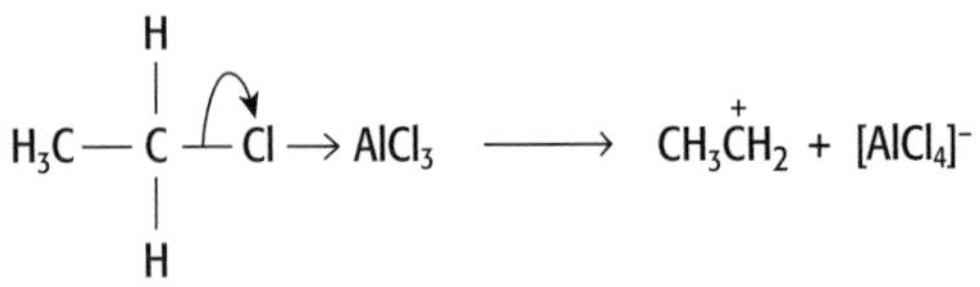

The carbocation electrophile then attacks the benzene ring:

2nd step

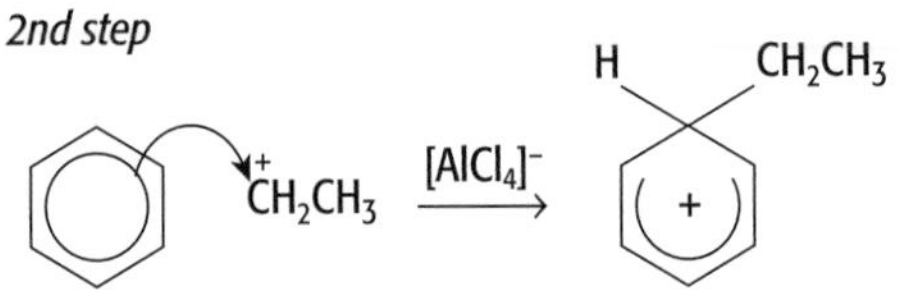

The aluminium chloride catalyst is regenerated in the final step:

3rd step

$$\text{(benzene ring with H and CH}_2\text{CH}_3\text{, +)} + [\text{AlCl}_4]^- \longrightarrow \text{(benzene ring with CH}_2\text{CH}_3\text{)} + \text{HCl} + \text{AlCl}_3$$

Further alkylation of the benzene ring can take place as the reaction proceeds.

Oxidation of the side-chain in arenes

The presence of the benzene ring in an alkylarene, such as methylbenzene, can affect the characteristic reactions of its alkyl side-chain. For example, alkanes are not usually oxidised by a chemical oxidising agent such as potassium manganate(VII). However in alkylarenes, the alkane side-chain is oxidised to form a carboxylic acid. For example, methylbenzene produces benzoic acid when refluxed with alkaline potassium manganate(VII), and then acidified with dilute sulfuric acid, or another strong oxidising agent such as acidified potassium dichromate(VI):

$$\text{(benzene ring with CH}_3\text{)} + 3[\text{O}] \longrightarrow \text{(benzene ring with COOH)} + \text{H}_2\text{O}$$

QUESTIONS

5 a Copy and complete the two equations below, which can be used to show the alkylation and acylation of benzene, to produce the mono-substituted products.

   i $C_6H_6 + CH_3CH_2CH_2Cl \longrightarrow$ _____ + _____

   ii $C_6H_6 + CH_3CH_2CH_2CH_2COCl$
       $\longrightarrow$ _____ + _____

   b i   Name the mono-substituted organic product in part **a i**.

      ii What class of compound is formed in part **a ii**?

6 Hexylbenzene is refluxed with alkaline potassium manganate(VII) and then acidified with dilute sulfuric acid. The same experiment is carried out using hexane and the oxidising agent. Compare what would happen in these experiments.

Phenol

Phenol, C_6H_5OH, is a crystalline solid that melts at 43 °C. It is used to manufacture a wide range of products (Figure 25.5). Its structure is:

$$\text{(benzene ring with OH)}$$

Figure 25.5 Araldite adhesive, compact discs and TCP® antiseptic (which contains 2,4,6-trichlorophenol, as does Dettol®) are all manufactured using phenol as a starting material.

The melting point of phenol is relatively high for an aryl compound of its molecular mass because of hydrogen bonding between its molecules. However, the large non-polar benzene ring makes phenol only slightly soluble in water, as it disrupts hydrogen bonding with water molecules.

Phenol is weakly acidic, losing an H⁺ ion from its hydroxyl group:

$$C_6H_5OH(aq) \rightleftharpoons C_6H_5O^-(aq) + H^+(aq)$$
$$\text{phenoxide ion}$$

The position of this equilibrium lies well over to the left-hand side. However, phenol is still a stronger acid than water or an alcohol. The values of pK_a are shown in Table 25.3. Remember: the higher the value of pK_a, the weaker the acid (see page 307).

387

Weak acid	Dissociation in water	pK_a at 25 °C
phenol	$C_6H_5OH(aq) \rightleftharpoons C_6H_5O^-(aq) + H^+(aq)$	10.0
water	$H_2O(l) \rightleftharpoons H^+(aq) + OH^-(aq)$	14.0
ethanol	$C_2H_5OH(aq) \rightleftharpoons C_2H_5O^-(aq) + H^+(aq)$	16.0

Table 25.3 Comparing the acidity of phenol, water and ethanol.

Phenol is more acidic than water, with ethanol being the least acidic of the three compounds. We can explain this by looking at the conjugate bases formed on the right-hand side of the equations in Table 25.3. The phenoxide ion, $C_6H_5O^-(aq)$, has its negative charge spread over the whole ion as one of the lone pairs on the oxygen atom overlaps with the delocalised π bonding system in the benzene ring.

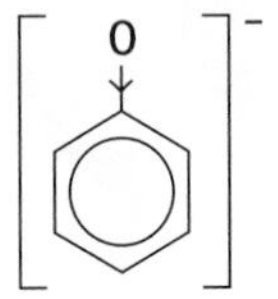

phenoxide ion, with negative charge spread over the whole ion

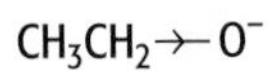

ethoxide ion, with negative charge concentrated on the oxygen

This delocalisation reduces the charge density of the negative charge on the phenoxide ion compared with $OH^-(aq)$ or $C_2H_5O^-(aq)$. Therefore $H^+(aq)$ ions are not as strongly attracted to the phenoxide ion as they are to hydroxide or ethoxide ions, making phenoxide ions less likely to re-form the undissociated molecules.

Alternatively, we can explain the greater acidity of phenol by saying that phenol ionises to form a more stable negative ion, so the ionisation of phenol is more likely. This results in the position of equilibrium in the phenol equation in Table 25.3 lying further to the right-hand side (i.e. more molecules donating an H^+ ion) than the other equations.

Ethanol is a weaker acid than water because of the electron-donating alkyl (ethyl) group attached to the oxygen atom in the ethoxide ion. This has the effect of concentrating more negative charge on this oxygen atom, which more readily accepts an H^+ ion. This explains why the position of equilibrium lies further to the left-hand side, favouring the undissociated ethanol molecules.

388

QUESTION

7 a Place the following molecules in order of their acidity, starting with the most acidic:

CH_3COOH C_6H_5OH HCl C_3H_7OH H_2O

b Would you expect methanol to be more or less acidic than phenol? Explain your answer.

Reactions of phenol

We can divide the reactions of phenol into those involving the hydroxyl group, OH, and those involving substitution into the benzene ring.

Breaking of the OH bond in phenol

Although phenol is only slightly soluble in water, it dissolves well in an alkaline solution. As you have just learnt, phenol is a weak acid so it will react with an alkali to give a salt plus water:

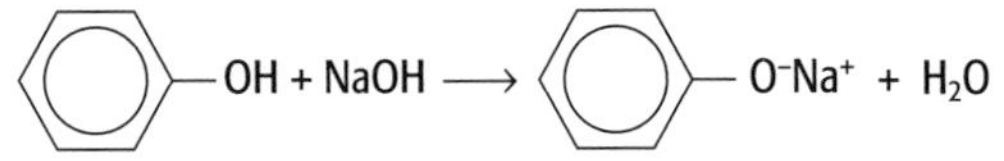

The salt formed, sodium phenoxide, is soluble in water.

Phenol also reacts vigorously with sodium metal, giving off hydrogen gas and again forming sodium phenoxide:

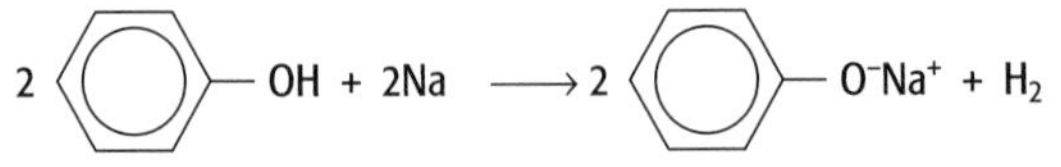

Substitution into the benzene ring of phenol

Compared with benzene, phenol reacts more readily with electrophiles. The overlap of one of the lone pairs of electrons on the oxygen atom in the OH group with the π bonding system increases the electron density of the benzene ring in phenol. This makes the benzene ring more open to attack from electron-deficient electrophiles. It 'activates' the benzene ring, especially at positions 2, 4 and 6 (see Table 25.4, page 390).

BROMINATION OF PHENOL

Phenol undergoes similar reactions to benzene, but phenol does so under milder conditions. For example, bromine water will not react with benzene at room temperature. To produce bromobenzene we need pure bromine (not a solution) and an iron(III) bromide catalyst.

However, bromine water reacts readily with phenol, decolorising the orange solution and forming a white precipitate of 2,4,6-tribromophenol (see Figure 25.6):

OH   + 3Br$_2$ $\longrightarrow$ Br—OH—Br, Br   + 3HBr

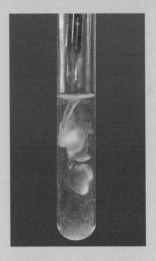

Figure 25.6 Bromine water is added to aqueous phenol.

Similar reactions happen between phenol and chlorine or iodine.

This activation of the benzene ring is also shown in the nitration of phenol. With benzene, we need a mixture of concentrated nitric and sulfuric acids to reflux with benzene at about 55 °C for nitration to take place (see page 385). However, the activated ring in phenol readily undergoes nitration with dilute nitric acid at room temperature:

OH $\xrightarrow{\text{dil. HNO}_3}$ OH, NO$_2$ + OH, NO$_2$

If we use concentrated nitric acid we get 2,4,6-trinitrophenol formed, shown below:

OH, O$_2$N, NO$_2$, NO$_2$

QUESTION

8 a Place these molecules in order of ease of nitration, with the most reactive first:

C_6H_6 $C_6H_5CH_3$ C_6H_5COOH C_6H_5OH

b i Write a balanced equation to show the reaction when excess chlorine is bubbled through phenol at room temperature.

ii How would the reaction conditions differ from those in part **b i** if you wanted to make chlorobenzene from benzene and chlorine?

Summary

- The benzene molecule, C_6H_6, is symmetrical, with a planar hexagonal shape.

- Arenes have considerable energetic stability because of the six delocalised π bonding electrons that lie above and below the plane of the benzene ring.

- The main mechanism for arene reactions is electrophilic substitution. This enables arenes to retain their delocalised π electrons. Hydrogen atoms on the benzene ring may be replaced by a variety of other atoms or groups, including halogen atoms and nitro ($-NO_2$) groups, as well as alkyl or acyl groups in Friedel–Crafts reactions.

- Despite the name ending in -ene, arenes do not behave like alkenes. Arenes undergo **electrophilic substitution**, whereas alkenes undergo electrophilic addition.

- Sometimes the presence of the benzene ring affects the usual reactions of its side-chain, e.g. methylbenzene is oxidised by refluxing with alkaline potassium manganate(VII) to form benzoic acid.

- When the $-OH$ group is joined directly to a benzene ring, the resulting compound is called a phenol.

- Phenols are weakly acidic, but are more acidic than water and alcohols. The acidity of phenol is due to delocalisation of the negative charge on the phenoxide ion into the π bonding electron system on the benzene ring.

- When reacted with sodium hydroxide, phenol forms a salt (sodium phenoxide) plus water. The reaction of sodium metal with phenol produces sodium phenoxide and hydrogen gas.

- The OH group enhances the reactivity of the benzene ring towards electrophiles. The $-OH$ group is said to activate the benzene ring. For example, bromine water is decolorised by phenol at room temperature, producing a white precipitate of 2,4,6-tribromophenol.

- Table 25.4 summarises the positions activated by different substituents in a benzene ring:

Substituent groups in the benzene ring that direct the in-coming electrophile to attack the 2, 4 and/or 6 positions. These groups activate attack by electrophiles (because they tend to donate electrons into the benzene ring)	Substituent groups in the benzene ring that direct the in-coming electrophile to attack the 3 and/or 5 positions. These groups de-activate attack by electrophiles (because they tend to withdraw electrons from the benzene ring)
$-NH_2$, $-NHR$ or $-NR_2$	$-NO_2$
$-OH$ or $-OR$	$-N^+H_3$
$-NHCOR$	$-CN$
$-CH_2$, $-$alkyl	$-CHO$
$-Cl$	$-COOH$, $-COOR$

Table 25.4 Summary of positions attacked in electrophilic substitution into substituted benzene compounds.

End-of-chapter questions

1   **a**   What is the empirical formula of benzene?   [1]

    b   What is the molecular formula of benzene?   [1]

    c   **i**   Draw the full displayed formula of the Kekulé structure of benzene, showing all atoms and using double bonds and single bonds.   [1]

        ii   Draw the skeletal formulae for the Kekulé and delocalised structures of benzene.   [2]

                                                  Total = 5

2   Benzene reacts with bromine.

    a   Write a balanced chemical equation for this reaction.   [1]

    b   Name the catalyst used.   [1]

    c   What visual observations could be made during the reaction?   [2]

    d   Benzene will also react with halogenoalkanes. This is called a Friedel–Crafts reaction.

        i   Using 1-chloropropane, write the formula of the catalyst needed to start the reaction with benzene.   [1]

        ii   Write the structural formula of the electrophile in this Friedel–Crafts reaction.   [1]

        iii   Name the organic product of this reaction.   [1]

        iv   There are three steps in the mechanism of this Friedel–Crafts reaction. Draw the three steps in the mechanism to show the formation of the electrophile, the attack on the benzene ring by the electrophile and the formation of the products of the reaction (to include the regeneration of the catalyst).   [4]

                                                  Total = 11

3   Phenol is an aryl compound.

    a   **i**   What is the molecular formula of phenol?   [1]

        ii   What is the empirical formula of phenol?   [1]

    b   Molten phenol reacts with sodium metal. Give one observation and write a balanced chemical equation for the reaction.   [2]

    c   Phenol reacts with sodium hydroxide solution. Name the type of reaction and write a balanced chemical equation for the reaction.   [2]

    d   The reactions in parts **b** and **c** both give the same organic product. Name it.   [1]

    e   Phenol reacts with bromine water. Give the name of the product, two visual observations and a balanced chemical equation, and comment on how this shows that phenol is more reactive than benzene.   [7]

    f   Explain why phenol is more reactive than benzene. Your answer must include reference to the model used for the arrangement of electrons.   [4]

                                                    Total = 18

4   Benzene can be nitrated to give nitrobenzene.

    a   Name the mechanism for this reaction.   [2]

    b   The species attacking benzene in the reaction is NO_2^+. How is this generated in the reaction mixture? (Name the substances used and give a chemical reaction leading to the formation of NO_2^+.)   [3]

    c   Suggest a suitable temperature for this reaction.   [1]

    d   Use curly arrows to show the mechanism of how benzene reacts with NO_2^+ to produce nitrobenzene.   [3]

e The structure of a common household substance is given below:

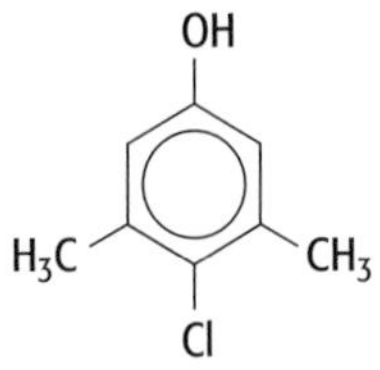

i Give the molecular formula of the compound. [1]

ii Suggest a use for this compound in the home. Explain your suggestion. [2]

iii When bromine water is added to a solution of the compound, it is decolorised. Suggest two structures for the product of the reaction. [2]

Total = 14

5 a Describe the bonding in benzene. Include a description of the model used for the arrangement of electrons in the molecule. [5]

b Cyclohexene decolorises bromine water; benzene has no effect on bromine water. Explain the difference in reactivity towards bromine water. [5]

Total = 10

Chapter 26:
Carboxylic acids and their derivatives

Learning outcomes

You should be able to:

- explain the relative acidity of carboxylic acids and of chlorine-substituted ethanoic acids
- describe how some carboxylic acids, such as methanoic acid and ethanedioic acid, can be further oxidised
- describe the reactions of carboxylic acids in the formation of acyl chlorides

- describe the hydrolysis of acyl chlorides
- describe the reactions of acyl chlorides with alcohols, phenols and primary amines
- explain the relative ease of hydrolysis of acyl chlorides, alkyl chlorides and aryl chlorides, including the condensation (addition-elimination) mechanism for the hydrolysis of acyl chlorides.

Introduction

We use several carboxylic acids around our homes and in our food. Vinegar is used as a preservative and in cooking. Other common carboxylic acids are citric acid, which gives citrus fruits their sharp taste, and ascorbic acid, which is the vitamin C in the same fruits.

Figure 26.1 Vinegar contains about 7% ethanoic acid – a carboxylic acid.

The acidity of carboxylic acids

Carboxylic acids display the typical reactions of all acids due to the presence of excess $H^+(aq)$ ions in their aqueous solutions (see page 307). For example, they react with bases to form a salt plus water. Their salts are called carboxylates. The carboxylate salt formed by the reaction of ethanoic acid with sodium hydroxide is called sodium ethanoate, $CH_3COO^-Na^+$.

The carboxylic acids are weak acids. The majority of their molecules are undissociated in water. For example:

$$CH_3COOH(aq) \rightleftharpoons CH_3COO^-(aq) + H^+(aq)$$
$$\text{ethanoic acid} \qquad \text{ethanoate ion}$$

The position of this equilibrium lies well over to the left-hand side. The dissociation constant, K_a, of ethanoic acid at 25 °C is 1.7×10^{-5} mol dm^{-3} (see page 308). Remember that the smaller the value of K_a, the weaker the acid.

The carboxylic acids are stronger acids than alcohols.

■ The O—H bond in the carboxylic acid is weakened by the carbonyl group, C=O.

electrons in the C—O bond are drawn towards the C=O bond

electrons are drawn away from the O—H bond

■ The carboxylate ion is stabilised by the delocalisation of electrons around the —COO$^-$ group. This delocalisation spreads out the negative charge on the carboxylate ion, reducing its charge density and making it less likely to bond with an $H^+(aq)$ ion to re-form the undissociated acid molecule.

negative charge is spread over the whole —COO$^-$ group (the bond lengths of both carbon–oxygen bonds are equal)

Electron-withdrawing groups bonded to the carbon atom next to the —COOH group make the acid stronger. There are two reasons for this:

■ electron-withdrawing groups further weaken the O—H bond in the undissociated acid molecule

■ electron-withdrawing groups extend the delocalisation of the negative charge on the —COO$^-$ group of the carboxylate ion, further increasing the stabilising of the —COO$^-$ group and making it less likely to bond with an $H^+(aq)$ ion.

Chlorine atoms are an example of an electron-withdrawing group. The dissociation constants of ethanoic acid and its three substituted chloro derivatives are shown in Table 26.1.

Acid	K_a at 25 °C / mol dm^{-3}
ethanoic acid, CH_3COOH	1.7×10^{-5}
chloroethanoic acid, $CH_2ClCOOH$	1.3×10^{-3}
dichloroethanoic acid, $CHCl_2COOH$	5.0×10^{-2}
trichloroethanoic acid, CCl_3COOH	2.3×10^{-1}

Table 26.1 The larger the value of K_a, the stronger the acid.

Trichloroethanoic acid, CCl_3COOH, has three strongly electronegative Cl atoms all withdrawing electrons from the —COOH group, weakening the O—H bond more than the other acids in Table 26.1. Once the O—H bond is broken, the resulting anion is also stabilised more effectively by its three electron-withdrawing Cl atoms, making it less attractive to $H^+(aq)$ ions. This makes the CCl_3COOH the strongest of the acids listed in Table 26.1 as it has most Cl atoms (see Figure 26.2).

394

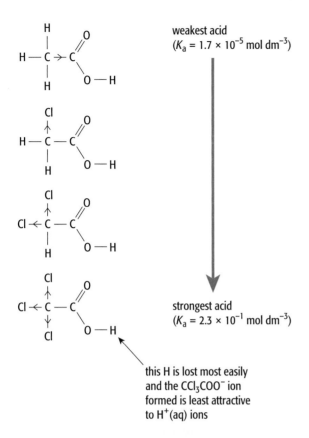

weakest acid
($K_a = 1.7 \times 10^{-5}$ mol dm^{-3})

strongest acid
($K_a = 2.3 \times 10^{-1}$ mol dm^{-3})

this H is lost most easily
and the CCl$_3$COO$^-$ ion
formed is least attractive
to H$^+$(aq) ions

Figure 26.2 The more electron-withdrawing groups on the C atom in the COOH group, the stronger the acid.

Ethanoic acid is the weakest acid in Table 26.1, as the methyl group is electron donating. This has the opposite effect to electron-withdrawing groups:

■ it strengthens the O—H bond in the acid's —COOH group
■ it donates negative charge towards the —COO$^-$ group of the carboxylate ion, making it more likely to accept an H$^+$(aq) ion.

QUESTION

1 a Place the following acids in order of strength, starting with the strongest acid first.

CH$_3$CH$_2$COOH   CH$_3$CCl$_2$COOH   CH$_3$CHClCOOH

b Explain why ethanoic acid is a stronger acid than ethanol.

c Predict which would be the stronger acid – methanoic acid or ethanoic acid – and explain your reasoning.

Oxidation of two carboxylic acids

You saw in Chapter 17 that primary alcohols can be oxidised by acidified potassium dichromate(VI) solution to form aldehydes and then further oxidation produces carboxylic acids (see page 236). The carboxylic acids prepared are not usually oxidised any further.

However, methanoic acid (HCOOH) is a stronger reducing agent than other carboxylic acids, so it can undergo further oxidation.

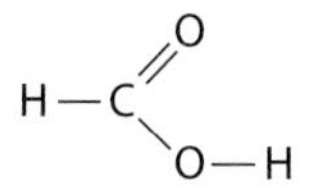

Figure 26.3 The displayed formula of methanoic acid.

This involves the oxidising agent breaking down the methanoic acid molecule, forming **carbon dioxide.** This oxidation can be carried out even by warming with mild oxidising agents (such as the Fehling's or Tollens' reagents used to distinguish between aldehydes and ketones – see page 239).

In a positive test for an aldehyde, the Cu^{2+} ion in Fehling's solution is reduced to the Cu$^+$ ion, which precipitates out as red copper(I) oxide. When methanoic acid is oxidised by Fehling's solution, the same positive test result is obtained. With Tollens' reagent, the silver ion present, Ag$^+$, is reduced to silver metal when it oxidises methanoic acid (also as in the positive test for an aldehyde).

The half-equation for the oxidation of methanoic acid can be written in terms of electron transfer to an oxidising agent as:

$$\text{HCOOH} \xrightarrow{\text{oxidation}} \text{CO}_2 + 2\text{H}^+(\text{aq}) + 2\text{e}^-$$
oxidation number   +2   +4

or in terms of the addition of oxygen from an oxidising agent as:

$$\text{HCOOH} + [\text{O}] \longrightarrow \text{CO}_2 + \text{H}_2\text{O}$$

This oxidation of methanoic acid will also occur with stronger oxidising agents such as acidified solutions of potassium manganate(VII) – decolorising the purple solution – or potassium dichromate(VI) – turning the orange solution green.

395

Another common example of a carboxylic acid that can be oxidised by these stronger oxidising agents is ethanedioic acid (a dicarboxylic acid). Its molecular formula is $H_2C_2O_4$. Its structural formula is HOOCCOOH or $(COOH)_2$, and its displayed formula is shown in Figure 26.4.

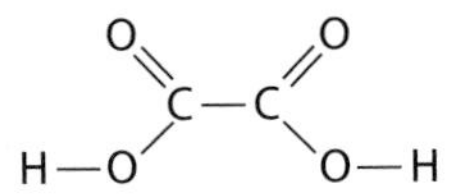

Figure 26.4 The displayed formula of ethanedioic acid.

A solution of ethanedioic acid (with sulfuric acid added) can be used in titrations to standardise a solution of potassium manganate(VII). As with methanoic acid, the oxidation results in the formation of carbon dioxide and water. The solid ethanedioic acid can be weighed out accurately to make a standard solution of known concentration. This is warmed in a conical flask and the potassium manganate(VII) solution to be standardised is run in from a burette. The end-point of the titration is identified when the addition of a drop of the purple manganate(VII) solution turns the solution pink. This happens when all the ethanedioic acid has been oxidised.

The balanced ionic equation for this redox reaction is:

$$2MnO_4^- + 6H^+ + 5H_2C_2O_4 \longrightarrow 2Mn^{2+} + 10CO_2 + 8H_2O$$

The manganese(II) ions formed catalyse the reaction. This is an example of autocatalysis, in which one of the products of the reaction acts as a catalyst for that reaction.

> **QUESTION**
>
> 2 a Why is methanoic acid never prepared by refluxing methanol with acidified potassium dichromate(VI) solution?
>
> b Look back at the two half-equations for the oxidation of methanoic acid. Write two similar equations representing the oxidation of ethanedioic acid.
>
> c i In a titration between ethanedioic acid and potassium manganate(VII) solutions, ethanedioic acid is heated in its conical flask before adding the potassium manganate(VII) solution from the burette. Suggest why.
>
> ii In an experiment to standardise a solution of potassium manganate(VII), $25.0\,cm^3$ of a standard solution of $0.0500\,mol\,dm^{-3}$ ethanedioic acid was fully oxidised by a titre of $8.65\,cm^3$ of potassium manganate(VII) solution. What was the concentration of the potassium manganate(VII) solution?

Acyl chlorides

Making acyl chlorides

An acyl chloride is similar in structure to a carboxylic acid but the —OH group has been replaced by a Cl atom. The displayed formula of ethanoyl chloride is:

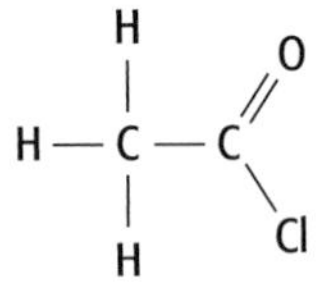

ethanoyl chloride

The structural formula of ethanoyl chloride can be written as CH_3COCl.

We can prepare acyl chlorides from their corresponding carboxylic acid using phosphorus(V) chloride, phosphorus(III) chloride or sulfur dichloride oxide ($SOCl_2$).

With phosphorus(V) chloride:

$$CH_3COOH + PCl_5 \longrightarrow CH_3COCl + POCl_3 + HCl$$

No special conditions are required for this reaction.

With phosphorus(III) chloride:

$$3CH_3COOH + PCl_3 \longrightarrow 3CH_3COCl + H_3PO_3$$

Heat is required for this reaction.

With sulfur dichloride oxide:

$$CH_3COOH + SOCl_2 \longrightarrow CH_3COCl + SO_2 + HCl$$

No special conditions are required for this reaction.

> **QUESTION**
>
> 3 Write a balanced equation, using structural formulae for the organic compounds, and state any conditions necessary, to show the formation of:
>
> a propanoyl chloride from a suitable carboxylic acid and $SOCl_2$
>
> b methanoyl chloride from a suitable carboxylic acid and PCl_3
>
> c butanoyl chloride from a suitable carboxylic acid and PCl_5.

Reactions of acyl chlorides

Many useful compounds can be synthesised from carboxylic acids. However, the synthetic reactions that are needed can be difficult to do because carboxylic acids are quite unreactive. One way round this is to first convert the carboxylic acid into an acyl chloride. Acyl chlorides are much more reactive than carboxylic acids.

As we saw on page 396, an acyl chloride is similar in structure to a carboxylic acid, with the —OH group replaced by a Cl atom. So the —COOH functional group is changed to the —COCl group. The structural formula of acyl chlorides can be written as ROCl, where R is an alkyl or aryl group. For example, propanoyl chloride can be written as CH_3CH_2COCl.

The structural formulae of benzoic acid and its derivative benzoyl chloride are shown in Figure 26.5.

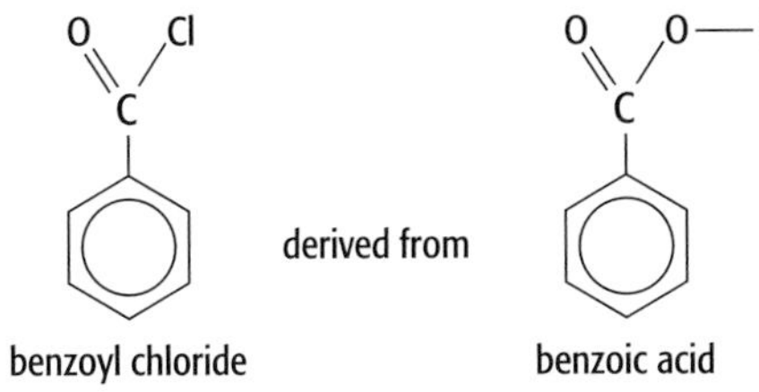

Figure 26.5 Benzoyl chloride is the acyl chloride derived from benzoic acid.

Acyl chlorides are reactive compounds. The carbonyl carbon has electrons drawn away from it by the Cl atom as well as by its O atom, and both are strongly electronegative atoms. This gives the carbonyl carbon a relatively large partial positive charge and makes it particularly open to attack from nucleophiles.

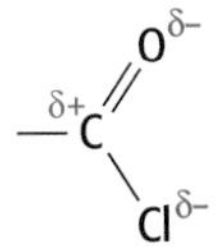

The acyl chlorides are reactive liquids. When they react with nucleophiles the C=Cl bond breaks and white fumes of hydrogen chloride, HCl, are given off. To generalise their reactions, we can write:

$$ROCl + HZ \longrightarrow ROZ + HCl$$

where HZ can be water, an alcohol, ammonia or an amine. Notice that HZ contains either an oxygen or nitrogen atom with a lone pair of electrons that can be donated. HZ can therefore act as a nucleophile.

HYDROLYSIS OF ACYL CHLORIDES

Water is a suitable nucleophile to attack an acyl chloride molecule. A lone pair on the oxygen atom in water initiates the attack on the $\delta+$ carbonyl carbon atom. The reaction produces a carboxylic acid and hydrogen chloride. It is an example of a hydrolysis reaction, i.e. the breakdown of a compound by water. For example:

$$CH_3CH_2COCl + H_2O \longrightarrow CH_3CH_2COOH + HCl$$
propanoyl chloride   propanoic acid

The acyl chloride can be added to water using a dropping pipette. The reaction is immediate and white fumes of HCl are observed rising from the liquid.

Figure 26.6 shows the mechanism of the hydrolysis, showing the initial attack by a water molecule, acting as a nucleophile, followed by the elimination of a molecule of hydrogen chloride.

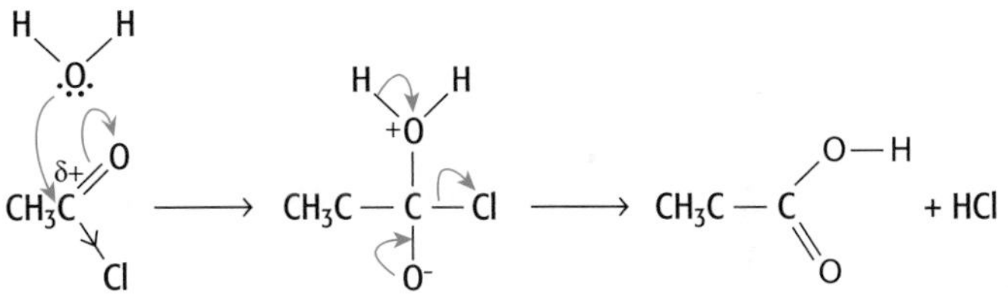

Figure 26.6 The condensation (addition-elimination) mechanism of hydrolysis of ethanoyl chloride.

The hydrolysis can be classified as a condensation reaction, as there is an initial addition reaction of water across the C=O bond, followed by elimination of a small molecule, in this case HCl.

This reaction is far more vigorous than the hydrolysis of chloroalkanes (see page 219). The hydrolysis of chloroalkanes needs a strong alkali, such as aqueous sodium hydroxide, to be refluxed with the chloroalkane to hydrolyse it. The nucleophile needed to hydrolyse a chloroalkane is the negatively charged hydroxide ion, OH^-. However, a neutral water molecule is sufficient to hydrolyse an acyl chloride quickly at room temperature. This difference is due to the carbon bonded to the chlorine atom in a chloroalkane not being as strongly $\delta+$ as the carbon atom in an acyl chloride. Remember, in an acyl chloride the carbon bonded to the chlorine atom is also attached to an oxygen atom. It has two strongly electronegative atoms pulling electrons away from it. Therefore the attack by the nucleophile is much more rapid.

Aryl chlorides, such as chlorobenzene, will not undergo hydrolysis. The carbon atom bonded to the chlorine atom is part of the delocalised π bonding system of the benzene ring. The p orbitals from the Cl atom tend to overlap with the delocalised p electrons in the benzene ring. This causes the C—Cl bond to have some double bond character, making it stronger, and hydrolysis does not occur.

> The ease of hydrolysis, starting with the compounds most readily broken down, is:
>
> acyl chloride > chloroalkane > aryl chloride

QUESTIONS

4 In its reaction with a nucleophile, explain why an acyl chloride reacts faster than an alcohol.

5 a Name the products of the hydrolysis of propanoyl chloride.

  b i Place the following compounds in order of ease of hydrolysis, starting with the most reactive first.

   C_6H_5Cl CH_3CH_2COCl $CH_3CH_2CH_2Cl$

   ii Explain your answer to part i.

   iii If a reaction occurs with water, what will you see in part i?

Reaction with alcohols and phenol

When acyl chlorides react with alcohols and phenol, we get esters (and HCl) formed. The reactions happen more quickly than the reactions of alcohols or phenol with carboxylic acids. The acyl chloride reactions also go to completion and do not form an equilibrium mixture. Therefore they are useful in the synthesis of esters in the chemical industry.

Ethanoyl chloride will react vigorously with ethanol to form an ester:

ethanoyl   ethanol   ethyl
chloride   ethanoate

With phenol, the reaction with an acyl chloride proceeds if warmed. There is no reaction between phenol and carboxylic acids, so acyl chlorides must be used if you want to make phenyl esters. The reaction takes place in the presence of a base. The initial reaction between phenol and the base creates the phenoxide ion, $C_6H_5O^-$, which acts as the nucleophile to attack the acyl chloride.

phenyl ethanoate

benzoyl   sodium   phenyl
chloride   phenoxide   benzoate

Reaction with amines

Amines contain nitrogen atoms with a lone pair of electrons. This lone pair of electrons is available to attack the carbonyl carbon atom in acyl chlorides. The reaction is vigorous and the organic product is a substituted amide. For example:

N-methylethanamide

QUESTION

6 a Using an acyl chloride as a starting compound in each case, name the reactants you would use to make:

   i   ethyl ethanoate

   ii methyl butanoate

   iii phenyl benzoate.

  b Complete the following equation:

   $CH_3CH_2COCl + CH_3CH_2CH_2NH_2$

   $\longrightarrow$ _____ + _____

Summary

- Carboxylic acids are weak acids. Their strength is increased if the carbon atom next to the COOH group has electron-withdrawing atoms, such as chlorine, bonded to it.

- Acyl chlorides (RCOCl) are made by reacting carboxylic acids with PCl_5, PCl_3 or $SOCl_2$.

- Acyl chlorides react with amines to give substituted amides. They are more reactive than their corresponding carboxylic acids.

- Acyl chlorides are reactive liquids. They are easily hydrolysed by water, forming a carboxylic acid while giving off white fumes of hydrogen chloride.

- Acyl chlorides also react with alcohols and phenols to give esters. They are more reactive than their corresponding carboxylic acids.

End-of-chapter questions

1 Acyl chlorides and carboxylic acids can both be used to prepare esters.

   a i Give the reagents and conditions required to make ethyl ethanoate directly from a carboxylic acid.   [3]

      ii Write an equation to show the formation of ethyl ethanoate in part **a i**.   [1]

   b i Give the reagents and conditions required to make phenyl benzoate from an acyl chloride.   [3]

      ii Write an equation to show the formation of phenyl benzoate in part **b i**.   [1]

                                          Total = 8

2 a Draw the displayed formula of butanoyl chloride.   [1]

   b i Give the name and formula of a reagent that can be used to prepare butanoyl chloride from butanoic acid.   [2]

      ii Write a balanced equation for the reaction in part **b i**.   [1]

      iii Butanoic acid is a weaker acid than 2-chlorobutanoic acid. Explain why.   [2]

      iv Draw the skeletal formula of 2-chlorobutanoic acid.   [1]

      v Name a chloro-substituted butanoic acid that is a stronger acid than 2-chlorobutanoic acid.   [1]

                                            Total = 8

Chapter 27:
Organic nitrogen compounds

Learning outcomes

You should be able to:

- describe the formation of:
  - alkyl amines (by the reaction of ammonia with halogenoalkanes or the reduction of amides with $LiAlH_4$ or the reduction of nitriles with $LiAlH_4$ or H_2/Ni)
  - phenylamine (by the reduction of nitrobenzene with tin/concentrated HCl)
- describe and explain the basicity of amines and the relative basicities of ammonia, ethylamine and phenylamine
- describe the reaction of phenylamine
  - with aqueous bromine
  - with nitrous acid to give the diazonium salt

- and phenol, followed by the coupling of benzenediazonium chloride and phenol to make a dye
- describe the formation of amides from the reaction between RNH_2 and $R'COCl$, and the hydrolysis of amides by aqueous alkali or acid
- describe the acid/base properties of amino acids and the formation of zwitterions
- describe the formation of peptide bonds between amino acids to give di- and tri-peptides
- describe simply the process of electrophoresis and the effect of pH, using peptides and amino acids as examples.

Introduction

Amines and their derivatives are examples of organic nitrogen compounds. They are used in drugs to treat many diseases such as malaria and sleeping sickness.

Figure 27.1 Doctor administering treatment for malaria.

Amines

Classes of amines

There are three classes of amine: primary, secondary and tertiary.

■ Primary amines have an NH_2 group bonded to an alkyl or aryl group, e.g. ethylamine, $C_2H_5NH_2$ (Figure 27.2), or phenylamine, $C_6H_5NH_2$. Note that some primary amines do not have the NH_2 group at the end of an alkyl chain. We indicate the position of the NH_2 group on the hydrocarbon chain by numbering from the nearest end of the molecule. In these cases we refer to the NH_2 group as the 'amino' group, e.g. $CH_3CH_2CH(NH_2)CH_2CH_2CH_3$ is called 3-aminohexane.

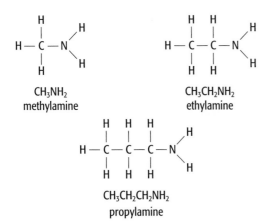

Figure 27.2 Three primary amines.

■ Secondary amines have two alkyl or aryl groups attached to an NH group, e.g. dimethylamine, $(CH_3)_2NH$ (Figure 27.3).

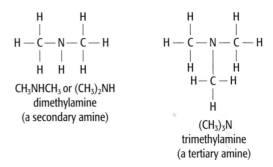

Figure 27.3 A secondary amine and a tertiary amine.

■ Tertiary amines have three alkyl or aryl groups attached to the same nitrogen atom, e.g. trimethylamine, $(CH_3)_3N$ (shown in Figure 27.3).

The basicity of amines

We can think of the amines as substituted ammonia (NH_3) molecules. For example, a primary amine is an ammonia molecule with one of its H atoms replaced by an alkyl or aryl group. Ammonia and the amines act as bases because of the lone pair of electrons on the nitrogen atom. Remember that a base is a proton (H^+ ion) acceptor. The nitrogen atom donates its lone pair to an H^+ ion, forming a co-ordinate (dative) bond.

For ammonia:

$$NH_3 + H^+ \longrightarrow NH_4^+$$

401

For a primary amine:

$$RNH_2 + H^+ \longrightarrow RNH_3^+$$

Dilute hydrochloric acid reacts with ammonia and with amines to produce salts.

For ammonia:

$$NH_3 + HCl \longrightarrow \underset{\text{ammonium chloride}}{NH_4^+Cl^-}$$

For a primary amine:

$$CH_3NH_2 + HCl \longrightarrow \underset{\text{methylammonium chloride}}{CH_3NH_3^+Cl^-}$$

Ammonia and the amines have different strengths as bases.

> The strength of ammonia and amines as bases depends on the availability of the lone pair of electrons on their N atom to bond with an H^+ ion.

Let us consider ammonia, ethylamine and phenylamine as examples. We find that the strongest base of the three is ethylamine, followed by ammonia and, finally, phenylamine.

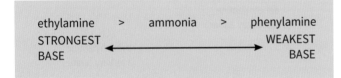

Ethylamine is a stronger base than ammonia because the ethyl group is electron-donating in nature (see Figure 27.4). By releasing electrons to the N atom, the ethyl group makes the lone pair more readily available to bond with an H^+ ion than it is in ammonia. Ammonia has three H atoms bonded to the N atom.

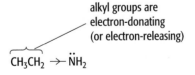

Figure 27.4 Ethylamine is a stronger base than ammonia.

Ammonia is a stronger base than phenylamine because one of the p orbitals on the nitrogen atom in phenylamine overlaps with the π bonding system in the benzene ring. This causes the lone pair of the N atom in phenylamine to be delocalised into the benzene ring. This then makes the

lone pair less available to form a co-ordinate bond with an H^+ ion than it is in ammonia (see Figure 27.5).

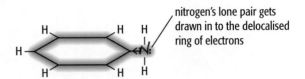

Figure 27.5 Phenylamine is a very weak base.

QUESTION

1 a Name the following compounds:
     i $CH_3CH_2CH_2CH_2CH_2NH_2$
     ii $(CH_3CH_2CH_2)_2NH$
     iii $C_2H_5NH_3^+Cl^-$
   b Predict whether diethylamine is a stronger or weaker base than ethylamine. Explain your reasoning.

Formation of amines

Making ethylamine

1 In Chapter 16 (page 218) you learnt how bromoethane undergoes nucleophilic substitution with ammonia to form a mixture of amines. In order to prepare ethylamine (while avoiding the formation of secondary and tertiary amines and ammonium salts) we use excess hot ethanolic ammonia:

$$CH_3CH_2Br + NH_3 \longrightarrow \underset{\text{ethylamine}}{CH_3CH_2NH_2} + HBr$$

Hydrogen bromide, HBr, which could react with the ethylamine, is removed by the excess ammonia. It forms ammonium bromide, NH_4Br. The excess ammonia also reduces the chances of bromoethane being attacked by ethylamine; ethylamine is also a nucleophile.

2 We also learnt in Chapter 16 (pages 219–220) about the formation of nitriles by reacting a halogenoalkane with the CN^- ion. To carry out the reaction, a solution of potassium cyanide, KCN, in ethanol is heated under reflux with the halogenoalkane:

$$\underset{\text{bromomethane}}{CH_3Br} + CN^- \longrightarrow \underset{\text{ethanenitrile}}{CH_3CN} + Br^-$$

Note that we start with bromomethane, not bromoethane, as the cyanide group adds a carbon atom to the alkyl group. We can then reduce (add hydrogen to) the ethanenitrile to make ethylamine. The nitrile vapour and hydrogen gas are passed over a nickel catalyst or $LiAlH_4$ (lithium tetrahydridoaluminate) in dry ether can be used for the reduction:

$$CH_3CN + 4[H] \longrightarrow \underset{\text{ethylamine}}{CH_3CH_2NH_2}$$

3 We can also use $LiAlH_4$ in dry ether to reduce amides to amines. So ethanamide will be reduced ethylamine.

$$\underset{\text{ethanamide}}{CH_3CONH_2} + 4[H] \longrightarrow \underset{\text{ethylamine}}{CH_3CH_2NH_2} + H_2O$$

Preparing phenylamine

Phenylamine is made by reducing nitrobenzene. This reduction is carried out by heating nitrobenzene with tin (Sn) and concentrated hydrochloric acid:

The phenylamine is separated from the reaction mixture by steam distillation (Figure 27.6).

Figure 27.6 Steam generated in the round-bottomed flask is passed into the reaction mixture and phenylamine is distilled off and collected.

QUESTION

2 a i Give the reagents and conditions needed to make butylamine from butanenitrile.

   ii Name the bromoalkane that can be used to make the butanenitrile in part **a i**.

   iii Name two types of organic compound that can be reduced by $LiAlH_4$ to form an alkyl amine.

b i Give the name and structural formula of the aryl amine formed when 2-nitrophenol reacts with tin and concentrated hydrochloric acid.

   ii What type of reaction does 2-nitrophenol undergo in part **b i**?

Reactions of phenylamine

Phenylamine with aqueous bromine

The reaction of aqueous bromine with phenylamine is similar to the reaction of aqueous bromine with phenol (see page 389): a white precipitate is formed. The nitrogen in the $-NH_2$ group in phenylamine has a lone pair of electrons that can be delocalised into the benzene ring so that the π bonding system extends to include the C—N bond. The extra electron density in the benzene ring makes it more readily attacked by electrophiles. Remember that the 2, 4 and 6 positions around the benzene ring are activated when electron-donating groups, such as $-NH_2$ or $-OH$, are attached to the ring:

2,4,6-tribromophenylamine

This reaction is called **diazotisation**. Note that the positive charge on the diazonium ion ($C_6H_5N_2^+$) is on the nitrogen atom shown with four bonds in the equation above.

The reaction mixture must be kept below 10 °C using ice. This is because the diazonium salt is unstable and will decompose easily, giving off nitrogen gas, N_2, at higher temperatures.

DIAZOTISATION

Phenylamine is an important compound in the synthesis of dyes. The first step is the reaction between phenylamine and nitrous acid (nitric(III) acid), HNO_2, to give a diazonium salt. Nitrous acid is unstable, so it has to be made in the test tube, then the phenylamine added. We can make the nitrous acid using sodium nitrite (sodium nitrate(III)) and dilute hydrochloric acid:

$$NaNO_2 + HCl \longrightarrow \underset{\text{nitrous acid}}{HNO_2} + NaCl$$

The first step in the synthesis of a dye is the production of benzenediazonium chloride:

benzenediazonium chloride

In the second step, the diazonium ion reacts with an alkaline solution of phenol in a **coupling** reaction:

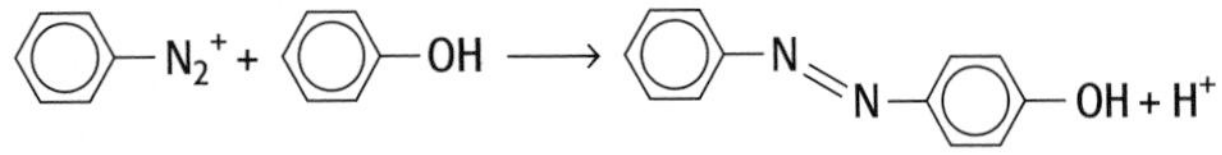

The positively charged diazonium ion acts as an electrophile. It substitutes into the benzene ring of phenol at the 4 position. An orange dye is formed, called an **azo dye**, or diazonium dye. The delocalised π bonding system extends between the two benzene rings through the NN group, which acts like a 'bridge'. This makes the azo dye, called 4-hydroxyphenylazobenzene, very stable (an important characteristic of a good dye). The azo dye forms immediately on addition of the phenol to the solution containing the diazonium ion (Figure 27.7).

Figure 27.7 The azo dye (also called a diazonium dye) forms in a coupling reaction between the diazonium ion and an alkaline solution of phenol.

By using alternative aryl compounds to phenol, we can make a range of brightly coloured dyes. For example, Figure 27.8 shows a molecule of a compound used as a yellow dye.

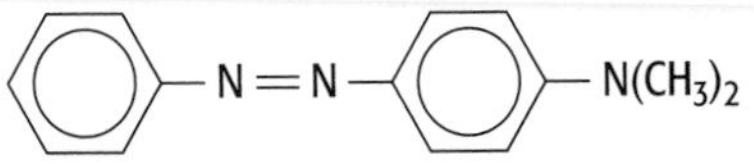

Figure 27.8 A molecule of a yellow azo dye. Instead of phenol, C_6H_5OH, the reactant used in the coupling reaction is $C_6H_5N(CH_3)_2$.

3 a i Which would be more readily attacked by an electrophile – benzene or phenylamine? Explain your answer.

   ii Write a general equation to show the equation for the reaction of phenylamine with excess of an electrophile, represented as X^+.

   b i Why is the reaction of phenylamine to make the diazonium ion carried out below 10 °C?

   ii Write a balanced equation to show how nitrous acid is made for the reaction in part **b i** to take place.

   iii Show the two steps that would be used to make the yellow dye shown in Figure 27.8, starting from phenylamine.

Amino acids

Amino acids are an important group of compounds that all contain the amino group ($-NH_2$) and the carboxylic acid group ($-COOH$). One type of amino acid has the $-NH_2$ group bonded to the C atom next to the $-COOH$ group. These 2-amino-carboxylic acids are the 'building blocks' that make up proteins.

The general structure of a 2-amino-carboxylic acid molecule is shown in Figure 27.9.

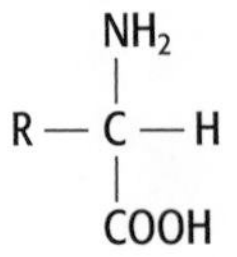

$$R-\underset{\underset{COOH}{|}}{\overset{\overset{NH_2}{|}}{C}}-H$$

Figure 27.9 The general structure of a 2-amino-carboxylic acid.

The general structural formula of a 2-amino-carboxylic acid is $RCH(NH_2)COOH$.

The R group is the part of the amino acid that can vary in different amino acids. The simplest amino acid is glycine (systematic name aminoethanoic acid) in which R is an H atom:

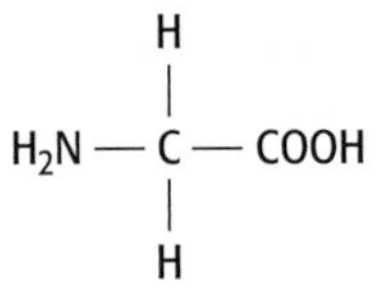

$$H_2N-\underset{\underset{H}{|}}{\overset{\overset{H}{|}}{C}}-COOH$$

glycine (aminoethanoic acid)

Alanine (systematic name 2-aminopropanoic acid) is an amino acid in which the R group is the methyl group, $-CH_3$.

The R group can be acidic (e.g. it contains another carboxylic acid group, $-COOH$ group), basic (e.g. it contains another amine group, —NH$_2$ group) or neutral (e.g. when R is an alkyl group).

Amino acids will undergo most reactions of amines and carboxylic acids. However, each molecule can interact within itself due to its basic —NH$_2$ group and its acidic —COOH group:

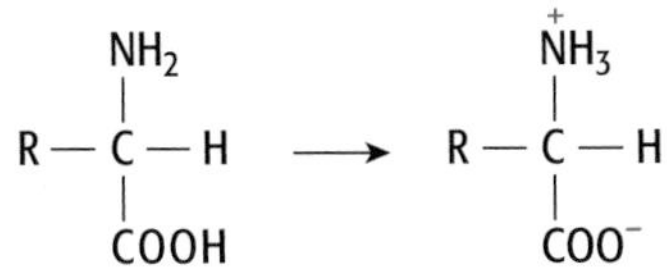

The ion is called a zwitterion (from the German 'zwei' meaning 'two') as it carries two charges: one positive (—NH$_3$$^+$) and one negative (—COO$^-$). The ionic nature of the zwitterions gives amino acids relatively strong intermolecular forces of attraction. They are crystalline solids that are soluble in water.

A solution of amino acids contains zwitterions that have both acidic and basic properties (i.e. they are amphoteric). They will resist changes in pH when small amounts of acid or alkali are added to them. Solutions that do this are called buffer solutions (see pages 313–5).

If acid is added, the —COO$^-$ part of the zwitterion will accept an H$^+$ ion, re-forming the undissociated —COOH group. This leaves a positively charged ion:

If alkali is added, the —NH$_3$$^+$ part of the zwitterion will donate an H+ ion to the hydroxide ion (H$^+$ + OH$^-$ $\longrightarrow$ H$_2$O), re-forming the amine —NH$_2$ group. This leaves a negatively charged ion:

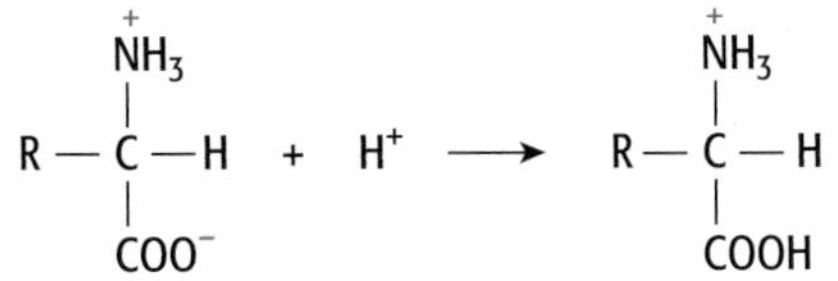

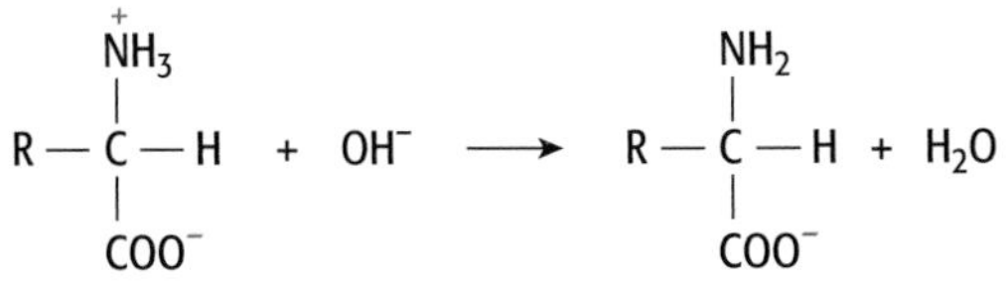

4 a i What is the general structural formula of a 2-amino-carboxylic acid?

　　ii Why are all amino acids solids at 20 °C?

b i Draw the displayed formula of the 2-amino-carboxylic acid called serine, in which the R group is HO—CH$_2$—.

　　ii Draw the structure of the zwitterion of serine.

　　iii Draw the structure of the ion of serine present in acidic conditions.

　　iv Draw the structure of the ion of serine present in alkaline conditions.

Peptides

Amino acid molecules can also react with each other; the acidic —COOH group in one molecule reacts with the basic —NH$_2$ group in another molecule. When two amino acids react together, the resulting molecule is called a **dipeptide**:

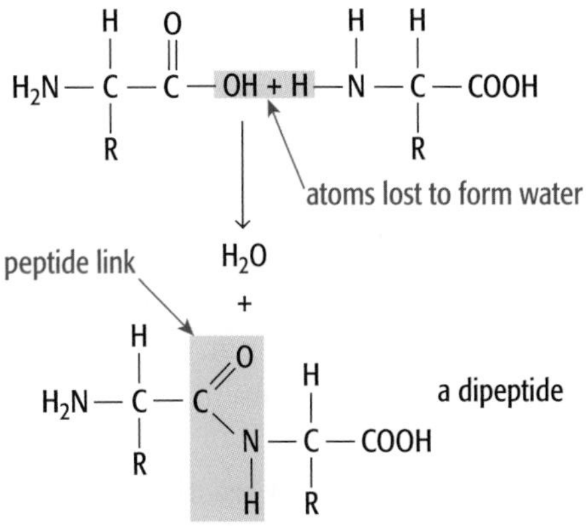

Note the amide link between the two amino acids. An amide link between two amino acid molecules is also called a peptide link. The reaction is a **condensation reaction** as a small molecule, in this case water, is eliminated when the reactant molecules join together.

You can see that the dipeptide product still has an —NH$_2$ group at one end and a —COOH group at the other end. Therefore the reaction can continue, to form a **tripeptide** initially, and then ever-longer chains of amino acids. The longer molecules become known as polypeptides, and then **proteins** as they get even longer sequences of amino acids (see pages 413 and 415 in Chapter 28).

405

QUESTION

5   The R groups in the 2-amino-carboxylic acids alanine and valine are —CH_3 and $(CH_3)_2HC$—, respectively.

   a   Draw the structures of both these amino acids.

   b   Give an equation to show the formation of a dipeptide made from alanine and valine.

Reactions of the amides

The amide group is represented in structural formulae by $CONH_2$. For example, ethanamide can be shown as CH_3CONH_2. Its displayed formula is:

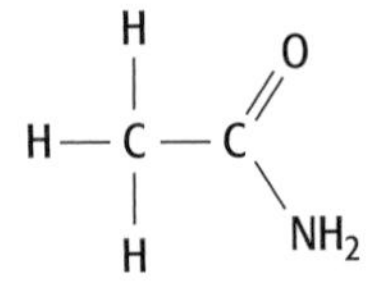

ethanamide

Unlike the basic amines met at the start of this chapter, the amides are neutral compounds. The presence of the electron-withdrawing oxygen atom in the amide group means that the lone pair on an amide's nitrogen atom is not available to donate to electron deficient species, such as H^+ ions.

Making an amide

The acyl chlorides are more reactive compounds than the carboxylic acids they are made from (see page 397) and are used for synthesising other useful compounds, such as amides.

Ethanamide can be made by reacting ethanoyl chloride with concentrated ammonia solution:

$$CH_3COCl + NH_3 \longrightarrow CH_3CONH_2 + HCl$$

A primary amine, such as ethylamine, reacts with an acyl chloride to produce a substituted amide.

$$C_3H_7COCl + C_2H_5NH_2 \longrightarrow C_3H_7CONHC_2H_5 + HCl$$

Both these reactions occur at room temperature, releasing white fumes of hydrogen chloride as soon as the reactants are added together. If there is an excess of the amine, it will react with the HCl formed to make its salt. For example, in the previous reaction ethylamine will form ethylammonium chloride, $C_2H_5NH_3^+Cl^-$.

The italic letter N is used in naming substituted amides to denote which alkyl (or aryl) group or groups are bonded to the nitrogen atom. For example, in N-ethylbutanamide, $C_3H_7CONHC_2H_5$, the ethyl (C_2H_5—) group has replaced an H atom in the amide group. If the H atom on the nitrogen in this molecule is replaced by another alkyl or aryl group, two N's are used in the name, e.g. $C_3H_7CON(C_2H_5)_2$ is called N,N-diethylbutanamide.

Hydrolysis of amides

The characteristic —CONH— group in substituted amides links the two hydrocarbon sections of their molecules together. This link can be broken by hydrolysis with an acid or an alkali. The amide is refluxed with, for example, hydrochloric acid or sodium hydroxide solution, to hydrolyse it:

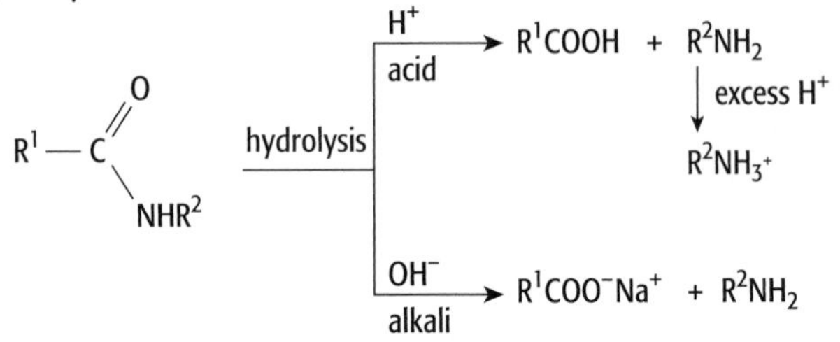

The products of hydrolysis of a substituted amide with acid are a carboxylic acid (R^1COOH) and a primary amine (R^2NH_2). The amine formed will react with excess acid in the reaction vessel to make its ammonium salt, e.g. $R^2NH_3^+Cl^-$ with excess hydrochloric acid.

With an alkali, such as aqueous sodium hydroxide, the products are the sodium salt of the carboxylic acid ($R^1COO^-Na^+$) and the primary amine (R^2NH_2).

If we reflux an unsubstituted amide ($RCONH_2$) with acid, the products are the corresponding carboxylic acid and ammonia. The ammonia in solution reacts with excess acid to make an ammonium salt. With an alkali, the products are the salt of the carboxylic acid and ammonia.

QUESTION

6   a   Write an equation to show the formation of the following compounds using an acid chloride:

     i   propanamide

     ii   *N*-ethylpropanamide.

   b   Write an equation to show the hydrolysis of:

     i   butanamide by refluxing with dilute hydrochloric acid

     ii   *N*-ethylbutanamide by refluxing with aqueous sodium hydroxide.

Electrophoresis

How electrophoresis works

Electrophoresis is used extensively in biochemical analysis. It can be used to separate, identify and purify proteins. We can use it with amino acids and peptides obtained when a protein is hydrolysed.

The analytical technique of electrophoresis is based on separating ions placed in an electric field. If a sample is placed between two electrodes, positively charged ions will move towards a negatively charged electrode. Negatively charged ions will move towards a positively charged electrode (Figure 27.10).

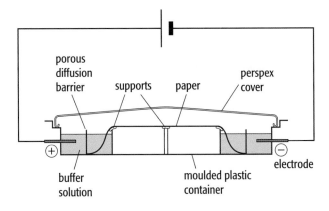

Figure 27.10 This apparatus shows how paper electrophoresis is carried out.

The sample is placed on absorbent paper or on a gel supported on a solid base such as a glass plate. A buffer solution carries the ions along. The rate at which the ions move towards the oppositely charged electrode depends, among other things, on the size and charge on the ions: larger ions will move more slowly; highly charged ions will move more quickly. Therefore the ions are separated as the electric field is applied. You get a series of lines or bands on the paper or gel once a chemical is applied. Sometimes ultraviolet light is used to show the bands up. The series of bands is called an **electropherogram** (Figure 27.11).

Let us consider a simple example of how a mixture of three amino acids undergoes separation. Amino acid A could have a side-chain that is positively charged in a certain buffer solution, amino acid B could be neutral and amino acid C could be negatively charged (Figure 27.12).

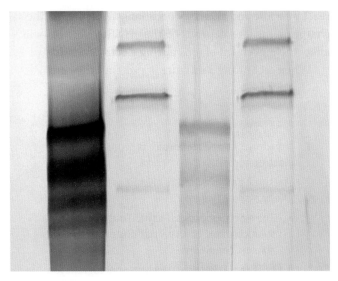

Figure 27.11 Comparing electropherograms.

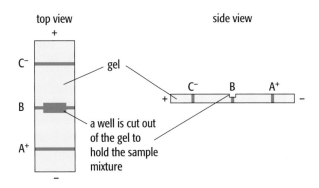

Figure 27.12 The principle of gel electrophoresis.

At a pH of 7, the amino acid species present in samples of A, B and C are shown in Figure 27.13.

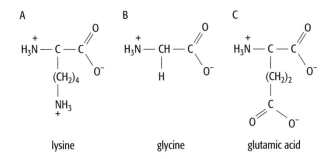

Figure 27.13 The charge on amino acids depends on the pH of the solution.

In Figure 27.10 you will notice the use of a buffer solution in the electrophoresis apparatus. The chemical structures in Figure 27.13 show why we need to control the pH in electrophoresis. On page 405 we saw how amino acids

407

react in acidic and alkaline conditions to form ions. The charge on the ions depends on the pH. Therefore pH will affect the movement of ions during electrophoresis.

When separating a mixture of proteins, they are usually first treated with a chemical that makes them all negatively charged. A dye can also be added. All the proteins then migrate in the same direction, towards the positive electrode, but larger proteins move more slowly.

QUESTION

7 A mixture of three amino aids is separated by gel electrophoresis.

The three amino acids are glycine, valine and phenylalanine (Figure 27.14).

a The electrophoresis is carried out in a buffer solution of pH 10. Draw the ions present in these alkaline conditions.

b i Draw a sketch of the electropherogram you would expect (viewed from above), labelling the amino acids as Gly, Val and Phe.

ii Explain your answer to part **b i**.

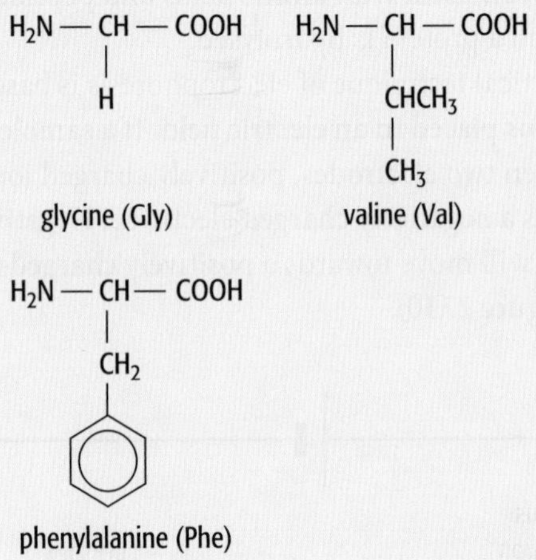

Figure 27.14 Three amino acids to be separated by electrophoresis.

Summary

- Primary amines contain the NH_2 group.

- Ethylamine is prepared either by reducing ethanenitrile, e.g. with hydrogen gas using a nickel catalyst, or by treating bromoethane with an excess of hot, ethanolic ammonia.

- Phenylamine is prepared by reducing nitrobenzene using tin and concentrated hydrochloric acid.

- Like ammonia, amines behave as bases. Because of the lone pair of electrons on their nitrogen atom, they can readily accept protons (H^+ ions), reacting to form salts.

- Ethylamine is a stronger base than ammonia because of the electron-releasing ethyl group.

- Phenylamine is a weaker base than ammonia because the lone pair on the N atom of phenylamine is delocalised into the benzene ring.

- Phenylamine reacts with nitrous acid (nitric(III) acid) below 10 °C, to form benzenediazonium chloride and water; this reaction is called diazotisation.

- Diazonium salts react with other aromatic compounds (such as phenol) to form dyes; this is known as a coupling reaction. Diazonium dyes are commercially important.

- The stability of diazonium dyes arises from the extensively delocalised π bonding electron system.

- There are about 20 naturally occurring amino acids (2-amino-carboxylic acids) with the general formula $RCH(NH_2)COOH$, where R may be H, CH_3 or another organic group.

- The amino group of an amino acid interacts with the acid group to form a zwitterion.

- Amino acids react with both acids and bases to form salts.

- Two amino acids react together in a condensation reaction, bonding together by a peptide (amide) link to form a dipeptide and water. Three amino acids form a tripeptide, and repetition of this condensation reaction many times leads to the formation of polypeptides and proteins.

Amides are prepared by reacting acyl chlorides with ammonia or amines.

Amides can be hydrolysed by aqueous alkali or acid. With aqueous alkali the products are the salt of a carboxylic acid and a primary amine. With acid

hydrolysis the products are a carboxylic acid and a primary amine.

Electrophoresis uses an electric field to separate the compounds in a mixture. It is used widely in analysing the sequence of amino acids in proteins.

End-of-chapter questions

1   Ethylamine and phenylamine are two organic nitrogen compounds. Both compounds are basic.
   a Draw the displayed formula of each compound, including lone pairs. [2]
   b Write a balanced symbol equation for the reaction between one of these compounds and an acid to form a salt. [2]
   c Which structural feature of each compound accounts for the basicity? [1]
                          Total = 5

2   Phenylamine can be made using nitrobenzene as starting material.
   a Name this type of reaction. [1]
   b What reagents are used to bring about this change? [2]
   c Write a balanced symbol equation for this reaction. The conventions [O] or [H] may be used if necessary. [2]
                          Total = 5

3   Phenylamine reacts with nitrous acid (nitric (III) acid) to form a diazonium salt.
   a Which two reagents would you use to prepare the nitrous acid? [2]
   b What are the essential conditions for the reaction? [1]
   c Give the displayed formula of the diazonium salt. [3]
   d Write a balanced symbol equation for this reaction. [2]
                          Total = 8

4   The diazonium salt formed in question **3** reacts with phenol to form a useful substance, X.
   a What are the essential conditions for the reaction? [2]
   b Give the displayed formula of X. [2]
   c Write a balanced symbol equation for this change. [1]
   d Give a possible use for X. [1]
                          Total = 6

5   The formulae of two amino acids, glycine (Gly) and alanine (Ala), are given here:
   glycine is H_2NCH_2COOH   **alanine is $H_2NCH(CH_3)COOH$.**
   a i   Give the systematic names of both amino acids. [2]
      ii Draw their skeletal formulae. [2]
   b Alanine can exist as two stereoisomers.
      i   Draw these two stereoisomers, showing how they differ in their spatial arrangements. [2]
      ii Explain why glycine does not have stereoisomers. [2]
                          Total = 8

6   Both glycine and alanine are amphoteric.
   a   Explain the term **amphoteric**.   [1]
   b   Explain the structural features of both glycine and alanine that enable them to be amphoteric.   [4]
   c   i   Amino acids form zwitterions. Using glycine as an example, explain the term **zwitterion**.   [1]
      ii   State and explain two physical properties of amino acids that can be explained by the existence of zwitterions.   [4]
   d   Draw the two different dipeptides that can be formed when alanine and glycine react together through a condensation reaction.   [4]

   Total = 14

7   The structure of a certain tripeptide is shown here:

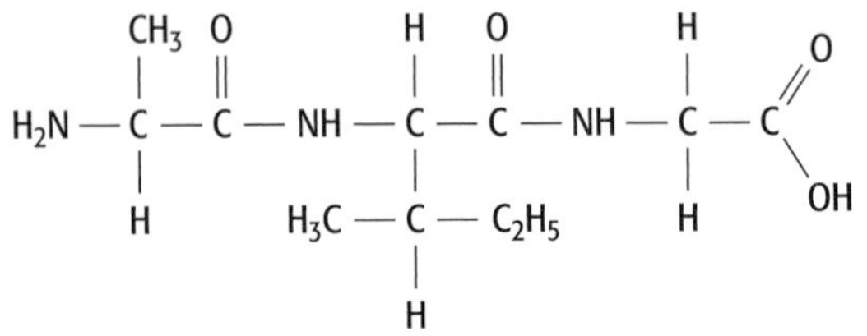

   a   i   Draw the displayed formulae of the three amino acids that make up the tripeptide.   [3]
      ii   Which of these amino acids has two chiral carbon atoms?   [1]
   b   This tripeptide can be split up into the three amino acids by refluxing with aqueous hydrochloric acid.
      i   Which bond is broken in this reaction?   [1]
      ii   The reaction can be described as hydrolysis. Explain why, using a diagram.   [3]
      iii   Name the method commonly used to separate mixtures of amino acids.   [1]
      iv   Explain how to set up the method used to separate amino acids.   [4]
      v   Explain how the method to separate amino acids works.   [5]

   Total = 18

Chapter 28:
Polymerisation

Learning outcomes

You should be able to:

- describe the characteristics of condensation polymerisation in polyesters and polyamides

- distinguish between the primary, secondary and tertiary structures of proteins and explain the stabilisation of secondary structure and tertiary structure

- deduce repeat units, identify monomer(s) and predict the type of polymerisation reaction which produces a given section of a polymer molecule

- discuss the properties and structure of polymers based on their methods of formation, and how the presence of side-chains and intermolecular forces affect their properties

- explain the significance of hydrogen-bonding in the pairing of bases in DNA and describe the hydrolysis of proteins

- recognise that polyalkenes are chemically inert and therefore nonbiodegradable but that polyesters and polyamides are biodegradable, either by acid hydrolysis or by action of light

- describe how polymers have been designed to act as non-solvent-based adhesives and conducting polymers.

Introduction

Polymers are made up of thousands of repeat units made when small, reactive molecules combine in polymerisation reactions. You have met addition polymerisation reactions in Chapter 15. In this chapter you will find out more about another type of polymerisation reaction called condensation polymerisation.

Figure 28.1 Some useful everyday products made from polymers (also see Chapter 15, page 211).

Condensation polymerisation

In Chapter 27 (page 405) we saw how amino acids can react together to form peptides. The reaction is called a **condensation** reaction. We can think of it as an addition reaction (in which reactant molecules bond to each other), followed by an elimination reaction (in which a small molecule is released). For example, the following equation shows how three amino acid molecules can react to make a tripeptide:

$$H_2N - \underset{\underset{H}{|}}{\overset{\overset{R}{|}}{C}} - COOH \ + \ H_2N - \underset{\underset{H}{|}}{\overset{\overset{R}{|}}{C}} - COOH \ + \ H_2N - \underset{\underset{H}{|}}{\overset{\overset{R}{|}}{C}} - COOH$$

amino acid

$$\downarrow$$

$$H_2N - \underset{\underset{H}{|}}{\overset{\overset{R}{|}}{C}} - \overset{\overset{O}{||}}{C} - \underset{\underset{H}{|}}{\overset{\overset{}{|}}{N}} - \underset{\underset{H}{|}}{\overset{\overset{R}{|}}{C}} - \overset{\overset{O}{||}}{C} - \underset{\underset{H}{|}}{\overset{\overset{}{|}}{N}} - \underset{\underset{H}{|}}{\overset{\overset{R}{|}}{C}} - COOH \ + \ 2H_2O$$

a tripeptide

A large protein molecule, formed by condensation polymerisation, can contain thousands of amino acid monomers. As each amino acid monomer joins the chain a peptide link forms, and an H_2O molecule is also produced (see page 405).

- Condensation polymerisation is characterised by monomers that contain two different functional groups capable of reacting with each other. This occurs in two ways:
  - the two different functional groups are found within the same molecule, as in amino acids; each amino acid monomer molecule has an $-NH_2$ functional group and a $-COOH$ functional group
  - the two different functional groups are found in two different molecules; for example, nylon 6,6 is made from two different monomers – one monomer has two $-NH_2$ functional groups and the other monomer has two $-COOH$ functional groups.
- Condensation polymerisation also leads to the formation of small molecules such as H_2O or HCl.

QUESTION

1 **a** Which of these monomers form addition polymers and which form condensation polymers?

  i $NH_2CH(CH_3)COOH$

  ii $H_2C = CHC_6H_5$

  iii $H_2C = CHCOOH$

  iv NH_2CH_2COOH

  v $CH_3CH(OH)COOH$

  b Explain the basis of your decisions in part **a**.

  c **i** Write an equation to show the polymerisation reaction between propene molecules.

  ii What type of polymerisation reaction is shown in part **c i**?

  iii What is the repeat unit of poly(propene)?

412

Synthetic polyamides

Proteins have their monomers bonded to each other via peptide links (also called amide links in synthetic polymers such as nylons). This means that polypeptides and proteins are types of **polyamide**.

For the last 80 years, chemists have used condensation polymerisation to make synthetic polyamides. Nylon is a polyamide. Nylon can be made from a variety of monomers, but all nylons are made in reactions between the amine group ($-NH_2$) and a carboxylic acid ($-COOH$) or acyl chloride group ($-COCl$).

For example, 1,6-diaminohexane reacts with hexanedioic acid to make nylon 6,6:

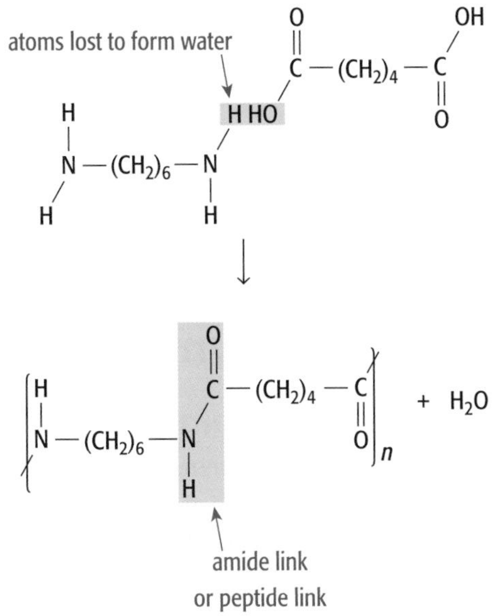

atoms lost to form water

amide link or peptide link

The numbers used in nylon 6,6 refer to the number of carbon atoms in each monomer unit.

Hexanedioyl dichloride, $ClOC(CH_2)_4COCl$, can be used as a more reactive, but more expensive, monomer than hexanedioic acid.

Nylon 6 is the only example of a nylon polymer that is not formed by a condensation reaction; instead it is made from the compound caprolactam, which is a cyclic amide. When heated in an atmosphere of nitrogen the ring breaks open at the amide group. The resulting chains join together to make nylon 6 (Figure 28.2).

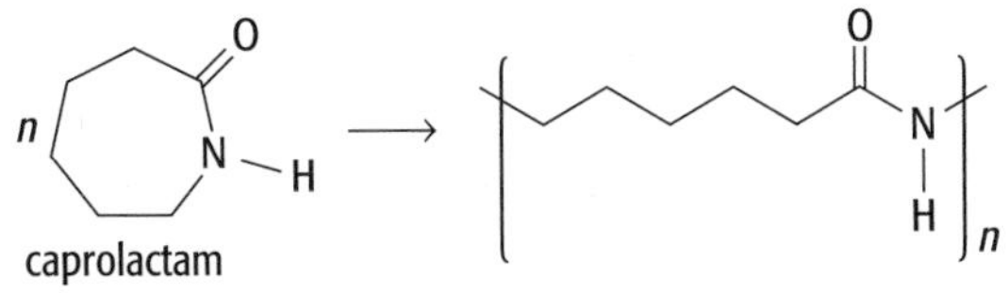

caprolactam

Figure 28.2 Nylon 6 is not formed by condensation polymerisation as no small molecule is given off. The reaction is called 'ring-opening' polymerisation.

Note that caprolactam is made from 6-aminohexanoic acid, with its NH_2 group and COOH group at either end of the molecule. They react with each other in a condensation reaction, releasing water. It is easier to visualise the formation of nylon 6 as the condensation polymerisation of 6-aminohexanoic acid (which would follow the usual pattern of condensation polymerisation to form a polyamide).

Nylon's low density, its strength and its elasticity make it a very useful fibre in the clothing industry. These properties also make it ideal for climbing ropes (Figure 28.3). During the manufacturing process, the nylon is forced out of nozzles and pulled into long fibres. This is called 'cold drawing'. It lines up the nylon polymer chains along the length of the fibre. Strong hydrogen bonds form between neighbouring chains, accounting for nylon's high tensile strength and elasticity.

413

Figure 28.3 Climbers rely on nylon's elasticity and high tensile strength to minimise the effects of a fall.

Kevlar®

Kevlar is a polyamide, containing benzene rings. It is very strong, but flexible. It is also resistant to fire and abrasion. It has these properties because of its structure.

Its long, linear polymer chains can line up next to each other in a regular pattern. This results in extensive hydrogen bonding between the polymer chains of Kevlar®.

The formula and structure of Kevlar® is shown in Figure 28.4.

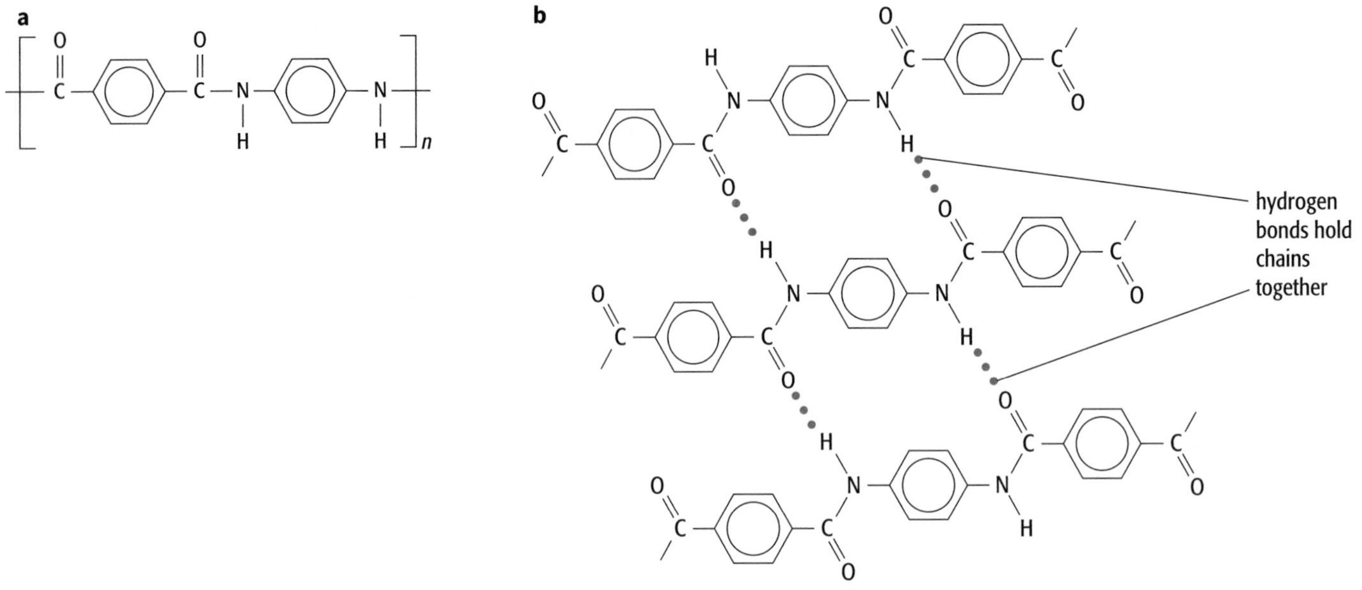

Figure 28.4 a The formula showing the repeat of Kevlar®. **b** The hydrogen bonding between chains of the polyamide. The latest tennis rackets contain Kevlar®, where its low density and strength are important. The wings of fighter jets can also be made of Kevlar®.

The exceptional properties of Kevlar® have led to its use in making bullet-proof vests, ropes, fire-protective clothing (as used by Formula 1 racing drivers) and modern 'leathers' worn by motorcycle riders. It is also used to reinforce other materials, such as the rubber in tyres.

QUESTION

2   Different types of nylon are identified by the number of carbon atoms in each of its monomers, with the diamine quoted first, followed by the dicarboxylic acid.

   a Draw the skeletal formula of each monomer used to make nylon 6,10.

   b Use the skeletal formulae in part **a** to draw an equation showing the condensation polymerisation to make nylon 6,10 from a diamine and a dicarboxylic acid.

   c i Draw the skeletal formula of an alternative monomer to the dicarboxylic acid drawn in part **a** to make nylon 6,10.

   ii What would be the other product of the polymerisation reaction using the alternative monomer?

   d Explain in terms of structure and intermolecular forces why Kevlar® is such a strong material.

Biochemical polymers

Proteins are made from amino acids

The amino acids found in proteins are α-amino acids (Figure 28.5). The names of the amino acids found in proteins can be written in a shorthand form containing three letters. For example, Ala is alanine, Try is tryptophan and Gln is glutamine.

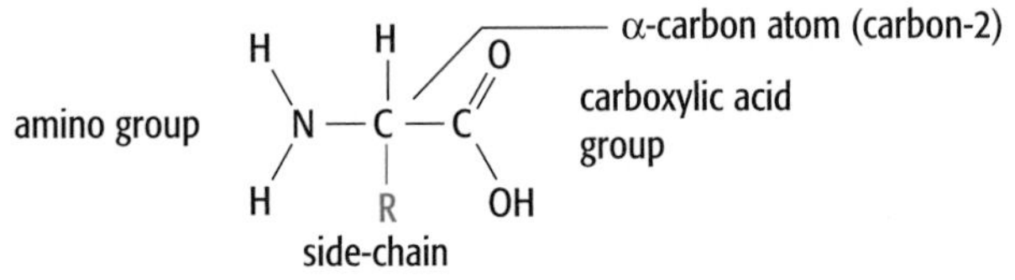

Figure 28.5 The generalised structure of an amino acid, highlighting the key features.

The 20 different amino acids that cells use to build proteins are distinguished by their side-chains (R groups). The side-chains can be classified as non-polar, polar or electrically charged (acidic or basic). Table 28.1 shows some examples.

Table 28.1 Examples of the three different classes of side-chains (in red) in the amino acids found in proteins.

Type of side-chain	Example	Structure
non-polar	alanine (Ala)	$NH_2 — C — COOH$ with H above and CH_3 below
	valine (Val)	$NH_2 — C — COOH$ with H above, CH below, and CH_3 CH_3
polar	serine (Ser)	$NH_2 — C — COOH$ with H above and CH_2OH below
electrically charged (acidic or basic)	aspartic acid (Asp)	$NH_2 — C — COOH$ with H above and CH_2COOH below
	lysine (Lys)	$NH_2 — C — COOH$ with H above and $(CH_2)_4NH_2$ below

Amino acids are amphoteric – they show both acidic and basic properties, depending on conditions. The pH of many body tissues is near pH 7. At this pH both the NH_2 and the COOH groups of the amino acid are ionised. So at pH 7 an amino acid, e.g. glycine, exists in a charged form in which the + and − charges are balanced:

$$^+NH_3CH_2COO^-$$

- in acidic conditions amino acids become positively charged (see page 405)
- in alkaline conditions amino acids become negatively charged.

Proteins are condensation polymers

On page 405 you learned that the NH_2 group of one amino acid can react with the COOH of another amino acid to form a dipeptide by a condensation reaction. The covalent bond formed is called a peptide bond (amide link). Additional amino acids can then react to form a tripeptide, a tetrapeptide, and so on. Eventually a **polypeptide**, containing many **peptide bonds**, is formed.

QUESTION

3 a Name and give the formulae of the two functional groups present in all amino acids.

b Name an example of an amino acid with a non-polar side-chain.

c Draw a diagram of two molecules of serine to show the formation of hydrogen bonds between the OH groups of the side-chain.

A polypeptide chain may contain 50 to 2000 amino acids. An amino acid unit within a polypeptide chain is called an **amino acid residue**. We draw the amino acid sequence in a polypeptide starting from the end that has a free NH_2 group (the N-terminal end).

$$NH_2–\square–CONH–...–\square–CONH–\square–COOH$$

Proteins may contain one or more polypeptide chains. Some important facts about proteins are:

- proteins are formed by condensation polymerisation
- the polypeptide chain in proteins is unbranched
- each protein has a unique sequence of amino acids
- the sequence of amino acids is determined by DNA
- each protein has a particular biological function.

Primary, secondary and tertiary structure

The structure of a protein molecule is described in three parts, or levels.

- **Primary structure:** the sequence of amino acids in the polypeptide chain.
- **Secondary structure:** a regular structural arrangement stabilised by hydrogen bonding between the NH group of one peptide bond and the CO group of another peptide bond.
- **Tertiary structure:** the further folding of the polypeptide chain into a three-dimensional (3-D) shape. This 3-D shape is stabilised by attractive forces and bonding between the amino acid side-chains (R groups).

Each protein has its own, unique, function because each protein has its own, unique, 3-D shape.

Primary structure

The primary structure is the order in which the amino acids are linked together. The primary structure of one of the polypeptide chains of insulin is shown in Figure 28.6.

415

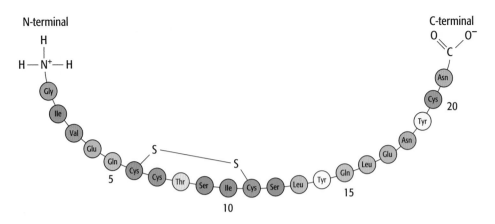

N-terminal

C-terminal

Figure 28.6 The primary sequence of the insulin A chain, a short polypeptide of 21 amino acids.

The primary structure of a protein:

- is written with the amino acids numbered from the N-terminal end
- determines the way that the protein can fold to form its secondary and tertiary structure
- is held together by covalent bonds. These bonds are found within amino acid residues, and between the residues as peptide linkages.

(In Figure 28.6 there are —S—S—links (disulfide bridges) between two amino acid residues. These help maintain the **tertiary** structure.)

Secondary structure

Secondary structure describes regions of the polypeptide chain in which there is a particular arrangement of the amino acid residues. The structure is stabilised by hydrogen bonding between the —NH group of one peptide bond and the —CO group of another peptide bond. The side-chains of the amino acids are not involved. Two types of secondary structure are:

- the α-helix (alpha-helix)
- β-pleated sheet (beta-pleated sheet).

The α-helix

Each polypeptide chain has a 'backbone' of atoms (—C— C—N—C— C—N—) that runs along the chain. Some points on the chain are flexible and allow free rotation around the bonds (Figure 28.7).

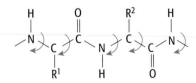

Figure 28.7 There is free rotation around the bonds either side of the peptide group. R^1 and R^2 represent the amino acid side-chains.

In the α-helix the backbone twists round in a spiral so that a rod-like structure is formed. All the —NH and —CO groups of each peptide bond are involved in hydrogen bond formation. The hydrogen bonds lie parallel with the long axis of the helix with each —NH group forming a weak intermolecular link to a —CO group four amino acid residues further along the backbone (Figure 28.8). The large number of hydrogen bonds in the same direction stabilises the structure. The side-chains of the amino acid residues stick out on the outside of the helix.

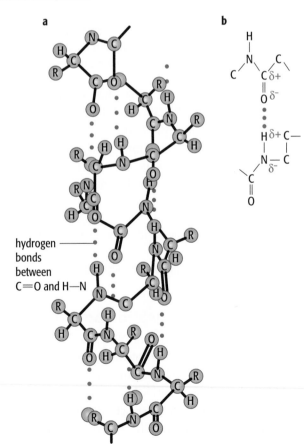

Figure 28.8 a An α-helix. **b** Detail of one hydrogen bond in the α-helix.

416

The β-pleated sheet

In a β-pleated sheet, hydrogen bonds are formed between —NH and —CO groups in different polypeptide chains or different areas of the same polypeptide chain. Figure 28.9 shows the β-pleated sheet in the structural protein, silk. A fairly flat sheet-like structure is formed.

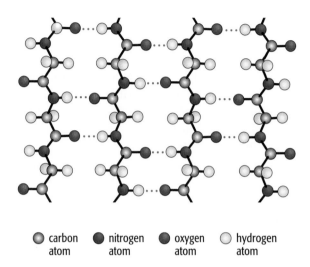

carbon atom   nitrogen atom   oxygen atom   hydrogen atom

Figure 28.9 A β-pleated sheet in silk. The hydrogen bonds are formed between separate polypeptide chains.

Proteins may have a mixture of secondary structures

Regions of regular secondary structure occur in many proteins. Figure 28.10 shows a computer graphic of pepsin, a digestive enzyme found in the stomach.

The structure of pepsin has:

■ α-helical regions (represented by the cylindrical rods)
■ β-pleated regions (represented by arrows).

Between the regions of secondary structure there are bends (β turns) and apparently randomly coiled regions.

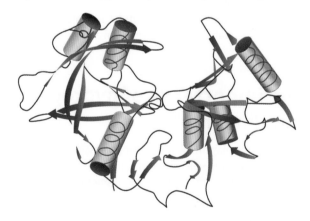

Figure 28.10 A computer graphic model of the structure of pepsin.

Tertiary structure

The tertiary structure involves further folding of the polypeptide chain. The complex 3-D shape (see Figure 28.11) is stabilised by:

■ **disulfide bridges** – these are covalent (S—S) bonds (also see synthetic rubber in Figure 28.22)
■ weak van der Waals' forces
■ relatively weak hydrogen bonds
■ ionic bonds (salt bridges).

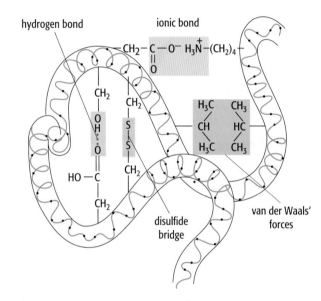

Figure 28.11 A diagram illustrating the nature of the interactions responsible for protein tertiary structure. The forces and bonds stabilising the tertiary structure have been exaggerated in size.

Disulfide bridges are usually found in proteins that function outside the body cells; for example, digestive enzymes.

Disulfide bridges can be formed within the same polypeptide chain or between different polypeptide chains. The disulfide bridges help maintain the tertiary structure by 'locking' the polypeptide chains in place (see Figure 28.12 on page 418).

Dipole-induced dipole forces (van der Waals' forces) are formed when non-polar amino acid residues are close to one another. A large proportion of the amino acid residues in the 'centre' of many proteins are non-polar. So, although van der Waals' forces are weak, the stabilisation of tertiary structure due to total van der Waals' forces may be considerable.

Hydrogen bonds are formed between polar side-chains having hydrogen atoms attached to the highly

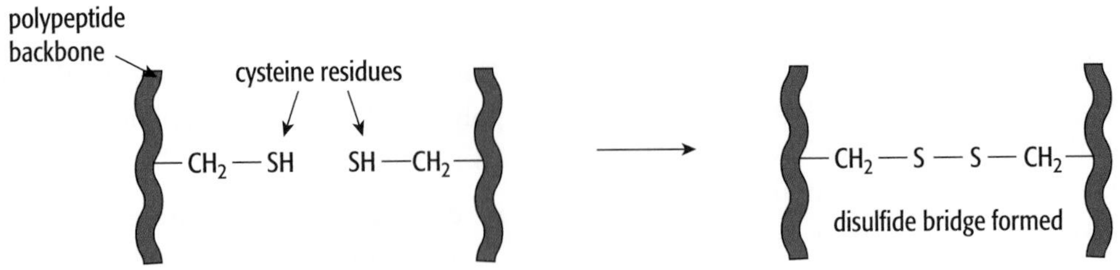

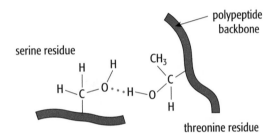

Figure 28.12 The formation of a disulfide bridge from two cysteine residues.

electronegative atoms nitrogen or oxygen. Figure 28.13 shows hydrogen bonds formed between serine and threonine residues.

Figure 28.13 A hydrogen bond (shown by three red dots) formed between serine and threonine residues.

Ionic bonds are formed between ionised acidic side-chains and ionised basic side-chains. Figure 28.14 shows the ionic bonds that form between the negatively charged aspartate side-chain and the positively charged lysyl side-chain.

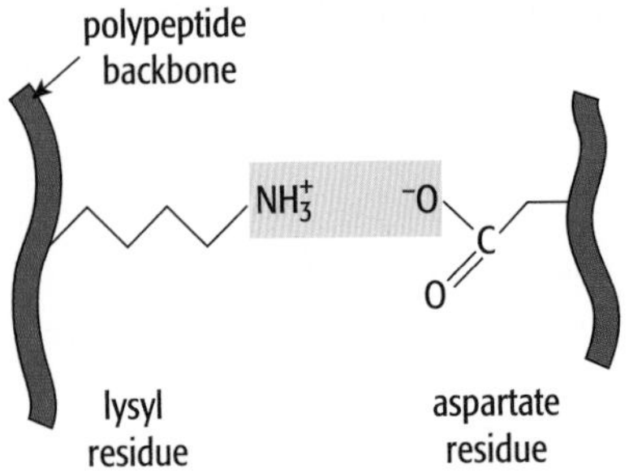

Figure 28.14 An ionic bond formed between an aspartate residue and a lysyl residue (from lysine).

Hydrolysis of proteins

As you learnt on page 406 the amide or peptide link can be broken down by hydrolysis. In the laboratory we can break down polypeptides and proteins by refluxing them with strong acid or alkali. We can show the hydrolysis of the peptide link as:

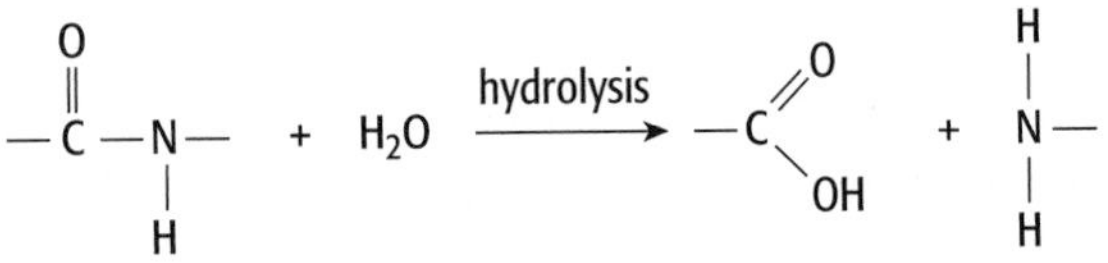

With acid reflux, the products of hydrolysis of a peptide are its original 2-amino-carboxylic acids. The amine ($-NH_2$) groups will react with excess acid in the reaction vessel to make their ammonium salts. For example, when hydrolysed with excess hydrochloric acid $Cl^-H_3N^+-RCH-COOH$ will form.

With an excess of alkali, such as aqueous sodium hydroxide, refluxing produces the sodium salts of the original 2-amino-carboxylic acids. For example, $H_2N-RCH-COO^-Na^+$ will form.

QUESTION

4 a A polypeptide is said to have direction. How are the two ends of the chain described?

  b What type of chemical bonding is responsible for maintaining the primary structure of a protein?

  c What is meant by the term **amino acid residue**?

  d Draw a diagram to show how a hydrogen bond may be formed between two peptide bonds in a polypeptide chain.

  e List the different types of interaction responsible for stabilising the tertiary structure of a protein.

  f What is the major difference in the position of the hydrogen bonds in the secondary and tertiary structures of a protein?

  g i Name the amino acid that gives rise to a disulfide bridge.

   ii What part do disulfide bridges play in stabilising the structure of a protein?

The importance of hydrogen bonding in DNA

Nucleic acids play an essential role in passing on genetic information from generation to generation. This genetic information determines the structure of living things and the nature of the chemical reactions that go on inside them. The two main types of nucleic acid are deoxyribonucleic acid (DNA) and ribonucleic acid (RNA). The structure of DNA contains a genetic code that determines the specific amino acid sequence for all the proteins in the body. Both DNA and RNA are polynucleotides. They are made by condensation polymerisation of units called **nucleotides**.

The structure of DNA

Deoxyribonucleic acid (**DNA**) has two important functions in living organisms.

- DNA can make copies of itself so that the genetic information can be passed on from generation to generation.
- DNA contains a sequence of bases that form a genetic code used to synthesise proteins.

The nucleotides in DNA are made up of three components (Figure 28.15). These are:

- a sugar called deoxyribose (which has a five-membered ring)
- a phosphate group (attached by a phosphoester link to deoxyribose)
- a nitrogen-containing base (of which there are four types).

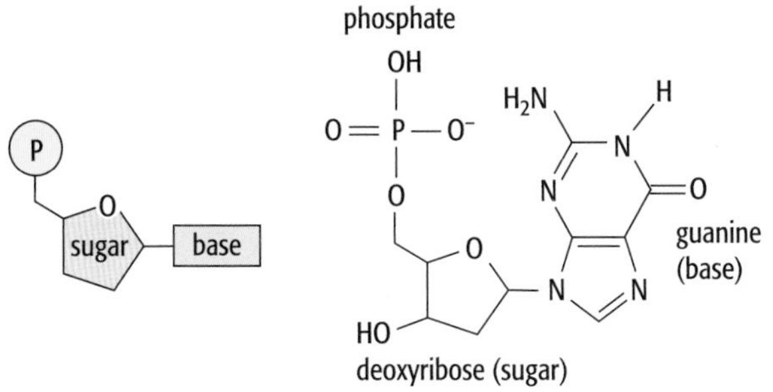

Figure 28.15 The three components that make up a nucleotide. You do not need to recall the detailed structure shown in the displayed formula.

The nitrogen-containing bases (with their abbreviations) are:

- adenine (A)
- guanine (G)
- thymine (T)
- cytosine (C).

Adenine and guanine have a planar structure with two rings; thymine and cytosine have a planar structure with a single ring.

The DNA molecule consists of a double helix made up of two strands which are kept in place by hydrogen bonding between pairs of bases (Figure 28.16). The main points about the structure of DNA are:

- each strand has a backbone of alternating sugar and phosphate units; this is on the outside of the structure
- the two strands run in opposite directions to each other (compare the 3' and 5' positions of the deoxyribose sugar units in the two chains in Figure 28.16b)

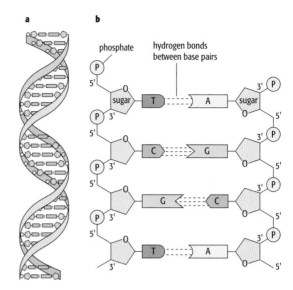

Figure 28.16 a Part of the DNA double helix. **b** An outline structure of DNA, showing base pairing. The chain has been 'straightened out' to make the base pairing clearer.

- the two strands are twisted to form a double helix
- the nitrogen-containing bases link the two strands
- the bases are positioned at right angles to the long axis of the helix (rather like a pile of coins)
- the bases are linked by hydrogen bonds.

The base pairs fit into the space between the two backbones so that the helix has a regular shape. In order to do this the bases pair up so that:

- A always pairs with T (forming two hydrogen bonds between them)
- G always pairs with C (forming three hydrogen bonds between them).

The bases on one strand always link to a particular base on the other strand. We say they form **complementary base pairs**.

You do not have to know the detailed structure of the bases. They can be represented by blocks, as in Figure 28.16.

The structure of DNA is kept stable by:

- hydrogen bonds between the base pairs
- van der Waals' attractive forces between one base pair and the next.

Figure 28.17 shows the hydrogen bonding between the base pairs in DNA in more detail. You can see that the hydrogen bonding is not as regular as indicated in Figure 28.16. In reality, the base pairs on each strand are not completely in line with each other; rather they are slightly twisted out of line. This allows the DNA double helix to be able to bend, rather than being a straight rod-like structure.

419

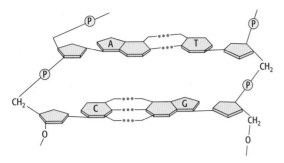

Figure 28.17 The detailed structure of part of a DNA molecule, showing the hydrogen bonding between the base pairs.

QUESTIONS

5 The diagram here represents the basic chemical unit from which DNA is formed.

   a State the name of:

      i   the whole unit   ii X   iii Y

   b Name the four nitrogen-containing bases present in DNA.

6 a Representing the nitrogen-containing bases by 'B', sugars by 'S' and phosphate groups by 'P', show how these are linked in a short length of double-stranded DNA. Use full lines (——) to show covalent bonds and dots (•••) to show hydrogen bonds.

   b i   How do the two backbones in DNA differ?

      ii State how this difference is shown on diagrams of DNA.

How DNA replicates

The chromosomes in the cell nucleus contain DNA. The DNA in almost every cell in our body is identical. When a cell divides, both the new cells need a complete copy of all of this DNA because DNA contains the information for all the cell's activities. The information is provided by the sequence of bases in DNA. The process of copying DNA during cell division is called **replication**.

Replication is a complex process requiring a number of different enzymes and other compounds. Although you do not need to explain this process in detail, it is interesting to see how it works. A simplified model of replication is shown in Figure 28.18.

- The hydrogen bonds and van der Waals' forces between the base pairs in part of a DNA molecule are broken.
- This part of the double helix unwinds.
- Nucleotide triphosphates are brought up one by one to the separated part of the chain.
- Enzymes catalyse the polymerisation reaction..

Each new strand contains a sequence of bases that is complementary to the original strand. So if the order of bases in part of the original strand is:

—A T G C C G T T A A G T—

then the complementary sequence on the new strand is:

—T A C G G C A A T T C A—

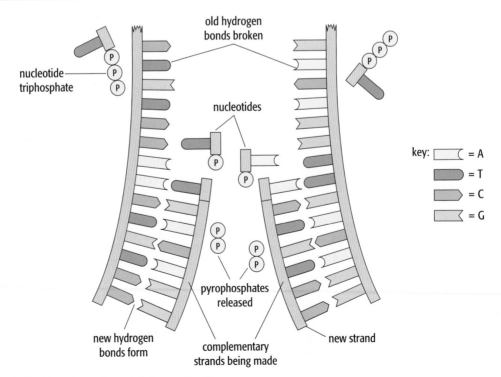

Figure 28.18 A strand of DNA acting as template for replication.

The two double helices formed are identical. Each double helix contains one strand from the old DNA and one newly synthesised strand. This is called semi-conservative replication (Figure 28.19).

DNA carries the genetic information for the production of proteins. Particular sections of the DNA chain (genes) store the information as a sequence of bases to make particular polypeptide chains. These specific sequences are decoded to enable the synthesis of particular proteins.

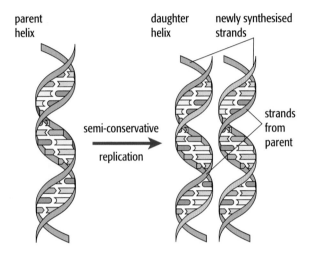

Figure 28.19 Semi-conservative replication.

QUESTION

7 a An analysis of the bases in a sample of double-stranded DNA gave the partial result: adenine 23 mol % and guanine 27 mol %. What would you expect the rest of the analysis to show? Explain your answer.

   b What role do hydrogen bonds play in the accurate replication of DNA?

   c The base sequence in part of the 5' to 3' parent strand of DNA is

   —TAGAAAGCTCAG—

   What is the DNA sequence in the corresponding part of the new strand made during replication?

Polyesters

Polyesters are another type of condensation polymer. As you learnt in Chapter 17 (page 229), esters are made by reacting carboxylic acids with alcohols:

carboxylic acid + alcohol ⟶ ester + water

Therefore, polyesters can be made by reacting dicarboxylic acids with diols, e.g. propanedioic acid and ethane-1,2-diol. The most common polyester fibre is Terylene®. Terylene® is made from benzene-1,4-dicarboxylic acid and ethane-1,2-diol. The conditions required are a catalyst such as antimony(III) oxide at a temperature of about 280 °C:

Poly(lactic acid), PLA, is another polyester. However, PLA is made using just one monomer, lactic acid. Its systematic name is 2-hydroxypropanoic acid. The monomer contains the carboxylic acid and alcohol groups within each molecule:

lactic acid

poly(lactic acid)

The polyester PLA, whose raw material is starch from crops such as corn, is now being used as a biodegradable alternative to oil-based plastics. The ester links can be hydolysed in acidic conditions to break down the polymer chains when used items containing polyesters are dumped in land-fill sites. Alcohol and carboxylic acids will be the products of the acid hydrolysis of polyesters.

QUESTION

8 a Draw the repeat unit of the polyester, PLA (shown above).

   b Draw the repeat unit of Terylene®.

421

Designing useful polymers

Low-density and high-density poly(ethene)

In the 1930s the first type of polyalkene formed was low-density poly(ethene) (LDPE) and it is still useful today. Its non-polar polymer chains interact with each other by van der Waals' forces. As the chains are heavily branched, not straight chains, these intermolecular forces are relatively weak for such large molecules. The random branching makes it impossible for the polymer chains to pack neatly together and accounts for its low density and low melting temperature (see Figure 28.20).

Then in the 1950s a chemist called Karl Ziegler discovered a catalyst that helped produce poly(ethene) consisting of straight chains, showing that reaction conditions can affect the nature of the polymer formed. This new type of poly(ethene) had different properties. Its unbranched polymer chains could pack closely together (see Figure 28.21) and formed high-density poly(ethene) (HDPE).

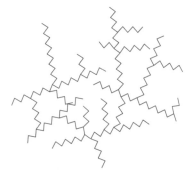

Figure 28.20 The branched chains of LDPE. The van der Waals' forces between the non-polar polymer chains are affected not only by the size of the chains but also their inability to pack closely together, reducing the effectiveness of instantaneous dipoles in one chain to induce dipoles on neighbouring chains.

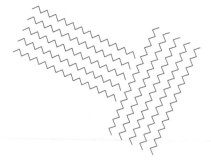

Figure 28.21 The unbranched chains of HDPE can pack closely together in regions of regular patterns, increasing the surface area of contact between neighbouring chains resulting in stronger van der Waals' forces being set up between chains.

This is a much stronger plastic and has a higher melting temperature. Therefore HDPE can be used to make water pipes and containers that can be sterilised with boiling water. This demonstrates the importance of the intermolecular forces between polymer chains when considering the properties of polymeric materials.

Another example of this is the difference in properties between natural rubber and synthetic rubbers. From the 1930s, chemists have tried to mimic natural polymers. Finding synthetic substitutes for rubber and silk, for example, offered the chance to produce cheaper materials with improved properties. Neoprene, a synthetic rubber, and nylon, a synthetic polyamide, were both products discovered at that time. Neoprene was made from the polymerisation of the monomer 2-chloro-1,3-butadiene in an addition reaction:

$$n \; \underset{H}{\overset{H}{\diagup}} C = C \overset{Cl}{\underset{\;}{|}} - C \overset{H}{\underset{\;}{|}} = C \underset{H}{\overset{H}{\diagdown}} \longrightarrow \left[- \underset{\underset{H}{|}}{\overset{\overset{H}{|}}{C}} - \underset{\;}{\overset{Cl}{\underset{\;}{|}}} C = C \overset{H}{\underset{\;}{|}} - \underset{\underset{H}{|}}{\overset{\overset{H}{|}}{C}} - \right]_n$$

neoprene

The monomer of natural rubber is 2-methyl-1,3-butadiene, which is very similar to the monomer for neoprene. The intermolecular forces between natural rubber polymers are van der Waals' forces. A process called vulcanisation was invented to make rubber tyres more resilient and hardwearing. This links rubber polymer chains by covalent bonds across 'sulfur bridges' (Figure 28.22).

QUESTION

9 **a** The word 'resilient' means to return to the original form or position after being bent, compressed or stretched. Explain why the process of vulcanising makes rubber 'more resilient'.

   b Give an equation to show the polymerisation of 2-methyl-1,3-butadiene to form rubber.

   c Using the concept of intermolecular forces, explain why HDPE could be used to make containers that can be sterilised by boiling water but LDPE cannot.

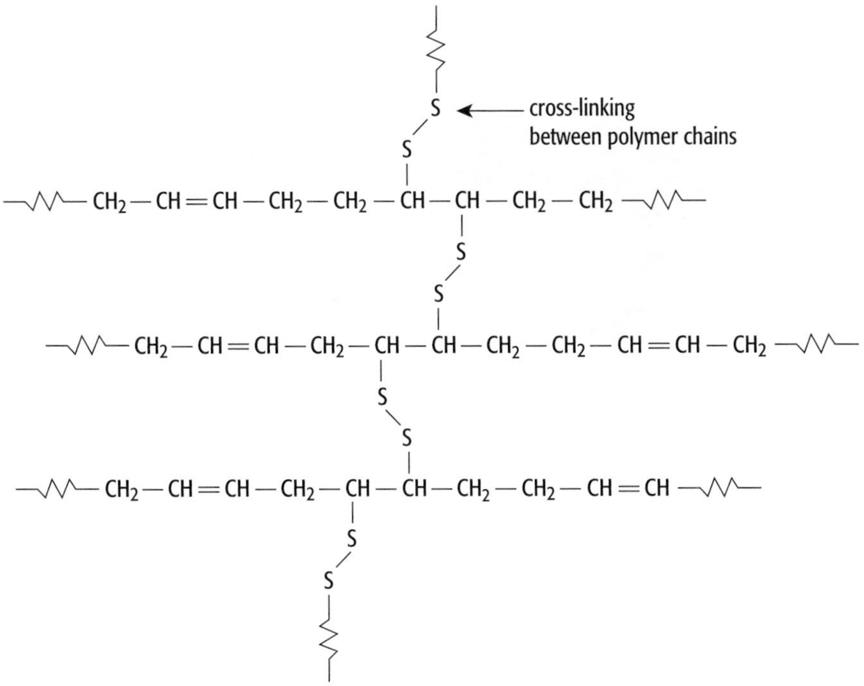

Figure 28.22 The sulfur bridges between polymer chains make rubber more resilient.

Non-solvent-based adhesives

Traditional adhesives (glues) use an organic solvent to dissolve a polymer that will stick two surfaces together. After applying the adhesive, the solvent evaporates off and the solid polymer is left behind and acts as the glue. The solvent used is often the ester, ethyl ethanoate, as it has a low toxicity and is volatile. However, it is flammable and other organic solvents used in adhesives are harmful to health. Therefore chemists have developed glues that do not rely on organic solvents that are a source of pollution.

The main component of non-solvent-based adhesives is often a polymer that contains silicon bonded to oxygen. They set (or cure) by reacting with the moisture present in air. The water hydrolyses the silicon–oxygen parts of the polymer chain, which form cross-linkages between each other. This effectively bonds the polymer chains to each other with strong covalent bonds. The cross-linking siloxane grouping is $-Si-O-Si-$, which is the equivalent of an ether functional group in carbon chemistry (see Figure 28.23).

$$2RSi(OCH_3)_2R' + H_2O \rightarrow [RSi(OCH_3)R']_2O + 2CH_3OH$$

The polymers are called 'silyl modified polymers' (SMPs) and are non-toxic and environmentally friendly, and they

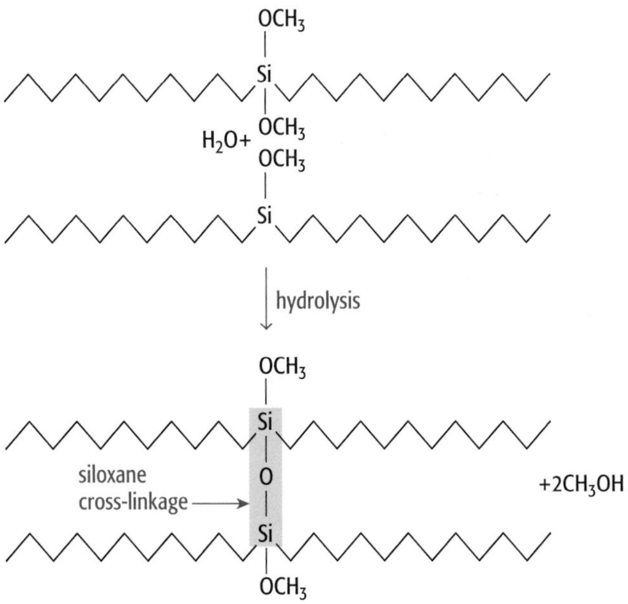

Figure 28.23 This shows how hydrolysis of a $Si-O-CH_3$ grouping can form a siloxane cross-link between polymer chains. As an adhesive sets (cures) many of these strong covalent links will be formed to produce a giant network.

set quickly. They perform well with most materials under a wide range of conditions (see Figure 28.24).

423

Figure 28.24 Silyl modified polymers (SMPs) are a safer option than traditional adhesives, which use potentially harmful organic solvents.

Polymers that form extensive networks of covalent cross-links are called thermosets. They are very strong and cannot be melted and remoulded. Epoxy resins are common examples of these macromolecules formed by condensation polymerisation. These thermosetting glues

are formed when the two reactants, one derived from epoxyethane (a reactive, triangular molecule, CH_2CH_2O) and a diamine, are mixed as pastes. For example, a monomer with reactive epoxy groups at either end could have the structure shown in Figure 28.25.

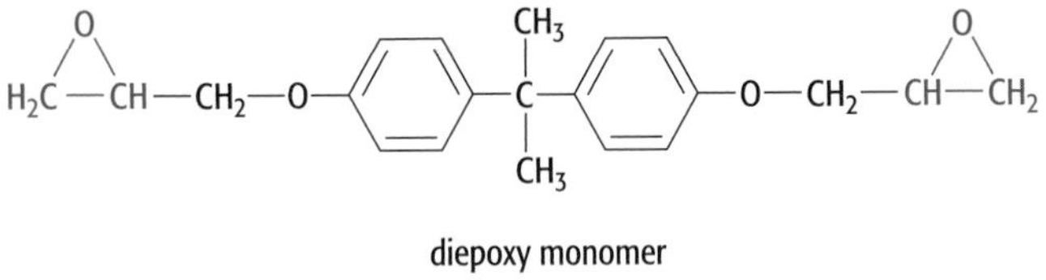

diepoxy monomer

Figure 28.25 A diepoxy monomer.

This can be reacted with a diamine, $H_2N—R—NH_2$, to form a hard, strong epoxy resin with a giant network of cross-linking (see Figure 28.26).

In contrast to the condensation polymerisation reaction for epoxy resins, another fast-acting fixing agent, Super Glue®, uses an addition reaction to stick objects together. The monomer is $CH_2=C(CN)COOCH_3$, methyl cyanoacrylate, and the addition takes place across the carbon–carbon double bond. The polymerisation reaction is initiated by the presence of moisture.

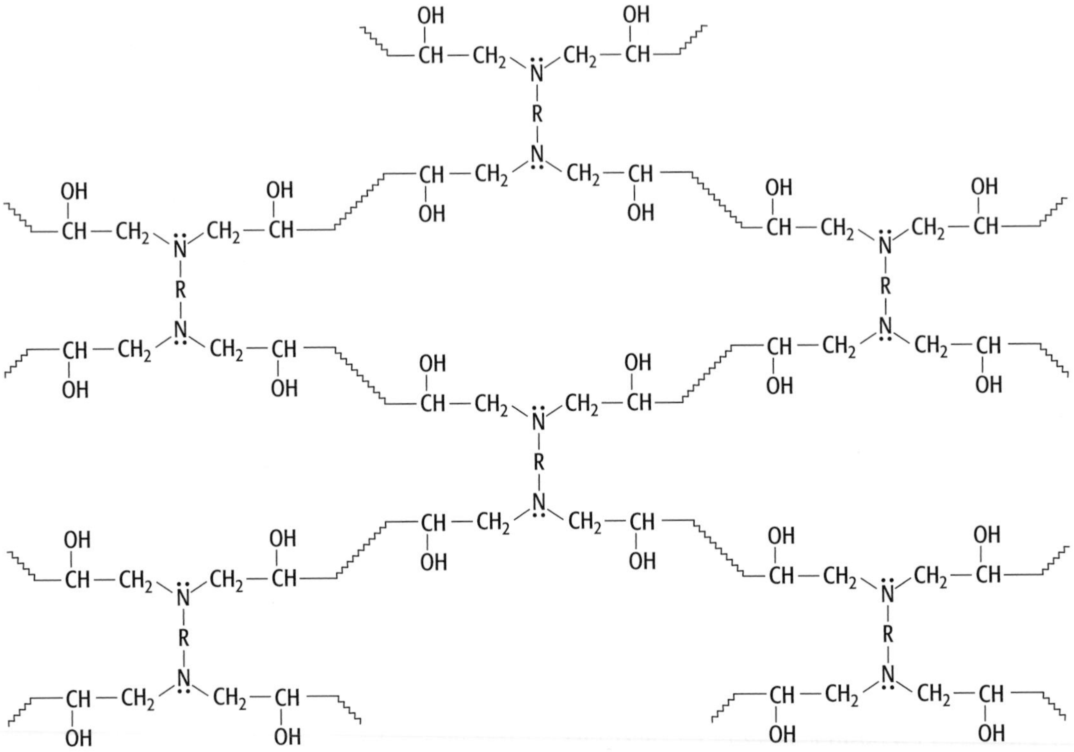

Figure 28.26 The extensive cross-linking in a thermosetting epoxy resin.

10 **a** How does a non-solvent-based adhesive, such as an SMP, set to become a solid?

b What type of monomers react together to form an epoxy resin?

c **i** Draw the displayed formula of the monomer used in Super Glue®.

ii Draw two of these monomers in a Super Glue® polymer chain.

iii How do the polymerisation reactions differ when epoxy resins and Super Glue® set?

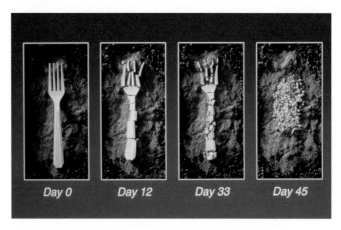

Figure 28.27 Chemists are devising plastics that can be broken down by microorganisms in soil or by light.

Degradable polymers

Chemists are now developing degradable plastics that break down when they are discarded. The use of degradable plastics is becoming more common as people start to realise the issues related to the disposal of polyalkenes as a result of their non-biodegradability caused by their lack of reactivity (see page 212). Here are two developments to help solve the disposal problem: **biodegradable plastics** and **photodegradable plastics**.

Biodegradable plastics

Some plastics, when buried for many years, eventually become brittle and break down into smaller pieces that can be decomposed naturally by microorganisms in soil. If the surface area of the plastic being buried could be increased, then it could degrade much more quickly. Scientists have developed plastics that contain small amounts of starch granules that the bacteria and fungi in moist soil can break down. So the plastic is broken into smaller pieces, with a larger surface area for decomposition to occur faster. Other plastics are now made from monomers derived directly from plant materials, such as PLA, which soil microorganisms can digest easily (Figure 28.27).

In polyamides, such as nylon, the amide links, — CO — NH —, can be broken down by hydrolysis in acidic conditions found in land-fill waste dumps with rotting vegetation. You can see the hydrolysis reaction on page 406, in which carboxylic acids and amines are formed.

In polyesters, the ester links are similarly broken down by acid hydrolysis, forming alcohols and carboxylic acids (see page 229). This susceptibility to hydrolysis makes both polyamides and polyesters biodegradable, unlike the non-biodegradable polyalkenes.

Photodegradable plastics

Polymer chains also have been designed that incorporate carbonyl groups ($C = O$) at intervals down their length. These carbonyl groups absorb energy from the ultraviolet region of the electromagnetic spectrum. This causes the bonds in the region of the carbonyl group to weaken and break down. As the polymer breaks into smaller fragments, the plastic will biodegrade much more quickly if it is not chemically inert.

There is some debate as to whether photodegradable plastics are better for the environment or not. In a land-fill site, the plastic waste is often buried under other rubbish and eventually soil – so there is no light available to trigger the breakdown of the polymer chains. They also make recycling plastics problematic, as they could weaken a recycled mixture of different plastics when it is put to a new use.

Conducting polymers

Most polymers are electrical insulators, which makes them very useful for making plugs, sockets and light switches. However, a group of polymers have been developed that can conduct electricity. One of the first was the polymer formed from the hydrocarbon called ethyne (also still know by its old name, acetylene). Its molecular formula is C_2H_2 and its displayed formula is:

$$H - C \equiv C - H$$

425

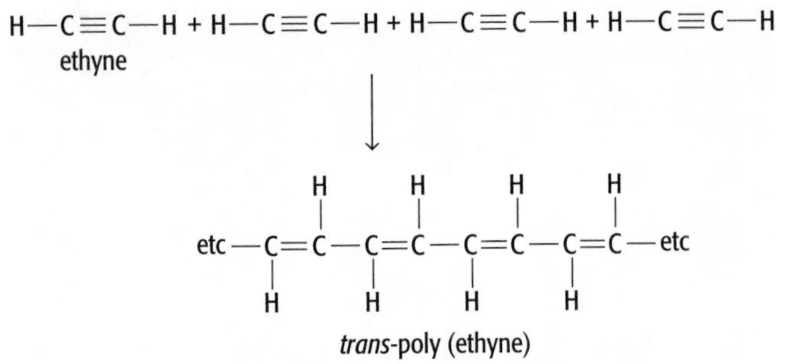

ethyne

$$H-C\equiv C-H + H-C\equiv C-H + H-C\equiv C-H + H-C\equiv C-H$$

trans-poly (ethyne)

Figure 28.28 The polymerisation of ethyne (acetylene) to form a conducting polymer.

We can represent the formation of poly(ethyne) from its ethyne monomers as shown in Figure 28.28.

As drawn in Figure 28.28, the poly(ethyne) is in the *trans*- configuration as opposed to the *cis*- form of the polymer. Figure 28.29 shows how to represent both forms. A polymer chain with mixture of *cis*- and *trans*- sections can be made by varying the reaction conditions.

Note the alternate double and single carbon–carbon bonds in poly(ethyne). It can conduct electricity because its π bonding spreads down the length of the polymer chain. The overlapping p orbitals on neighbouring carbon atoms result in long bands of delocalised electrons that are free to move along the length of the polymer chains (see pages 80 and 383).

Lots of research has been carried out to produce other conducting polymers with extended π bonding systems. Poly(ethyne) and some other examples are shown by their skeletal formulae in Figure 28.29.

Conducting polymers usually have other substances, such as iodine, added to improve their electrical conductivity. This is called 'doping'. They have a number of advantages over the metal conductors that they can potentially replace. They do not corrode, are much less dense, and can be shaped more easily. For example, they can be made into thin sheets to make flat panels that light

trans-poly(ethyne)   *cis*-poly(ethyne)

poly(1,6-heptadiyne)   poly(phenylene)   poly(pyrrole)

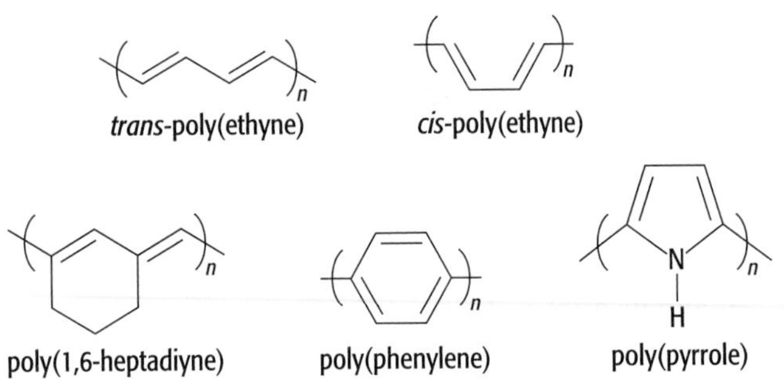

Figure 28.29 Some examples of conducting polymers – note the alternate double and single carbon–carbon bonds.

up. They can also now be used in LED lighting. They are ideal in situations where saving weight is important, such as in satellites and aeroplanes.

Polymer deductions

You may encounter a variety of different problems about polymers to solve:

1 predict the type of polymerisation reaction for a given monomer or pair of monomers

2 deduce the repeat unit of a polymer obtained from a given monomer or pair of monomers

3 deduce the type of polymerisation reaction that produces a given section of a polymer molecule

4 identify the monomer(s) present in a given section of a polymer molecule.

Predicting the type of polymerisation reaction for given monomer(s)

i Addition polymers

Given a monomer that contains the C=C double bond, it will undergo addition polymerisation. Many addition polymers are made using one type of monomer, e.g. poly(propene) from propene monomers. However, co-polymers can also be produced by using more than one type of unsaturated monomer, e.g. $H_2C=CH_2$ and $H_2C=CHCOOH$.

ii Condensation polymers

When identifying monomers used in condensation polymerisation, look out for the presence of two functional groups that will react with each other, giving off a small molecule in the reaction. These two functional groups can be in the same molecule, as in the case of poly(lactic acid) on page 421, or at either end of two different monomers, as in nylon 6,6 on page 413. The functional groups involved in condensation polymerisation are usually:

■ amines (—NH_2) and carboxylic acids (—COOH) producing a polyamide and H_2O

■ amines (—NH_2) and acyl chlorides (—COCl) producing a polyamide and HCl

■ carboxylic acids (—COOH) and alcohols (—OH) producing a polyester and H_2O

■ acyl chlorides (—COCl) and alcohols (—OH) producing a polyester and HCl

Deducing the repeat unit of a polymer for given monomer(s)

i Addition polymers

Given a monomer with a C=C bond, simply turn the double bond into a C—C single bond and show the bonds either side of the two C atoms that would continue the chain:

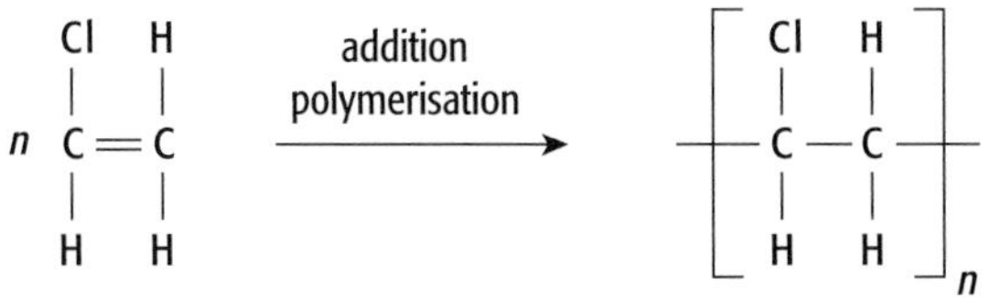

ii Condensation polymers

Given monomers with two reactive functional groups, draw the product formed when two monomers react together. Then take off the atoms at both ends that would be lost if another two monomers were to react with those groups:

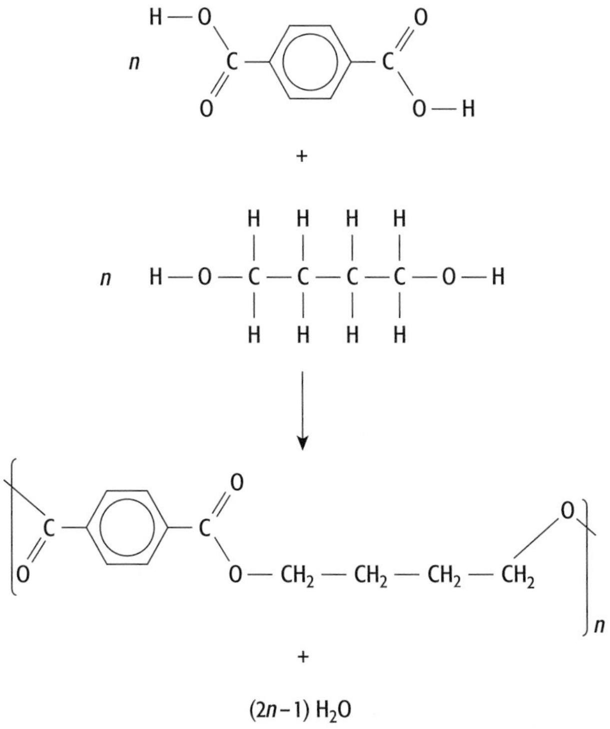

Deducing the type of polymerisation reaction for a given section of a polymer chain

i Addition polymers

Polymers resulting from addition polymerisation will have repeat units with no functional groups in the actual chain

of carbon atoms that forms the 'backbone' of the polymer. Poly(phenylethene) is an example:

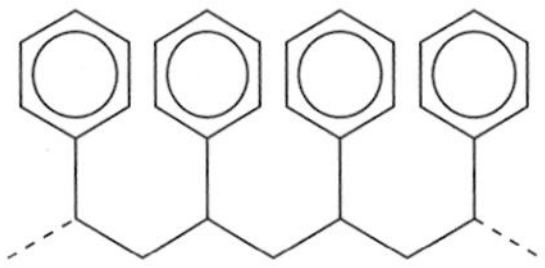

poly(phenylethene)

Note that functional groups may be present on the side-chains, such as the nitrile group, —CN. However, the 'backbone' in addition polymers usually consists of a chain of carbon atoms.

ii Condensation polymers

Polymers resulting from condensation polymerisation will have amide links (—CONH—) or ester links (—COO—) in the 'backbone' of the polymer chain. For example:

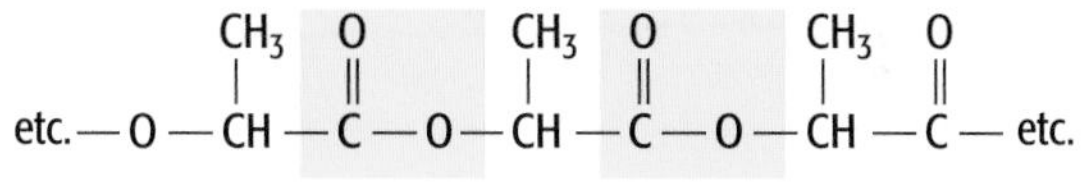

Identifying the monomer(s) present in a given section of a polymer chain

This is an extension of the approach above. Having decided whether the polymer was made in an addition or a condensation polymerisation, you can then split the polymer chain into its repeat units.

i Addition polymers

With an addition polymer, you need to put the C=C double bond back into the monomer:

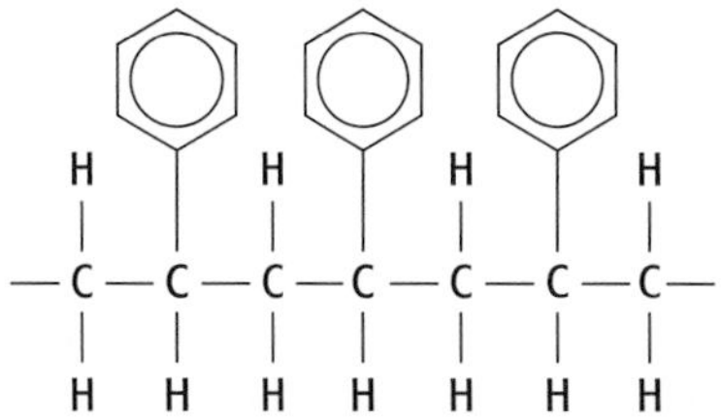

part of addition polymer

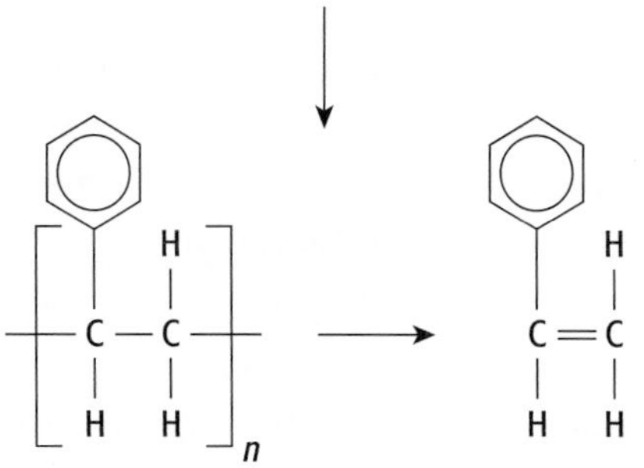

427

ii Condensation polymers

With condensation polymers, you need to identify the atoms from the small molecules given off in the polymerisation reaction and replace them on the reactive functional groups in the monomers.

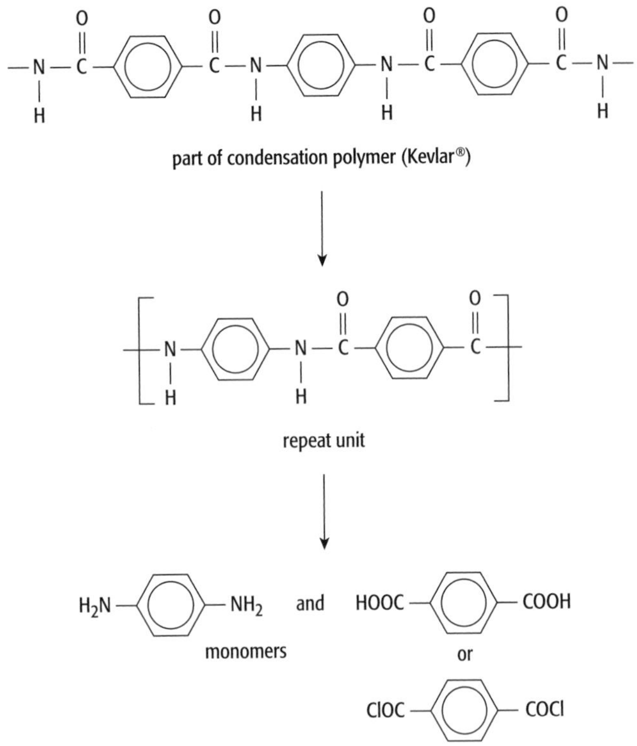

part of condensation polymer (Kevlar®)

repeat unit

monomers

QUESTION

11 a What type of polymerisation reaction formed the polymer shown below?

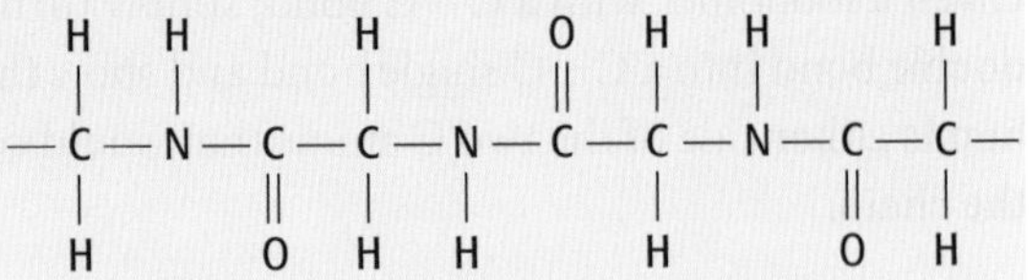

b Draw the displayed formula of the single monomer used to make the polymer shown in part **a**.

Summary

- Polymers are very large molecules that are built up from a very large number of small molecules known as monomers.

- Remember from Chapter 15 that addition polymerisation occurs when an unsaturated monomer, such as an alkene, bonds to itself in an addition reaction. Poly(ethene), poly(chloroethene) and poly(phenylethene) are all addition polymers.

- Condensation polymerisation involves the loss of a small molecule (usually water) in the reaction between two monomer molecules. Both polyesters and polyamides are formed by condensation polymerisation.

- Polyamides are formed by condensation polymerisation between an amine group and a carboxylic acid group. These groups may be in the same monomer or on different monomers. Nylon 6,6

is formed in a condensation polymerisation between 1,6-diaminohexane and hexanedioic acid. Nylon 6 is formed by heating caprolactam, which is produced from 6-aminohexanoic acid in a condensation reaction. The numbers in the name of a particular nylon refer to the number of carbon atoms in the monomers.

- Condensation polymerisation between the amino and carboxylic acid groups in amino acids produces a polypeptide or protein. The amide links in these polymers are known as peptide links (also known as peptide bonds).

- The polyester called Terylene® is formed by condensation polymerisation of benzene-1,4-dicarboxylic acid with ethane-1,2-diol. H_2O is also produced in the reaction.

- There are 20 different amino acids used by cells to build proteins.

- The amino acids found in proteins contain a carboxylic acid, an amino group and a side-chain (represented by R) all attached to the same carbon atom. They have the general formula $NH_2CH(R)COOH$.

- The R groups may be classified as polar or non-polar, and as acidic, basic or neutral.

- The primary structure of a protein chain is the sequence of amino acids in the chain.

- The secondary structure of a protein arises from the folding of the polypeptide backbone into α-helices or β-pleated sheets and their stabilisation by hydrogen bonding between N—H and C=O groups in different peptide bonds.

- The tertiary structure of a protein arises from further folding of the secondary structure and its stabilisation by bonds and intermolecular forces between the R groups (disulfide bonds, ionic bonds, hydrogen bonds and van der Waals' forces).

- The functioning of proteins depends on their three-dimensional structure (which is determined by their amino acid sequence).

- Proteins and polypeptides can be hydrolysed by refluxing in a strong acid, such as HCl(aq), forming 2-amino-carboxylic acids.

- Deoxyribonucleic acid (DNA) is a condensation polymer consisting of:
  - two chains of sugar–phosphate backbone (the sugar is deoxyribose)
  - nitrogen-containing bases attached to each sugar; the bases are adenine (A), guanine (G), cytosine (C) and thymine (T).

- The two sugar–phosphate chains run in opposite directions (they are anti-parallel) with the two chains twisted round each other to form a double helix.

- Pairs of bases (complementary pairs) are stacked at right angles to the long axis of the helix. A always pairs with T and C always pairs with G by hydrogen bonding. This helps stabilise the helix.

- DNA produces new copies of itself during cell division. This is called replication.

- When DNA replicates itself identical copies of the base sequence are produced. After cell division the new DNA molecules consist of one parent DNA strand and one 'new' strand.

- Complementary base pairing is the molecular basis for DNA replication.

- DNA carries the genetic information for the production of proteins. Each gene stores the information for a polypeptide chain.

- Poly(alkene)s are chemically inert and therefore non-biodegradable. The van der Waals' forces between their polymer chains depend on the reaction conditions chosen, which can affect chain length and extent of branching. The longer the polymer chains and the less branching, the stronger the van der Waals' forces – increasing the strength and melting temperature of the plastic.

- Polyesters and polyamides are biodegradable by acid hydrolysis and by the action of light, breaking their ester or amide links between their monomers in the polymer chains.

- Chemists have designed polymers to act as non-solvent-based adhesives, for example epoxy resins and superglues, as well as conducting polymers, for example poly(ethyne) – also known as polyacetylene.

429

End-of-chapter questions

1 a Explain the term **condensation polymer**. [2]

   b Kevlar is a condensation polymer that is used for making bullet-proof vests. Here are two monomers that could be used for making Kevlar:

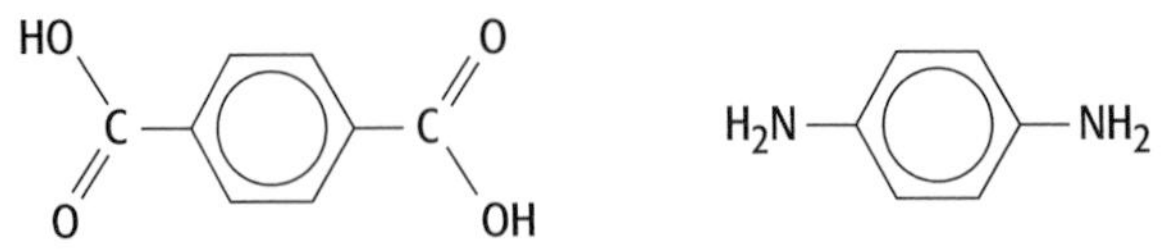

      i Explain the term **monomer**. [1]

      ii Give the structure of Kevlar, showing the repeat unit. [2]

      iii What type of condensation polymer is Kevlar? [1]

   c Explain how the chains of Kevlar are held together to make such a strong material. [3]

                                                         Total = 9

2 a Polyesters are condensation polymers. Give the structures of two monomers that could be used to give a polyester. [2]

   b Give the structure of the polyester formed from these two monomers. [2]

                                                           Total = 4

3 a Glycine is an amino acid with the formula H_2NCH_2COOH.

      i Give the systematic name for glycine. [1]

      ii Give the structure of the polymer that could be formed from glycine, showing at least two repeat units. [2]

      iii Name the linkage between the repeat units. [1]

      iv What type of attractive force forms between the chains of poly(glycine)? [1]

   b 3-hydroxypropanoic acid is capable of forming polymers.

      i Give the structure of 3-hydroxypropanoic acid. [1]

      ii Give the structure of the polymer formed from this acid, showing at least two repeat units. [2]

      iii Name the linkage present in the polymer. [1]

      iv What type of attractive force forms between chains of poly(3-hydroxypropanoic acid)? [1]

                                                       Total = 10

4 Sections of some polymers are shown below. For each polymer:

   i identify the repeat unit

   ii give the structures of the monomers used to make the polymer.

    a

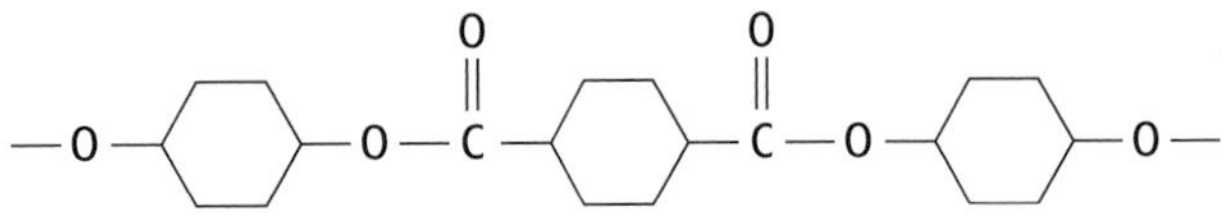

[3]

    b

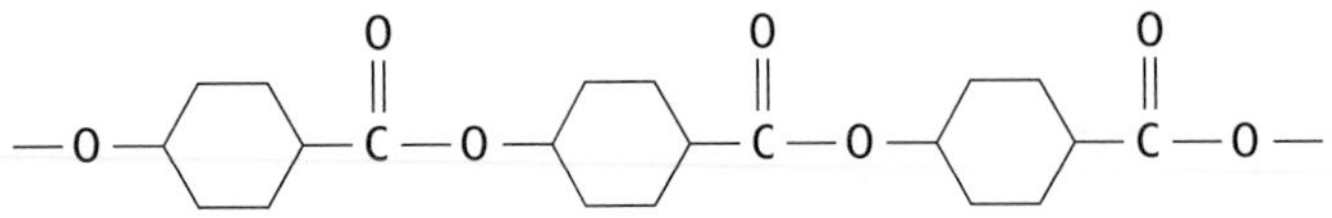

[3]

c

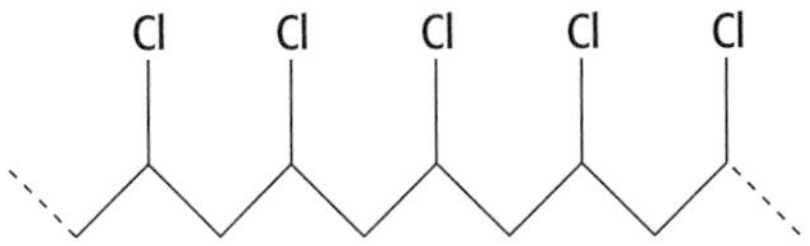

[2]

d

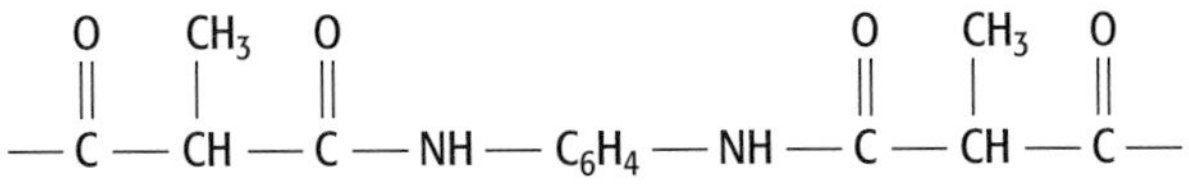

[3]

e

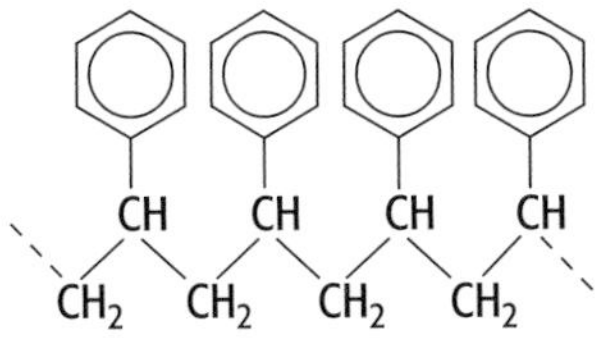

[2]

Total = 13

5 Give the structures of the polymers formed from the monomers given below, showing at least two repeat units. For each polymer identify the following:

i the repeat unit

ii the type of linkage present

iii the attractive force between the polymer chains.

a

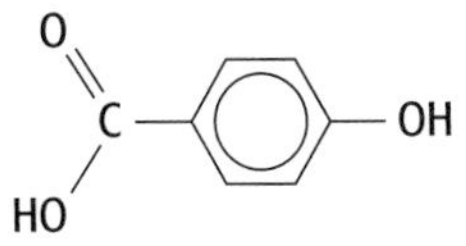

[3]

b

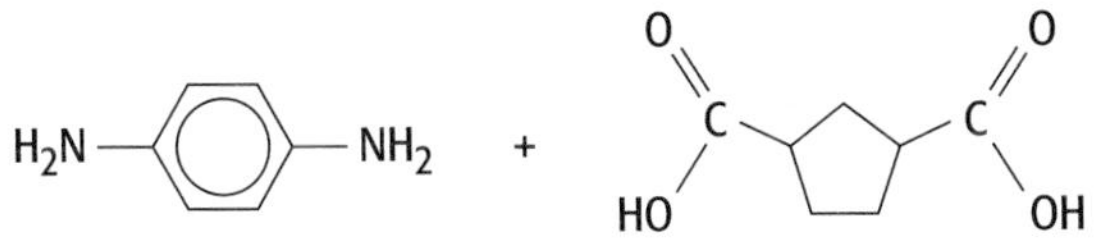

[3]

Total = 6

6 a Explain the term **biodegradable**. [2]

b Explain how the production of biodegradable polymers has lessened the impact of polymers on the environment. [3]

c Poly(L-lactic acid) is a biodegradable polymer. Give two uses of poly(L-lactic acid) and explain how its properties make it suitable for each use. [4]

Total = 9

7 Ribonuclease is an enzyme. Its secondary structure contains both α-helices and β-pleated sheets.

a i Describe the structure of a typical α-helix. [5]

ii Describe the structure of a typical β-pleated sheet. [4]

b The single polypeptide chain of ribonuclease contains four disulfide bridges. Draw the structure of a disulfide bridge. [1]

c Describe how van der Waals' forces between amino acid side-chains help to stabilise the tertiary structure of a protein. In your answer refer to the type of side-chains involved. [3]

Total = 13

8   The structure of DNA is stabilised by hydrogen bonding.
   a   Give the full name of DNA.   [1]
   b   Write the names of the bases A, C, G and T.   [2]
   c   Explain, in terms of intermolecular bonding, how the structure of DNA is stabilised   [6]
   d   Explain the importance of hydrogen bonding of specific base pairs in the replication of DNA.   [6]

Total = 15

9   Three levels of protein structure are primary, secondary and tertiary.
   a   Describe the primary structure of a typical protein containing one polypeptide chain. Name the type of chemical bonding involved in the primary structure of a protein.   [4]
   b   Describe how hydrogen bonding stabilises the α-helical secondary structure of a protein.   [4]
   c   The tertiary structure of a protein is stabilised by interactions between the side-chains of particular amino acids. Describe **four** different types of interactions that maintain the tertiary structure of a protein. For each type of interaction give an explanation of how the attractive forces arise.   [8]

Total = 16

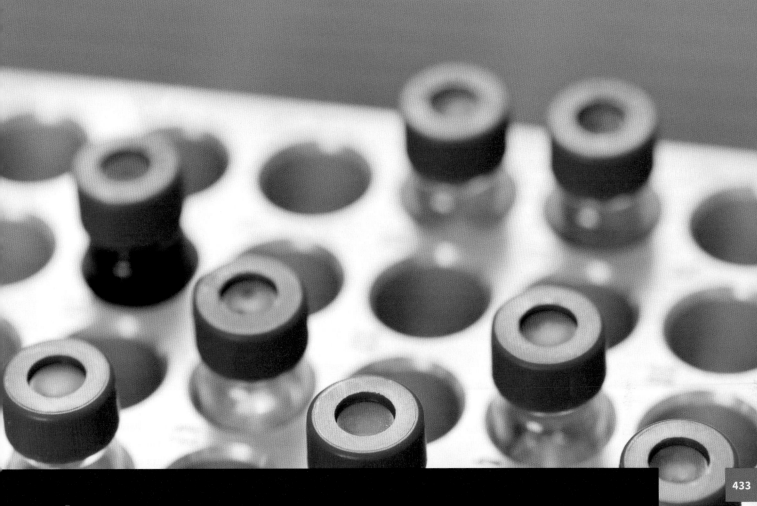

Chapter 29:
Analytical chemistry

Learning outcomes

You should be able to:

- explain and use the terms R_f value in thin-layer chromatography and retention time in gas–liquid chromatography, and interpret gas–liquid chromatograms to find the percentage composition of a mixture
- use a mass spectrum to deduce the molecular mass of an organic molecule, the number of carbon atoms in a compound using the $M + 1$ peak, and the presence of bromine and chlorine atoms in a compound using the $M + 2$ peak
- suggest the identity of molecules formed by simple fragmentation in a given mass spectrum
- analyse a carbon-13 NMR spectrum of a simple molecule to deduce the different environments of the carbon atoms present and the possible structures for the molecule

- predict the number of peaks in a carbon-13 NMR spectrum for a given molecule
- analyse and interpret a proton NMR spectrum of a simple molecule to deduce the different types of proton present, the relative numbers of each type of proton present, the number of non-equivalent protons adjacent to a given proton and the possible structures for the molecule
- predict the chemical shifts and splitting patterns of the protons in a given molecule
- in obtaining an NMR spectrum, describe the use of tetramethylsilane, TMS, as the standard for chemical shift measurements, and the need for deuterated solvents, e.g. $CDCl_3$
- describe the identification of O—H and N—H protons by proton exchange using D_2O.

Introduction

We can detect and identify any chemical substance using a range of different techniques. Specialised instruments have been developed to carry out tests, such as gas-liquid chromatography, nuclear magnetic resonance (NMR) spectroscopy and mass spectrometry. The instruments used are often very sensitive, so chemical substances can be detected at very low concentrations.

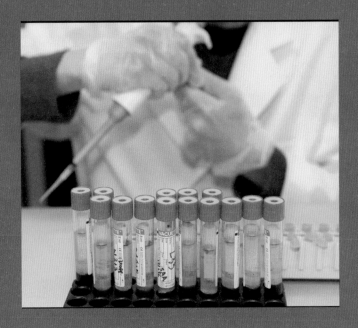

Figure 29.1 Instrumental analysis can quickly detect tiny traces of banned substances in a urine sample taken from an athlete during random testing. These checks are used to monitor many sportspeople around the world and ensure that competition is fair on the sportsfield.

Chromatography

Paper chromatography

You will be familiar with the technique of paper chromatography. It is used to separate mixtures as a solvent moves up a piece of absorbent paper. We call the solvent the **mobile phase**, and water trapped between the cellulose fibres of the paper is the **stationary phase**. The substances in the mixture will have different affinities for the solvent and for the water, and so they move at different rates over the paper (Figure 29.2).

The R_f **values** (retardation factors) of substances are calculated as shown in Figure 29.3. The conditions must be identical to those quoted in the R_f data table, e.g. the same temperature and the same solvent used.

Coloured substances can be seen directly on the paper but others are sprayed with a chemical that forms coloured compounds on the chromatogram. For example, amino acids can be revealed as bluish spots by ninhydrin spray.

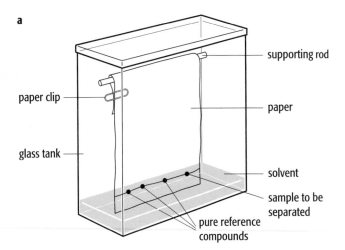

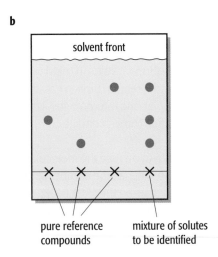

Figure 29.2 a Paper chromatography. **b** The chromatogram produced. Components of the mixture can be identified by comparison with pure reference compounds or by calculating R_f values (see Figure 29.3) and comparing these values with those in tables of data.

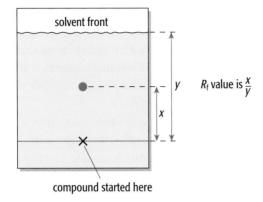

Figure 29.3 How to calculate R_f values, which are then compared with reference values obtained under identical conditions.

Two-way chromatography

Sometimes two or more components in a mixture can have similar R_f values in a particular solvent. This means that their spots on the paper chromatogram will overlap and separation will be poor. This can happen when we hydrolyse a protein and try to identify the amino acid residues present. This is when **two-way chromatography** is useful. In this technique, paper chromatography is carried out as normal but then the chromatogram produced is rotated by 90° and re-run in a different solvent. It is unlikely that the R_f values will coincide in two different solvents, so separation takes place (Figure 29.4).

Making a two-way paper chromatogram

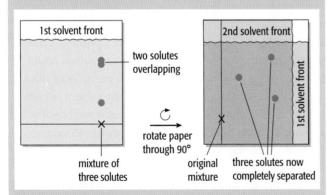

Figure 29.4 Two-way paper chromatography to separate solutes with similar R_f values in a solvent. The technique can also be used with thin-layer chromatography (see page 436).

Partition coefficients in chromatography

The principle of partition of a **solute** between two solvents (see page 319) helps us to understand more fully how the components in a mixture are separated in chromatography.

In paper chromatography the different partition coefficients of the components in a mixture correspond to their relative solubilities in the two solvents. The mobile phase is the solvent chosen. The other solvent is the water trapped in the paper's structure, which is the stationary phase. Figure 29.5 shows solute molecules partitioned between the mobile phase and a stationary liquid phase on a solid support.

The solutes in the mixture being separated are partitioned to different extents between the solvents in the mobile and stationary phases. The greater the relative solubility in the mobile phase, the faster the rate of movement as the mobile phase passes over the stationary phase.

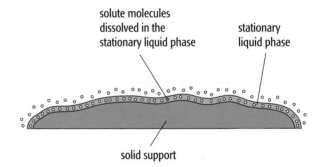

Figure 29.5 Partition chromatography. The mobile phase moves over the stationary liquid phase, carrying solute particles with it. The filter paper is the solid support in paper chromatography.

QUESTION

1 Look at this paper chromatogram:

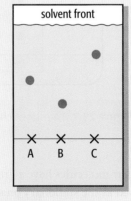

a The solvent used was ethanol. Which sample of ink, A, B or C, has the greatest relative solubility in ethanol?

b Work out the R_f value of the ink whose partition coefficient in ethanol and water lies between the values of the other two inks.

435

Thin-layer chromatography

In thin-layer chromatography, referred to as **TLC**, the stationary phase is a solid that adsorbs solute molecules onto its surface (Figure 29.6).

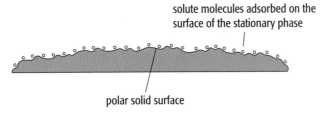

solute molecules adsorbed on the surface of the stationary phase

polar solid surface

Figure 29.6 Adsorption chromatography. The mobile phase moves over the stationary solid phase.

The solid stationary phase is usually alumina (Al_2O_3) or silica (SiO_2), which is made into a slurry with water and spread onto a microscope slide. This is then put into an oven, where it dries out into a solid white coating on the glass. A chromatogram is then made in a similar way to paper chromatography (Figure 29.7).

Making a thin-layer chromatogram

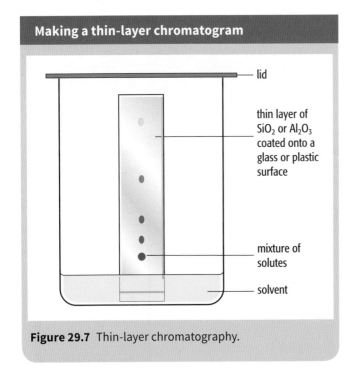

lid

thin layer of SiO_2 or Al_2O_3 coated onto a glass or plastic surface

mixture of solutes

solvent

Figure 29.7 Thin-layer chromatography.

Polar molecules have a greater attraction for a polar solid used as the stationary phase, and they are adsorbed more strongly onto its surface. Therefore they travel more slowly up the thin layer of alumina or silica, and separation occurs. Solutes are located on the chromatogram and identified by comparing with standard known substances or by calculating R_f values.

Note that although TLC is normally described as adsorption chromatography, some partitioning does occur if water is present. Both dried alumina and silica can become rehydrated. When this happens, water also acts as a partitioning stationary phase together with the adsorbing stationary solid phase.

TLC is quicker than paper chromatography and can be used on smaller samples, making it useful in forensic science, where it can be used to identify drugs and explosive residues. For example, TLC is used for the analysis of a substance that is suspected to be cannabis. The stationary phase is silica sprayed with silver nitrate solution, which is then dried. The mobile phase is methylbenzene.

QUESTION

2 a TLC can separate mixtures of components. What do we call the mechanism of separation usually at work in TLC?

  b A mixture of propanone and hexane was separated on a TLC chromatogram using alumina as the stationary phase and methylbenzene as the solvent. Which substance would you expect to rise further up the chromatogram? Explain why.

High-performance liquid chromatography

High-performance liquid chromatography, referred to as **HPLC**, uses partitioning to separate and identify the components in a mixture. The stationary phase is a non-volatile liquid, such as a long-chain hydrocarbon liquid, bonded onto a solid support, e.g. small particles of silica. This is packed tightly into a column. The solvent chosen for the mobile phase is usually polar, e.g. a methanol/water solvent. This has to be forced under pressure through the densely packed column where separation occurs (Figure 29.8).

The tiny solid particles in the column have a very large surface area over which partitioning can occur, resulting in excellent separation. The more polar components in the mixture have a greater relative solubility in the polar solvent. Therefore they are carried through the column faster than components whose molecules are more non-polar (which dissolve better in the non-polar stationary phase in the column). The detector records **retention times**, i.e. how long it takes each component to pass

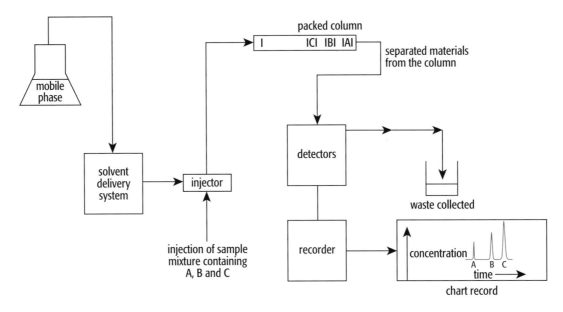

Figure 29.8 High-performance liquid chromatography.

through the column. The area under each peak recorded is proportional to the amount of solute emerging from the column (Figure 29.9).

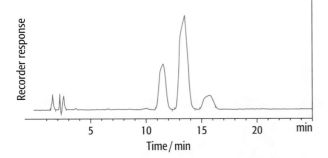

Figure 29.9 The chromatogram from a vitamin E HPLC analysis carried out by a food scientist investigating chilli peppers.

HPLC is used:

- in medical research to separate peptides and proteins
- to analyse urine samples from athletes for banned substances such as steroids or stimulants
- for monitoring pollutants in the atmosphere and in rivers, e.g. measuring levels of pesticides
- by food standards agencies to check the accuracy of the data on food labels.

Gas–liquid chromatography

Gas–liquid chromatography, which is referred to as **GLC**, is similar to HPLC but a gaseous sample enters the column. The column contains the stationary phase and the sample is moved through by an inert carrier gas. This method is used with gases, liquids and volatile solids (as they must be in the form of a vapour). The apparatus is shown in Figure 29.10.

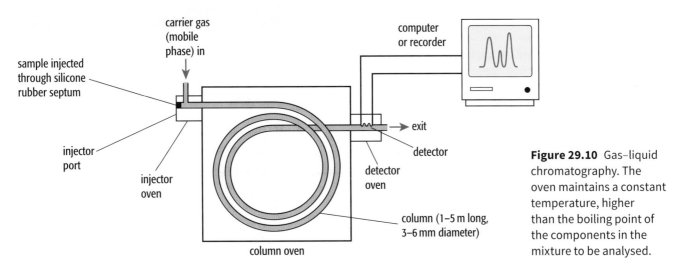

Figure 29.10 Gas–liquid chromatography. The oven maintains a constant temperature, higher than the boiling point of the components in the mixture to be analysed.

As in all chromatography, the conditions must be controlled in order to make comparisons with published databases. The chromatogram must be obtained using the same carrier gas, flow rate, stationary phase and temperature that were used when the standard data was obtained. Figure 29.11 shows a chromatogram obtained using GLC.

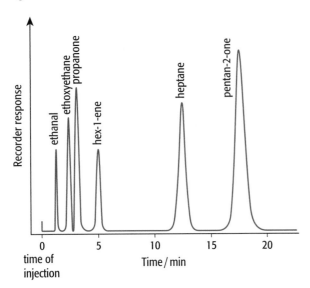

Figure 29.11 A gas chromatogram from a mixture of volatile organic compounds.

Analysis by gas–liquid chromatography does have some limitations. For example, similar compounds will have similar retention times and if a newly discovered compound is detected it will not have a match in the computer's database of retention times.

Determination of the percentage composition of a mixture by GLC

For quantitative analysis, the component peaks are first identified and then the area of each is measured. The peaks are roughly triangular in shape so their area is approximately:

$\frac{1}{2} \times$ base $\times$ height (i.e. the area of a triangle)

The GLC machine usually measures the area of the peak automatically and can print the results with the chromatogram. If the peaks are very narrow or have similar base widths, then peak height may be used instead of peak area to estimate the proportion of components in a mixture.

For this method:

- the chromatogram must show peaks for all the components in the mixture
- all the components of the mixture must be separated
- the detector must respond equally to the different components so that peak area is directly proportional to the component concentration.

The amount of each component in a mixture is found by expressing it as a percentage of the sum of the areas under all the peaks. For example, for a mixture of three esters A, B and C:

(approx.) % of ester A

$$= \frac{\text{peak area (or height) of A}}{\text{sum of the areas (or heights) of A, B and C}} \times 100$$

GLC is used in testing for steroids in competing athletes and for testing the fuels used in Formula One motor racing (Figure 29.12). It is also used for medical diagnosis in analysing blood samples. With GLC it is possible to determine the percentages of dissolved oxygen, nitrogen, carbon dioxide and carbon monoxide in blood samples as small as $1.0\,cm^3$. GLC is often combined with mass spectrometry (see later in this chapter) to separate then rapidly identify the components of a mixture.

Figure 29.12 GLC is used to check that the components in the fuel used in Grand Prix cars conform to strict regulations.

QUESTION

3 a For GLC separations explain:

  i   how retention time is measured

  ii how the areas under the component peaks are used.

  b What can you use as an approximate measure of the proportion of a component in a mixture from a GLC chromatogram which produces sharp peaks?

Proton (^{1}H) nuclear magnetic resonance

How NMR works

Nuclear magnetic resonance (**NMR**) spectroscopy is a widely used analytical technique for organic compounds. NMR is based on the fact that the nucleus of each hydrogen atom in an organic molecule behaves like a tiny magnet. The nucleus of a hydrogen atom consists of a single proton. This proton can spin. The spinning motion of the positively charged proton causes a very small magnetic field to be set up.

In NMR we put the sample to be analysed in a magnetic field. The hydrogen nuclei (protons) either line up with the field or, by spinning in the opposite direction, line up against it (Figure 29.13).

There is a tiny difference in energy between the oppositely spinning ^{1}H nuclei. This difference corresponds to the energy carried by waves in the radiowave range of the electromagnetic radiation spectrum. In NMR spectroscopy the nuclei 'flip' between the two energy levels (Figure 29.14). Only atoms whose mass number is an odd number, e.g. ^{1}H or ^{13}C, absorb energy in the range of frequencies that are analysed.

The size of the gap between the nuclear energy levels varies slightly, depending on the other atoms in the molecule (the molecular environment). Therefore, NMR can be used to identify ^{1}H atoms in different parts of a molecule. This is easier to visualise by looking at an example. If we look at a molecule of methanol, CH_3OH, we can see that there are ^{1}H atoms in two different molecular environments. We have the ^{1}H atoms in the $—CH_3$ group and the ^{1}H atom in the $—OH$ group. The energy absorbed by the $—CH_3$ ^{1}H atoms is different from the energy absorbed by the ^{1}H atoms in $—OH$.

In NMR spectroscopy, we vary the magnetic field as that is easier than varying the wavelength of radiowaves. As the magnetic field is varied, the ^{1}H nuclei in different

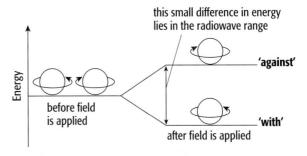

Figure 29.14 Hydrogen (^{1}H) nuclei will absorb energy in the radiowave range when they 'flip' from the lower energy level, lining up with the applied magnetic field, to the higher energy level, lining up against it.

molecular environments flip at different field strengths. The different field strengths are measured relative to a reference compound, which is given a value of zero. The standard compound chosen is tetramethylsilane (**TMS**). TMS is an inert, volatile liquid that mixes well with most organic compounds. Its formula is $Si(CH_3)_4$, so all its H atoms are equivalent (i.e. they are all in the same molecular environment). TMS only gives one, sharp absorption, called a peak, and this peak is at a higher frequency than most other protons (Figure 29.15). All other absorptions are measured by their shift away from the TMS line on the NMR spectrum. This is called the chemical shift (δ), and is measured in units of parts per million (ppm).

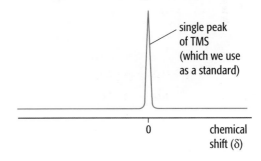

Figure 29.15 The standard TMS peak used as a reference on NMR spectra.

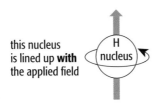

Figure 29.13 Hydrogen (^{1}H) nuclei will line up with or against an applied magnetic field.

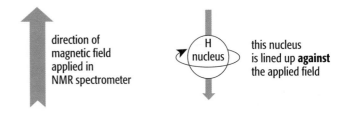

439

4 a Explain why tetramethylsilane (TMS) is used as a standard in NMR spectroscopy.

b In NMR we use solvents such as tetrachloromethane to prepare samples for the machine (Figure 29.16).

Figure 29.16 Samples dissolved in a solvent in narrow tubes ready for NMR analysis.

i What is the molecular formula of tetrachloromethane?

ii Why do you think tetrachloromethane is used as a solvent?

iii Solvents that contain deuterium, D, are also used as solvents in NMR. Deuterium is the isotope ^2H. A substance in which ^1H is replaced by ^2H is said to be deuterated. Why would the deuterated solvent $CDCl_3$ be used instead of $CHCl_3$?

Low-resolution NMR

A low-resolution NMR spectrum shows a single peak for each non-equivalent hydrogen atom; an example is shown in Figure 29.17.

Note how the zero point on the x-axis, chemical shift (δ), is on the right of the spectrum and the shift increases in value going left.

There are three peaks on ethanol's low-resolution NMR spectrum. These correspond to the ^1H atoms in $-OH$, $-CH_2-$ and $-CH_3$. Note how the heights of the peaks vary. The area under each peak tells us the relative number of equivalent ^1H atoms responsible for that particular chemical shift. The largest peak will be from the $-CH_3$ hydrogen atoms, the middle peak from the $-CH_2-$ hydrogen atoms and the smallest peak from the $-OH$ hydrogen. The relative areas under the peaks are shown on the NMR spectrum by the labels 1H, 2H and 3H (Figure 29.17).

The type of H atom present can be checked against tables of data (Table 29.1) if you are using NMR to identify unknown organic compounds.

Using Table 29.1 we can see that the peak at about 1.2 ppm is caused by the $-CH_3$ hydrogen atoms (range 0.7–1.6 ppm), the peak at about 3.7 ppm corresponds to $-CH_2-$ hydrogen atoms (range 3.3–4.3 ppm) and the peak at about 5.4 ppm is due to the $-OH$ hydrogen atom.

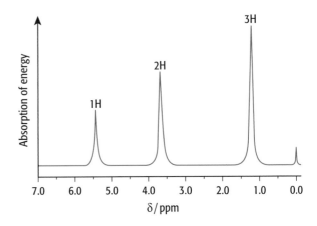

Figure 29.17 The low-resolution NMR spectrum of ethanol, CH_3CH_2OH.

Table 29.1 ^{1}H NMR chemical shifts relative to TMS. Chemical shifts are typical values that can vary slightly depending on the solvent, concentration and substituents. $^{(a)}$OH and NH chemical shifts are very variable (sometimes outside these limits and are often broad. Signals are not usually seen as split peaks).

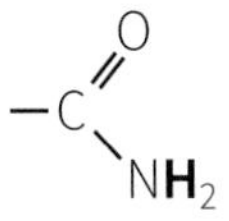

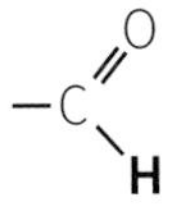

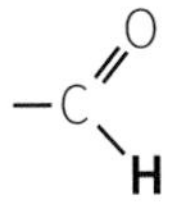

Type of proton	Chemical shift, δ / ppm
R—CH$_3$	0.7–1.6
N—H R—OH	1.0–5.5$^{(a)}$
R—CH$_2$—R	1.2–1.4
R$_3$CH	1.6–2.0
H$_3$C—C(=O) RCH$_2$—C(=O) R$_2$CH—C(=O)	2.0–2.9
C$_6$H$_5$—CH$_3$ C$_6$H$_5$—CH$_2$R C$_6$H$_5$—CHR$_2$	2.3–2.7
N—CH$_3$ N—CH$_2$R N—CHR$_2$	2.3–2.9
O—CH$_3$ O—CH$_2$R O—CHR$_2$	3.3–4.3
Br or Cl—CH$_3$ Br or Cl—CH$_2$R Br or Cl—CHR$_2$	3.0–4.2
C$_6$H$_5$—OH	4.5–10.0$^{(a)}$
—CH=CH—	45.–6.0
—C(=O)NH$_2$ —C(=O)NH—	5.0–12.0$^{(a)}$
C$_6$H$_5$—H	6.5–8.0
—C(=O)H	9.0–10
—C(=O)H	11.0–12.0$^{(a)}$

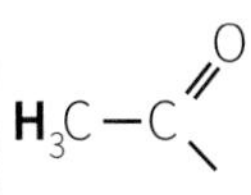

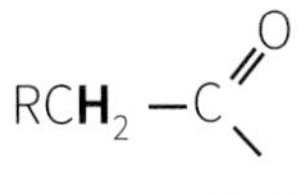

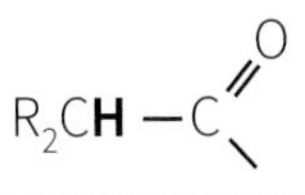

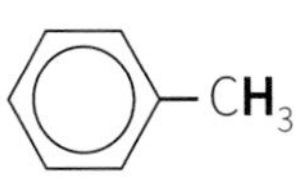

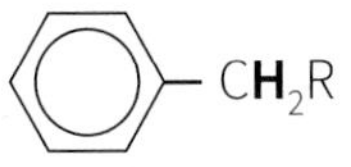

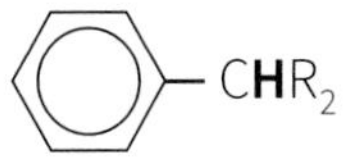

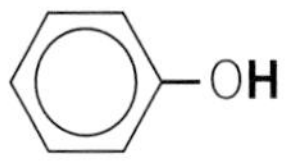

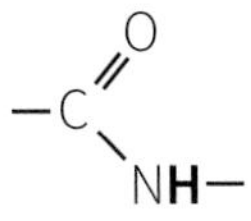

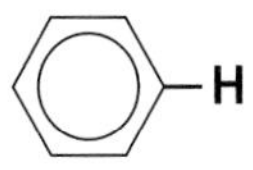

QUESTION

5 Predict the number of peaks and the relative areas under each peak, where appropriate, on the low-resolution proton NMR spectrum of:

a methanol, CH$_3$OH
b benzene, C$_6$H$_6$
c chloroethane, C$_2$H$_5$Cl
d propan-1-ol
e propan-2-ol
f propanone.

High-resolution NMR

As you can see in Table 29.1, the chemical shifts are given over ranges, and the ranges for different types of hydrogen atoms do overlap. In some molecules where there is heavy shielding of the hydrogen nuclei by lots of electrons in surrounding atoms, peaks are shifted beyond their usual range. In such cases high-resolution NMR is useful. High-resolution NMR gives us more information to interpret. Peaks that appear as one 'signal' on a low-resolution NMR spectrum are often revealed to be made up of a cluster of closely grouped peaks. This is because the magnetic fields generated by spinning nuclei interfere slightly with those of neighbouring nuclei.

This interference is called spin–spin coupling. The exact **splitting pattern** of a peak depends on the number of hydrogen atoms on the adjacent carbon atom or atoms.

> The number of signals a peak splits into equals $n + 1$ where n is the number of ^1H atoms on the adjacent carbon atom.

The high-resolution NMR spectrum of ethanol illustrates this $n + 1$ rule used to interpret splitting patterns (Figure 29.18).

■ The —CH_3 peak is split into three because there are two ^1H atoms on the adjacent CH_2 group. $n + 1 = 3$ (as $n = 2$); this is called a triplet.

■ The —CH_2— peak is split into four because there are three ^1H atoms on the adjacent —CH_3 group. $n + 1 = 4$ (as $n = 3$); this is called a quartet.

■ The —OH peak is not usually split as its ^1H atom is constantly being exchanged with the ^1H atoms of other ethanol molecules and any water present. This results in one average peak being produced.

Table 29.2 shows the relative intensities and distribution of the splitting patterns you are likely to meet.

Figure 29.19 shows another high-resolution NMR spectrum. You should try to interpret it by following these steps:

Step 1 Use δ values to identify the environment of the equivalent protons (^1H atoms) present at each peak (remembering the peak at zero is the TMS standard reference peak).

Step 2 Look at the relative areas under each peak to determine how many of each type of non-equivalent protons (^1H atoms) are present.

Step 3 Apply the $n + 1$ rule to the splitting patterns to see which protons (^1H atoms) are on adjacent carbon atoms in the unknown molecule.

Step 4 Put all this information together to identify the unknown molecule.

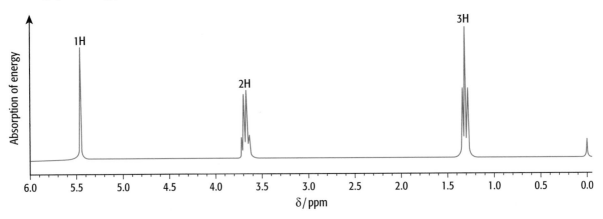

Figure 29.18 The high-resolution NMR spectrum of ethanol, showing the splitting pattern in two of the peaks. The area under each series of peaks still represents the number of equivalent ^1H atoms in the molecule, as in low-resolution NMR.

Number of adjacent ^1H atoms	Using the $n + 1$ rule, the peak will be split into ...	Relative intensities in the splitting pattern	Observed on the NMR spectrum as ...
0	1 peak, called a singlet	1	
1	2 peaks, called a doublet	1:1	
2	3 peaks, called a triplet	1:2:1	
3	4 peaks, called a quartet	1:3:3:1	

Table 29.2 Splitting patterns in high-resolution NMR spectra.

WORKED EXAMPLE

1   An ester is used as a solvent in a glue. A chemist was given a sample of the ester to analyse. The NMR spectrum of the ester is shown in Figure 29.19.

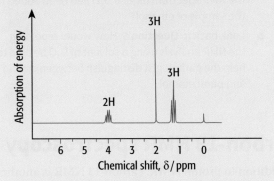

Figure 29.19 The high-resolution NMR spectrum of an unknown ester in a glue.

Step 1   Identify possibilities for the three major peaks that appear at chemical shifts of 1.3, 1.9 and 4.1 ppm. Using Table 29.1, these could be:

1.3 ppm $R—CH_3$, $R—CH_2—R$

1.9 ppm R_3CH (possibly $H_3C—CO—$, $RCH_2CO—$ or $R_2CH—CO—$)

4.1 ppm $—O—CH_3$, $O—CH_2R$, $O—CHR_2$

Step 2   Use the relative numbers of each type of proton (^1H atom) labelling each major peak to narrow down possibilities.

1.3 ppm   labelled 3H, so could be $R—CH_3$

1.9 ppm   labelled 3H, so could be $H_3C—CO—$

4.1 ppm   labelled 2H, so could be $O—CH_2R$

Step 3   By applying the $n+1$ rule to the splitting patterns we can see which protons (^1H atoms) are on adjacent carbon atoms.

1.3 ppm   labelled 3H and split into triplet, so $R—CH_3$ would be next to a C atom bonded to two ^1H atoms ($2+1=3$, triplet).

1.9 ppm   labelled 3H and a singlet, so $H_3C—CO—$ would be next to a C atom with no ^1H atoms attached ($0+1=1$, singlet). It could well be next to the C—O, with the carbonyl carbon also bonded to an O atom, as in an ester, i.e. $H_3C—COOR$.

4.1 ppm   labelled 2H and split into quartet, $O—CH_2R$ would be next to a C atom bonded to three ^1H atoms ($3+1=4$, quartet).

Step 4   Putting this information together we get the ester ethyl ethanoate, $CH_3COOCH_2CH_3$.

QUESTION

6   A pathologist was given a sample of a white tablet found at the scene of a suicide. In order to complete her report the pathologist received an NMR spectrum of the sample (Figure 29.20a) and information from the police that the tablets involved were either aspirin or paracetamol. The displayed formulae of both drugs are also shown in Figure 29.20b.

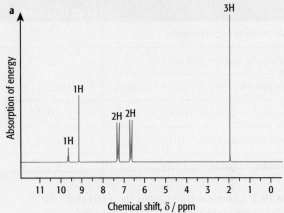

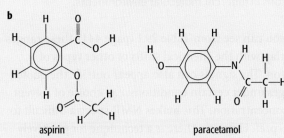

Figure 29.20 a NMR analysis of the unknown drug sample. **b** Aspirin and paracetamol.

a   Using this information, which drug was in the white tablet? Explain your answer.

b   Sketch the NMR spectrum you would expect to see if the other drug had undergone NMR analysis. Label each peak with its relative area and the type of proton that caused it.

Identifying the —OH or —NH— signal in an NMR spectrum

The —OH signal in the high-resolution NMR spectrum of ethanol appears as a single peak. As we have seen on page 442, the peak is not split by the ^1H atoms (protons) on the neighbouring —CH_2— group. The reason for this is that the —OH proton exchanges very rapidly with protons in any traces of water (or acid) present, as follows:

$$CH_3CH_2OH + H_2O \rightleftharpoons CH_3CH_2OH + HOH$$

443

The hydrogen atoms involved in this reversible proton exchange have been coloured red and blue. The exchange takes place so rapidly that the signal for the —OH protons becomes a single peak. This exchange also happens in amines and amides which contain the —NH— group.

Table 29.3 shows the chemical shift ranges for the different —OH and —NH— signals.

Different OH and NH protons	Range of chemical shift (δ) / ppm
in alcohols, R—OH protons	1.0–5.5
in phenols, arene—OH protons	6.5–7.0
in carboxylic acids, R—COOH protons	11.0–11.7
in amines, —NH_2 / —NH—	1.0–5.5
in aryl amines, arene—NH_2	3.0–6.0
in amides, —$CONH_2$—, —CONH—	5.0–12.0

Table 29.3 Chemical shift ranges for —OH and —NH— protons in different molecular environments.

As you can see from Table 29.1 (page 441), these ranges overlap with the chemical shifts of other types of proton. The signals can also appear outside the quoted ranges under certain conditions, e.g. choice of solvent or concentration. This makes NMR spectra difficult to interpret. However, there is a technique for positively identifying —OH or —NH— groups in a molecule. Their peaks 'disappear' from the spectra if you add a small amount of deuterium oxide, D_2O, to the sample. The deuterium atoms (^2H) in D_2O, called 'heavy water', exchange reversibly with the protons in the —OH or —NH— groups. For example:

$$\text{—OH} + D_2O \rightleftharpoons \text{—OD} + HOD$$

$$\text{—NH—CO—} + D_2O \rightleftharpoons \text{—ND—CO—} + HOD$$

The deuterium atoms do not absorb in the same region of the electromagnetic spectrum as protons (^1H atoms). This makes the —OH or NH signal disappear from the NMR spectrum. By checking against the peaks in the original NMR spectrum, without D_2O, we can tell if the —OH or —NH— groups are present in the sample. The ^1H atom in the —OH or —NH— group is referred to as a 'labile' proton.

QUESTION

7 a Look back to Figure 29.18 on page 442. The high-resolution NMR spectrum shown is from a sample of ethanol containing traces of water. How would the NMR spectrum differ if D_2O had been added to the sample of ethanol?

  b Look back to **Question 6**. How would repeating the NMR analysis using a solvent of D_2O be able to help the pathologist distinguish between aspirin and paracetamol?

Carbon-13 NMR spectroscopy

In addition to proton NMR. carbon-13 NMR is another analytical tool used frequently by organic chemists. The vast majority of carbon atoms in any organic compound will be the carbon-12 isotope. This isotope has an even mass number (12). Therefore it has no signal on an NMR spectrum, as NMR only works with atoms with an odd mass number (such as ^1H, as we have already seen). However, about 1% of the carbon atoms in any sample of an organic compound will be the carbon-13 isotope. Its nuclei will interact with the magnetic field applied in NMR analysis so can produce a NMR spectrum.

Carbon-13 NMR produces a spectrum with different chemical shifts for non-equivalent carbon atoms in a molecule. Typical carbon-13 NMR shifts are shown in Table 29.4. As in proton NMR, the chemical shifts are measured with reference to the TMS peak at 0 ppm on the spectrum (see page 439).

Analysis of carbon-13 NMR spectra is similar to that of proton NMR, looking to match different chemical shifts to characteristic molecular environments. However, the signals produced in carbon-13 NMR appear as discrete vertical lines on the spectra (without the complication of the splitting patterns caused by the protons in ^1H atoms within the molecules). Take care in interpreting the carbon-13 NMR spectra because the heights of the lines are **not** usually proportional to the number of equivalent ^{13}C atoms present.

The solvent used to prepare samples for ^{13}C NMR analysis is $CDCl_3$. This accounts for the small signal near 80 ppm that can be ignored when interpreting a spectrum, as it is caused by the atoms of ^{13}C in the solvent molecules.

Hybridisation of carbon atom	Environment of carbon atom	Example structures	Chemical / ppm shift range (δ)
sp³	alkyl	CH_3-, CH_2-, $-CH-$	0–50
sp³	next to alkene/arene	$-CH_2-C=C$, $-CH_2-$⬡	10–40
sp³	next to carbonyl/carboxyl	$-CH_2-COR$, $-CH_2-CO_2R$	25–50
sp³	next to nitrogen	$-CH_2-NH_2$, $-CH_2-NR_2$, $-CH_2-NHCO$	30–65
sp³	next to chlorine ($-CH_2-Br$ and $-CH_2-I$ are in the same range as alkyl)	$-CH_2-Cl$	30–60
sp³	next to oxygen	$-CH_2-OH$, $-CH_2-O-CO-$	50–70
sp²	alkene or arene	$-C=C-$, (benzene ring of C)	110–160
sp²	carboxyl	$R-CO_2H$, $R-CO_2R$	160–185
sp²	carbonyl	$R-CHO$, $R-CO-R$	190–220
sp	alkyne	$R-C\equiv C-$	65–85
sp	nitrile	$R-C\equiv N$	100–125

Table 29.4 Typical ^{13}C chemical shift values (δ) relative to TMS = 0. Note that chemical shifts are typical values and can vary slightly depending on the solvent, the concentration and substituents present.

445

Figure 29.21 shows the ^{13}C NMR spectrum for propanone, $(CH_3)_2CO$.

Note that there are only two peaks: one for the carbon atom in the carbonyl group, C=O, and the other for the carbon atoms in the methyl groups, $-CH_3$. Although there are two $-CH_3$ groups in propanone, they are both equivalent and so appear as only a single peak (just as equivalent H atoms do in proton NMR).

Figure 29.22 shows another example of a carbon-13 NMR spectrum, that of ethylbenzene, $C_6H_5CH_2CH_3$.

The carbon atoms in the benzene ring are almost equivalent but will be affected to slightly different extents by the presence of the ethyl group in the molecule. Hence the series of lines clustered near 125 ppm.

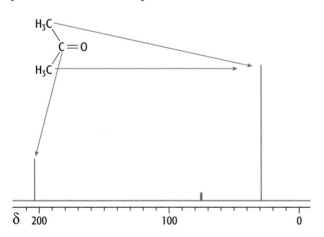

Figure 29.21 The carbon-13 NMR spectrum of propanone.

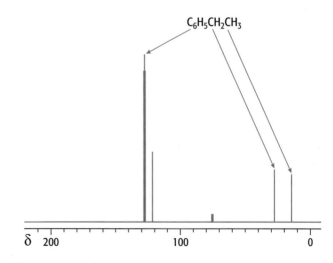

Figure 29.22 The carbon-13 NMR spectrum of ethylbenzene.

QUESTION

8   **a**   Look at the series of lines clustered at about 125 ppm in Figure 29.22.

   i   One line is separated slightly from the main cluster – explain which carbon atom in ethylbenzene is most likely to have produced that signal.

   ii   Predict how many lines make up the tightly clustered grouping of the tallest line on the ^{13}C spectrum and explain your reasoning.

   b   Predict the number and location of signal lines in the carbon-13 NMR spectrum of benzene, C_6H_6.

   c   Explain the number of signal peaks you would expect to see in the carbon-13 NMR spectrum of:

   i   propan-1-ol

   ii   propan-2-ol.

Mass spectrometry

You have already seen how a mass spectrometer works (see page X). The mass spectrum of an element can be used to measure relative isotopic masses and their relative abundances. This information is used to calculate relative atomic masses. However, the main use of mass spectrometry is in the identification of organic compounds. As in other forms of spectroscopy, a substance can be identified by matching its spectrum against the spectra of known substances stored in a database. This technique is known as 'fingerprinting'.

In a mass spectrometer the sample is first vaporised. When vapour from the sample enters the machine it is bombarded by high-energy electrons. This knocks electrons from the molecules and breaks covalent bonds, fragmenting the molecule. Figure 29.23 shows the mass spectrum produced by propanone.

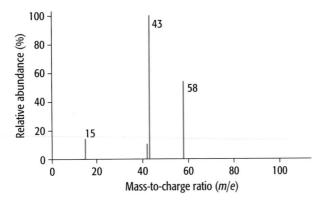

Figure 29.23 The mass spectrum of propanone.

The peak at the highest mass-to-charge ratio is caused by the **molecular ion (M⁺)**. This ion is formed by the sample molecule with one electron knocked out. It gives us the relative molecular mass of the sample. We can assume the ions detected carry a single positive charge, so the reading on the horizontal axis gives us the mass. In the case of propanone, CH_3COCH_3, the molecular ion has a relative mass of 58.0. This corresponds to $CH_3COCH_3^+$, with a mass of $(3 \times 12.0) + (1 \times 16.0) + (6 \times 1.0)$.

We also get large peaks at 15 and 43 on the mass spectrum. These peaks are due to fragments that are produced when propanone molecules are broken apart by the electron bombardment. Knowing the structure of propanone we should be able to identify the fragment responsible for each peak (Figure 29.24).

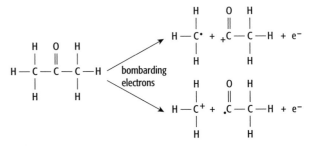

Figure 29.24 The fragmentation of propanone: $^+CH_3$ causes the peak at 15 and CH_3C^+O causes the peak at 43.

The electron bombardment has caused the C—C single bonds in the propanone molecules to break. This has resulted in the fragments at m/e 15 and 43 that are observed in Figure 29.22. The breaking of single bonds, such as C—C, C—O or C—N, is the most common cause of **fragmentation**.

QUESTION

9   Look at Figure 29.25 on page 447, which shows the mass spectrum of ethanol, C_2H_5OH. A structural isomer of ethanol is methoxymethane, an ether with the formula CH_3OCH_3.

   a   Predict the mass-to-charge ratio of a fragment that would appear on the mass spectrum of methoxymethane but does not appear on ethanol's mass spectrum.

   b   Give the formula of the ion responsible for the peak in your answer to part **a**.

QUESTION (CONTINUED)

c Look at the mass spectrum of ethanoic acid:

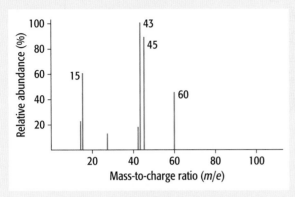

Identify the fragments with mass-to-charge ratios of:

i 15   **iii** 45

ii 43   **iv** 60.

High-resolution mass spectra

High-resolution mass spectrometers can distinguish between ions that appear to have the same mass on a low-resolution mass spectrum. Table 29.5 shows the accurate relative isotopic masses of the most common atoms found in organic molecules.

Isotope	Relative isotopic mass
^1H	1.007 824 6
^{12}C	12.000 000 0 (by definition)
^{14}N	14.003 073 8
^{16}O	15.994 914 1

Table 29.5 Accurate masses of isotopes.

These accurate isotopic masses enable us to measure the mass of the molecular ion so accurately that it can only correspond to one possible molecular formula. For example, a molecular ion peak at 45 could be caused by C_2H_7N or CH_3NO. However, a high-resolution mass spectrum would show the $C_2H_7N^+$ peak at 45.057 846 and the CH_3NO^+ peak at 45.021 462. We can, therefore, be sure which molecule is being analysed.

Using the [M + 1] peak

There will always be a very small peak just beyond the molecular ion peak at a mass of [M + 1]. This is caused by molecules in which one of the carbon atoms is the ^{13}C isotope. This is shown in the mass spectrum of ethanol in Figure 29.25.

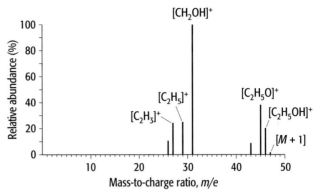

Figure 29.25 The mass spectrum of ethanol, showing the [M + 1] peak.

In any organic compound there will be 1.10% carbon-13. We can use this fact to work out the number of carbon atoms (n) in a molecule. We apply the equation:

$$n = \frac{100}{1.1} \times \frac{\text{abundance of } [M + 1]^+ \text{ ion}}{\text{abundance of } M^+ \text{ ion}}$$

WORKED EXAMPLE

2 An unknown compound has a molecular ion peak, M^+, with a relative abundance of 54.5% and has an $[M + 1]^+$ peak with a relative abundance of 3.6%. How many carbon atoms does the unknown compound contain?

Substituting the values of relative abundance into the equation:

$$n = \frac{100}{1.1} \times \frac{\text{abundance of } [M + 1]^+ \text{ ion}}{\text{abundance of } M^+ \text{ ion}}$$

we get:

$$n = \frac{100}{1.1} \times \frac{3.6}{54.5} = 6.0$$

There are **6 carbon atoms** in each molecule.

QUESTION

10 A hydrocarbon has a molecular ion peak at a mass-to-charge ratio of 84 (relative abundance of 62.0%) and an [M + 1] peak with a relative abundance of 4.1%.

a How many carbon atoms are in the hydrocarbon?

b What is its molecular formula?

c The hydrocarbon does not decolourise bromine water. Name the hydrocarbon.

447

Using [M + 2] and [M + 4] peaks

If the sample compound contains chlorine or bromine atoms, we also get peaks beyond the molecular ion peak because of isotopes of chlorine and bromine. Chlorine has two isotopes, ^{35}Cl and ^{37}Cl, as does bromine, ^{79}Br and ^{81}Br. Table 29.6 shows the approximate percentage of each isotope in naturally occurring samples.

Isotopes	Approximate %
^{35}Cl	75
^{37}Cl	25
^{79}Br	50
^{81}Br	50

Table 29.6 Naturally occurring isotopes of chlorine and bromine.

One Cl or Br atom per molecule

Imagine a sample of chloromethane, CH_3Cl. We will have molecules of $CH_3{}^{35}Cl$ (75%) and molecules of $CH_3{}^{37}Cl$ (25%). The molecular ion will be $CH_3{}^{35}Cl^+$, and two units beyond that on the mass spectrum will be the peak for $CH_3{}^{37}Cl^+$. The peak for $CH_3{}^{37}Cl^+$ will be one-third the height of the molecular ion. This is the [M + 2] peak.

In the mass spectrum of bromomethane, CH_3Br, we will have two molecular ion peaks of approximately the same height – one for $CH_3{}^{79}Br^+$ and the other for $CH_3{}^{81}Br^+$ (the [M + 2] peak).

You should look out for the relative heights mentioned here when interpreting mass spectra.

■ if the [M + 2] peak is one-third the height of the M peak, this suggests the presence of one chlorine atom per molecule
■ if the [M + 2] peak is the same as the height of the M peak, this suggests the presence of one bromine atom per molecule.

An example of the [M + 2] peak is shown on the mass spectrum of chlorobenzene (Figure 29.26).

Two Cl or Br atoms per molecule

The situation is a little more complex with two chlorine atoms in a molecule, as there are three possibilities. Considering dichloromethane, CH_2Cl_2, we have:

$^{35}ClCH_2{}^{35}Cl^+$	the M peak
$^{35}ClCH_2{}^{37}Cl^+$	the [M + 2] peak
$^{37}ClCH_2{}^{35}Cl^+$	the [M + 2] peak
$^{37}ClCH_2{}^{37}Cl^+$	the [M + 4] peak

The relative heights of the peaks must take into account the natural abundances: it works out as 9:6:1 for molecules with two Cl atoms.

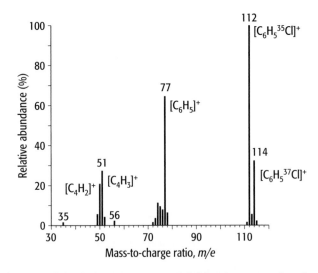

Figure 29.26 The mass spectrum of chlorobenzene, showing the [M + 2] peak. (Note that there are also tiny [M + 1] and [M + 3] peaks corresponding to ^{13}C in the molecule.)

The M, [M + 2] and [M + 4] peaks also occur in dibromomethane but the relative heights of peaks are easier to work out. Because the ratio $^{79}Br:{}^{81}Br$ is 1:1, the M : [M + 2] : [M + 4] height ratio is 1:2:1.

11 a List the ions responsible for the M, [M + 2] and [M + 4] peaks in a mass spectrum of dibromomethane.

b What would be the mass-to-charge ratio and relative abundances of the major peaks with the highest charge-to-mass ratios in the mass spectrum of chloroethane?

c How many peaks would you see beyond the molecular ion peak in 1,1-dibromoethane? What would be their mass-to-charge ratios and abundances relative to the molecular ion? (Ignore peaks due to ^{13}C.)

Applications of the mass spectrometer

To identify the components in a mixture, we can link gas–liquid chromatography (GLC) or high-performance liquid chromatography (HPLC) apparatus directly to a mass spectrometer.

This combined technique is very sensitive, and any two solutes that can be separated with a time gap of 1 second on a GLC column can be identified almost instantly by the mass spectrometer without the need to be collected. Identification is by comparing the mass spectrum of each solute with the mass spectra of known compounds, using a computer's spectral database. The data generated is complex. There can be many components in a mixture, each with a peak at its particular retention time on the chromatogram, and each peak will generate its own characteristic series of lines in the mass spectrometer. We can combine the chromatogram and the mass spectra to display the data on a three-dimensional (3-D) graph (Figure 29.27).

GLC linked to a mass spectrometer (GLC–MS) is used for analysing complex mixtures, for example the identification of the hydrocarbons in a sample of crude oil. The combined technique is fast and gives reliable results that can identify trace quantities of pollutants, drugs, biochemical molecules and toxins. This means it is used in:

- forensics
- environmental monitoring of pollutants
- drug testing in sport
- geological and archaeological dating
- airport security.

Mass spectrometry has even been used on space probes to analyse rocks on Mars and in 2005 a mass spectrometer was used to analyse the frozen hydrocarbon surface of Titan, one of Saturn's moons. The technique is also used to analyse the isotopes in the solar wind on board the Solar and Heliospheric Observatory (SOHO) satellite.

QUESTION

12 Look at Figure 29.27.

   a What is the retention time of the compound shown?

   b What is the approximate relative molecular mass of the compound shown?

   c How would the compound be identified?

As with electrophoresis and NMR spectroscopy, mass spectrometry is also helping in medical research – to both identify and research the amino acid sequences in proteins. It can be used to analyse the whole protein molecule or the peptides left after breaking down the protein with specific enzymes. Figure 29.28 shows the mass spectrum of a pentapeptide that is made into a charged compound by the addition of a proton, hence the MH^+ peak.

In research laboratories synthesising new compounds, a combination of instrumental techniques will need to be used to confirm the structure of a previously undiscovered molecule (as no spectral records exist in databases, so identification by 'fingerprinting' is not an option).

449

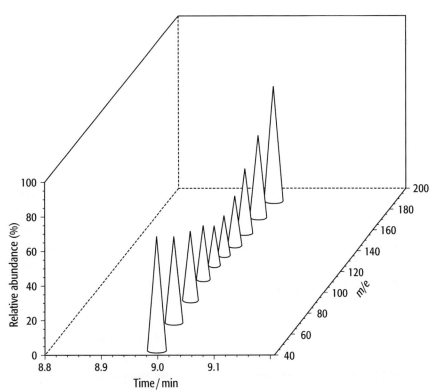

Figure 29.27 The *x*-axis shows retention time, the *y*-axis the amounts and the *z*-axis is the charge/mass ratio of the mass spectra. These 3-D data show the peaks on a mass spectrum for one component in a gas–liquid chromatogram.

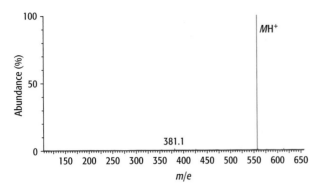

Figure 29.28 The mass spectrum of leucine enkephalin ($C_{28}H_{37}N_5O_7$), a peptide made up of five amino acids. It has been charged by adding a proton instead of by ionisation by high-energy electrons (which would fragment the molecule). This is known as a 'soft ionisation' method.

QUESTION

13 Look at Figure 29.28.

    a Calculate the relative molecular mass of leucine enkephalin ($C_{28}H_{37}N_5O_7$) using relative atomic masses.

        (A_r values C = 12.0, H = 1.0, N = 14.0, O = 16.0)

    b i How is the peptide ionised before detection in the mass spectrometer?

       ii Why is this known as 'soft ionisation'?

    c Why is there a peak at [MH + 1]?

    d An unexpected peak occurs at charge-to-mass ratio 578.1. This is caused by ionisation of the pentapeptide by a metal ion instead of an H^+ ion. Which metal ion is responsible for this ionisation?

Summary

- Chromatography separates mixtures of substances for identification. In chromatography, the mobile phase moves the components of a mixture through or over the stationary phase. Separation occurs by the transfer of the components to the stationary phase either by:
    - partition between two liquids (due to the different solubility of solutes in the mobile phase and stationary phase)
    - partition between a gas and a liquid
    - adsorption on a solid surface.

- The stationary phase may be solid or liquid; the mobile phase may be liquid or gas.

- In paper and thin-layer chromatography (TLC) the components of a mixture are identified by their R_f values.

- In gas–liquid chromatography (GLC) and high-performance liquid chromatography (HPLC), the components of a mixture are identified by their retention times; the amount of each component is found by measuring the area of each peak (estimates can be made from peak heights).

- The proton NMR spectrum of a compound provides detailed information about the structure of the compound. In particular, the spectrum for the protons, ^1H, in a compound can provide a complete determination of the compound's structure.

- Protons in different chemical environments produce signals at different chemical shifts. The chemical shift provides information about the proton's environment.

- Protons on neighbouring carbon atoms cause signals to be split. The splitting pattern establishes which groups of protons are on adjacent carbon atoms. The $n + 1$ rule predicts the splitting pattern.

- Protons on —OH and —NH— can be identified by the addition of D_2O to the NMR sample, which collapses the peak due to an —OH or an —NH— proton.

- Carbon-13 NMR can also help to determine the structure of organic molecules.

- The mass spectrum of a compound enables the relative molecular mass of the compound to be determined using the molecular ion peak. The molecular ion peak, M, is the peak produced by the loss of one electron from a molecule of the compound.

- We can deduce the number of carbon atoms in a compound using the [M + 1] peak and the presence of a single bromine or chlorine atom using the [M + 2] peak (and two Cl or Br atoms by the [M + 4] peak as well).

- We can also use mass spectroscopy to identify unknown organic compounds by 'fingerprinting' (matching the spectrum to other known spectra). The fragmentation peaks give us clues as to the structure of the original molecule.

■ Gas–liquid chromatography/mass spectrometry (GLC–MS) provides a more powerful tool for identifying the components in a mixture than GLC alone (compounds can have similar retention

times but can be 'fingerprinted' by their unique mass spectra). It is used in airport security checks, food industries and in forensic, environmental and medical testing.

■ A combination of techniques (such as infra-red, NMR and mass spectroscopy) must be used to confirm the structure of newly discovered compounds.

End-of-chapter questions

1 a Identify the fragments that would cause peaks in the mass spectrum of $HOCH_2COCH_3$ with the following m/e values:

   i $m/e = 15$ [1]

   ii $m/e = 17$ [1]

   iii $m/e = 31$ [1]

   iv $m/e = 43$ [1]

   v $m/e = 57$ [1]

   vi $m/e = 59$ [1]

  b At what value for m/e would you find the molecular ion peak? [1]

Total = 7

2 The gas–liquid chromatogram for a mixture of organic compounds is shown below.

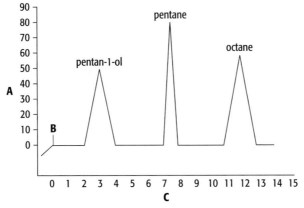

  a Give the correct labels for **A**, **B** and **C**. [3]

  b What percentage of the mixture is pentan-1-ol? [6]

  c Give an explanation for the different retention times. [3]

  d i How would the chromatogram change if the liquid in the stationary phase was much more polar? [1]

    ii Explain your answer. [2]

  e Why is gas–liquid chromatography useful in testing for anabolic steroids in the blood of athletes? [2]

  f Explain why the use of gas–liquid chromatography linked to a mass spectrometer is so useful. [2]

  g Why is it difficult to separate dyes using gas–liquid chromatography? [2]

Total = 21

3   Paper chromatography was used to separate a mixture of amino acids. The mixture was run in two dimensions using two different solvents. The chromatogram obtained is shown below.

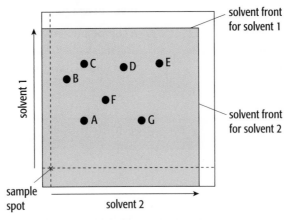

a   Explain briefly how the chromatography was carried out.   [4]
b   Which amino acids were inseparable using solvent 1? (Give just the corresponding letters.)   [2]
c   How could the amino acids be located?   [1]
d   Give the R_f value for amino acid C in each solvent.   [2]
e   Which amino acids would have been inseparable by solvent 2 alone?   [1]
f   In another experiment, a mixture of radioactively labelled amino acids was separated using paper chromatography. The results obtained are shown below.

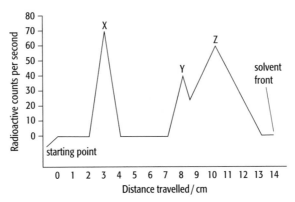

i   Find the R_f values for acids X, Y and Z. Show your working.   [3]
ii   Explain how paper chromatography is used to separate the components of a mixture.   [4]

Total = 17

When answering questions 4–7, you will need to use the values in Table 29.1 (page 441).

4   Compound B has the composition 62.1% carbon, 10.3% hydrogen and 27.6% oxygen. Its mass and ^{1}H NMR spectra are shown below.

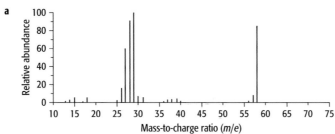

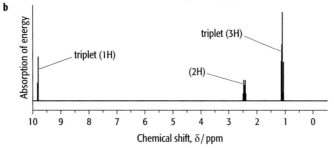

a   Calculate the empirical formula of B.   [2]
b   From the mass spectrum, find the molecular mass of B and hence its molecular formula.   [2]
c   i   Draw displayed formulae for the possible isomers of B which contain a carbonyl group.   [2]
    ii   Use the ^{1}H NMR spectrum of B to decide which isomer is B.   [1]
    iii Explain your reasoning.   [3]
d   Explain what caused the peak at $\delta = 1.1$ ppm and why it is split into a triplet in the ^{1}H NMR spectrum of B. [2]
e   Predict the number of signal lines present on the carbon-13 NMR spectrum of:
    i   compound B, stating the origin of each line   [2]
    ii   the isomer of compound B identified in your answer to **c** part **i**, stating the origin of each line. [2]

                                                                                                     Total = 16

5   Arene C has the composition 90.6% carbon and 9.4% hydrogen. Its mass and ^{1}H NMR spectra are shown below.

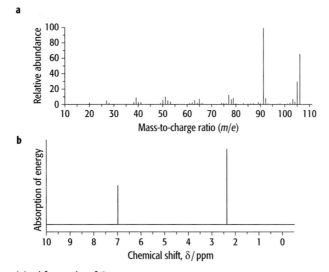

a   Calculate the empirical formula of C.   [2]
b   From the mass spectrum, find the molecular mass of C and hence its molecular formula.   [2]

c i Draw displayed formulae for the possible aromatic isomers of C. [4]

ii When C is treated with chlorine in the presence of $AlCl_3$ it undergoes electrophilic aromatic substitution. In this reaction one of the hydrogen atoms bonded directly to the benzene ring is replaced with one chlorine atom, and one single aromatic product is formed. Use this evidence and the NMR spectrum of C to decide which isomer is C. [5]

d Explain the main features of the ^1H NMR spectrum of C. [4]

Total = 17

6 Compound D has the composition 77.8% carbon, 7.41% hydrogen and 14.8% oxygen. It mass and ^1H NMR spectra are shown below.

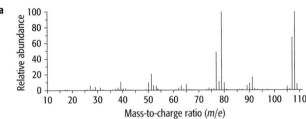

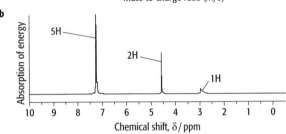

a Calculate the empirical formula of D. [2]

b From the mass spectrum, find the molecular mass of D (ignoring the ^{13}C peak) and hence its molecular formula. [2]

c i Draw displayed formulae for five possible isomers of D that contain a benzene ring. [5]

ii Use the ^1H NMR spectrum of D to decide which isomer is D. [1]

iii Explain your reasoning. [3]

d Explain the main features of the NMR spectrum of D. [4]

Total = 17

7 Compound E has the composition 69.8% carbon, 11.6% hydrogen and 18.6% oxygen. Its mass and ^{1}H NMR spectra are shown below.

a
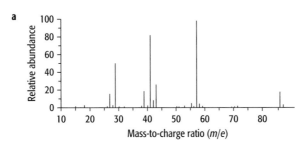

b
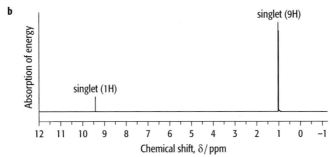

a Calculate the empirical formula of E. [2]

b From the mass spectrum, find the molecular mass of E (ignoring the ^{13}C peak) and hence its molecular formula. [2]

c Compound E reacts with 2,4-dinitrophenylhydrazine to give a yellow-orange precipitate. Draw displayed formulae for the seven possible isomers of E. [7]

d Compound E gives a silver mirror with Tollens' reagent. Identify the functional group in E. [3]

e Use the ^{1}H NMR spectrum to identify E. Explain your reasoning. [4]

Total = 18

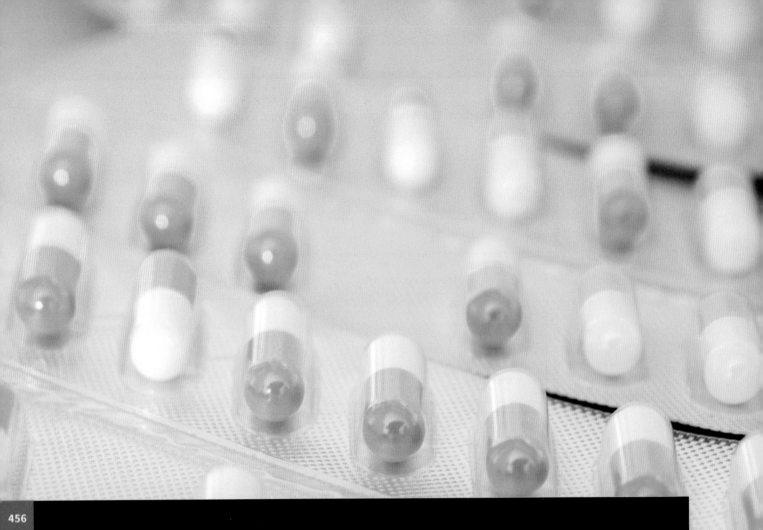

Chapter 30:
Organic synthesis

Learning outcomes

You should be able to:

- state that most chiral drugs extracted from natural sources often contain only a single optical isomer
- state reasons why the synthetic preparation of drug molecules often requires the production of a single optical isomer, e.g. better therapeutic activity, fewer side effects

- for an organic molecule containing several functional groups:
  - identify organic functional groups using key reactions
  - predict properties and reactions
- devise multi-stage synthetic routes for preparing organic molecules using key reactions.

Introduction

Chemists play a vital role in developing new materials to improve our lives. In this chapter you can find out about their work in developing new medicinal drugs.

Figure 30.1 Chemists around the world work in large teams to model, develop and test new medicines.

Designing new medicinal drugs

How do we go about designing new molecules to fight diseases? One way is to identify the structural features the new drug will need to stop particular bacteria or viruses working. The structural features may be associated with the active site on a particular enzyme needed for an essential function of the pathogen. Once these structural features have been identified we can then predict the shape of a molecule that would fit into, and hence block, the active site.

The functional groups present would also be crucial to ensure the drug could bind into the active site effectively. The intermolecular bonds formed between the drug and its target molecule could involve:

- hydrogen bonding
- ionic attraction
- dipole–dipole forces
- instantaneous dipole–induced dipole forces (van der Waals' forces, see Chapter 4, page 62).

Computers are now used to judge the fit between a potential drug molecule and a receptor site on its target molecule. Such **molecular modelling** has greatly speeded up the process of designing new medicines. The interactions and fit of a potential medicine with a biological receptor molecule can be studied before the medicine is ever made in the lab. Before molecular modelling became available, the synthesis of a new

medicine involved far more trial and error. Chemists had to prepare many more possible medicines for testing. With molecular modelling, only those molecules that are definite possibilities are made and tested. Molecular modelling on a computer is now a powerful tool, used when designing medicines and many other compounds (e.g. pesticides and polymers).

This type of research was used in the fight against AIDS in the late 1980s and 1990s. Scientists using X-ray crystallography (a method in which a sample is irradiated with X-rays and the pattern is analysed by computer) worked out the shape of HIV protease in 1988 (Figure 30.2). This enzyme plays an important role when the virus becomes infectious. Researchers realised that, if a molecule could be discovered that could block its active site, this might be one step on the route to finding a cure for AIDS. Knowing the molecule that the enzyme worked on (its substrate), researchers were able construct similar molecules on the computer screen to fit the active site.

The first attempts fitted perfectly, but were not water soluble. This meant the drug could not be delivered to its target, the HIV protease. Eventually a soluble molecule that would interfere with the enzyme was found. In less than 8 years pharmaceutical companies had developed three new anti-viral drugs for people with HIV/AIDS. This would have taken about twice as long if the structure of HIV protease had not been determined. Traditional

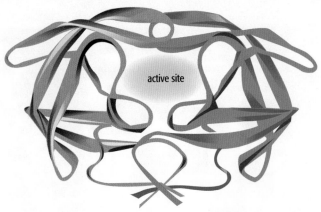

Figure 30.2 A symmetrical HIV protease molecule, with its active site in the centre of the molecule. Knowing its structure made the search for a drug to fight AIDS much quicker and cheaper than traditional trial-and-error methods.

trial-and-error methods involve the testing of many thousands of possible drugs.

The death rate from AIDS dropped significantly. However, the virus developed resistance to the new drugs as it mutated. So scientists now have to model the new drug-resistant strains of the infection and are developing new drugs to inhibit the mutant versions of HIV protease. These inhibitors are one part of a cocktail of drugs that can be used to treat the disease now.

Identifying macromolecules

NMR spectroscopy is also used extensively in finding out the structures of biological macromolecules such as proteins and nucleic acids. As well as identifying the different types of ^{1}H atoms present, more sophisticated data can yield, for example, the distance between atoms in macromolecules. Large amounts of data are collected and analysed by computer programs to reveal the shape of the molecules under investigation.

Figures 30.3 and 30.4 show images obtained from NMR analysis of two protein molecules made up from over 100 amino acids. These are called **ribbon diagrams**.

Figure 30.3 A protein made up of 106 amino acid residues.

Figure 30.4 A protein made up of 153 amino acid residues.

This NMR analysis takes place in solution, so it is particularly useful for medical research. Many human proteins exist in solution in the body so we can mimic the interactions that take place in cells or in the bloodstream.

QUESTION

1 a Which method was used to determine the structure of HIV protease in 1988?

   b Which method could be used to show the shape of the enzyme in solution?

   c What type of natural polymer is an enzyme such as HIV protease?

   d How did the new anti-viral drugs work?

Chirality in pharmaceutical synthesis

The pharmaceutical industry is constantly searching for new drugs. Their research chemists have discovered that most of these drugs contain at least one chiral centre (see page 195). Remember that a molecule containing a carbon atom bonded to four different atoms or groups of atoms can exist as two non-superimposable mirror images. These two isomers are called enantiomers and they will be optically active. They differ in their ability to rotate the plane of polarised light to the left or to the right.

Using conventional organic reactions to make the desired product will yield a 50 : 50 mixture of the two enantiomers. We call this a racemic mixture. Although the physical properties of the enantiomers will be identical, each differs in its 'pharmaceutical activity', i.e. the effect the drug has on the body. For example, naproxen is a drug used to treat the pain caused by arthritis (Figure 30.5). One enantiomer will ease the pain but the other can cause liver damage.

As another example, one enantiomer of a drug used to treat tuberculosis (TB) is effective, whereas the other can cause blindness. Therefore, chemists ideally need a single pure enantiomer to put in their drug product. Note that about 80% of new drugs patented are single enantiomers.

Using pure enantiomers will be beneficial as it:

■ reduces the patient's dosage by half as the pure enantiomer is more potent, i.e. has better therapeutic activity (thereby cutting costs of production)
■ minimises the risk of side effects (thereby protecting patients from further problems and drugs companies from possible legal action for damages if serious side effects do occur).

There are three ways to prepare pure enantiomers:

■ optical resolution
■ using optically active starting materials
■ using a chiral catalyst.

Optical resolution

This method involves the chemists following a traditional synthetic route to make the compound, resulting in a racemic mixture. Then they separate the two enantiomers in a process called **optical resolution**. This involves using a pure enantiomer of another optically active compound (called a chiral auxiliary) that will react with one of the isomers in the mixture. The new product formed will now have different properties and so can be separated by physical means. For example, the solubility in a given solvent will differ so the unwanted enantiomer and the new product can be separated by fractional crystallisation. The new product is then converted back to the desired enantiomer in a simple reaction (e.g. by adding dilute alkali).

The crystallisation is repeated many times to ensure purity. This method is difficult, time-consuming, uses extra reagents and involves the disposal of half the original racemic mixture.

Large volumes of organic solvents (often harmful to the environment) are used in the process. However, chemists are now using supercritical carbon dioxide as a solvent, which is much safer. At 31 °C and 73 atmospheres pressure, CO_2 is a suitable non-polar solvent for many drug derivatives in the racemic resolution process. The solubility of the derivatives can be changed, simply by varying the density of the solvent. The solvent, which is non-toxic, is easily removed by reducing the pressure and then recycling it to use in the process again.

We can also use high-performance liquid chromatography (HPLC, see page 436) to separate a racemic mixture, as long as the stationary medium (e.g. the solid that packs the column) is itself optically active.

Using optically active starting materials

This technique uses starting materials that are themselves optically active and in the same orientation as the desired product. These are often naturally occurring compounds such as carbohydrates or L-amino acids. The biochemist will choose from this 'chiral pool'. The synthetic route is designed to keep any intermediates and the final product formed in the same enantiomeric form. As a result, there is no need to carry out the costly separation process needed when a racemic mixture is produced.

Chiral catalysts

Chemists are also developing new chiral catalysts that ensure only one specific enantiomer is formed in a reaction. The benefits of these catalysts are that only small quantities are needed and they can be used over and over again, although the catalyst itself can be expensive. A ruthenium (Ru) organometallic catalyst is used in the production of naproxen (see Figure 30.5).

Often a combination of optical resolution and chiral synthesis is needed in the production of a pharmaceutically active, pure enantiomer.

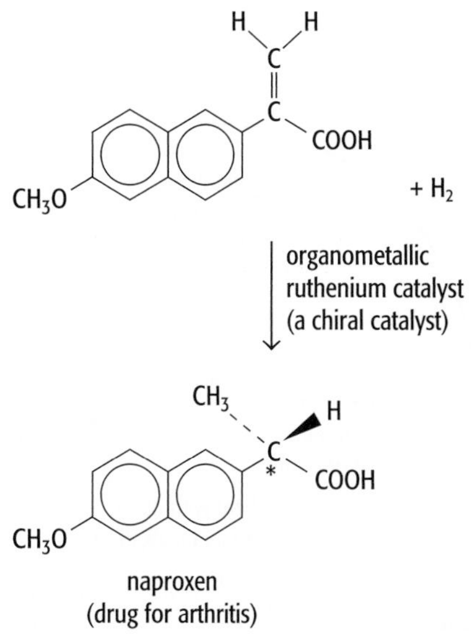

Figure 30.5 The chiral catalyst (an organometallic ruthenium compound) ensures only the desired enantiomer is formed – in this case, naproxen for the treatment of arthritis. The chiral centre in naproxen is marked with an asterisk. The marked carbon atom is known as an 'asymmetric carbon'.

459

The pharmaceutical industry can also use enzymes to promote stereoselectivity and produce single-enantiomer products. The specific shape and the nature of the molecular interactions at the active site of an enzyme ensure only one enantiomer will be formed (as in living things). The enzymes are often immobilised (fixed in place) on inert supports. This enables the reactants to be passed over them without the need to separate the product from the enzymes after the reaction.

However, it can be expensive isolating enzymes from living things. Using whole organisms, such as bacteria, can reduce this cost. Nowadays, synthetic enzymes can also be made, designed for a particular synthesis. Therefore a search for a suitable enzyme from the limited pool available from natural sources is not always necessary.

Overall, using an enzyme process might take longer to develop than a conventional synthetic route, but in the long run the benefits generally outweigh the disadvantages. There are fewer steps needed in the synthesis route, resulting in a 'greener' process.

> **QUESTION**
>
> **2 a** Why are pure enantiomers rather than racemic mixtures the better option for use as pharmaceutical drugs from the point of view of:
>
>   **i** a patient
>
>   **ii** a pharmaceutical company?

> **QUESTION (CONTINUED)**
>
> **b** Why are modern enzyme-based processes for manufacturing pure enantiomers more sustainable (environmentally friendly) than traditional synthetic routes used by the pharmaceutical industry?
>
> **c** Find out why the drug thalidomide resulted in legal action against its manufacturer.

Synthetic routes

When research chemists want to make a new compound, they usually work backwards from the desired compound to create a series of reactions, starting with a compound extracted from a commonly available raw material. In industry, common starting materials are hydrocarbons from crude oil and its refining, and compounds extracted from plants, such as esters from fats and vegetable oils.

You will need some of the skills of a research chemist when tackling questions that involve:

- predicting the reactions of complex molecules you have never seen before, containing more than one functional group
- suggesting a series of reactions to make a given compound from a given starting compound.

In order to be successful in answering these questions, you will need to be familiar with all the reactions and conditions of each homologous series mentioned in the syllabus. The flow chart in Figure 30.6 is a summary of

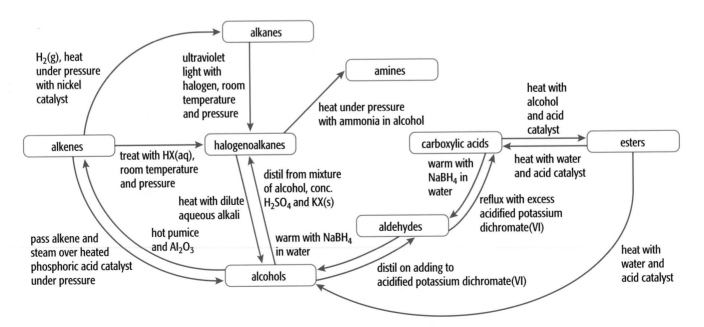

Figure 30.6 Some of the important organic reactions you have to remember.

some of the most useful reactions you need to know, but you could be asked about others, so it is a good idea to make your own summary spider charts for all the reactions in Chapters 15 to 28. For example, for Chapter 16 write the word 'Halogenoalkane' in a box and draw arrows radiating out from the box to the products made in their reactions, labelling the arrows with other reactants and the reaction conditions. Displaying these on a wall and using different colours will help you remember them.

Adding carbon atoms

Sometimes the starting compound from a raw material does not have enough carbon atoms in its molecules to make the desired product. An extra carbon atom can be added by adding the nitrile functional group, $-C\equiv N$. Remember that these can be made from halogenoalkanes:

$$RBr + HCN \xrightarrow{\text{reflux with ethanolic KCN}} RCN + HBr$$

where R is an alkyl group, so RCN has an extra carbon atom.

The RCN molecule can be either **hydrolysed** to make a carboxylic acid (by refluxing with dilute hydrochloric acid) or reduced to make an amine (by adding $LiAlH_4$ in dry ether).

We can add an alkyl or acyl side-chain to a benzene ring by carrying out a Friedel–Crafts reaction, which is another useful reaction when planning synthetic routes. For example:

$$C_6H_6 + CH_3CH_2Cl \xrightarrow{\text{AlCl}_3 \text{ catalyst}} C_6H_5CH_2CH_3 + HCl$$
benzene   ethylbenzene

QUESTION

3 a Name the functional groups in the molecules of:

   i aspirin

   ii paracetamol.

aspirin   paracetamol

b i Both the molecules in part **a** are broken down when refluxed with dilute hydrochloric acid. Write an equation each for the reaction of aspirin and paracetamol with H_2O.

  ii What do we call the type of reaction in **b i**?

4 a Name the organic products A to D in the synthetic route below:

$$C_2H_5COOC_3H_7 \xrightarrow{\text{boil with NaOH(aq)}} A \xrightarrow{\text{add excess HCl(aq)}} B$$

$$\xrightarrow{\text{add PCl}_5} C \xrightarrow{\text{add conc. ammonia}} D$$

b i Devise a three-stage synthetic route to convert benzene into benzenediazonium chloride.

  ii How would you convert the benzenediazonium chloride into an orange dye?

Summary

- Both natural biochemicals and modern medicinal drugs contain chiral molecules. Generally, only one of the enantiomers of a drug is beneficial to living organisms and the other isomer may have undesirable effects. The beneficial isomer has the appropriate shape and pattern of intermolecular forces to interact with a receptor molecule in a living organism.

- Chemists are now producing drugs containing single enantiomers rather than a racemic mixture of isomers. This enables the dose to be halved, improves pharmacological activity (behaviour of molecule in an organism), reduces side effects and minimises litigation against manufacturers.

- Molecular design of a new medicinal drug is made possible with a sound understanding of the structural features that produce beneficial effects. The computerised study of the interactions between molecules and biological receptors has become a powerful tool in the search for new medicines.

- Recognising the functional groups in a given organic molecule enables us to predict its reactions.

- Knowing the reactions of the different functional groups in organic reactions enables us to devise synthetic routes to make given compounds.

End-of-chapter questions

1 A sample of lactic acid ($CH_3CH(OH)COOH$) was extracted from a natural source and found to be optically active. It was then subjected to two reactions, as shown below.

$$CH_3CH(OH)COOH \xrightarrow{\text{step } \textbf{A}} CH_3COCOOH \xrightarrow{\text{step } \textbf{B}} CH_3CH(OH)COOH$$

sample 1   sample 2

Sample 1 was optically active but sample 2 was not optically active.

a   i   Give the systematic name for lactic acid. [1]

    ii The structure of one optical isomer of the lactic acid is:

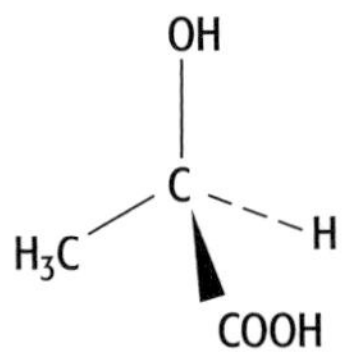

        Draw the other optical isomer. [1]

    iii Explain why lactic acid can form optical isomers. [1]

b   i   Give the reagents and conditions necessary for step **A**. [2]

    ii Give the balanced equation for the reaction. [2]

c   i   Give the reagents and conditions necessary for step **B**. [2]

    ii Give the balanced equation for the reaction. [2]

d   i   Give the mechanism for step **B**. The first step involves nucleophilic attack on the carbon of the ketone group by an H^- ion from $NaBH_4$. [5]

    ii Explain why sample 2 does not show any optical activity – it does not rotate plane-polarised light. [3]

e   i   Explain why lactic acid can be polymerised. [2]

    ii State the type of polymerisation reaction that this an example of. [1]

    iii Draw the repeat unit of poly(lactic acid). [1]

Total = 23

2   Explain how 2-aminopropanoic acid can be prepared from lactic acid in two steps. You should give
    the reagents and conditions necessary plus balanced symbol equations for the reactions taking place.   [9]

Total = 9

3   Write short notes on the following methods of synthesising chiral molecules:
    a   using a chiral auxiliary   [3]
    b   use of a chiral pool.   [3]

Total = 6

4   The structure of the compound known as thalidomide can be shown as:

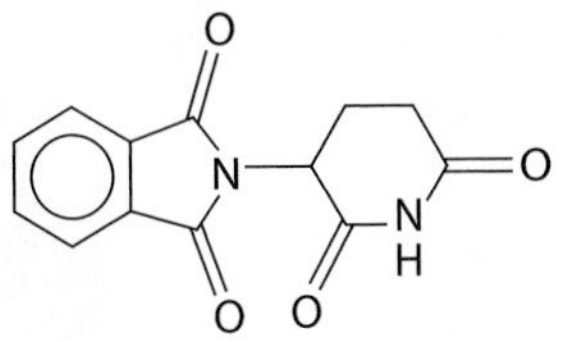

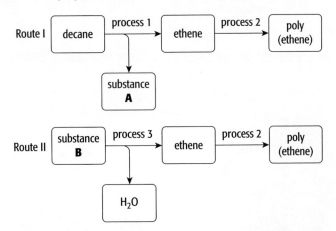

    a   Copy the molecule and mark the chiral centre on your drawing.   [1]
    b   Name two functional groups found in a molecule of thalidomide.   [2]
    c   Suggest the type of reaction that might change the molecule into an alcohol and any reagents needed.   [2]
    d   Explain why the chirality of drugs has been such an important issue in the pharmaceutical industry,
        giving one benefit to patients and one benefit to pharmaceutical companies of using pure enantiomers.   [3]

Total = 8

5   The flow charts below show how poly(ethene) can be obtained by two different routes.

Route I   decane — process 1 → ethene — process 2 → poly (ethene)
                      ↓
                 substance **A**

Route II   substance **B** — process 3 → ethene — process 2 → poly (ethene)
                         ↓
                      H_2O

    a   i   Identify substance **A** and give the equation for the reaction taking place in process 1.   [3]
        ii   What term is used to describe process 1?   [1]
    b   i   Name substance **B** and give the equation for the reaction taking place in process 3.   [3]
        ii   What term is used to describe process 3?   [1]

Total = 8

463

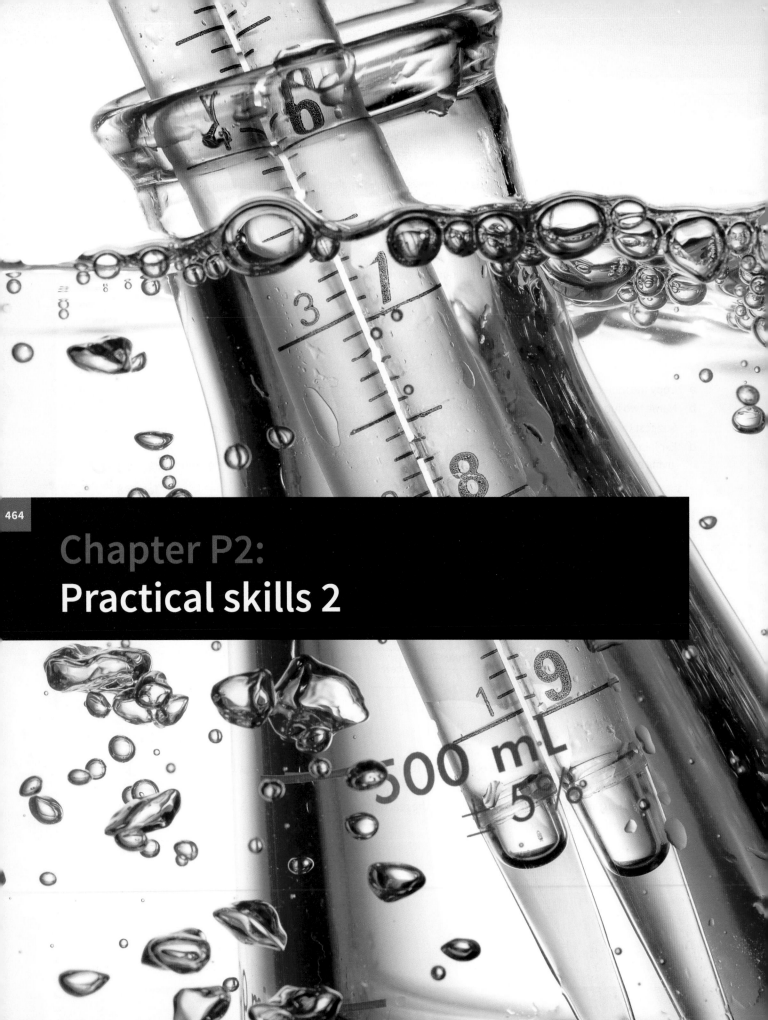

Chapter P2:
Practical skills 2

Introduction

The ability to plan, analyse and evaluate practical work requires higher-order thinking skills. You will need plenty of practice in carrying out tasks requiring these skills as you progress through your course.

Figure P2.1 Many chemists are employed to plan, carry out and evaluate tests on substances found in the environment.

Written examination of practical skills

Paper 5 in the Cambridge International Examinations International A Level Chemistry syllabus is the written examination of practical skills. It focuses on the higher-order experimental skills of planning, analysis and evaluation. Some questions on this paper may be set in areas of chemistry that are difficult to investigate experimentally and may be based on novel situations. However, no question will require knowledge of theory or equipment that is beyond the syllabus.

Before going through the following section, it would be a good idea to read Chapter P1, Practical skills 1, pages 246–256. This will remind you of the structure of investigations – which is essential to understand before you can apply the higher-order practical skills tested in Paper 5.

Planning

Expectations

You should be able to:

Defining the problem

- identify the independent variable in the experiment or investigation
- identify the dependent variable in the experiment or investigation
- formulate the aim in terms of a prediction or hypothesis, and express this in words or in the form of a predicted graph
- identify the variables that are to be controlled.

Methods

- describe the method to be used to vary the independent variable, and the means that you propose to ensure that you have measured its values accurately
- describe how you will measure the dependent variable
- describe how you will control each of the other key variables
- explain how you will use any control experiments to verify that it is the independent variable that is affecting the dependent variable and not some other factor
- describe the arrangement of apparatus and the steps in the procedure to be followed
- suggest appropriate volumes and concentrations of reagents
- assess the risks of your proposed methods
- describe precautions that should be taken to keep risks to a minimum
- draw up tables for data that you might wish to record
- describe how the data might be used in order to reach a conclusion.

As the expectations above show, all plans contain two distinct sections:

- defining the problem – this is worth 4 marks
- the actual method – this is worth a further 8 marks.

Defining the problem

The question generally begins with a stem, which will contain information relevant to the plan and the aim of the investigation. The context of the task to be covered may or may not be familiar to you, but the stem will contain all of the detail required.

Almost invariably, a prediction is required together with an explanation of the basis of the prediction, forming a hypothesis to test. For example, in a question about rate of reaction, you might make a quantitative prediction, such as the direct proportionality between the rate and concentration. Here, the supporting explanation would need to be given in terms of the doubling of the frequency of particle collisions as a result of doubling the concentration. The planning question might also ask for a supporting graph to be given.

You will have to specify the independent and the dependent variables. You might also have to consider the need to control other variables.

In a 'rate' exercise, the independent variable might be the concentration of a reactant or the temperature. The measured rate of the reaction at different values of the independent variable is the dependent variable. Alternative ways of measuring the rate of reaction, such as the time to collect a set volume of gas (giving average rates) or the monitoring of gas released over time (then calculating the initial gradient of lines on a graph to measure initial rates), are acceptable.

Methods

When creating a method, you should produce one that can be followed by another student without the need to ask any extra questions. This means that fine detail is required and nothing should be omitted on the basis that it is 'obvious'.

The question might provide further information that builds on the stem, but you are expected to have experience of basic laboratory apparatus. The best way to achieve this is to follow a programme of experimental work throughout the course. This also has the advantage of promoting the understanding of concepts underlying the practical work.

Basic techniques, such as titrations, standard solution production and rate measurement, should be thoroughly understood in detail. You also need to be aware of the various methods of measuring volume and mass available in a laboratory. For example, an experiment involving the production and collection of a gas, such as the effect of heat on nitrates, would require you to be aware that gas syringes usually have a maximum capacity of $100\,cm^3$ and that the alternative of collecting the gas over water in a burette would allow for the collection of only $50\,cm^3$. This example shows how it is important to perform meaningful practical work in order to prepare for Paper 5. There is no substitute for familiarity in handling real apparatus.

On occasion, a diagram of the apparatus to be used is requested and you need to be able to represent the apparatus in a simple and understandable format. It is essential that each piece of equipment can be easily recognised in the diagram. Practice drawing sessions are a very good idea.

Relevant calculations are an almost routine requirement, and these must be logically presented, step by step.

The preparation of a standard solution of a solid acid, such as ethanedioic acid, requires the calculation of the mass to be dissolved in a chosen volumetric flask in order to produce the required concentration. The described procedure should indicate that the solid needs to be dissolved completely in distilled water before adding the solution to the volumetric flask (see Figure P2.2). You should make clear how you can ensure that all of this solution is transferred successfully to the volumetric flask – for example, by rinsing any solution stuck on the inside of the original container into the volumetric flask using distilled water. Once in the volumetric flask, the solution is made up to the required mark, and must then be thoroughly mixed.

You are expected to calculate the amounts of substance used to suit the volume or size of the apparatus that you specify. For example, if the plan involves collecting a gas from the decomposition of a carbonate in a $100\,cm^3$ gas syringe, the calculated mass of the solid heated should be such as to produce slightly less than $100\,cm^3$ of the gas.

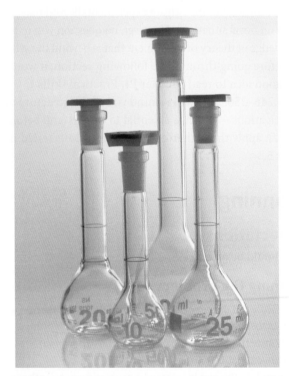

Figure P2.2 Volumetric flasks are used to make up standard solutions of known concentration accurately.

An integral part of any plan is the collection and presentation of results. Any processing of the results must be specified, and the figures obtained should also be presented as the 'derived results'. The derived results may then be processed in order to confirm or deny (falsify) the original prediction or hypothesis. This processing may involve calculating means of repeat readings and the graphical presentation of results.

The recorded results are those collected from the various steps taken in carrying out the procedure. For example, in an exercise to find the enthalpies of solution of Group 1 hydroxides, the necessary results columns to be recorded are:

- the name or nature of the hydroxide
- the mass of a weighing bottle
- the mass of the weighing bottle and a sample of the hydroxide
- the initial temperature of the water
- the final temperature of the solution.

If you plan to repeat any tests to get replicate results, extra columns must be incorporated into the results table. Each column should have the correct units – represented as either '/ g' or '(g)' for any mass, for example.

The next stage is to process the results:

1 to calculate the mass of hydroxide used
2 to calculate the number of moles of hydroxide used
3 to calculate the number of joules of energy released into the solution
4 to use the results to parts **2** and **3** to deduce the standard enthalpy change per mole of hydroxide.

All plans have to be assessed for risk. Examination questions can ask for:

- an assessment of the risks involved in a particular experiment
- how to deal with the risks
- both of the above.

In an exercise to determine the enthalpy of neutralisation of hydrochloric acid (the question will tell you that this is 'harmful') and sodium hydroxide (which is 'corrosive'), you could be asked about a suitable precaution. Alternatively, an experiment on solubility may have hot water as a possible hazard or if a toxic gas is formed, as in the decomposition of Group 2 nitrates, the investigation should be carried out in a fume hood.

Points to remember

- When planning an investigation, your method must be ordered in a logical sequence, so you might prefer to make some rough notes at the back of the examination paper before writing a bullet pointed list or flow chart that explains exactly how you would carry out the investigation. These could include diagrams of assembled apparatus that can save complicated written explanations of the set-up.
- When describing how to vary your independent variable, ensure you consider how to measure its values accurately. For example, in a rate of precipitation investigation, when varying the concentration of a solution you might choose to measure volumes of water and solution using volumetric pipettes and fillers rather than just using a measuring cylinder (see Figure P2.3). You should also be familiar with the volumes and masses of reagents that are reasonable to use in normal everyday laboratory work. For example, a volume of $15\,cm^3$ of solution would be suitable for an experiment in a boiling tube but not in a $250\,cm^3$ conical flask.
- When deciding how to measure the dependent variable, you should also consider accuracy – how you intend to measure its 'true' value. In a rate of precipitation investigation you might choose to carry out the reaction in a conical flask on top of a piece of paper with a pencil mark drawn on it. You could then time how long it takes for the pencil mark to be no longer visible when viewed from above the flask. This will involve a subjective judgement by the observer. If you have done an experiment like this before, you will know just how difficult it is to decide the exact moment when you can no longer see through the solution. So including a

467

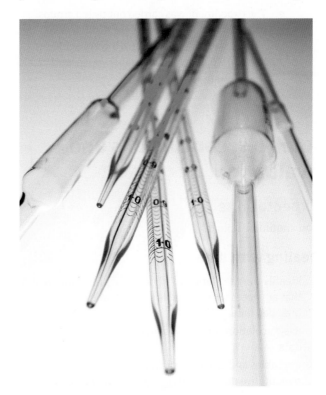

Figure P2.3 Volumetric and graduated pipettes are used to transfer accurate volumes of liquid. Volumetric pipettes give greater accuracy than graduated pipettes, due to the single line to measure to on the thin section above the bulge.

very accurate timing device, reading to one-thousandth of a second, would not be appropriate for this method.

■ You might also be required to sketch the axes you would use to graph the data collected and describe how you would use the data to draw a conclusion.

QUESTION

1 In an experiment to determine the formula of an oxide of copper, the copper oxide was reduced by hydrogen gas. The hydrogen was passed over the oxide of copper in a boiling tube with a hole near its end. The excess hydrogen was burnt off at this hole. The copper oxide was placed inside the boiling tube, which was clamped in a horizontal position, in a porcelain boat and was heated strongly.

a Name the products of the reaction.

b Draw a labelled diagram of the apparatus.

c Make a list of the measurements you would make to find the formula of the oxide of copper.

d Using the measurements made, how would you work out the mass contained in the oxide of copper of:

  i copper

  ii oxygen

e The experiment was carried out by ten groups of students, each with a different initial mass of the oxide of copper. Sketch a graph with the line you would expect to enable you to work out the formula.

Analysis, conclusions and evaluation

Expectations

You should be able to:

Dealing with data

■ identify the calculations and means of presentation of data that are necessary to be able to draw conclusions from provided data

■ use calculations to enable simplification or explanation of data

■ use tables and graphs to draw attention to the key points in quantitative data, including the variability of data.

Evaluation

■ identify anomalous values in provided data and suggest appropriate means of dealing with such anomalies

■ within familiar contexts, suggest possible explanations for anomalous readings

■ identify the extent to which provided readings have been adequately replicated, and describe the adequacy of the range of data provided

■ use provided information to assess the extent to which selected variables have been effectively controlled.

Conclusions

■ draw conclusions from an investigation, providing a detailed description of the key features of the data and analyses, and considering whether experimental data supports a given hypothesis

■ make detailed scientific explanations of the data, analyses and conclusions that you have described

■ make further predictions, ask informed and relevant questions and suggest improvements.

The three remaining skills are Dealing with data, Evaluation and Conclusions cover these areas. You should also revise the equivalent section in Chapter P1 on pages 251–253 before reading the following advice.

Dealing with data

In a written practical paper, typically you will be presented with some data, usually in a table, derived from an experiment. The details of the experiment are given to you, and then you will be asked to process the data and produce a system that incorporates all the results and allows not only correct patterns to become apparent but also detects anomalous results. The tabulated results will be the measured quantities of the processes carried out in a laboratory.

For example, in an experiment to confirm the formula of zinc iodide by reacting excess zinc with iodine, the measurements would be:

■ mass of an empty test tube

■ mass of the test tube and zinc powder

■ mass of the test tube, zinc powder and iodine

■ mass of the test tube and excess of zinc.

From these you would calculate:

■ the mass of zinc used

■ the mass of iodine that reacted with that mass of zinc.

These results would be tabulated, possibly alongside the original data, with each column showing the appropriate units and an expression to show how the values were calculated.

All calculations should be correct and recorded to an appropriate number of significant figures and/or decimal places. The question will on occasion tell you the degree of accuracy required, but often you will need to decide this yourself.

Many balances weigh to the nearest 0.01 g, and hence masses should be recorded to 2 decimal places, remembering that whole number masses should be recorded to the same accuracy, e.g. 4.00 g. In other circumstances, derived data should be recorded to the same number of significant figures as the least accurate item of supplied data. Where you are in doubt, 3 significant figures are appropriate for most calculations.

Having processed the raw data, the next step involves either a series of calculations to be averaged or some form of graphical plot.

In the zinc iodide experiment already discussed, the ratio of the number of moles of iodine to the number of moles of zinc can be used to produce a series of ratios.

These ratios can either then be averaged, excluding any anomalies to produce an appropriate result, or a graph could be plotted of the two molar values. In this case the appropriate gradient of the line would indicate the formula of zinc iodide. For example, if you plot the number of moles of zinc on the x-axis, and the moles of iodine on the y-axis, the gradient of the line on the graph should be 2. This shows that the formula of zinc iodide is ZnI_2.

The first step in plotting a graph is an appropriate choice of scales for the two axes, with the independent variable along the x-axis (the horizontal axis). When choosing a suitable scale it is useful to remember that the plotted points should be spread over at least half of each axis.

You must decide whether or not the origin (0,0) is a point on your graph. Whether or not to include the origin will usually be clear from the nature of the results. For example, if the concentration of a reactant is shown to affect the rate of a reaction, it is reasonable to assume that if the reactant were absent the reaction would not occur, so the rate would be zero when the concentration was zero. The origin can then provide a further useful point to be plotted. Chosen scales should be easily readable, but errors are counted if unhelpful scales are used. For example, the division of each of the two-centimetre squares on the graph grid into three makes accurate plotting very difficult.

Plotted points are best shown as small crosses, made with a hard, sharp, pencil.

Most plotted points will show a clear trend, indicating whether the graph should be a straight line or a curve; a straight line is the more usual. The plotted points must first be assessed to identify any anomalous points. If any anomalous points are identified, they should be clearly labelled as such. The line of best fit is then drawn, either as a curve or straight line. This line may not pass through all, or indeed any, of the plotted points. As a rough guide, an equal number of points should lie on the left of the line and on the right of the line, producing an 'average' line.

Evaluation

The evaluation of a set of results can be approached in a number of ways. The aim of any experiment is to draw an appropriate conclusion, either to verify a relationship or to establish a new relationship. This is accomplished by looking at the nature of the results and the quality of the experiment itself.

When anomalous results are identified, they should be clearly labelled as such. The source of the anomaly will often need to be identified and will usually fall into one of two categories: either a positive or a negative deviation from the general trend.

In a reaction involving the reduction of a metal oxide, the anomaly might arise because the reduction was incomplete, leading to a larger than expected mass of metal. The excess mass is the unreacted oxide.

If the reaction involves the thermal decomposition of hydrated iron(II) sulfate two, opposite, errors are possible:

- insufficient heating – this will cause the residual mass to be too great
- overheating – this will cause the residual mass to be too small.

The former result corresponds to the incomplete removal of the water of crystallisation, whereas the latter relates to the decomposition of the iron(II) sulfate into iron oxide.

You may be called upon to consider whether the actual experiment data under consideration is of high enough quality to produce reliable results, and appropriate improvements may be requested. If the results provide poor support for a conclusion, it may be that further repeats are needed, or that the range of results needs to be extended.

Apparatus may need to considered from two viewpoints:

- is it appropriate?
- is it accurate?

In the measurement of volume, burettes and pipettes are intrinsically more accurate than measuring cylinders, but if the volume to be measured is large, for example, a measuring cylinder could be perfectly adequate.

An experiment measuring a small temperature change in an enthalpy exercise often involves volumes of the order of 25 cm^3 to 50 cm^3 and a typical temperature change of the order of 5 °C to 10 °C, using a thermometer accurate to the nearest degree. In this case, the volumes could safely be measured with a measuring cylinder, as the percentage error of the temperature change will be greater than that of the measuring cylinder.

The volumes measured during titrations are about as accurate as simple exercises can be. If these are involved in an experiment the source of any error is likely to be elsewhere.

Measuring small volumes or masses generally produces high percentage errors, whichever item of simple laboratory apparatus is used. As an example, an experiment to investigate the rate of reaction between hydrochloric acid and magnesium by measuring the volume of hydrogen produced requires less than 0.10 g of magnesium if the gas produced is to be collected in a 100 cm^3 syringe. This is a very small mass of magnesium. Using a typical balance accurate to 0.01 g would give a 10% error and consequently the accuracy of the syringe is of negligible significance. The error in measuring the mass of the magnesium will be the greatest percentage error.

Conclusions

The conclusion of an exercise draws upon the key features of data collected and the subsequent analyses. Usually the data given will support a given hypothesis. However, it must be clearly understood that data that do not support an initial suggestion might also have to be considered.

In the magnesium/acid reaction, processing could involve plotting a graph of rate against the relative concentration of the acid. Inspection of the graph would allow a deduction to be made about the order with respect to [H$^+$] in the rate equation. This conclusion would then be considered in the light of an original hypothesis. This, in turn, could lead to further predictions and experiments (see page 253 in Chapter P1).

If the experiment is considered to be too approximate, suggested improvements to the exercise might be requested.

Points to remember

- Calculations involving data collected may ask for the mean, median, mode, percentage loss or percentage gain.
- To calculate the mean, add up the individual values in a set and divide by the number of values. Take care not to quote the mean to an unrealistic number of significant figures – the mean should reflect the precision of the measurements from which it was calculated.
- The median is the middle result when all the results are put in order of magnitude.
- The mode is the most common value.
- Percentage loss or gain is calculated by dividing the actual loss or gain by the original value, then multiplying by 100.
- The interval of the independent variable can be consistent when planning an investigation, but additional values can be selected to look more closely where a pattern seems to change (e.g. the gradient of a line changes on a graph of your results) or to extend the limits of your original range below its minimum value or above its maximum value. For example, you might decide to test a much lower dilution of 0.01 mol dm^{-3} when investigating the effect of concentration on the rate of reaction. This would enable you to test if the trend seen within your original range of data continues as expected.

QUESTION

2 a In the experiment described in **Question 1** on page 468, a student weighed a mass of 11.35 g of the oxide of copper on a balance reading to the nearest 0.05 g. What was the percentage error in this measurement?

   b Another group of students carrying out the same experiment found that their sample of the oxide of copper contained 13.24 g of copper and 3.26 g of oxygen. What is the most likely formula of the oxide of copper? (Relative atomic mass of Cu = 63.5; O = 16.0.)

   c Nine out of the ten groups who tackled the experiment obtained results consistent with those of the group described in part **b**. The other group's measurements resulted in a ratio that suggested the formula of the oxide was Cu$_2$O.

      i   What do we call their result when plotted on a class graph of moles of oxygen against moles of copper?

      ii How would you deal with this result when drawing the line of best fit?

      iii Give a possible explanation for the Cu$_2$O result obtained.

Summary

■ The following table summarises the breakdown of skills and the marks allocated to each skill area as it is assessed in the Cambridge International A Level Chemistry Planning, Analysis and Evaluation examination (Paper 5).

Skill		Breakdown of marks[a]	
Planning	12 marks	Defining the problem	4 marks
		Methods	8 marks
Analysis, conclusions and evaluation	12 marks	Dealing with data	6 marks
		Evaluation	4 marks
		Conclusion	2 marks

[a]The remaining 6 marks will be allocated across the skills in this grid and their allocation may vary from paper to paper.

End-of-chapter question

1   Diffusion in a gas is the random motion of particles involved in the net movement of a substance from an area of high concentration to an area of low concentration. The process of diffusion also takes place in solution. Medical scientists are interested in the rate of diffusion of pharmaceutical compounds through tumours. They can model the factors that affect the rate of diffusion of these drugs by conducting investigations using coloured compounds (to model the drugs) and gelatin, a jelly-like substance (to model the tumours).

The kinetic energy of particles depends on their mass and the speed they travel at. So at a given temperature, large particles will travel slower on average than smaller particles.

Imagine that you are a member of a research team trying to find out how the rate of diffusion through gelatin depends on the relative molecular mass (M_r) of a drug.

a   i   Predict how you think that the rate of diffusion will be affected as the relative molecular mass of a drug **increases**. Explain your reasoning.

    ii   Display your prediction on a sketch graph, including any relevant units.   [4]

b   In the experiment you are about to plan, identify the:

    i   the independent variable

    ii   the dependent variable.   [2]

c   The research team can make thin discs of gelatin to cover the central area of Petri dishes, leaving space around the edge of each disc to place a solution of the coloured dyes under investigation:

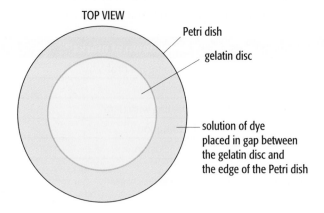

TOP VIEW

Petri dish

gelatin disc

solution of dye placed in gap between the gelatin disc and the edge of the Petri dish

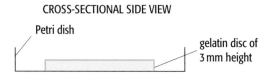

CROSS-SECTIONAL SIDE VIEW

Petri dish

gelatin disc of 3 mm height

You have been given five coloured powders of dyes, labelled A to E, to test. These have relative molecular masses of 486, 534, 686, 792 and 886, respectively. You are also provided with a stopclock/watch and a ruler with a millimetre scale. You can also use any other common laboratory apparatus needed to complete the investigation. The diffusion is a slow process and the team carry out some trial runs to get a rough idea how quickly the dyes diffuse through the gelatin. They decide to monitor the experiment for 72 hours.

Describe how you would carry out the experiment, making sure that you include how to:

- ensure the same number of dye molecules is used in each test
- ensure that the Petri dish is kept under the same conditions throughout all of the experiments
- measure the rate of diffusion
- produce reliable results. [6]

d   Two of the dyes are classified as 'harmful' and are hazardous if absorbed through the skin or are inhaled. State any precautions you would take to minimise the risk. [2]

e   Draw a table with headings that show clearly the data you would record when carrying out your experiments and any values you would need to calculate in order to construct a graph to check your prediction in part **a**. The headings **must** include the appropriate units. Ensure that the table covers all the detail relating to the five dyes listed in part **c**. [2]

Total = 16

Appendix 1

The Periodic Table of the Elements

key

atomic number
atomic symbol
name
relative atomic mass

Period	Group 1	2	3	4	5	6	7	8	9	10	11	12	13	14	15	16	17	18
1	1 **H** hydrogen 1.0																	2 **He** helium 4.0
2	3 **Li** lithium 6.9	4 **Be** beryllium 9.0											5 **B** boron 10.8	6 **C** carbon 12.0	7 **N** nitrogen 14.0	8 **O** oxygen 16.0	9 **F** fluorine 19.0	10 **Ne** neon 20.2
3	11 **Na** sodium 23.0	12 **Mg** magnesium 24.3											13 **Al** aluminium 27.0	14 **Si** silicon 28.1	15 **P** phosphorus 31.0	16 **S** sulfur 32.1	17 **Cl** chlorine 35.5	18 **Ar** argon 39.9
4	19 **K** potassium 39.1	20 **Ca** calcium 40.1	21 **Sc** scandium 45.0	22 **Ti** titanium 47.9	23 **V** vanadium 50.9	24 **Cr** chromium 52.0	25 **Mn** manganese 54.9	26 **Fe** iron 55.8	27 **Co** cobalt 58.9	28 **Ni** nickel 58.7	29 **Cu** copper 63.5	30 **Zn** zinc 65.4	31 **Ga** gallium 69.7	32 **Ge** germanium 72.6	33 **As** arsenic 74.9	34 **Se** selenium 79.0	35 **Br** bromine 79.9	36 **Kr** krypton 83.8
5	37 **Rb** rubidium 85.5	38 **Sr** strontium 87.6	39 **Y** yttrium 88.9	40 **Zr** zirconium 91.2	41 **Nb** niobium 92.9	42 **Mo** molybdenum 95.9	43 **Tc** technetium –	44 **Ru** ruthenium 101.1	45 **Rh** rhodium 102.9	46 **Pd** palladium 106.4	47 **Ag** silver 107.9	48 **Cd** cadmium 112.4	49 **In** indium 114.8	50 **Sn** tin 118.7	51 **Sb** antimony 121.8	52 **Te** tellurium 127.6	53 **I** iodine 126.9	54 **Xe** xenon 131.3
6	55 **Cs** caesium 132.9	56 **Ba** barium 137.3	57–71 lanthanoids	72 **Hf** hafnium 178.5	73 **Ta** tantalum 180.9	74 **W** tungsten 183.8	75 **Re** rhenium 186.2	76 **Os** osmium 190.2	77 **Ir** iridium 192.2	78 **Pt** platinum 195.1	79 **Au** gold 197.0	80 **Hg** mercury 200.6	81 **Tl** thallium 204.4	82 **Pb** lead 207.2	83 **Bi** bismuth 209.0	84 **Po** polonium –	85 **At** astatine –	86 **Rn** radon –
7	87 **Fr** francium –	88 **Ra** radium –	89–103 actinoids	104 **Rf** rutherfordium –	105 **Db** dubnium –	106 **Sg** seaborgium –	107 **Bh** bohrium –	108 **Hs** hassium –	109 **Mt** meitnerium –	110 **Ds** darmstadtium –	111 **Rg** roentgenium –	112 **Cn** copernicium –		114 **Fl** flerovium –		116 **Lv** livermorium –		

lanthanoids

57 **La** lanthanum 138.9	58 **Ce** cerium 140.1	59 **Pr** praseodymium 140.9	60 **Nd** neodymium 144.4	61 **Pm** promethium –	62 **Sm** samarium 150.4	63 **Eu** europium 152.0	64 **Gd** gadolinium 157.3	65 **Tb** terbium 158.9	66 **Dy** dysprosium 162.5	67 **Ho** holmium 164.9	68 **Er** erbium 167.3	69 **Tm** thulium 168.9	70 **Yb** ytterbium 173.1	71 **Lu** lutetium 175.0

actinoids

89 **Ac** actinium –	90 **Th** thorium 232.0	91 **Pa** protactinium 231.0	92 **U** uranium 238.0	93 **Np** neptunium –	94 **Pu** plutonium –	95 **Am** americium –	96 **Cm** curium –	97 **Bk** berkelium –	98 **Cf** californium –	99 **Es** einsteinium –	100 **Fm** fermium –	101 **Md** mendelevium –	102 **No** nobelium –	103 **Lr** lawrencium –

Appendix 2

Selected standard electrode potentials

Electrode reaction	$E^{\ominus}/V$	Electrode reaction	$E^{\ominus}/V$
$Ag^+ + e^- \rightleftharpoons Ag$	$+0.80$	$Mn^{2+} + 2e^- \rightleftharpoons Mn$	-1.18
$Br_2 + 2e^- \rightleftharpoons 2Br^-$	$+1.07$	$MnO_4^- + 8H^+ + 5e^- \rightleftharpoons Mn^{2+} + 4H_2O$	$+1.52$
$Ca^{2+} + 2e^- \rightleftharpoons Ca$	-2.87	$Ni^{2+} + 2e^- \rightleftharpoons Ni$	-0.25
$Cl_2 + 2e^- \rightleftharpoons 2Cl^-$	$+1.36$	$NO_3^- + 2H^+ + e^- \rightleftharpoons NO_2 + H_2O$	$+0.81$
$ClO^- + H_2O + 2e^- \rightleftharpoons Cl^- + 2OH^-$	$+0.89$	$NO_3^- + 10H^+ + 8e^- \rightleftharpoons NH_4^+ + 3H_2O$	$+0.87$
$Cr^{2+} + 2e^- \rightleftharpoons Cr$	-0.91	$O_2 + 4H^+ + 4e^- \rightleftharpoons 2H_2O$	$+1.23$
$Cr^{3+} + 3e^- \rightleftharpoons Cr$	-0.74	$O_2 + 2H_2O + 4e^- \rightleftharpoons 4OH^-$	$+0.40$
$Cr_2O_7^{2-} + 14H^+ + 6e^- \rightleftharpoons 2Cr^{3+} + 7H_2O$	$+1.33$	$Pb^{2+} + 2e^- \rightleftharpoons Pb$	-0.13
$Cu^+ + e^- \rightleftharpoons Cu$	$+0.52$	$PbO_2 + 4H^+ + 2e^- \rightleftharpoons Pb^{2+} + 2H_2O$	$+1.47$
$Cu^{2+} + e^- \rightleftharpoons Cu^+$	$+0.15$	$Sn^{2+} + 2e^- \rightleftharpoons Sn$	-0.14
$Cu^{2+} + 2e^- \rightleftharpoons Cu$	$+0.34$	$Sn^{4+} + 2e^- \rightleftharpoons Sn^{2+}$	$+0.15$
$F_2 + 2e^- \rightleftharpoons 2F^-$	$+2.87$	$SO_4^{2-} + 4H^+ + 2e^- \rightleftharpoons SO_2 + 2H_2O$	$+0.17$
$Fe^{2+} + 2e^- \rightleftharpoons Fe$	-0.44	$S_2O_8^{2-} + 2e^- \rightleftharpoons 2SO_4^{2-}$	$+2.01$
$Fe^{3+} + e^- \rightleftharpoons Fe^{2+}$	$+0.77$	$S_4O_6^{2-} + 2e^- \rightleftharpoons 2S_2O_3^{2-}$	$+0.09$
$Fe^{3+} + 3e^- \rightleftharpoons Fe$	-0.04	$V^{2+} + 2e^- \rightleftharpoons V$	-1.20
$2H^+ + 2e^- \rightleftharpoons H_2$	0.00	$V^{3+} + e^- \rightleftharpoons V^{2+}$	-0.26
$2H_2O + 2e^- \rightleftharpoons H_2 + 2OH^-$	-0.83	$VO^{2+} + 2H^+ + e^- \rightleftharpoons V^{3+} + H_2O$	$+0.34$
$H_2O_2 + 2H^+ + 2e^- \rightleftharpoons 2H_2O$	$+1.77$	$VO_2^+ + 2H^+ + e^- \rightleftharpoons VO^{2+} + H_2O$	$+1.00$
$I_2 + 2e^- \rightleftharpoons 2I^-$	$+0.54$	$VO_3^- + 4H^+ + e^- \rightleftharpoons VO^{2+} + 2H_2O$	$+1.00$
$K^+ + e^- \rightleftharpoons K$	-2.92	$Zn^{2+} + 2e^- \rightleftharpoons Zn$	-0.76
$Mg^{2+} + 2e^- \rightleftharpoons Mg$	-2.38		

Appendix 3

Qualitative analysis notes

1 Reactions of aqueous cations

Cation	Reaction with	
	NaOH(aq)	NH$_3$(aq)
aluminium, Al^{3+}(aq)	white precipitate soluble in excess	white precipitate insoluble in excess
ammonium, NH$_4^+$(aq)	no precipitate NH$_3$ produced on heating	–
barium, Ba^{2+}(aq)	faint white precipitate is nearly always observed unless reagents are pure	no precipitate
calcium, Ca^{2+}(aq)	white precipitate with high [Ca^{2+}(aq)]	no precipitate
chromium(III), Cr^{3+}(aq)	grey-green precipitate soluble in excess	grey-green precipitate insoluble in excess
copper(II), Cu^{2+}(aq)	pale blue precipitate insoluble in excess	pale blue precipitate soluble in excess giving dark blue solution
iron(II), Fe^{2+}(aq)	green precipitate turning brown on contact with air insoluble in excess	green precipitate turning brown on contact with air insoluble in excess
iron(III), Fe^{3+}(aq)	red-brown precipitate insoluble in excess	red-brown precipitate insoluble in excess
magnesium, Mg^{2+}(aq)	white precipitate insoluble in excess	white precipitate insoluble in excess
manganese(II), Mn^{2+}(aq)	off-white precipitate rapidly turning brown on contact with air insoluble in excess	off-white precipitate rapidly turning brown on contact with air insoluble in excess
zinc, Zn^{2+}(aq)	white precipitate soluble in excess	white precipitate soluble in excess

2 Reactions of anions

Ion	Reaction
carbonate, $CO_3^{2-}(aq)$	CO_2 liberated by dilute acids
chloride, $Cl^-(aq)$	gives white precipitate with $Ag^+(aq)$ (soluble in $NH_3(aq)$)
bromide, $Br^-(aq)$	gives cream precipitate with $Ag^+(aq)$ (partially soluble in $NH_3(aq)$)
iodide, $I^-(aq)$	gives yellow precipitate with $Ag^+(aq)$ (insoluble in $NH_3(aq)$)
nitrate, $NO_3^-(aq)$	NH_3 liberated on heating with $OH^-(aq)$ and Al foil
nitrite, $NO_2^-(aq)$	NH_3 liberated on heating with $OH^-(aq)$ and Al foil; NO liberated by dilute acids (colourless NO → (pale) brown NO_2 in air)
sulfate, $SO_4^{2-}(aq)$	gives white precipitate with $Ba^{2+}(aq)$ (insoluble in excess dilute strong acids)
sulfite, $SO_3^{2-}(aq)$	SO_2 liberated on warming with dilute acids; gives white precipitate with $Ba^{2+}(aq)$ (soluble in excess dilute strong acids)

3 Tests for gases

Gas	Test and test result
ammonia, NH_3	turns damp red litmus paper blue
carbon dioxide, CO_2	gives a white precipitate with limewater (precipitate dissolves with excess CO_2)
chlorine, Cl_2	bleaches damp litmus paper
hydrogen, H_2	'pops' with a lighted splint
oxygen, O_2	relights a glowing splint
sulfur dioxide, SO_2	turns acidified aqueous potassium manganate(VII) from purple to colourless

Glossary

acid a proton (hydrogen ion) donor.

acid–base indicator a substance that changes colour over a narrow range of pH values.

acid dissociation constant, K_a the equilibrium constant for a weak acid:

$$K_a = \frac{[H^+][A^-]}{[HA]}$$

activation energy the minimum energy that colliding particles must possess for a successful collision that results in a reaction to take place.

active site (of an enzyme) the 'pocket' on an enzyme surface where the substrate binds and undergoes catalytic reaction.

acyl chloride a reactive organic compound related to a carboxylic acid, with the —OH group in the acid replaced by a —Cl atom, for example ethanoyl chloride, CH_3COCl.

addition polymerisation the reaction in which monomers containing carbon-to-carbon double bonds react together to form long-chain molecules called polymers.

addition reaction an organic reaction in which two reactant molecules combine to give a single product molecule.

adsorption (in catalysis) the first stage in heterogeneous catalysis – molecules of reactants (usually gases) form bonds with atoms on the surface of the catalyst.

alkali a base that is soluble in water.

alkaline earth metals the elements in Group 2 of the Periodic Table.

alkanes saturated hydrocarbons with the general formula C_nH_{2n+2}.

alkenes unsaturated hydrocarbons with a carbon–carbon double bond. Their general formula is C_nH_{2n}.

allotrope different crystalline or molecular forms of the same element. Graphite and diamond are allotropes of carbon.

alloy a mixture of two or more metals or a metal with a non-metal.

amino acid residue an amino acid unit within a polypeptide chain.

amphoteric able to behave as both an acid and a base. Aluminium oxide is amphoteric.

anion a negatively charged ion.

anode the positive electrode.

arenes hydrocarbons containing one or more benzene rings.

atomic orbitals regions of space outside the nucleus that can be occupied by one or, at most, two electrons. Orbitals are named s, p, d and f. They have different shapes.

average bond energy a general bond energy value used for a particular bond, e.g. a C—H, when the exact bond energy is not required. Average bond energies are often used because the strength of a bond between two particular types of atom is slightly different in different compounds.

Avogadro constant the number of atoms (or ions, molecules or electrons) in a mole of atoms (or ions, molecules or electrons): its numerical value is 6.02×10^{23}.

azo dyes coloured compounds formed on the addition of phenol (or another aryl compound) to a solution containing a diazonium ion. They contain the —N=N— group.

base a proton (hydrogen ion) acceptor.

bidentate ligands that can form two co-ordinate bonds from each ion or molecule to the central transition metal ion.

biofuels renewable fuels, sourced from plant or animal materials.

boiling point the temperature at which the vapour pressure is equal to the atmospheric pressure.

Boltzmann distribution a graph showing the distribution of energies of the particles in a sample at a given temperature.

bond energy/bond enthalpy the energy needed to break 1 mole of a particular bond in 1 mole of gaseous molecules.

Born–Haber cycle a type of enthalpy cycle used to calculate lattice energy.

Brønsted–Lowry theory of acids acids are proton donors and bases are proton acceptors.

buffer solution a solution that minimises changes in pH when moderate amounts of acid or base are added. Common forms of buffer consist of either a weak acid and its conjugate base or a weak base and its conjugate acid.

carbocation an alkyl group carrying a single positive charge on one of its carbon atoms, e.g. $^+CH_2CH_3$

catalyst a substance that increases the rate of a reaction but remains chemically unchanged itself at the end of the reaction.

cathode the negative electrode.

cation a positively charged ion.

chiral centre a carbon atom with four different groups attached, creating the possibility of optical isomers.

closed system a system in which matter or energy is not lost or gained, e.g. gases in a closed vessel.

cofactor a small molecule that is not a substrate but that is essential for an enzyme-catalysed reaction.

common ion effect the reduction in the solubility of a dissolved salt by adding a compound that has an ion in common with the dissolved salt. This often results in precipitation of the salt.

competitive inhibition enzyme inhibition by molecules that bind to the active site, preventing the normal substrate from reacting. They have a structure similar to the substrate molecule. The inhibition is reversible.

complementary base pairing In nucleic acids, bases are said to be complementary to each other if they form specific hydrogen-bonded pairs. In DNA adenine (A) always pairs with thymine (T) and cytosine (C) always pairs with guanine (G).

complex a central transition metal ion surrounded by ligands.

compound a substance made up of two or more elements bonded (chemically joined) together.

condensation the change in state when a vapour changes to a liquid.

condensation reaction a reaction in which two organic molecules join together and in the process eliminate a small molecule, such as water or hydrogen chloride.

conjugate pair (acid/base) an acid and base on each side of an equilibrium equation that are related to each other by the difference of a proton; e.g. the acid in the forward reaction and the base in the reverse reaction or the base in the forward reaction and the acid in the reverse reaction.

co-ordinate bond a covalent bond in which both electrons in the bond come from the same atom.

co-ordination number the number of co-ordinate (dative) bonds formed by ligands to the central transition metal ion in a complex.

coupling reaction when a diazonium ion reacts with an alkaline solution of phenol (or similar compound) to make an azo dye.

covalent bond a bond formed by the sharing of pairs of electrons between two atoms.

cracking the process in which large, less useful hydrocarbon molecules are broken down into smaller, more useful molecules.

dative covalent bond another name for a co-ordinate bond.

degenerate orbitals atomic orbitals at the same energy level.

dehydration a reaction in which a water molecule is removed from a molecule, e.g. in the dehydration of an alcohol to give an alkene.

delocalised electrons electrons that are not associated with a particular atom – they can move between three or more adjacent atoms.

denaturation the process by which the three-dimensional structure of a protein or other biological macromolecule is changed, often irreversibly. Relatively high temperatures, extremes of pH and organic solvents often cause denaturation.

desorption the last stage in heterogeneous catalysis. The bonds holding the molecule(s) of product(s) to the surface of the catalyst are broken and the product molecules diffuse away from the surface of the catalyst.

diazotisation the reaction between phenylamine and nitrous acid (nitric(III) acid), HNO_2, to give a diazonium salt in the first step in making an azo dye.

dipeptide the product formed when two amino acids react together.

dipole a separation of charge in a molecule. One end of the molecule is permanently positively charged and the other is negatively charged.

discharge the conversion of ions to atoms or molecules at electrodes during electrolysis, for example, during the electrolysis of concentrated sodium chloride solution, chlorine is discharged at the anode by the conversion of Cl^- ions to Cl atoms, which then combine to form Cl_2 molecules.

displayed formula a drawing of a molecule that shows all the atoms and bonds within the molecule.

disproportionation the simultaneous reduction and oxidation of the same species in a chemical reaction.

dissociation the break-up of a molecule into ions, for example, when HCl molecules dissolve in aqueous solution, they dissociate completely into H^+ and Cl^- ions.

disulfide bridge an S—S bond formed when the —SH groups on the side-chain of two cysteine residues in a protein combine. Disulfide bridges help maintain the tertiary structure of some proteins.

DNA (deoxyribonucleic acid) a polymer with a double helical structure containing two sugar–phosphate chains with nitrogenous bases attached to them. The sequence of bases forms a code, which is used to form more DNA by replication or to encode mRNA (transcription).

dot-and-cross diagram a diagram showing the arrangement of the outer-shell electrons in an ionic or covalent element or compound. The electrons are shown as dots or crosses to show their origin.

double covalent bond two shared pairs of electrons bonding two atoms together.

dynamic (equilibrium) in an equilibrium mixture, molecules of reactants are being converted to products at the same rate as products are being converted to reactants.

electrochemical cell two half-cells in separate compartments joined by a salt bridge. When the poles of the half-cells are joined by a wire, electrons travel in the external circuit from the half-cell with the more negative $E^{\ominus}$ value to the half-cell with the more positive $E^{\ominus}$ value.

electrode a rod of metal or carbon (graphite) which conducts electricity to or from an electrolyte.

electrode potential the voltage measured for a half-cell compared with another half-cell.

electrolysis the decomposition of a compound into its elements by an electric current.

electrolyte a molten ionic compound or an aqueous solution of ions that is decomposed during electrolysis.

electron tiny subatomic particles found in orbitals around the nucleus. They have a negative charge but have negligible mass.

electron affinity (first electron affinity) $\Delta H^{\ominus}_{ea1}$; the enthalpy change when 1 mole of electrons is added to 1 mole of gaseous atoms to form 1 mole of gaseous 1– ions under standard conditions.

electron affinity (second electron affinity) $\Delta H^{\ominus}_{ea2}$; the enthalpy change when 1 mole of electrons is added to 1 mole of gaseous 1– ions to form 1 mole of gaseous 2– ions under standard conditions.

electronegativity the ability of an atom to attract the bonding electrons in a covalent bond.

electronic configuration a way of representing the arrangement of the electrons in atoms showing the principal quantum shells, the subshells and the number of electrons present, e.g. $1s^2\,2s^2\,2p^3$. The electrons may also be shown in boxes.

electropherogram the physical results of electrophoresis.

electrophile a species that can act as an acceptor of a pair of electrons in an organic mechanism.

electrophoresis the separation of charged particles by their different rates of movement in an electric field.

electrovalent bond another name for an ionic bond.

element a substance made of only one type of atom.

elimination a reaction in which a small molecule, such as H_2O or HCl, is removed from an organic molecule.

empirical formula the formula that tells us the simplest ratio of the different atoms present in a molecule.

endothermic term used to describe a reaction in which energy is absorbed from the surroundings: the enthalpy change is positive.

energy levels (of electrons) the regions at various distances from the nucleus in which electrons have a particular amount of energy. Electrons further from the nucleus have more energy. See principal quantum shells.

enhanced global warming the increase in average temperatures around the world as a consequence of the huge increase in the amounts of CO_2 and other greenhouse gases produced by human activity.

enthalpy change of atomisation $\Delta H^{\ominus}_{at}$; the enthalpy change when 1 mole of gaseous atoms is formed from its element under standard conditions.

enthalpy change of hydration $\Delta H^{\ominus}_{hyd}$; the enthalpy change when 1 mole of a specified gaseous ion dissolves in sufficient water to form a very dilute solution.

enthalpy change of solution $\Delta H^{\ominus}_{sol}$; the energy absorbed or released when 1 mole of an ionic solid dissolves in sufficient water to form a very dilute solution.

enthalpy change the energy transferred in a chemical reaction (symbol ΔH).

enthalpy cycle a diagram showing alternative routes between reactants and products that allows the determination of one enthalpy change from other known enthalpy changes by using Hess's law.

enthalpy profile diagram a diagram showing the enthalpy change from reactants to products along the reaction pathway.

entropy a measure of the dispersal of energy or disorder of a system. The system becomes energetically more stable when disordered.

enzyme a protein molecule that is a biological catalyst. Most act on a specific substrate.

enzyme activity a measure of the rate at which substrate is converted to product in an enzyme-catalysed reaction.

equilibrium constant a constant calculated from the equilibrium expression for a reaction.

equilibrium expression a simple relationship that links K_c to the equilibrium concentrations of reactants and products and the stoichiometric equation.

479

equilibrium reaction a reaction that does not go to completion and in which reactants and products are present in fixed concentration ratios.

esterification the reaction between an alcohol and a carboxylic acid (or acyl chloride) to produce an ester and water.

eutrophication an environmental problem caused by fertilisers leached from fields into rivers and lakes. The fertiliser then promotes the growth of algae on the surface of water. When the algae die, bacteria thrive and use up the dissolved oxygen in the water, killing aquatic life.

exothermic the term used to describe a reaction in which energy is released to the surroundings: the enthalpy change is negative.

Faraday constant the charge carried by 1 mole of electrons (or 1 mole of singly charged ions). It has a value of 96 500 coulombs per mol ($C\,mol^{-1}$).

Faraday's laws first law: the mass of a substance produced at an electrode during electrolysis is proportional to the quantity of electricity passed in coulombs. Second law: the number of Faradays needed to discharge 1 mole of an ion at an electrode equals the number of charges on the ion.

feasibility (of reaction) the likelihood or not of a reaction occurring when reactants are mixed. We can use $E^{\ominus}$ values to assess the feasibility of a reaction.

Fehling's solution an alkaline solution containing copper(II) ions used to distinguish between aldehydes and ketones. A positive test is one in which the clear blue solution gives a red/orange precipitate when warmed with aldehydes, but no change is observed with ketones.

fragmentation the breaking up of a molecule into smaller parts by the breaking of covalent bonds in a mass spectrometer.

free energy see Gibbs free energy.

free radical very reactive atom or molecule that has a single unpaired electron.

free-radical substitution the reaction in which halogen atoms substitute for hydrogen atoms in alkanes. The mechanism involves steps in which reactive free radicals are produced (initiation), regenerated (propagation) and consumed (termination).

Friedel–Crafts reaction the electrophilic substitution of an alkyl or acyl group into a benzene ring.

fuel cell a source of electrical energy that comes directly from the energy stored in the chemicals in the cell, one of which is oxygen (which may come from the air).

functional group an atom or group of atoms in an organic molecule that determine the characteristic reactions of a homologous series.

gene a length of DNA that carries a code for making a particular protein.

general formula a formula that represents a homologous series of compounds using letters and numbers; e.g. the general formula for the alkanes is C_nH_{2n+2}. By substituting a number for n in the general formula you get the molecular formula of a particular compound in that homologous series.

general gas equation an equation relating the volume of a gas to the temperature, pressure and number of moles of gas. Also called the ideal gas equation.

$$pV = nRT$$

genetic code a code made up of sets of three consecutive nitrogenous bases that provides the information to make specific proteins.

genetic engineering the deliberate alteration of one or more bases in the DNA of an organism, leading to an altered protein with improved properties. Scientists hope to be able to use genetic engineering to eliminate genetic diseases which are caused by mutations in DNA.

genetic fingerprinting a technique based on matching the minisatellite regions of a person's DNA to a database of reference samples.

giant molecular structure/giant covalent structure structures having a three-dimensional network of covalent bonds throughout the whole structure.

Gibbs free energy the energy change that takes into account both the entropy change of a reaction and enthalpy change. Reactions are likely to be feasible if the value of the Gibbs free energy change of reaction is negative. The Gibbs free energy change of reaction is given by the relationship

$$\Delta G^{\ominus} = \Delta H^{\ominus} - T\Delta S^{\ominus}$$

GLC gas–liquid chromatography.

GLC/MS a technique in which a mass spectrometer is connected directly to a gas–liquid chromatograph to identify the components in a mixture.

haemoglobin the iron-containing protein found in red blood cells that transports oxygen around the body.

half-cell half of an electrochemical cell. The half-cell with the more negative $E^{\ominus}$ value supplies electrons. The half-cell with the more positive $E^{\ominus}$ value receives electrons.

half-equation in a redox reaction, an equation showing either an oxidation or a reduction.

half-life the time taken for the amount (or concentration) of the limiting reactant in a reaction to decrease to half its value.

halogens Group 17 elements.

Hess's law the total enthalpy change for a chemical reaction is independent of the route by which the reaction takes place.

heterogeneous catalysis the type of catalysis in which the catalyst is in a different phase from the reactants. For example, iron in the Haber process.

homogeneous catalysis the type of catalysis in which the catalyst and reactants are in the same phase. For example, sulfuric acid catalysing the formation of an ester from an alcohol and carboxylic acid.

HPLC high-performance liquid chromatography.

hybridisation of atomic orbitals the process of mixing atomic orbitals so that each has some character of each of the orbitals mixed.

hydrocarbon a compound made up of carbon and hydrogen only.

hydrogen bond the strongest type of intermolecular force – it is formed between molecules having a hydrogen atom bonded to one of the most electronegative elements (F, O or N).

hydrolysis the breakdown of a compound by water, which is often speeded up by reacting with acid or alkali.

hydrophobic the non-polar part of a molecule that has no attraction for water molecules ('water hating').

hydroxynitrile an organic compound containing both an —OH and a —CN group, e.g. 2-hydroxypropanenitrile, $CH_3CH(OH)CN$.

ideal gas a gas whose volume varies in proportion to the temperature and in inverse proportion to the pressure. Noble gases such as helium and neon approach ideal behaviour because of their low intermolecular forces.

infra-red spectroscopy a technique for identifying compounds based on the change in vibrations of particular atoms when infra-red radiation of specific frequencies is absorbed

initiation step the first step in the mechanism of free-radical substitution of alkanes by halogens. It involves the breaking of the halogen–halogen bond by UV light from the Sun.

intermolecular forces the weak forces between molecules.

ion polarisation the distortion of the electron cloud on an anion by a neighbouring cation. The distortion is greatest when the cation is small and highly charged.

ionic bond the electrostatic attraction between oppositely charged ions.

ionic product of water, K_w the equilibrium constant for the ionisation of water.

$$K_w = [H^+][OH^-]$$

ionisation energy, ΔH_i the energy needed to remove 1 mole of electrons from 1 mole of atoms of an element in the gaseous state to form 1 mole of gaseous ions.

isotopes atoms of an element with the same number of protons but different numbers of neutrons.

kinetic theory the theory that particles in gases and liquids are in constant movement. The kinetic theory can be used to explain the effect of temperature and pressure on the volume of a gas as well as rates of chemical reactions.

lattice a regularly repeating arrangement of ions, atoms or molecules in three dimensions.

lattice energy the enthalpy change when 1 mole of an ionic compound is formed from its gaseous ions under standard conditions.

le Chatelier's principle when any of the conditions affecting the position of equilibrium are changed, the position of that equilibrium shifts to minimise the change.

ligand a molecule or ion with one or more lone pairs of electrons available to donate to a transition metal ion.

lock-and-key mechanism a model used to explain why enzymes are so specific in their activity. It is suggested that the active site of the enzyme has a shape into which the substrate fits exactly – rather like a particular key fits a particular lock.

lone pairs (of electrons) pairs of electrons in the outer shell of an atom that are not bonded.

mass number see nucleon number.

mass spectrometer an instrument for finding the relevant isotopic abundance of elements and to help identify unknown organic compounds.

metabolism the series of linked chemical reactions taking place in living organisms.

metalloid elements that have a low electrical conductivity at room temperature but whose conductivity increases with increasing temperature. Metalloids are found in a diagonal band running from the top left to nearly the bottom right of the p-block in the Periodic Table.

mobile phase the solvent in the chromatography process, which moves through the column or over the paper or thin layer.

molar mass the mass of a mole of substance in grams.

481

mole the unit of amount of substance. It is the amount of substance that has the same number of particles (atoms, ions, molecules or electrons) as there are atoms in exactly 12 g of the carbon-12 isotope.

molecular formula the formula that tells us the actual numbers of each type of atom in a molecule.

molecular ion the ion that is formed by the loss of an electron from the original complete molecule during mass spectrometry and that gives us the relative molecular mass of an unknown compound.

monodendate ligands, such as water and ammonia, that can form only one co-ordinate bond from each ion or molecule to the central transition metal ion.

monomer a small, reactive molecule that reacts to make long-chain molecules called polymers.

nanotechnology the design and production of machines that are so small we measure them in nanometres (nm), where $1\,nm = 1 \times 10^{-9}\,m$.

Nernst equation an equation used to predict quantitatively how the value of an electrode potential varies with the concentration of the aqueous ion.

neutron a subatomic particle found in the nucleus of an atom. It has no charge and has the same mass as a proton.

nitrogenous bases nitrogen-containing bases found in DNA and RNA. In DNA they are adenine (A), guanine (G), thymine (T) and cytosine (C). In RNA uracil (U) replaces thymine.

NMR nuclear magnetic resonance spectroscopy.

non-degenerate orbitals atomic orbitals that have been split to occupy slightly different energy levels.

non-polar (molecule) a molecule with no separation of charge; it will not be attracted to a positive or negative charge.

nucleon number the total number of protons and neutrons in the nucleus of an atom.

nucleophile species that can act as a donor of a pair of electrons.

nucleophilic addition the mechanism of the reaction in which a nucleophile attacks the carbon atom in a carbonyl group and adds across the C=O bond, e.g. aldehydes or ketones reacting with hydrogen cyanide.

nucleotide a compound consisting of a nitrogenous base, a sugar (ribose or deoxyribose) and a phosphate group. Nucleotides form the basic structural units of DNA and RNA.

nucleus the small dense core at the centre of every atom, containing protons (positively charged) and neutrons (no charge). Nuclei are therefore always positively charged.

open system a system in which matter is lost or gained, e.g. a mixture of solids and gases in an open beaker.

optical isomers stereoisomers that exist as two non-superimposable mirror images.

optical resolution the separation of optically active isomers (enantiomers) from a mixture.

order of reaction the power to which the concentration of a reactant is raised in the rate equation. If the concentration does not affect the rate, the reaction is zero order. If the rate is directly proportional to the reactant concentration, the reaction is first order. If the rate is directly proportional to the square of the reactant concentration, the reaction is second order.

oxidation the addition of oxygen, removal of electrons or increase in oxidation number of a substance; in organic chemistry refers to a reaction in which oxygen atoms are added to a molecule and/or hydrogen atoms are removed from a molecule.

oxidation number (oxidation state) a number given to an atom in a compound that describes how oxidised or reduced it is.

oxidising agent a reactant that increases the oxidation number of (or removes electrons from) another reactant.

partial pressure the pressure that an individual gas contributes to the overall pressure in a mixture of gases.

partition coefficient the ratio of the concentrations of a solute in two different immiscible solvents when an equilibrium has been established.

peptide bond the link between the amino acid residues in a polypeptide or protein chain. The link is formed by a condensation reaction between the —NH_2 group of one amino acid and the —COOH group of another amino acid.

periodicity the repeating patterns in the physical and chemical properties of the elements across the periods of the Periodic Table.

permanent dipole–dipole forces a type of intermolecular force between molecules that have permanent dipoles.

pH the hydrogen ion concentration expressed as a logarithm to base 10.

$$pH = -\log_{10}[H^+]$$

pi (π) bonds multiple covalent bonds involving the sideways overlap of p atomic orbitals.

pK_a values of K_a expressed as a logarithm to base 10.

$$pK_a = -\log_{10}K_a$$

polar (covalent bond) a covalent bond in which the two bonding electrons are not shared equally by the atoms in the bond. The atom with the greater share of the electrons has a partial negative charge, δ−, and the other has a partial positive charge, δ+.

polarising power (of a cation) the ability of a cation to attract electrons and distort an anion.

polyamides polymers whose monomers are bonded to each other via the amide link, —CONH—.

polyesters polymers whose monomers are bonded to each other via the ester link, —COO—.

polymer a long-chain molecule made up of many repeating units.

polypeptides natural polymers whose monomers are bonded to each other via the amide link, —CONH—, and whose monomers are amino acids.

primary alcohol an alcohol in which the carbon atom bonded to the —OH group is attached to one other carbon atom (or alkyl group).

primary structure (of proteins) the sequence of amino acids in a polypeptide chain.

principal quantum shells, *n* regions at various distances from the nucleus that may contain up to a certain number of electrons. The first quantum shell contains up to 2 electrons, the second up to 8 and the third up to 18.

propagation step a step in a free-radical mechanism in which the radicals formed can then attack reactant molecules generating more free-radicals, and so on.

protein condensation polymer formed from amino acids and joined together by peptide bonds. Proteins can be structural (e.g. cartilage), catalysts (enzymes), hormones (e.g. insulin) or antibodies.

proton a positively charged subatomic particle in the nucleus.

rate constant the proportionality constant in the rate equation (see rate equation).

rate equation an equation showing the relationship between the rate constant and the concentrations of those reactants that affect the rate of reaction. The general form of the rate equation is:

$$\text{rate} = k[\text{A}]^m[\text{B}]^n$$

where k is the rate constant, [A] and [B] are the concentrations of those reactants that affect the rate of reaction, m is the order of the reaction with respect to A and n is the order of reaction with respect to B.

rate of reaction a measure of the rate at which reactants are used up or the rate at which products are formed. The units of rate are $\text{mol}\,\text{dm}^{-3}\,\text{s}^{-1}$.

rate-determining step the slowest step in a reaction mechanism.

real gases gases that do not obey the ideal gas law, especially at low temperatures and high pressures.

redox reaction a reaction in which oxidation and reduction take place at the same time.

reducing agent a reactant that decreases the oxidation number of (or adds electrons to) another reactant.

reduction the removal of oxygen, addition of electrons or decrease in oxidation number of a substance; in organic chemistry it is the removal of oxygen atoms from a molecule and/or the addition of hydrogen atoms to a molecule.

relative atomic mass the weighted average mass of the atoms of an element, taking into account the proportions of naturally occurring isotopes, measured on a scale on which an atom of the carbon-12 isotope has a mass of exactly 12 units.

relative formula mass the mass of one formula unit of a compound measured on a scale on which an atom of the carbon-12 isotope has a mass of exactly 12 units.

relative isotopic mass the mass of a particular isotope of an element on a scale in which an atom of the carbon-12 isotope has a mass of exactly 12 units.

relative molecular mass the mass of a molecule measured on a scale in which an atom of the carbon-12 isotope has a mass of exactly 12 units.

residue see amino acid residue.

retention time the time taken for a component in a mixture to travel through the column in GLC or HPLC.

reversible reaction a reaction in which products can be changed back to reactants by reversing the conditions.

R_f value the ratio of the distance a component has travelled compared with the distance travelled by the solvent front during paper chromatography or TLC.

salt bridge a piece of filter paper soaked in potassium nitrate solution used to make electrical contact between the half-cells in an electrochemical cell.

saturated hydrocarbons compounds of hydrogen and carbon only in which the carbon–carbon bonds are all single covalent bonds, resulting in the maximum number of hydrogen atoms in their molecules.

secondary alcohol an alcohol in which the carbon atom bonded to the —OH group is attached to two other carbon atoms (or alkyl groups).

secondary structure (of proteins) the second level of protein structure. The folding of a polypeptide chain into specific structures (e.g. α-helix and β-pleated sheet), which are stabilised by hydrogen bonds formed between —CO and —NH groups in peptide bonds.

shielding the ability of inner shells of electrons to reduce the effective nuclear charge on electrons in the outer shell.

sigma (σ) bonds single covalent bonds, formed by the 'end-on' overlap of atomic orbitals.

single covalent bond a shared pair of electrons bonding two atoms together.

skeletal formula a simplified version of the displayed formula that has all the symbols for carbon and hydrogen atoms removed, as well as the carbon to hydrogen bonds. The carbon to carbon bonds are left in place as are the bonds to other atoms.

S_N1 mechanism the steps in a nucleophilic substitution reaction in which the rate of the reaction (which is determined by the slow step in the mechanism) involves only the organic reactant, e.g. in the hydrolysis of a tertiary halogenoalkane.

S_N2 mechanism the steps in a nucleophilic substitution reaction in which the rate of the reaction (which is determined by the slow step in the mechanism) involves two reacting species, e.g. in the hydrolysis of a primary halogenoalkane.

solubility product, K_{sp} the equilibrium expression showing the product of the concentrations of each ion in a saturated solution of a sparingly soluble salt at 298 K, raised to the power of the relative concentrations:

$$K_{sp} = [C^{y+}(aq)]^a[A^{x-}(aq)]^b$$

where a is the number of C^{y+} ions in one formula unit of the compound and b is the number of A^{x-} ions in one formula unit of the compound.

solute a substance that is dissolved in a solution.

specific most enzymes are described as specific because they will only catalyse one reaction involving one particular molecule or pair of molecules.

spectator ions ions present in a reaction mixture that do not take part in the reaction.

spin-pair repulsion electrons repel each other as they have the same charge. Electrons arrange themselves so that they first singly occupy different orbitals in the same sublevel. After that they pair up with their spins opposed to each other.

splitting pattern the pattern of peaks that main signals are divided into in high-resolution NMR.

stability constant, K_{stab} the equilibrium constant for the formation of the complex ion in a solvent from its constituent ions or molecules.

standard cell potential the difference in standard electrode potential between two half-cells.

standard conditions conditions of temperature and pressure that must be the same in order to compare moles of gases or enthalpy changes accurately. Standard conditions are a pressure of 10^5 pascals (100 kPa) and a temperature of 298 K (25 °C).

standard electrode potential the electrode potential of a half-cell when measured with a standard hydrogen electrode as the other half-cell.

standard enthalpy change an enthalpy change that takes place under the standard conditions of pressure (10^5 Pa) and temperature (298 K).

standard hydrogen electrode a half-cell in which hydrogen gas at a pressure of 1 atmosphere (101 kPa) bubbles into a solution of 1.00 mol dm^{-3} H$^+$ ions. This electrode is given a standard electrode potential of 0.00 V. All other standard electrode potentials are measured relative to this value.

state symbol a symbol used in a chemical equation that describes the state of each reactant and product: (s) for solid, (l) for liquid, (g) for gas and (aq) for substances in aqueous solution.

stationary phase the immobile phase in chromatography that the mobile phase passes over or through. Examples are the surface of the thin-layer particles in TLC or the involatile liquid adsorbed onto the column in GLC or HPLC.

stereoisomers compounds whose molecules have the same atoms bonded to each other but with different arrangements of the atoms in space.

stoichiometry the mole ratio of the reactants and products in the balanced equation for a reaction.

strong acid/base an acid or base that is (almost) completely ionised in water.

structural formula the formula that tells us about the atoms bonded to each carbon atom in an organic molecule, e.g. $CH_3CH{=}CH_2$.

structural isomers compounds with the same molecular formula but different structural formulae.

subshells regions within the principal quantum shells where electrons have more or less energy depending on their distance from the nucleus. Subshells are given the letters s, p, d and f.

substitution a reaction that involves the replacement of one atom, or group of atoms, by another.

substrate a molecule that fits into the active site of an enzyme and reacts.

successive ionisation energy ΔH_{i1}, ΔH_{i2}, etc.: the energy required to remove the first, then the second, then the third electrons and so on from a gaseous atom or ion, producing an ion with one more positive charge each time. Measured in kJ per mole of ions produced.

surroundings in enthalpy changes, anything other than the chemical reactants and products, for example the solvent, the test tube in which the reaction takes place, the air around the test tube.

termination step the final step in a free-radical mechanism in which two free radicals react together to form a molecule.

tertiary alcohol an alcohol in which the carbon atom bonded to the —OH group is attached to three other carbon atoms (or alkyl groups).

tertiary structure (of proteins) the third level of protein structure. It involves further folding of the polypeptide chain, which is stabilised by interactions between the amino acid side-chains (ionic interactions, hydrogen bonding, van der Waals' forces and disulfide bonds).

titre in a titration, the final burette reading minus the initial burette reading.

TLC thin-layer chromatography.

TMS tetramethylsilane. An inert, volatile liquid used as a reference in NMR, given a chemical shift of zero.

Tollens' reagent an aqueous solution of silver nitrate in excess ammonia solution, sometimes called ammoniacal silver nitrate solution. It is used to distinguish between aldehydes and ketones. It gives a positive 'silver mirror' test when warmed with aldehydes, but no change is observed with ketones.

triple covalent bond three shared pairs of electrons bonding two atoms together.

two-way chromatography a technique used in paper or thin-layer chromatography in which one spot of a mixture is placed at the corner of a square sheet and is developed in the first solvent as usual. The sheet is then turned through 90° and developed in the second solvent, giving a better separation of components having similar R_f values.

unsaturated hydrocarbons compounds of hydrogen and carbon only whose molecules contain carbon-to-carbon double bonds (or triple bonds).

van der Waals' forces the weak forces of attraction between molecules caused by the formation of temporary dipoles.

vaporisation the change in state when a liquid changes to vapour.

vapour pressure the pressure exerted by a vapour in equilibrium with a liquid.

weak acid/base an acid or base that is only slightly ionised in water.

X-ray crystallography an analytical technique that uses the diffraction pattern of X-rays passed through a solid sample to elucidate its structure.

Index

acid dissociation constant (K_a), 307–9
acid rain, 184–5, 205, 341–2
acid–base equilibria, 130–4
acid–base indicators, 309–10
acids, definitions of, 130–4
activation energy, 100, 141–5, 182, 340
active site, 457–8
acyl chlorides, 396–8, 406, 410, 416
addition polymerisation, 211–3, 426–7
addition reactions, 198, 208–12, 237, 383, 397, 412, 422, 424
addition reactions of alkenes, 198, 208–12
adsorption, 342–3
adsorption chromatography, 436
alanine, 404, 415
alcohols, formation of, 219
alcohols, reactions of, 226–31
aldehydes, formation of, 210, 236
aldehydes, reactions of, 225, 237–40
alkalis, definition of, 130
alkaline earth metals, 164–167
alkanes, reactions of, 204–7
alkanes, sources of, 202–3
alkenes, production of, 207–8
alkenes, reactions of, 208–12
allotropes, 80, 82
alloys, 79–80
aluminium, 53–4, 79–80, 84, 153
aluminium, reactions of, 154–6
aluminium–air batteries, 293
amides, formation of, 398
amides, reactions of, 406
amines, basicity of, 401–2
amines, classes of, 401
amines, formation of, 402–3
amines, reactions of, 403–4
amino acid residues, 416–7, 435
amino acids, 404–5, 407, 414–6, 434
ammonia, basicity of, 130, 134
ammonia, hydrogen bonding and, 64
ammonia, production of, 122, 128–9, 182
ammonia, reactions of, 101, 401–2, 406
ammonia, shape of, 52, 53, 55–6
ammonium compounds, 182–4
amphoteric materials, 131, 156, 405, 415
anions, 151, 263, 266, 295–6
anodes, 275, 295–7

arenes, 382
arenes, reactions of, 384–7
aromatic hydrocarbons, 203, *see also* arenes
aryl compounds, 193, 382–3
atomic mass, 2–5
atomic orbitals, 37–8, 57–8
atomic structure, 25–9
atoms, 2, 5–9, 25–6, 28
average bond energies, 100
Avogadro number or Avogadro constant, 5–6, 277–8
Avogadro's hypothesis, 18–19
azo dyes, 403–4

base units, SI, 5
bases, definitions of, 130–4
benzene, 193, 382–3
benzene, reactions of, 384–7
benzene, structure of, 382–3
benzene, nitration of, 385
benzene, π bonding in, 383
bidentate ligands, 372–3, 376
biochemical analysis, 407
biochemical polymers, 414–8
biochemical reactions, 145
biofuels, 227
bleach, 178
boiling points, trends in, 62–65, 66
Boltzmann distribution, 143–4
bonds, breaking and making of, 99–100, 196
bond energy, 54, 100–1
bond length, 54–6, 382
Born–Haber cycle, 259–62
boron trifluoride, structure and shape of, 51–2, 56
bromoethane, 209, 218, 220, 227, 373
Brønsted–Lowry theory of acids and bases, 131–2
buckminsterfullerene, 82–3
buffer solutions, 313–5, 405, 407

calcium chloride, 50
calorimetry, 94
carbocations, 197, 209–10, 221–2, 386
carbon dioxide, structure and shape of, 52–3, 56
carbon-neutral fuel, 227
carbonyl group, testing for, 238–9
carboxylic acids, acidity of, 394–5
catalysis, 142, 144–5, 340–3

catalysts, definition of, 142
catalytic converters, 184, 205, 343
catalytic crackers, 208
cathode ray tube, 26
cathodes, 275, 295
cations, 151, 295–6, 316, 384
cells and batteries, 293–5
ceramics, 158
CFCs, *see* chlorofluorocarbons, 222–3
chain isomerism, 195
chemical bonding, types of, 49–55
chemical equations, balancing of, 12, 97–8, 108, 112, 117–8
chemical formulae, 10–12
chiral catalysts, 459
chiral centres, 195–6
chiral drugs, 458–9
chlorides, of Period 3 elements, 158–60
chlorine, disproportionation of, 177
chlorobenzene, 382, 384, 398, 448
chlorofluorocarbons (CFCs), 222–3
chromatography, 319–20, 434–8
cis–trans isomerism, 195, 373
closed system, 119
collision theory, 141–2
combustion, enthalpy change of, 92–3
combustion, in determination of empirical formulae, 9
combustion, of alcohols, 226
combustion, of alkanes, 204–5
combustion, of fuels, 90–1
common ion effect, 318–9
complementary base pairs, 419
complex ions, 176, 369, 371–8
complexes, colour of, 376–8
compounds, properties of covalent, 66–7
compounds, properties of ionic, 66–7
compounds, naming of, 10–11
concentration, effects on equilibrium, 120, 126
concentration of reactant against time graphs, 332–4
condensation polymerisation, 412–4, 419, 424
condensation polymers, 412, 415, 421, 426–8
condensation reactions, 238–9, 397, 405, 412–3, 415
conjugate acids, 132–3, 314,
conjugate bases, 132–3
conjugate pairs, 132–3
Contact process, 129, 185
co-ordinate bonds, 53–4, 371–2, 376–7
co-ordination number, 372
copper, colour of complex ions of, 368, 374
copper, in electrolysis, 122
copper, uses of, 367

coupling reaction, 404
covalent bonding, 51–5
covalent bonds, dative, 53–4
covalent bonds, multiple, 52–3
covalent compounds, 11, 66–7, 109, 263
crude oil, 185, 202–3, 207, 227, 449, 460–1
cycloalkanes, 202

dative covalent bonds, 53–4
degenerate orbitals, 376–7
dehydration reactions, 230
delocalised electrons, 59–60, 383–5, 398, 402–4
desorption, 342–3
diamond, 81–2, 352
diazonium dyes, 403–4
diazotisation reactions, 403–4
diffusion, 342–3, 351
dipeptides, 405
displacement reactions, 174
displayed formula of compounds, 53, 190, 194
disproportionation, 177–8
DNA (deoxyribonucleic acid), 418–20
dot-and-cross diagrams, 50–4
drugs, delivery of, 83
drugs, designing new, 457–9
drugs, testing for, 449
dynamic equilibrium, 117–8, 319

$E^\ominus$ values, defining standard electrode potentials, 279, 281
$E^\ominus$ values, for oxidising and reducing agents, 284
$E^\ominus$ values, impact of ion concentration on, 280–1
$E^\ominus$ values, measuring standard electrode potentials, 282
$E^\ominus$ values, table of, 474
$E^\ominus$ values, use of, 284–8
electrical conductivity, improving through doping, 426
electrical conductivity, patterns of, 67, 83, 151-2, 326, 369

electrochemical cells, 280–1, 284–8, 293–4
electrode, pH, 306, 311
electrode, standard hydrogen, 279
electrode potentials, 278–88, 296
electrode reactions, 275, 474
electrodes, 275–6, 407
electrolysis, 84, 275
electrolysis, of aqueous solutions, 295–6
electrolysis, of brine, 296–7
electrolysis, of molten electrolytes, 295
electrolysis, quantitative, 276–8
electrolytes, 275–6, 293–6
electrolytic cells, 275

electrolytic purification of copper, 84

electron affinity, definition of, 258–9

electronegativity, 60–61, 64, 204, 209, 220, 238, 394, 397

electronic configurations of atoms and ions, 11, 33–4, 38–40, 164–5, 172–3, 193

electronic configurations of transition elements, 367–8, 377

electronic structure, 33–4, 38–40

electron-pair repulsion theory, 55–6

electrons, 26–9

electropherograms, 407

electrophiles, 197, 204–9, 384–6, 388, 403–4

electrophilic addition, 209–10

electrophilic substitution, 384–6

electrophoresis, 407–8

electrovalent bond, 50

elements, 2–4

elimination reactions, 222, 230, 397, 412

empirical formulae of compounds, 9–10, 190

endothermic reactions, 90–1, 99, 122, 141–2, 265, 354, 358

energy changes, 90

energy levels (quantum shells), 33

enthalpy change, calculation using bond energies, 99–101

enthalpy change, definition of, 90

enthalpy change, Hess's law of, 97

enthalpy change, measurement of, 94–6

enthalpy change, of atomisation, 93

enthalpy change, of combustion, 92, 95, 98

enthalpy change, of formation, 92, 98

enthalpy change, of hydration, 93–4, 99

enthalpy change, of neutralisation, 93, 94

enthalpy change, of reaction, 92

enthalpy change, of solution, 93, 95

enthalpy change, of vaporisation and boiling point, 65, 77

enthalpy change, standard conditions for, 92–4

enthalpy change, types of, 92–5

enthalpy cycles, 97–100, 259–260, 266

enthalpy profile diagrams, 91

entropy, 350–3

entropy, and free energy, 357–8

entropy, and temperature, 357

entropy, calculating changes in, 354–7

enzymes, 145

enzymes, digestive, 417

enzymes, in DNA replication, 420

equilibria, acid–base, 130–4

equilibrium, 117–135

equilibrium, dynamic, 118

equilibrium, position of, 119–23

equilibrium and ammonia production, 129

equilibrium and sulfuric acid production, 129–30

equilibrium constant (K_c), 123–6

equilibrium constant (K_p), 127–9

equilibrium expressions, 123

equilibrium reactions, 117

esterification reactions, 229–30

esters, 229–30

ethane, 58, 193

ethanoic acid, 229, 231–2

ethene, 53, 58, 193–4

ethylamine, 220, 241, 401–3

eutrophication, 183–4

exothermic reactions, 90–1, 99, 122, 126, 141–2, 258, 265, 266, 354, 357–8

faraday, unit (F), 276

Faraday constant, 277–8

Fehling's solution, 239, 395

forensic science, use of chromatography in, 436, 449

free-radical substitution reactions, 207, 385

free radicals, 196, 206–7, 223

fullerenes, 82–3

functional group isomerism, 195

functional groups, 192, 412, 426

gas reactions, equilibria in, 127–8

gas volumes and stoichiometry, 19

gaseous state of matter, 73–7

gas–liquid chromatography (GLC), 437–8, 448–9

gasohol, 227

gel electrophoresis, principles of, 407–8

general formulae of compounds, 192

general gas equation, 75–6

genetic code, 419

genetic information, 421

giant molecular structures, 80–2

Gibbs free energy, 357–60

Gibbs free energy, calculating changes in, 360–2

global warming, 84, 205–6, 212

graphene, 83

graphite, 80–1

greenhouse gases, 205

Group 2 carbonates and nitrates, thermal decomposition of, 168

Group 2 compounds, uses of, 169

Group 2 elements, physical properties of, 164–5

Group 2 elements, reactions of, 165–8

Group 17 elements, physical properties of, 172

Group 17 elements, reactions of, 173–5

Group 17 elements, uses of, 178

Haber process, 101, 129, 182, 183, 342–3

haemoglobin, 204–5, 315

half-cells, 279–85, 290

half-equations, 108–9, 177, 274, 279–85, 369–70

half-life, 335–6

halide ions, reactions of, 174–6, 290–1

halogenoalkanes, elimination reactions, 222

halogenoalkanes, nucleophilic substitution
    reactions, 220–1

halogenoalkanes, uses of, 222–3

halogens, 172–8, 206–7, 209

halogen compounds, uses of, 178, 222–3

Hess's law, 97–9, 259–62, 266

heterogeneous catalysis, 144–5, 340, 342–3

heterolytic fission, 196–7

high-performance liquid chromatography (HPLC), 436–7,
    448–9, 459

homogeneous catalysis, 145–6, 340–2

homolytic fission, 196, 206,

hydrocarbon fuels, 204

hydrocarbons, 19, 189–190, 192, 202, 213, 460

hydrocarbons, saturated, 202

hydrocarbons, unsaturated, 207

hydrofluorocarbons (HFCs), 223

hydrogen bonding, 64–7, 226, 242, 387, 413–21

hydrogen electrode, standard, 279

hydrogen–oxygen fuel cells, 294–5

hydrolysis, 67, 198

hydrolysis, of acyl chlorides, 397

hydrolysis, of amides, 406, 425

hydrolysis, of esters, 229

hydrolysis, of halogenoalkanes, 219

hydrolysis, of nitriles, 231

hydrolysis, of phosphorus(V) chloride, 159

hydrolysis, of proteins, 421

hydroxynitrile, 238

ice, structure of, 66

ideal gas laws, limitations of, 75

ideal gases, 74–6

intermolecular forces, 49, 60–6, 74–8, 152, 405, 422

iodine–peroxodisulfate reaction, 341

ion polarisation, 263–4

ionic bonding, 49–50, 60, 77, 158, 258

ionic compounds, 13, 49–51, 66–7, 77–8, 295, 316

ionic equations, balancing of, 13–14

ionic lattices, 50, 78–9, 258, 263–4

ionic product of water, 304

ionic radii, periodic patterns of, 151

ionisation energies, 34–6, 41–2, 153, 260, 369

isotopes, 2–4, 28–9

isotopes, and mass spectrometry, 3–4, 446–8

isotopic mass, 2–3

ketones, 235

ketones, reactions of, 237–8

ketones, preparation of, 210, 230, 236–7

ketones, testing for, 238–40

kinetic theory of gases, 73–5

lattice energy, definition of, 258

lattice energy, and Born–Haber cycles, 259–63

lattice enthalpy, *see* lattice energy

lattice structures, 78–80

Le Chatelier's principle, 119–23

lead–acid cells, 293

ligands, 371–8

liquid state of matter, 77–8

liquids, behaviour of, 77–8

lone pairs, and bonding, 51, 53, 64, 384, 397–8, 402,

lone pairs, and ligands, 376–8

lone pairs, and molecular shapes, 56, 182, 388

macromolecules, 424, 458

mass, 2

mass, molar, 5–7

mass, percentage composition by, 8

mass, relative atomic, 2–5

mass, relative formula, 3

mass, relative isotopic, 2–3

mass, relative molecular, 3, 76–7

mass spectrometry, 3–4, 446–50

medicinal drugs, design of, 457–61

metallic bonding, 58–60

metallic lattices, 79

metals, electrical conductivity of, 67

metals, properties of, 59–60, 66–7

metals, solubility of, 67

molar gas volume, 18–19

molar mass, 5–7

molecular formulae, of compounds, 9–10, 190

molecular ions, 446

molecular lattices, 80

molecular modelling, 457

molecules, shapes of, 55–6

moles, 5–6

moles, calculations of, 6–10

monodendate ligands, 372

monomers, 211–13, 412–14, 421–8

nanotechnology, 25
neutrons, 2, 26–9
nickel–cadmium cells, 293
nitrate fertilisers, 183–4
nitrogen, 181–4
nitrogen oxides, 182–5, 205, 343
NMR (nuclear magnetic resonance) spectroscopy, 439–45
non-degenerate orbitals, 376–8
non-polar alkanes, 204
nuclear magnetic resonance (NMR) spectroscopy, 439–45
nucleic acids, 418–9, 458
nucleon number, 2, 28
nucleons, 25–6, 28
nucleophile, definition of, 197
nucleophilic addition reactions, 237–8
nucleophilic substitution reactions, 218–22, 227
nucleus, atomic, 25–6
nucleus, cell, 420
nucleus, in NMR, 439–40
nylons, 413

open system, 119
optical isomerism, 195–6
optical resolution, 459
orbitals, atomic, 37–8
order of reaction, 330–1, 333–7
order of reaction, calculation of, 334–7
order of reaction, prediction of, 340
organic compounds, techniques for identification of, 241–2, 439–50
organic compounds, naming of, 192–3
organic molecules, bonding in, 193–4
organic molecules, representation of, 189–91
organic molecules, shapes of, 57–8, 189–91
organic reactions, mechanisms for, 196–7
organic reactions, types of, 198
Ostwald, Friedrich, 307
oxidation, 107–12, 184, 198, 205, 210–11, 230–1, 236–7, 242–3, 275, 387, 395
oxidation numbers, 110–111, 156, 158, 177, 340–1, 368
oxidation states, 113, 368
oxides, of Period 3 elements, 156–8
ozone layer, 206, 223

paper chromatography, 320, 434–6
partial pressure, 127–8
partition coefficients, 319–20, 435
pepsin, 417
peptides, 405, 412–3
Period 3 chlorides, 158–60

Period 3 oxides, 156–8
Periodic Table, 10–11, 28, 149, 150, 473
Periodic Table, patterns in, 40–2, 149–60
periodicity, 149–60
periodicity, of chemical properties, 154–60
periodicity, of physical properties, 149–53
permanent dipole–dipole forces, 60, 63–4
pH, definition of, 305
pH calculations, 305–6
pH change, monitoring of, 309–13
pH of buffer solution, 313
pH of strong acids, 306
pH of strong bases, 306
pH scale, 305
pharmaceuticals, synthesis of, 457–61
phenol, 387–8
phenol, reactions of, 388–9
phenylamine, 401–4
pi (π) bonds, 54, 57–8, 193–4
pickling, 185
pK_a values, 307–8, 315, 387–8
polarising power of cations, 263
polarity and chemical reactivity, 61
polarity in molecules, 60–1
pollution, 204–6, 314
poly(alkene) plastics, disposal of, 212
polyamides, 413–4, 422, 425–6
polyesters, 421, 425–6
polymer deductions, 426–8
polymerisation, addition, 211–3, 426–7
polymerisation, condensation, 412–4, 419, 424
polymers, 211–13, 412, 414–5, 422–4
polymers, degradable, 425–6
position isomerism, 194
primary alcohols, 226
primary alcohols, oxidation of, 230–1
principal quantum shells, 33–4, 37
proteins, 182, 404–5, 407–8, 413–8
proteins, hydrolysis of, 418
proteins, structure of, 415–8
proteins, synthesis of, 414–5
proton number, 28, 35
protons, 2, 25–9

quantitative electrolysis, 276–8
quantum shells, principal, 33–4, 37
quantum sub-shells, 37–8

rate constant (K) 330
rate constant, calculations involving, 334–5

490

rate constant, units of, 331
rate equations, 330–4
rate of reaction, 141–5, 248, 325–43
rate of reaction, factors influencing changes in, 325–9
rate of reaction, graphical calculation of, 332–4
rate-determining step, 338–40
reacting masses, 6–8
reaction kinetics, 141–5, 325–43
reaction mechanisms, 196–7, 220–2, 338–43
reaction mechanisms, predicting order of reaction from, 340
reaction mechanisms, verification of, 338–9
reaction rate against concentration graphs, 332
real gases, 74–5
rechargeable cells, 293
recycling of materials, 84, 425
redox reactions, 107–10, 274–5, 280
redox reactions, and electrode potential, 280
redox reactions, in electrolysis, 275
reduction, 107–12, 177, 198, 232, 237, 275, 280, 289–90, 403
relative atomic mass, 2–5
relative formula mass, 3
relative isotopic mass, 2
relative molecular mass, 3, 76–7
retention times, 436–7
reversible reactions, 117–9
ribosomes, 407, 428–9
RNA (ribonucleic acid), 418–20

saturated hydrocarbons, 202
secondary alcohols, 226, 230–1, 235–6
secondary alcohols, oxidation of, 236
shielding effect, 35, 41–2, 151–3, 165, 173, 369, 441
sigma (σ) bonds, 54, 57, 193, 383
significant figures, 8
silicon(IV) oxide, 81–2
silk, 417
skeletal formula of compounds, 190
S_N1 mechanism, 221
S_N2 mechanism, 220–1
sodium chloride lattice, 258
solid state cells, 293
solid state of matter, 78–82
solubility, 66–7
solubility, equilibrium and, 316
solubility, of Group 2 hydroxides, 167
solubility, of Group 2 sulfates, 267–8
solubility product, 316–8
solubility product, calculation of, 317–8

solubility product, for predicting precipitation, 318
solute, 320, 435–7, 448
solute, and partition coefficients, 319
solution concentration, calculation of, 17
solution concentration, by titration, 17–18
spectator ions, 13, 93, 176
spin-pair repulsion, 42
splitting pattern, 442
standard electrode potentials, 279, 281–4, 286, 290, 370, 474
standard enthalpy changes, 92–3
state symbols, 12
states of matter, 73–84
stereoisomerism, 195–6
stereoisomerism, in transition metal complexes, 373
stoichiometry, 6–8, 17, 19
stoichiometry by titration, 17–18
storage cells, 293
strong acid–strong base titrations, 311–12
strong acid–weak base titrations, 312
strong acids, pH of, 306
strong base–weak acid titrations, 312
strong bases, pH of, 306
structural formulae of compounds, 190–1, 194
structural isomerism, 194–5
subatomic particles, 26–8
subshells, 37
substitution, of ligands, 374–5
substitution reactions, 198, 206–7, 218–9, 220, 227–8, 374–5, 384–5
substrates, 145
successive ionisation energies, 34–7
sulfur, oxides of, 185
sulfur dioxide, as pollutant, 206
sulfur hexafluoride, molecular shape of, 51–2, 56
sulfuric acid, production of, 129, 185
surface tension, 65
synthetic polymers, 413–5

tertiary alcohols, 226, 230
tertiary alcohols, testing for, 231
tetramethylsilane (TMS), 439
thermal decomposition, of Group 2 carbonates and nitrates, 168
thermal stability, of Group 2 carbonates and nitrates, 264
thermal stability, of hydrogen halides, 175
thin-layer chromatography (TLC), 436
titration, 2, 15–17, 466
titration, calculation of solution concentration by, 17
titration, deducing stoichiometry by, 17–18

TMS (tetramethylsilane), 439
Tollens' reagent, 239, 395
transition elements, 367–78
transition elements, common oxidation states of, 368
transition elements, electronic configurations of, 367–9
transition elements, ligands and complex formation, 371–8
transition elements, physical properties of, 369
transition elements, redox reactions involving, 369–71
transition elements, use as catalysts, 342–3
transition elements, use in catalytic converters, 343
tri-iodomethane (iodoform), 240–1
two-way chromatography, 435

unsaturated hydrocarbons, 207
unsaturated oils, 208

van der Waals' forces, 62–5, 75, 80–1, 149–50, 417–20, 422, 457

vaporisation, 77
vaporisation, enthalpy change of, 62, 65–6,
vapour pressure, 77–8
vinegar, 394
viscosity, 65–6

water, ionic product of, 304
water, properties of, 65–6
weak acids, acid dissociation constant of, 307–8
weak acid–strong base titration, 312
weak acid–weak base titration, 312–3
weak acids, pH of, 133, 309
weak bases, pH of, 134

X-ray crystallography, 457

zwitterions, 405

Acknowledgements

The authors and publishers acknowledge the following sources of copyright material and are grateful for the permissions granted. While every effort has been made, it has not always been possible to identify the sources of all the material used, or to trace all copyright holders. If any omissions are brought to our notice, we will be happy to include the appropriate acknowledgements on reprinting.

Cover isak55/Shutterstock; Chapter 1 Ryan McVay/Thinkstock; 1.1, 1.13 Martyn F Chillmaid/SPL; 1.2 Tek Images/SPL; 1.7 SPL; 1.8 Geoscience features; 1.9 Andrew Lambert/SPL; 1.10 Ben Johnson/SPL; 1.12, 1.15a-d David Acaster; 1.14 GP Bowater/Alamy; 1.16 MedicImage/Alamy; Chapter 2 Jose Antonio Nicoli Andonie/Thinkstock; 2.1 IBM Research/SPL; 2.2 NASA/JAXA; 2.4 Prof Peter Fowler/SPL; 2.6 University of Cambridge Cavendish Laboratory; Chapter 3 Kheng Guan Toh/Shutterstock; 3.1 Charles D Winters/SPL; 3.3 Sheila Terry/SPL; Chapter 4 Sunagatov Dmitry/Thinkstock; 4.1 Tony Camacho/SPL; 4.3, 4.7, 4.28 Charles D Winters/SPL; 4.28 Tom McHugh/SPL; 4.28, 4.46 Andrew Lambert/SPL; 4.30 Alfred Paseika/SPL; 4.31 Natural Visions/Alamy; 4.38 sciencephoto/Alamy; 4.45 Steve Allen/SPL; Chapter 5 eugenesergeev/Thinkstock; 5.1 foodfolio/Alamy; 5.1 D. Hurst/Alamy; 5.7 bigjo5/Thinkstock; 5.9 Wikipedia; 5.14 Roberto de Gugliemo/SPL; 5.18b ogwen/Shutterstock; 5.19 Burke/Triolo Productions/Getty Images; Chapter 6 Design Pics/Thinkstock; 6.1 Peter Menzel/SPL; 6.2 David R Frazier Photolibrary. Inc/Alamy; Chapter 7 DanielPrudek/Thinkstock; 7.1 NASA; 7.2 Mar Photographics/Alamy; 7.3x2 Charles D Winters/SPL; Chapter 8 Blazej Lyjak/Shutterstock; 8.1 Camera lucinda lifestyle/Alamy; 8.2 David Acaster; 8.7 Images of Africa Photobank/Alamy; 8.13 Linda Kennedy/Alamy; 8.13 Andrew Lambert/SPL; 8.14 mediablitzimages/Alamy; Chapter 9 Iculig/Shutterstock; 9.1 Cephas Picture Library/Alamy; 9.1 Sheila Terry/SPL; 9.11a GIPhotostock/SPL; 9.11b sciencephotos/alamy; Chapter 10 isak55/Shutterstock; 10.1a Wikipedia; 10.1b Gordon Woods, 3 Peterboro' Ave, LE15 6EB; 10.8, 10.9, 10.14 Andrew Lambert/SPL; 10.10 Phil Degginger/Alamy; 10.11 David R Frazier Photolibrary, Inc./Alamy; Chapter 11 E.R. Degginger/Alamy; 11.1 Avpics/Alamy; 11.5, 11.6, 11.7 Andrew Lambert/SPL; 11.8 Dirk Wiersma/SPL; Chapter 12 Roberto Anguita Escribano/Thinkstock; 12.1 africa924/Shutterstock; 12.2, 12.3, 12.4 Andrew Lambert/SPL; 12.6 Ron Bull/Alamy; Chapter 13 Nathalie Speliers Ufermann/Shutterstock; 13.1a Tor Eigeland/Alamy; 13.1b National Georgaphic Images Collection/Alamy; 13.3 Keith Kent/SPL; 13.6 Nigel Cattlin/SPL;

13.7 geophotos/Alamy; 13.8 CORDELIA MOLLOY/SPL; Chapter 14 Wildnerdpix/Thinkstock; 14.1 istock/Thinkstock; Chapter 15 think4photop/Shutterstock; 15.1 Stephane Compoint/eyevine; 15.5 Andrew Lambert/SPL; 15.6 dbimages/Alamy; 15.7 Tina Manley/Alamy; 15.8 National Geographic Image Collection/Alamy; 15.9 Document General Motors/Reuter R/Corbis Sygma; 15.11a Paul Rapson/SPL; 15.13 Realimage/Alamy; 15.19 Ashley Cooper/Alamy; Chapter 16 Ammit Jack/Shutterstock; 16.1 Caro/Alamy; 16.8 NASA/SPL; Chapter 17 PathomP/Thinkstock; 17.1 Bjorn Svensson/SPL; 17.3 AFP/Getty Images; 17.4, 17.5, 17.8 Andrew Lambert/SPL; 17.6 Goran Bogicevic/Shutterstock; Chapter 18 Jupiterimages/Thinkstock; 18.1a funkyfood London - Paul Williams/Alamy; 18.1b Art Directors & TRIP/Alamy; 18.3, 18.4, 18.5, 18.6 Andrew Lambert/SPL; Practice Test 1 luchschen/Thinkstock; P1.1 Decha Thapanya/Shutterstock; Chapter 19 FotoStocker/Shutterstock; 19.1 Scott Camazine/Alamy; Chapter 20 David Hanlon/Shutterstock; 20.1all, 20.6, 20.19, 20.21, 20.22 Andrew Lambert/SPL; 20.25 David J Green/SPL; 20.26 Michael Klinec/Alamy; Chapter 21 pixinoo/Shutterstock; 21.1 Bjorn Svensson/SPL; 21.2 Martin Shields/SPL; 21.3 Wikipedia; 21.4 Andrew Lambert/SPL; 21.12 CNRI/SPL; 21.13 Barry Slaven/Visuals Unlimited; 21.15 Douglas Faulkner/SPL; Chapter 22 Jupiterimages/Thinkstock; 22.1 Jack Finch/SPL; 22.2 Martyn F Chillmaid/SPL; 22.3 Andrew Lambert/SPL; 22.16 Roger Norris; 22.20 Elenac/BASF; Chapter 23 Martyn Vickery / Alamy; 23.1 Martyn F Chillmaid/SPL; 23.4 Korpithas/Sutterstock; 23.7 INTERFOTO/Alamy; Chapter 24 Ramon Espelt Photography/Shutterstock; 24.1 stock connection blue/Alamy; 24.1 Claire Dunn/Alamy; 24.1 moodboard/Alamy; 24.2, 24.3, 24.11, 24.12 Andrew Lambert/SPL; Chapter 25 zorandimzr/Thinkstock; 25.1 blickwimkel/Alamy; 25.5 Michael Brooke/SPL; 25.6 Andrew Lambert/SPL; Chapter 26 Khlongwangchao/Thinkstock; 26.1 Michael Rosenfeld/Getty Images; Chapter 27 Neale Cousland/Shutterstock; 27.1 Jake Lyell/Alamy; 27.6, 27.7 Andrew Lambert/SPL; 27.11 R.A Longuehaye/SPL; Chapter 28 Jozef Jankola/Shutterstock; 28.1 Charles D Winters/SPL; 28.3 Maxim Tupikov/Shutterstock; 28.24 Yganko/Shutterstock; 28.27 Roger Ressmeyer/Corbis; Chapter 29 Dmitry Kalinovsky/Shutterstock; 29.1 caro/Alamy; 29.12 speedpix/Alamy; 29.16 Colin Cuthbert/SPL; Chapter 30 MJTH / Shutterstock; 31.1 Bill Varie/Alamy; Practice Test 2 Jaroslav74/Thinkstock; P2.1 Radharc Images/Alamy; P2.2 Sealstep/Shutterstock; P2.3 Science Photo Library/Alamynds and undergoes catalytic reaction.

493

Terms and conditions of use

This is a legal agreement between 'You' (which for individual purchasers means the individual customer and, for network purchasers, means the Educational Institution and its authorised users) and Cambridge University Press ('the Licensor') for Cambridge International AS and A Level Chemistry Second edition Course book with CD-ROM. By placing this CD in the CD-ROM drive of your computer You agree to the terms of this licence.

1. **Limited licence**
   a) You are purchasing only the right to use the CD-ROM and are acquiring no rights, express or implied to it or to the software ('Software' being the CD-ROM software, as installed on your computer terminals or server), other than those rights granted in this limited licence for not-for-profit educational use only.
   b) Cambridge University Press grants the customer the licence to use one copy of this CD-ROM either (i) on a single computer for use by one or more people at different times, or (ii) by a single person on one or more computers (provided the CD-ROM is only used on one computer at any one time and is only used by the customer), but not both.
   c) You shall not: (i) copy or authorise copying of the CD-ROM, (ii) translate the CD-ROM, (iii) reverse-engineer, alter, adapt, disassemble or decompile the CD-ROM, (iv) transfer, sell, lease, lend, profit from, assign or otherwise convey all or any portion of the CD-ROM or (v) operate the CD-ROM from a mainframe system, except as provided in these terms and conditions.

2. **Copyright**
   a) All original content is provided as part of the CD-ROM (including text, images and ancillary material) and is the copyright of, or licensed by a third party to, the Licensor, protected by copyright and all other applicable intellectual property laws and international treaties.
   b) You may not copy the CD-ROM except for making one copy of the CD-ROM solely for backup or archival purposes. You may not alter, remove or destroy any copyright notice or other material placed on or with this CD-ROM.

c) The CD-ROM contains Adobe® Flash® Player. Adobe® Flash® Player Copyright © 1996–2010 Adobe Systems Incorporated. All Rights Reserved. Protected by U.S. Patent 6,879,327; Patents Pending in the United States and other countries. Adobe and Flash are either trademarks or registered trademarks in the United States and/or other countries.

3. **Liability and Indemnification**
   a) The CD-ROM is supplied 'as-is' with no express guarantee as to its suitability. To the extent permitted by applicable law, the Licensor is not liable for costs of procurement of substitute products, damages or losses of any kind whatsoever resulting from the use of this product, or errors or faults in the CD-ROM, and in every case the Licensor's liability shall be limited to the suggested list price or the amount actually paid by You for the product, whichever is lower.
   b) You accept that the Licensor is not responsible for the persistency, accuracy or availability of any urls of external or third party internet websites referred to on the CD-ROM and does not guarantee that any content on such websites is, or will remain, accurate, appropriate or available. The Licensor shall not be liable for any content made available from any websites and urls outside the Software.
   c) Where, through use of the CD-ROM and content you infringe the copyright of the Licensor you undertake to indemnify and keep indemnified the Licensor from and against any loss, cost, damage or expense (including without limitation damages paid to a third party and any reasonable legal costs) incurred by the Licensor as a result of such infringement.

4. **Termination**
   Without prejudice to any other rights, the Licensor may terminate this licence if You fail to comply with the terms and conditions of the licence. In such event, You must destroy all copies of the CD-ROM.

5. **Governing law**
   This agreement is governed by the laws of England, without regard to its conflict of laws provision, and each party irrevocably submits to the exclusive jurisdiction of the English courts.